A HISTORY OF
THE UNITED STATES

THE MACMILLAN COMPANY
NEW YORK · BOSTON · CHICAGO · DALLAS
ATLANTA · SAN FRANCISCO

MACMILLAN & CO., LIMITED
LONDON · BOMBAY · CALCUTTA
MELBOURNE

THE MACMILLAN COMPANY
OF CANADA, LIMITED
TORONTO

A HISTORY

OF

THE UNITED STATES

BY

EDWARD CHANNING

VOLUME IV

FEDERALISTS AND REPUBLICANS

1789–1815

New York

THE MACMILLAN COMPANY

1935

3.6.7 Macm.

5/9/40

19343

PRINTED IN THE UNITED STATES OF AMERICA BY
THE BERWICK & SMITH CO.

CONTENTS

MAPS

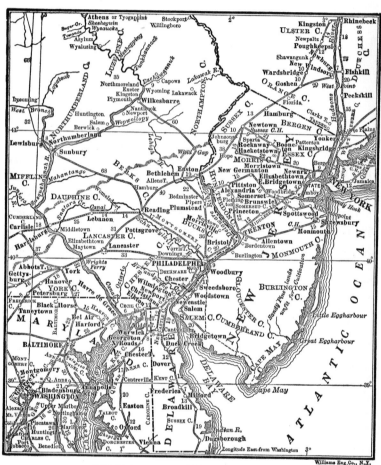

THE HEART OF THE UNITED STATES, 1796

(From Abraham Bradley Junr's *Map of the United States*, 1796)

viii

A HISTORY OF THE UNITED STATES

CHAPTER I

FROM THE OLD TO THE NEW

In 1789, a new era dawned on mankind. The inauguration of Washington as first President of the United States
(April 30) set a limit to the social and administrative systems
of colonial times and began a new national republican organization that was to reach fulfilment after three-quarters of a
century of striving. On May 5, 1789, the States General
met at Versailles and proceeded to the democratization of
France and of Europe.[1] Civil convulsions and wars followed.
Their influence extended westwardly across the Atlantic and
affected society, politics, commerce, and finance in America.
In England, the industrial revolution was vigorously proceeding. The high cost of the raw material hampered the
extension of the factory system; but the cultivation of the
short staple cotton in South Carolina and Georgia cut in
two the price of the fibre, made possible the development
of the textile industry in England and in America, and, in
consequence, fastened negro servitude on the southern United
States. The application of steam to transportation by
water and by land in the first half of the new century changed
the whole face of civilization by making practicable what had
before been impossible. The new conditions of living led

[1] See Lewis Rosenthal's *America and* *States on France in the XVIIIth Century*
France: The Influence of the United (New York, 1882).

to changed manners of thinking — to the liberalization of the mind, to scientific evolution, to the breaking down of religious barriers, to a radical alteration in the ethical outlook, and to the creation of a new literature.

The twenty-five years covered in the present volume were distinctly a period of transition from the old order of things to the new, from the modes of thought and action of the seventeenth and eighteenth centuries to those of our own times. At the moment, the future seemed full of doubt. There were most novel and urgent problems of administration and of finance to be settled at home; and the relations of the United States with the outer world were never more precarious than they were in this quarter of a century. Washington was ever accustomed to weigh with care all the elements in the problems that came to him for settlement, and his judgment was unrivalled. At no time in his career was he more oppressed by the gravity of the task [1] to which his countrymen had called him than he was when he rode away from Mount Vernon to take up his high office at New York in April, 1789.

Of all the things that stood in the way of a realization of the dreams of those who had made the Constitution none was more formidable than the difficulties of transportation which then beset the conveyor of men, goods, information, or administrative orders. Four million men, women, and children — white, black, and red — lived within the boundaries of the United States,[2] about four-fifths as many as now

[1] *Writings of Washington* (Ford), xi, 379, 388; Massachusetts Historical Society's *Collections*, Seventh Series, vol. vi, 192.

[2] The *Return of the Whole Number of Persons within the Several Districts of the United States*, Philadelphia, 1791 (often cited as *The First Census*) gives the total population as 3,929,326. S. N. D. North in *A Century of Population*

Growth, p. 54, including some guesses as to the population of unenumerated sections, states the total as 3,934,625. According to an analysis in the last-mentioned book (p. 121) at the time of the first census rather more than ninety-one per cent of the people were of British nationality — mostly English — judging by the names of the heads of the families. This table gives less than **two**

live within the limits of New York City. The four millions
in 1789 were scattered over the Atlantic seaboard from the
St. Croix and the Penobscot to the Savannah and the St.
Mary's, a distance of from twelve to thirteen hundred miles
from northeast to southwest. Inland, the farms and clear-
ings extended for nearly a thousand miles, beyond the Alleghanies into the Ohio Valley — into lands that were soon to
become the States of Kentucky, Tennessee, and Ohio. To
the northward, between the Connecticut River and Lake
Champlain, lived the Green Mountaineers, who were admitted into the Union as the fourteenth State in 1791.[1] A
thousand miles from north to south or from east to west are
formidable, even today; in 1789, they were well-nigh insu-
perable to the carrying on of any effective, centralized federal
control.

Any statement of distances conveys no idea to us of what
the problem really was, because nowadays we are habituated
to thinking in points of time or in costs of transportation.
It is only by translating facts, gleaned from old letters, account books, and newspapers, into hours and dollars that
one can bring these things within easy comprehension. Boston is now five hours and seven dollars distant from New
York on the fastest train, and Washington is likewise five
hours and something under seven dollars away from the
great metropolis in the other direction. In the last decade

per cent of the population as "Irish"
in 1790 and less than six per cent "German."   As to the accuracy of this mode
of computation, see the present work,
ii, 421. In 1790, the "settled area"
was a little over 200,000 square miles.

[1] The constitutional history of Vermont is complicated, as both New York
and New Hampshire laid claim to the
territory between Lake Champlain and
the Connecticut. In 1777, Vermont
set up for herself. From that time on,

for some years, Vermont was independent. She took no part in the Federal
Convention and was not asked to ratify
the Constitution. In 1790, New York
consented to the admission of Vermont
to the Union as a State, and this was
accomplished by act of Congress of
February   18,   1791.   See   Samuel
Williams's *Natural and Civil History of
Vermont* (Walpole, N.H., 1794), and R.
E. Robinson's *Vermont*, in the "Commonwealth Series."

of the eighteenth century, express riders, sparing neither horse nor man, covered the road from New York to Boston in ninety-six hours,[1] at what cost no letter writer tells us. The usual stage-coach fare was reckoned at six cents a mile, and a stage went about thirty miles a day, or somewhat more. Even so short a journey as that of forty miles from Providence to Boston was broken by a night's lodgings on the way. It took from eight to ten days and cost from twenty to twenty-five dollars to go from Boston to New York by land and about two-thirds as much in money and considerably more in time to go by stage to Providence and thence by sailing sloop to New York through Long Island Sound. Southward from the Hudson, wide and deep rivers and poor roads — beyond Philadelphia — made the journey to the Potomac much slower, thereby greatly adding to the number of lodgings and meals to be paid for. The United States mail made the distance in less than five days, but the traveller usually occupied at least ten, at a cost of thirty to forty dollars.[2]

The details just given relate to transportation for moderate distances along the seaboard, through the most travelled portion of the country. When the traveller turned his back to the ocean and essayed a journey westward for fifty or one hundred miles from tide-water, he found the problem much more serious. It was possible to go on horseback or by wagon from one part of the country to nearly every other

---

[1] C. R. King's *Life and Correspondence of Rufus King*, i, 391.

[2] In 1790, Jefferson took from March 12 to March 22 from the Potomac to New York, and in November of the same year, he left Monticello on the 8th, reaching Philadelphia on the 21st. Ten years later, in 1800, Gouverneur Morris was ten days on the road from New York to Washington. In 1806, by combining land and water transportation, the time from Philadelphia to Washington by way of Annapolis was reduced to less than four days, the fare being $12.25 and inn charges, as appears by an advertisement in the *Federal Gazette and Baltimore Daily Advertiser*, June 21, 1806. For an account of travelling comparable to "the limited" train of the present day, see the "Diary of the Hon. Jonathan Mason," 1804–1805, in Massachusetts Historical Society's *Proceedings* for March, 1885, pp. 5–34.

portion of it, but only with great expenditure of time and strength and with no small outlay of money. A few good roads led from Philadelphia into the interior, and from Boston to Worcester there was one of the best highways in the country. Elsewhere, when water routes could not be made to serve, progress was painful and slow. It took three weeks or a month to bring a wagon load of flour or tobacco from the Valley of Virginia or from Lynchburg to Richmond, and as much more to carry back the supplies for the plantations whence came the flour or the tobacco. Two trips a year were about the only communication that planters living fifty miles from Virginia's commercial town had with the store-keepers of that place whence came everything consumed in the household that was not produced or made on the plantation.

With land transportation so difficult and so expensive, water communication was availed of at every opportunity. Schooners and sloops plied along the coast or up and down the sounds, bays, and rivers, to an extent that is undreamed of nowadays, even with all the advantages of steel construction and of steam. Southern Congressmen came to New York and Philadelphia by water; Timothy Pickering sent his family by the Sound route from Pennsylvania to Salem, and practically all travel and commerce up and down the Hudson Valley was by the "safe, fast, and commodious" river sloops. On the removal of the government offices from Philadelphia to Washington in 1800, all the furniture and record books and files were sent by water, and so, too, was the printing equipment for the "National Intelligencer," which was from thirty to forty days on board ship.

Transportation was not only slow, expensive, and fatiguing, it was often positively dangerous. Of the Carolina Congressmen who came by water to Philadelphia in 1790, Thomas

Tudor Tucker sailed for sixteen days in perpetual storms, and Ædanus Burke was wrecked off the Capes of the Chesapeake. Two other Southerners, Jackson and Mathews from Georgia, were set on shore at Cape May and had to travel over land and across rivers one hundred and sixty miles further to Philadelphia.[1] Nor were land journeys to be lightly undertaken for two New Englanders coming by road were badly injured when the stage in which they were travelling was overset.

The poor transportation facilities were due in great part to the lack of demand for better means of communication in the years before the establishment of a strong federal government, in those days when each colony or State lived a life of its own and a very simple life at that. In 1789, there were only seventy-five postmasters in the whole country and the total receipts of the postal service were some twenty-five thousand dollars.[2] The growing business of the country and the increase in the speculative fever, together with a remarkable development in the interchange of ideas between persons in different parts of the country, all combined to create a demand for better facilities. The transmission of the mails was expedited and new post-offices were opened. In 1800, there were nine hundred and three of them, and in 1810, more than two thousand post-offices were open for business. One thing that greatly interfered with the development of the postal service was the high rate of postage coupled with the lavish use of the freedom of the mails given to officials and to members of Congress. The postage on a "single letter" weighing one-quarter of an ounce was

---

[1] Ulrich B. Phillips's "South Carolina Federalists," in *American Historical Review*, xiv, 779.

[2] D. D. T. Leech's *History of the Post Office Department, 1789–1879* (Washington, 1879), pp. 11–13. For the later figures, see *Gentleman's Annual Pocket Remembrancer*, for 1813, p. 122. Statistics for the years 1790–1809 may be found in a "Letter from the Post-Master General transmitting a Report" dated April 30, 1810.

ten cents from New York to Philadelphia — just under one hundred miles — and proportionately higher rates were charged for greater weight or longer distance. Newspapers were carried one hundred miles for one cent and for greater distances for one cent and a half. Magazines and printed matter of all kinds were shown no favor. By the law of 1792, they were not received at all, and the act of 1794 gave postmasters discretion as to whether they would take them or not. Under these circumstances, every effort was made to elude the necessity of paying postage by putting private mail matter with public despatches, by using the franking privilege of congressional friends, and by sending everything possible by private conveyance. In 1793, Pickering, who was then Postmaster General, estimated that fifteen thousand free letters had been posted at Philadelphia in the preceding year and eighteen thousand free letters received. At the same time the total expense of the local post-office at that place was thirteen hundred and fifty dollars.[1] Notwithstanding everything that had been done to quicken the postal service, it was not until the 19th of July, 1808, that New York newspapers contained the first announcement of a very destructive fire that had occurred at Savannah on July 5, and it took three days more for the news to get to Albany and find a place in the "Register" that was published there. Foreign news took a very long time to filter through war-stricken Europe and to cross the Atlantic, — the battle of Eylau that was fought on February 7, 1807 was

[1] These statements are from a memorandum in the "Pickering Papers," vi, 71. The rates of postage were settled by act of Congress in 1792 and were somewhat increased by the law of 1794. The act of 1792 provided for the transportation of letters, packets, and newspapers; the law of 1794 authorized the Postmaster General "where the mode of conveyance and the size of the mails will admit of it" to transport magazines and pamphlets, at the rate of two cents per sheet for one hundred miles or more. The postmasters were to keep separate accounts of the newspapers, magazines, and pamphlets, and local postmasters were to receive fifty per cent of the postage thereof, exclusive of other allowances.

not reported in the Charleston, South Carolina, "Times" until June 9, following.

Under these difficulties of transportation, the task of administering affairs of peace and war from any one city was certain to be great. In view of the divergent interests of the several parts of the country and of all the social and political prejudices that attended on these divergences, was it going to be possible to administer a constantly growing consolidated federal government for any length of time? Had not the steamboat, the railroad, and the telegraph come when they did would the Union have long continued? It is well to ponder these facts before condemning Patrick Henry or Samuel Adams for their opposition to the establishment of a national government, or Washington for his dismal forebodings as to his ability to carry on the work.

Men and women in those days lived a simple and natural existence, lacking the home conveniences and hygienic improvements of the present day. One's imagination finds it difficult to picture Washington in Robert Morris's mansion at Philadelphia, or Jefferson in the "President's Palace" at Washington City, without a lighting system — no gas, no electricity, not even kerosene — without plumbing, heating plant, or telephone, with nothing, indeed, but walls, floors, and ceilings, expensively decorated, to be sure, and filled with some of the best furniture of the time. Salaries and incomes were commensurate with this simplicity of living. The President of the United States received twenty-five thousand dollars each year and a residence which was partly furnished at public expense;[1] but no other compensation came anywhere near to this. An annual salary of four thousand dollars was allotted to the Chief Justice of the United States,

[1] The salaries paid to Washington, Jefferson, and Hamilton may be compared with the seventy-five thousand paid to President Wilson and the twelve thousand each paid to Secretaries Bryan and McAdoo.

while the Associate Justices and the Secretaries of State and
Treasury were given three thousand five hundred dollars each
in 1789; but this amount was somewhat increased before the
close of the century. Important clerks, who really were
assistant secretaries, were given eight hundred dollars a year
and minor clerks as little as five hundred.[1] The most prosperous lawyer in the country took in ten thousand dollars a
year.[2] Possibly this estimate was too high, for the largest
amount that John Marshall received as a practising lawyer
was not far from five thousand dollars. This was in 1798 or
1799 when he stood at the head of his profession in Virginia,
— a few years earlier his income was much smaller. The
compensation of clergymen, in those days, as in our own, was
much less than that paid to successful lawyers; but the parson
had a certain fixity of tenure in his place and his compensation. One of them, John Pierce of Brookline, Massachusetts,
was a painstaking and popular preacher and a most careful
keeper of accounts. He had a settled salary, a parsonage,
a farm, and an allowance for fuel, and, in addition, received
extra grants from his parish and a continuing flow of presents
from his parishioners. He carefully estimated the money
value of each gift and set it down in a book with the extra
grants and legacies. Lumping his receipts together, it appears that in cash or its equivalent, he took in from eight
hundred to a thousand dollars a year.[3] A minister similarly

---

[1] For the compensations of 1793, see
Hamilton's "Estimate of Appropriations" for that year in *Annals of Congress*, 2nd Cong., 1285. For increases see
act of March, 1799, in *ibid.*, 5th Cong.,
vol. iii, 3939. Collectors of customs
were compensated by "fees and percentage"; most of them got very little,
but the collector at Philadelphia took
in $12,000 in 1801 and those at Boston,
New York, and Charleston about $8000
each. See "Letter of the Secretary of
the Treasury" dated February 27,

1802. The governor of Massachusetts
in 1814 was paid $2666.67, the chief
justice of the State $3500. I. Thomas,
Jr.'s *Town and County Almanack* for
1814.

[2] Timothy Pickering to John Adams,
September 20, 1798.

[3] The Reverend John Pierce kept
most detailed books. One set was devoted to his presents, a money value
being affixed to each. The total of
the presents varied from $153.00 in 1803
to $618.00 in 1813, averaging in the later

circumstanced today receives five or six thousand dollars
annually. The incomes of business men are impossible of
computation now and were then, but the diaries tell us something as to the wages of working men. A man who could do
rough carpentry in rural New England received about eighty
cents a day. In addition he had a little farm of his own and
a house, which possibly had come down to him from his
father. His total income might be estimated as the equivalent of four hundred and fifty or five hundred dollars a year.
A man of the same grade in the labor scale in our own time
would earn two dollars and a half to three dollars a day. In
domestic service, one can take as a standard the old-fashioned
New England general houseworker. In those days she received about thirty-nine or forty dollars a year, or twenty
shillings New England currency a month. These incomes
seem very small indeed, and one is tempted to moralize on the
insufficiency of compensation to all but the highest placed
and most successful men in the country.

In 1800 the hand-worker labored twelve or thirteen hours
a day, the merchant and the professional man worked from
nine in the morning until his dinner at two or three in the
afternoon. For a hundred years the hand-worker has constantly diminished his hours of labor and now ceases produc-
tive employment in the middle of the afternoon; whereas
the professional man has elongated his period of daily money-
getting to ten, twelve, or fourteen hours. Meantime the
laborer's wages have tripled or quadrupled, but the brain-
worker and master of finance or administration takes in ten,
twenty, or fifty times as much as he did in 1800. Whether
there is any relation between these various factors and what
it is, is a subject for debate; but it would seem that the in-

years of his pastorate about $400.00
annually. He probably was one of the
best paid ministers in New England;

Brookline, then as now, being the
chosen place of residence of rich men.

come of the laboring man as measured in purchasing power
has diminished relatively to that of the head-worker. The
efficiency of machinery and attendance due to division of
labor, to shorter hours, and to increased speed is one of the
marvels of modern times. Might it not be worth discussion,
however, as to whether the introduction of some diversity of
employment, some lengthening of hours, and some lessening
of tension would not lead to greater efficiency of the human
race in the long run of years. Or, recurring to Adam Smith's
classic example of the pin-maker, in this search for "efficiency," has there not been too much consideration for the pin
and too little for the maker, — for the man and woman?

Before the epoch of cities and railroads, almost nothing was
paid for the transportation and distribution of the necessities of life. The people then lived on farms and plantations
or in small groups in villages and in towns, and few of them
in anything that could be likened to the present ever thicken-
ing congeries of humanity. In other words they lived near
to the source of supplies and they paid nothing for delivery.
With the exception of flour and a few tropical commodities
and some manufactured goods, the New Englander bought
almost nothing that was not produced or made within five
miles of his house. The case was even truer of the farmer of
the Middle States or the planter of the South. Contrast this
simplicity of existence for a moment with the complexity of
city dwelling today. Take the New Yorker, and think of
him as he sits down to his breakfast. His grape-fruit comes
from Cuba, Florida, or California, his cereal from Ohio, his
chop from Montana, his bread from Minnesota, and his
butter, milk, and eggs from nobody knows where, but a long
way from Fifth Avenue. And so it is with everything.
Nothing that a man eats or drinks is grown on Manhattan
Island. All this concentration of food-stuffs at a given point

and prompt distribution of them cost a great deal of money and take up a large part of the increased incomes of the people. Another portion goes for the daily transportation of the worker. In 1800, men and women, except a few of the richest sort, lived within easy walking distances of their employments. Now every one pays for miles of travel daily, and an expenditure such as millions make each year for automobiles was then undreamed of. Almost no one then, except ministers, politicians, lawyers, and sailors, ever went twenty miles from home.

Running over diaries, letters, and account books and utilizing whatever "prices current" have come down to us and such advertisements as one can find in the newspapers, it is possible to reach a rough approximation of something like a chart of prices. Taking five commodities that may fairly be classed among the necessities, — flour, beef, coffee, sugar, and butter, — let us compare prices in 1800 and in 1900. In April, 1800, a householder at Boston could buy one pound of each of these things for eighty cents;[1] his successor a

[1] Before 1800 prices were ordinarily stated in shillings and pence of the local currency; after 1800 they are more and more often given in dollars and cents. The following table — confessedly imperfect — will give some idea of the range of prices in these years : —

	Flour, Bbl.	Beef, Lb.	Coffee, Lb.	White Sugar, Lb.	Butter, Lb.	Molasses, Gal.	Upland Cotton, Lb.
Boston, 1790 . .	$ 7.67	—	—		—	.29	
Boston, 1800 . .	10.25–12.50	.08	.25	.18	.16–.20	.45	.40
Boston, 1810 . .	8.25–11.25	.07–.10	.24–.25	.12½	.16–.23	.67	.16
New York, 1790 .	—		—		—	—	
New York, 1800 .	$ 9.50–10.50	.08–.10	.23–.27	.15–.17½	.16–.18	.56	.28–.32
New York, 1810 .	7.75–10.75	—	.18–.24	—	—	.60	.15–.18
Philadelphia, 1790	$ 5.73–8.26	—	.16–.18	.10+		.35	—
Philadelphia, 1800	10.00–11.50	.08	.25	.14		.48	.40
Philadelphia, 1810	7.00–10.50	.10	.18–.24	.12–.14		.85	—

In gathering these statistics, I have been greatly assisted by Mr. Herman H. Haskins of Winchester, Massachusetts.

hundred years later would have paid one hundred and ten
cents or about one-quarter more. A century ago, beef and
mutton were cheap, costing about eight cents a pound.
Breadstuffs, on the other hand, were high; corn bringing
seventy-five cents a bushel or more and flour costing from
eight to ten dollars a barrel. Coffee was a little cheaper than
it is now, but sugar cost from fifteen to twenty cents a pound,
instead of five or six; and butter brought twenty cents instead of about thirty-five for the same grade and season.
There was considerable variation in prices in different parts
of the country, owing to the crudities of the transportation
system. Breadstuffs were noticeably cheaper outside of New
England, but imported foods were as a rule more expensive, in these early years, at New York and Philadelphia
than they were at Boston and Salem. One of the things that
surprises a student is the constancy of the yearly average of
food prices at any one place and the seasonal variations
which are repeated year after year. Turning now from
food to clothing, it appears that it cost about as many dollars and cents to provide a suit of clothes or a dress as it does
at the present time. Fashions in clothing and nomenclature
of goods change so rapidly that it is impossible to construct
anything like a chart of prices of textiles. Cottons had not
begun to take the place of woollens and linens in 1790, or even
in 1800, and the price of fabrics had not yet been affected
by the introduction of cheap manufacturing processes, cheap
fibre, or the production of ready-made clothing of all prices
and qualities. John Pierce valued a broadcloth suit, which
a parishioner had given him, at forty-four dollars, and Jefferson paid twenty-eight dollars each for the liveries that were
worn by the servants at the President's Mansion. Foot-
wear appears to have been much cheaper then than now;
ladies' slippers costing less than two dollars a pair. As soon,

however, as one gets away from the everyday things that one associates with human existence, prices are out of all comparison with those of the present day.

Up to 1800, house warming was by means of wood fires in the old-fashioned fireplaces, although Franklin and Count Rumford had already designed more effective means for utilizing the heat of burning wood and coal. About 1809 advertisements of stoves and furnaces begin to appear in the newspapers.[1] Jefferson used coal brought from Richmond by water to heat the presidential mansion during a part of his term of office,[2] and not many years were to pass away before John Pierce was having semi-bituminous coal delivered at his house in Brookline for twelve dollars a ton. Taking everything into consideration and making all possible allowances for the imperfection of such records as are accessible, it seems that the difference in the cost of living between the beginning and the ending of the nineteenth century was due to the confinement of one's expenditures — in 1800 — for the most part to things that were produced near at hand, and to the great paucity of opportunity for expenditure on amusements and other accessories of existence.

There were theatres at New York and Philadelphia and plays were enacted at other places, even at Boston and Salem.[3] Side by side with these, and often in connection

---

[1] See *Columbian Centinel*, Jan. 11, 1809.

[2] A side-light on expenses is given by Jefferson's board bills at Philadelphia while Vice-President. In 1798 and again in 1799, he paid $26.00 a week for himself and servant, $13.00 being for the rooms; besides, his candles cost him .27 a week, his fire-wood from $3.60 a week to $4.00. In 1799, President Smith of Princeton sent an estimate to Madison as to the yearly expenses of a student. In this he gives board as $2.33 a week, wood at $4.67 a cord, and candles at .16½ a pound. The total necessary expenses for a year including matriculation and tuition are set down at $176.35. Besides, a student provided his own bed and furniture, and President Smith stated that voluntary expenses for dress and horses are generally made considerably more, especially for southern students. These figures are borne out by the statement of John Quincy Adams that $300.00 would pay for a year at Harvard College.

[3] William Dunlap's *History of the American Theatre* (New York, 1832; London, 1833) sets forth at length the vicissitudes of the drama in early

with them, were exhibitions of agility and athletic performances; then there were displays of horsemanship and cir-
cuses and fireworks and the showing of strange animals.
Among the last was a beautiful African lion, as he appeared in
one advertisement, or a "tyger," as he was shown in another,
and a "cassawary." The most noticeable of them all was
an elephant whose movements may be traced up and down
the coast. In 1797, he was at Providence on his way to the
approaching Commencement at Cambridge, and the next
year was being exhibited at Richmond.[1] Besides these,
there were representations of famous men and women and
historic events. The human beings were represented by wax
figures; the events by panoramas, and an attempt was made
to combine the two by mechanical means. The most elaborate thing of the kind was a representation of the last days
of Louis XVI and Marie Antoinette, ending with the execution of the queen — life size and dressed as she was on the
scaffold. She was represented before the guillotine and
then as "laying herself in the guillotine." The executioner
was shown in the act of releasing the knife and the head of
Marie Antoinette was seen falling into a basket. This representation was "performed by an invisible machine." It
had been admired at London, according to the advertisement,
and admission was at the high price of fifty cents. There
was great eagerness to see wild animals in captivity, repre-

America; J. N. Ireland's *Records of
the New York Stage from 1750 to 1860*
(New York, 1866), i, 1–364; G. O. Seil-
hamer's *History of the American Theatre*
(3 vols., Philadelphia, 1891) brings the
story only to 1797. William B. Wood's
*Personal Recollections of the Stage . . .
during a Period of Forty Years* (Philadelphia, 1854) is life-like and interesting,
but is confined to Philadelphia, Baltimore, and Washington. A work that
gives a similar outlook for Boston and
New York is John Bernard's *Retrospec-
tions of America, 1797–1811* (New York,
1887), but it lacks the authoritative personality of Wood's book.

[1] Dr. Bentley saw him and gives one-
third of a page to a description. *Diary*,
ii, 235. In the same volume he also
notes the attempts of the play actors to
interest the people of Salem in their
performances. The examples in the
text are taken from the newspapers of
the time.

sentations of horrible scenes, and theatrical performances. Dr. Pierce viewed all the animals that came to Boston, at twenty-five cents apiece; Washington and Mrs. Washington went to the theatre, both at New York and at Philadelphia. They also visited the circus and went to other public entertainments.

As things were, the easiest way to forget one's self was to take to alcoholic stimulants. Wines and liquors were consumed in almost fabulous quantities. Jefferson in his eight years of the presidency spent $10,855.90 for wines and liquors, besides at least another thousand for "syrup of punch" and other stimulants that were consumed at Monticello. Washington's presidential wine bill has not been preserved, but his inventory of the contents of the President's House at Philadelphia notes punch urns valued at £143, bottle stands at £12, and bottle rollers at £99. Other evidence of the drinking habits of those days comes out in letters and receipted bills. Margaret Bayard Smith's husband, Samuel Harrison Smith, writing to her while absent, told of a dinner party at General Dearborn's, the Secretary of War, at which Madison, the Secretary of State, and Gideon Granger, the Postmaster General, were present. It was Saturday night. After one or two bottles of champagne the conversation turned on the effects of that wine on the human head. Dearborn produced bottle after bottle from the cellar and the next day being Sunday, they decided to experiment upon themselves and did so.[1] In 1785, Nathan Dane, the supposed author of the anti-slavery clause in the Ordinance of 1787, was at New York on official business for the State of Massachusetts. He lodged with Elbridge Gerry and Rufus King. After a two weeks' stay he paid the bill for all three,

[1] Margaret Bayard Smith's *Forty Years of Washington Society* (ed. by Gaillard Hunt), p. 35.

which included charges for three dozen bottles of porter, six gallons of madeira, four gallons of spirits, and five dozen bottles of claret. Far away from New York in a little inland town in Georgia, two New Englanders opened a general store and like all of their kind sold liquor, — sometimes as much as thirty pounds sterling worth in one day. Practically all of the rum sold at this store was consumed within one rod of the door, there being sometimes fifty men drinking at once.[1] There were not wanting people even in those days to urge reform in drinking habits. Among others, was Dr. Benjamin Rush. In 1788, he wrote that in 1915, a century and a quarter later, an habitual drunkard would be held, he hoped, as infamous in society as a liar or a thief.[2]

Dr. Rush was as far in advance of his times in this thought as he was behind in some others. At the moment, intoxication was regarded rather as an accomplishment than a disgrace, and alcoholic stimulant was looked upon as a necessity. It is one of the most curious pursuits of the historian to seek to relate cause and effect. There is little doubt of the preeminence of Jefferson and Madison in the office of Secretary of State, and we have had few better representatives at London than Rufus King. Whether alcohol quickened or dimmed their intellects would probably best be left for decision to others. What effect it produced on their bodily

[1] *The Alexander Letters, 1789–1900*, p. 16. In 1787, Andrew Ellicott starting on a surveying expedition into the western country and expecting to be away about four months, took for the use of the party 176 gallons of rum, 64 of whiskey, and 16 of brandy. On the other hand, it is worth noting that when Dane was in New York in 1790 with his wife, he paid for only one bottle of wine; but he may have spent some part of his time with Gerry and King, both of whom were now members of Congress.

[2] Massachusetts Historical Society's *Collections*, Sixth Series, iv, 417. There were other advocates of temperance, but they were not many. In Thomas's *Almanac for 1806*, there is an exhortation on the dangers of flip, toddy, and milk punch, and an advocacy of switchel, cider, and pure water and the statement that the rum drunk by three hands in the haying season would purchase three calves or pay the taxes of a small farmer.

health is also an interesting inquiry and one upon which conclusion would be quite as difficult. King died at the age of seventy-two, Jefferson at eighty-three, and Madison at eighty-five, after years of service unsurpassed each in his way.

Those days were certainly unlike our own in the simplicity of living and in the attitude of society toward the use of alcoholic drinks. They were also very unlike our own in the modes of thinking and in the attitude toward many things that are now looked upon as ethically wrong. As to the use of deductive reasoning, the difference is possibly nowhere better seen than in the rudeness of the treatment of disease and in the failure to relate cause to effect, while the ethical dissimilarity is well illustrated by the attitude of society toward lotteries then and now. There were old men to be found in nearly every town and village. In Salem, Massachusetts, in 1811, on one street within a distance of three hundred and fifty feet, there were thirteen persons whose aggregate years numbered one thousand and twelve, the youngest being seventy years of age and the oldest ninety-five.[1] On the other hand, it is noticeable that men of fifty regarded themselves as beginning the evening of their days or as verging on the decline of life. There was a great deal of solicitude as to the state of one's "health." Letters begin with inquiries as to the other's health and with statements as to the writer's own condition of body.

Mortality statistics were published in the newspapers much more widely than now, but owing to the difficulty of getting at complete files of papers whatever figures are available are necessarily fragmentary. A few conclusions may be reached with some degree of safety. One is that the rate of mortality was approximately the same as today, but was differently distributed. The proportion of deaths of children to the

---

[1] *Salem Gazette* for Friday, May 3, 1811. See also *ibid.*, for January 10, 1812.

whole number was shocking. One-half of the deaths in
New York and Philadelphia in portions of 1804 and 1808 were
of children under ten years of age. Apart from infantile disorders and from the ravages of epidemics, consumption accounted for the greatest number of deaths. On the average
from one-fifth to one-quarter of the total yearly deaths
in Boston were from this disease as compared with eleven
per cent in that city in 1910. Of course something may be
attributed to difference of diagnosis, but most of the deaths
from consumption were due to ignorance of the proper mode
of treatment. In those days, a fever was a fever, no matter
what its origin, and the way to treat it was to reduce it by
bleeding the patient and by purgings. As one lay scoffer
wrote of a noted physician, "If they [his patients] are not
quite gone, he bleeds them to death." Many other modes
of treatment of tuberculosis were proposed. One of them
consisted in a temperate mode of living, the avoiding of
liquors, wearing flannel next the skin, and a morning draught
of "half a pint of new milk, mixed with the expressed juice
of green hoarhound." Doubtless this was more efficacious
than giving oil of earthworms for colic or an emulsion of
dried rattlesnake for rheumatism, but its effect on a tubercu-
lous person could not have been very great. Cancer figures
very slightly in the early lists, but from the frequency of
remedies for it advertised in the papers, there may have
been more of it than appears on the surface.

Doctors and patients had no idea of the part played by
sanitation and personal hygiene, or of the influence of micro-
scopic organisms. When the yellow fever came to Philadelphia, it was accounted for in all manner of ways. Some
thought that it came from the offensive smell emitted from a
cargo of putrid coffee. Others held that it was a pestilential
poison brought from the West Indies or was due to a peculiar

condition of the atmosphere which was shown by the swarms of grasshoppers, flies, and mosquitoes.[1]   It came year after year in the summer, and was confined to certain limited areas in Philadelphia and other cities.   It disappeared with the first cold weather and could be avoided by moving a short distance away.[2]

Dr. Benjamin Rush, one of the foremost physicians of the day, in letters to his wife, whom he had promptly sent out of town, gives a picture of the horrors of the epidemic of 1793 that reminds one of Daniel Defoe's "Journal of the Plague Year."   For days and weeks, his house was crowded at all hours, — "It is not yet five o'clock [A.M.] and I have had seven calls already."   Two to six persons were sometimes ill in one family at a time.   Parents deserted their children and children thrust their parents out into the streets as soon as they complained of a headache.   Rush's sister and one of his apprentices died in his house, his mother and two apprentices were stricken with the fever, and he, himself, was greatly worn by his responsibilities, fatigues, and inevitable sympathizings.   Morning after morning, he awakened surprised to find himself still alive.[3]   Most of the officials

---

[1] Jean Devèze, a French physician from Cap Française, was certain it was not contagious and attributed it to some change in the air, *Recherches et Observations, Sur les Causes et les Effets de la Maladie Épidémique qui a régné à Philadelphie, depuis le mois d'Août jusques vers le milieu du mois de Décembre de l'année 1793* (Philadelphia, 1794). Dr. J. L. E. Wm. Shecut of Charleston, in his "Essay on the Yellow Fever," attributed it to a "specific gaseous poison" which came from an "impaired state of the atmospherical air." Dr. Rush thought it came from "putrid exhalations from vegetable and animal substances." He protested vigorously against the belief that it was imported. Noah Webster thought it was caused by earthquakes, storms, dead fish, or black worms.   Doctor Brown of Boston held that "Septic poison (venim septique)" was responsible for many human plagues which "are generally said to have been imported in ships from the coasts of Africa." For the outbreak of 1798, see Condie and Folwell's *History of the Pestilence, commonly called Yellow Fever, which almost desolated Philadelphia in . . . 1798.*

[2] See the very interesting *Extracts from the Journal of Elizabeth Drinker, from 1759 to 1807*, edited by Henry D. Biddle (Philadelphia, 1889) ; and *Memoirs of Matthew Clarkson . . . and Gerardus Clarkson*, 57–74.

[3] *Old Family Letters relating to the Yellow Fever*, Series B., 26, 31, 32, 58, 81 ; Benjamin Rush's *Enquiry into the Origin of the late Epidemic Fever in Phil-*

fled to Germantown or to Trenton, but Oliver Wolcott remained at his post. In September, he wrote: "Every face is sad, all conversation is avoided except at a distance, a great part of the houses are shut up — & the Citizens fled, the Streets in the buisy parts of the City where I now write are as silent as at midnight." [1] More than thirty-five hundred persons perished of the fever before the cold weather put a stop to the infection; on one day one hundred and thirty-seven bodies were buried by the public authorities besides those who were interred by their families or friends. Other towns endeavored to keep the plague away from them by instituting quarantines which were enforced by military guards.

The case was very similar with consumption. There was a Virginia clergyman in whose family and in that of his wife consumption had been very fatal. He, himself, was attacked by the disease. In desperation he abandoned his home and lived in the open. He soon got better, returned to his house, and again had to seek safety in the woods. No one undertook an investigation of the flora and fauna of Philadelphia, or of the environment of the consumptives. Very likely they could not have gone far with the instruments at their disposal, but it would certainly seem that by experimentation and exercising their powers of deduction, they might have stumbled upon the reason of both of these disorders or, at any rate, have removed the cause of them.[2]

adelphia, and the papers controverting his position by Mathew Carey, William Currie, and others, all printed in Philadelphia in 1793, and Rush's *Observation upon the Origin of the . . . Yellow Fever* (Philadelphia, 1799). For Rush's career as a whole see David Ramsay's *Eulogium* (Phila., 1813); an *Elegiac Poem, on the Death of Dr. Benjamin Rush* (Phila. 1813); and *A Memorial of . . . Dr. Benjamin Rush Written by himself* (Lanoraie, 1905).

[1] Skeel's *Noah Webster*, i, 369. Timothy Pickering also described the pestilence in a letter dated Philadelphia, Oct. 1, 1793; see Upham's *Life of Pickering*, iii, 55. The letter is at greater length in "Pickering Papers," vol. 35, fo. 177. S. J. Harrison wrote a graphic account of his own case (*The Harrisons of Skimino*, 63).

[2] G. Brown Goode gave some facts as to scientific thinking in the United States in the earlier period in his "Be-

Instead of so doing, they dosed and bled the victim of yellow fever and "peri-pneumonia" and carefully nursed the consumptive in the warmest and tightest room in the house.

One of the greatest scourges of those days was small-pox. Any one familiar with the history of the Revolutionary War realizes what terrible ravages this disease made with the soldiers. The only remedy for it was inoculation, or giving the actual small-pox to a patient in health and under the most favorable possible circumstances. Small-pox came in waves. At its worst it was very fatal, attacking all ranks of society. Inoculation lessened the mortality; but it was always very disagreeable, frequently brought about deformities, and was sometimes fatal. In 1799, Dr. Waterhouse of Cambridge learned of Jenner's discovery of the relation of cow-pox to small-pox and procured some vaccine matter from him. With this he vaccinated four of his own children, and three other members of his family. A month later, these were taken to a small-pox hospital and inoculated. All came out at the end of ten days without any signs of infection. Jefferson was one of the first to welcome the new discovery. He obtained some of the matter from Dr. Waterhouse and caused eighty or ninety persons to be vaccinated at Monticello and vicinity.[1] The belief in the new prophylactic spread very slowly. In 1802, the Boston Board of Health permitted an experiment to be tried on a group of children. Twelve of these had been vaccinated and two others had not had either cow-pox or small-pox. The whole fourteen were inoculated with small-pox, and the

ginnings of Natural History in America" in the *Proceedings* of the Biological Society of Washington, iii.

[1] Letter from Jefferson dated Monticello, September, 1801, stating that he had received vaccine matter from Dr. Waterhouse and had inoculated twenty members of his family, his sons-in-law inoculating sixty or seventy more.

twelve who had been vaccinated, showing no signs of the small-pox, were again inoculated with it. They all remained together in one room, oftentimes sleeping in the same bed, without producing the least appearance of small-pox in those who had been vaccinated. The report of this experiment was published by the authorities and seems to have produced conviction of the efficacy of vaccination.[1]

Doctors went their rounds with lancet and physic.[2] No visit was complete without leaving a vial of medicine, for which the physician charged more ungenerously than he did for his own services. Calomel, jalap, salts, and ipecac with preparations of mercury and opium were administered in combination with bleeding by day and by night. The papers had columns of advertisements of patent medicines, for the taking of these avoided the doctor and his lancet. The list is long and elaborate; from "Bateman's Drops" and "Botanical Tea" to "Dr. Robertson's Celebrated Elixir of Health" and "Dr. Coolidge's Anti-Pestilential Pills." The advertisements ran to column length with statements of virtues and warm testimonials of cures effected. Newspapers all over the country contained them, showing how widespread was the habit of medicine taking. Sometimes they occupied one-half of a page of a four-paged paper or one-eighth of the whole printed space, which would be equiva-

---

[1] See letter of Dr. Waterhouse to President Dwight of Yale, printed in the Norfolk, Va., *Epitome of the Times*, July 7, 1800. The account of the experiment at Boston is taken from the "Report of the Board of Health" of Dec. 15, 1802, printed in broadside. By 1805 doctors in several parts of the country were advertising that they were prepared to vaccinate. There is an interesting account of small-pox in the *Columbian Centinel* of Oct. 28, 1809.

[2] Doctors' bills were left unpaid sometimes for years. Many of them have been preserved and tell how great a part bleeding and purging played in the physician's life. In 1808, Dr. Foushee presented a bill to a Richmond merchant of seventy entries, some sixty were for bleeding or purging. One charge in 1803 was for a night visit for the purpose of bleeding the debtor's spouse, for which a charge of eighteen shillings was made; but a day visit to the sister-in-law for the same purpose was set down at six shillings. These charges were in Virginia currency and were equal to three dollars and one dollar in silver.

lent to five or six pages of a present-day Sunday issue. Of all the patent medicines, none were more persistently advertised and presumably in greater demand than those of Dr. Hamilton. His "Elixir" cured colds, obstinate coughs, and approaching consumption. Luther Martin, the Attorney General of Maryland, gave his testimonial of its worth in relieving him of a "painful and troublesome affection of the breast, accompanied with soreness and obstructed and difficult breathing." Even more efficacious was Dr. Hamilton's "Grand Restorative." It actually cured consumption and melancholy, — in the advertisments, — his "Essence of Mustard" disposed of gout and sciatica, while his "Worm Lozenges" were truly wonderful in their advertised operation. These advertisements are found in papers all over the country, and patent medicines ordinarily formed a part of the stock in trade of the general store-keeper. Next to proprietors of patent medicines, the lottery brokers contributed most largely to the finances of the owners and publishers of newspapers.

Business men and speculators with money and credit found ample uses for their funds in investment in government bonds and bank stock, in land promoting, and in commercial ventures to the far East and to Russia. For those with small sums of money to invest, there were few opportunities before the days of industrial and public service corporations, with their multitudinous bonds and stocks. The small investor and the lesser speculator found in lottery tickets their only chance of gain or loss.[1] Lotteries go back in American history to the beginning of colonization, when the Virginia Company was authorized to secure funds in this

---

[1] The first advertisement of a sale of shares in private corporations that I have seen is in the *Salem Gazette* for March 20, 1812, and included shares in nine separate corporations, one bank, one aqueduct, two turnpike, and five insurance companies.

way. They remained in good public odor until the second
third of the nineteenth century, when the moral reaction of
that time made people look at them somewhat askance.[1]
Washington bought lottery tickets at various times.[2] Jefferson sought to rehabilitate his lost fortunes by selling some of
his lands through a lottery; and Dr. Bentley, of Salem in
Massachusetts, wrote that the building of colleges and meeting houses "seems [to be] a public licence to the clergy for
speculation, which many of them chearfully embrace."[3]
The newspapers contain one advertisement after another of
lotteries, sometimes even three columns of them, and posters
were printed by promoters and ticket brokers, as W. and T.
Kidder and Gilbert and Dean — two enterprising Boston
firms. One issue of the Philadelphia "Aurora" advertised
four church lotteries: the Holy Trinity, the Fourth Presby-
terian, the Second Baptist, the African Episcopal, as well as
the "Lottery for the Encouragement of the Useful Arts."
To this list of church lotteries might be added from other
papers the German Evangelical Reformed Church of Philadelphia and the Catholic Cathedral Church of Baltimore.
Educational institutions found this the most feasible means
of raising money. From Dartmouth College in New Hampshire to William and Mary College in Virginia and Vincennes
University in Indiana, they employed this mode of financial
relief. Turnpikes, as the Bustleton and Smithfield road near
Philadelphia, and canals, as the South Hadley Canal, were
built or dug at the expense of the buyers of lottery tickets.
Money was raised in this way for a monument to Washington

---

[1] The following matter on lotteries is
made up mainly from the newspapers, as
the *Baltimore American* and the *Kentucky Gazette*. See also J. R. Tyson's
*Brief Survey of the Great Extent and evil
Tendencies of the Lottery System* (Philadelphia, 1833); *Picture of a Factory
Village* (Providence, 1833, p. 118), and

A. R. Spofford's article in American
Historical Association's *Report* for 1892,
p. 173.

[2] In 1794, he paid $188.00 for 20
tickets in "P. Fitzburgh's lottery,"
Pennsylvania Magazine of History, xxx,
161.

[3] *Diary of William Bentley*, ii, 97.

and also for the "Society for the Relief of Poor Widows with small children."

A simple form of lottery was that advertised in the "Baltimore American" in 1808 for "A College in Baltimore." In this case there were twenty-two thousand tickets at ten dollars each which should bring in two hundred and twenty thousand dollars. Prizes were offered to this total amount, but fifteen per cent was deducted at the time of payment. This left thirty-three thousand dollars for expenses and the college. The Bustleton and Smithfield turnpike lottery was one of the largest and most elaborate. There were to be eighty drawings in all, three in each week and at least four hundred tickets at each drawing. The greatest prize was drawn on the forty-fifth day, but there then remained several prizes of one thousand dollars or over and the scheme of the lottery provided that the first drawn of the last two hundred and fifty tickets should get a prize of ten thousand dollars. The price of tickets in this lottery started at ten dollars apiece; on the forty-second day it was raised to thirteen dollars, on the sixty-sixth day to fifteen dollars, on the seventieth to twenty dollars, and on the seventy-fifth to thirty. The Harvard College Lottery was perhaps the most widely advertised, even as far afield as Charleston, South Carolina. The record books of some of the drawings of this lottery are still preserved. It went on from year to year, the total amount taken for each class varying from seventy thousand to eighty thousand dollars. Two-thirds of the tickets were doomed to draw blanks; the prizes, going to the holders of fortunate numbers, ranged from six dollars to twenty thousand; the last drawn number taken from the wheel being entitled to five thousand dollars. The expenses of this lottery were deducted from the prizes, the net profit realized in each year being about fifteen thousand dollars. In connection with

lotteries as well as with patent medicines, one comes nearer
to modern advertising methods than anywhere else. In
"Relfs Philadelphia Gazette" for September 7, 1808, "Hope
and Company" invite the ladies, who are not obliged to "consult their cautious plodding husbands" to buy tickets in the
Universalist Church lottery or in the Holy Trinity lottery
and thus gain "one or more of the many dazzling prizes"
which await "the claim of beauty." Brokers sometimes
offered to receive worn-out bills at a small discount or even
approved promissory notes in exchange for lottery tickets.
These glimpses into the past certainly give us a feeling of
queerness; but, before we sit too tight with our consciences, we
would do well to picture to ourselves what those purchasers
of lottery tickets would have thought of Wall Street or of the
Chicago Wheat Pit. It is quite evident that when Washington took the oath of office in New York on the last day of
April, 1789, living and ideas of life were far removed from
ours, materially, morally, and mentally. In actual number
of days, months, and years that time was only a century and a
quarter away, but in essentials that epoch belonged to the
days of Commissary Blair and the Earl of Shaftesbury. In
the quarter century before 1815, the national life was reorganized and the American mind prepared to take advantage
of the opportunities which the application of steam to modes
of transportation and to the moving of machinery were to
place within the people's grasp.

NOTE

I. **General Bibliography.** — The Second Series of Hildreth's *United States* [1] remains to this day the most satisfactory account of the administrations of Washington and John Adams, although written three-quarters of a century ago. The book has no pretensions to literary merit, is a mere annal, and is prejudiced; but it gives the facts accurately and in usable form. The first volume of James Schouler's *History of the United States . . . under the Constitution* (5 vols., Washington, 1880–1891) was printed in 1880, some thirty years later than Hildreth's original edition. In the intervening time a great deal of material had been made accessible. Schouler's sympathies are with Jefferson rather than with the Federalists, but his style is as dry as that of Hildreth. Very different from these books in point of view and in use of material is McMaster's *History of the People of the United States* (8 vols., New York, 1884–1913). As the title implies, this work goes far beyond the merely political and seeks to bring to view the reasons for political action. McMaster used the newspapers with great effect, but, sometimes, without the exercise of the critical care which this class of material peculiarly demands. There is also a certain metallic quality to the style and a lack of variation which makes the book difficult reading in any quantitative manner. As a storehouse and index to material, it is unsurpassed, — but sometimes it is difficult to verify the citations.[2] Of the smaller and more recent books, Professor J. S. Bassett's *Federalist System*, forming the eleventh volume of Albert Bushnell Hart's *American Nation* series, is an excellent piece of work, bearing in mind the limited space at the author's disposal.

[1] Richard Hildreth's *History of the United States from the Adoption of the Federal Constitution to the end of the Sixteenth Congress* (3 vols. New York, 1851).
[2] H. von Holst's *Constitutional and Political History of the United States* (8 vols. including index, Chicago, 1877–1892) enjoyed great vogue when it appeared; but owing to his doctrinaire treatment of our history has since lost favor.

CHAPTER II

ORGANIZATION OF THE GOVERNMENT

THE fourth day of March, 1789, was the time appointed, and New York the place, for beginning operations under the new Constitution.[1] Ever since September, 1788, when the demise of the old Confederation had been settled without reclaim, Congress had led a lingering and stuporous existence. October 10, 1788, was the last time that a quorum of States had attended. Enough members appeared every now and then, thereafter, to go through the form of adjournment and to give Charles Thomson the chance to add a name or two to the roll. The last entry was made on March 2, 1789, and noted the coming of "Mr Philip Pell from New York."[2] For the next week or two

[1] *Resolved*, That the first Wednesday in January next, be the day for appointing electors in the several states, which before the said day shall have ratified the said constitution; that the first Wednesday in February next, be the day for the electors to assemble in their respective states, and vote for a president; and that the first Wednesday in March next, be the time, and the present seat of Congress the place for commencing proceedings under the said constitution. *Journal of the United States in Congress Assembled*, September 13, 1788 (John Dunlap edition, vol. xiii, p. 141).

[2] 1789 Thursday Jany 1 M^r J R. Reid from Pensylvania

Mr R. Barnwell from South Carolina
Thursday Jany 8 M^r A Clarke from New Jersey

Saturday Jany 10 Mr T. Coxe from Pensylvania

Monday Jany 26 M^r N Gorham from Massachusetts

Thursday Jany 29 M^r G Thatcher from Massachusetts

Friday Feby 6 Mr D. Ross from Maryland

Thursday Feby 12 Mr G. Gardner from Rhode island

Wednesday Feby 18 M^r D Gelston from New York

Thursday Feby 19 M^r N Gilman from Newhampshire

Monday, March 2 Mr Philip Pell from New York

On March 9, 1789, Jay wrote to Jefferson (*Diplomatic Correspondence, 1783–1789*, iv, 43) that at no time after

there was no federal government of any kind anywhere. Wednesday, March 4, only twenty-one members of the new Congress were present, eight Senators and thirteen Representatives, not a quorum of either House.   Day after day, and week after week, the members repaired to the Federal Hall, a building that had been made over for their accommodation, but it was not until the first day of April that thirty members of the House appearing, that body organized by the choice of a Speaker.   On April 6, enough Senators answered to their names to choose a temporary presiding officer — whose sole duty should be to open and count the electoral votes. Washington had the vote of every elector and was therefore President; but the second votes of the electors were widely scattered.   John Adams had the next largest number and was, therefore, Vice-President, although he did not get a majority of the whole number of electors appointed.   Two more weeks elapsed ere Washington could be apprized of his election and reach the seat of government.   He had been very unwilling to allow his name to be placed before the electors, as he had hoped to pass the evening of his days in the midst of domestic felicity at Mount Vernon.   He was now in his fifty-eighth year and, after the mode of the day, regarded himself as an old man.   He distrusted his administrative powers.   He was painfully conscious of his financial poverty and realized that only persistent personal oversight of his plantations could place him on his feet.   Hamilton and Madison convinced him that it was his duty to accept the place, because the expectation that he would be the first President was the

October 10, 1788, was there a quorum of the Congress present.   That enough members came to New York to keep the Confederation alive is an interesting example of the tenacity of even the most feeble and undesirable institutions.   At least one of these Congressmen obtained an office under the new government.

one thing that had induced many good people to acquiesce in the ratification of the Constitution. He bowed to the call of duty, borrowed six hundred pounds Virginia money from a neighbor, — at six per cent interest, — paid off his outstanding debts, and with some money in his pocket set out for New York, leaving his household and the members of his family to follow.[1]

From Mount Vernon to New York was one continued ovation. Washington's mansion had hardly faded from sight, when the citizens of Alexandria welcomed their illustrious neighbor. Across the Potomac at Georgetown, an address and a banquet awaited him. Everywhere there were breakfasts and dinners, processions of civilians and militiamen; every now and then the roads and bridges were carpeted and festooned with flowers; singing children, pealing bells, and roaring cannon welcomed him and sped him on his way. At the Jersey waterside, he entered a barge rowed by thirteen ship captains and safely crossed the river to Manhattan Island. He, himself, has told us how his mind was oppressed with anxious and painful sensations when he left Mount Vernon. All these rejoicings only served to deepen the gloom with which he rode forward to

[1] See Washington to Captain Richard Conway, March 4, 1789, in *Pennsylvania Magazine of History*, xix, 325, stating that short crops and other causes incline him to borrow money on interest. He asked for £500. Conway lent him this amount at six per cent on March 6, and on March 13, lent him an extra £100, on the same terms. Washington gave "bonds" to secure the repayment of these sums, which was accomplished in December, 1790. See the "Washington Ledger" in Library of Congress, fo. 299. Of this sum he used a part to pay current accounts at Mount Vernon. He bought a bill of exchange on Baltimore for £100 and one on New York for £205. These with cash in his own pocket, £60 or so that he gave to Mrs. Washington and £20 to Tobias Lear to take him and a servant to New York, used up the balance. From a note in Ford's edition of Washington's *Writings*, xi, 399, it appears that he failed to secure other loans.

In September, 1788, Edmund Randolph wrote to Madison that the scarcity of money in Virginia can hardly be conceived by those dwelling in a large city; "tithable negroes sell under executions for fifteen pounds [Virginia currency] and the approach of british debts thickens the horror of the prospect."

take upon himself the weighty and untried task to which his country had called him.

The inaugural proceedings at New York on April 30, 1789, were fully described by Don Diego Gardoqui, the Spanish minister, in a letter to his chief, the Count Florida Blanca. The State troops, so he wrote, with the "high constable" on horseback, and distinguished gentlemen in carriages, escorted "his Excellency" from his residence to the Federal Hall. Committees of the two Houses led him to the Senate Chamber, where he was received by John Adams, who had already taken the chair as Vice-President.[1] Shortly afterwards the party proceeded to a gallery which opened on the street. There Robert R. Livingston, Chancellor of the State of New York, administered the oath of office, after which he proclaimed in a loud voice, "Long live George Washington, the President of the United States!" Huzzas and acclamations followed, and then salutes, among them fifteen guns from the Spanish ship-of-war, *Galveston*, at anchor in the stream. The party returned to the Senate Chamber, where the President delivered the first inaugural address.[2] Fisher Ames, one of the Representatives from Massachusetts, described this part of the proceedings. The scene, he says, was quite of the solemn kind. Washington's aspect was grave, almost to sadness, and his voice so low as to call for close attention. William Maclay,

---

[1] Adams reached New York on April 20, 1789. On the following day he was met on the floor of the Senate Chamber by Mr. Langdon, who had been chosen Vice-President pro tempore. He conducted Adams to the chair. Washington reached New York two days later. He took the oath of office prescribed in the Constitution on April 30, and delivered the First Inaugural Address. President Washington approved the act to regulate the administering certain oaths on June 1, 1789.

In conformity with this, on June 3, Langdon administered the oath to John Adams as Vice-President. This interesting sequence of events was called to my attention by Mr. H. Barrett Learned, who has studied most thoroughly the details of the history of the administration of our government.

[2] C. W. Bowen (editor), *History of the Centennial Celebration of the Inauguration of George Washington* (New York, 1892), p. 46.

Senator from Pennsylvania, was not so merciful. He thought Washington agitated and embarrassed and described him as putting the fingers, first of one hand, then of the other, into his breeches' pockets, and wished he could have been first in speech making as in everything else.[1] After expressing gratitude to Heaven for watching over American affairs, Washington adverted to the high character of those whom the voters had intrusted with the organization of the government. He made no suggestions with regard to the policy of the new organization, but the question of amendments to the new Constitution evidently aroused great interest in his mind.

George Washington's face and figure are more familiar than are those of any other of our greatest men, — with the possible exception of Abraham Lincoln, — but as to the inner man we are even now strangely ignorant. For fifteen years, Washington lived in public gaze. During the war, he fought and marched over the country from Boston to Yorktown; while President he journeyed up and down the land from Portsmouth in New Hampshire to Charleston in South Carolina. In the course of a busy life, he wrote thousands of letters, military orders, and state papers — of these volumes have been printed and other volumes are accessible in manuscript. He stands in a peculiar place in the World's Annals, as a king enshrined in the imagination and veneration of his people, "unsullied by a throne!" [2] His tall, spare frame and set features are stereotyped on

[1] Seth Ames's *Works of Fisher Ames* (2 vols., Boston, 1854), i, 34 and *The Journal of William Maclay*, 9. This volume was published at New York in 1890. A much less extended compilation from the same manuscripts was privately printed in 1880 at Harrisburg as *Sketches of Debate in the First Senate of the United States, in 1789–90–91, by William Maclay*. The description portions which give life to the history of these years are greatly toned down in the latter, or omitted altogether. Maclay writes that Washington was "dressed in deep brown, with metal buttons, with an eagle on them, white stockings, a bag [for his queue], and sword."

[2] From the ode written to celebrate Washington's arrival at New York.

the American retina. This is the heroic figure, the peripheral man ; when one seeks beneath these exterior shroudings to find the living, breathing, human being, one soon comes to realize that no more elusive personality exists in history.

The turning over of masses of manuscripts, the perusal of countless printed books, yields some human notes ; but they are few. Once, writing to Madison at midnight, Washington complained of "an Aching head" and added, "I am ashamed to send such a letter, but cannot give you a fairer one — G. W.";[1] but this confession of human ailment stands almost alone. Writing familiarly to Jefferson — in those days when the two men trusted each other — Washington referred to himself as "the P." Another time, he informed the Secretary of State that the British minister "starts three to one against you." Stopping one night at a roadside tavern, Washington was assigned to a room with two or three other persons ; on entering, he turned to the next in line, and offered him the choice of beds. At Mount Vernon, he lighted at least one guest to his bedroom with a candle and poked the fire into a blaze before wishing him goodnight. A few stories of tempestuous laughter and fewer tales of righteous wrath complete the list. Otherwise, he stalked impassive through his world, inspiring awe and trust wherever he went.[2]

As a politician, Washington was a strong partisan. He thought that only persons of "sound politics" should be appointed to civil offices or be given commissions in the

1789. It was sung to the air of "God save the King."

> "These shores a Head shall own,
> Unsullied by a throne —
> Our much-loved Washington,
> The Great, the Good."

Clarence W. Bowen's *Centennial Celebration of the Inauguration of George Washington*, p. 29.

[1] "Madison Manuscripts" in the Library of Congress, xiv, 4.

[2] See bibliographical note at end of chapter.

army. His methods were sometimes devious. On one occasion, he directed a correspondent to show his letter to another person as coming from himself and not from the writer; and, on another, he ordered the recipient to "burn this letter!" which was by no means an unusual direction in those days and was disobeyed on this and other occasions. Socially, Washington was a man of his day; wine was served at his table, he had no scruples as to lotteries or land speculations, and lost no opportunity to engage in dancing and other festivities at which the presence of ladies, especially of youthful age, was a necessary adjunct. He was excessively fond of outdoor excursions and had a craving for the sight of strange beasts and abnormal living beings. From 1775 to the end, he made the fullest use of the phrasings and advisings of others, so much so that his identity seems often merged in that of Hamilton or of Madison; but he had a mind of his own, capable of accurate thinking, and of correct expression, more correct perhaps in his later than in his earlier years.[1] He was by no means a man of books, but in his library were technical works on war and agriculture, which he seems to have purchased and certainly studied.

Looking backward and thinking of the long life that the Constitution has enjoyed, and remembering how immediate

---

[1] For example, he wrote under circumstances which make it seem hardly possible that he had help from another, — "The science of figures, to a certain degree, is not only indispensably requisite in every walk of civilized life, but the investigation of mathematical rules accustoms the mind to method and correctness in reasoning, and is an employment peculiarly worthy of rational beings. . . . It is here that the rational faculties find a firm foundation to rest upon." *Catalogue of Washington Collection in Boston Athenæum*, 165.

Washington's library was large in numbers and wide in range. Many of the books were technical works on war and agriculture, as Hanson's *Prussian Evolutions in actual Engagements* (Philadelphia, 1775); *The Manual Exercise as ordered by his Majesty in 1764* (Boston, 1774); Thos. Hale's *Compleat Body of Husbandry* (London, 1758); and Commerell's *Account of the Culture and Use of the Mangel Wurzel* (London, 1787). There were also some works of literature as Smollett's *Adventures of Peregrine Pickle* and Barlow's *Vision of Columbus*.

and great were the successes attending the organization of the new government and Hamilton's financial measures, one can hardly imagine the chaotic condition of affairs that confronted Washington when he took the oath of office in the spring of 1789. The strongest men of the country were behind him: Hamilton, Madison, Robert Morris, James Wilson, and those who had worked with them in the Federal Convention; John Jay, Thomas Jefferson, and John Adams, who had no part in the actual framing of the document; even Patrick Henry, George Clinton, and Samuel Adams, who had opposed its adoption, — all these men and many others in the second rank were anxious to see the new system given a full and fair trial. They cannot be said to have formed a political party, for they were held together by no organic bond, except that of patriotic desire for their country's welfare. The only organized body extending through the country as a whole was the Society of the Cincinnati.[1] This comprised the officers of the Revolutionary armies. Very many of them held offices under the local governments, a large number of which would be merged in the general administration. Alongside were the civilian leaders in the

[1] The Society of the Cincinnati was formed in consequence of proposals that were circulated among officers of the American army, then encamped on the banks of the lower Hudson. It was to be partly benevolent and partly to transmit their glory as a heritage to their descendants. It was this latter function that aroused hostility which took the form of anathema of hereditary orders and everything of the kind, and provoked a considerable literature. The original proposals are printed in fac-simile in F. S. Drake's *Memorials of the Society of the Cincinnati of Massachusetts*, following p. 6; as revised and adopted they are printed in *ibid.*, p. 8, and in many other places. They were again altered and amended to do away with the objectionable features and were adopted in their final form on May 15, 1784; see *A Circular Letter addressed to the State Societies of the Cincinnati*, Philadelphia, 1784. The letter is dated May 15, 1784, and is signed G. Washington, President. It is printed in all the state histories of the Cincinnati. The leading paper in opposition was by Judge Ædanus Burke of South Carolina and was entitled "Considerations on the Society or Order of Cincinnati" and was published anonymously in Philadelphia, 1783. See also *Writings of Washington* (Ford), x, 387 and note on p. 388.

separation from England. These, too, were to a very considerable extent office-holders and many of them were likely to be affected in the shift from the old system to the new. Practically all these men looked toward Washington as their chief and very many of them relied upon him for new appointments upon which their livelihood depended. These men would have rallied to Washington's summons and, in fact, they formed something like a party organization, but it had no directive machinery. It may be said, therefore, that Washington came forward to seize the fruits of revolution — for the adoption of the Constitution was nothing else — without an army at his back, or a political organization supporting him. And among his supporters were many powerful men whose ideas were so unlike his own that a disruption into two political parties was certain. Probably never in modern history has a successful revolutionary leader been so bereft of any tangible means of compulsion as was Washington in April, 1789.

The organization of the general government under the Articles of Confederation, if one can use such a title for so helpless a thing, had been most imperfect. There was a department of foreign affairs presided over by John Jay, but this had been little more than a letter-writing organization; for, in the disjointed condition of government, American ministers abroad had accomplished very little, except to send home voluminous reports of their disappointments. There was a Board of Treasury composed of three members with William Duer as secretary. This was hardly more than an accounting department, registering the amounts due to the States and especially those due from the States, but unpaid. This Board had very little money at its disposal, and at the end of 1788, the treasury seems to have been absolutely empty. There was a War

Department presided over by Henry Knox. He had under his orders a few soldiers on the western frontier, an arsenal with arms and ammunition in it at Springfield, Massachusetts, and some recruits in the State of Connecticut. He also appears to have had a little money at his disposal [1] which had been raised in Connecticut at the time of the Shays Rebellion and had not yet been expended. It formed the only financial resource of the federal government until a few thousand dollars were borrowed from the banks at New York and Philadelphia.[2] Charles Thomson had performed the function of chancellor or Secretary of State, as the custodian of public papers, and as testifying to the genuineness of resolutions and commissions.[3] Putting them all together, there were fifteen or twenty employees of the old government who went over into the new, struggling on for months with little money laid by and no wages coming in. Under the former organization all the machinery for collecting and caring for public moneys had been within the control of the States. With the downfall of the old organization, this collecting machinery came to an end and nothing could be substituted for it until the new Congress should pass an administrative law. There would be nothing to collect until general legislation should be passed and no law could be enforced, until courts were established, and judges and all the ministerial officers

[1] "Knox Papers," xxv, 1, 66, 68, and *Journal of the House of Representatives*, under date of April 15, 1789. For eulogistic reviews of Knox's career, see F. S. Drake's "Life and Correspondence of Major-General Henry Knox" in his *Memorials of the Society of the Cincinnati of Massachusetts*, pp. 91–205, and also printed separately; and Noah Brooks's *Henry Knox, A Soldier of the Revolution*.

[2] For information as to the finances of these early years, see *A Summary Statement of the Receipts and Expendi-* *tures of the United States, from the commencement of the present government to the end of the year 1793. Published by order of the House of Representatives —* and printed by Childs and Swaine.

[3] In informing Washington of his election as President, Charles Thomson described himself as "having been long in the Confidence of the late Congress charged with the duties of one of the principal civil departments of Government." "Washington Manuscripts" in Library of Congress.

of the law — marshals and district attorneys — appointed. Under any circumstances, this would have been a matter of weeks and months. The new Congress, as the successor of the old, in its first days seems to have inherited many of the vices of its predecessor. It was difficult for the Senators and Representatives to realize that they were no longer delegates from the States, for most of them had seen service in the old days. They certainly proceeded with great deliberation in the beginning. When they once got fairly at work, one thing after another thrust itself in to interfere with the speedy passage of the most necessary laws. There were the rules of debate and the modes of addressing one another and the executive officers to be decided. Mingled with those who represented the reactionary or conservative ideas that had predominated in the Federal Convention, there were some ardent radicals. These came to New York full of suspicion and prepared to see potential kings and peers everywhere. Then there was the question of the place of residence for the federal government. This intruded itself at all possible angles and in every possible shape. There was certain to be difficulty in the passing of any financial legislation, for this would at once arouse sectional interests and prejudices, none more violent than those connected with the importation of negro slaves. The revenue bill did not become law until July 4, 1789,[1] and the administrative law was not approved by the President until July 31. The first department to be established was that of Foreign Affairs. It was a continuation of the old department and speedily became en-

---

[1] This is the date on the enrolled bill; in the edition of the *Acts passed at a Congress of the United States of America, begun and held at the city of New York, on Wednesday, the Fourth of March, in* *the Year M, DCC, LXXXIX* and printed by Childs and Swaine, "Printers to the United States," the date of approval is given as June 1, 1789.

larged to include also all those things that had been performed by the Secretary of Congress, with the designation
of Department of State.[1] The act for the establishment
of the Treasury Department, involving the organization of a
whole new system, took a good deal of time and did not
finally become law until September 2. The Judiciary Act
was even more difficult to draft because there were grave
differences in the jurisprudence of the several sections.
Henry Lee, viewing the conduct of affairs from Virginia,
wrote to Knox, his old comrade in arms, that the doings
of the first Congress furnished no ground for hope of prosperity to "the federated nation"[2] and regretted that the
Constitution had not given the President power to dissolve an ignorant and vicious legislature. The framework
of government being outlined by these acts and by others
of similar import, Washington proceeded to organize or
reorganize the official force. For Secretary of State he
picked out Thomas Jefferson, a Virginian like himself and
then minister to France. When Jefferson first heard of
the making of the Constitution, he was greatly alarmed by
the vigor of the proposed government. He thought it
was "setting up a kite [a hawkish bird] to keep the hen-
yard in order." He especially disliked the permanency of
the presidential office, there being no limit set upon the
number of times that the chief magistrate might be
reëlected; for, having viewed stadtholders, kings, and

[1] On the "Creation of the Department of State," see Gaillard Hunt in
American Journal of International Law,
July, 1908; in book form as *The Department of State of the United States*.

[2] Lee's letter is dated Stratford, Va.,
10 Oct., 1789. He asks Knox whether
"the second revolution will produce
half the good predicted by its friends
and whether the eastern conspiracy in
the house of representatives declared

afterwards on the floor respecting the
permanent seat of gov[t] will not prove
the simplicity of associating with them
in a form of gov[t] where they possess a
majority. . . . In as many words
might the member on the floor have
said, spend no more time in discussing
this public question, we have determined to go to —— & no where else."
"Knox Papers," xxv, 13.

princes at close range, he was anxious that nothing of the kind should be instituted in America.[1] As soon as Jefferson realized that the Constitution could be amended by legislative action, he abandoned opposition and advised its ratification.[2] In November, 1788, he applied for a leave of absence for five or six months, that he might return to America and attend to "matters of great moment to others as well as myself."[3] The inefficiency of the old government had prevented the granting of permission to leave his post, so that it was not until a year later that he returned to Virginia. He found Washington's offer of the position of Secretary of State awaiting him. His letters to the President and to Madison clearly show that he would have preferred to return to France, but he yielded to Washington's wish.[4] For the next twelve or eighteen months Jefferson and the President were on intimate confidential terms. In offering this position to Jefferson, Washington

---

[1] Jefferson's first letters were widely used by Patrick Henry to bring about the defeat of the Constitution in Virginia. See Jefferson to Col. Forest, Paris, Dec. 31, 1787 (*Writings of Jefferson* (Ford), iv, 484) ; to John Adams (Nov. 13, 1787, *Diplomatic Correspondence of the United States, 1783–1789*, iii, 337); to Wm. Carmichael (Dec. 11, 1787, *ibid.*, iii, 342) ; to Madison (Dec. 20, 1787, *ibid.*, iii, 347) ; to Carmichael (May 27, 1788. *ibid.*, iii, 410). On the other hand, Jefferson's commendations of the "Federalist" and of Adams's "Defence of the Constitutions," which he declared would be "an institute for our politicians old as well as new," were rather in the nature of compliments. At this time (1788) the Jeffersons and the Adamses were quite intimate.

[2] *Writings of Jefferson* (Ford), v, 2, 4, 5, 7, 8, 19, 25, 53, 77, 82, 89.

[3] *Diplomatic Correspondence, 1783–1789*, vol. iv, 8.

[4] See *Writings of Jefferson* (Ford ed.), v, 56, 107, 128, 134, 140, 143. The letter on p. 140 was written at "Chesterfield," Virginia, Dec. 15, 1789, to Washington, expressing a distinct preference for a continuance in the French mission. See also letter to Madison of January 9, 1790, in "Madison Manuscripts," vol. xvii, fo. 57, in Library of Congress. It is in this letter that Jefferson informed his most intimate friend that he expected with anxiety the President's ultimate determination, adding, "I cannot bring myself to be indifferent to the change of destination, tho' I will be passive under it." At the moment, Jefferson had no feeling of hostility whatsoever toward Hamilton and there is no basis for the surmise that Washington appointed Jefferson to this place to "keep him out of mischief." He would have been politically innocuous in the legation at Paris. H. B. Learned has brought together a mass of references on this subject in his *President's Cabinet*, 115 and 132.

undoubtedly was influenced by his knowledge of Jefferson's tact in dealing with men and by the fact that he already had had experience in a diplomatic station. John Jay would have been the natural appointee to the office, but Washington wished to place him as Chief Justice of the Supreme Court. For the twelve months between the inauguration of Washington and Jefferson's assuming office, Jay transacted whatever foreign business there was to be done.

For the Treasury Department, Washington selected Alexander Hamilton who, with Madison and Jay and himself, had been most responsible for the birth of the new government. The presence of both Washington and Hamilton at New York prevented the interchange of letters like those which have thrown so much light on the appointment of Jefferson. There is a story that Robert Morris, replying to Washington's inquiry as to what could be done with the heavy national debt, answered, there is but one man who can tell you; that is Alexander Hamilton.[1] At this time, Washington was undoubtedly in close intimacy with Morris, and the latter's fame would seem to have pointed to him as the man to organize the new financial department. Washington had lived with the Morrises at the time of the Federal Convention. Even then Morris's creditors were pressing for payment, although he was reputed to be the richest man in America. He also had been unable to secure a settlement of his accounts as Superintendent of Finance. Either one of these facts would probably have prevented Washington offering the position of head of the financial department to Robert Morris.

[1] This is given on the authority of Bishop White, Morris's brother-in-law; see Hamilton's *History of the Republic,* iv, 30. G. W. P. Custis gives this story in a somewhat different form in his *Recollections and Private Memoirs of Washington,* 349.

Next to him, Alexander Hamilton seemed to be the man for the place. His great organizing faculties were well known to Washington, who had already used them extensively. The other important offices were filled by continuing Henry Knox at the War Department, and Samuel Osgood in the Post Office, and by appointing Edmund Randolph, Washington's protégé, as Attorney General.

Washington desired, whether general or President, to consider every question as it arose with the greatest possible thoroughness and from every point of view. The Constitution gave the President power to require the written opinion of the principal officer in each executive department upon any subject relating to that department.[1] With the advice and consent of the Senate, he had the appointing power, and, provided two-thirds of the Senators concurred, the power to make treaties. In the Federal Convention, various propositions had been made for the establishment of some kind of a council, either advisory or executive or both. They had all been voted down, the clauses just noted were the residuum. It was upon these, in connection with another constitutional anomaly, known as the Vice-President, that Washington proceeded to evolve a council that has existed to this day under the inappropriate name of "cabinet," thus suggesting to the country and to

[1] George Mason, Washington's friend and nearest political neighbor, had brought forward a measure for the establishment of a directory or council something after the English model. This had been voted down, but Mason was still eager for the establishment of an elected council. The kind that was established seemed to him to be "the worst and most dangerous of all ingredients in a free country." See K. M. Rowland's *George Mason*, ii, 113, 289.

Charles Pinckney, in his "Observations on the Plan of Government," states that the President "will have a right to consider the principals of these departments as his council, and to acquire their advice and assistance, whenever the duties of his office shall render it necessary. By this means our government will possess what it has always wanted, but never yet had, a cabinet council." This seems to be the earliest use of the word "cabinet" in connection with the new government, and was probably written in 1787; see Max Farrand's *Records of the Federal Convention of 1787*, iii, 111, and Frank Moore's *American Eloquence*, 364.

its members that it has some relation to the English Cabinet which belongs to an entirely different species of government,[1] and has an entirely different evolutionary history. The vice-presidency grew out of the desirability of providing for the succession to the chief magistracy in time of difficulty or danger. At first it was proposed that the Senate should select its presiding officer and that he should succeed the President in case of the latter's death or inability. Difficulties were at once suggested, and in the end it was provided that the person having the next largest number of electoral votes to the President should be Vice-President and presiding officer of the Senate. This arrangement would provide a second officer representing the whole nation and would, moreover, give the smaller States an indirect and slight chance at the presidency. These were the constitutional provisions and ideas that governed Washington in trying to provide something in the way of a council.

At first, Washington seems to have expected to advise personally with the Senate. There were only twenty-two members of that body and the phrase "advise and consent" may have seemed to him to mean what the words usually imply. Twice he repaired to the Senate Chamber with a Secretary and papers, prepared to discuss business with the assembled Senators; but there was so much talking and so much friction that this trial was enough.[2] Again, at a somewhat later time (April 10, 1792), he tried to induce the Senate to promise to advise and consent in advance to a proposed treaty with Algiers.[3] It was suggested that forty thousand dollars should be given to the Algerians to keep them quiet. Washington asked the Senate if this

---

[1] The word cabinet was not recognized by law until 1907.

[2] E. S. Maclay's *Journal of William*

Maclay, 128, 131.

[3] "Washington Manuscripts" in Library of Congress under date.

sum appeared too large to state what lower limit it would approve. This seems to have been the last endeavor to get advice. Washington and later Presidents have had to content themselves with consent or disapproval. In the first two years of his presidency, Washington advised with leading men connected with the government, not only with the executive part of it, but with the Senators, individually, and with members of the House of Representatives. In 1790, when the Nootka Sound controversy raised several critical questions, he asked the opinions of the Vice-President and the Chief Justice in addition to those of the three Secretaries and the Attorney General. On other occasions, the Chief Justice was invited to give advice, but it was given so unwillingly that Washington soon stopped asking it. In a somewhat similar manner, Congress placed some executive functions on the members of the Supreme Court, but after preliminary skirmishing, these withdrew[1] within the fence of their strictly judicial functions.

One of the problems of writers on the American system of government has been to provide something for the Vice-President to do. The Constitution devolves the powers and duties of the presidency upon the Vice-President in case of the removal, resignation, or death of the President, or his inability to discharge the powers and duties of his

---

[1] The Invalid Pension Act of March, 1792, directed the federal circuit courts to decide upon applications for pensions and submit their decisions to the Secretary of War. Within two weeks the Chief Justice with his associates on the circuit court for New York expressed themselves as willing to act in the capacity of commissioners, but protested and asked to have their protest communicated to Congress, and at the next session of Congress another method of dealing with pensions was adopted. In Pennsylvania, the circuit court declined to proceed under the act at all. See Max Farrand's "First Hayburn Case" in *American Historical Review*, xiii, 281.

The Chief Justice and the Vice-President were appointed Trustees of the Sinking Fund, according to the act of Congress; but Jay attended only two or three meetings.

office. Washington was away from the seat of government
a large part of the time, either in his progresses to the eastward or the southward, or else at Mount Vernon looking
after his crops. On all these occasions he certainly was
unable to discharge such of the powers and duties of the
presidential office as required his presence at the seat of
government. Why at such times did not the administration naturally and constitutionally devolve on the Vice-
President? Or was it only in cases of incapacity from
mental or physical illness that he should step into the
first place?[1] At the outset, Washington consulted Adams
frequently. In 1791, at the time of his southern journey,
he directed the three Secretaries to consult together if anything serious should arise and determine whether his return
was necessary, — if the Vice-President were in town, they
were to call him into consultation. These seem to be
almost the only cases in which the Vice-President was
utilized as an administrative officer. John Adams was one
of the most honest and highest-minded men who have ever
been elected to office; but he had infirmities of temper
and habits of expression that made him an unpleasant team-
mate. For this or for some other reasons, those in authority soon ceased to consult him. And for this or some other
reason, when Adams was President and Jefferson Vice-
President, consultations between them soon came to an
end, Jefferson determining to his own satisfaction that his
duties were legislative.[2] By a process of elimination,
therefore, Washington was confined to the Secretaries and
the Attorney General for his advisers. The Postmaster
General was not then, nor for years thereafter, looked upon
as on a footing of equality with these four, although he

[1] There is an interesting series of
articles on "Presidential Inability" in
the *North American Review*, for November, 1881.

[2] *Writings of Jefferson* (Ford), vii,
120.

actually enjoyed in many respects greater influence than
all of them put together, because he had so many offices in
his gift. The year 1793, with the great strain of foreign
affairs, owing to the war between Great Britain and revolutionary France, brought Washington and his leading advisers into intimate working relations. On February 25,
they met at his house,[1] at which time certain questions
were proposed and answers given. Forty-five other meetings were held during that year, and this may be regarded
as the beginning of the Cabinet as an executive council.[2]
Thus was established a council that was not elected, that
was appointed by its presiding officer — with the advice
and consent of the Senate — and was removable by him,
— actually an institutional monstrosity.

The phraseology of the Constitution is vague as to appointments and removals, as it is in so many other matters.
Was the power of removal a part of the general executive
function belonging to the President unless otherwise provided for? Or did it go hand in hand with the process of
appointment and was it shared with the Senate? The
question came before Congress, when the establishment of
a Department of Foreign Affairs was under discussion.
After several days' debate the bill passed the House of
Representatives with an acknowledgment, in so many
words, that the power belonged to the President without
the Senate. When the bill came before the Senate, there
was further discussion. Eighteen members voted on the
question whether the bill should be passed, nine on either
side. John Adams then performed one of the most im-

[1] See "Washington Manuscripts" in
Library of Congress under date of Feb.
23, 1793.
[2] For the origin and history of the
American cabinet system, see Henry
Barrett Learned's *The President's Cab-*
inet (New Haven, 1912); "Some As-
pects of the Cabinet Meeting" in
Columbia Historical Society's *Proceed-*
ings, xviii, p. 95; and "Shall Cabinet
Officers Have Seats in Congress?" in
The Nation, Feb. 11, 1915.

portant acts of his life by giving his casting vote as presiding officer for the passage of the bill [1] and thus made it
possible for the presidency to develop as it did from the
time of Washington to the end of the Civil War.

Any one familiar with the writings of the first ten or
dozen men of that time is impressed by the distaste for public employment that constantly comes out in them.[2] In
the case of Washington, Hamilton, and Jefferson, pecuniary
reasons were undoubtedly at the bottom of it. The salaries
provided by Congress did not repay the expenses of the
President, Vice-President, and Secretaries. In his inaugural address, Washington had declined to receive any
emolument for his services, but had expressed a desire that
his expenses should be repaid. It proved to be more convenient to allot him a settled salary of twenty-five thousand dollars a year, which he might spend or not as he
chose. He was also given the use of furniture that had
already been purchased, and a house, rent free, was provided for him. He used every cent of the twenty-five
thousand dollars and his enemies insisted that he drew
more than the yearly stipend.[3] When he retired from the

[1] For the debate in the House, see
Annals of Congress, 1st Cong., vol. ii,
455 and fol. ; for the proceedings in the
Senate, see *Journal of the First Session
of the Senate of the United States* (New
York, Greenleaf, 1789), p. 65, under
date of July 18; *Works of John
Adams*, iii, 407; Maclay's *Journal*,
109–121. The Vice-Presidents have
given the casting vote 179 times up to
March, 1915; see H. B. Learned's
"Casting Votes of the Vice-Presidents,
1789–1915" in *American Historical Review* for April, 1915, and "Some Aspects of the Vice-Presidency" in the
Proceedings of the American Political
Science Association for 1912, p. 162.

[2] The desire of spending the "evening of life" in retirement was not peculiar to Americans. French pre-revolu-

tionary philosophy may have had
something to do with it as we find
Moustier, the French minister, writing
to Knox that he would fain pass the
remainder of his days "dans un *log-
house* Americain."

[3] October 26, 1795, Hamilton wrote
to Washington as to the attack made
by a writer who signed himself "Calm
Observer" in a recent number of the
Aurora: "Should you think it proper
to meet the vile insinuation in the close
of it — by furnishing for one year the
account of expenditure of the salary"
he, Hamilton, would make the necessary explanation which he did in a
paper with that title. See Hamilton's
Works (Lodge), vii, 81, viii, 364. It
appears from this paper that at one
time an advance had been made to the

presidency, he certainly believed himself to be poorer than when he entered it. His last years were clouded by borrowings from the banks and sales of lands to pay up past debts and even to provide for current expenses. Jefferson had the same story to tell, and the close of his life was financially tragic. John Adams, when he realized that five thousand was to be the vice-presidential fee, cut down his expenses, and with the aid of the "excellent Mrs. Adams" undoubtedly came through the vice-presidential and presidential periods without having incurred debt and probably with money in his pocket. Hamilton remained at the Treasury for rather less than six years and greatly to his financial undoing. His salary of thirty-five hundred dollars did not pay his living expenses, and the stress of his work prevented him from prosecuting his profession. At his death, he was probably insolvent and his friends were obliged to come to the aid of his family; all of which explains his refusal to accept an appointment to the New York senatorship in 1798.[1] Unquestionably, these men were genuinely unwilling to enter the public service, if it could be honorably avoided. They gave their lives, their properties, and their reputations to their country.

Going from these greatest men of their time to those of lesser clay, one is impressed with directly the opposite,

---

President to the extent of $6154, but that taking the years together the total appropriations for the President's compensation had not been exceeded. The "Explanation" was printed in the newspapers of the day. See also "Washington's Household Account Book, 1793–1797" in *Pennsylvania Magazine of History*, vols. xxix–xxxi.

[1] "There may arrive a crisis," he wrote, "when I may conceive myself bound once more to sacrifice the interest of my family to the public call. But I must defer the change as long as possible." "Hamilton Manuscripts" in Library of Congress. At his death his property was valued at $80,000 including a "country establishment" appraised at $25,000. The whole property was unproductive and the debts amounted to $55,000. Considering the difficulty of disposing of the real estate, Oliver Wolcott wrote to Rufus King on July 30, 1804, "It is questionable if the estate can be rendered solvent." A fund was raised by subscription to alleviate the financial distress of his widow and children.

with their craving for public office, sometimes even when the assured income was painfully small. Public office in the olden time was looked upon as a free-hold designed by nature for the care of certain families. This idea came to America with the settlers and held firm place throughout the colonial era. The theory did not depart with the Loyalists. The radicals, who had had slight chance of office, were glad to see the Tories go and helped them off. They seized their offices and adopted their ideas as to office-holding. After having once fed at the public crib, it seemed a perfectly natural thing to continue feeding there. Families remained in office from father to son and grandson. In Rhode Island, there were the Ellerys; in Massachusetts, the Warrens; in Delaware, the McLeans; in Virginia, the Pages; in South Carolina, the Pinckneys. William Ellery, a signer of the Declaration of Independence, was appointed collector of customs in 1790. He held the place until 1820, when he died in his ninety-third year. Not long before his death, he wrote that the office was a very troublesome one and "if it did not furnish me and my children with the necessaries of life, I would resign it at once." As soon as the ratification of the Constitution was known, applications for office began to come in. They were made to Washington, whom everybody expected would be President, and to the actual occupants of office, who seemed likely to continue in their present positions or secure others. The holders of State offices that would cease or would be merged in corresponding federal offices naturally felt anxious as to their future and took to letter writing. Many of these places had been filled for years by one or more members of some family of influence. It seemed to the neighbors that now was the time for a new distribution, and they applied to the most likely person. There was

the case of the collectorship at Norfolk, Virginia. Upon
the approaching demise of the collector, application was
made for the office for a certain Francis S. Taylor, who had
been performing the duties as deputy and was about to marry
the daughter of the dying collector.[1] By succeeding to the
office "the means of comfort and happiness would be afforded the Family" which consisted of "an amiable Lady and
Six children," one of them being the prospective Mrs. Taylor.

The officers of the Revolutionary Army occupied many
of these places, but some of them had no positions of any
kind and very small incomes. These sent in their applications. One of these was from Thomas McKean, a patriot
of the Revolution. Now he had "an ambition to take a
share in Your Excellency's administration" in the judicial
line. He had lost by depreciated "Congress-money" upwards of six thousand pounds which he wished to recover in
some honorable way for the sake of his eight promising
children, — all of whom later, either by themselves or
through their husbands, occupied public offices.[2] Obtaining no place from Washington, McKean continued in
office as chief justice of Pennsylvania and, in 1799, was
elected Democratic governor of the State. General Henry
Knox, Secretary at War under the Confederation, was one
of those marked out by office-seekers for high place in the
new government, and letters came to him, some of them by
no means welcome. One of these was from Mrs. Mercy
Warren, who was once regarded as a famous historian
and was justly feared by her correspondents. She now
wrote that she thought Knox would not forget Winslow

[1] Gaillard Hunt's "Office-seeking
during the Administration of John
Adams" in *American Historical Review*,
ii, 247–254.
[2] Later the McKeans were known
to their political opponents as the
"royal family"; see list of offices held
by them in R. Buchanan's *Life of the
Hon. Thomas McKean, LL.D.*, p. 97.
McKean's application is in *Amercian
Historical Review*, ii, 98.

Warren in the "arrangement of the military department" and confidently sought the position of collector of customs for the "port of plimouth & Duxborough" for Major Henry Warren. With military precision Knox retreated behind Washington, advising Mrs. Warren to send her papers to him direct. Nathaniel Gorham, once president of Congress, desired the place of naval officer at Boston. General Benjamin Lincoln, a Massachusetts man who had held high rank in the Revolution, wrote to Knox that "after forty Years close application to business" he must either get an appointment or begin life anew in the wilderness. He had invested some of the continental certificates, that had been given him in the settlement of his arrears of pay, in wild lands for which there was no sale and he also had some Massachusetts securities for which there was no market. He was appointed collector at Boston and held his office until within two or three years of his death, in 1810. The increase in the value of public securities and lands was so great that ten years later, Lincoln was able to repay Knox for his aid by indorsing his note for fifty thousand dollars.

Washington seems to have laid down in his own mind certain definite principles as to appointments.[1] He took over the old staff in the offices of the Secretaries of Congress, and of Foreign Affairs, and of War, and also provided for the Board of Treasury and its employees. In general,

[1] See Gaillard Hunt's "Office-seeking during Washington's Administration" in *American Historical Review*, i, 270; "The Adjustment of Rhode Island into the Union, 1790" in Rhode Island Historical Society's *Publications*, viii, 104–135. In the "Pickering Manuscripts" are dozens of letters addressed to Pickering after his appointment as Postmaster General. One of these is an application for the postmastership at Boston, but this candidate was willing to take anything else, even the inspectorship of distilleries at Haverhill would suit him. An interesting light is thrown on the whole subject by a pencilled note in Pickering's handwriting on an application for the postmastership at Charleston, S. C., to the effect that the compensation was scarcely sufficient to pay the office rent.

he required applicants to send him letters of recommendation from well-known characters in their States. Practically all of these were friends of the Constitution and favorable to the administration. Undoubtedly a few persons,
who were hostile to the new order of things, were appointed
to office; but Senator Maclay tells us that he could not get
his friends appointed because he was a republican. On
September 27, 1795, after opposition had become crystallized,
Washington wrote to Timothy Pickering that he would
not knowingly appoint a man to an important office "whose
political tenets are adverse to the measures wch the general
government are pursuing, for this, in my opinion, would be
little better than political suicide." [1] Of men of equal
abilities and political soundness, preference should be given
to him against whom the least clamor can be excited. For
this reason, Washington was opposed to the appointment
of persons who had been defeated at the polls, because the
mere fact that a man could not obtain a majority of votes
showed that his constituents were opposed to him on personal grounds. At all events the offices became filled with
friends of the Constitution and of the administration. Not
many new offices were created, but when the positions in
the customs service, post-office, and judiciary that had
formerly been local appointments were included in one list,
the size of it alarmed many persons, among others, Senator
Maclay who declared that before long offices would be provided for the whole Cincinnati.

The desire for government employment with the sure income and the permanence that then went with it did not in
any way diminish as the years went by. The civil service
was filled when the government was transferred from Wash-

[1] "Pickering Manuscripts," xx, 62.   *Washington*, xi, 74, and by Ford in his
This is printed in substance in Sparks's   *Writings of Washington*, xiii, 107.

ington to Adams, so that the latter had no opportunity to reward those who had fought and worked with him. Whenever a vacancy occurred there was no dearth of candidates. In September, 1797, on the death of the treasurer of the mint, no less than ten applicants presented themselves for the place. Four of these are set down as "Dr.," one was a clergyman, one a colonel, and four were untitled. Pickering, who was then Secretary of State, submitted the names to Adams for his selection with some notes that throw a good deal of light on ideas as to qualifications for federal appointments. One of the applicants had no special claim to public office, because he was in "easy circumstances" and was a "warm Democrat." Another had lived splendidly in France, but was a bankrupt, and few of them "are free from stain"; ostensibly he was a Federalist, but evidently not a "warm" one. The clergyman had a parish at Trenton which was too small for his support, and rheumatism prevented his supplying an extra pulpit in winter. He was of unblemished integrity, attached to the present Constitution, and, if he lived in Philadephia, could add to his mint duties by occasional preaching for pay. One of the untitled ones, Mr. Caldwell, was a decided Federalist and of "fair moral character." He was brother-in-law of Pickering's colleague, McHenry, the Secretary of War, and it might be expedient to appoint him. The job was given to Dr. Rush, one of the ten, who happened to be a firm personal friend of the President, although he and Adams disagreed most violently on the virtues and failings of theoretical democracy. Family relationships and connections and personal friendship played their parts and did not stop with the close of Adams's administration. In fact the most remarkable case of the kind occurred in the presidency of Thomas Jefferson, his successor.

John Page of Virginia was the friend of Jefferson's youth, and the recipient of his effusions as to "Belinda,"— one of the loves of his early days. Like most Virginians Page was often in need of funds. While they were both at Philadelphia, he induced Jefferson to indorse a note, which he discounted at the Bank of the United States. Just before this became due Jefferson indorsed another note which Page discounted at the Bank of North America. With the proceeds he paid off the first note, and by this process of alternation, provided for himself and Mrs. Page until a remittance came from Virginia. In 1802, Page being out of place and quite poor, Jefferson suggested to him that the collector of customs at Petersburg would have to be removed on account of the fury of his Federalism. The office was worth from two to three thousand dollars a year. The responsibility was very great; but if one were careful, there would be no danger. He would be glad to appoint Page to this or to some other office. An attack of illness with "vertiginous symptoms" compelled Page to resign this commission before he had entered on the discharge of the duties of this office; and an election as governor of Virginia at the end of the year relieved his financial necessities for a time. In 1806, he was again out of a job and in need of money. Jefferson then appointed him Commissioner of Loans at Richmond. In 1808, Page's health had become so infirm that he discharged its duties with difficulty. Jefferson then suggested that the office might be transferred to his son, Francis, "for your use with an understanding that it should afterwards continue with him for the benefit of the family." The letter found Page on his death bed. Mrs. Page answered it about two weeks before her husband's death. She wrote that Francis Page, who was a son by a former wife, declined to accept the appointment on the terms mentioned by Jefferson. She suggested that Thomas Taylor or Benjamin Harrison, the latter a relation of Mr. Page's, son of the late Governor Harrison, and "educated in Republican principles, to which he strictly adheres," would be willing to accept the office, and hold it in trust for her benefit and that of her children. If this were done, she pledged herself to use the money for that purpose and also to take care of the only one of her step-children who was in needy circumstances.[1] Jefferson nominated Harrison to this office, but the Senate refused to confirm the appointment.[2] The "spoils system," indeed, instead of being an invention of Jacksonian Democrats or Jeffersonian Republicans, was an inheritance from the Federalist Presidents and by them had been built up on colonial and English precedents.

[1] See *Writings of Jefferson* (Ford), viii, 85, 132 and fol. "The Jefferson Papers" in Massachusetts Historical Society's *Collections*, Seventh Series, i, 120; and the "Jefferson Manuscripts" in the cabinet of that Society. See also Dice R. Anderson's *William Branch Giles*, 92; Letter of Margaret Page (wife of John Page) to Thomas Jefferson, dated Rosewell, Aug. 23, 1802, in Library of Congress. This incident truly "deserves to be told at length," as Paul Leicester Ford suggested.

[2] *Executive Journal of the Senate*, ii, 88.

NOTES

I. President Washington. — The traditional Washington is mainly the work of two Scottish men of genius, Gilbert Stuart and Mason L. Weems. The Stuart head as we have it in the Athenæum original has served as a model for countless duplications; but how closely it resembles the actual Washington is extremely doubtful.[1] It certainly is difficult to reconcile the Stuart type of face with the bust by Houdon that is still to be seen, somewhat restored, at Mount Vernon. The Washington of the cherry tree and hatchet comes from the imagination and pen of Mason L. Weems and is a most striking example of the pseudo-historical art which some persons confuse with history. In the original edition of Weems's *Washington* (Georgetown, (1800), the author reproduced the conception of the recently deceased President that he had gained from conversation with the neighbors at Mount Vernon, for he was never personally acquainted with him. The book at once found a market, and Weems, recognizing the opportunity, rewrote the narrative, putting in the " hatchet story " and the rest, that have given to the legendary Washington whatever vivacity there is. The new version appeared in the fifth edition (Augusta, 1806). The book proved very popular and persistent, the seventieth edition being printed in 1861.

The first serious memoir of Washington was the work of Chief Justice John Marshall.[2] It was laboriously compiled from original material and is now regarded as a source rather than as literature. The political portion of Washington's career was treated by Marshall from an exclusively Federalist standpoint. Irving's *Washington* [3] has literary charm, but lacks historical distinction. Many attempts

[1] Charles Henry Hart has contributed notes on the portraits of Washington to *Harper's Magazine* (August, 1896) and *The Century* (April, 1889, p. 860, and February, 1902); and see the "Proem" to his *Catalogue of the Engraved Portraits of Washington* published by the Grolier Club of New York in 1904. It would seem that in the "Lansdowne Washington," the arm and hand were painted from Stuart's own, and his boarding house keeper, a man named Smith, posed for the body and legs; or possibly they represent those of Colonel W. S. Smith, John Adams's son-in-law. All portraits painted after the inauguration were affected by the experiments made by John Greenwood, the dentist.

[2] *Life of George Washington, Commander in Chief of the American Forces, . . . and First President of the United States* (5 vols., Philadelphia, 1804–1807). This was reprinted almost simultaneously at London.

[3] *Life of George Washington* (5 vols., New York, 1855–1859).

have been made to produce something more satisfying to the historical conscience by giving some attention to literary expression and not occupying too much space. None of these attempts succeeded, partly because Washington's career was so long drawn out and so important and so various that it does not lend itself to any brief artistic treatment. Paul Leicester Ford's *True George Washington* best reproduces the man for us ; [1] but it is difficult to enlarge on the social and human side of Washington's career without undue accentuation, for, after all, his life from 1774 to the end was so burdened with weighty cares that it is the serious side that shows us the man as he really was.

Two sets of Washington's *Writings* have been printed, — edited by Jared Sparks and by Worthington Chauncey Ford. Sparks's editorial methods were those of his day and he corrected the matter taken from Washington's letter-books, — as some of the earlier letter-books were corrected by Washington, himself, in his latest years. Sparks deserves the gratitude of all students of American history for his assiduity in collecting material and in making so much of it accessible. Ford's edition of Washington's *Writings* omits some of the matter that Sparks printed and contains other material.[2] W. S. Baker's *Bibliotheca Washingtoniana* contains titles of 502 books, essays, and sketches relating to Washington and printed before 1890. Of these, one might almost say that Theodore Parker's " Character of Washington " is to this day the clearest summation of that great man's career. Possibly the most interesting insight into Washington's home life is to be found in " A Few Pages of an Unpublished Diary of the Polish Poet J. U. Niemcewicz " (*The Century*, New Series, xli, 510).

II. Public Documents. — General A. W. Greely has described the " Public Documents of the Early Congresses with special reference to Washington's Administrations " in American Historical Association's *Reports* for 1896, i, pp. 1111–1248. This has three appendixes, the second giving the most important publications containing reprints and indexes. J. D. Richardson's *Compilation of the Messages and*

---

[1] Two attempts have been made in recent years to depict Washington's private life, P. L. Haworth's *George Washington: Farmer* and Paul Wilstach's *Mount Vernon*. They repeat much of the same matter, but certainly give life to our first President.

[2] For a criticism of Ford's editorial method see Herbert B. Adams's *Life and Writings of Jared Sparks*, i, p. xxxix.

Papers of the Presidents 1789–1897 (10 vols., Washington, 1896–1899), Wait's *State Papers*,[1] the great series known as *American State Papers* in 38 volumes,[2] and the *Annals of the Congress of the United States* serve as guide-posts and indexes to the student; but any one engaged in anything more than superficial research will have to go beyond these volumes, for Richardson, in many cases, did not print the documents accompanying the messages and the two collections of the *State Papers* were censored so that the careful student is obliged to go to the original papers themselves. Gales and Seaton's *Annals of Congress*[3] is a most useful compilation containing, besides debates in the two Houses, documentary appendixes reprinting masses of matter of all kinds so far as such was included in the Presidents' messages and also giving the acts passed during each session; but here again the careful student will go to originals, to supplement and verify all this printed matter.

[1] *State Papers and Publick Documents of the United States;* published under the patronage of Congress and printed by T. B. Wait and Sons, 1st ed., 6 vols. (Boston, 1815); 2nd ed., 10 vols. (Boston, 1817); 3rd ed., 12 vols. (Boston, 1819).

[2] *American State Papers. Documents, Legislative and Executive, of the Congress of the United States. . . . Selected and edited under the authority of Congress* (38 vols., Washington, Gales and Seaton, 1832–1861). Six of these volumes are entitled *Foreign Relations;* one, *Claims;* two, *Commerce and Navigation;* five, *Finance;* two, *Indian Affairs;* seven, *Military Affairs;* two, *Miscellaneous;* four, *Naval Affairs;* one, *Post-Office Department;* and eight, *Public Lands.*

[3] *The Debates and Proceedings in the Congress of the United States; with an Appendix, containing Important State Papers and Public Documents, and all the Laws of a Public Nature* (Washington, 1834–1856, 42 vols.). This is usually cited as *Annals of Congress* from the binder's title; there are 28 volumes to 1815. It is sometimes indexed under the name of Gales and Seaton, the printers and publishers.

CHAPTER III

CREDIT AND COMMERCE

MONEY was the first necessity to the new government. The United States owed between fifty and seventy-five million dollars to creditors at home and abroad.[1] The daily expenses began on March 4, 1789, and went on with ever increasing volume; officials, from the President to the poorest paid clerk, had to be supported, while Senators and Representatives needed to be reimbursed their mileage and paid their daily wage. Many of the Senators had private means, for then, as now, they were drawn from the richer classes of the community; otherwise, few Congressmen and government employees had enough money in hand to pay their living expenses for more than a few weeks. Recognizing this, on April 8, the day on which the Representatives took the oath of office, James Madison, one of the members from Virginia, moved that a temporary revenue should be provided by substantially enacting, as a national law, the propositions made by the Congress of the Confederation in 1783. These had secured the approbation of most of the States, but not being approved by all had not gone into effect. The duties proposed under this plan had been a very low percentage on the value of the goods. The amount of revenue to be brought in by Madison's plan would not be large; but a temporary tariff on this basis might be passed

---

[1] D. R. Dewey's *Financial History of the United States*, § 39. The figures are given in Hamilton's report on the public credit which is printed in many places; among others in *Annals of Congress*, 1st Cong., ii, 1991.

in time to assess the new duties on the spring importations from Europe.

No sooner had the debate begun on Madison's revenue resolution than Thomas Fitzsimons of Philadelphia asserted that specific imposts were more suitable than ad valorem duties. He represented the manufacturing and commercial interests of Pennsylvania. He wished to establish a system to encourage American productions and more especially to "protect our infant manufactures." He moved to substitute certain resolutions embodying his ideas for those that Madison had introduced. This proposal defeated the purpose of Madison's resolution, for no such scheme could be adopted off-hand; but Fitzsimons thought that it would be well to take whatever time was required to formulate a plan that would be in some degree adequate to the situation. He had served with Robert Morris and Alexander Hamilton in the Old Congress, and had acted with them in pushing important financial measures. Morris was now one of the Senators from Pennsylvania, and Hamilton was in New York, although he did not enter office until some months later than the time now under review. Nevertheless, it may reasonably be supposed that Fitzsimons acted in harmony with them.

Madison's and Fitszimons's financial plans were referred to a committee of one from each State, on which their authors represented Virginia and Pennsylvania.[1] The actual framing of the resolutions seems to have been left to Fitzsimons. He took the Pennsylvania tariff of 1785 as a basis. This law had been originally adopted for the protection of Pennsylvania manufacturing industry and had served its purpose well. An effective argument for the passage of a national protective act was now made: Pennsylvania and some other

[1] *Journal of the House of Representatives*, April 11, 1789.

States, while they were possessed of the taxing power, had offered inducements to capitalists to invest their funds in manufacturing enterprises, and this they had done by imposing duties on articles imported from foreign countries. It would be only right to continue this protection now that the States had confided the taxing power to the national government.

As soon as the debate was renewed in earnest, it was evident that the framing of any protective measure and even of any general impost law would be a very difficult matter. It was easy enough for a State legislature to pass such a law, because it represented a limited number of local interests, but a national tariff had to take cognizance of the various industries of the different sections. New Englanders wanted one thing, Pennsylvanians another, South Carolinians a third, and no one of them wished what the others desired. Take molasses and nails, as examples of New England's needs. Her distilleries turned the molasses into rum and the making of nails was a household industry that could be carried on when outdoor work was slack. Enough rum was distilled in New England to satisfy the drinkers of that section and of the others, too, and nails were made in such abundance that they were beginning to find their way into the Middle States. The New Englanders asked for a low rate on molasses,[1] a high rate on competing West Indian rum, and a moderate duty on nails, which, with the freight, would discourage the importation of them from England. The Pennsylvanians had made considerable progress in the working up of the rich iron ores

[1] At one time it was proposed to put a rather high duty on molasses, which aroused discontent in Massachusetts. See Nathaniel Gorham to Alexander Hamilton, Charlestown, Mass., April 21, 1789, in which he states that the people are "alarmed" at the proposed duty. "Hamilton Manuscripts" in the Library of Congress.

of that region.   Their tariff of 1785 had placed an ad valorem duty of ten per cent on British steel and on the rougher forms of manufactured iron.   They now wanted to have a similar duty inserted in the national tariff act and they also wished to have protection continued to textile industries which had already made progress in their State.   The South Carolinians had no distilleries, naileries, iron mills, or manufacturing establishments.   They thought they ought to have protection, if the others had it, and suggested that a duty be laid on all hemp imported for the purpose of encouraging the hemp industry in the South.   All these desires were laudable and each of them was opposed to the interests of the other sections.   The Pennsylvanians and the South Carolinians liked Jamaica rum.   They were using nails every day in the construction of houses and vessels and did not want to pay any more for them than they could help.   The New Englanders and the South Carolinians were united in opposing duties on iron that the Pennsylvanians asked for, because these duties would increase the cost of ship-building in the North and of agricultural implements in both sections.   Finally, the New Englanders and Pennsylvanians had no desire for any duty on hemp, for that would increase the cost of rigging for their ships.   Log-rolling began with the beginning of the government; the New Englanders, if they got the duties on molasses, rum, and nails that they wished, were willing to vote for the imposts that the Pennsylvanians and South Carolinians asked for, and so it was all the way round.   The interests were so diverse that it took months of discussion before the first tariff act was passed.   It was approved by the President on July 4, 1789, and was to go into effect on the first day of the following August.   This law was followed by one levying duties on tonnage (July 20), by another providing the machinery for the collection of duties (July 31), and a fourth establishing the Treasury Department (September 2). All these laws and one to promote the settlement of accounts between the national government and the several States (August 5) were passed before Hamilton became Secretary of the Treasury; but he was undoubtedly consulted as to them all, and they represented his wishes and constructive genius.

The duties provided in the First Tariff Act were very low and they were soon increased to bring in more revenue. The act was not divided into schedules, but the articles were grouped something after the manner of the Pennsylvania law. A few duties may be noticed: that on molasses was two and a half cents a gallon, which may be compared with the one penny duty that was levied in the years just preceding the Revolution [1] and with the duty of ten cents a gallon on Jamaica rum. Seven and a half per cent ad valorem was laid on rough manufactures of iron and one cent per pound on nails and spikes. Upon hemp the impost was sixty cents per hundred and twelve pounds weight, and manufactures of wool, cotton, and linen and other unspecified goods were taxed five per cent ad valorem. A determined attempt was made to levy discriminating duties upon British goods, but this was not successful. The Tonnage Act, however, imposed a duty eight times heavier upon all foreign vessels than it did upon American. This tonnage duty was to be paid upon foreign vessels at every entry into a port of the United States; as American vessels were liable for the duty only once in each year, this clause practically excluded all foreign vessels from the coastwise trade.[2]

---

[1] See the present work, vol. iii, p. 85, note 1.

[2] There has been some discussion as to whether this First Tariff Act can be described as a protective measure. From the debates, it clearly appears that the framers of the law intended that it should work for the

The act establishing the Treasury Department provided that the Secretary of the department should report to either House of Congress on financial matters when required so to do. Alexander Hamilton assumed the duties of head of the Treasury Department in the middle of September. Born in the West Indies on the island of Nevis of Scottish and French parents, Hamilton embodied in his own person something of the ardent temperament and business capacity which one associates with such an origin. He had come to New York to complete his education; and, on the outbreak of the Revolutionary troubles, had ardently espoused the American cause. He had come directly under Washington's eye, had lived in his military family for years, and had greatly attracted him by his mental gifts and his facility in making use of them. Hamilton had no faith in the people, but believed in vigorous government and in rallying to the support of authority all the strongest elements in society by appeals to their interest. He was of too sanguine a temperament to have joined with George Cabot, the first of American conservatives, in "letting the world ruin itself in its own way." [1] On the contrary, Hamilton would have striven, and did strive according to the best of his lights, to rescue the people from the inevitable results of their

protection and encouragement of American industry, and the preamble of the law declares this to be the purpose of the act. On the other hand, the rates were so low that the amount of protection afforded by the law taken by itself was very slight and, therefore, it was not protective in our use of the word. See William Hill's "The First Stages of the Tariff Policy of the United States" in American Economic Association's *Publications*, viii, 559, and his "Protective Purpose of the Tariff Act of 1789" in the *Journal of Political Economy*, ii, 54. On the other side, see H. C. Adams's "Taxation in the United States, 1789–1816," p. 8, in Johns Hopkins University *Studies in Historical and Political Science*, Second Series.

[1] George Cabot held "democracy in its natural operation to be *the government of the worst.*" He thought that no government could be relied on that had not "a material portion of the democratic mixture in its composition"; but it was absurd to suppose that mankind would "cease to act from impulse and habitually act from reflection." These phrases are taken from a letter written by Cabot in 1804, Lodge's *George Cabot*, p. 341.

lack of qualities which were to be found only in "the best" and "the good." It is impossible to overstate the debt of the American people to this far-seeing fearless statesman, but it is well also to remember that he made some of the cruelest political blunders in our history. Apart from administration, Hamilton had extraordinary intuition in forecasting with a statesman's imagination the material development of America. He organized the assets of the nation, calling to his aid all the elements that were in the future to exploit the resources of the country. He was the organizer of exploitation, the originator of monopoly; but he did his work at the precise moment that exploitation needed to be organized and human ingenuity required excitation by hope of monopoly.

When Hamilton took control of the Treasury Department, he found there was a great amount of work to be done in organizing the collecting and disbursing force throughout the country.[1] The difficulties of formulating any plans for dealing with the outstanding debt were most formidable. Hamilton took until January 9, 1790, to consider all the details of the subject and draw up his first report on the public credit. When one reflects that his whole life since coming to man's estate had been passed in the discharge of military duties and in fitting himself

---

[1] Hamilton undertook to manage, not only his own department, but the whole government. In the summer of 1792, he wrote to Washington that Knox would not take his advice as to issuing military supplies and suggested that the President should call for reports on the subject from both the Secretary of War and the Secretary of the Treasury. This Washington did in two letters, embedding his demand for information in each case in extraneous matter. See J. C. Hamilton's *Writings of Alexander Hamilton*, iv, 226, 238, and *Writings of Washington* (Ford),

xii, 152.

Another example of the great interest that Hamilton took in starting the government comes out in a letter he wrote to Rufus King, July 15, 1789, saying that Burr had secured the nomination of Duane for the national Senate to which he was opposed because "some very unfit character [possibly Burr] would be his successor." Rufus King was chosen somewhat later. On the retirement of General Schuyler, Hamilton's father-in-law, at the end of the second year, Burr was elected his successor.

for the practice of the law and that he had no personal
experience with the administration of financial affairs, this
report is certainly a most remarkable document. There
is no doubt, whatever, of the great influence exercised upon
him by a study of the English financial system as it had been
developed up to that time by William Pitt. In point of
fact that system was the only successful working financial
machine in existence, and it must be remembered that the
tremendous strain of the French wars had not then induced
Pitt to adopt some of the hazardous schemes that were
later connected with his name.[1] After some preliminary
observations as to the diffidence he felt in his own qualifications, Hamilton adverted to the necessity of borrowing
that a modern nation must face and to the necessity, therefore, of maintaining the public credit.[2] It merited particular attention, he said, that among the most enlightened
friends of good government are those who had the most
confidence in the good faith of the American people. After
this opening, he went on to consider the case of the United
States. The foreign debt amounted in principal and interest to nearly twelve million dollars. This must be provided
for, according to the precise terms of the contracts relating
to it. There was no difference of opinion on that subject.
The principal of the domestic debt, or that which had been
contracted at home, amounted to more than twenty-seven
million dollars, and the accumulated unpaid interest to
thirteen millions more. Besides this, there were two millions of "unliquidated claims," bringing the whole amount
that was owed at home to over forty-two millions, and with

[1] On this subject, see Charles F.
Dunbar's "Some Precedents Followed
by Alexander Hamilton" in the *Quarterly Journal of Economics*, iii, 32.

[2] *Report of the Secretary of the Treas-*

*ury . . . for the Support of the Public
Credit of the United States* (New York,
Childs and Swaine, 1790); reprinted
without date in *Annals of Congress*,
1st Cong., ii, 1991–2022.

the foreign debt to something like fifty-four million dollars
in round numbers. Besides these obligations which had
been inherited from the Confederation, there were the debts
of the individual States. These amounted to some twenty-
five millions of dollars, principal and interest. Hamilton
thought that the whole debt, including the State debts,
should be taken care of by the national government. There
should be no discrimination anywhere. Some persons
thought that the original holders of the domestic debt
should receive preferential treatment in comparison with
that accorded to recent purchasers. Among those to hold
this opinion was James Madison. He and Hamilton had
worked together harmoniously and successfully to bring
about the establishment of the government. Now they
disagreed. The Secretary was opposed to any preferential
treatment being given to the "primitive possessors" of the
public securities. The present holders of the certificates
had acquired them in conformity with the provision contained in each certificate that the amount was payable by
the United States to the first holder or to his assignee. To
pay the latter less than the former would be inconsistent
with justice and a breach of contract. Another point that
had been urged in the public prints was that the overdue
and unpaid interest had less claim to consideration than
the original capital. Hamilton insisted that the accrued interest should be regarded as equally entitled to fair treatment with the principal. The credit of the United States
would be firmly established only by funding the whole
amount, principal and accumulated interest together.
Moreover, the Constitution itself provided that all debts
contracted and all engagements entered into before the
adoption of that instrument "shall be as valid against the
United States under it, as under the Confederation." The

national debt was the price of liberty, the public faith had been repeatedly pledged for it. Moreover, a properly funded public debt answers most of the purposes of money, for the public stock passes current as specie. As to the assumption of the State debts, Hamilton contended that the establishment of the national credit required that also. The central government was even then taking possession of the taxes on goods imported, which had hitherto been collected by the States and had formed one of the most fruitful sources of revenue. It was only right, therefore, that it should also assume the responsibility of the State debts. If this were not done, the States would compete with one another and with the United States to seek new sources of revenue from which these obligations might be met, — such competition would injure the credit of the national government and of the States also.

Probably not one Congressman in ten had come to New York with any other expectation than that of scaling down the public debt. Continental loan certificates had sold as low as three shillings eight pence in the pound as recently as January, 1786, — that is, within four years of the date of this report. Since then, they had risen rapidly, but had sold for eight shillings in the pound in 1789. Why would it not be possible to make some arrangement by which the government could issue new bonds for the old certificates at the highest price that they had brought in the market before some given date, say before January 1, 1790? To many members of Congress and to the people at large, Hamilton's proposition to fund the domestic debt and the arrears of interest at the face value of the certificates and the interest indents seemed to be an act of quixotic generosity, to be in the nature of a free gift to speculators and capitalists. Hamilton had declared the public credit to be a nation's most precious possession, and that the ability to borrow money in time of necessity might be equivalent to salvation. After a great deal of discussion, it was decided to fund the whole of the old Continental debt, including accrued interest to the actual possessor at its face value.

The burden of interest on the new securities would be heavy, especially until the new national taxing system should be fully established and the commerce and industry of the country should begin to develop under the stimulus of the new conditions. Hamilton, therefore, proposed various schemes to avoid paying full interest on the whole sum at once. Terminable annuities might be issued, part of the debt might be funded in land warrants, or interest might be deferred on a portion of the debt. Land warrants did not appeal to the members of Congress, but they adopted in effect one of the Secretary's alternative propositions. This was to fund two-thirds of the principal of the domestic debt in six per cent stock on which no more than eight dollars on the hundred of the sum mentioned in such certificate could be paid in any one year, including principal and interest. On the other third, interest would not begin until 1800, and the accrued interest should be funded in full, but with interest at three per cent.[1] There was a fair amount of agreement as to these points in the funding scheme after they had been thoroughly discussed; but as to the assumption of the State debts, the Houses were more equally divided.

The assumption of State debts by the general government was no new matter. As far back as the Revolutionary War itself, Congress had recognized that the interests of the States and of the Continent were inextricably bound

---

[1] Sections 4 and 5 of the act of Aug. 4, 1790 in *Annals of Congress,* 1st Cong., ii, 2245, and *Statutes at Large,* etc.

together. Commissioners had been appointed to settle
the accounts between the United States in Congress Assembled and the several States, and in 1784 elaborate rules
had been drawn up for their guidance.[1] The matter had
come up in the Federal Convention and a proposition had
been brought forward that the general government should
provide for the State debts as well as for the debts of the
Union.[2] This had been opposed because it did not extend
far enough, — to the repayment of all that "the States
had sunk, as well as that which remained unpaid."[3] It was
also thought that it would be well to make the matter one
of administration, instead of putting it into the Constitution and thereby increasing the "obstacles to its reception
on collateral details."[4] The commissioners on accounts
had been working over the matter, but so far without any
very tangible result. Hamilton now proposed that the
United States should assume such part of the debts of the
States as should before a certain day be subscribed towards
a loan to the United States.[5] In other words that it should
assume whatever portion of the State debts should be converted into United States securities. Whatever sums were
thus converted should be charged in the final settlement
against the respective States.

The question of assuming the State debts or portions of
them soon took on a distinctive sectional phase. The States
that had the largest unpaid debts were Massachusetts and
South Carolina. On the other hand, Virginia and New

---

[1] See *Journal of the United States in Congress Assembled*, ix, 305–308.

[2] See Farrand's *Records of the Federal Convention*, ii, 322, 327, 328, 352, etc., using index.

[3] Speech of Elbridge Gerry in the House of Representatives, Feb. 25, 1790 in Farrand's *Records of the Federal Convention*, iii, 361.

[4] Alexander Hamilton to Edward Carrington, May 26, 1792 in Farrand's *Records of the Federal Convention*, iii, 366. My attention was called to this and the preceding citation from Far-rand's *Records* by Mr. Frederick E. Malick of Shamokin, Penn.

[5] Hamilton's "Report," *American State Papers, Finance*, i, 18, 25; *Annals of Congress*, 1st Cong., vol. ii, 2001, 2021.

York had very small debts remaining unpaid, while Pennsylvania's debt was not large. It seemed to the Virginians that if the assumption were carried out, they would be taxed to pay a part of the interest and, ultimately, a part of the principal of the debts of Massachusetts and South Carolina and the other States that had balances to their credit against the United States as a whole. The Pennsylvanians calculated that they would receive about as much as they would be called upon to pay out and therefore took little interest in the matter. Congress had already in the first session provided for the continuance of the commission to ascertain and settle the accounts between the national government and the States. Why not wait until this commission completed its labors and then assume only the amounts that were then due from the United States to the several States? The answer to this was ready: that any such putting off the day of assumption would tend to keep down the price of the State securities, which would in that case pass into the hands of foreign capitalists who could easily afford to buy up these obligations at a low rate and keep them until they should appreciate. A similar argument was also advanced against all propositions to provide a low rate of interest for the national securities. Four per cent had been thought of, but any such low rate would prove reasonably attractive to foreigners, but would not be attractive to home investors. In order to keep the securities in America, it was essential that they should at once command a good price in the market, and this could only be accomplished by making them attractive to home investors. In the act as passed, it was provided that two-thirds of the principal of the domestic debt should be funded at six per cent and should be irredeemable except that the government might at its pleasure pay off in each year two per cent of the face value of the bond. This payment was not obligatory upon the government, but, on the other hand, confining the amount that could be paid on the principal to only two per cent per annum, guaranteed a reasonably long life to this part of the debt. The objection to the plan was that it was in reality the creation of eight per cent annuities which would cease in 1818, provided the government was able to make full payments in each year. It was really a "wasting security" because unless the holder promptly each quarter reinvested the portion of the principal reimbursed, he was insensibly consuming his capital without being fully aware of the fact.[1] The other third of the principal of the domestic debt should likewise be funded at six per cent, but no interest should be paid until 1800. The arrears of interest were to be funded with interest at three per cent and without any provision for redemption, leaving it to the government to purchase them whenever it could, at whatever price the holders would part with them. Congress refused to accept Hamilton's assumption plan in the form in which he proposed it; but the bill contained a provision for the assumption of a certain sum for each State amounting in all to over twenty-one millions. The amounts allowed for the several States were the result of bargaining, and were equivalent to giving a douceur to the States that had small balances in their favor. Holders of State securities could exchange them for United States bonds —

[1] The way in which this provision might work was pointed out in a letter from Oliver Wolcott, dated March 8, 1796, from which it appears that the principal might be extinguished in 1818 or 1819, by yearly payments of eight dollars on each one hundred dollars of face value. This process of extinguishment was so insidious and so invisible that Gallatin proposed to stamp on the face of each certificate as it came into the hands of the treasury officials "the true amount of the annuity due, and of the time when it shall cease." See *American State Papers, Finance*, i, 404; ii, 213. These documents may be conveniently consulted in Jonathan Elliot's *Funding System*, which is printed in the *House Executive Documents*, 28th Cong., 1st Sess., vol. ii.

provided they accomplished their purpose before the State's quota was exhausted. This was only part of the consideration that was paid for the passage of this act; the other portion consisted in a southern location of the federal capital and in yielding to the Southerners on the subject of slavery.

The slavery question had interjected itself into the debates of the Federal Convention. To placate the Southerners, the slave trade had been permitted until 1808, and to please the Northerners, Congress had been authorized to levy a small tax upon imported slaves, not exceeding ten dollars a head. The proposition was now brought forward to levy this duty. The South Carolinians and Georgians most vehemently opposed this, and its advocacy by some of the Virginia members did not in any way lessen their wrath. The matter was put aside, but it undoubtedly helped to increase sectional animosities. Much more important at the moment was the dispute over the location of the seat of government of the infant republic.

Nowadays, the precise location of the federal offices and of the halls of Congress does not much matter. If so much money had not been expended in buildings and monuments at Washington, it is conceivable that there would be no violent objection on the part of dwellers on the Atlantic slope to Congress holding its deliberations in the Mississippi Valley, or even in the heart of the Rockies. In the days of which we are now writing, the subject seemed to be of great importance. It was partly a matter of sentiment. Other nations had capital cities; Britain had its London, France its Paris, Russia its Petrograd. Why should not America likewise have its centre of government, art, and social life? As far back as the days of the Revolutionary

War,[1] when Congress could not provide the means for meeting everyday expenses, propositions had been made for the establishment of the seat of government outside of any existing large municipality.[2] Later the disorderly behavior of some Pennsylvania soldiers had driven Congress from Philadelphia to Princeton in New Jersey. There the members found themselves straitened for accommodations, and the place was exceedingly inconvenient for the few representatives of foreign powers who then attended the motions of Congress. The next move was to New York, and there Congress was when the Constitution was ratified. A lively debate had arisen over the question of holding the first meetings of the new Congress at some other place, but the expense of removal had forbidden this and procured for New York the honor of the first inauguration. Congress had appointed March 4 as the day to begin operations under the new instrument. Why so inclement a date had been picked out remains still a mystery. Travelling by sea in a coasting schooner in the last week in February and the first week in March from Savannah, Charleston, Newbern, and Norfolk to New York was not lightly to be undertaken by a Congressman journeying alone and was still less desirable for his women people, children, and servants. By land the journey was somewhat safer, perhaps, but not much more agreeable, whether made by horseback or by stage-coach. The roads were likely to be fully as bad at this time of the year as they were in mid-winter, when Jef-

[1] In 1783 Jefferson, writing to General G. R. Clark from Annapolis — where Congress then was — describes an intrigue not unlike that of 1790. *American Historical Review*, iii, 673.

[2] The early history of propositions looking toward a permanent residence is traced in detail with abundant citations by Wilhelmus Bogart Bryan in his *History of the National Capital*, i, ch. i. On May 10, 1787, a motion was made in Congress for the erection of public buildings at Georgetown on the "Potowmac" for the accommodation of Congress, that being "a permanent situation most central to all parts of the union." *Journal of Congress*, xii, 75.

ferson was obliged to abandon his horses and take to the
stage between Alexandria and Philadelphia. The New
Yorkers had made great preparations for the entertainment
of the Congress and executive officers, but New York does
not seem to have been a very comfortable place of residence.
The old town had been badly wrecked by fire during the
war, and the more eligible residential places were outside
of the thickly inhabited region. Moreover, board and
lodging were expensive at New York in comparison with
Philadelphia and with southern towns like Williamsburg
and Charleston. Sentiment, convenience, and personal
economy all urged some other location and some location
to the southward of Sandy Hook. Had this matter come
up by itself, the New England members of Congress would
no doubt have been glad to further the convenience of Southern Representatives and Senators; combined with threats
of disunion over slavery and with charges of undue grasp-
ing in the matter of assumption, the Northerners were not
inclined to do anything to meet the wishes of the Southerners. At this point the Pennsylvanians entered into the
fray with a proposition for making Philadelphia the temporary seat of government at any rate. Place after place
was now suggested in combination with a few years on the
Delaware. The Southerners plainly desired to have a
capital city built on the banks of the Potomac; the New
Englanders would have preferred the Susquehanna. In
the midst of the discussions over assumption, slavery, and
the site of the capital, Representatives appeared from North
Carolina and gave the majority to the Southern side.

North Carolina and Rhode Island had resolutely refused
to come into the new confederation. In the case of the
former, there seems to have been no real reason for holding
aloof, apart from the fact that ratification had been advo-

cated by politicians who were, for the moment, not in the ascendency. The Rhode Islanders, on the other hand, were disaffected, owing to the unpleasant way in which their financial policy had been received by neighboring States. Rhode Island radicals had overreached themselves in almost every way and were now reaping the results. It was not until a bill had actually passed the Senate prohibiting all commercial intercourse with that State and calling upon it for a prompt payment of its portion of the Continental debt, that it ratified the Constitution on May 29, 1790, but only by vote of thirty-four to thirty-two.[1] North Carolina had already come into line in the preceding November, her representatives reaching New York in June (1790), just in time to turn the majority of the House of Representatives against assumption.

In the final settlement of assumption and the national residence, there was a good deal of intrigue. The whole story has never been told and probably never can be. A few facts that have come out in the publications of letters and diaries are certainly suggestive of the motives of our ancestors and of their modes of transacting business. In May, 1789, John Adams wrote to Dr. Benjamin Rush that he saw no unusual symptoms of corrupt influence in New York.[2] His eyes were not so keen as those of Senator Maclay, or it may be that, having no financial interest in the matter, he did not fully realize what was going on around him. Maclay's "Journal" has several entries as to bargainings. On June 14, 1790, he recorded that, on the preceding Friday, Jackson, of the President's family, and Coxe, of the Treasury, had been to see Clymer and Fitzsimons to negotiate a bargain giving Pennsylvania the

[1] See F. G. Bates's *Rhode Island and the Formation of the Union*, p. 200 (Columbia University's *Studies in History,* *Economics and Public Law,* x, No. 2).

[2] *Old Family Letters copied for Alexander Biddle,* Series A., pp. 34, 35.

capital in return for votes for assumption.[1] He relates that
Robert Morris thereupon made an appointment with Hamilton to meet him as if by accident. The meeting came off,
and Maclay said that Hamilton offered to give the permanent residence to Pennsylvania, if Morris would procure
him one vote in the Senate and five in the House for the
assumption. The next day, Maclay entered in his journal
that Morris had a communication from Mr. Jefferson suggesting a temporary residence at Philadelphia for fifteen
years and a permanent residence at Georgetown on the
Potomac. Fifteen days later Rufus King, then Senator
from New York, made a "memorandum" to the effect
that during the interval of voting on assumption, a bargain
had been made between Pennsylvania, Delaware, Maryland, and Virginia by which the capital was to be at Philadelphia for ten years and afterwards to be located permanently on the Potomac.[2] Later, he says that Hamilton
informed him that the combination was likely to fail, owing
to an apprehension that the assumption could not be carried.
Jefferson's own account of his part in the affair gives one
the impression of guileless simplicity and general gullibility
that one does not usually associate with him. He represents himself as on his way to the President's, when, by
chance, he came across Hamilton, who walked him "backwards & forwards before the President's door" and for
the first time he learned of the critical condition of the proposed assumption law.[3] Jefferson had not favored assumption, but had recognized the necessity of passing the measure for the preservation of harmony and union. He now
suggested that Hamilton should dine with him and discuss

[1] William Maclay's *Journal*, 291,
292, 321, 333, etc. (index under "Residence bill").

[2] Charles R. King's *Life and Correspondence of Rufus King*, i, 383, 384.

[3] Jefferson's "Anas" in his *Writings*
(Ford), i, 162–164; and vi, 173. Neither
of these accounts is contemporaneous,
so far as is known.

the political situation with some of the Virginia members. Hamilton came. The dinner proved successful. Two Virginians changed their votes on assumption and Hamilton rounded up enough New Englanders to carry the Potomac site for the national city.[1] Whichever account is true, that of Maclay written at the time, or that of Jefferson, probably written years afterwards, it is certain that the assumption-national city deal went through. It does not appear that the change of the two Virginia votes on assumption was essential to the carrying of the measure; but it may be noted that the assumption as passed "removed almost the whole of her [Virginia's] outstanding debt."[2] It is also certain that Jefferson never forgave himself for having thus contributed to the consummation of this part of Hamilton's plan for building up an energetic government under the Constitution,[3] even though, by doing this, he secured what was most dear to Virginia hearts, the placing of the federal city on the banks of the Potomac.

The first part of what slowly developed into Hamilton's complete financial scheme was thus in great measure adopted. Congress, however, had not been willing to authorize levying as large excise duties on distilled liquors as he had wished, and the rates provided in the first tariff were too low to bring in much revenue. Owing to the slowness with which governmental machinery was organized and to the delays that necessarily took place in the conversion of the old debt into the new, it was impossible to begin the payment of interest on the new obligations for some time. The smallness of the revenue, for the moment, mattered little; but,

---

[1] The votes on assumption are tabulated by Professor Orin G. Libby in "Political Factions in Washington's Administrations" in the *Quarterly Journal of the University of North Dakota*, iii, 298.

[2] W. F. Dodd's "Virginia Finances, 1776–1790" in *Virginia Magazine of History*, x, 370.

[3] Jefferson to Washington, September 9, 1792, *Writings of Jefferson* (Ford), vi, 102.

with 1791, when the payment of interest would begin, and especially, with 1792, when the payment of interest on the assumed State debts would begin, more funds must be provided.[1] Moreover, a part of Hamilton's scheme contemplated the early redemption of a portion of the public debt to form the beginning of a sinking fund. By an act passed August 10, 1790, the rates levied on about half of the commodities by the first tariff were considerably increased, experience having shown that with the establishment of a national customs service the irregularities of the old State services could be avoided. In the autumn of 1789, Hamilton and Madison had exchanged ideas on the subject of supplementary taxes. Madison suggested an excise upon home distilleries regulated according to size and an augmentation of duties on imported liquors or a land tax. He wrote that a general stamp tax would be obnoxious to prejudices that were not yet worn out and, therefore, does not seem to have advised any such being established. Madison hoped that some part of the domestic debt might be extinguished by the sales of western lands and thought that at all events it should be put in a manifest course of extinguishment or it would pass into the hands of foreigners. Hamilton had suggested an excise on distilled liquors in his report on the

[1] SOME EXPENDITURES OF THE NATIONAL GOVERNMENT

	1791	1792	1791–1796
War Department	$ 632,804	$ 1,100,702	
Interest on Debt	1,177,863	2,373,611	
Total Expenditures of National Government	3,134,150	8,324,400	
Average Annual Expenditures .			$ 5,854,172

This table is compiled from "Expenditures of the United States Government 1791–1907" (60th Cong., 1st Sess., Sen. Doc. No. 528), pp. 7, 39. This was prepared by the director of the census in 1908, and printed by order

funded debt, but Congress had refused to accept that part of his plan. In December, 1790, he returned to the matter in a second report on public credit. He argued powerfully in favor of a modified tax on domestic distilled liquors, coupled with additions to the duties on imported spirits, and argued against the attempt to levy a land tax. This seems to have been a favorite idea with the Congressmen from the uncommercial States. They pointed to England as a country where a tax on land had worked exceedingly well and for a long time. Hamilton was able to point out that in a new country there was no such stability in land values like that which made the collection of a tax of this kind in England so economical and so easy. In answer to this report, which also set forth the urgent need of more revenue in the immediate future, Congress passed an act (March 3, 1791) providing for the assessment and collection of internal revenue duties on distilled liquors and also for additional duties on imported spirits.[1] As no one had any experience with the levying of taxes of this kind in America, the mode prescribed proved to be impossible of execution; it had to be modified a year later,[2] and even then brought on an insurrection in western Pennsylvania and western Virginia. The revolt of the western frontiersmen was no unmixed evil, although it occurred at a very critical time in our relations with Great Britain, because it enabled the federal government to show its power and to prove that

of the Senate. These figures do not show the whole expenditures as we would regard them nowadays, because at that time and for many years thereafter the local custom collectors and other officials were paid by fees. A table of these fees is given in Thomas Cooper's *Some Information respecting America*, 175. Necessarily under such a system the compensation of collectors varied greatly. Owing to the different modes of compensation and of bookkeeping no valid comparison can be made between these figures and later ones.

[1] *Statutes at Large* (ed. 1850), i, 199; *Annals of Congress*, 1st Cong., vol. ii, 2320.

[2] Act of May 3, 1792 in *Statutes at Large*, i, 267; and *Annals of Congress*, 2nd Cong., 1374.

it was no mere rope of sand that could be easily dissolved.

Hamilton's original plan had provided for something in the way of a "sinking fund." Provision was made looking toward the immediate extinguishment of a part of the debt by the first Congress. This was done by handing over to a committee, comprising the Chief Justice, the Vice-President, the Secretaries of the Departments of State and Treasury, and the Attorney General, whatever balance should remain after providing for the appropriations of the year and also two million dollars that were to be raised by loan. These sums were to be applied under the direction of this committee or commission to the purchase of public securities. When bought, these securities were not to be cancelled or destroyed, but were to be held. The interest on them was to be used to repay this loan and then to buy other securities. Whatever the virtues or defects of a sinking fund may be or may not be, this arrangement at this precise time had very great advantages. As soon as the United States stepped into the market for the purchase of its own bonds, it greatly accelerated the progress of those securities towards par, and thus prevented them being absorbed at a low rate by Englishmen and Dutchmen. All in all the success of the plan so far was remarkable and was so remarkable as to arouse the envy of those who for one reason or another were not its beneficiaries. This is well put in an anonymous note to Hamilton saying that the funding system is "as much abused as if it were criminal in a Government to provide for the payment of a Nation."

So far, Hamilton's plan of providing a living capital for that which was dead had borne fruition. His further task was to make this capital active or fluid by providing a nation-wide banking system. At the moment there were only three banks in the country: at Philadelphia, New York, and Boston, although a fourth was on the point of starting at Baltimore. The combined capital of these institutions was about two million dollars. If a national bank should be established with branches in the more important centres of commerce and industry, the transaction of business of all kinds would be made very much more easy, the collection and disbursement of government money could be carried on much more conveniently and with much less disturbance, the hidden hoards of the country would come to light, and foreign capital would be induced to cross the Atlantic to take part in building up the financial fabric that would surely follow the successful establishment of such a national institution. Until this were done no rapid development of the country's resources, no great increase in manufacturing, no rapid and substantial settlement of the lands on the frontiers could be expected. Finally, the acceptance of United States securities instead of money for a portion of the subscriptions to the capital of the proposed bank would greatly help to increase the selling price of government bonds and also interest the conservative portion of the community in the stability of the new federal government.

Hamilton signed his report on the national bank on December 13, 1790.[1] Following his usual method, he began with a recital of the utility of such an institution and then took up the arguments that might be advanced against him. These were the increase of usury, the temptation to over-trading, and giving a fictitious credit to bankrupts. He was confident that these disadvantages would be found to be less than they appeared, and would be more than

---

[1] See *American State Papers, Finance*, i, 67–76; *Annals of Congress*, 1st Cong., vol. ii, 2032–2059.

counterbalanced by the advantages which would follow the creation of such an institution. The proposition to establish a national bank resembling in great measure the Bank of England aroused as great an interest in Congress as the proposal to assume the State debts had brought forth. The project was finally passed by both Houses in practically the form that Hamilton had suggested and came before Washington for his approval (January 20, 1791). So loud had been the clamor that the President felt doubts as to the power of Congress to incorporate such an institution. He called upon the heads of departments and upon the Attorney General for their opinions. Those given by Jefferson and Hamilton [1] remain to this day among the most important expositions of our constitutional law and practice. Jefferson objected to the measure, because it formed the subscribers into a corporation and established something approaching a monopoly. He considered the foundation of the Constitution to be laid in the Tenth Amendment, which, by the way, was not yet adopted.[2] The language of this amendment, that all "powers not delegated to the United States by the Constitution, nor prohibited by it to the States, are reserved to the States respectively, or to the people," is worth noting, nevertheless, as both Hamilton

[1] Jefferson's opinion is dated February 15, 1791, and is in the "Memorial edition" of his *Works*, iii, 145; Hamilton's is dated February 23, 1791 and is in Lodge's edition of his *Works*, iii, 180.

[2] There is some question as to when the first ten amendments went into force. August 8, 1791, Jefferson wrote to Christopher Gore, stating that he understood Massachusetts had ratified some of the amendments. If this was so, those amendments would be in force, as Massachusetts, being the tenth State, would make the necessary three-fourths (*Documentary History of the Constitution*, v, 244). Virginia ratified the first amendment November 3, 1791. This amendment therefore was certainly in force on and after that day. Some writers, as Farrand in his *Framing of the Constitution* (p. 252), say that these amendments "appear to have been in force" from November 3, 1791. Alexander Johnston (*History of American Politics*, ed. 1880, p. 252) gives the date as December 15, 1791; but these authorities give no citations. At all events it is certain that the Tenth Amendment was not in force in February, 1791, when Jefferson and Hamilton presented their letters on the constitutionality of the national bank to President Washington.

and Jefferson use it in their arguments. Jefferson declared that the power to incorporate a bank had not been delegated to the United States by the Constitution. It was not among the powers especially enumerated of laying taxes, borrowing money, regulating commerce, nor is it within the scope of the general phrases authorizing Congress to lay taxes to pay the debts and to provide for the general welfare. Jefferson restricts this grant of power to laying taxes for the purpose of providing for the general welfare. He would limit both parts of the phrase, thus confining the laying of taxes to paying the debts or providing for the general welfare and, in a like manner, confining the provision for the general welfare to laying of taxes for that purpose. To consider the latter phrase as not describing the purpose of the first would give a distinct and independent power to Congress to do any act which it held might be for the general welfare and would thus reduce the whole instrument to one single phrase. Jefferson then passes to the other general phrase in the Constitution authorizing Congress "to make all laws necessary and proper for carrying into execution the enumerated powers." As to this he says, as all these powers can be carried into execution without the incorporation of a bank, a bank is not necessary and, therefore, not authorized. It was true that the establishment of such a financial corporation would facilitate the collection of taxes, but the Constitution does not allow those things which are merely "convenient," but only those which are "necessary." To permit such a latitude of construction in this phrase would swallow up the delegated powers and reduce the whole to one power, as had been observed in the discussion of the other general phrase.[1]

[1] Only ten or eleven weeks earlier Jefferson had argued for a very liberal construction of the Act of Congress for the establishment of a national

Washington turned Jefferson's opinion over to Hamilton, who set forth with all his skill the opposing arguments.[1] He based his discussion upon the general principle that is inherent in the very definition of government, that every power vested in it is in its nature sovereign and includes the right to employ all the means requisite and fairly applicable to the attainment of the end of such powers which are not forbidden by the organic law or contrary to the essential ends of political society. The government of the United States is sovereign, for the Constitution expressly declares that laws and treaties made pursuant to it shall be the supreme law of the land. The power of erecting corporations is a sovereign power and is unquestionably incident to that of the United States in relation to the object intrusted to the management of the government. As to the argument from the Tenth Amendment, the main proposition is not to be questioned; but how much is delegated in each case is to be made out by fair reasoning and construction. There are both implied powers and expressed powers, the former equally delegated with the latter. As to the meaning of the word "necessary," it often means no more than needful, requisite, incidental, useful, or conducive to. It is a common mode of expression to say that it is

capital. The expression "such quantity of land as the President shall deem *proper for the United States*" used in the law "is vague," wrote Jefferson. "It may therefore be extended to the acceptance or purchase of land enough for the town; and I have no doubt it is the wish, and perhaps expectation. In that case, it will be to be laid out in lots and streets." *Writings of Jefferson* (Ford ed.), v, 252. And accordingly the city of Washington was laid out at considerable expense and the construction of the "President's palace" and the capitol begun without any other authorization from Congress.

[1] The opinions of Jefferson and Hamilton were not known at the time, or for years afterward. Extracts from Hamilton's letter were first printed in the appendix to the fifth volume of Marshall's *Washington* that was published in 1807; the whole letter apparently was first printed in 1810. Professor MacDonald notes similarities between Hamilton's argument and Marshall's in the opinion given in the case of McCulloch *vs.* Maryland (Massachusetts Historical Society's *Proceedings* for May, 1913; the first draft of Hamilton's opinion is in *ibid.* for November, 1909).

necessary for a government or a person to do this or that when nothing more is understood than that the interests of the government or the person will be promoted by doing this or that. The whole turn of the clause shows that it was the intention of the framers to give a liberal latitude to the exercise of the specified powers. On the other hand, the restrictive interpretation of the word "necessary" is contrary to sound interpretation. A bank has a natural relation to the power of collecting taxes — to that of regulating trade, to that of providing for the common defence, and as the bill under consideration contemplates the government in the light of a joint proprietor of the stock of the bank it thus brings the case within the provision of the clause of the Constitution which immediately respects the property of the United States.

Hamilton's arguments convinced Washington of the constitutional propriety of the measure. He approved the bill, February 25, 1791. The subscription books were opened on July 4, following, and within two hours, the whole capital was subscribed for and many persons who had hoped to get the right to take up stock found themselves left out. Never in the course of history has there been so immediate and permanent a financial foundation laid for any country's prosperity as that which was built by Hamilton, the men of the First Congress, and President Washington.[1] It is true that they had in their hands an opportunity greater than was ever vouchsafed to any other beginners of a State. There were no national financial institu-

---

[1] It was the confidence of the legislators, voters, and people generally in Washington's integrity and judgment that made this legislation possible. Per contra, Senator Maclay, in his desperation at seeing affairs go in a direction contrary to that he desired, wrote he hoped it was not treason, but he wished that Washington were in heaven, that his name might not be used as a constant cover to every "irrepublican act." This was in 1790. The idea became a favorite one with the opposition.

tions to hamper them; there were no laws, regulations, or traditions to hinder them from pursuing the path of wisdom. The slate was perfectly clean. They might establish the credit of the government of the United States on a firm basis; or they might give it an insufficient underpinning that would collapse under the weight of the superstructure of later years. They acted with a sagacity that the world has seldom seen. The fabric that they wrought has been changed and mended from time to time to meet the needs of succeeding generations, but the framework is even now essentially as they left it.

NOTES

I. Books on Hamilton. — Henry Cabot Lodge's *Alexander Hamilton* in the " American Statesmen " series is one of the most artistic bits of biographic-historical writing ever done in this country, — and, for that reason, one of the most dangerous for any except the most erudite. Of the half dozen other biographies, those by J. T. Morse, Jr., and W. G. Sumner may be mentioned. John C. Hamilton's *History of the Republic of the United States of America, as traced in the Writings of Alexander Hamilton*, etc. (6 vols., New York, 1857–60) is really a biography of the first Secretary of the Treasury by his son. Lodge's edition of the complete *Works* of Alexander Hamilton (9 vols., New York, 1885–86) is now generally used, but some persons find the earlier edition in seven volumes edited by J. C. Hamilton (New York, 1850–51) more satisfying. Paul Leicester Ford printed a *Bibliotheca Hamiltoniana* (New York, 1886).

II. Assumption. — The gross claims of Massachusetts amounted to $26,000,000. A large part of this sum disappeared by the easy process of reducing it from a paper currency to a specie basis. The final depreciation arranged for by Congress for the old continental money was forty for one; but this would have been an unfair rule to apply to portions of the Massachusetts claims. In writing to Governor Hancock in 1791, Dane thought that Massachusetts' claim of nine and one-half million dollars appeared to be well supported by acts of Congress and proper vouchers. Granting that this was so, the interest on each item to date of payment would have to be calculated and added to the principal, and then over against the gross sum thus found there would be many offsets. Wherever one turned, there were troubles, — in settling the scale of depreciation, in computing the interest, in finding the voucher, in producing the act of Congress. The accounts were stated in thirty-two books and were placed before the commission with a mass of justifying papers. See Dane's letter of February 17, 25, 1791, February 4, 1793, and Massachusetts Archives in the State House at Boston. "Papers relating to Resolves of 1791, January Sess.," chap. 160. This material was brought to my attention by Mr. Adolf A. Berle, Jr., who has helped me in other ways.

CHAPTER IV

HIGH FINANCE, 1789–1800

IN August, 1791, six months after the passage of the Bank Act, Henry Lee journeyed from Philadelphia to Alexandria. The whole way, he wrote, was "one continued scene of stock gambling; agriculture commerce & even the fair sex relinquished, to make way for unremitted exertion in this favorite pursuit." [1] Ever since 1785, and probably before that year, the accumulation of public securities in the hands of a few persons, — from Lord Timothy Dexter of Newburyport, Massachusetts, to William Loughton Smith of Charleston, South Carolina — had been steadily proceeding.[2] In 1785, agents from New York went among the Connecticut farmers, buying their Continental and State certificates as quietly as

[1] To Madison, August 14, 1791, "Madison Manuscripts" in Library of Congress, xviii, 58.

[2] See W. C. Ford's *Correspondence and Journals of Samuel Blachley Webb*, iii, 40, 45, 53, 55, 59. In 1788, Duer and his friends were buying securities in South Carolina. See "Duer Manuscripts" in the New York Historical Society's library (letters in volume ii). In January, 1790, Madison informed Jefferson that "emissaries are still exploring the interior and distant parts of the Union in order to take advantage of the ignorance of holders" of public securities (*Writings of Madison*, i, 502). Later on, there was a good deal of protest against the method by which securities had been segregated in a few hands. W. L. Smith, one of the South Carolina Representatives, found it necessary to declare publicly that he had never speculated in the funds until every man in the United States knew of the assumption law. He had informed his correspondents in the State that the law would be passed. Local speculators had bought stocks from the original holders at far below their real value and the blame for this had been put on members of Congress and on the capitalists of Philadelphia, New York, and Boston. Professor Ulrich B. Phillips kindly communicated this note to me from the *City Gazette and Daily Advertiser*, Charleston, October 3, 1794.

possible and for the smallest sums of hard money that the holders would take. The progress of legislation was watched most narrowly, as it seemed to be generally recognized that the establishment of confidence in the government would be the signal for a sharp rise in the price of public funds, in the value of lands, and for an outburst of activity in commerce, manufacturing, and trade. It is not only among merchants, financiers, and politicians that the gambling fervor is found; Noah Webster, of the "Speller" and the "Dictionary," was kept from speculating simply by the fact that he had no money,[1] and the Reverend Doctor Jeremy Belknap, founder of the Massachusetts Historical Society, was in constant receipt of information as to the progress of events by letters from Senator Paine Wingate. The lawyers caught the infection. James Kent, afterwards the famous Chancellor,[2] purchased land in western New York and made money by it, while James Wilson, one of the "Fathers of the Constitution" and Associate Justice of the Supreme Court of the United States, bought so much wild land in Pennsylvania, North Carolina, and Kentucky, that he died prematurely, a bankrupt. The most unexpected of these early speculators was Patrick Henry. With a few Virginia associates, he obtained an extensive grant of land in the Yazoo-Mississippi country from the State of Georgia. The associates then bought up Georgia paper money and certificates at a very low rate and

[1] E. E. F. Skeel's *Noah Webster*, i, 203, 204, 207. On September 20, 1789, Webster informed James Greenleaf, whose sister he was about to marry, of what he called "the outdoor talk of Col. Duer, the Vice-Secretary" that the debt will be funded and "it is in contemplation to establish a National Bank." "This," he wrote, "will be the time for your speculations."

[2] William Kent's *Memoirs and Letters of James Kent*, 75. As showing the extent of land speculations in this period, it may be noted that fifteen million acres of lands in Kentucky in the names of non-residents were offered for sale in 1800 for non-payment of taxes, J. H. Daveiss to R. and S. Smith, Lexington, Ky., November 16, 1800. Ten years later on November 6, 1810, the *Albany Register* printed a twenty page *Supplement* advertising lands for sale in default of taxes.

turned them into the State treasury at par in payment of the lands. The treasurer received some of them, refused to receive any more, and the legislators granted the lands to another Yazoo Company. For a time the Virginians thought of contesting the matter in a court of law, but the assumption of State debts made it more profitable to exchange Georgia certificates for United States bonds, par for par, than for wild Yazoo lands, and contributed to make Patrick Henry financially independent[1] at the moment when so many of the foremost planters of the Old Dominion were beginning to feel the first pinches of poverty, for they had already invested so heavily in lands and slaves that they had no money to put into new forms of speculation.

Before the establishment of a national financial system, interstate commerce and speculative enterprises had been carried on with great difficulty owing to the varying standards of money[2] and to the practical impossibility of establishing credits in different colonies or States. When a Philadelphian made a purchase of rice at Charleston, he had to pay for it either by shipping commodities vendable at that place or by getting together whatever gold and silver he could find, — moidores, johannes, half-joes, pieces-of-eight, and bags of clippings, — or he could buy exchange on England, if he could find it, for that had a market everywhere. Even after the establishment of the new government, until the banking system got into working order, the remittance of funds was no easy matter.[3] In one of his first circulars,

---

[1] W. W. Henry's *Life and Letters of Patrick Henry*, ii, 512; *American State Papers, Public Lands*, i, 156; C. H. Haskins's "Yazoo Land Companies" in American Historical Association's *Papers*, v, 395; and *Writings of Jefferson* (Ford), v, 250. See also *Report of the Secretary of the South-Carolina Yazoo Company* in three parts.

[2] See the present work, vol. ii, 497–504.

[3] The origin of the suggestion of dividing the dollar into one hundred units, represented by a copper cent, seems to be obscure, — it may have come from China. Possibly the two Morrises, Robert and Gouverneur, and Jefferson all had a hand in it, or they

Hamilton directed the collector at Boston to forward funds
by the medium of notes of the Bank of North America or the
Bank of New York. These were to be cut in halves, each half
to be signed by the collector and then the two were to be sent
by successive posts. It would be well to secure a receipt from
the postmaster which would serve as a voucher.[1] After 1793,
the use of cheques and drafts on the Bank of the United
States, or on State banks, became more and more frequent
and greatly facilitated the carrying on of business and the
promotion of speculative ventures.

By 1790 the advantages arising from speculation in the
public funds had turned everything into that channel : "The
Merchant, the man who lives upon the interest of his bonds,
the tradesman, and the farmer convert their whole into
money, to engage in this lucrative business." In the summer
of 1790, speculation was even more widely spread among the
people of Boston than of New York, and pervaded the whole
town. The result of speculative activity in different parts
of the country is seen in the figures that Professor Beard compiled from the treasury books. In 1795, citizens of Massachusetts received over three hundred thousand dollars in

---

may have borrowed the idea of a deci-
mal division. The Congress of the
Confederation adopted measures looking toward the establishment of an
American coinage, but nothing tangible
was done until after the act of April 2,
1792, establishing a mint and regulating
the coins of the United States. And
then the actual striking of gold, silver,
and copper coins was a very slow matter.
See the writings connected with the
names of Jefferson and the Morrises.
McMaster has summarized the matter
in his *United States*, iv, 283 and fol.

[1] See "Custom House Papers" in
Library of Congress under date of
October 14, 1789. In January, 1792,
the Bank of the United States was
added to the list. Bank cheques seem
to have been in use as early as April,
1792, for then Robert Carter of Virginia
inquires "if printed checks only will
be taken up" at the Bank of Maryland.
They were sparingly used before 1800
and 1805. One device was called a
"post-note." This was equivalent to
a cashier's cheque to order, dated ahead.
Timothy Pickering stated that the
British postmaster general had advised
the cutting bank notes in halves and
sending them by successive posts so
that the practice was not peculiar to
America. See Skeel's *Noah Webster*, i,
320 ; Murray's *New English Dictionary*,
vii, Pt. 2, p. 1175. Mr. Albert Mathews
of Boston most kindly brought Robert
Carter's letter to my attention.

interest on United States securities, while only sixty-two thousand dollars were paid to Virginians on that account. Indeed, Virginia was seventh on the list of holders of public securities, Massachusetts, Connecticut, New York, Pennsylvania, Maryland, and South Carolina all standing before her.[1]

The rise in prices was great and the increase in the volume of transactions in stocks and bonds was astonishing. The rights to subscribe to the stock of the Bank of the United States sold at above par before they were issued, and within six months a share that was issued at four hundred dollars could be sold for six hundred. The rise in the price of the public funds of the United States and of the several States was even more remarkable. In April, 1786, one of Nathan Dane's clients living in Essex County paid thirteen hard dollars for four thousand three hundred and sixty-two dollars of the "Old Emission" of Massachusetts paper.[2] In March, 1788, New Loan certificates had risen at Philadelphia from their lowest point of one and two shillings in the pound to four shillings and sixpence. In the following May, when the ratification of the Constitution had become almost a certainty, they went up another sixpence to five shillings or twenty-five per cent of their face value. The actual acceptance of the new fundamental law by nine States did not at once bring about a further increase in the selling price of public securities. From June, 1788, to September, 1789, there is a rise of only three pence in the pound. The actual payment of money by the government in October, 1789, aroused renewed confidence. In three months, public securities nearly

[1] These figures are from Professor Charles A. Beard's article in *American Historical Review*, xix, 294.

[2] "Nathan Dane Manuscripts" in the cabinet of the Massachusetts Historical Society. In March, 1787, Dane paid eighteen shillings hard money for eighty-four shillings of "New Emission"; in October, 1790, he paid $928.00 for $1468.00 in Final Settlement Certificates and Indents.

doubled in price, — the New Loan certificates selling in
December, 1789, for ten shillings.[1] The new national bonds
at once secured public favor. In January, 1791, the six per
cents were selling at eighty-five cents on the dollar, or seventeen shillings in the pound. In the following December,
they went above par, the highest point for the movement
being one hundred and twenty-five in the spring of 1792.[2]
One of the most interesting things connected with this whole
matter is the credit enjoyed by American funds in England and
Holland. Bird, Savage, and Bird of London became very
active in the buying and selling of United States securities.
By August 12, 1791, they had disposed of several million
dollars worth of them in London. These securities were then
selling for one hundred and five, a month later they brought
one hundred and seven and a half, and in October, they actually
brought one hundred and fifteen in London. The success
of speculation in government securities induced men to go into
other things, — into buying lands or buying more lands, into
building ships or starting manufacturing establishments,

[1] The following table showing the
prices of securities in shillings and pence
at Philadelphia is compiled from the
Columbian Magazine for 1788, 1789 : —

1788	Mar.	Apr.	May	June	July	Aug.	Sept.	Oct.	Nov.	Dec.
New Loan Certificates.	4/-4/6	4/-4/4	4/6-5/	4/6-5/	4/6-5/	4/6-5/	4/6-5/	4/6-5/	4/-4/4	4/9-5/
Continental Certificates.	3/-3/4	2/8-3/2	2/8-3/2	4/-4/2	4/-4/6	4/-4/6	4/-4/6	4/-4/6	3/9-4/	3/9-4/
1789										
New Loan Certificates.	6/-6/6	6/-6/8	4/10-5/4	4/8-5/3	4/8-5/3	4/8-5/3	4/8-5/3	5/3-6/	6/-7/6	8/-10/
Continental Certificates.	4/2	4/8	4/8-5/	4/8-4/9	4/8-4/9	4/8-4/9	4/8-4/9	5/2-5/4	6/6-7/6	8/4-9/6

[2] The appreciation of national securities was greatly helped by purchases
for the "sinking fund." These were
authorized by the "Trustees of the
Sinking Fund" and were made by the
Treasurer of the United States either
in the open market or by sealed proposals in Philadelphia or New York —
at the latter place under the direction
of the "Cashier of the Office of Discount
and Deposit of the Bank of the United
States," see *Report of the Board of Trustees of the Sinking Fund*, dated Philadelphia, February 25, 1793.

into the organizing and carrying on of banks. In 1788, there were only three banks in the country with a capital of a little over two millions; by 1800 the number had increased to twenty-eight, counting the national bank and all its branches as one institution, and the total capital had increased to twenty-one million dollars.

At New York and at Philadelphia, while he was occupying the office of Secretary of the Treasury as well as before and after that period, Alexander Hamilton was on friendly terms and was even intimate with members of the first well-defined group of speculators in our history. One of these was Robert Morris, the prince of plungers; another was Alexander Macomb; a third was William Duer, — all of them foreign born. The relations between Hamilton and Morris were very close, while the latter represented Pennsylvania in the Senate. Their unpublished correspondence contains many references to financial transactions of one sort or another, in which Hamilton ultimately seems to have lost as did so many others.[1] One of the most interesting speculations of the time was the purchase of ten townships on the southeastern shore of the St. Lawrence. Among the associates in this venture were Hamilton, his father-in-law, General Philip Schuyler, Henry Knox, and Alexander Macomb. The last named acted as "trustee."[2] William Duer had been Secretary of the old Treasury Board and had been taken over as Hamilton's assistant, or "Vice-Secretary," as he was sometimes called. Duer's speculative ventures will be presently noted in detail; at this place, it will only be pointed out that he

---

[1] See Morris to Hamilton, November 13, 1789, in the "Hamilton Manuscripts."

[2] "Knox Papers," xxii, fo. 58; xxiii, fo. 47. In the "Hamilton Manuscripts" is a letter from Schuyler, dated January 29, 1792, informing Hamilton that he had been asked to draft a bill to prevent any more such sales as that to Macomb, which possibly refers to the "Ten Townships." In 1791, G. Morris was in London trying to sell this tract of land, "Knox Papers," xxviii, fo. 149.

was the first "governor" of the Society for Establishing Useful Manufactures at Paterson, New Jersey, which was distinctly a Hamiltonian scheme.[1] There are entries in the records and in letters connecting Hamilton's name with the sale of bank stock. It is not at all certain that these shares belonged to Hamilton himself; in some of these transactions he seems to have been acting for Mrs. Hamilton's sister Angelica's husband, J. B. Church. In August, 1792, William Seton, the government agent at New York, wrote to Hamilton that he had been an improvident steward with "your Bank Stock," having sold it at one hundred and thirty when he might have realized four or five per cent more on it, if he had only held it for a few days longer.[2] Outside of his family, Hamilton was circumspect, refusing point blank to give even so good a Federalist as Henry Lee information as to the probable future operations of the Treasury Department. The speculation in the certificates of bank stock troubled Hamilton, because "a bubble connected with my operations is of all the enemies I have to fear, in my judgment, the most formidable." He let it be known that he thought the "Stocks are all too high" and at once received a letter from Rufus King advising him to be careful as to speaking of the value

[1] See Levi R. Trumbull's *History of Industrial Paterson*, W. Nelson's "Founding of Paterson as the Intended Manufacturing Metropolis of the United States" in New Jersey Historical Society's *Proceedings*, 2nd series, ix, 177. In getting the historical setting for this chapter, I have been greatly aided by the perusal of two unpublished papers by Dr. Joseph S. Davis. One of these has to do with early American corporations, the other with the Paterson scheme. Hamilton, Knox, Duer, Flint, and Macomb were all interested in this venture.

[2] This was probably stock in the Bank of the United States because the shares were $400 each and were selling at 130, as appears from a pencilled note at the bottom of Seton's letter of August 6, 1792. Probably in this case, as in others, Hamilton was acting for some one else, as it was then a common practice for treasury officials to transact business, more or less connected with the government, for their relatives and friends.

Upon being charged with using his official position for purposes of speculation, Hamilton, to preserve his professional honor, confessed to having illicit relations with a certain Mrs. Reynolds. See Hamilton's *Observations on Certain Documents contained in . . . " The History of the United States for the Year 1796 "* (Philadelphia, 1797).

of securities, because his utterance was used to depress prices.[1]

William Duer was of good English stock.[2] After some time spent in India, he resided at Antigua, where he had inherited an estate. Coming to the continent before the outbreak of the Revolutionary War, he took the radical side, served in the army, was elected to Congress, and married Katherine Alexander, daughter of the claimant of the Stirling peerage, for which reason she was called Lady Kitty Duer. Knox and Duer became financially intimate some time about the year 1786, at least that is the first time that we find them swapping cheques and promissory notes.[3] It was then, too, that Duer obtained a contract for furnishing supplies to the United States forces in the western country. In 1791, they embarked on what they expected would be a most profitable speculation. The idea was to purchase from one million to four million acres of land in Maine, then a part of Massachusetts. Knox and Duer were to have the exclusive direction of the enterprise and those who "held Subordinate Interests of the Purchases" were to be bound by regulations

---

[1] King's note is in the "Hamilton Manuscripts"; the reply, dated August 17, 1791, is in C. R. King's *Correspondence of Rufus King*, i, 402.

[2] Mrs. John K. Van Rensselaer's *New Yorkers of the XIX. Century*, p. ix. There is an article about Duer in the *Knickerbocker Magazine* for 1852, containing information that cannot now be found elsewhere. From a letter in the "Duer Manuscripts" (No. 188) in January, 1789, Duer was negotiating with the Spanish minister as to a settlement on the western side of the Mississippi. Archer B. Hulbert takes a hostile view of Duer's western activities in his "Andrew Craigie and the Scioto Associates" in American Antiquarian Society's *Proceedings* for 1913. Letters in the "Duer Manuscripts" seem to show that both Duer and Barlow were acting in good faith, and sundry entries in Rowena Buell's *Rufus Putnam*, pp. 110, 111, 116, add to this impression. In 1790, provisions were so scanty that Putnam wrote that it was impossible to take a party of Frenchmen across the mountains, until the new crops should be harvested. For a French view, see N. F. Jacquemart's *Le Nouveau Mississippi, ou les dangers d'habiter Les Bords du Scioto* (Paris, 1790).

[3] January 29, 1790, Knox wrote to Duer as to a note which he gave him in September, 1789, for $2000 and had received from him cancelled notes for $1000 and $990. April 27, 1791, Duer asks Knox to "lend him a check" for $6000 until the following Saturday; "Knox Papers," xix, fo. 99; xxv, fo. 114; xxvi, fo. 103; xxviii, fo. 43, etc.

which the directors might make at any time. They could
not sell their lands without first offering them to the directors
and the lands might be bought from the "Subordinates" at
any time at an agreed on price, which was not to exceed three
hundred per cent of the purchase money. In 1791, negotiations with the Massachusetts authorities were begun. The
agents were instructed to lose no time and to employ counsel
if it were necessary. If the committee seemed indisposed to
sell so large a tract as two or three million acres "from a
jealousy of monopoly," or for any other reason, "names may
be made Use of [to] obtain the whole Land we want by Different Applications varying in some Instances in order to
avoid Suspicion of Combination." It might be necessary to
apply to the legislature directly in which case their agents
should secure "an Interest favorable to our Object," which,
presumably, would be very necessary, as four million acres
well located would include very nearly all the cultivable land
in the District of Maine that was not already occupied.[1]
Duer and Knox had very slight personal resources, but they
had influential friends and at this time enjoyed credit with
the banks. There has come down to us an undated scrap of
paper which probably throws some light on their financial
hopes and modes of thought. The plan, so this memorandum reads, was to sell a million acres more or less for a dollar
or so an acre. The deeds were to be given at once and the
lands put into the hands of the purchasers. Of the money
taken in, sixty per cent should be invested in United States
three per cent bonds, the par value of which would equal
the amount of money realized from the sale of the lands.
These bonds were to be placed in the hands of trustees. For
ten years the interest was to be paid to the purchaser as a
bonus for taking up the land. At the end of that time the

[1] "Knox Papers," xxviii, fo. 81, 122.

bonds, principal and interest, were to revert to the proprietors.
If everything went well, Duer and Knox and their associates
would sell a million acres for a million dollars. They would
pay one hundred and fifty thousand dollars to the State and
to individuals and six hundred thousand more for the three
per cents, leaving a quarter of a million to be divided between
the associates. At the end of the ten year period, the associates would come into possession of the three per cents which
by that time would probably be worth a good deal more than
the six hundred thousand dollars that they would cost. As
to the additional expenses, it appears that in 1792, Jackson
discovered that he and William Tudor were working against
one another and were running up the price of wild lands from
ten cents to twenty cents per acre. Thereupon Jackson gave
Tudor a note for one thousand guineas on condition that he
would stop bidding against him.[1] Ultimately, the Duer and
Knox associates secured preëmption rights to three million
acres of land in the central part of Maine. For this they were
to pay twenty-one cents per acre, something down, and the rest
in instalments at six per cent interest [2] and there were other
expenses to be met, whenever the lands should be taken up
for actual settlement. The amount of money involved was
very large for two men who had nothing or next to nothing,
but Duer and Knox were not in the habit of borrowing
trouble. They even secured additional lands on Mount
Desert and the neighboring mainland,[3] agreeing to pay six

[1] "Knox Papers," liii, fo. 166. They
ultimately agreed to pay 21 cents per
acre for 2,839,453 acres and actually
paid $5000 down as "earnest," "Re-
port of the Committee for the Sale of
Eastern Lands . . . 1783–1795," nos.
xxiii and xxiv.

[2] In the end, Jackson was obliged to
appeal to the legislature for a release
from the obligation to carry out his
contract in its entirety. See *Resolves*
of the *General Court of the Commonwealth of Massachusetts, respecting the
Sale of Eastern Lands* (1803), pp. 242,
269.

[3] "Knox Papers," xxix, fo. 31, 35, 69,
76, etc. This purchase was made from
M. and Mme. de Gregoire; see G. E.
Street's *Mount Desert*, 133 note. The
western portion was confirmed to Sir
John Bernard, son of Sir Francis sometime governor of Massachusetts, to whom

pence ha'penny per acre for them, the payments to extend
over two years.

A great deal of money had been made in land speculations
in the Genesee Valley and in the upper Mohawk region.   For
a time it seemed as if this success might be repeated in Maine.
Many French refugees were coming to America either singly
or in groups.   Some of these were fugitives from the wrath of
the Parisian mob, others had been driven out of San Domingo
by the rebellious mulattoes or negroes, who, even then, were
more or less guided by Toussaint Louverture.   Among the
refugees were Madame de la Val and Monsieur de la Roche.
They fell into the hands of Duer, probably with a view to settling within the Scioto country, but he turned them and their
friends toward Mount Desert.   He wrote to Knox that the
climate of Maine might not be so congenial as that of the
Scioto, but there were other superior advantages.   For
the present, he thought that the change of the course of the
French immigration would better be kept a secret, but a successful settlement on Mount Desert Island would give éclat
to the whole Maine speculation.   Knox was also interested
in the settlement of a great tract on the coast between the
Penobscot and Kennebec rivers, which had come to Mrs.
Knox from her father.   She and General Knox had bought
out the other claimants to it and had also purchased several
islands in the neighboring Penobscot Bay.   The tract was
already partly occupied by squatters and it was only very
slowly and with a great deal of trouble that General Knox
was able to bring them to a realizing sense of the insufficiency
of their titles and of the necessity of paying money to him to
secure good ones.

Besides his various interests in Maine, the Mississippi

the whole island had been granted ; see   references, under date of August 27,
Barrington-Bernard Correspondence, 50,   1791, and on, in the "Knox Papers" to
56, 66, etc.   There are a good many   this French settlement in Maine.

Valley and New York, Duer entered into an agreement with Alexander Macomb for "making speculations in the Debt of the United States." [1] This document was dated December 29, 1791, and the association was to continue for twelve months. Duer and Macomb took others into this "blind pool" which was known at the time as the "Six Per Cent Club" and extended their operations to the manipulation of bank stock and manufacturing shares. When this syndicate was formed, the price of securities was rising rapidly. Rumor had already pointed to Duer as being particularly engaged in raising the price of the certificates and of the rights to subscribe to the capital of the Bank of the United States; but King wrote to Hamilton that Duer's conduct "had been as correct as any Buyer's and seller's could be." Within three months after the formation of the Six Per Cent Club, Duer was finding it difficult to secure funds. It is said that an ambitious zealot in the Treasury Department [2] gave the first stab to his credit by asserting that he was behind in his accounts with the government to the extent of a hundred thousand dollars or so. Duer was able to explain this away, but he was soon paying five and six per cent a month for small sums of money: "Butchers, mechanics, old batchelors & old maids, all lent him their cash." [3] He was said to have entered into negotiations for five million dollars. In March, 1792, Duer found it impossible to go on and his "stoppage" created great distress at New York, as there was scarcely a capitalist who was not concerned with him. His friends

---

[1] "Duer Manuscripts" in New York Historical Society, nos. 245, 247.

[2] Something of the other side of this matter is contained in a "Report from Committee of the House of Representatives to whom was referred the petition of Theodosius Fowler presented the 3rd of February, 1801." It appears from this that Fowler and Duer were im-

plicated in what had been looked upon as an overdraft in connection with Duer's contract to supply the army on the frontier in the year 1791.

[3] Letter of William L. Smith, Philadelphia, March 24, 1792, to Gabriel Manigault, "Jenkins Manuscripts," communicated to me by Professor Ulrich B. Phillips.

tried to tide him over, but it soon appeared that all his marketable securities had been assigned for certain preferred creditors. This meant that those who had loaned him small sums of money at usurious rates were excluded from all hope of repayment and they were indignant. Securities were pressed for sale and money could not be obtained at any interest. At one moment it was said that as high as one per cent per day [1] was tendered for funds and in vain, although the best bonds and stocks were tendered as collateral security. Hamilton now interfered by authorizing William Seton to purchase public stocks to the amount of one hundred and fifty thousand dollars. He bought bonds from no less than eighty persons which no doubt did something toward restoring confidence. It then appeared that the Six Per Cent Club was deeply involved. Macomb had bought half a million dollars worth of securities on which only part payment had been made, he was liable for the difference in the price to the holders. In the end the company paid only five per cent on its obligations.[2] Duer was now in the city jail, where he was physically safe from his creditors. He begged Macomb to send him money which was "essential to preserve the Peace of the City, and to prevent the Industrious and Malignant Efforts of our Enemies. . . . For Heavens, Sake, for your own, if not for Friendship for me — Send this Sum." He would be personally responsible for the return of the money within a fortnight. "Do not, again, let the Bearer Return without the only thing Needful — with this Aid all Violence can be prevented; without it it is absolutely Impossible."

[1] A letter from Elbridge Gerry, dated Philadelphia, 19th March, 1792, in the "Wendell Papers."

[2] See Henry Remsen to Jefferson, April 11, 1792, in the "Jefferson Manuscripts," Washington; Hamilton to Seton, April 4, 1792; and Seton to Hamilton, April 9 and 11, in "Hamilton Manuscripts" at Washington; Duer to Macomb, April 11, 1792, "Washburn Autograph Collection," fo. 43. See also Upham's *Life of Timothy Pickering*, iii, 27.

But Macomb who had come to New York with a fortune of sixty thousand pounds sterling, like Duer, was at the end of his resources.[1]

The panic that followed on Duer's downfall was of short duration. By the autumn of 1792, speculation was again proceeding with vigor. Of all the operations of the next few years, none stands out more prominently than that connected with the building of the City of Washington, partly because the whole affair has somewhat the appearance of a miracle and partly because it was so intimately connected with the catastrophe of Robert Morris's fortunes. In providing for the establishment of a permanent seat of government, Congress had no thought of expending any of the nation's money. Virginia had already voted one hundred and twenty thousand dollars as an aid to the enterprise to which Maryland added seventy-two thousand. With this money and such as might be obtained from interested persons in the future, the Federal City was to be built. Washington was authorized to select the actual site, anywhere along the Potomac, between the Eastern Branch and the Conogocheague, an affluent of the main stream which joined it about seventy miles higher up, and only about thirty miles south of the Pennsylvania line. Washington viewed the whole tract ostentatiously, being banqueted at various places, but already he had fixed upon the territory near Alexandria, Virginia, the nearest town to Mount Vernon. The site selected has been described as consisting of two hills, separated by a morass, and there are those who assert that a more salubrious situation might easily

---

[1] On April 12, 1792, one of Knox's correspondents wrote to him from New York: "No place was ever in such a state of distress as this — Poor Macomb stoped Yesterday — He is gone beyond redemption, and must begin the World again — This last failure has involved everybody — It is expected that before Saturday upwards of Forty persons of considerable Note will stop — God knows where it will end! Mrs Colden stoped Yesterday and had process served on Her." "Knox Papers," xxxi, fo. 38.

have been picked out higher up the river. Washington was undoubtedly influenced by the expectation that the new city just below the falls of the Potomac would in no long time rival Philadelphia, New York, and Baltimore as a centre of industry and would become the continental mart for ocean borne commerce, — would be, in short, the metropolis of the Western World.[1] It would be at the changing place of ocean and river borne commerce, for the Potomac was then looked upon as one of the gateways of the Ohio Valley. At that time few people in Virginia — and not many others anywhere — had any other idea than that the easiest route to the rapidly growing western country would be by the way of the Potomac or the James. No one had then thought of the line of the Erie Canal through central New York as the economic approach to "The West."

Having determined upon the general location of the Federal District, Washington appointed commissioners to secure for the United States whatever lands were needed between Georgetown and the Eastern Branch. There was some dickering and the President was finally obliged to use his personal influence. Ultimately all the holders of lands within the chosen limits agreed to turn them over to the federal authorities, who were to lay out the city. The original proprietors were to contribute whatever land was needed for streets, but were to be paid for whatever other lands should be taken for public purposes at the rate of twenty-five pounds per acre, and each was to receive back one-half of the lots

[1] See Jonathan Elliot's *Historical Sketches of the Ten Miles Square* (Washington, 1830), p. 320. The acts for establishing the seat of government are chapter xxviii of the acts of the second session of the First Congress and chapter xvii of the third session. The latter extended the limit of choice to include the town of Alexandria, in Virginia, which was practically Washington's home town; but the capital city was to be laid off on the Maryland side of the river. It is only by a stretch of the imagination that these acts can be construed as giving authority to lay out a city and to undertake expenditures that would inevitably run up to over a million dollars.

laid out on his land in absolute possession, — which he could retain or sell as he pleased.   If everything went well each one of these lots would be worth as much as the original cornfield. In this planning of the new city, Washington was greatly helped by Jefferson, who had a good deal of artistic sense and had distinct memories of many foreign towns.   Some of his suggestions were not practical, but his sketch of the new city with the President's House at one end of a public walk and the capitol at the other was the origin of one of the distinctive features of the Federal City.[1]   For a paid assistant, Washington picked out Major Pierre Charles L'Enfant,[2] who possessed original genius together with some of the qualities that often go with it, and intrusted the actual survey to Andrew Ellicott.   L'Enfant soon evolved the scheme upon which the City of Washington was actually built with some few changes,[3] mainly in the direction of restricting the size of pub-

---

[1] This is reproduced in W. B. Bryan's *History of the National Capital*, i, 130. The original plan is in the "Jefferson Papers" at Washington, Series 4, vol. i, 121. An instance of Washington's reliance on Jefferson, occurred on June 30, 1793, when objections were raised to Thornton's plan of the capitol on the ground of practicability, time, and expense. Washington desired Jefferson to hear both sides and "report your opinion on the case and the plan which ought to be executed. . . . Your own knowledge of this and judgment will decide." Somewhat differently phrased, this letter appears in Glenn Brown's *History of the United States Capitol*, i, 10.

[2] For interesting memorials about L'Enfant, see *Records* of the Columbia Historical Society, ii, 26–157 ; this includes articles by John Stewart, W. B. Bryan, and J. D. Morgan.   For Ellicott, see C. Van C. Mathews's *Andrew Ellicott, His Life and Letters*.

[3] Glenn Brown thinks that L'Enfant was influenced by a plan for rebuilding the burned portion of London that was drawn by Sir Christopher Wren, but not used at that time. He also points out that a combination of radial and right angular streets was actually in existence at Annapolis.   See his article in Columbia Historical Society's *Records*, vi, 1.

Following is L'Enfant's own description of the method which he pursued: "Having first determined some principal point, to which I wished making the rest subordinate, I next made the distribution regular with streets at right angles, north-south and east-west.   But afterwards I opened others in various directions as avenues to and from every principal place, wishing by this not merely to contrast with the general regularity nor to afford a greater variety of pleasant seats and prospects, . . . but principally to connect each part of the city with more efficacy by, if I may so express, making the real distance less from place to place." (W. Bogart Bryan's *History of the National Capital*, i, 148).   He wrote to Washington that he "could discover no one [site] so advantageously to greet the congressional building as is that on the west end of Jenkins heights which stand as a pedestal waiting for a monument, and I am confident, were all the

lic reservations.   The plan may be described as following the
lines of a gridiron, like the streets of Philadelphia, with the
stiffness relieved by a series of broad radiating avenues, with
sumptuous open circles at important intersections, — a series
of cartwheels superimposed on a checker-board.   Today
after a century and a quarter of existence, Washington is the
most attractively planned city in the world, — whose qualities
are both accentuated and marred by sudden transitions from
palace to hovel, from the abode of aristocracy to that of the
negro.   That the city exists at all is due very largely to the
financial genius of Robert Morris and his associates, all of
whom passed their declining years in penury.

Robert Morris was brought from England by his father in
his early boyhood.[1]   In youth, he showed remarkable business acumen and was taken by his employer, Thomas Willing
of Philadelphia, into the firm of which he was the head.
Morris's part in the Revolution is well known.   During and
after the Revolutionary War he engaged in most profitable
transactions with the Farmers General of France and with
other foreigners and became interested in promoting the
settlement of wilderness lands.   He acquired great tracts in
central and western New York and sold them for a million or
more than they had cost him.   This success impelled him to
buy wild lands in all directions: in North Carolina, Kentucky, the Northwest Territory, Georgia, and Pennsylvania,
and he retained some of his early holdings in New York.   At
an evil hour for himself, Morris listened to the urgings of
James Greenleaf and became interested in building Washington City [2] as the national capital was known after 1791.

wood cleared from the ground no situation could stand in competition with
this." Columbia Historical Society's
Records, ii, 35.
    [1] Charles Henry Hart has brief
articles on Robert Morris and his wife

in *Pennsylvania Magazine of History*, i,
333; ii, 157.
    [2] On September 9, 1791, the Com-
missioners wrote to Major L'Enfant
that they had agreed to call the federal
district the Territory of Columbia and

When L'Enfant had evolved the main features of his scheme and Ellicott had made progress in running the lines of the streets and squares, the commissioners advertised the first sale of building lots. Their hopes were great. They seem to have expected an influx of buyers, but the results were not at all commensurate with their anticipations. They offered to sell house lots on easy terms, the condition being that dwellings of a standard size and construction should be erected on a certain portion of each purchase within a limited time, and the period of payment was prolonged. Nevertheless the sales were disappointing and the amount of money taken in far below what the commissioners required. It was in these early years of discouragement that James Greenleaf [1] of Boston and New York came forward with a proposition for the purchase of lots by the thousand. This remarkable man was American consul at Amsterdam and was brother-in-law of Noah Webster, the lexicographer. Greenleaf had a Dutch wife and expected to procure the necessary funds for this enterprise through his friends and his wife's connections in Holland. He was already associated with Robert Morris and John Nicholson [2] of Pennsylvania in the North American Land Company, which had been formed to take over some of Robert Morris's promotions. The three now joined in a syndicate to carry through the Washington venture. Greenleaf had contracted for three thousand lots. The syndicate now doubled this amount, offering to pay an average price of

the capital, the City of Washington. Another early mention of these names occurs in a letter from Daniel Carroll of Georgetown, dated December 12, 1791, in "Madison Manuscripts," xviii, 90.

[1] See Allen C. Clark's *Greenleaf and Law in the Federal City* (Washington, D. C., 1901) ; W. B. Bryan's *History of the National Capital* (New York, 1914), vol. i, ch. ix, "The Early Realty Oper-

ators." Mr. Clark has a succinct account of James Greenleaf in Columbia Historical Society's *Records*, v, 212.

[2] Nicholson had been comptroller general of Pennsylvania and was said to have held grants of one-seventh of the surface of that commonwealth. See Columbia Historical Society's *Records*, vi, 217.

eighty dollars per lot.   The six thousand taken by the syndicate comprised more than one-half of the total number owned by the government.   In addition the associates secured the option on twelve hundred and thirty-four other lots owned by private proprietors.[1]   In all Morris and his partners agreed to pay to the Commissioners of the national city nearly half a million dollars.   They actually paid over one hundred thousand as against less than that sum paid and promised by all other purchasers put together up to 1796.   In that year the Commissioners reported to Congress that their total resources were something over three-quarters of a million[2] including the sums which the syndicate had contracted to pay but had not yet paid and the one hundred and ninety-two thousand that Virginia and Maryland had appropriated to the carrying out of the enterprise.

Morris, Greenleaf, and Nicholson had gone into this speculation as they had into many others in perfectly good faith. The country was growing rapidly, European capital was seeking investment in America, and the future seemed to every one to be full of promise.   They had calculated without taking into account the tremendous social and financial convulsions that were to overtake Europe and Great Britain during the next few years following on the French Revolution.   And who can blame them?   What statesman or man of business in America, or anywhere indeed, in 1792 foresaw, or could foresee, what the next few years were to bring forth? Instead of flowing into Washington City to pay for house lots

---

[1] W. B. Bryan's *History of the National Capital*, i, 219.

[2] See a report of the Commissioners of the Federal City in 1796 (" Papers of the House of Representatives," No. 4, in Library of Congress).   Somewhat different figures are in *American State Papers, Miscellaneous*, i, 136.   In 1798, the Commissioners asked for an appropriation of $200,000 for public buildings, but only one-half that sum was voted because Northern Congressmen thought that Virginia and Maryland ought to supply the money and also objected to the style of buildings that were being put up in the Federal City.

Dutch gold went to finance the French revolutionary armies.[1] Excepting a few French refugees and a few fugitives from Ireland, hardly any colonists came to America in the following decade. There were no immigrants to settle on the domains of the North American Land Company in Georgia, North Carolina, or elsewhere ; to buy the millions of acres that Knox and Duer had acquired in Maine ; or to occupy the newly sur· veyed house lots of Washington City. The peasants, who in other times would have thronged the decks of emigrant ships bound for the New World, now instead, turned their faces away, and marched to unknown graves on battlefields associated with the names of Napoleon, Wellington, Massena, Soult, and the rest, or fought the guns of the ships at Camperdown, at Aboukir, and at Trafalgar.

At Philadelphia there were many men of large means ; in the front rank was William Bingham. He was influential politically, succeeding Morris as Senator from Pennsylvania and was director in the Bank of the United States of which his father-in-law, Thomas Willing, was president. After Duer's failure, Knox induced him to take over Duer's share in the two million acre purchase in Maine, and, as a part of the price of letting him in to the "deal," induced him to agree to pay the sums that Knox still owed on the contract. By 1795, Bingham was beginning to feel the financial pressure of the times. At this moment Alexander Baring came to the rescue.[2] He was in America as agent for his father, Sir

---

[1] Dr. H. T. Colenbrander tells us that one hundred million guilders (*American Historical Review*, xix, 619) went from Holland to France as the price of liberty and equality. See also Ford's *Writings of J. Q. Adams*, i, 319, 329 ; John Marshall reported the amount at forty to sixty million dollars or one hundred to one hundred and fifty million florins.

[2] Alexander Baring was the founder of the great banking house of Baring Brothers of London. He was a steadfast friend of the United States. It was he who financed the Louisiana Purchase and as Lord Ashburton negotiated the treaty of 1842. For half a century and more, the Barings received income from the lands in Maine. The "Heirs of William Bingham" even now have an office at Bar Harbor, Maine.

Francis Baring, and for other English capitalists. He made his headquarters at Bingham's house and in a year or two married his eldest daughter, the younger becoming the wife of his younger brother. Alexander Baring paid a quarter of a million dollars and loaned Knox fifty thousand in addition. Had it not been for this help, both Bingham and Knox would have been unable to meet their obligations in 1796. The former's letters to his partner are filled with accounts of the distress at Philadelphia. The immense speculations in lands and in the China trade had exhausted the resources of the banks and money was at a premium of two per cent a month and remained at about that rate for three years. Bingham had not eight thousand dollars free capital at his disposal; but some of his friends hearing that he was about to receive one hundred thousand guineas from Mr. Baring had applied to him for temporary loans which he had been obliged to make to save his credit. Even Philadelphia city lots were unsalable. A few months later in April, 1797, Edward Shippen,[1] also writing from Philadelphia, declared that the spirit of enterprise had lately stalked with such gigantic strides as to infatuate all people, and there is by no means "such Confidence in men of reputed fortunes and prudence as used to exist."

Of the reputed rich men who were no longer to be so regarded, Robert Morris was undoubtedly the first in Shippen's mind. Morris, Nicholson, and Greenleaf had struggled strenuously to secure funds, but everything had gone against them. Possibly as one means of bolstering up his fallen

---

[1] Bingham's letters are in the "Knox Manuscripts." Shippen's letter is in *Pennsylvania Magazine of History*, xxvi, 228. In 1797, Duer was again in trouble "owing to An Unfortunate Connection with J. Greenleaf" and implored Knox to come to New York, secretly and at once, to "concert Arrangements for securing the little Wreck of what may remain for my Wife's Dower &c from Destruction"; "Knox Manuscripts," no. 40, fo. 66. There are several references to the bankruptcies of this later time in the *Writings of Jefferson* (Ford), vii, 73, 127, 133, 188, 314.

credit, in 1795 Morris had begun the erection of a house on a lot that occupied a whole square, the house in which he formerly dwelt being then occupied by the President of the United States. L'Enfant had been employed to draw the plans and to oversee the construction. After three years' time and the expenditure of much money, or possibly only promissory notes, the roof was not on. The unfinished house and lot were sold at auction in December, 1797, for forty-six thousand dollars, "whereas," according to Bingham, "the Lot alone would have Sold for nearly double the Amount twelve months ago." It was the horrid usury of the times, Morris informed Hamilton, that made it impossible to pay what he owed, adding that he had frequently been without what was necessary to buy his daily food. Morris retired to a country house and fortified himself there, holding out for months against creditors, collectors, and constables. Nicholson did the same in another house not far away. Greenleaf pursued a different course and sought refuge in the poor debtors' prison on Prune Street in the city, where the others joined him in 1798. Greenleaf was released in that year, having been declared a bankrupt ; and Nicholson died in jail in 1800. Morris remained in confinement until August, 1801, when some arrangements having been made as to an annuity for his wife, he was declared a bankrupt and regained his liberty. Republics are proverbially ungrateful ; but, considering Robert Morris's services to the United States, it should never have been possible for him to write the following sentences,[1]

[1] Robert Morris's "Private Letter Book" in Library of Congress, iii, 28. Long quotations from these letters are given in Clark's *Greenleaf and Law in the Federal City*, pp. 30–34, and in Oberholtzer's *Robert Morris, Patriot and Financier*, 343. Sumner takes a rather unfriendly view of Morris in his *Financier and the Finances of the American Revolution*. Morris's accounts as Financier were not settled until 1790; see Michael Nourse in *The Bankers' Magazine*, new series, ix, 577. William B. Wood, the actor-manager, met Morris in the yard of the Prune Street gaol where Gouverneur Morris dined with him. See Wood's *Personal Recollections of the Stage*, 36–42, and *Diary*

no matter what his short-comings. They occur in a letter
to Nicholson who had asked when the selling of their property
would cease. "I answer," wrote Morris, "that they will
have done . . . after it is all sold and gone. . . . By heaven
there is no bearing with these things, I believe I shall go mad,
every day brings forward scenes and troubles almost unsup-
portable and they seem to accumulate so that at last they
will like a torrent carry everything before them. God help
us, for men will not."

of Gouverneur Morris, ii, 378, etc. O.
Turner's *Pioneer History of the Holland
Purchase* and his *Phelps and Gorham's
Purchase* contain much useful matter
on the New York land speculations;
and there are some curious entries
as to Robert Morris in Boogher's
Miscellaneous Americana, 51.

After his release from the debtors'
prison, Morris and his wife lived on
$1500 a year that was paid to them
by the Holland Land Company as the
price of Mrs. Morris's assignment of
dower.

NOTE

Office Holding and Personal Business. — As was several times noted in the third volume of the present work, office holding in the eighteenth century was not looked upon as separating a man from ordinary business pursuits. Members of Parliament were usually men of means and had to be, as they received no compensation for their services in that body. Contractors for public service were oftentimes members of that Parliament until the century was nearing its close, and officials who had the handling of public money were quite in the habit of diverting interest on the balances in their hands into their own pockets. Moreover, it was not customary to settle accounts every month or every year. Sometimes, where there was a dispute as to an item, a large sum of public money remained in private hands for many years. So it was in America. Timothy Pickering's accounts as Quartermaster General of the Revolutionary armies were still unsettled in 1797.[1] It seems to have been customary in those days to credit the Heads of Departments with considerable sums of money for paying expenses arising within their Department, thus we find Pickering reporting to President Adams that money which had been apportioned to Edmund Randolph as Secretary of State for payment of diplomatic expenses had not been remitted to London when he, Pickering, took possession of the Secretary of State's office.[2] James McHenry, after he resigned from the Department of War, found himself seriously indebted to the government, — owing to carelessness in book-keeping in the Department.[3] One of the most curious examples of the blending of public and private interests occurred as to the purchase of wine for President Washington in 1790. The business was confided to Jefferson, who was a connoisseur. He turned it over to William Short, Chargé of the United States at Paris. Washington had gone off to Mt. Vernon without leaving funds for the wine, and Jefferson had none. The United States had a balance in Holland. He told Short to draw on that for payment, assuring him that bills of exchange would be sent to cover all costs of the transaction.[4]

[1] *Pickering Manuscripts*, vi, fo. 237. In 1802, Gallatin reported that a suit was then pending against Randolph for a deficit of $51,000, *ibid.*, i, 757.

[2] "John Adams Manuscripts" under date of Philadelphia, September 5, 1796.

[3] Steiner's *Life and Correspondence of James McHenry*, 512.

[4] *Writings of Jefferson*, v, 242.

Other instances of somewhat different commingling of private and official interests were the pecuniary dealings between government officials. Thus we find James Monroe, Senator from Virginia, asking the Secretary of War for a loan of six or seven hundred dollars for a few months, — which Knox politely declined. In the summer of 1789, when the clerks were unusually straitened for funds, Isaac Sherman, one of the employees in the Treasury and son of the redoubtable Roger, borrowed one hundred and fifty dollars from Alexander Hamilton which he did not repay until January, 1792. Another and more interesting loan was one that Hamilton made to Washington in February, 1793, of two thousand dollars, which was repaid forty days later, on March 11.[1] Personal influence was also sometimes asked and used, as in August, 1794, when Senator Bingham of Pennsylvania requested Knox to bring forward his business at the " Council," if he could without showing too much friendliness, assuring him that Col. Hamilton will do everything in his power to " effectuate this Business." Still another example is that of John Adams and the loans negotiated in the Netherlands. As the loan was filling slowly, Adams to inspire confidence subscribed for a considerable sum in his own name.[2] In 1803, Bird, Savage, and Bird of London became insolvent. At the moment they had in their hands funds arising from the redemption of United States loans in Holland which should have gone to Adams. Eventually the money was repaid, but the last instalment was not received until after the death of John Adams, twenty-three years later.

[1] *Pennsylvania Magazine of History,* **xxix**, 386.

[2] *Writings of J. Q. Adams* (Ford), iii, 13 note.

CHAPTER V

THE promulgation of the Neutrality Proclamation on April 22, 1793, gave the signal for America's withdrawal from Old World politics. No event in Washington's administration aroused more interest, few of the deeds that are associated with his name had more lasting consequences, and not one of them demanded greater courage or betokened more thoughtfulness and foresight. In the first quarter-century of our national history, the fate of America was bound up with that of Europe to an extent that nowadays seems almost incredible. The War for Independence had freed America from the yoke of British misrule. In the minds of European chancelleries, it had done nothing more; the newly enfranchised States belonged to the Concert of Nations after 1783 fully as much as the English colonies had belonged to it before Lexington and Bunker Hill. Washington, Jefferson, Hamilton, John Adams, and those who worked with them, liberated the United States from this European thraldom, — for a century, the American people lived a life apart from the rest of the world.

In 1789, the external outlook was as unpleasing as was the internal. Great Britain had not obeyed the Treaty of Paris of 1783, except as it suited her interest so to do. She had given Americans important trade privileges in the ports of Great Britain, but had closed the British West Indies to American vessels and had refused to enter into negotiations for a commercial treaty. The French Revolution was in full sweep, the revolutionists were looking to America for sympathy and were certain to ask for more than sympathy whenever the inevitable war with Britain should begin. The Spaniards, too, had no thought of complying with the settlement of 1783, so far as it restricted their American territory and imposed obligations upon them. This led to serious uneasiness among the settlers of the western country, for they could only market the bulkier produce of their farms by way of the Mississippi River. English and Scottish moneylenders, merchants, traders, and factors were to be found in every commercial centre. British consuls were stationed at New York and Philadelphia, and official emissaries of one sort or another came to spy out the land. These all consorted with the more conservative elements in the population. They imbibed the pessimism of their hosts and reported to their employers that the American States were helpless, that the American people was divided by discordant political sentiments, and that the country was ripe, or nearly so, for the reëstablishment of monarchy or aristocracy. The Americans seemed to be relapsing into the colonial condition from sheer inability to keep out of it.[1] The ministers at Downing Street, therefore, paid no attention to John Adams's groping for a commercial treaty, or to his inquiries as to violations of the Treaty of 1783 except to make inconvenient assertions as to the weakness of the American government. So hopeless did the outlook in London seem that Adams announced his intention of returning to America at the end of his term of office.[2]

---

[1] In 1789, Vermont was as sovereign and independent as Massachusetts or South Carolina before the ratification of the federal Constitution. Her trade relations were with the St. Lawrence rather than with the Hudson, and her political leaders turned to the English authorities in Canada for aid and encouragement, — but got very little of either. It was under these circumstances that Vermont joined the United States in 1791, as the fourteenth state. See S. F. Bemis's introductory remarks to documents found by him in London and printed in *American Historical Review*, xxi, 547, and see also *Canadian Archives*, 1889, pp. 53–58; 1890, p. 210.

[2] Adams to Jay, January 24, 1787

The French contempt for America is shown in the Consular Convention of 1788, which conferred upon French officials in the United States powers not dissimilar to those given to our own consuls in more recent days in China and Siam.[1] Even Jefferson was unable to secure any important concessions at Paris. The Spanish representative in the United States, Don Diego Gardoqui, like the French and British agents, felt to the full the helplessness and inefficiency of the government of the Confederation. He reported likewise these impressions to his employers in Spain, with the result that they showed no desire to give satisfaction to the United States. Such were the relations of the United States to foreign powers when Washington took the oath of office on April 30, 1789.

A few days later (May 5, 1789) a Spanish ship let go her anchor in the quiet waters of Friendly Cove, an inlet of Nootka Sound, on the western coast of Vancouver Island. This port had been a convenient rendezvous for American and British vessels engaged in the fur-trade of the Northwest Coast. Before long several of these vessels appeared. The Spaniards seized two of the British ships and carried them with their crews to Mexico. In January, 1790, news of this affair reached London. Soon afterward came a demand

(*Diplomatic Correspondence, 1783–1789*, v, 164).

[1] An example of French high-handedness is seen in the case of Captain Joseph Marie Anne Ferrier of the French brig *David*, who was placed in irons by the French vice-consul at Norfolk for some alleged infringement of French regulations. The only thing that saved him from being sent to Nantz for trial was the appearance of a Virginia sheriff with a writ for his arrest as a debtor. He was liberated on bail by the resident magistrate and the French consul could get no satisfaction from John Jay, who was then in charge of foreign affairs, or from Governor Randolph of Virginia. See *Diplomatic Correspondence, 1783–1789*, i, 353–381. For the Consular Convention of 1788, see *ibid.*, i; *Writings of Jefferson* (Ford), i, 117; and Trescott's *Diplomatic History of the Administrations of Washington and Adams*, 31. Mr. S. E. Morison copied figures from *Tableau Général des Consulats suivant leur Formation Actuelle, et les Changements Proposés* (Paris, 1792), from which it appears that the cost of the French consular service in the United States was greater than that in any European country and was exceeded only by that of the Levant and the Barbary coast.

from Spain that the British authorities should give the
strictest orders prohibiting ships of their nation from resorting to Nootka Sound and its neighborhood. The government at London refused to enter upon any discussion of the
matter until satisfaction should have been made for a proceeding so injurious to Great Britain.[1] Note and reply
followed as rapidly as the distance between London and
Madrid and Spanish dignity permitted. On the night of
May 4th, or the morning of the 5th (1790), residents of London and other seacoast towns were "suddenly surprised by a
hot press, which like an explosion swept between 3 & 4000
seamen" from the houses on the shore and the merchantmen
at anchor in the harbor to the decks of British ships-of-war.
Before long thirty-five ships of the line with accompanying
frigates were cruising off Cape St. Vincent.   The Spaniards
replied as well as they could, but they could do little to curb
the insolence of the British seamen.   Orders were sent to
British commanders in various parts of the world to prepare
to attack the nearest Spanish possession.   Francisco de
Miranda, a mysterious Spanish-American character, was
even then striving to induce the British government to aid
him in revolutionizing Spanish America.[2] He now found
favor ; many conferences and meetings were held with him,
and some money was furnished to him as a sort of revolutionary retainer.   Sir Guy Carleton, now Lord Dorchester
and Governor General of Canada, was on the point of leaving

[1] The details of this controversy are
set forth at length from the original
sources in W. R. Manning's "Nootka
Sound Controversy" in the *Reports* of
the American Historical Association for
1904, pp. 279-478. A contemporaneous
and exceedingly useful publication is
*Official Papers Relative to the Dispute
between the Courts of Great Britain and
Spain, . . . on the subject of . . .
Nootka Sound*, London [1790].

[2] See William S. Robertson's *Francisco de Miranda and the Revolutionizing of Spanish America*.
    There is an interesting letter from
Miranda to Pitt in the documents
printed in the *American Historical Review* under the title "English Policy
toward America in 1790-1791" (vii, 706-
735 ; viii, 78-86 ; the Miranda letter is
in the earlier volume, p. 711).

Quebec for a visit to England. He was directed to remain in Canada, do what he could to strengthen his military forces, and make friendly overtures to the new American government.

The important bearing that this friction between Great Britain and Spain over the Nootka Sound affair might have on Anglo-American relations was fully recognized by both the American and British governments. Pitt and his colleagues realized that they must yield to American desires, send a minister to Philadelphia, make a commercial treaty, and hand over the Northwestern posts. The agent chosen by Lord Dorchester to make friendly overtures at Philadelphia was Major George Beckwith.[1] On his arrival at Philadelphia in July, 1790, he conferred with Hamilton, whom he had previously known; but the conversations were carefully reported to the President, and Jefferson was present at the later ones. Beckwith suggested that the United States would probably take part with Great Britain rather than with Spain. The Secretary of the Treasury in return gave the Englishmen to understand that while the United States had no engagement with Spain and, indeed, had some matters to adjust with her, the Americans would dislike a British occupation of New Orleans. This was about all that Beckwith got from Hamilton and Jefferson and about all that Hamilton and Jefferson got from him; but, out of doors, it was supposed that things had gone a good deal farther. In the spring of 1791, it was reported that the Indians were receiving ammunition from the British. Thereupon, Washington asked Adams and the three Secretaries to confer to-

---

[1] Beckwith went up rapidly in the military scale, being termed "Major," "Lieutenant Colonel," and "Colonel" during these conferences. During the French Wars, he rose to the rank of "Lieutenant General," having command of all the British forces in the Lesser Antilles. In 1809, he was created Knight of the Bath on account of his conquest of Martinique. As to his doings at Philadelphia, see *Canadian Archives*, 1890, pp. xxxvi-xlii, 121 and fol.; *Writings of Jefferson* (Ford), i, 172, 173; J. C. Hamilton's *Works of Alexander Hamilton*, iv, 30–34.

gether as to whether some kind of representation might not be made to Lord Dorchester through Beckwith. On the evening of April 11, happening to be at Knox's house, Beckwith hinted that the assertions might be unfounded because the British government had a system of managing the Indians by distributing presents and goods.[1]

William Stephens Smith, John Adams's son-in-law, was in England in the spring of 1791. He was politely entertained by Lord Grenville and, returning to Philadelphia, tried to convince the government of the friendly disposition of the British. Robert Morris, who was at this time in the Senate, was in confidential communication with Patrick Colquhoun, a Glasgow merchant, who acted as go-between for the British government. Through this channel, Morris had been assured that a British minister would be sent to Philadelphia, and he had been asked to state his ideas as to the commercial relations between the two countries. It was in one of his letters that Colquhoun hazarded the supposition that "the President and Mr. Secretary Hamilton are among the number who will feel satisfaction"[2] at the settlement of difficulties between Great Britain and the United States.

[1] "Memorandum of a conversation which passed between the subscriber and Lt. Colonel Beckwith who seems charged with some fact of an informal political commission by Lord Dorchester," April 11, 1791, in "Knox Papers," xxviii, 23. Beckwith and Knox had become intimate, the former believing that the promotion of "the benign purposes of peace" could not be better concluded "than by a little eating and drinking." Major General Maunsell, an officer in the British army, on October 20, 1791, handed to Knox — whom he seems to have known — an unsigned paper to the effect that Mr. Pitt had authorized him to declare that Great Britain was anxious to establish and preserve the strictest amity and friendship with the United States. He,
Maunsell, was not diplomatically employed; but he hoped that the United States would be satisfied of the friendly disposition of the Court of London, ibid., xxix, 153.

[2] See The Manuscripts of J. B. Fortescue, Esq., preserved at Dropmore, ii, 145, 157, 197, 228, 263. These volumes are included in the Reports of the Royal Historical Manuscripts Commission and are often cited as Dropmore Manuscripts. They form the basis of Ephraim D. Adams's Influence of Grenville on Pitt's Foreign Policy, 1787–1798 (Washington, 1904). It appears that Phyn and Ellis, London merchants engaged in the Canadian trade, in 1791, were advised to secure their property at Niagara and Detroit, because those post were to be delivered to the United States.

While the negotiations were proceeding between Great Britain and Spain, Jefferson inquired of the President as to the policy of the United States in case the British should ask permission to march a military force through the western country toward Louisiana and Florida ; and what should be done in case the British passed through American territories without asking permission or in defiance of the expressed wishes of the United States government. Washington, thereupon (August 27, 1790), requested the Vice-President, the Chief Justice, and the three Heads of Departments to give their written opinions. Their replies were promptly returned with the exception of Hamilton's, which was delayed for a couple of weeks, owing to the pressure of other business. They all held much the same tone.[1]   On one point, they were in absolute accord : the United States should keep out of war as long as possible, neutrality as between European combatants was clearly the policy of the new nation.   Jefferson also tried to utilize the temporary embroilment of Spain with Great Britain to settle the disputes that had existed ever since 1783 between the United States government and the Court of Madrid ; but it took so long to communicate with William Carmichael, the United States representative in Spain, that nothing was accomplished.[2]

For some months, even for more than a year, the harmonious relations between the United States and Great Britain continued. Then everything changed and the old friction and policy of do nothing returned. In their helplessness, the Spaniards had applied to France for aid under the terms of the treaty of many years ago, known as the Family Compact, by which either branch of the Bourbon family was obliged to go to the assistance of any other member who

---

[1] Worthington C. Ford's *The United States and Spain in 1790* (Brooklyn, 1890).

[2] *American State Papers, Foreign Relations*, i, 130, 131; *Writings of Jefferson* (Ford), v, 407, 408.

asked for aid. As things were at Paris, this demand was necessarily submitted to the National Assembly and much discussion ensued.[1] In the end it was voted to place a great French fleet in commission and to inform the Spanish government that it would be well to negotiate a new treaty obliging either nation to go to the aid of the other, when unjustly attacked. Forty-five French battleships [2] would have been a potent addition to Spanish armadas, but the suggestion that treaties and alliances were national affairs frightened the Spaniards. They had been given ten days in which to make up their minds whether they would accept the British terms or not. They needed only five to consent to everything that was asked of them. The Nootka Treaty was signed on October 28, 1790. The pressure on both Spaniards and Englishmen relaxed and the international horizon of the United States became even more clouded than it had been in 1789.

One of Washington's first acts as President was to ask Gouverneur Morris, who was then in France on private business, to cross the Channel and find out why the British government refused to carry out the provisions of the Treaty of Peace.[3] Morris reached London in March, 1790, but the

[1] The "Report of the Diplomatic Committee on the Family Compact . . . addressed to the National Assembly" by M. Mirabeau and the "Decree of the National Assembly of France, on the Family Compact" are in *Official Papers relative to . . . Nootka Sound.*

[2] Benjamin Bailey to Christopher Champlin, L'Orient, September 10, 1790, in *Commerce of Rhode Island*, ii, 421 (Massachusetts Historical Society's *Collections*, vol. 70).

[3] On the condition of trade between the United States and the British Empire in this period, see *Collection of Interesting and Important Reports and Papers on the Navigation and Trade of Great Britain . . . printed by order* of "*The Society of Ship-Owners of Great Britain*" in 1807. This is said to have been edited by Nathaniel Atcheson. The second document in this *Collection* is "The Report of the Lords of the Committee of the Privy Council of January 28, 1791." Worthington Ford found a copy of this in the State Department at Washington and printed it in 1888 as *Report of a Committee of the Lords of the Privy Council on the Trade of Great Britain with the United States.* A useful compendium manual is W. W. Bates's *American Navigation* (Boston, 1902). A comparative statement of the duties paid in British ports on goods imported in "American, Foreign, and British" ships since January 5, 1798, so far as

British ministers would not talk freely with him because they thought he was too familiar with Luzerne, the French ambassador at London, and also with Mr. Charles James Fox.[1] In one of his conversations with the British foreign minister, Morris observed that the press gangs had " entered American vessels with as little ceremony as those belonging to Britain." He also hinted that if the greatest care were not used, ship captains, on returning home, "will excite much heat in America, 'and . . . will perhaps occasion very disagreeable events.'" He suggested that certificates of citizenship might be issued to American seamen for their protection.[2] The British government approved of this idea, but nothing was done. The net result of the Nootka Sound controversy was to lay down the doctrine that neutrality was the best policy for the United States and to add impressment of American seamen to the grievances already existing against Great Britain.

Meantime, in America, increased irritation against the British had been aroused by the constantly growing trouble with the Indians of the Northwest and the belief which grew into conviction that British officials made their murderous activities [3] possible by supplying the natives with food, clothing, arms, and ammunition. Washington had inherited these troubles from the Confederation. In 1789, General Harmar was conducting a campaign in the Indian country.

---

the same respects the commerce of the United States is given in a printed "Letter of [the] Secretary of State" dated January 5, 1802.

[1] *Canadian Archives, 1890*, xxxviii. It appears that the British government was well informed, for Morris noted in his diary that he had told Luzerne of his errand at London because he thought it prudent to be able to say to the French court that every step in the negotiations had been taken with their privity. Anne C. Morris's *Diary and Letters of Gouverneur Morris*, i, 310.

[2] *Ibid.*, i, 327, 328.

[3] Professor A. C. McLaughlin has studied this subject with industry and care. He has absolved the British government from the charge of encouraging the Indians to war against the Americans; but supplies of food and clothing and, in 1794, of military equipment — obtained from British colonial officials — made it possible for the Indians to wage war on the United States. See his "The Western Posts and the British Debts" in American Historical Association's *Reports*, 1894, p. 413.

The President did not augur much good from this, because, as he wrote, Harmar was a drunkard.[1] His prediction was amply justified by the event, for the American expedition was obliged to withdraw (October, 1790) without producing other result than a series of court martials. It was impossible to leave affairs in this position. A new force was fitted out. The command was given to Arthur St. Clair, governor of the Northwest Territory. For one reason or another St. Clair's career had been a series of misfortunes, although he had, notwithstanding, risen to high position. In the present case, besides Indian hostility, he was afflicted by jealousies and insubordination among his officers, and he himself was ill and unable to overlook in person all the arrangements. The result was a crushing defeat (November 4, 1791).[2]

On the 21st day of January, 1793, Louis XVI perished by the guillotine. Eleven days later France declared war against Great Britain and Holland and turned over a new page in the history of mankind on both sides of the Atlantic. The progress of the French Revolution had been followed in America with great interest. To Jefferson and to those whose thoughts were like his, the millennium seemed to be

[1] *Writings of Washington* (Ford), xi, 506; *Annals of Congress*, 2nd Cong., 1113.

[2] St. Clair's official report is printed in *American State Papers, Indian Affairs*, i, 137, and in many other places. The disaster naturally aroused interest and led to publication. The second volume of the *St. Clair Papers* arranged and annotated by W. H. Smith contains a mass of material which may be supplemented by the *Diary of Col. Winthrop Sargent during the Campaign of MDCCXCI*, of which forty-six copies were printed at "Wormsloe" in 1851. The St. Clair side of the case is set forth in *A Narrative of the manner in which the campaign against the Indians was conducted under the command of Major General St. Clair together with his Observations . . . and the Reports* (Philadelphia, 1812). There is a memoir of St. Clair prefixed to the *St. Clair Papers*, but it deals mainly with the earlier period of his life. In some respects a much shorter sketch by A. B. Rorison and J. N. Boucher is more satisfactory. It is entitled *Major-General Arthur St. Clair*. In the "Knox Papers" vol. xxxi, 81, there is a copy of the "Report of the Committee of the House of Representatives" with manuscript notes by Knox or some one else. In the same collection, vol. **xxx**, 12, there is an interesting letter from Col. William Darke, dated Fort Washington, Nov. 9, 1791. For all practical purposes Denny's "Diary" and St. Clair's letter of November 9 are adequate (*St. Clair Papers*, ii, 251–267).

not far away. When the movement turned into massacre
and the crowds became masters of the leaders, he retained
his faith that all would be for the best, — if kings and aristocrats were eradicated, the lives of a thousand or a million
men and women would be well spent. Conservatives, like
Washington, looked with dismay upon the course of events
in France, especially after the guillotine had begun its bloody
work. When Lafayette was forced to fly from Paris and the
royal family was imprisoned, they took a more gloomy view;
when the propagandist nature of the Revolution was forced
upon them, they actively turned against the former allies of
America. Earlier, Frenchmen by the hundreds had given
their personal help to the struggling colonists, but, now, few
Americans sought the shores of France to aid in the contest
for the rights of man against the Bourbon monarchy. In the
War for American Independence the French government had
loaned money and had given arms and accoutrements to the
rebellious colonists. The interest of the Bourbon monarchy
had been partly, perhaps mainly, due to the fact that American success would greatly weaken the strength of perfidious
Albion, — the hereditary and natural foe of France and
Frenchmen. The present movement at Paris had no such
elements of interest for America, the contest was one for abstract right. It was an idealistic conflict, until the declaration of war against Great Britain brought it within the range
of practical politics. Frenchmen now looked to America to
repay a part of these obligations, and did not for one moment
doubt that the American people would fully and actively
respond.

The government of His Britannic Majesty held much the
same view. They thought that the Americans would
naturally side with the French Republic. Moreover, they
would be obliged to do so because by the terms of the Treaty

of Alliance of 1778 between the United States and France, the former had guaranteed the French West Indian possessions against all comers. Moreover this treaty contained an ill-worded provision that no privateers of other nationalities should receive hospitality in United States ports, — implying, thereby, that French privateers would be sheltered. The British government took it for granted that when France declared war, she would call upon her American ally to protect her islands in the West Indies and that her ally would faithfully respond, — which meant that war between Great Britain and the United States was only a few months away. The authorities at London, therefore, directed the capture of American vessels in the West Indies whenever they seemed to be in any way infringing British laws and regulations. In Canada, Lord Dorchester addressed a gathering of Indian chiefs at Quebec in language that was only fitting on the supposition that war with the United States was on the point of breaking out. On April 8, 1793, Citizen Genêt, representative of the ruling powers in France, landed at Charleston, and ten days later, Washington called upon his advisers for their counsels as to the obligations of the United States under the French treaty.

However divided American statesmen were on other subjects, they were unanimous as to the necessity of keeping the United States out of the vortex of European politics. In 1785, John Adams had written to John Jay that the friendship of France, Holland, and Spain should be fostered, and, in case of a war between France and England, the United States should preserve her neutrality, if possible.[1] In 1787, Jefferson had conferred with William Eden, who was then in France, as to the effect of the Treaty of 1778 in case of war,[2]

---

[1] *Diplomatic Correspondence, 1783–1789*, ii, 168.
[2] Jefferson to W. Carmichael, *Diplomatic Correspondence, 1783–1789*, iii, 341.

and had told him that it obliged the United States to receive armed vessels of France with their prizes and to refuse to admit prizes made by her enemies and that the United States guaranteed the American possessions of France in case they were attacked. "Our dispositions would be to be neutral," he asserted, and that would be for the interests of both powers because it would relieve them of anxiety as to providing their West Indian plantations with food. The next year Jefferson informed Washington [1] he was decidedly of opinion that the United States should take no part in European wars. Now, in April of 1793, Jefferson wrote to Madison that he favored neutrality, although it might "prove a disagreeable pill to our friends." [2] There was no difference of opinion as to the desirability of neutrality; there was disputation as to whether the treaty with France had come to an end with the destruction of the Bourbon monarchy. Jefferson was willing to look upon it as suspended, until the French government should make a categorical demand upon the United States for the performance of its obligations and then there would be ample time to issue a statement as to the duties and obligations of American citizens. Moreover, it would be well not to do anything at present, but to keep the British government in a state of anxiety as to the policy of the United States. It might even turn out that the authorities at London would adopt a more friendly tone to prevent the United States from taking part with France. Hamilton argued that the treaty had been made with the king of France, and the king being dead and the monarchy destroyed, the treaty had come to an end.[3] Washington determined to disregard the treaty for the time being. He issued a proclamation [4] declaring the duty and interest of the United States

---

[1] *Writings of Jefferson* (Ford), v, 57.

[2] *Ibid.* vi, 232.

[3] J. C. Hamilton's *Writings of Alexan-*

der *Hamilton*, iv, 362, 382.

[4] The Proclamation is in countless places; among others in *Annals of Con-*

require that they should "pursue a conduct friendly and impartial toward the belligerents" (April 22, 1793) ; but this did not interfere with the sale and exportation of munitions of war.[1] Jefferson's sensibilities were somewhat mollified by not using the word "neutrality" in the proclamation. Three weeks later, Citizen Genêt arrived at Philadelphia.

Edmond Charles Genêt came of a notable family.[2] Although only thirty years of age, he had had much diplomatic experience and was a man of very considerable abilities. He was received with effusion at Charleston, to which harbor his vessel had been driven by the winds of the Atlantic. In some sort he replied by fitting out a privateer from that port, a few of her crew being American citizens. He then journeyed overland to Philadelphia, arriving there early in May. He was fêted and banqueted here and there along the way, and was met at Gray's Ferry across the Schuylkill by a delegation from the Quaker City.[3] From the federal authorities, however, even from Jefferson himself, he received one rebuff after another. The Neutrality Proclamation was issued before he reached the seat of government. Soon after his arrival at Philadelphia, captive British vessels were brought into harbor as prizes of Genêt's privateers or of French men-

---

gress, 3rd Cong., 1285 ; *American State Papers, Foreign Relations*, i, 140 ; *Messages and Papers of the Presidents*, i, 156.

[1] On August 4, 1793, Hamilton issued a "Circular Letter" to the collectors of the customs, instructing them as to the enforcement of neutrality. The following two sentences are taken from this paper : "The purchasing within, and exporting from, the United States *by way of merchandize* articles commonly called contraband (being generally warlike instruments and military stores) is free to all the parties at War, and is not to be interfered with. If our own Citizens undertake to carry them to any of those parties they will be abandoned to the penalties which the Laws of War authorize." "Customs House Papers" in the Library of Congress, under date. The letter is printed in *Annals of Congress*, 3rd Cong., 1286.

[2] L. Didier's "Le Citoyen Genêt" in *Revue des Questions Historiques*, xcii, 62, and xciii, 5 ; George Clinton Genêt's *Washington, Jefferson and "Citizen" Genêt, 1793* [New York, 1899].

[3] McMaster's *History of the People of the United States*, ii, 101. This account is based on contemporary newspapers. G. C. Genêt gives an entirely different account of Genêt's coming to Philadelphia, but does not state his authority.

of-war. George Hammond, the first British minister of his
type to reside at the American seat of government, was
greatly excited by these seizures. He demanded the return
of the vessels to their owners and asked that the neutrality of
the United States should be made more evident. The position of the government was very difficult. It had no armed
force with which to make its orders respected. The best that
it could do was to appeal to the governors of the States to use
militiamen and constables to prevent French aggressions [1] on
British commerce in American waters and to compel French
captains to observe the neutrality of the United States.

Besides using the United States as a basis for an attack on
British commerce, Genêt proposed to utilize American territory for the purpose of organizing expeditions to seize Spanish and British lands to the south and to the north, — for the
Spaniards by this time were also in conflict with the French
Republic. Genêt had little difficulty in securing the aid of
prominent characters in South Carolina and Kentucky, or in
enlisting men for these proposed expeditions.[2] His trouble
consisted in finding the money necessary to procure supplies
and to pay the wages of those whom he employed. It occurred to him that possibly the government might be willing

[1] An example of the aggressiveness
of French officials is seen in a letter from
Jefferson to Genêt, dated Germantown,
November 5, 1793. The French consul at Baltimore was proposing to collect
a force of French ships in Chesapeake
Bay to protect French property against
the designs of the British. Jefferson
asks Genêt to curb the consul's activities, reminding him that Great Britain
had never violated the sovereignty of
the United States. "Jefferson's Private
Papers" under date.

[2] By the summer of 1794, there was a
revulsion of feeling at Charleston owing
to the "diabolical decree of the national
convention which emancipates all the
slaves in the french Colonies, a circumstance the most alarming that could
happen to this country." In the early
autumn, a gentleman terming the crew
of a French vessel a "lawless band of
pirates" was himself called a liar and
scoundrel, but instead of a duel taking
place the utterer of these latter epithets
was bound over to keep the peace.

Professor F. J. Turner has printed a
mass of original material relating to
Genêt's activities in the American Historical Association's *Reports*, 1896, i, pp.
930–1107; 1897, pp. 569–679; 1903,
ii. He has stated the result of his re-
searches in *American Historical Review*,
iii, 650. See also *ibid.*, ii, 474; iii, 490;
xviii, 780; the *St. Clair Papers*, ii, 322
note; and Skeel's *Webster*, i, 371.

to advance the remainder of the payments due to France on
the Revolutionary loans. He laid this proposition before
Jefferson under the guise of relief for the victims of the long-
drawn-out tragedy of San Domingo. Genêt's predecessor,
Jean de Ternant, had used payments made by the government on account, for this purpose. Jefferson fell into the
trap, but Hamilton's consent was necessary. On laying the
matter before the Secretary of the Treasury, objections at
once arose. Already Hamilton had had doubts as to the
validity of receipts given by the existing authorities in France.
Moreover, the French revolutionists had issued large quantities of paper money or assignat, which had greatly depreciated. If a valid receipt could be obtained, how was the
amount of the payment to be determined? Finally, he declared that there was not money enough in the treasury to
anticipate payments of any kind. The result was that Genêt
and those whom he had commissioned were brought to a
standstill.

Genêt also applied directly to the government for muskets,
cannon, and ammunition which might be supplied from the
public arsenals and the value deducted from the debts still
due to France. He said France realized that by nature
Guadaloupe and Martinique — he did not say San Domingo
— were connected with this country. The authorities at
Paris, therefore, had put commerce with them upon the same
footing for the United States as for France, and consequently
any assistance the United States might render would be, in
fact, aiding itself. He added that the administration must
be sensible that France had the right to demand our guarantee of these islands. She had waived that demand and only
asked for a supply of arms and ammunition which might be
furnished as secretly as possible. This communication was
first made to Knox. He replied that as a matter of fact the

United States arsenals were very deficient, but if they were filled with arms and ammunition, it might be doubted whether these could be alienated without an act of the legislative authority; and, besides, such an act would be considered as very unfriendly to Great Britain and could scarcely be kept a secret. After some further debate, it was agreed that Knox should submit the matter to the President. This he did in the presence of the Secretary of the Treasury. Washington agreed with Knox that the request could not be complied with, but told him to lay the whole matter before Jefferson, who at once declared that it was inadmissible.[1] Before leaving this part of the subject, it is well to recall that Genêt, with all his activity, hardly went beyond what Franklin, Deane, and Lee had done in France before the signing of the Treaty of Alliance, and that the French government had in effect done for the Americans in the matter of military equipment exactly what Genêt had asked Knox to do for him.

The attitude of the American government was beyond Genêt's comprehension. The people everywhere, so far as he had anything to do with them, seemed to be very friendly to French principles and to France. The government took an entirely different attitude. Even Jefferson, whom Genêt supposed to be a friend to liberty and to France, was constantly advising him to be moderate and even imploring him to pursue other courses. It is true that Jefferson was a friend of France and the rights of man, but he was also an American politician of unparalleled skill in assessing the public mind. In one letter after another to his intimates,

[1] "Knox Papers," xxxiv, fo. 48. William Stephens Smith seems to have been in collusion with Genêt, as he was with Grenville and Miranda, for he writes to Knox that Citizen Genêt was disposed to leave him in the lurch relative to the accoutrements provided for his nation and asks Knox to take them, — cartridge boxes with belts and sword belts with bayonet scabbards. *Ibid.*, xxxiv, fo. 146.

he declared that Genêt was alienating public opinion and strengthening the position of the Hamiltonians. How far Jefferson was cognizant of Genêt's plans for the seizure of Louisiana and Florida is not clear from his published or unpublished papers; but it is inconceivable that a man of Jefferson's resources and one so well acquainted with the politicians of Kentucky and Tennessee should not have had some inkling of what was going on. In December, 1793, Genêt determined to cut the knot by appealing to the representatives of the people. He sent a letter enclosing certain documents which he asked to have transmitted to the two Houses of Congress. This was the parting stroke. Jefferson, by order of the President, returned Genêt's communication with a curt and severe reminder [1] of his place as a diplomatic representative. Before this, the administration had asked for his recall. No difficulty was made in complying with this request, but it was coupled with a similar demand that Gouverneur Morris, who had been at Paris for some time as American minister and had more than sympathized with the misfortunes of the Bourbons, should likewise be recalled. This was also acceded to; but Genêt never returned to France, and it was years before Morris came back to America.[2]

Jefferson no less vigorously upheld the rights of the United States in a correspondence with George Hammond,[3] the British minister. His letter of May 29, 1792,[4] is one of the most

[1] *Writings of Jefferson* (Ford), vi, 495. For earlier depreciatory opinions of Genêt, see *ibid.*, vi, 338, 398, 419.

[2] Genêt married a daughter of Governor Clinton of New York and became an American citizen, and Morris travelled over Europe partly, at least, as the unaccredited though confidential representative of the British foreign minister.

[3] Hammond was descended from a Pennsylvania loyalist family. He was only twenty-eight years of age when he

came to Philadelphia in 1791. After his unfortunate experiences in America he was appointed an under-secretary in the British Foreign Office, for he had strong friends among the politicians. For years he remained a disagreeable thorn in the side of successive American ministers at London.

[4] The original draft of Jefferson's letter is printed in Paul Leicester Ford's edition of the *Writings of Jefferson*, vi, 7, with all the changes and suggestions made by Hamilton. The letter as sent

memorable documents that ever came from his pen. It should be read by every one who is interested in Jefferson or in the international history of the United States. It is in the form of a reply to a previous letter from Hammond, stating in detail British views as to the misdoings of America. Jefferson rehearsed at great length the legislation by the States and the action by the courts as to British debts and loyalists. He reiterated the demand for the surrender of the Northwestern posts and compensation for slaves taken away at the time of the evacuation of New York and Charleston. Hammond was so impressed with the formidableness of Jefferson's array of facts that he was incapable of reply. He forwarded the letter to London and, upon Jefferson's urgent desire, stated that the communication had brought up so many new points that he could not reply to it without further instructions from home. It is not necessary to go further into these controversial writings, because documents unknown to Jefferson, and only recently accessible to any one, show conclusively that before the ratifications of the treaty were exchanged and before it became obligatory upon either party, the British government had determined to retain the posts in the Northwest as a species of hostage for the future performance of the provisions of the treaty by the Americans. This comes out in a letter from Lord Sydney, then Secretary of State, to Frederick Haldimand, Governor General of Canada. It was dated April 8, 1784, the day before the British ratification of the definitive treaty was signed at London, and more than a month before the exchange of the ratifications took place at Paris.[1]   In this letter, the official mouthpiece

---

is in the Congress edition of the *Writings of Jefferson*, iii, 365–429, and in *American State Papers, Foreign Relations*, i, 201. See also *Diplomatic Correspondence of the United States, 1783–1789*, v, 259 and fol.

[1] *Canadian Archives*, 1885, p. 286. Professor McLaughlin pointed out this sequence of dates in his "The Western Posts and the British Debts" in American Historical Association's *Reports*, 1894, p. 413. (This article is

of the British government declared that the "posts in the United States will not be evacuated till the Articles of the Treaty of Peace are complied with."

Expecting the United States to fulfil its obligations to France,[1] the British government ordered the seizure of all vessels carrying provisions to the French West Indies. Hundreds of American vessels were captured, a very large proportion of them being condemned by prize courts at Jamaica [2] and other British islands.   Besides the hardships and losses inevitable to the carrying out of any such policy, the prize courts were very harsh and indiscriminate in their condemnations, and there was a good deal of unjustifiable plundering.[3]   In some sort as a makeweight, the ports of Jamaica were opened for all kinds of American produce which might be brought in American vessels ; these could also take away Jamaican produce as freely as British ships.[4]   This permission was given for six months, but the ports of the island were not again closed for years.   Under these varying regulations and orders, American ship owners suffered great losses ; but they must also have made great gains or there would not have been so many of them resorting to the West Indies.

Years before, John Adams had struck the true note in a

---

substantially repeated in *Yale Review* for February and May, 1895.) An analysis of the chronology of this matter is in the Note at end of the present chapter.

[1] Two of Knox's correspondents undoubtedly reflected public opinion in America. Henry Jackson wrote to him from Boston in March, 1794, as to the captures and depredations made on our commerce by the British and declared that "most of our cool good men think War inevitable." S. Ogden, writing to him from Newark, N. J., about two months later, declared that he feared the British Court intended to wage war in order to secure an alteration of the western boundary line.

"Knox Papers," xxxv, 64, 119.

[2] Grenville certainly tried to improve the situation in the West Indies ; see *Dropmore Manuscripts*, iii, 533. Five months later, in March, 1795, Jay wrote to Grenville that "If America was set right as to the affair of the Indians, and relieved from West India judges and privateers not better than Indians, ill humour, having nothing to feed upon, would die away." *Ibid.*, iii, 39.

[3] Samuel Lawton to Christopher Champlin, Kingston, Jamaica, March 16, 1794, in *Commerce of Rhode Island*, ii, 466 (Massachusetts Historical Society's *Collections*, vol. 70).

[4] Massachusetts Historical Society's *Collections*, vol. 70, p. 470.

letter which he wrote to John Jay from Auteuil near Paris, on April 24, 1785. In this he advocated the punctual execution of the Treaty of Peace by the United States. "If we establish the principle," he wrote, "that we have a right to depart from the treaty in one article, because they have departed from it in another, they will certainly avail themselves of the same principle," [1] and probably extend it farther. The true policy of both countries was to take up all the subjects [2] in dispute and refer them to commissions to arrange for something like an equitable settlement. In 1794, Washington asked James Monroe of Virginia to go to Paris as successor to Gouverneur Morris, and Chief Justice John Jay to go to England as special envoy for the purpose of negotiating a treaty. Thomas Pinckney, who was already in London as representative of the United States, was to go to Spain and endeavor to bring about a settlement of all existing disputes with that country.

Jay found the English ministers distinctly favorable toward his mission. They were conscious that a new page had opened in American history with the establishment of the government under the Constitution. One thing that had shown this was the firmness with which the administration compelled obedience to its policy of neutrality. There are also hints, which are not entirely conclusive, that some approaches had been made to the United States by Sweden and Denmark with a view to the inclusion of the United States in a new league for the enforcement of neutral rights upon the

[1] *Diplomatic Correspondence, 1783–1789*, ii, 171.

[2] There were matters discussed in these negotiations, other than those noted in the text, as to the boundary line between the United States and British America, the impressment of American seamen, the settlement of commercial difficulties, and the regulation of contraband. See J. B. Moore's *Digest of International Law*, v, 699; J. C. B. Davis's "Notes" in the Appendix to *Treaties and Conventions concluded between the United States and Other Powers*. In preparing this chapter I have been greatly aided by the perusal of an unpublished essay on "The History and Diplomacy of the Jay Treaty, 1789–1794" by Samuel Flagg Bemis of Medford, Mass.

sea.[1] Were America to join with the Baltic powers in carrying out any such plan, it would have been very difficult for Great Britain to starve France and the French colonies. It may be also that the government at London had come to realize the magnitude of the task which lay before it in attempting to stifle French propagandism. Jay himself had had long diplomatic experience, had known many Englishmen, and, as Chief Justice, occupied a position of great dignity. He and Lord Grenville, who was now in charge of foreign affairs, at once became friends.[2] Negotiations proceeded rapidly, and in November, 1794, a treaty was signed at London which won most unenviable notoriety for its American negotiator.

According to the provisions of Jay's Treaty, Great Britain was to turn over the Northwestern posts by the first day of June, 1796, and the questions of debts, boundaries, and compensation for unlawful captures were to be referred to commissions or to be made subjects of future negotiations. As to the Loyalists, no objection of alienage [3] should interfere with the possession of lands within the dominions of either power by subjects or citizens of the other. In case of future war between the two countries, no debts should be confiscated whether public or private. Hereafter, American vessels were to have the same privileges as British in Great Britain and in the East Indies, but, like British vessels, should be subject to the regulations of the East India Company within the limits of its territories. American vessels under seventy tons might engage in trade with the British

---

[1] *Writings of John Quincy Adams* (Ford), ii, 304.

[2] Lord Auckland to Grenville, June 23, 1794, *Dropmore Manuscripts*, ii, 578. He wrote that Jay had great appearance of coolness, was a patient hearer, with a good memory, argued closely, but was "long-winded and self-opinioned." Like every man, he has a "weak and assailable quarter, and Mr. Jay's weak side is *Mr. Jay.*"

[3] See F. G. Franklin's *Legislative History of Naturalization in the United States*, 9. The provision on this subject in the treaty was not so much an act of favor toward America as it was a means of protecting what was left of loyalist property in the United States.

West India Islands; but, while this privilege continued, no cotton or any other of the principal West Indian staples should be exported from the United States to Europe. Moreover, the right of the British government to lay countervailing duties to overcome the discriminations of the American tonnage and tariff acts was distinctly recognized, and it was further provided that no additional tonnage duties should be imposed by the United States. Something was done toward the definition of contraband: articles serving directly as equipment for war vessels were so marked and provisions and some other things might be seized by either party on condition that full compensation was made. There were many other regulations as to the treatment of vessels and prizes, but these were not to interfere with the obligations of existing treaties.

By the time Jay's Treaty reached America and, indeed, for that matter before it was signed, the position of the national government had greatly improved. In August, 1794, General Wayne had inflicted a crushing defeat on the Indians of the Northwest in the battle of Fallen Timber and had pursued them under the guns of a fort that the British had built at the foot of the rapids of the Miami, or Maumee as that river came to be called in the next century. Moreover, in November of the same year the Whiskey Insurrection in western Pennsylvania had been put down by federal activity. The excise tax levied upon domestic distilled liquors had excited great discontent in the settlements beyond the Alleghanies.[1] The farmers of western Pennsylvania and the

---

[1] In a private and confidential letter to Knox, written on June 11, 1794, Wayne enclosed an abstract of a letter from the Deputy Quartermaster General showing the temper of the people of Kentucky. This describes a meeting at Lexington where most inflammatory language was used, one speaker declaring that he would not be displeased to see the British in possession of the northwest shores of the Ohio River. The inhabitants also refused to take United States Bank notes and demanded specie. "Knox Papers," xxxv, fo. 129.

adjoining country had found it much easier to take their surplus grain to market in the form of whiskey than in bulk. Whether there was any real hardship inflicted by the excise law may be questioned, but the inquisitorial methods that were necessarily employed in its enforcement were foreign to existing American notions of liberty, — especially among frontiersmen. They held meetings, mobbed federal officials, and showed a disposition to nullify the enforcement of the law. Among the earlier acts to be passed by Congress was one authorizing the President to call out the militia of the several States to repel invasion, or to put down insurrection whenever a federal judge certified that the courts were unable to enforce the law.[1] Such a certificate was now given by the judge of the United States district court in Pennsylvania. Governor Mifflin of that State denied the necessity of action by the federal government,[2] but himself did not do anything to bring about the enforcement of the law. Upon this Washington issued a proclamation, ordering the insurgents to retire to their homes and calling for fifteen thousand men from New Jersey, Pennsylvania, Maryland, and Virginia. At first there was some backwardness in Pennsylvania, but it was only temporary. The troops were easily assembled and marched in good order over the mountains to the western country. They met with no opposition in the field. The ringleaders were seized and handed over to the judiciary for trial. Most of the soldiers then returned to their homes, but a few passed the winter in the disturbed area.

---

[1] *Acts Passed at the Second Congress of the United States* (Philadelphia, 1795, p. 112). This law is ch. xxviii of the First Session of the Second Congress. It may conveniently be found in *The Public Statutes at Large of the United States* (Boston, 1850, vol. i, p. 264).

[2] See his letter to Washington of August 5, 1794 in *Pennsylvania Archives*, Second Series, iv, 104. The first five hundred and fifty pages of this volume are occupied entirely with documents relating to the Whiskey Insurrection. See also *American State Papers, Miscellaneous*, i, 83–113. There is interesting matter on the subject of the insurrection in Henry Adams's *Life of Albert Gallatin;* for other references see *Guide to American History*, § 182.

There were not wanting people at the time to assert that Hamilton had seized upon this opportunity to show the strength of the new government, and certainly whether necessary or not, the raising so many soldiers in so short a time and using them so effectively did greatly strengthen the administration.

As to Indian affairs, it was impossible to permit them to remain in the condition that they were in after the St. Clair expedition. It was necessary to raise a new army and to appoint a new commander. The raising of the army was merely a matter of money which Congress was obliged to vote, but the appointment of a suitable leader was a matter of difficulty. At length Washington pitched upon Anthony Wayne. He was distinctly averse to accepting a commission [1] that would place him under any one except the President and the Secretary at War. In the end he was given the supreme command of a new expedition and was convinced that he would enjoy the necessary support of the administration. In the Revolution, Wayne had received the sobriquet of "Mad Anthony"; such a designation may have been undeserved at that time, it certainly had no relation to his conduct in the discharge of the delicate and important duties that now fell to him. He took abundant time to recruit and train the new army and, when all was ready, marched forward with deliberation and with every precaution. In April, 1794, Lieutenant Governor Simcoe, who had charge of the interior Canadian affairs,

[1] Wayne to Henry Knox, Philadelphia, April 1, 1792, "Knox Papers," xxxi, fo. 13. After the close of the campaign, charges were made against Wayne, probably by General James Wilkinson, whose schemes appear to have been interfered with by Wayne. From a letter written by Wayne in October, 1796, it seems not unlikely that the attempt to supersede him was a part of Wilkinson's conspiracy with the Spanish authorities at New Orleans. Owing to Wayne's early death, they were never investigated officially, but from a letter in the "Knox Papers" (xxxvi, 114) it would appear that Washington was disturbed by the charges, whatever they were. Knox writes to Wayne that the differences between him and Wilkinson "afford no pleasing sensations" and would better be compromised, if possible, and closes with the statement, "You see the footing upon which his charges are placed by the President."

established, or reëstablished, a British post at the falls of the Miami, or Maumee, sixty miles and more to the southward of Detroit.[1] He asserted that this plain violation of the territory of the United States was necessary for the defence of Detroit, — and very likely it was if the Indians of that part of the United States were to continue to remain under British guardianship. Probably the real reason for this move was Simcoe's belief that by the time the news of his doings reached the seaboard, his country and the United States would be at war. On the morning of August 20, 1794, Wayne's men came within touch of the Indians. Every care was taken to avoid ambushes and surprises, but in the end the battle was not at all as Wayne had planned it, for his first line was so rapidly and thoroughly successful that the second line never had a good chance at the enemy. The Indians were pursued and their cornfields destroyed to within sight of the British fort. Their loss was never ascertained, but it was so heavy that the next year they entered into a treaty at Greenville by which they ceded lands to the United States and promised to keep the peace.[2] Among the prisoners taken in this Battle of the Fallen Timber were some members of the Detroit Volunteers, and there can be no doubt that on this occasion the British agent at Detroit furnished military equipment to the natives.[3] Fortunately Jay's Treaty came in time to save

[1] On Simcoe's fort at the Miami Rapids, see his letters of October and December, 1794, in D. B. Read's *Life and Times of Simcoe*, 233, and D. C. Scott's *John Graves Simcoe*, 143–154. These letters are calendared in *Canadian Archives* for 1891, "State Papers — Upper Canada," 40, 42, 46. A good compendious account of this period from the local point of view is that by C. E. Slocum in *The Ohio Country between the Years 1783 and 1815*. Slocum treated at length this whole period of northwestern Ohio history in his *History of the Maumee River Basin from the Earliest Account to Its Organization into Counties* (Defiance, Ohio, 1905).

[2] *American State Papers, Indian Affairs*, i, 562.

[3] See Wayne's report in *ibid.*, i, 491. Professor McLaughlin pointed out these facts in his "Western Posts and the British Debts"; but he likewise insisted that the government at London was not privy to this breach of international and human obligation.

William Clark's journal of this campaign is printed, with elaborate annotations, in the *Mississippi Valley Historical Review*, i, 418. Lieutenant

these unfriendly acts from being new causes of discord between the United States and Great Britain.

The arrival of the treaty in America — in March, 1795 — aroused a storm of indignation[1]; even good Federalists considered it disgraceful, mortifying, and injurious to the country. Everywhere public meetings were held which passed condemnatory resolutions. In the Senate there was much opposition to it, and its ratification was advised by a very close vote and then only on condition that the clause as to trade with the West Indies should be stricken out. At the time and since, it has seemed remarkable that so high-minded and patriotic a man as John Jay should have signed an instrument containing so disastrous a stipulation. In a few years after 1795, the United States was exporting cotton by the thousand bales, sugar by the tons, and molasses and rum by the thousands of hogsheads. A study of the statistics available to Jay will show, however, that the exportation of these articles before 1794 was in trifling volume.[2] The perfection of the cotton gin and the indirect trade which sprang up between the French islands and the mother country by way of the United States resulted in an enormous export business,

Boyer's "Journal of Wayne's Campaign" was printed in the *American Pioneer*, i, 315, 351, and in the 1866 edition of J. J. Jacob's *Biographical Sketch of Captain Michael Cresap*, and there is something in the contemporary "Narrative of John Brickell's Captivity" in the *American Pioneer*, i, 51. An excellent modern account is in W. A. Brice's *History of Fort Wayne*.

The frontier attitude towards Wayne is well expressed in the following lines that were printed in the *Staunton Gazette* for January 11, 1797: —

Brave, honest soldier, sleep —
And let the dews weep over thee,
And gales that sigh across the Lake;
'Till men shall recognize thy worth,
And coming to this place, shall ask,
"Is this where Wayne is buried?"

[1] Nathaniel Ames, brother of Fisher Ames, and of diametrically opposite politics, wrote in his diary, August 14, 1795 : "Washington now defies the whole Sovreign that made him what he is — and can unmake him again. Better his hand had been cut off when his glory was at its height before he blasted all his Laurels!" *Dedham Historical Register*, vii, 33. See also *The Letters of Curtius, written by the late John Thomson of Petersburg* (Richmond, 1804). The Federalist side is well set forth in *An Address from Robert Goodloe Harper, of South-Carolina, to his Constituents* (Boston, 1796).

[2] The following table, which is compiled from Pitkin's *Statistical View* (ed. 1817, p. 59 and fol.) shows the exports of West Indian staples from the United

— but this would have been entirely a matter of prophecy at the time of the negotiations between Jay and Grenville. A statesman should have foreseen that the Revolutionary and Napoleonic wars would inevitably open a new commerce to America. That Jay did not foresee it must be ascribed to ignorance, to error in judgment, but not to any purpose of sacrificing the interests of this country.

Meantime, great changes had taken place among Washington's official advisers; Jefferson retired at the close of 1793 and Hamilton and Knox in the winter of 1794–95. In their places, Washington appointed Edmund Randolph to the State Department, Oliver Wolcott to the Treasury, and Timothy Pickering to the War Office; but Hamilton unofficially continued to act as adviser in all difficult matters. The English government was anxious to secure a ratification of Jay's Treaty, but British vessels continued to seize American ships, and while the treaty was still under debate, the government at London renewed its orders as to the seizure of provisions on the way to enemies' ports.[1] This was per-

States before and after the outbreak of the war between Great Britain and France and before and after the making of Jay's Treaty : —

	1791	1793	1797	1799
Coffee, lb.	962,977	17,580,049	44,521,887	31,987,088
Cocoa, lb.	8,322	234,875	875,334	5,970,590
Molasses, gal.	12,721	28,733	48,559	61,911
Sugar, brown and other clayed, lb.	74,504	4,539,809	38,366,262	78,821,751
Cotton, lb.	189,316	487,600	3,788,429	9,532,263

[1] It is a striking commentary upon the lack of correlation between the different departments of the British government that the signing of Jay's Treaty did not put a stop to British maritime aggression. In July, 1795, two British ships of war and a Bermudian privateer were capturing vessels right and left off Boston Light and sending them to Halifax for adjudication. Grenville certainly did what he could to curb naval activity against the Americans, but he first had to convince the Lords of the Admiralty of the soundness of his position and then these had to restrict the operations of naval men scattered far and wide over the seas, reached only by sailing vessels, and all of them hungry for prize money.

mitted by the terms of the recently signed treaty providing
that full compensation must be given for such seizures, —
but there was a good deal of doubt as to how complete this
compensation would be.   Unlike the British the French
desired to postpone or defeat the ratification of the treaty.
Genêt's successor at Philadelphia, Joseph Fauchet, was
greatly aided in this endeavor by the impecuniosity of Edmund
Randolph, the new Secretary of State.[1]   It does not seem
certain that Randolph accepted money from Fauchet, but
there is a good deal that is dark and unexplained in his conduct and he did everything that he could to put off the actual
signing of the ratification by the President.   The crisis came
while Washington was at Mount Vernon, when Liston, the
new British minister, showed Wolcott copies of despatches
from Fauchet to the government at Paris.   These had been
rescued from the water by British seamen after the capture
of the French corvette, *Jean Bart*.   Wolcott and Pickering
made a rough translation of the documents, from which it
appeared that Randolph's conduct had been equivocal.   They
consulted the Attorney General and urged Washington to
return at once to Philadelphia, which he did on August 11,
1795.   In due course, he put the French despatches into
Randolph's hands, who at once resigned.   Later, after a correspondence with Washington, in which Randolph appears to
distinctly bad advantage, he issued a long statement explaining and defending his conduct,[2] — but unsuccessfully.

[1] Randolph is said to have owed
nearly thirty thousand dollars to the
United States at the time of his resignation.   He was still owing it in 1805,
as appears from a letter from Gallatin
to W. C. Nicholas advising him not to
indorse Edmund Randolph's notes.
Replying (April 18, 1805), Nicholas
shows no doubt as to Randolph's in-
debtedness and writes that he has
always advised him to pay it as speedily

as possible and with "as few circumstances of mortification as practicable."
See also a "Letter from the Comptroller
of the Treasury," dated December 1,
1809.

[2] For details of this episode, see M.
D. Conway's *Edmund Randolph*, 270–
289; C. W. Upham's *Timothy Pickering*,
iii, 209–229; *Writings of Washington*
(Ford), xiii, 87 and fol.; Gibbs's *Administrations of Washington and John*

Pickering succeeded Randolph as Secretary of State, James McHenry of Maryland coming into the administration as Secretary of War.

The last scene in the drama of Jay's Treaty was the attempt of the House of Representatives to interfere in the conduct of diplomatic affairs. After the ratifications had been exchanged at London and the President had proclaimed the treaty to be the law of the land, a motion was made in the House calling upon the President for the papers relating to Jay's negotiation (March, 1796). After a lively debate the motion was carried. Washington, as was his wont, consulted his advisers, and then in a message refused to send the papers, as the assent of the House of Representatives was not necessary and the treaty itself made perfectly clear what legislation must be passed in order to carry out its provisions. He also stated that having been a member of the Federal Convention he had no doubt whatever that the treaty-making power was exclusively invested in the President with the advice and consent of two-thirds of the Senators present. This statement aroused Madison, who was still a member of the House of Representatives. He declared in debate that opinions drawn from the discussions of the Convention meant nothing. The Constitution as it came from that body was a mere bit of writing; vitality was breathed into it by the people speaking through the ratifying conventions. It was to these bodies and not to the Federal Convention itself that one must go for the interpretation of the federal organic law. The greatest speech that was made in this debate — and one of the greatest speeches ever made in Congress — was that of Fisher Ames, Representative from Massachusetts. He

Adams, i, 239 and fol. ; "Edmund Randolph on the British Treaty, 1795" in *American Historical Review,* xii, 587 and fol. Randolph's *Vindication of*

Mr. Randolph's Resignation was printed more than once at Philadelphia in 1795, and was several times reprinted elsewhere.

declared that the opposition to the treaty was political, was not based upon the provisions of the instrument, but was due to desire to inflame the public passions against the government. The opposition was not to this treaty, but to any treaty with Great Britain. None should be made with a monarch or a despot, there would be no naval security while those sea robbers domineer on the ocean. "It has been said the world ought to rejoice if Britain was sunk in the sea — if where there are now men and wealth and laws and liberty, there was no more than a sand bank for sea monsters to fatten on ; a space for the storms of the ocean to mingle in conflict."[1] The effect produced by this oration was such that the opposition moved an adjournment before the vote should be taken. *Per contra,* John Adams, who did not hear the speech, called Ames "the pretty little warbling Canary Bird." The resolution providing for carrying into effect the treaty with Great Britain was finally passed by three votes.

Monroe was well received at Paris, but the story of his abortive mission would better be described in connection with the complications that arose with France a few years later. Thomas Pinckney was more successful in Spain than was Jay in England or Monroe in France. He arrived at Madrid at the psychological moment when the Spanish government was disturbed by Jay's successful negotiation with England.[2] He speedily concluded a treaty by which the Spaniards conceded everything to the United States. They agreed to accept the thirty-first parallel as the northern boundary of Florida and acknowledge the rights of the United States to the free navigation of the Mississippi.

[1] *Speech of Mr. Ames in the House of Representatives . . . April 28, 1796,* p. 26. See also Seth Ames's *Works of Fisher Ames,* i, 12; ii, 51.

[2] G. L. Rives's "Spain and the United States in 1795" in *American Historical Review,* iv, 62 · Mississippi Historical Society's *Publications,* i, 50; ix, 255; *Memoirs of Don Manuel de Godoy, Prince of the Peace, written by himself* (London, 1836), ii, 458.

More than this, they acceded to the request of the United States for the right of deposit, that is to say, for the right to land goods within the Spanish limits free of duty while awaiting transshipment. This was a most important concession, for, without it, freedom to navigate the Mississippi in its course through Spanish Louisiana was of very much less value, as the goods were brought down stream in river boats and had to be transferred to seagoing vessels for transportation to all parts of the world.[1] With the signing of this treaty with Spain and with the ratification of the British treaty, the first chapter in the international history of the United States closed[2]; but the political differences that had appeared within Congress marked the formation of the first great party organizations in our history.

---

[1] See *Memoirs of Don Manuel de Godoy, Prince of the Peace, written by himself* (London, 1836), i, 459. Godoy states that in this treaty "we realized the first application of modern ideas respecting the equality of maritime rights, and the measures which humanity enjoins in order to lessen the evils of war." For the treaty, see *Treaties and Conventions*, 776. He had not read the treaty with Prussia of 1785, *ibid.*, 710.

[2] It proved to be very difficult to get possession of the country down to the thirty-first parallel. See *The Journal of Andrew Ellicott, . . . Commissioner on Behalf of the United States . . . for determining the Boundary between the United States and the Possessions of his Catholic Majesty* (Philadelphia, 1803); C. Van C. Mathews's *Andrew Ellicott, his Life and Letters* (New York, 1908); and F. L. Riley's "Transition from Spanish to American Rule in Mississippi" in Mississippi Historical Society's *Publications*, iii, 261.

NOTE

American and British Infractions of the Treaty of 1783. — To apportion the blame for the frictions and misunderstandings that arose over the enforcement, or lack of enforcement, of the treaty, an examination of the following dates will be helpful. The Preliminary Articles were signed at Paris on November 30, 1782. On February 14, 1783, an agreement for the cessation of hostilities was signed at Paris. Six days later, February 20, the American commissioners in France issued a proclamation in conformity thereto and this was published at the head of the army in America on April 19 following. The British proclamation of the cessation of hostilities with America and also with France was issued on February 27, 1783, and went into effect at once. Hostilities between the United States and Great Britain ceased therefore in April, 1783. The Definitive Treaty of Peace, however, was not signed by the ministers of the two powers until September 3, 1783. It was not ratified by Congress until January 14, 1784. The British monarch seems to have waited for action by America, for the British ratifications were not signed until April 9 and it was not until May 12, 1784, that the ratifications were exchanged at Paris and the treaty became a solemn binding compact that both nations were bound to respect and enforce. Previously, on April 4, 1782, orders had been issued to Carleton to evacuate New York, Charleston, and Savannah. These orders had been given because the troops stationed at those places were needed elsewhere. No orders had been sent to Haldimand at Quebec to evacuate any post within the limits of his command, because whatever troops were stationed at those places would continue to be needed in Canada. The provisions of the treaty as to Loyalists were not obligatory until the exchange of ratifications; but nearly a year before, on May 30, 1783, Congress recommended to the States to carry out the preliminary articles relating to the Loyalists. The evacuation of New York was delayed by various circumstances, especially by lack of transport; but was finished on November 25, 1783, — before the signing of the Definitive Treaty by the commissioners in Paris was known in America. On January 14, 1784, when Congress ratified the Definitive Treaty, it again urged the just treatment of the Loyalists on the attention of the States.

As to the retention of the posts, we find Haldimand writing to Lord North on November 27, 1783, that they should be retained for the present to avoid an Indian war. On April 8, 1784, Lord Sydney had written to Haldimand that the posts would not be given up until the articles of the treaty, which had not then been ratified, should be complied with. This letter, on its way to Quebec, crossed one from Haldimand, dated May 12, 1784, stating that the posts ought not to be given up until the agreement as to the Loyalists had been carried out by the United States. On June 14, 1784, Haldimand informed Sir John Johnson that Lord Sydney had approved of his refusal to give up the posts "as America has not complied with even one article of the treaty." Whatever one may think of Haldimand's opinions, his refusal to give up the posts until he was ordered so to do by his superiors in England, or was compelled to by force of arms, was entirely correct. The moving cause for the retention of the posts was the influence of British merchants engaged in the Canadian trade. These put pressure upon the government, while Hartley, Franklin, and Adams were vainly trying to revise the preliminary articles. They were reënforced by those who had debts owing to them by residents of America and also by the complaints and petitions of the Loyalists. These last were led by persons of influence in England as James Wright, Thomas Boone, and Lord Dunmore, three former governors of American provinces, and George Chalmers and Guy Johnson. These five names were signed to a petition that was presented at this time. With them were also the names of five American-born refugees, — Joseph Galloway, William Franklin, William Pepperrell, Paul Wentworth, and George Rome. It is to be remembered that the treaty obliged Congress to make a recommendation only, but the meaning of this does not seem to have been understood by any one. According to Jefferson's view, no British creditor had any cause for complaint until he had exhausted all means of judicial relief and this had been denied him in accordance with some State law. The subject at best is a very intricate one. Possibly a good way to leave it will be with the statement that Jefferson made the best possible showing for the United States; but that there was ground for complaint on the other side. As to taking away negroes at the time of the evacuation, the British were clearly in the wrong, but it is difficult to see how Sir Guy Carleton, as an honorable man, could have acted in any other way.

CHAPTER VI

THE RISE OF POLITICAL PARTIES

THERE were no national political parties in the United States in 1789, — as we use the term today. Some leading men, working together, had brought about the formation of the new government; others had opposed it. For the time being, the latter were quite willing to see the new system put into operation, and many of them were willing to aid in its organization. In the new administration and in Congress were many men who had either taken no part in the recent contest or had been in opposition; among these were some of the chiefs of the party that was to overthrow Hamiltonianism at the close of the century. Outside of political life, but not by any means hostile to the administration, were Patrick Henry, who ended his life as a Federalist, and Charles Pinckney, who fought Jefferson's battle in South Carolina in 1800, but would now have been glad to accept an office from Washington. Even the New York politicians — George Clinton, Aaron Burr, and the Livingstons — were satisfied to see the new organization perfected. From the beginning, there were differences of opinion among the executive officers and among the members of both Houses of Congress.[1] Some Congressmen

[1] In the first Congress, ten or a dozen members supported the measures advocated by Hamilton and another dozen opposed them. During the life of the second Congress, Jefferson gathered to himself 23 members of the House of Representatives, and the Hamiltonians numbered 32; but the balance of power was held by 14 who voted first one way and then the other.

stood firmly by Washington and Hamilton and others as
firmly opposed them; but between these extremes were
the mass of Senators and Representatives who voted sometimes one way, sometimes the other, as their interests or
their convictions compelled them. By 1793, opinion began
to crystallize, and by 1796, a definite party alignment had
taken place, but it was on new lines. The differentiation
grew out of varying conceptions of the character of the new
government and was accentuated by the sectionalism due
to divergent industrial conditions, the ever present contests
between capitalism and agrarianism, and between conservatism and radicalism. Moreover, the line of cleavage,
between those who had and those who had not, had been
widened by the disorders of the preceding decade and by
the reaction which had placed the propertied classes in
power.[1]

No one, at this distance of time, can for a moment maintain that Washington and Hamilton and Adams and their
supporters had any immediate expectation of reviving mon-

This solidarity, such as it was, soon
disappeared and in the third Congress
only 17 members consistently supported
Hamiltonian policies and 8 represented
all that was left of Jeffersonianism,
while 76 voted as their wills or their
interests dictated, or did not vote at all.
These figures are taken from a very
useful tabulation that was made by
Professor Orin G. Libby (*Quarterly
Journal of the University of North
Dakota*, iii, no. iv; and see also an
article by the same author in *ibid.*, ii,
no. iii). These articles are the result
of prolonged research and are stimulating, but it is impossible to agree
with many of Professor Libby's de-
ductions, or to accept all the facts as
he has stated them. Professor Charles
A. Beard has likewise tabulated the
votes in both Houses of Congress on
the Assumption according as to whether
a member held public securities or not.
This interesting and painstaking sum-

mation proves conclusively that the
statesmen in that time were actuated
by very much the same motives as
statesmen of later days and, indeed, of
all times and places. See *American
Historical Review*, xix, 282–298.

[1] Charles A. Beard's *Economic Interpretation of the Constitution of the
United States* (New York, 1913) is a
most valuable contribution to our
knowledge of the mainsprings of political activity in this epoch.

Chief Justice William Cushing of
Massachusetts, in a charge to the grand
jury of Bristol County in October, 1787,
favored the adoption of the Constitution
from "the well grounded fear that we
might yet lose our Freedom for want of
Government"; and Henry Knox declared, a few months later, that if it
were rejected, "we shall have to encounter a boisterous and uncertain
Ocean of events."

archy in America; but we must remember that monarchy
then was the general habit of mankind. Hamilton certainly looked upon the English system with its king, lords,
and commoners, with its aristocracy, its middle class, and
lower sort of people, as the most perfect system to be found
anywhere, but he knew full well that nothing of the kind
could be openly set up in the United States. Adams maintained that men were more easily governed when trained
to habits of respect to those in high station. He would
have honored the chief magistrate with some such title as
"His Majesty, the President." He constantly used the
words monarchical, aristocratic, and democratic to describe
a government by three branches. He had no idea that a
limited monarchy would be established in the United States
in his time; but he believed it would come eventually
because jealousy, envy, and ingratitude had ruined every
democracy and every aristocracy and every mixture of the
two. America would be no exception to the march of
history in other lands and in other times.[1] Adams's opinions were well known and found favor in the eyes of Hamilton and his friends and were greatly disliked by many
others.[2] Washington's ideas on monarchy, as on most
things, are locked up in his remarkable reticence. He had
once put aside the allurements of a crown; but now he
took part, with every appearance of willingness, in cere-
monials that dismayed and disgusted many persons of
republican and democratic proclivities. He had asked the
advice of Adams and Hamilton as to what kind of station
he should keep, and the reply of the latter became the basis

[1] See *Old Family Letters copied for Alexander Biddle*, Series A., especially p. 60.

[2] As early as June, 1789, Senator Grayson of Virginia inquired of Patrick Henry if it were not strange that "Mon-archy should issue from the East? Is it not still stranger that John Adams, the son of a tinker, and the creature of the people, should be for titles and dignities and preheminencies?"

of his official conduct.[1] He decided not to maintain an open table, as the presidents of Congress had done. He determined to make no visits and not to receive callers, except on certain stated public occasions. These came to be called "levees," where there was a good deal of stately precision. Mrs. Washington also held her "drawing-rooms," and both the President and his wife were present at public balls.[2] Washington drove about the capital city, whether New York or Philadelphia, in a coach drawn by four cream-colored horses, quite after the Guelphic manner. He made three journeys over the country, which might fairly be likened to royal progresses. An ancient farmer greeted him with "God bless your reign"; a gratulary poet [3] recited to him : —

"Thy Glory beams to Eastern skies,
  See! Europe shares the sacred flame —
And hosts of patriot heroes rise,
  To emulate thy glorious name."

The people, having few days of relaxation and missing their colonial habit of celebrating the natal day of the reigning monarch, kept Washington's birthday as a festival, and this

---

[1] For their replies see *Works of John Adams*, viii, 491 ; and J. C. Hamilton's *Writings of Alexander Hamilton*, iv, p. 1.

[2] Jefferson's account of the inaugural ball, or what served as such, with the President and Mrs. Washington seated on a couch on a raised dais seems to be incorrect ; Mrs. Washington did not reach New York until May 28. See Elizabeth B. Johnston's *Washington Day by Day*, 68, 79 ; and Rufus W. Griswold's *Republican Court*, 156. Some such arrangement may very well have been observed at later balls and been confused in Jefferson's memory with the earlier function which took place before he left France.

[3] For the other side of the picture, see St. George Tucker's *Probationary Odes*, which were first published in Freneau's *Gazette* in 1793 and were gathered into book form with additions in 1796, as, for instance: —

" *Go on, Great* CHIEF, *to make us all,*
Nor from *your shoulders* cast the ball,
    Lest we, like worms, should drop,
Who on a *golden* pippin *prey,*
Till haply on some stormy day
    'Tis shaken from the top."

A suggestion which brings Washington rather near to the "common clay" is found in a letter, written by him December 21, 1794, and printed in *Bulletin of the New York Public Library,* ii, 118.

was enumerated in the opposition newspapers as one of the "Forerunners of Monarchy and Aristocracy in the United States." The establishment instituted by Washington would have fitted well the sovereign of some lesser European principality. It was entirely beyond the views of those who arranged the salary list, and it aroused the suspicions of very many persons who had nearly made up their minds to support the new government.

Sectionalism had begun with the first settlement of the country, owing to the different industrial conditions of the regions then occupied. The same sort of people went to Virginia and to New England; they desired to do similar things, but were forced to adapt themselves to their natural environments. The Virginians tried to introduce concentrated municipal life, entirely without success; the Massachusetts leaders attempted to work their lands in large units; they were obliged to content themselves with farming on a moderate scale and to utilize the rest of their strength in commerce and in the rougher forms of manufacturing. The separation between agrarian and capitalistic effort was not so pronounced in New York and Pennsylvania, or, perhaps, it would be better to say that both were present in the Middle Colonies. These primal differences were soon greatly accentuated by the introduction of black servile labor, which proved to be unsuited to the North and most congenial to the South. With the development of slavery the southern agriculturist became a magnate, the white race an aristocracy, and its more prosperous and stronger men a true landed oligarchy, — the "Virginia Lordlings," as Stephen Higginson termed them.[1] They

---

[1] American Historical Association's *Reports*, 1896, p. 836. Virginia presented the interesting spectacle of a landed aristocracy on all fours with that of England, between the days of the "robber barons" and the brewery

soon came to have the contempt of their class for trade, for shop-keepers and mechanics; and they feared capitalists. Whether the people of these several sections could ever work together in reasonable harmony was distinctly a question for the future in 1789.

Nowadays "secession" and "disunion" have a dreadful sound, but then they had nothing of the kind. The relative advantages and disadvantages of working together or in two or three groups was a subject for discussion and correspondence. Every now and then the putting an end to the existing constitutional arrangement came before the politicians as a practical question for peaceful solution. In 1790, the assuming or not assuming State debts was generally recognized as involving a continuation or a dissolution of the federal system. In 1792, the ending of the Union is constantly mentioned in letters, and Daniel Carroll of Georgetown, one of the commissioners for the Federal City, declared that Congress was unwilling to vote money for carrying out the plans for laying out a city, because there was so strong a disposition to dissolve the government.[1] In 1795, the Reverend John Pierce, noticing the sumptuousness of the new capitol at Hartford, Connecticut, wrote that it "excites the suspicion . . . that it is contemplated by some to make this a Capitol, should there be a division of the Northern from the Southern States." [2] The next

---

earls, — the principal difference being that sixteenth century English aristocrats lived on the exploitation of white workingmen, while those of eighteenth century Virginia were sustained by the labors of black slaves.

[1] Oliver Wolcott, writing to his father, February 8, 1793, declared that the pressure of debts made the Virginia planters unquiet. If the Union with the Southerners should now prove to be unsuccessful, the two sections ought to part like good friends, but "the separation ought to be eternal." Gibbs's

Administrations of Washington and John Adams, i, 86.

[2] Massachusetts Historical Society's *Proceedings*, Second Series, iii, 49. In 1794, John Taylor of Caroline, Senator from Virginia, drew up a memorandum as to the disunion sentiment in Congress, from which it would seem that the Northerners at that moment felt despondent and were not averse to a separation from the South; see Gaillard Hunt's *Disunion Sentiment in Congress in 1794*.

year, Washington devoted a large portion of the farewell address to his "Friends, & Fellow-Citizens" to arguing for the continuance of the "Unity of Government." [1] In the first writing of the address, he adverted to the constant assertions that were made as to the small amount of affection of the several parts of the United States for each other, and that the Union would be dissolved if this measure or that measure were passed. These intimations were indiscreet, he thought, and tended to teach the minds of men to consider the Union as an object to which they ought not to attach their hopes and fortunes. The most notable deliverance on the subject of disunion came from Jefferson in 1798 in a letter to John Taylor of Caroline. Taylor had suggested to a common friend [2] that the way out of all the difficulties that were besetting the South was for that section to separate from the North. Jefferson acknowledged that they were then under "the saddle of Massachusetts and Connecticut," but the temporary superiority of one portion of the country over the rest was no justification for "a scission of the Union." If the New England States were cut off, a Pennsylvania and a Virginia party would

---

[1] This address has been printed over and over again, nowhere better than in Avery's *History of the United States* (vii, 407). Washington looked upon the federal system as the "palladium of your political safety and prosperity." He thought the people should "reverence the Union," suit their actions to that idea, and discountenance any suspicion that it can be abandoned. As to the authorship of the address, see *Works of Alexander Hamilton* (Lodge), vii, 143 note, and Horace Binney's *Inquiry into the Formation of Washington's Farewell Address* (Philadelphia, 1859).

[2] June 4, 1798, Jefferson at Philadelphia wrote to John Taylor as follows: —

"Mr. New shewed me your letter on the subject, of the patent, which gave me an opportunity of observing what you said as to the effect with you of public proceedings, and that it was not unusual now to estimate the separate mass of Virginia and N. Carolina, with a view to their separate existence."

See the letter in the "Washburn Collection of Autographs" in the cabinet of the Massachusetts Historical Society, and printed in its *Collections*, as above, with trifling differences (7th Series, i, 61, 62). As printed in Ford's *Jefferson* (vii, 263) the words "not unusual" are given "not unwise." A note pasted into some copies states that the correct reading is "not usual" and refers to the *Southern Literary Messenger* for May, 1838 (iv, 344), which states correctly the reading, "it was not unusual now."

immediately arise in the "residuary confederacy." It was convenient to have some one to quarrel with and the New Englanders were good for that purpose. "A little patience and we shall see the reign of witches pass over" and the South will come into its own.

One thing that postponed attempts to divide the Union into two or three portions was the adoption of the first eleven amendments.[1] In their eagerness for ratification, Washington and Madison had practically pledged themselves to labor for the passage of amendments that would make the Constitution more palatable. Washington in his inaugural had earnestly set forth the need of attending to this at once; but, after the new machinery began to work, the pressure for amendments entirely died away. Nevertheless, Madison brought the matter forward by proposing a set of amendments founded on those that had been suggested by the ratifying conventions. A committee was appointed to report on these resolutions, but there was no interest displayed. The only thing that attracted attention was as to what form the changes should take : Should there be an actual change in the wording of the Constitution or should the proposed amendments be placed by themselves at the end of the document? Some of the State constitutions, like that of Virginia, were merely parts of the statute law and could be amended by ordinary legislative act. The new national Constitution was plainly very different, for one reason, because Congress and the

[1] H. V. Ames brought together a mass of matter in his *Proposed Amendments to the Constitution of the United States* (American Historical Association's *Report* for 1896, vol. ii). In the *American Historical Review* (ii, p. 100) he has printed a report from a committee from the Massachusetts legislature in 1790 on additional amendments to the Constitution which is very interesting. Considering the importance of the first ten amendments, it is astonishing how little one can find about them in the documentary sources or in the writings on the Constitution and the works of those who secured their consideration and adoption.

government itself owed its very existence to that organic law. By changing the words of the original instrument, the constitutional status of the government might be imperilled. It was decided, therefore, to place the amendments by themselves at the end of the document. Twelve amendments were adopted by Congress and submitted to the States (September 25, 1789). Two of the twelve were rejected because they dealt with matters of detail. Of the ten that were adopted, the first eight had to do with the rights of individuals and were restrictions upon the exercise of power by the central government. The other two amendments, the ninth and the tenth, were actual changes in the nature of the fundamental law and were intended to place a limitation on the strong nationalistic tendency of the Constitution. In none of these amendments was any attempt made to define the word "power" and the phrase "necessary and proper" used in section eight of the first article of the Constitution itself. Yet that was the moment for the enemies of a strong central government to carry their point. The Constitution is hardly more than paragraphs of precepts which are to be defined and executed according to a strict or liberal interpretation. It was inevitable that if the strict interpretation was not insisted upon at the beginning, the other would become the accepted canon.

On one subject connected with the general distributions of powers, there soon came to be a reasonable amount of unanimity. A clause that had suddenly appeared in the draft of the Constitution, on its emergence from one of the committees [1] to which it was referred, was that which provided for the suability of a State by a citizen of another

[1] Oliver Ellsworth, in his old age, declared that "he himself was one of the five who drew up that Constitution." W. G. Brown's *Oliver Ellsworth*, 170.

State. Before long three or four suits were entered under this clause. Patrick Henry and the Virginia Yazooites had thought of suing the State of Georgia because of its cavalier treatment of their claims.[1] George Mason, too, had taken steps looking toward testing the right of Virginia to repudiate her contract with the Indiana claimants,[2] and suits had actually been entered against Massachusetts, New Jersey, and Georgia. The last of these had been brought by the heirs of Alexander Chisholm to enforce the payment of certain claims that had come down from Revolutionary days. Georgia refused to appear. The Supreme Court of the United States ordered judgment by default to be entered against the State at the next term, unless Georgia should appear, or show cause to the contrary. As Georgia remained contumacious, judgment was entered for Chisholm, February, 1794. No actual writ of execution was ever issued, partly, no doubt, because the State legislature by law declared it to be a felony to proceed any further in this matter, thus nullifying the decision of the Supreme Court, the Judiciary Act passed by Congress, and the provision of the Constitution itself.[3] Congress at once adopted an amendment to the Constitution, — which was later ratified,[4] — declaring that that instrument should not be construed to permit any suit to be brought against a State by a citizen of another State or of a foreign

---

[1] See W. W. Henry's *Patrick Henry*, ii, 514.

[2] See K. M. Rowland's *Life of George Mason*, ii, 343.

[3] The opinions of the judges are in *A Case decided in the Supreme Court of the United States, in February, 1793. In which is discussed the question—"Whether a state be liable to be sued by a private citizen of another state?"* (Philadelphia, 1793).

[4] It is difficult to account for the working of cause and effect in the adoption of the first eleven amendments. In Congress, Madison seemed to be almost the only one who had any interest in the first batch of amendments, but ten of the twelve were almost at once adopted by three-fourths of the State legislatures. In the case of the Eleventh Amendment, the States had appeared to be greatly interested in securing it; but when Congress fell in with their wishes, it took no less than four years for three-quarters of the States to vote in favor of ratification.

country, thus reëstablishing the sovereign irresponsibility of the States.

When Jefferson came to New York in March, 1790, he looked upon Hamilton with favorable eyes as the co-worker with Madison, his own most intimate friend. For some months the two labored in harmony to organize the new system. The first hint of distrust of Jefferson on Hamilton's part is in a memorandum made by Colonel Beckwith, in which the Secretary of the Treasury is represented as speaking of Jefferson's opinions respecting the British government and "possible predilections elsewhere," namely, in favor of France.[1] Jefferson, at very nearly the same point of time, began to question Hamilton's financial doings. Sundry accounts had been printed from the Treasury Department. Few dates were given to the separate items and some of them were very vaguely stated.[2] Jefferson asked Hamilton for something more definite, as he had a right to do as one of the trustees of the sinking fund. He got no satisfaction. As time went on, he became greatly distressed at the extent to which speculation ran. From this beginning, he became thoroughly distrustful, especially as he was convinced that the capital that so eagerly went into the bank, into commerce, and into speculative ventures of all kinds was so much drawn from agriculture. Worthington Ford, in one of his illuminating and elusive editorial notes, declares that the trouble with the Virginians was that in estimating the produce of their tobacco crops they added two and two together to make five, while their agents

[1] This comes out in a memorandum made by Colonel Beckwith; see *Canadian Archives*, 1890, p. 148; for the identification of persons, see *ibid.*, xli.

[2] Joseph Jones, another Virginian, had similar trouble. He found Hamilton's report on the sinking fund "intricate and so complicated it appears to one to require some time and attention to understand. At first view I think it well calculated to keep us all in the dark excepting those . . . who thrive on speculation." Massachusetts Historical Society's *Proceedings*, Second Series, xv, 122n, 140.

in England could only make three by the same process. There was something hopelessly optimistic in a Virginia planter's calculations as to the profits that were coming to him and something hopelessly pessimistic as to the business performances of other persons.

In the spring of 1792, Jefferson stated his opinions as to public policies in a letter to Washington. The public debt, he declared, was greater than could possibly be paid. It had been created by adding together the creditor and debtor sides of the accounts and other projects were on foot to increase the mass of the debt. The ultimate object was to pave the way for the establishment of monarchy. The financial system had already produced a mass of speculators who had got into Congress and made a majority in both Houses. Jefferson had been communicating these thoughts to his confidential correspondents for some time. In writing to Washington, he fully realized that his letter would at once be turned over to Hamilton, which was exactly what happened. Replying to Jefferson, Washington deplored the dissensions that had taken place among his advisers. In rejoinder, Jefferson denied that he had ever intrigued with the legislative department and he had meddled with the other executive departments as little as possible. At the time of the assumption of the State debts, Hamilton had made a tool of him and he had then interfered with legislation; but he had never used his influence to defeat the Secretary's plans. Jefferson admitted that he had expressed disapproval of the Hamiltonian system in private conversations; but this was because it flowed from principles adverse to liberty and calculated to undermine the republic. In the circumstances, he implored the President to serve another term, and Washington consenting, Jefferson, himself, agreed to remain at the Department of State for the coming year, 1793. Jefferson had analyzed correctly enough the motives that actuated Hamilton and the means by which he was carrying out his policy. Not being able to secure a "strong government" directly through the Federal Convention, Hamilton was gradually building up such an organization by a liberal interpretation of the Constitution and by executive action. Years afterward, in his old age, Madison accounted for the breach between Jefferson and himself, on the one side, and Washington and Hamilton, on the other, by Hamilton's making perfectly plain "his purpose and endeavour to *administration* [administer] the Government into a thing totally different from that which he and I both knew perfectly well had been understood and intended by the Convention who framed it, and by the People adopting it." [1]

Jefferson undertook the task of consolidating and harmonizing the forces that were opposed to Hamilton and all his works. Superficially Jefferson would seem to be far removed from the successful politician. He was an idealist, a believer in the perfectability of human nature, and a student of prehistoric beasts. His earlier life in the remoter parts of Virginia had freed his mind from many of the shackles of civilization, the struggles of the American Revolution had strengthened his radicalism, and intercourse with the leaders of the first phases of the French Revolution had intensified it. To Jefferson the people

[1] Nicholas P. Trist to Martin Van Buren, May 31, 1857, "Van Buren Manuscripts" in Library of Congress. This paper was brought to my attention by Mr. Gaillard Hunt, to whom I am indebted for many courtesies. In a somewhat similar vein, in a letter to Lafayette, dated December 25, 1798, Washington charged the Republicans with the intention to "oppose the government in all its measures, and . . . by clogging its wheels indirectly to change the nature of it, and to subvert the constitution." *Writings of Washington* (Ford), xiv, 123. There is a keen and discriminating analysis of Hamilton's motives in W. G. Sumner's *Alexander Hamilton* in the "Makers of America" series.

were the only sure reliance for the preservation of liberty. They should be educated and informed, so that they might see it was for their interest to preserve peace and order. For monarchies and aristocracies and oligarchies, he had dread and contempt. There should be a rebellion every twenty years to warn rulers that the people have preserved the spirit of resistance. "The tree of liberty must be refreshed, from time to time, with the blood of patriots and tyrants. It is its natural manure." [1] "Were there but an Adam & an Eve left in every country, & left free, it would be better than as it now is." [2] What were the tranquillity and ease of a few years in comparison with the happiness of millions to come? In the existing condition of human depravity — due to ignorance — there must be government by compulsion. There should be as little of it as possible, — just enough to keep men from interfering with the rights of others to life, liberty, and the pursuit of happiness. Jefferson had some small faith in representative institutions, but charters, constitutions, and laws had no sanctity in his eyes. He even advocated the ending of all constitutions and laws at stated periods that the people might begin again with a clean slate.[3] Coupled with these extremely radical notions, one finds some things more nearly allied to his social position on the fringe of the Virginia aristocracy. Thus in 1788, the Paris world seemed to him politically mad and the French people not yet ripe for receiving the blessings to which they were entitled by the laws of nature.[4]

[1] To W. S. Smith, and to Madison, Paris, November and December, 1787; *Diplomatic Correspondence, 1783–1789*, iii, 340, 353.

[2] *Writings of Jefferson* (Ford), vi, 154
[3] *Ibid.*, v, 115–124.
[4] *Ibid.*, v, 9, 53. Fourteen years after this time, when the holding of high office may have temporarily sapped his theoretical radicalism, he wrote to Peale, the artist, whose son was to take the bones of a mammoth to Europe for exhibition, that he would better divide the spectators into three groups to keep

In 1793, the war between England and France came into
American politics, greatly complicating the issues. The
"monocrats," as Jefferson dubbed the followers of Hamilton, strove vigorously for justice to England; American
citizens, they agreed, ought to reject "all novelties and
innovations" and guard against "any deterioration of our
principles."[1] They held that modern French ideas were
inconsistent with the present state of society in America,
— as, indeed, they were. The Hamiltonians, or Federalists,
as they were now called, believed in aristocracies and looked
upon themselves as the best people and the wisest. As one
of the other side put it: "Fedralism" charmed by the
allurements of its melody "the learned, the wise, the polite,
the reputable, the honorable, and virtuous:" all the rest
of the world were "poor, ignorant asses." George Cabot
— the Sage of Massachusetts Federalism — had no faith
whatever in the rule of the people; his panacea for the
ills assailing American society was to confine the franchise
to those possessing a considerable amount of landed property. Other Federalists would not have gone as far as
this, but that party was reactionary and aristocratic from
start to finish and became more reactionary and more aristocratic with each successive year.

At the opposite end of the line, the radicals warmly
welcomed French revolutionary ideas and adopted Parisian
modes with startling alacrity. They mounted the cockade,
wore the red cap, sang the "Ça ira," and formed democratic
societies. They were most forward in Pennsylvania, for
there radicalism was the most rampant. The formation
of societies spread to other parts of the country, and a sort
of organization of the whole was on the point of being effected when the yellow fever at Philadelphia in the sum-

"the decent part of them" from being   etc. *Ibid.*, viii, 152.
mixed with pickpockets, chimney sweeps,   [1] Skeel's *Noah Webster*, i, 383.

mer of 1793 carried off so many of the leaders that the
project came to an abrupt ending.

As the years went by, Jefferson became more and more
the leader of the opposition. His political methods were
inscrutable. By inheritance, he was a plantation magnate,
by nature he was a scholastic hermit, living a life of retirement on his estate — or wherever he chanced to be. He
charmed both men and women by his talk, but could not
make a speech to a crowd of his assembled fellow citizens.
He lacked the particular kind of personal magnetism that
is nowadays looked upon as essential to a political leader.
Apparently, Jefferson was as unfitted to found and drill
a great party as any man who has appeared in the front
rank of American history. He early realized that the newspapers were essential to the formation of public opinion.
Indeed, if he had had his choice between government by
publicity and government by compulsion, he would have
taken the former. He found his self-imposed task very
difficult, for the success of the new government which
alarmed him did not arouse misgivings in the minds of a
large portion of his countrymen.[1] To focus public opinion
in opposition to the evil acts of the Hamiltonians, he established, or helped to establish, a newspaper at Philadelphia.
This was the "National Gazette," which was edited by
Philip Freneau, who is best known as a writer of verse.[2]

[1] See letters from Joseph Jones to
Madison in Massachusetts Historical
Society's *Proceedings* for June, 1901,
pp. 117–161. In the introduction to
these letters, Worthington C. Ford has
given one of the best and briefest accounts of the origin of the Jeffersonian
party.

[2] See P. L. Ford's "Freneau's National Gazette" in *The Nation* for February 21, 1895. *Writings of Madison*
(Hunt), vi, 46 and note, 117 ; *Writings
of Jefferson* (Ford), v, 330, 373 ; letter

of Ædanus Burke in G. Hunt's "Office-
Seeking during Jefferson's Administration" in *American Historical Review*,
iii, 279. In the "Hamilton Manuscripts" at Washington are two bits of
information which seem to show that
Hamilton got his idea that Jefferson
was at the bottom of the founding of the
National Gazette from Francis Childs,
the New York printer, through Jonathan
Dayton ; see Hamilton to Rufus King,
July 25, 1792, and Dayton to Hamilton,
Aug. 26, 1792.

Jefferson's connection with this undertaking is obscure, as is pretty much everything else in his political career. He welcomed Freneau, gave him a small clerkship in the Department of State, did what he could to promote the circulation of the paper, and contributed to it indirectly. Freneau's "Gazette" had only a short life, but its place was more than filled by the "General Advertiser" or "Aurora," as it was termed after the first year or so. Its first editor was Benjamin Franklin Bache, grandson of Dr. Franklin, and inheritor of his prejudices. The "Aurora" soon developed a feature of personal abuse which had hitherto been absent, but was to be wofully extended by William Duane, who succeeded to the paper and to the prejudices. The obstacles to the establishment of an influential newspaper were the small amount of advertising and the high cost of delivery. The latter led to the establishment of countless local papers. These copied extensively from the leading city papers and thus transmitted, though very slowly, news and partisan opinions from one end of the country to the other.

On his retirement from the Department of State [1] to Monticello, Jefferson was a disheartened man; so far he had made very little headway in his opposition to Hamilton, who had vexed him by referring to the Republican Party as a faction. The friction with Britain preceding Jay's Treaty seemed to him to give a new lead. He now redoubled his efforts to discredit the Hamiltonians by connecting them with the speculation and with the British. He talked and wrote about a "corrupt squadron" that existed in Congress to carry through Hamilton's plans, and

---

[1] Paul Leicester Ford (*Writings of Jefferson*, vi, 116 note) writes that class feeling in Philadelphia was so keen that only three of Jefferson's equals would have him at their houses. It was at about this time that Jefferson asked Madison if it would be wise to coalesce with the democrats?

asserted over and over again that the Federalists were
under British influence.[1] There was a groundwork of
truth in both assertions. Senator Bingham, one of the
most influential men in that party, was closely connected
with American financiers and with the Barings of London,
as has already been noted, and the same thing was true
of Robert Morris, Bingham's predecessor in the Senate.
Gouverneur Morris had taken a very prominent part in
the framing of the Constitution and had then gone to
Europe to represent the financial interests of Robert Morris,
Henry Knox, and other Americans. In an audience with
King George he reminded the monarch that his own eldest
brother was the husband of the Duke of Gordon's daughter,
a lieutenant-general in the British army, and at that very
moment in command of the fortress at Plymouth. In the
latter half of this decade, Gouverneur Morris travelled over
central Europe, seemingly as the confidential, though
unofficial, representative of Lord Grenville, the head of the
British Foreign Office.[2] It is worth noting, too, that the
sister of William Duer, whose name has so often appeared
in these pages, was the wife of George Rose, Secretary of
the British Lords of the Treasury, and one of William Pitt's
right-hand men. There is little doubt as to the interlock-
ing of the financial and political interests of the rulers of the
Federalist party, and little doubt of their close connection
with persons high in finance and politics in Great Britain.
There were English and Scottish commercial firms and
agencies at Richmond and Charleston and other places
in the South as well as in the commercial centers of the
North; but they had no such relations with their Southern

---

[1] One of the earliest asseverations as
to British influence was made by Genêt
in August, 1793, according to Noah
Webster. See Skeel's *Webster*, i, 370.

[2] See *Dropmore Manuscripts*, iii, 87,
226, 563 in Royal Historical Manuscripts Commission's *Report* for 1899.

customers and neighbors as existed between the London
capitalists and their Northern customers. They bought
tobacco, rice, and flour from the planters and marketed
them in Europe; or sold them on commission. They also
supplied the planters with imported goods. With few
exceptions Virginians were indebted to the commission
merchants, who were disliked as creditors and also as having a commercial monopoly.[1] The cry of British influence,
therefore, found ready listeners in the Southern States.

Jefferson soon found himself at the head of what may
well be called a political organization, although the connecting bonds were vague, and, for the time being, the
number of persons taking part was distinctly limited. They
were men of remarkable political astuteness, and many of
them achieved great success in the eyes of the world. Two
of them, Madison and Monroe, occupied the President's
office in succession to Jefferson; and a third, Albert Gallatin, was only second to these, if he was that. The others
occupied important political stations, either in the national
government or in their States. Occasionally, Jefferson
consulted with his most intimate political friends. Otherwise, he carried on his work by correspondence and by writings in the political press which he drew from his friends.
So far as can be seen, the Republican Party had no other
organization; but in every State and in every important
town by 1796, there were to be found men who looked to
Jefferson for their political salvation and for the salvation
of their country, and waited the opportunity to carry out

---

[1] As a means of finding employment for the slaves on his plantations, in the off season of field work, Jefferson began the manufacture of nails. He procured nail rods from Philadelphia and had them beaten into proper shape at Monticello and then found it impossible to sell his product at Richmond, because the hardware dealers there were afraid to handle any nails except those of the British forwarders to whom they necessarily looked for financial favors. *Writings of Jefferson* (Ford), vii, 50.

his wishes. Almost never has a political party been so efficiently and so secretly marshalled and led. Much of this success was due to the wise counsel and skill displayed by Albert Gallatin as leader of the opposition in Congress. This extraordinary man was a Swiss from Geneva. He had crossed the Atlantic in pursuit of "Liberty." After participating in the Revolutionary contest in eastern Maine, he had taught French at Harvard College, had lived a year or two in Virginia, and had then turned farmer and store-keeper in western Pennsylvania. According to his own account, he was a bad farmer and a poor merchant, and spent more of his time in reading than he did in business.[1] He had been involved in the Whiskey Insurrection and largely for this reason had been denied a seat in the national Senate. In 1795, however, he was permitted to enter the House of Representatives. He at once took the lead of the opposition, Madison turning over to him the power that hitherto he had wielded.

The Federalists had more organization than the Republicans. For one thing they had the advantage of occupying nearly all of the federal offices. Then, too, presiding over the party's destinies were a dozen men of great ability and administrative experience. Three things were in the way of their continued success. The first was the undoubted unpopularity which Jefferson had managed to cast about several of their measures. Another was the autocratic tone of the leaders. A Federalist letter always begins "It is decided" or "It has been determined," — the "it" meaning that either Hamilton, or two or three men guided

---

[1] For Gallatin's early career, see Henry Adams's *Life of Albert Gallatin*, 1–75. The statements given in the text as to Gallatin's lack of success in business are taken from a letter that he wrote to Lewis F. Delesdernier, dated Philadelphia, May 25, 1798; see Maine Historical Society's *Collections*, vi, 100, 101.

by him, had come to a certain conclusion. In similar cases, on the other side of the political boundary, Jefferson's commands take the form of "Our friends think;" the difference was wide and was vital. The third obstacle to the long-continued predominance of the Federalist party was the lack of harmony within its ranks which clustered about the person and pretensions of John Adams.

As far back as the days of the Revolution, when Adams was a member of the Continental Congress, he had fallen under suspicion of the military group,[1] some of the members of which were now at the head of the Federalist party. He had opposed the permanency of military appointments and had also upheld democratic principles. A wider acquaintance with the world had changed his outlook. He was known to be opposed to the calling of a general convention to change the Constitution, and, besides, as the President was to come from the South, it was only right that the Vice-President should come from the North, — and supporting Adams for the second place would cast the weight of Massachusetts into the federal scale. These were the reasons[2] that led Madison, the Morrises, and Hamilton to advocate the election of John Adams to the vice-presidency in 1788. As the State elections proceeded, Hamilton became alarmed lest Adams should receive more electoral votes than Washington. He wrote to influential persons in Connecticut and New Jersey to induce them to see to it that some of the electoral votes in their State were cast

---

[1] John Adams to Nathanael Greene in C. F. Adams's *Works of John Adams*, i, 263; J. C. Hamilton's *Life of Alexander Hamilton*, i, 419; Madison to Jefferson, October 17, 1788 in Madison's *Writings* (Congress Ed.), i, 423, and also in Hunt's edition, v, 270.

[2] W. A. Duer's *Constitutional Jurisprudence of the United States*, 370. The original letter is in the "Madison Papers" in the Library of Congress and is dated only 1788 as in the printed text. In a postcript Duer writes that he had no objection to "R. & G. Morris seeing this letter," — a significant indication of the political method of the time. Duer writes on the authority of Henry Knox that Adams will strenuously oppose calling another general convention.

away from Adams.[1] The upshot was, that while Washington received one vote from every elector, Adams had only thirty-four out of the sixty-nine second electoral votes. A little later, when some busy-body carried the news of this diversion of electoral votes to the Vice-President, it assumed in his mind the shape of "a dark and dirty intrigue . . . to spread a panic lest John Adams should be President."[2] At first Adams had been consulted on affairs; but before long Washington seems to have ceased advising with him. Moreover, the Vice-President's eagerness for high-sounding titles and for the establishment of a strong government alienated many persons who had expected to find in him an apostle of democracy. They stigmatized him as a foe to liberty and, garbling his printed statements, declared that he wished to set the rich and the well-born by themselves in a Senate.[3] Nevertheless, his honesty and open ways gave John Adams continued place in the affections of his countrymen, and, besides, there was no other man in the Federalist party to compete with him. He was reëlected

---

[1] This comes out in a letter from Jeremiah Wadsworth to Hamilton, dated "Hartford, February, 1789." He acknowledged the receipt of Hamilton's letter of January 25, which came in good time — "Our votes were given agreeably to your wishes — Washington, 7; Adams, 5. Governor Huntington, 2." J. C. Hamilton's *Works of Alexander Hamilton*, i, 492.

[2] Adams to Benjamin Rush, June 9, 1789 in *Old Family Letters: copied from the Originals for Alexander Biddle*, Series A. (Philadelphia, 1892), p. 37.

[3] John Adams's words are: "The rich, the well-born, and the able, acquire an influence among the people, that will soon be too much for simple honesty and plain sense, in a house of representatives. The most illustrious of them must therefore be separated from the mass, and placed by themselves in a senate: this is, to all honest and useful intents, an ostracism. A member of a senate, of immense wealth, the most respected birth, and transcendent abilities, has no influence in the nation, in comparison of what he would have in a single representative assembly. When a senate exists, the most powerful man in the state may be safely admitted into the house of representatives, because the people have it in their power to remove him into the senate as soon as his influence becomes dangerous." This occurs on the 13th page of the preface to the original edition of Adams's *Defence of the Constitutions of Government of the United States of America* (London, 1787). The whole essay seems to be rather innocuous and, indeed, hardly to deserve the place that has been given it. See, however, C. M. Walsh's *The Political Science of John Adams* (New York, 1915).

to the second place, in 1792, and when Washington announced his determination to retire from public life in 1796, no other Federalist stood a chance against John Adams for the first place.

It must not be supposed that Jefferson had it all his own way in the opposition party, although he was distinctly the leader. There were the Pennsylvania democrats with whom he had hesitated to coalesce; and then there were the New York politicians, who always had their own ideas as to their merits and due rewards. Among these was Aaron Burr, one of the most extraordinary and lamentable figures of American political history. He was of good Connecticut family. His wife was the widow of an officer in the British army. At the outset, Burr, like so many others, was disposed to support Washington and the administration, but like nearly every one else, he expected to be recognized by those in power. Burr and Hamilton were rivals in law and local politics, and Burr was the more dextrous. He thought his friends should have some part in the new arrangements; but Hamilton was determined to fill every place, elective or appointive, and Burr was forced into opposition with the Livingstons and the Clintons. In 1791, he caused himself to be chosen to the national Senate. He made such skilful use of all the opportunities that came in his way that he was unquestionably the second personage in the opposition, and was, therefore, necessarily the candidate of the Republican party for Vice-President in 1796, so far as there was any.

As the year 1796 drew on, it became evident that four candidates would gain nearly all the electoral votes. On the Federalist side, John Adams and Thomas Pinckney [1] were most prominent. The latter had gained considerable

---

[1] For a differentiation of the Pinckneys, see Note on p. 210.

applause, especially in the South, by the negotiation of the Spanish treaty of 1795. The other two most prominent personages in the minds of the electors were Jefferson and Burr. There were thus two Southerners and two Northerners on whom the voting was certain to be concentrated. In the lax party ties of the time, sectional preferences were likely to exercise a powerful influence, especially as Burr was as obnoxious to Jefferson as Adams was to the Hamiltonians. As the months went by there was strong probability that many Southern electors would vote for Pinckney and Jefferson, thus leaving out of account both Adams and Burr. For fear that something of this kind might happen eighteen Northern electors gave their second votes to some one other than Pinckney. On the other hand, the eight South Carolinians voted solidly for Pinckney and Jefferson. When the votes were counted, it was found that Adams had seventy-one votes, Jefferson sixty-eight, Pinckney fifty-nine, and Burr thirty. This gave the presidency to Adams, the vice-presidency to Jefferson, and showed that Burr would have to be seriously reckoned with in the future.

While the election was still in doubt, Jefferson wrote to Madison authorizing him in case of a tie between himself and Adams to solicit votes for the latter, as he was the senior and had always preceded him in the march of public life. He also wrote a friendly letter to Adams which Madison might deliver or not as he thought best. One of the most dramatic moments in our history was at the close of the inauguration or instalment of John Adams on March 4, 1797. It occurred after the ending of his inaugural address, when, descending to the floor, he started to leave the hall, first stepping back to give his predecessor the precedence. This Washington declined and went down the hall following the new President and the new Vice-President of the United

States.   It was not in a similar spirit that the radical Republicans hailed Washington's departure from office: "'Lord,
now lettest thou thy servant depart in peace, for mine
eyes have seen thy salvation' . . . for the man, who is
the source of all the misfortunes of our country, is this day
reduced to a level with his fellow-citizens." [1]   This classic
of unseemly libel, as Worthington Ford has so aptly termed
it, was merely a repetition, unconscious probably, of what
Jefferson had written in the preceding year to Madison:
"I wish that his [Washington's] honesty and his political
errors may not furnish a second occasion to exclaim, 'curse
on his virtues, the've undone his country!'"

[1] *The Aurora* of March 6, 1797.
These words were written by Franklin's
grandson, B. F. Bache, and reflect the
family resentment at the chilling treatment of the venerable sage by Washington. See W. C. Ford's *Spurious Letters
Attributed to Washington*, 158. Duane
disclaimed the authorship in *New-England Historical and Genealogical Register*,
xxv, 386.

As very few copies of this number of
The Aurora have stood the rack of time,
the passage is here given in full : —

"'Lord, now lettest thou thy servant
depart in peace, for mine eyes have seen
thy salvation,' was the pious ejacula-
tion of a man who beheld a flood of
happiness rushing in upon mankind.
If ever there was a time that would license the reiteration of the exclamation,
that time is now arrived ; for the man
who is the source of all the misfortunes
of our country, is this day reduced to
a level with his fellow citizens, and is no
longer possessed of power to multiply
evils upon the United States. If ever
there was a period for rejoicing, this is

the moment — every heart, in unison
with the freedom and happiness of the
people, ought to beat high with ex-
ultation that the name of WASHINGTON
from this day ceases to give a currency
to political iniquity, and to legalize
corruption. A new æra is now opening
upon us, an æra which promises much
to the people ; for public measures
must now stand upon their own merits,
and nefarious projects can no longer be
supported by a name. When a retrospect is taken of the WASHINGTONIAN
administration for eight years, it is
a subject of the greatest astonishment,
that a single individual should have
cankered the principles of republicanism in an enlightened people, just
emerged from the gulph of despotism,
and should have carried his designs
against the public liberty so far, as to
have put in jeopardy its very existence.
Such however are the facts, and with
these staring us in the face, this day
ought to be a JUBILEE in the United
States."

NOTE

Political Manners. — With the halos that now illumine the heads of Washington and Adams, it is difficult to understand the language that was applied to them in the last years of the eighteenth century and also the language that they themselves sometimes employed. Bache's valedictory has been given in the text. Jefferson, writing to Mazzei [1] and plainly referring to Washington, told him that he would be surprised to learn the names of those " who were Samsons in the field & Solomons in the council, but who have had their heads shorn by the harlot England." Paine's letter [2] to Washington went beyond all bounds, even beyond Bache: " And as to you, sir, treacherous in private friendship, and a hypocrite in public life, the world would be puzzled to decide, whether you are an apostate or an imposter; whether you have abandoned good principles, or whether you ever had any." Washington, on his part, held a vigorous pen. He described himself as having been attacked " in such exaggerated and indecent terms as could scarcely be applied to a Nero, a notorious defaulter, or even to a common pickpocket." [3]

Among the most picturesque figures was Matthew Lyon, an Irishman of Ulster stock, from county Wicklow, who was in Congress from the State of Vermont.[4] He refused to march in the procession to present an address to Washington and, later getting into controversy with Representative Griswold of Connecticut, spat in his face, and the two of them took to sticks and tongs on the floor of the House. Lyon later became a Kentucky frontiersman, — the " Beast of Vermont prowls in the western wilderness." He turned upon some of his old friends with verbal ferocity. Indignantly denying Randolph's charge that he had been bribed, Lyon thanked his " Creator that he gave him the face of a man, not that of an ape or a monkey."

[1] *Writings of Jefferson* (Ford), vii, 72, **74** note, 76. The letter is dated Monticello, April 24, 1796. Jefferson's earlier letter is printed in *ibid.*, vii, 69.

[2] See *Alexandria Gazette*, February 18, 1797.

[3] *Writings of Washington* (Ford), xiii, 231.

[4] See J. Fairfax McLaughlin's *Matthew Lyon, The Hampden of Congress* (New York, 1900); *Annals of Congress*, 8th Cong., 2nd Sess., 1126.

CHAPTER VII

AN INTERLUDE

BETWEEN the acts of the political and financial drama in America, the X, Y, Z affair and the quasi-war with France came on the stage to add to the strain of domestic strife. When James Monroe arrived at Paris in August, 1794, he found the French Revolutionary kaleidoscope turning with great rapidity. He took a most fraternal tone toward the powers that happened to be at the moment; but found it difficult to keep up with the ever changing colors and arrangements of parties. Revolutionists of every hue were hungry for money, partly to line their own pockets and partly to wage war against surrounding enemies. Frenchmen had helped the American people to get on their feet, and to thrust out their ancient governor. Why should not they reciprocate and aid their fellow-citizens of France in dealing another stroke at perfidious Albion and all its allies? It would be undesirable for them to take an open part in the conflict on the side of France, because the moment their neutral character was violated the navies of Britain would put an end to their supplying Frenchmen with food. Would it not be possible for the United States to anticipate payment of the rest of the debt still owing to France and, perhaps, even to lend their fellow republicans some new money? Monroe apparently left the United States with assurances from Randolph, who was then Sec-

retary of State, that Jay's mission to England had no other
purpose than to put an end to the existing friction with
that country. French spies at London reported that the
new treaty would not be so innocuous as Monroe asserted.
He applied to Jay for information. This Jay was perfectly willing to give, provided Monroe would keep it to himself; but this was precisely what Monroe could not and
would not promise to do. When the treaty was published,
Pickering sent it to him with a long despatch directing him
to assure the French authorities that it had nothing to do
with previous treaties and to lay before them a long list of
grievances on the part of Americans against France. Instead of doing this, Monroe tried to palliate what seemed to
him to be the ill faith of his superiors at Philadelphia and
their envoy at London. There was a good deal to be said
for the French view of the treaty, for any settlement of the
existing friction between the United States and Great
Britain would be of assistance to the latter and, therefore,
hostile to the interests of France. Moreover, although Jay's
Treaty contained a clause saying in so many words that none
of the new conditions in it were to interfere with the obligations of preëxisting treaties, the arrangement that the
British might seize provisions on their way to France on
condition of making payment was likely to be of great
service to Britain and correspondingly harmful to France.
It was difficult for Monroe to explain away this actual,
though not technical, extension of the rule as to contraband. The suggestions that were made as to supplying
money to the Revolutionary cause seemed to him to be
reasonable; but the ceaseless fallings of the guillotine had
alienated the sympathies of great numbers of persons in
America and had made Americans unwilling to give aid
and comfort to the French revolutionists. Gouverneur

Morris reported to the Federalist leaders the weakness of Monroe's action.[1] They, after their habit, put pressure upon Washington to remove him and appoint another person who would ascertain the views of the French government and faithfully report them to the President.

Washington yielded to the promptings of Hamilton and Pickering, recalled Monroe (August, 1796), and sent in his place Charles Cotesworth Pinckney of South Carolina,[2] — a stiff-necked Federalist. As between Britain and France all his predilections were for the former, for he and his brother, Thomas Pinckney, had been educated at Westminster School and had grown up in intimate intercourse with Englishmen. Thomas Pinckney, in 1795, had been in Paris on his way to Madrid. He had with him a copy of the project of Jay's Treaty, but did not show it to Monroe. He also held himself aloof from the French authorities and did his own negotiating in Spain without asking their intercession. Charles Cotesworth Pinckney was one of the best examples of the Southern slave-holding aristocracy, but his appointment at this precise moment to the French mission was most unfortunate. Washington might as well have sent Jay or Hamilton to Paris in 1796 as to have sent him there. Pinckney landed at Bordeaux, and made the best of his way to the French capital, which he reached

---

[1] See letters from Hamilton to Washington in the Library of Congress. One of these is dated May 5, 1796; the other has no date, but is indorsed as received on June 23, 1796. For a more favorable view of Monroe's early diplomatic career, see Beverly W. Bond's "The Monroe Mission to France" in *Johns Hopkins University Studies*, xxv, 55. Monroe's own account is in his *View of the Conduct of the Executive in Foreign Affairs of the United States* (Philadelphia, 1797). This is reprinted in *Writings of Monroe*, iii,

383. In the "Washington Manuscripts" in the Library of Congress, there is a copy of this paper containing Washington's own comments on Monroe's statements. This is printed in Sparks's *Washington*, xi, 504. It is one of the few documents wherein Washington does not seem to be entirely ingenuous and possibly reflects the impairment of his faculties upon which his enemies so frequently insisted during his presidency.

[2] James Monroe's *View of the Conduct of the Executive*, 392.

early in December. The Directory was now in power. It refused to have anything to do with him and gave increased point to its refusal by an affectionate adieu to Monroe. Relations with France were in this trim when Washington handed over the administration of the government to Adams.

Schism in the Federalist party was probably inevitable. Adams personified the opposition to militarism in any form, — standing armies, or the existence of an official or semi-official military clique. Hamilton, Pickering, and McHenry had either been in Washington's military family or on his staff. They naturally looked to him and not to Adams, who had persistently opposed in the old days nearly every proposition that they had thought was necessary for the efficiency of the army. Next to Washington, or possibly even before him in the minds of Pickering and McHenry, was Hamilton, who had bound to himself by the brilliancy of his genius and the charm of his personal manner a small but extremely faithful band of followers. Pickering was Secretary of State and McHenry Secretary of War. The Secretary of the Treasury was Oliver Wolcott. He had not served in the Revolutionary War, but belonged to a coterie of Connecticut men who were very close to the army. Wolcott was a person of fair ability and skilled in routine ; Pickering was a most industrious second-rate character ; while McHenry was distinctly third-class. In all matters of policy they looked to Hamilton for inspiration. Adams committed the blunder of retaining these men in office. Probably in view of the still existing confusion as to party government, he did not in any way regard himself as the official head of the Federalist party and still less could he have looked upon himself as the chief of a group or clique. These men had served Washington well.

Why should they not serve him equally well? Nowadays, we recognize that it was Washington's personality that made it possible for him to consult Hamilton, make Hamilton's suggestions his own, and work in harmony with men who likewise in every event consulted the same oracle.[1] Adams should have recognized that he was not Washington and must necessarily adopt other methods and work with other men; but it is exceedingly difficult for any one to realize his own limitations. Before leaving this part of the subject, it seems desirable to say that Adams must have been fully cognizant of the part played by Hamilton. For eight years he had been close to the actual administration and could hardly help knowing that Hamilton was consulted on all important matters, not only by Washington, but by the Heads of Departments. Nor was there anything strange or out of the way in thus appealing for aid to the man of greatest intellect and insight within the Federalist ranks. When the time came for Adams to prepare his first message to Congress, he asked the Heads of Departments and the Attorney General for suggestions as to what should be put into it. Wolcott and McHenry at once wrote to Hamilton and, on receiving his reply, incorporated his ideas into their own answers to Adams's request, and Adams repeated a part of them in his speech to the two Houses. This was almost exactly what Washington had done time and again. There does not seem to have been any attempt at concealment, and any one as familiar with Ham-

---

[1] As an example of the position assumed by Hamilton and accorded to him by the leading Federalists, the following extract is given from his letter to Oliver Wolcott, dated New York, June 5, 1798: "Hitherto I have much liked the President's answers. . . . But there are limits which must not be passed, and from my knowledge of the ardour of the President's mind, and this specimen of the effects of that ardour, I begin to be apprehensive that he may run into indiscretion. This will do harm to the government, to the cause, and to himself. Some hint must be given, for we must make no mistakes." George Gibbs's *Administrations of Washington and John Adams*, ii, 50.

ilton's mode of reasoning as Adams must have been, must have known whence these suggestions came, and recognized them. As to the other side, the Hamiltonians, who formed the only organization that the Federalist party had, advocated Adams's election, because he was the only candidate whom the Federalists could possibly have elected. They knew his foibles and all the weaknesses of his character before the election. Having ranged themselves behind him, they should have given him their most loyal and thorough support.

Soon after Adams's inauguration, the newspapers printed letters to the effect that the French Directory would not receive Pinckney.[1] Already, Adams had thought of sending Jefferson to Paris[2] and no fitter appointment could possibly have been made. The project was opposed by Pickering and was vetoed by Jefferson himself. Considering the relationship of the Vice-President to the succession and the difficulty of trans-Atlantic communication in those days, it would doubtless have been unwise and perhaps against the spirit of the Constitution for the Vice-President to have gone so far away from the seat of government. It is interesting to speculate, nevertheless, as to what might have happened had Jefferson, with his experience with Frenchmen, his sympathy for the rights of man, and his great power of dealing with individuals, gone to France, — all the troubles of the next few years might have been avoided. And had Adams and Jefferson worked together in a non-partisan administration, how different the history of the next few years might have been! But the Hamiltonians would have none of it and Adams, instead of then asserting himself, yielded to the wishes of those who

[1] See *The Columbian Mirror and Alexandria Gazette*, March 15, 1797.

[2] Adams to Gerry, Philadelphia, 6 April, 1797, *Works of John Adams*, viii, 538.

had placed him in office.   It is difficult to account for his
untimely meekness.   He may have felt some of the same
misgivings that had influenced Washington eight years
earlier as to his administrative ability.   It is certain that
the serious illness of Mrs. Adams greatly affected him,
for she had for many years been his chief counsellor.   The
perusal of hundreds of pages of printed matter and a mass
of manuscripts has served to relieve John Adams of much
of the prejudice that an acquaintance with the annals of
his earlier life and the most unfortunate literary performances of his later years had left on the present writer's
mind.   Whether he was chastened by his wife's illness, or
whether he was mellowed by the responsibility of his high
office, he certainly subordinated his opinions to those of
Pickering and the rest, placed responsibilities upon them
which very likely they should not have borne, had no suspicion of their good faith, and showed truly marvellous
patience under great provocation.

The appointment of Jefferson being out of the question,
it was determined [1] to send a commission to Paris to be
composed of three members, one of them being Charles C.
Pinckney.   For the others, Adams selected John Marshall
of Virginia, and Francis Dana of Massachusetts.   Marshall accepted, but Dana refused to go.   Adams, thereupon, suggested the appointment of his old friend and fel-
low-worker, Elbridge Gerry.   His services in Congress and
in the Federal Convention had been great, but as Representative from Massachusetts he had voted against some
of the Hamiltonian measures and was not trusted by the

[1] On March 20, 1797, Adams asked
the three Secretaries and the Attorney
General to take into consideration our
relations with France and report in
writing their opinions on fourteen stated
questions.   It was in conformity with
these opinions that Adams appointed
the first Commission and prepared their
instructions.   "John Adams Manuscripts" under date.

Federalists. Pickering opposed the appointment, Adams insisted upon it, and Gerry was confirmed by the Senate. Marshall and Gerry crossed the ocean, were joined by Pinckney, and on October 5, 1797, announced their arrival to the Directory.[1] The moment was most inopportune. Just a month earlier, the Directory had been revolutionized by the ejectment of its more moderate members. The battles off Cape St. Vincent in February and off Camperdown in this very month of October temporarily put an end to continental sea-power; but French armies had been victorious on land [2] and time had not diminished French resentment against the negotiation of Jay's Treaty. This feeling had been heightened by the seeming acquiescence of the United States in the most recent British Order in Council directing the capture of ships carrying provisions to the Continent. Rufus King had by this time succeeded Thomas Pinckney as minister to England. He was soon on most friendly terms with Grenville. The British were capturing American provision ships, right and left, and British Admiralty courts in the West Indies were enforcing Jay's Treaty as to contraband with the utmost rigor and, indeed, without justification. On the other hand, the British were paying for the confiscated provisions and also for the freight of the captured vessels, and Grenville was doing everything in his power to restrain the activities of the West Indian prize courts.

[1] See *American State Papers, Foreign Relations* (folio ed.), ii, 153–182, 185–201, 204–238; writings, papers, and memoirs of the American negotiators, and Raymond Guyot's *Le Directoire et la Paix de l'Europe* (Paris, 1911), pp. 559–565. Marshall's "Journal" describing his experiences in France is in the "Pickering Papers" in the cabinet of the Massachusetts Historical Society. Large extracts from it are printed in Beveridge's *Life of John Marshall*, ii, 257–335. The best short account of this episode is in the "Notes" to the *Treaties and Conventions between the United States and Other Powers* (ed. 1873), p. 996.

[2] The Treaty of Campo Formio on October 17, 1797, placed the French Republic in a distinctly better international position.

The French government had tried to put pressure upon America by ordering the seizure, sequestration, and confiscation of American vessels bound to or from British ports or having British goods on board. French privateers swarmed in the Mediterranean and in the West Indies.[1] American vessels were captured in all directions and confiscated with their cargoes. One of these was the schooner *Sally* of Plymouth, Massachusetts. She was taken by a French privateer while on her homeward voyage from Demerara in July, 1798. All her crew, except the mate, were taken out and seven Frenchmen put on board. A week later, the mate, with a handspike, despatched the whole prize crew with the exception of one man and brought the schooner safely home. Insurance mounted to almost prohibitory figures, being no less than forty per cent of the value of ship and cargo for a voyage to Jamaica and back. Instead of convincing Americans of their helplessness, the Frenchmen only aroused a desire to come to some agreement with France like that which Jay had made with England.

Up to this time Frenchmen, in office or out, had been unable to take the Neutrality Proclamation seriously. They had refused to believe that the action of the government was approved by the people of the United States. French principles had been extended to the smaller European States, why should they not be propagated in America, — why should not America be freed from the yoke of its rulers as Holland and Hamburg had been? In each one of these also, the invaders or the saviours, whichever way one might regard them, had gathered up all the loose coin that there was and the Batavian Republic had also been

[1] On August 25, 1798, Benjamin Stoddert, Secretary of the Navy, reported that there were said to be sixty to eighty French privateers off Guadaloupe and that eighty American vessels were blocked at Havana.

compelled to hand over to the authorities at Paris several million florins in the form of bonds which were known as "Batavian rescriptions." About one-half of these Dutch securities had been worked off on the Hamburgers at double their real value as part of their city's contribution to the finances of the Directory and of France. Among the bankers who had handled these bonds was one Hottinguer, who was assisted in the deal by an American living in Hamburg, named Bellamy,[1] and by Charles Maurice de Talleyrand, once Abbé of Périgord and Bishop of Autun and now foreign minister of France and later Prince de Benevento. Like many another early revolutionist, Talleyrand[2] had fallen out with the Jacobins; but unlike many of his comrades, he had saved his head by timely departure. At first he found shelter in England, but, being ordered out of that country, came to America, which was then a haven of refuge for Frenchmen of all grades and opinions. After two years or so of exile, the fall of Robespierre made it possible for him to return to France, but he had prudently tarried at Hamburg for some months in order to make certain of his reception at Paris. In July, 1797, he was appointed Minister of Foreign Affairs, but for a year was hardly more than a clerk to the Directory.

In 1796, Pitt conceived the idea of making peace with France, impelled thereto by the financial and social conditions prevailing in England. His envoy, the Earl of Malmes-

---

[1] The intimacy of Talleyrand and Bellamy comes out in a letter from Joseph Pitcairn, United States consul at Hamburg, to Rufus King, dated 29 June, 1798. He writes that Talleyrand and Bellamy have made many bargains and the latter does not intend to permit the minister to sacrifice him. Bellamy admitted that he was not furnished with any writing from Talleyrand, but that he had clear author-ity from him in asking for money for Talleyrand's personal use.

[2] See Beaufort's translation of Broglie's *Memoirs of the Prince de Talleyrand*, i, 169, 173, 187, 190. An admirable brief and appreciative introductory notice of Talleyrand by Whitelaw Reid precedes the text of this work. On May 19, 1794, he had taken an oath of allegiance to Pennsylvania and to the United States.

bury, found the life of a diplomat at Paris very difficult, for his footmen and coachmen had to wear the tri-color cockade or keep off the streets. He returned to England in one of the last days of December. The negotiations were resumed at Lille in the summer of 1797. To that town came agents from the Directory, of all sorts and degrees. Their identities were concealed in the despatches under the names of William, Henry, Edward, etc. One of them is described as James Melvil, a "gentleman from Boston in America." Malmesbury did not see him, but Melvil told one of the embassy that he had recently negotiated a treaty with Portugal whereby the Directors had gained a million between them. He now offered for four hundred and fifty thousand pounds sterling to secure the signature of Barras, the first Director, to a treaty that would guarantee to England the colonies which her seamen had seized. Malmesbury being deaf to these proposals, "Mr. Melvil of Boston in America" went to London to see Mr. Pitt.[1] The Prime Minister thought well of the plan and wrote to the

[1] Raymond Guyot has elucidated this episode in his *Le Directoire et la Paix de l'Europe, 1795-1799* (Paris, 1911), ch. xi, § vi. This part of his study is based upon the archives at Paris and also upon the papers of Lord Grenville (*Dropmore Manuscripts*) and of William Pitt (*Chatham Correspondence*). These two have been used to good purpose by Professor Ephraim D. Adams in his essay on *The Influence of Grenville on Pitt's Foreign Policy, 1787-1798* in the publications of the Carnegie Institution. Rufus King was informed of this intrigue by some one who knew the facts and he forwarded the information to the commissioners at Paris. See the *Life and Correspondence of Rufus King*, ii, 261, 262, and *Diaries and Correspondence of First Earl of Malmesbury*, iii, 250 and fol. It also appears from entries in the *Dropmore Manuscripts* (iii, 356, 360, 369, 378) and in the *Correspondence of Rufus King* (i, 243) that the members of the Directory intended to share among themselves the money that was obtained from Portugal as they had already that which had been procured from Naples. A table printed in Beaufort's translation of Broglie's *Memoirs of Talleyrand*, i, xviii note, from Louis Bastide's biography of Talleyrand, gives the amount of that statesman's gains from foreign powers and from speculations in the three years following his return to France, at over fourteen million francs, and this amount does not include his gains from speculations at the time of Napoleon's accession to power. See also *The Official Correspondence relative to the Negotiation for Peace, between Great Britain and the French Republic, as laid before both Houses of Parliament* (London, 1797); and *Declaration of the Court of Great Britain, respecting the late Negotiation* (London, 1797).

king advocating it, even suggesting a mode by which the
money could be procured without the necessity of going to
Parliament. His Majesty had no objection to buying a
peace, but advised caution. The negotiations continued
for some time with other persons until Admiral Duncan's
victory over the Dutch off Camperdown made it quite un-
necessary to purchase Dutch colonies from the French, and
put an end to so many of Pitt's other anxieties that there
was no longer any thought of buying peace at any price.

Day after day, from October, 1797 onwards, the American commissioners at Paris waited for a communication
from the French government as to the date of their formal
reception and the beginning of negotiations. None came.
Instead, mysterious personages visited them. These were
two bankers, Hottinguer and Bellamy, and two other persons,
Monsieur Hauteval and a lady. These agents suggested
that the United States should lend money to the French
government and also pay a douceur to the Directors and
to their Minister of Foreign Affairs.[1] The commissioners
did not abhor the thought of buying the Directors and
Talleyrand any more than Pitt and King George had done;
but they refused point blank to involve the United States
in any breach of neutrality which would be the necessary
outcome of a loan to France. As one means of obviating

---

[1] The following statement is compiled from Marshall's "Journal," Oct.
18, 1797, in the "Pickering Papers": —
"He, Mr. Hortinguer, had had a
confidential conversation with a merchant of Hamburg who was the intimate & confidential friend of Talleyrand & who had directed him to communicate to Genl. Pinckney" that it
was "absolutely required" the United
States should give satisfaction for the
speech of the President, pay the debts
due by contract from France to American citizens, pay for the spoliations
committed on our commerce for which
France should be adjudged liable by
commissioners, and make a considerable loan. "Besides this added Mr.
Hortinguer there must be something
for the pocket. On being asked to
explain himself he said that there must
be a considerable sum paid for the
private use of the Directoire & minister under the form of satisfying claims
which did not in fact exist."
    Pinckney's expression in a later
conversation was "No. No. not a sixpence."

a breach of neutrality, it was suggested that America might buy the Batavian rescriptions that still remained in the French treasury. This would have been particularly convenient to Hottinguer and the Hamburg bankers, because with the credit of the United States behind them, these securities would promptly rise toward par. As the Americans would make no concessions and the Frenchmen were equally firm, the negotiations came to an abrupt ending in March, 1798. Marshall departed for home; Pinckney went to the south of France for his daughter's health, and Gerry, alone, remained at Paris, for Talleyrand had told him that France would at once declare war if he, too, abandoned the mission.

Twelve months later, Joel Barlow wrote to Washington [1] that the Directory had been prepared to negotiate with the American commissioners, "but from some unfortunate circumstances" did not believe that Pinckney and his companions desired to treat. What these unfortunate circumstances were has never been told. Barlow had very good means of information and Marshall and Pinckney had the preservation of the dignity of the United States and the carrying out of the policy of neutrality very much on their consciences. Gerry was more pliable and endeavored, with some loss of respect for himself and his country, to break down the reserve of his fellow commissioners and of the French rulers.[2] In the course of their proceedings, Marshall

[1] "Washington Manuscripts" in the Library of Congress; Charles B. Todd's *Life and Letters of Joel Barlow*, 156; and Sparks's *Washington*, xi, 399, 560. It was received by Washington, January 31, 1799, and was dated Paris, 2 October, 1798. Barlow enclosed the letter in one to Abraham Baldwin asking him to forward it to Mount Vernon after taking a copy and furthermore wrote: "If you find that neither this nor any other statement of facts is likely to calm the frenzy of him and

his associates; but that they continue running wild after a phantom to the ruin of their country, I should think it best to publish it with my name and his." "Barlow Papers" (No. 15) in the Harvard College Library. In 1799, Barlow printed a letter still further elucidating his ideas, under the title of *Joel Barlow to His Fellow Citizens, of the United States of America.*

[2] John Quincy Adams wrote to his father, September 25, 1798, that Gerry "had neither the spirit nor the pene-

drafted a paper reciting the misdeeds of the French toward America. It was a masterly and cold-blooded document and deserves a careful reading by any one who wishes to understand the attitude of France toward America; but it may well be doubted if it was entirely suited for the purpose in hand.

The arrival of the despatches from the envoys in France caused a revulsion of feeling in the United States. Adams, himself, was greatly stirred. In successive communications to Congress, he laid bare the perfidy of the Frenchmen, advocated preparations for war, and declared that he would "never send another minister to France without assurances that he will be received, respected, and honored as the representative of a great, free, powerful, and independent nation." The Jeffersonians doubted the exigencies of the case;[1] they reflected severely on the President for his intemperate and unconstitutional action and called upon him to justify himself by sending the report of the commissioners to Congress. He replied by sending all the papers, — the names of the French emissaries being replaced by letters, X, Y, and Z. The publication of the papers produced intense excitement in Congress and all over the country. "Millions for defence, but not one cent for tribute" became the prevailing sentiment. The Jeffersonian majority in Congress melted away, the members either going home or voting with the Federalists.

tration absolutely necessary for dealing with adversaries at once so bold, so cunning, and so false," as Talleyrand and his employers; and Jay wrote to Pickering that Gerry's conduct admitted of no excuse; "It would have been [more] reputable of him to have gone to the Temple on such an occasion" than to have acted as he did. Ford's *Writings of J. Q. Adams*, ii, 367; and "Pickering Manuscripts," xxiv, fo. 115.

[1] There is a printed letter in the "Madison Manuscripts," xxi, fo. 135, dated March 20, 1798, and signed by J. Dawson, one of the Representatives from Virginia, asking for an expression of sentiment on the President's "important, intemperate, and unconstitutional" message of the preceding day.

Adams recalled Gerry and preparations were begun for putting the country into a state of defence and for protecting American shipping in the West Indies. This sudden change of attitude compels one to ask how far sympathy for France and for Frenchmen really actuated the American people in the outbursts of 1793 and later. Was it not rather a general and genuine sympathy for the rights of individuals as opposed to the tyranny of king or nobility that impelled the radicals in America to shout, riot, and feast for France, to mount the tri-color cockade, and to form democratic societies?

In any scheme of defence the existing army could not be counted upon, because it was none too large for the police of the frontier. It was decided, therefore, to raise an entirely new army, infantry, cavalry, and artillery, and later in the year still further regiments were authorized. A naval force was also to be fitted out and, to increase both military and naval efficiency, the Navy Department was separated from the War Department and placed under the direction of a Secretary. Naturally, Hamilton and those in authority applied to Washington for advice and assistance. On the 19th of May, the former wrote to his old chief, that in case of hostilities, the country would demand his services. Washington replied that it would take an unequivocal manifestation of public opinion to compel him to leave Mount Vernon, that he would like to know whom his "coadjutors" would be and whether Hamilton himself would take an active part. Hamilton replied in the affirmative, stating that his preference would be for an appointment as Inspector General,[1] — a most admirable suggestion, for his administrative abilities would be most ser-

---

[1] There is no suggestion in this letter (June 2, 1798) that Hamilton should be appointed second in command.

viceable in the constructive work of raising and disciplining a new army. It was not until a month later (June 22) that Adams wrote to Washington that he wished he could in the present grave crisis turn the presidency over to him. He was at a loss to know, he wrote, whether he should call on the old generals or appoint a young set, for if the French came, it would be necessary to "march with a quick step" and to attack, for that was the only way in which the French could be met.[1]

Timothy Pickering also wrote to Washington, July 6, 1798, proposing that Hamilton should be placed second in command.[2] He thought the President seemed disinclined to make this appointment and added, "the weight of your opinion may be necessary." Replying at once to this letter, Washington declared that as the French would begin their invasions south of Maryland, it would be well to appoint Charles Cotesworth Pinckney to the second place, for his influence in the South would be of the greatest importance. Meantime, Adams had nominated Washington for chief command, apparently without having definitely ascertained whether he would accept.[3] He sent McHenry, the Secretary of War, to Mount Vernon with the commis-

[1] C. F. Adams's *Works of John Adams*, viii, 572.

[2] Sparks's *Washington*, xi, 530; Upham's *Life of Timothy Pickering*, iii, 419.

[3] McHenry had written to Washington on June 26, asking him if he would accept the chief command. He had replied to this on July 4, but neither of these letters had reached Philadelphia at the time of Washington's nomination and confirmation. In that to Adams, the master of Mount Vernon had stated that it would be difficult to find old generals of sufficient health and sound politics; recourse must be had, therefore, to the best officers of the late army without respect to grade. He would emerge from his retirement if it were necessary, but the officers of the general staff must be persons in whom the Commander-in-chief could place entire confidence; *Writings of Washington* (Ford), xiv, 18, 19. It is well again to state that Washington's nomination was made before this letter reached Adams. It is also well to bear in mind that it was written and sent off before Pickering's letter of July 6 came to Mount Vernon; but how many other letters, if any, may have passed between Washington, Hamilton, and Pickering and are no longer accessible in print or manuscript cannot be stated.

sion and also with a letter which he had written to McHenry, but which was to be shown to Washington.   In this Adams enumerated the names of those who might be appointed to the highest offices in the following order :   Lincoln, Morgan, Knox, Hamilton, Gates, Pinckney, Lee, Carrington, Hand, Muhlenberg, Dayton, Burr, Brooks, Cobb, and Smith.   McHenry also carried with him a letter from Adams to Washington,[1] stating that the Secretary would consult him upon the organization of the army and everything relating to it.   McHenry remained at Mount Vernon several days.   Washington showed him a copy of the letter he had written to him on July 4th, and another of the next day authorizing the Secretary to show the former to the President "as from yourself."   In this letter he reiterated that he must be allowed to choose such immediate associates as would be agreeable.[2]   Washington went over the names of possible appointments to the highest places and with McHenry's aid drew up a list which the Secretary submitted to Adams, with a statement, that unless confidential officers upon whom Washington could rely should be appointed, he thought he would not serve.[3]   The list as made up was rather indefinite.   Washington suggested Hamilton's appointment as Inspector General with the grade of major general.   Others suggested for the same rank were Charles C. Pinckney, Henry Knox, and Henry Lee.   For brigadiers, he proposed four names including that of Lee, if he were not given higher rank.   The third name of this group was that of William S. Smith, Adams's son-in-law, who was also placed third on Washington's list

---

[1] Sparks's *Washington*, xi, 531, 532 ; C. F. Adams's *John Adams*, viii, 574.

[2] See *Writings of Washington* (Ford), xiv, 19, 29; and also Bernard C. Steiner's *Life and Correspondence of James McHenry*, 310.

[3] McHenry to John Adams, Mount Vernon, July 12, 1798, in Sparks's *Washington*, xi, 534. See, however, Steiner's *McHenry*, 312 and note ; and Sparks's *Washington*, xi, 302.

of possible adjutant generals. In running one's eye over these names, it is noticeable that no mention is made of Muhlenberg or Burr,[1] both of whom had been suggested by Adams. Possibly Washington thought that they were not of "sound politics," but his reason for omitting them is otherwise unknown. Although no such statement was made, it is probable that Washington, after his conferences with McHenry, intended that the officers should rank in the order in which he placed them and that Hamilton should be second in command and actual chief while the army was being recruited.[2]

In general, Adams fell in with Washington's wishes, appointing Hamilton Inspector General and placing Lee at the head of the brigadiers. For Adjutant General he picked out William S. Smith. The nominations went to the Senate and so did Timothy Pickering, who lobbied so effectively against Smith that he received only five votes. Pickering carried on his intrigue so secretly that McHenry did not know why Smith had been rejected. He wrote to Washington that he thought it was "a hasty measure in the Senate"[3] and that Smith had not been confirmed be-

---

[1] In 1805, Adams wrote to Benjamin Rush that he had desired to make Burr a brigadier general and to give Peter Muhlenberg a commission also, but was prevented, and declared as President he "was only Vice Roy under Washington, and he was only Vice Roy under Hamilton, and Hamilton was Vice Roy under the Tories as you call them." He asks if Washington had consented to the appointment of Burr, would New York have been "democrified"? And if Muhlenberg had been given a commission, would not Pennsylvania have gone Federal in 1800? See Biddle's *Old Family Letters*, Series A., 76, 84, 457.

[2] On seeing this list, Pickering at once wrote to Washington that "Col? Hamilton's name occupied the station

in which the public voice, anticipating your opinion, had placed him." A few days later, evidently foreseeing trouble, Washington wrote to Knox that Hamilton "in the public estimation, as declared to me, is designated to be second in command." And he reiterated the same opinion not long afterwards; see "Pickering Manuscripts," ix, 261; *Writings of Washington* (Ford), xiv, 45, 60. As showing Federalist public opinion, John Jay wrote to Pickering, July 18, 1798, suggesting that Hamilton should be given a place measured by his merit and value. As this note is in the "Washington Manuscripts," it is probable that Pickering forwarded it to Mount Vernon.

[3] July, 1798. "Washington Manuscripts" in the Library of Congress.

cause of his embarrassed financial condition and also on account of rumors that he had not "conducted properly in some of his pecuniary engagements." Later in the year, when nominations for the additional regiments were being considered, Washington suggested the appointment of Smith to one of the colonelcies,[1] unless there were "just cause to impeach either his integrity, or his attachment to the measures of Government," adding that he had always viewed him "in the light of an Officer possessing military talents." Upon inquiry, it was found that the charges were groundless and Smith was given a regimental appointment.

Washington had set the example of visiting Mount Vernon, partly, at least, to look after his private affairs. Adams followed his predecessor in this regard, spending his summers on his farm at Quincy, Massachusetts. In 1798, Mrs. Adams was seriously ill, which induced the President to stay away from the seat of government, from midsummer to November. This was unfortunate, for these weeks were among the most critical in the history of his administration. General Knox at once raised the question of the relative rank of the major generals, refusing to serve under Hamilton, in case they should be ranked according to the order of the published list. He had been chief of artillery and major general in the Revolutionary War, while Hamilton had never gone beyond the grade of colonel. Nowadays, of course, it is perfectly clear that Hamilton and

The word that is given here as "hasty" may possibly be "party," for the manuscript is difficult to read.

[1] Washington to McHenry, Oct. 15, 1798 in Bernard C. Steiner's *Life and Correspondence of James McHenry*, pp. 346 note, 354. Long after this, John Adams wrote that Smith had always been his own worst enemy, — "an Enemy to no Man but himself." *Old Family Letters: copied . . . for Alexander Biddle*, Series A., p. 417. He may have been a heavy drinker, like so many historical personages of that day, but it is hardly likely that such was the case in 1798, in view of the strong indorsement he had received from Washington. See also C. F. Adams's *John Adams*, viii, 617.

Knox were not at all of the same grade of mentality; but it is also clear that Hamilton had never commanded any considerable body of men in battle, — nor had Knox. Federalist public opinion — as determined by Pickering, Jay, Bingham, and the rest — had pitched upon Hamilton for the first place next to Washington, and had convinced both Washington and Hamilton of the fact. Adams at Quincy was less accessible to "Federalist public opinion" and took Knox's part. In a memorandum that he drew up in September in the form of a letter to Wolcott, but did not send, he wrote that he and Knox were never intimate and that he had no kind of attachment to him or affection for him more than he had for Hamilton.[1] Indeed, when one comes to think of the two men, it is quite evident that Adams and Knox were very far apart in their general outlook and mode of life, while Hamilton with his keen mind would have been much more congenial to Adams had he not crossed his political path so frequently and so unreasonably. Adams directed that the commissions should be dated to give Knox the first rank. At once Federalist "public opinion" was turned vigorously upon both Washington and Adams. The former was worked upon so effectively that he actually declined to serve unless Hamil-

[1] This letter was dated Quincy, September 24, 1798. In it Adams states that at the time of Washington's nomination, he had evidence enough to convince him "that he expected it, that he wished it, and that he would accept it." As to the question of relative rank, he wrote, "it was never the advice of General Washington as I understood it, that the inspector general should be the First Major General. He never expressed any such idea to me. His list contained no such idea. When Mr. McHenry proposed to me to nominate him [Hamilton] to the senate as first Major General, I possitively refused to do it." Washington, Adams declared, expected that Pinckney would be first, but meant to leave the rank to be settled by friendly agreement. He reminded Wolcott that Hamilton was not a native of the United States, but a foreigner, and had not resided much longer in North America than Albert Gallatin. He concluded by saying that he had dated the commissions to Knox, Pinckney, and Hamilton all on the same day in the hope that "under the auspices of General Washington, the gentlemen may come to some amicable settlement of the dispute." "Adams Manuscripts"; printed with substantial correctness in C. F. Adams's *John Adams*, viii, 601 note.

ton were given first place.[1] As to Adams, Pickering wrote
to George Cabot and he to Higginson and Ames and Senator Goodhue — all staunch Hamiltonians in Massachusetts
— imploring them to write or call upon Adams.[2] The
President was obliged to give way before Washington's
threat of resignation;[3] but he cut the ground from under
the feet of the Hamiltonian military clique by sending in
the nomination of William Vans Murray as envoy to France.

One of the most interesting surmises that has been made
as to Hamilton in these years has to do with the projects
of Miranda for the revolutionizing of Spanish America.
It is represented that Hamilton pictured himself at the
head of an army of forty thousand men, abetted by a fleet
of British ships-of-war, liberating Louisiana, Florida,
Mexico, and whatnot from Castillian tyranny. Neces-

[1] In writing to Adams, Washington stated that as "principal and most confidential aid of the commander-in-chief" in the Revolutionary War Hamilton's position had afforded him the means of viewing everything on a large scale, although he had not exercised independent command. He added that former rank in the Revolutionary army ought not to have any influence in the present case, except in combination with brilliant exploits and extraordinary services. An interesting comment on this statement is the following extract from a letter in Washington's handwriting to McHenry, dated October 15, 1799: "Col⁰. Parker is stated to have been an older Captain in the Revolutionary War, than Col⁰. Bentley and they were accordingly marked by me in that order — vizt Parker the 9 and Bentley the 10 Lieut Colonel." "Washington Manuscripts" in Library of Congress. Washington's letter to Adams is printed in *Writings of Washington* (Ford), xiv, 92.

[2] These letters are in "Pickering Manuscripts," ix, 357, and xxiii, 159.

[3] C. F. Adams's *Works of John Adams*, viii, 601. Bernard C. Steiner's analysis of this whole episode is most helpful, accurate, and abundantly supplied with citations. See his *James McHenry*, pp. 309–349. In the "Letters to Adams" in the "Adams Manuscripts" is a letter from McHenry to Adams, dated Trenton, Sept. 21, 1798. It is the connecting link between the different parts of this episode and seems never to have been printed. In it McHenry informs Adams that he wrote to Washington on the 10th instant that the President thought it would be proper to arrange the ranks of the three major generals according to their standing in the Revolutionary Army. To this Washington replied on September 16, threatening to resign. These paragraphs McHenry quoted at length. He closed: "You will, Sir, I am sure feel for the situation in which I am placed, between your conceptions and General Washingtons . . . and cannot help retaining a hope, that you will upon a review of all circumstances, give your assent to his arrangement." This is indorsed "received Sept 29th Sent the 3 Commissions all dated 19 July on the 30. Sept^r."

sarily, the evidence on projects that never came to anything
is very vague and it is easy to make assertions which no
amount of research can prove to be false. In this instance,
there are several things that point to some kind of imaginary
scheme in Hamilton's mind. Writing to Knox in March,
1799, to mitigate his resentment on the ground that he
himself had yielded to the wishes of others and that great
public interests had been at stake,[1] he said there was a
moment when "their object" seemed to present itself as
not entirely chimerical. The "their" refers to a "package
of letters" on some unknown subject. Possibly this may
have had reference to coöperation with England, for Knox
had many British connections. Miranda had written to
Hamilton as early as February, 1798. On this letter there
is an indorsement in Hamilton's handwriting stating that
several years earlier, he had had frequent conversations
with Miranda, who was then "in America much heated with
the prospect of liberating S America from the Spanish
Domination," and had presumably expressed ideas favorable to his plan and possibly said that it was one that would
interest the United States. "He went then to England
upon it. Hence his present letter. I shall not answer
because I consider him as an intriguing adventurer."[2]
As the months went by Hamilton became more interested
in Miranda, now in the good graces of Rufus King, who
had great influence with the new Inspector General. In
March, Hamilton wrote to Pickering deprecating an immediate alliance with Great Britain, for her interest will
insure her coöperation, a treaty might entangle us and

---

[1] "Knox Manuscripts," xlii, 55.
A part of the letter is printed in F. S.
Drake's *Life and Correspondence of
Henry Knox* (Boston, 1873).
[2] "Hamilton Manuscripts" in the
Library of Congress. On August 22,
1798, in a letter to King, Hamilton
sounds a very different note. See J. C.
Hamilton's *Works of Alexander Ham-
ilton*, vi, 347.

public opinion is not prepared for it.[1] Great Britain might "lodge here powers commensurate with such arrangements as may be required." It would be a good plan to send a dozen frigates to the American coast to be placed under the orders of the United States government. This seems to have been as far as Hamilton ever went. Possibly a knowledge of Miranda's later visionary expedition when he sailed from England with scarcely any other means than "the resources of his own mind" may have led historians to attribute to Hamilton ideas that really belong to Miranda.[2] Danger from the French certainly brought the United States and Great Britain closer together in these years than they were to be again for a century. In October, 1798, the Duke of Gloucester,[3] deprecating the formation of an American navy, thought that the melancholy consequences which would surely follow might be obviated by loaning to the United States some line-of-battle ships, frigates, and smaller vessels, on condition that the Americans should pay a subsidy and man the ships, and should build no more war vessels of their own. In the autumn of that year, the British government consented to lend to the United States the guns of a captured French ship, the *Foudrouyant*,[4] then lying at Halifax, together with eighteen hundred shot. This was understood to be a loan, but the expectation clearly was that their return would never be

---

[1] "Pickering Manuscripts" xxii, 92.

[2] Documents in the *American Historical Review*, iii, 674, vi, 508 give interesting side-lights on this first filibustering expedition. Its interest now-a-days lies mainly in the trials of William S. Smith (John Adams's son-in-law) and S. G. Ogden under the "Neutrality Act" of June, 1794. See Moore's *Digest of International Law*, vii, 917 and citations therein.

[3] *Windham Papers*, ii, 81.

[4] Excerpts from the British Record Office MSS. are given in *Mississippi Valley Historical Review*, i, 51. Liston to Pickering, September 10, 1798; "Adams Manuscripts (Executive, State, Navy)" under date. See also C. F. King's *Rufus King*, ii, chs. xxviii — xxxiv. There are many suggestions in this volume that England offered convoy to American ships; but it is not certain that the offer was ever accepted.

asked. They were to be used for the defence of Charleston which was peculiarly exposed to attack from the West Indies. It is also noteworthy that the British minister handed to Pickering a list of signals which he had received from Admiral Vandeput, commanding the British naval forces on this side of the Atlantic,[1] that the vessels of the two countries might recognize one another. There were some disagreeable incidents as to impressment and the enforcement of the new rules as to contraband; but the correspondence between Grenville and Rufus King clearly showed every desire on the part of the British government to avoid any friction for the time being, at least.

The arrangements for recruiting the new army went forward very slowly. Washington and Hamilton were annoyed at the delay. They wrote to each other that McHenry was inefficient. They upbraided him and told him that he took too many details upon himself. In reply McHenry put the blame on the Treasury Department which had kept in its own hands the purchase of nearly everything that was used by the government. Wolcott really seems to have found difficulty in procuring materials for uniforms and military equipments. Without these things it was undesirable to embody large units of new soldiers. After he had been dragooned into appointing Hamilton to the second place, Adams evidently took very little interest in army matters. Washington reproached his successor for this lukewarmness, but Adams was immovable. Looking backward, the historical student finds himself wondering as to whether Adams was not gravely misunderstood by his contemporaries and by many who have come after him. Is it not likely, after all, that Adams was playing a diplomatic game, that he never intended to

---

[1] "Pickering Papers," ix, 84.

have an army, but was fully aware of the great effect that
would be produced by the passage of acts of Congress for
raising a military force and, especially by the appointment
of Washington to the chief command? All arguments as
to the necessity of drill and discipline had very little effect
upon him, for he had always been in favor of short enlistments and, now, could point to the victories of raw French
armies over the most highly trained soldiers of Europe.
At any rate, he took no active part in spurring Wolcott
and McHenry to action.

With the navy, the case was very different. Adams had
always been interested in maritime affairs and believed
firmly in the importance of sea-power. Moreover it was
on the water that the French were injuring the Americans,
and it was at sea that France was vulnerable. In Benjamin Stoddert, too, Adams had a capable Secretary of the
Navy. The result of presidential interest and secretarial
efficiency was that naval affairs went on with spirit and
success.[1] Three splendid frigates that had been on the
stocks for years were launched and fitted for sea, — the
United States, the *Constitution*, and the *Constellation*.[2]
More vessels were laid down and many were bought and
fitted out for war. In almost an incredibly short time,
half a dozen national ships got to sea, and others followed
in quick succession. They drove the French privateers off
the coast, followed them to the West Indies, and captured
many of them and several French national ships. They
also afforded convoys to American merchantmen.

[1] This episode in our annals has been admirably elucidated by Dr. Gardner W. Allen in one volume entitled *Our Naval War with France* (Boston, 1909). The Appendix contains an elaborate bibliography. This subject is also treated in Captain A. T. Mahan's volumes on *The Influence of Sea Power upon the French Revolution and Empire* (Boston, 1894). There is some original material of interest in Goldsborough's *United States' Naval Chronicle* (Washington City, 1824).

[2] These names were suggested by Pickering to Washington; as alternatives, he mentioned *Defender*, *Fortitude* and *Liberty*.

The emergence of Washington from his retirement at
Mount Vernon and the sudden appearance of the American
marine on the sea gave a shock to European public opinion.
Probably the French authorities were fully informed of the
new cordiality that prevailed between Americans and
Englishmen. Rumors of a possible naval alliance between them may have drifted across the water and may
well have alarmed the government at Paris, for it was in
August of this year (1798) that Nelson crashed down on
the French fleet at Aboukir, not far from the mouth of the
Nile. The union of British naval resources in ships and
money with the American supply of sea-fighters would
have been the one thing lacking to complete the destruction
of European sea-power. Whether the Frenchmen realized
their danger or not, it is certain that they changed their
tone. Talleyrand directed the French secretary of legation at the Hague to assure Vans Murray, the American
representative there, that if a new minister should come
from the United States to Paris, he would be respectfully
treated. From this beginning, assurances redoubled, although Talleyrand to the end tried to preserve an appearance of injured innocence. With this official protestation
of friendship, there came also unofficial information tending to the same end.

Among the curious by-products of combined Quakerism
and Pennsylvania politics was a certain Dr. George Logan,
grandson of William Penn's personal representative in the
province. Like all Quakers, he dreaded and disliked war
and like many democrats was fully convinced that "the
people of America" had not been and could not be properly
represented in France by Federalists. Armed with a
private letter from Thomas Jefferson certifying his American citizenship, Logan went to Paris, arriving there in

August, 1798. Jefferson afterwards most carefully explained that he had given Logan nothing in his character as Vice-President, but only as an American citizen and friend. The explanation was wholly unnecessary, for any note of introduction signed by Thomas Jefferson at that particular moment was equivalent to a declaration of friendship for France on the part of the bearer.[1] Logan had little trouble in opening communications with the Directors and returned to Philadelphia fully convinced of the pacific intentions of the authorities at Paris.[2] He had much more trouble in getting those in power in America to listen to him. Finally, he found his way into Washington's presence. The General received the physician most coldly; but as Logan refused to take his departure, Washington was obliged to hear his story and also became involved in more or less argument with his unwelcome guest. Congress conferred upon Logan the honor of an act, providing fine and imprisonment for any person who should undertake such unofficial negotiations in the future.[3] Nevertheless, Logan's mission contributed materially to turn the current of public opinion toward greater amiability to France and Frenchmen. Another private citizen to convey a similar pacific message was Joel Barlow, who had been living in France for ten or a dozen years, sometimes representing his country in minor negotiations. He had already informed several correspondents in America that the policy pursued toward France was entirely wrong. He now addressed Washington himself, declaring that the dispute with France was "simply and literally, a *misunder-*

---

[1] *Writings of Jefferson* (Ford), vii, 326.

[2] Deborah N. Logan's *Memoirs of Dr. George Logan of Stenton*, chs. iii and iv and Appendix ii.

[3] "An act for the punishment of certain crimes therein specified." Approved January 30, 1799. *Acts of the Fifth Congress*, ch. cvii. *Laws of the United States* (Philadelphia, 1799, vol. iv, p. 243).

standing" [1] and that the Directory sincerely wished to re-establish harmonious relations with the United States on terms honorable to both parties. Washington sent a copy of the letter to Adams stating that one could not presuppose ignorance on the part of Barlow or that the letter had been written without the knowledge of the French government. Talleyrand's assurances and Logan's and Barlow's statements coupled with the perilous condition of the Directory must have convinced anyone who was familiar with them all that the existing government in France was really desirous of coming to terms with the United States.

On February 18, 1799, Adams startled Congress and the country by sending to the Senate the nomination of William Vans Murray as minister to France. With this, he sent Talleyrand's latest letter declaring that if the United States should send another minister to Paris he would be received with the respect due to the representative of a free, independent, and powerful nation. As these assurances had come in a roundabout way, Adams suggested that Vans Murray should not actually go to Paris until direct and explicit confirmatory assurances were received.[2] The Hamiltonian Junto was rendered furious by the President's action. Their present power and popularity had grown out of the embroglio with France and was nearly certain to end

---

[1] See also seven reasons given by Tench Coxe for dissatisfaction on the part of France (*Pennsylvania Magazine of History*, xxx, 118). Dr. Morison has printed some exceedingly valuable documents throwing light on Talleyrand's action; Massachusetts Historical Society's *Proceedings*, xliv, p. 63.

[2] *American State Papers, Foreign Relations*, ii, 239. Charles Lee, Adams's Attorney General, writing to Adams from Philadelphia, March 14, 1799, enclosed a letter from John Marshall approving the appointment of Vans Murray. It is to be noted that this letter was written before the modification of the embassy was known in Virginia.

The Vans Murray papers are in the Library of Congress. The important ones were printed in the *Report* of the American Historical Association for 1912; a type-written calendar of these manuscripts is in the Harvard Library. In 1787, Vans Murray had "inscribed" a thin volume of *Political Sketches* to John Adams.

the moment that friendly relations were reëstablished.
A committee of five from the Senate waited on Adams to
persuade him to withdraw the nomination. Adams thought
this was a most unwarranted coercion of the executive.
He kept his temper, however, and suggested that a commission of three persons should be sent, Vans Murray to be
one of the three. The other two commissioners would be
appointed from persons actually residing in the United
States and their departure could be delayed until the requisite assurances were received from France. The committee grasped at this suggestion which might give opportunity for reconsideration and would delay matters.
Adams selected Oliver Ellsworth, the Chief Justice, and
Patrick Henry and they with Murray were confirmed by
the Senate. Henry refused to go on account of his age and
feeble health and William R. Davie, governor of North
Carolina, was appointed in his place. Talleyrand in the
name of the French government at once gave the required
assurance to Vans Murray, coupling it, however, with a
rather ungracious reference to the needlessness of the delay
thereby incurred.[1] While these details were being settled,
Adams asked his advisers to draw up the instructions for
the guidance of the commissioners whenever they should
go to France.

The required assurances reached America in mid-summer,
but the instructions were not completed until late in October, owing in part at least to Pickering's desire to delay the
departure of the commissioners as long as possible. They
were written in a rather peremptory strain, as were all of
Pickering's state papers. The commissioners were to require indemnity for spoliations and to secure a release from
the obligations imposed by the Treaty of Alliance with

---

[1] *American State Papers, Foreign Relations*, ii, 243.

France.[1] At this moment news reached America of the
downfall of the old Directory and the establishment of a
new one. The future of the French Republic appeared to
be very doubtful and the Hamiltonians seized upon this
fact as a reason for further delaying the departure of Ellsworth and Davie. Adams was now at last thoroughly
in earnest. He journeyed from Quincy, where he had
been for more than six months, to Trenton to which place
the government offices had been removed owing to the
reappearance of the yellow fever at Philadelphia. He
found Governor Davie at Trenton and Ellsworth soon arrived there rather unexpectedly. Adams conversed with
his official advisers and with the commissioners; and then
on his own responsibility directed them to embark [2] on the
frigate *United States* lying at Newport and proceed at once
to the execution of their mission. No event in John Adams's
whole career more certainly compels admiration than his
courage, in view of the critical condition of the affairs in
France and the hostility of his principal supporters at home,
in ordering the commissioners to proceed. It aroused a
storm of obloquy such as few American statesmen have had
to face and stands now as one of the most notable acts of a
remarkable man. Adams affected not to be disturbed by
the scurrility of his Federalist and Republican opponents.
He declared that even the "Spissitude of the black liquor"
dispensed by Thomas Paine [3] made no impression on him;

[1] *American State Papers, Foreign
Relations*, ii, 301–306.

[2] Stoddert and Lee, the Attorney
General, took a different view on most
subjects than the three Hamiltonian
secretaries. On October 6, 1799, the
former had written to Adams, without
any prompting from him, that he could
not perceive any sufficient reason for
suspending the mission to France.
Such a measure, he thought, would

disappoint the general expectation of
America and would excite suspicion of
the President's sincerity. There would
be no inconvenience even if the commissioners, on their arrival, found a
monarch on the throne of France.

[3] A few sentences from Paine's letter
to Jefferson of October 1, 1800, will
serve to show the latitude which Jefferson permitted his correspondents to
adopt as to his predecessors in the

but the constant references Adams made in the next few years to the events of these fourteen months would seem to show the contrary. And, indeed, John Adams experienced to the full that ingratitude for past services that is the fate of public men on their fall from power.

The *United States* made a prosperous voyage across the Atlantic, entering the Tagus on one of the last days of November, 1799. From that point her progress was slow and disagreeable, and, finally, after being buffeted about by a severe storm in the Bay of Biscay, the commissioners gave up trying to reach L'Orient and landed at a Spanish port near Corunna. From that place, after receiving passports and assurances of their proper reception, they journeyed to Paris where Vans Murray joined them.

Meantime, the coup d'état of the 18th Brumaire (November 9, 1799) had given the chief power in France to Napoleon Bonaparte with the title of First Consul. He fell in with his latest predecessor's policy as to America. The commissioners were welcomed by Talleyrand, were hospitably received by Napoleon, and three French commissioners were appointed to negotiate with them. There progress ceased. Ellsworth and his colleagues had been instructed to secure indemnities for French spoliations and on no account to protract the negotiations beyond the first of April, 1800. Up to this time no one had been able to extract indemnification from successive French revolutionary governments, and Napoleon, of all men of that time, was least likely to consent to pay anything of the kind. In the beginning, Joseph Bonaparte, the first of

presidential office. Paine referred to Adams's fractious, untractable disposition and wrote that, like Pickering, he mistook arrogance for greatness, and sullenness for wisdom; and added: "The silent hypocrisy of Washington,

. . . gave the first stab to the fame of America, and the entire nothingness of Adams has deepened the wound." *Massachusetts Historical Society's Proceedings*, 45, p. 25 and note.

the French commissioners, was stricken with sickness, or said that he was. Upon his recovery, one delay succeeded another. To hasten matters, the Americans prepared the project of a treaty which might serve as a basis for negotiation. Owing to the bad weather, Ellsworth and Davie had not reached Paris until the second day of March and Joseph Bonaparte's illness had put off the first meeting of the commission until the second day of April. Under these extraordinary circumstances the negotiations had to be prolonged beyond the time set in their instructions. Weeks went by and nothing was accomplished; then months passed away. Napoleon was in Italy and in his absence no one at Paris felt like taking any large amount of responsibility. After nearly half a year of dalliance, Ellsworth and his colleagues decided to throw overboard their instructions and try to make some temporary agreement with the French government that would put an end to the existing condition of quasi-war, deferring all discussions as to spoliations and guarantees to the future. In the convention that was finally agreed to it was provided that the two parties should treat each other's citizens and commerce fairly, and all national vessels that had been captured and all private vessels that had not been judicially condemned were to be restored. The Frenchmen fell in with these ideas and a treaty, or convention, embodying them was signed at Paris, September 30, 1800.[1]

[1] From a letter of Oliver Ellsworth, Jr. (W. G. Brown's *Life of Oliver Ellsworth*, 305) it appears that there was a second signing of the convention at Joseph Bonaparte's château at Mortefontaine on October 3 in connection with an elaborate fête at which Napoleon himself was present. In the official copies the convention is dated Paris, September 30, 1800. For the French side of these negotiations, see A. Du Casse, *Histoire des Négociations Diplomatiques relatives aux Traités de Mortfontaine, de Lunéville et d'Amiens pour faire suite aux Mémoires du Roi Joseph* (Paris, 1855), i, 177–380. The convention may most easily be found in *Treaties and Conventions concluded between the United States of America and Other Powers since July 4, 1776*, under France.

When the Convention of 1800, as the treaty is always
called in history, reached the United States, its provisions
seemed to go far towards justifying the hatred which the
Hamiltonians had maintained from the beginning toward
the commission and toward him who had sent it. In
reality it was one of the most fortunate bits of negotiation
that ever took place. While the consultations had been
proceeding at Paris in a very slow and disheartening manner, Napoleon had made his famous passage of the Alps,
and had won a great victory at Marengo. Before the
ratifications were exchanged (July 31, 1801), Moreau had
gained a bloody success at Hohenlinden and a little more
than two months later, the Treaty of Lunéville (February
9, 1801) marked the downfall of the Holy Roman Empire,
and not much more than a year afterwards the Peace of
Amiens put an end for a year or two to the contest between
Great Britain and France, and left the ocean open to the
navies of France and Spain. Had America still been in
conflict with the French Republic, there is no telling what
might have happened the moment the protection of the
British fleet was withdrawn. When the convention reached
the Senate, the Federalist majority insisted upon qualifying
their consent by omitting the paragraph which provided
for future negotiation as to spoliations and guarantees.
Instead, they inserted a provision limiting the duration of
the treaty to eight years. Napoleon consented to the
change provided the United States would say no more
about spoliations and guarantees.[1] And this was the way
the matter ended. At almost the same moment General
Berthier signed at San Ildefonso (October 1, 1800) pre-

[1] See the documents printed in *Annals of Congress*, 6th Cong., 1205–1207 ;
*American State Papers, Foreign Rela-
tions*, ii, 344. Brooks Adams has an
elaborate essay on the convention in
Massachusetts Historical Society's *Proceedings* for February, 1911.

liminary articles by which, after countless suggestions continued for many years, the Spanish king agreed to retrocede to France the colony and country of Louisiana, with
all its boundaries as it had been received from France in
1763.

NOTE

The Pinckneys. — Four Pinckneys or Pinkneys come into the history of this period. They are Charles, Charles Cotesworth, and Thomas Pinckney of South Carolina, and William Pinkney of Maryland. Of the Carolinians, Charles was adopted by Judge Pinckney, his uncle, to whom two sons, Charles Cotesworth and Thomas were born. Thus the Carolinians were cousins or, possibly, brothers. They were all three educated in England, as was also William of Maryland, who may have been related to them through some remote ancestor, for the slight difference in the spelling of their surnames meant nothing whatever in pre-Websterian days. All four of them were diplomats: Charles was sent as minister to Spain in 1801; Charles Cotesworth was minister to France in the X, Y, Z time; Thomas, minister to Great Britain, and negotiator of the 1795 treaty with Spain; and William, minister to Great Britain in the troublous embargo days. Both Charles Cotesworth and Thomas were presidential candidates, and both were generals; C. C. Pinckney having been appointed by Adams in 1798, and Thomas by Madison in 1812. And finally, Charles and Charles Cotesworth were both members of the Federal Convention. The doings of these remarkable men are spread at length upon the records of the United States, but their particular biographies are disappointing. See, however, Rev. C. C. Pinckney's *Life of General Thomas Pinckney*, Harriott Horry Ravenel's *Eliza Pinckney*, and Garden's and De Saussure's eulogies on General C. C. Pinckney. On William Pinkney, there are the biographies by Henry Wheaton and by the Rev. William Pinkney and articles in Sparks's *American Biography*, vol. vi, and W. D. Lewis's *Great American Lawyers*, ii, 177.

CHAPTER VIII

THE DOWNFALL OF FEDERALISM

THE election of 1800 turned upon New York, Pennsylvania, and South Carolina. In these States parties were so nearly equal that the change of two hundred and fourteen votes in New York City,[1] the sickness or death of a couple of assemblymen in Pennsylvania,[2] or the shifting of the political allegiance of half a dozen members of the South Carolina Assembly might have altered the whole course of political history and, indeed, of all kinds of history in America. In ten or eleven States presidential electors were chosen by the legislatures; in five by the voters directly, and in all public opinion was so evenly balanced that presidential elections were largely a matter of political accident, — the " people " had little to do with them.[3]

"The people" figure largely in the constitutions and political essays that are associated with the names of Jef-

[1] In New York in 1796 the electors had been appointed by the Assembly by a concurrent resolution. Since then futile efforts had been made to change to choice by the voters directly; but so far nothing had been accomplished.

[2] In Pennsylvania in 1796, the electors had been appointed by joint ballot of the two Houses of the legislature. Bills had been introduced to change this system, but, as in New York, nothing had been accomplished.

[3] A shift of public opinion was more easily discernible in the composition of the two Houses of Congress. In 1800, the Federalists and Republicans were evenly divided in the Representatives and stood 19 to 13 in the Senate; in 1801, there were 38 Federalist Representatives to 68 Republicans, and the figures in the Senate were almost exactly reversed. In calculating party allegiance for this tabulation great difficulty was found in assigning many men to one party or the other. These figures, therefore, must be taken with large measure of allowance.

ferson and his contemporaries;[1] but they were using the
phrase very differently from the way in which it is used by
later publicists. By "the people" the earlier writers meant
the active members of a political organization who were
supposed to speak for the whole number. The voter himself was a representative, and voting was a duty[2] which
must be performed like every other duty. The franchise
was rigidly circumscribed, only about one-fifteenth of the
white population being included in the voting classes.[3]
The number of votes actually cast in an election was often
much smaller. In some parts of the country, it was very
difficult to get to the polls. Oftentimes there was little
interest, as the result of the voting was a foregone conclusion
owing, partly at least, to the impossibility of appealing to
the voters in person or in printed argument; and, besides,
in those days one was obliged to have the courage of his
convictions, for he could not hide his political doings under
a bushel. In Virginia and some other States, the voter
announced his choice aloud and it was recorded in a polling
book which was open to public inspection, and a copy could
be obtained on payment of a fee. David Thomas, a Pennsylvanian temporarily residing in Virginia, described an
election in the Old Dominion in 1789. The candidate, he
wrote, "stands upon an Eminence thro which the people

[1] "We, the People of the United
States" is the opening phrase of the
Constitution; in the famous compact
contained in the Massachusetts constitution of 1780 the "people" covenant
to govern themselves for their good;
and the Virginia Bill of Rights of 1776
declares that "all power is vested in,
and consequently derived from, the
people."

[2] In Virginia every qualified elector
was obliged by law to attend all elections for delegates to the Assembly and
representatives to Congress and give
his vote or pay twenty-five per cent

additional in the tax levy. See Hening's *Statutes of Virginia*, xii, 122; and
Samuel Shepherd's *Statutes of Virginia*,
ii, 328.

[3] This estimate is based on a study
of early elections in the five States of
Massachusetts, New York, Pennsylvania, Virginia, and South Carolina.
In 1900, nearly fourteen million votes
were cast for McKinley and his opponents, — about one-fifth of the entire
population of the country. See Edward Stanwood's *History of the Presidency from 1897 to 1909*, pp. 74, 75.

pass to give their votes, viva voce, or by outcry" and begs, prays, and solicits the people's votes and "the poor wretched people are much difficulted by the prayers and threats of those Competitors, exactly similar to the Election of the corrupt and infamous House of Commons in England."

Apportionment of Representatives and Senators was as far away from adequately exhibiting the power and strength of the several parts of the different States as the "federal ratio" was of showing the relative power and strength of the several parts of the United States. In 1800, the North would have had twenty-three more presidential electors than it actually had — or the South correspondingly fewer — had the apportionment of electors been according to power and strength instead of desire to placate the delegates from the "small States" and the slave owners in the Federal Convention.[1] Representation in the lower House of the Massachusetts legislature was supposed to be according to the number of rateable polls and in the Senate according to the amount of taxes paid in; but there was no end of political jugglery — all of it designed to defeat the will of whatever "people" had the right to vote.[2] The most extraordinary example of manipulating the apportionment occurred in New York State, in 1808, when two counties that were separated by a third were placed in the same district.[3] In both these States presidential electors were chosen by the legislatures, and anything affecting the ap-

---

[1] "Boreas" in a pamphlet entitled "Slave Representation," printed in 1812 (p. 18), gives a table showing the number of added electors which the North ought to have had in each election from 1789 to 1833. The *Columbian Centinel* for Jan. 2, 1813 has an interesting article showing the disproportionate voting strength in Congress of the Northern and the Southern States. The representation was as five to four, but if it had been at all in proportion to efficient strength, it would have been as sixteen to four. See also *Salem Gazette*, Feb. 26, 1813.

[2] The town of Boston was then a "pocket borough," or as the Federalists termed it "the Headquarters of Good Principles"; S. E. Morison's *Harrison Gray Otis*, i, 296.

[3] See Elmer C. Griffith's *Rise and Development of the Gerrymander*, 58.

portionment, therefore, might be a determining factor in
the national election. The two most glaring examples of
inequality were to be found in the States of South Carolina
and Virginia.[1] In the former, the presidential electors were
appointed by the legislature in which the newly settled upland regions, where slaves were comparatively few, were
heavily discriminated against in favor of the older settled
country nearer the sea, where the blacks greatly outnumbered the whites. In Virginia, the Assembly reflected the
wishes of the slave owners of the tide-water counties, although the white population and the wealth were even
then greatest in portions of the State that had been settled
since 1700, — one hundred voters in the lower country having as much voice in the Assembly as one thousand in the
"Upper Regions." [2]

Ordinarily, throughout the country, the franchise was exercised by adult, free, white males who possessed a moderate amount of property either in lands or in movable goods.
The slightness of the landed restriction may be deduced
from the fact that in Virginia a voter need possess only
twenty-five acres of cleared land on which was a hovel of
at least twelve feet square; or fifty acres of wild land
without a hovel, or part of a town lot.[3] The white freeholder could vote in South Carolina,[4] or the man who had
paid a tax of three shillings. In Pennsylvania every tax-
payer could vote regardless of the amount paid.[5] Ken-

---

[1] See Note I at end of chapter.

[2] William Shelton's address to the
Freeholders of Louisa County in "Virginia Broadsides" in Library of Congress.

[3] Hening's *Statutes of Virginia*, xii,
120.

[4] J. F. Grimké's *Public Laws of South
Carolina* (Philadelphia, 1790), Appendix,
p. 37. In 1809, this act was amended
so that the franchise was extended to

all male whites of twenty-one and over,
except "paupers and non-commissioned
officers and private soldiers"; who had
resided in the district for six months;
see Brevard's *Digest of the Statute Law
of South Carolina*, ii, 270.

[5] In Pennsylvania, the sons of taxpayers between the ages of twenty-one
and twenty-two years also had the
right to vote although they had not
paid taxes. This was like the Rhode

tucky was the only State that gave the franchise [1] to free white male citizens without any property qualification whatever; but the State Senators were elected indirectly, thus curbing democracy to some extent. The framers of the New Jersey constitution omitted the word "male" in the usual description of those who were entitled to the franchise. Women took advantage of this omission to exercise the suffrage, and this was recognized by law in 1797. In 1807, the legislature passed another act which was euphemistically described as supplementary to this act. It provided that, in the future, no person should vote "unless such person be a *free, white, male citizen* of this state," twenty-one years of age, worth fifty pounds proclamation money, and resident of the county for twelve months.[2] Under these circumstances of apportionment and suffrage, it seems the height of futility to speak of the President as representing "the people."

Thomas Jefferson was the soul of the Republican party and its recognized head. He was its candidate for the presidency without any formalities of nomination or anything of the kind. There were, indeed, no nominating conventions, no primaries, nor anything that could be called a caucus, unless one uses that word in its generic sense. Leading Federalists in Congress and highly placed governmental officials met and talked over affairs, generally at

---

Island practice, where the oldest son of a freeholder possessed the franchise with his father. In New York, by the constitution of 1777, every male inhabitant of full age and resident for six months immediately preceding the election in any one county possessed the right to vote, provided he owned a £20 freehold or rented a tenement of the value of 40 sh., and had actually paid taxes; or was a freeman of the corporation of Albany or New York city.

[1] *Charters and Constitutions*, i, 651.

[2] The act of 1797 provided that every voter openly and in full view should "deliver his or her ballot, ... containing the names of the person or persons for whom he or she votes" to the election officer. *Laws of the State of New-Jersey* (ed. 1821), p. 275. The act of 1807 recites that doubts have been raised and great diversities in practice obtained "in regard to the admission of *aliens, females*, and *persons of color*, or *negroes*" to the franchise. *Laws of the State of New-Jersey* (ed. 1811), p. 33.

some social gathering. When these politicians had made up their minds as to candidates or policies, letters were written to foremost Federalists and in this way some sort of harmony of action was achieved. The fluidity of party organization comes out in a letter written by Jefferson in 1798.[1] "Two political Sects" have arisen, he says, one believing that the executive branch of the government needs support, the other that it is already too strong; "both parties claim to be federalists and republicans, and I believe with truth as to the great mass of them; these appellations therefore designate neither exclusively." The recognition of Burr as the Republican candidate for Vice-President illustrates the looseness of political methods.[2] It would seem that Albert Gallatin, the Republican leader in Congress, had written to James Nicholson, his father-in-law, who was at New York, requesting him to call upon Governor Clinton and Colonel Burr and "get their answer respecting being held up as Vice President." Gallatin also informed him that the Republican members of Congress understood Mr. Jefferson would be held up as President. Nicholson called on Clinton first, who stated many reasons why he should not be put forward for this office. He added that his love of country would compel him to accept in case his declining would cause serious injury to the Republicans. Nicholson made a memorandum of the conversation and then visited Burr. He showed him the paper and "requested his sense on the Subject." Burr declared that he would not give up the certainty of being

---

[1] *American Historical Review*, iii, 488, 489. As an example of the vagueness of party designations, it is suggestive that *The Epitome of the Times*, published at Alexandria in Virginia on Oct. 13, 1800, printed the "Form of the American Republican Ticket, or a list of those who will vote for John Adams"; but a later number of the same paper headed the ticket "Adams, Federal."

[2] Henry Adams's *Albert Gallatin*, 238–243. For Nicholson's recollection of the affair, written some three years later, see *American Historical Review*, viii, 512, 513.

chosen governor of New York for this honor, as the Southern States had not treated him well. Two unnamed gentlemen then appeared and all four talked the matter over, until Burr, with apparent reluctance, consented to be held up for the vice-presidency by the Republicans.

John Adams occupied a most perplexing political position. Nominally he was President by virtue of election by the Federalist party. He actually owed his place in 1796 to three nameless electors: one a Pennsylvanian, another a Virginian, and a third a North Carolinian. Why these electors, or any one of them, voted for Adams is unknown; but he plainly was President by accident. Adams began his term of office without the confidence of the leaders of Federalist opinion. His spirited opposition to French aggression gained him momentary applause. Then came the tragedy of Hamilton's military appointment, soon followed by the reopening of the negotiations with France. Hamilton and his following were beside themselves with resentment.[1] How long must a man live to be found out? Pickering asked. He answered it himself, that if such a man is an opinionist and inordinately vain, what mischief he might accomplish before he is found out. The Hamiltonians cast about for some other person to be held up for the votes of the Federalist electors. They appealed to Washington to allow his name to be used, but he refused as his candidacy would not "draw a *single* vote from the anti-Federal side."[2] Adams stood well with his fellow New Englanders who were likely to resent any slight put upon

[1] On one occasion Adams brought to McHenry's attention an anonymous letter advising the President to take the command of the army from Hamilton and give it to some one else. Upon this the Secretary of War straightened up and said the advice of the letter writer, if followed, would put eternal enmity between Hamilton and Adams. And others also wrote to the President warning him of the results of his opposition to Hamilton. See letters to Adams in "Adams Manuscripts."

[2] *Writings of Washington* (Ford), xiv, 192.

him. Hamilton journeyed through New England and returned to New York convinced that no one else had any hope of success. Unfortunately, at about this time it came to his ears that Adams had declared him to be under British influence. He wrote twice to the President on the subject, but received no answer to his letters. Thereupon, he proceeded to exhibit Adams in his true light in an essay. He showed him to be entirely unfit for the presidential office and then advised the Federalists to vote for him, because he was the only Federalist candidate who stood any chance of election. Cabot and other friends of Hamilton reflected severely upon this document, and it would probably have been suppressed had not Burr got hold of it and published it far and wide.[1]

For second place, the Federalists pitched upon Charles Cotesworth Pinckney, who had won some slight popularity by his doings in France and in the army. It occurred to the Hamiltonians that if a few Southern electors were to vote for Pinckney and not for Adams, the former might be brought in as President and the latter relegated to second place or left out of the running altogether. As part of the general campaign against Adams, there now appeared in print a letter that he had written in 1792, at the time of Thomas Pinckney's appointment to the British mission. In this he hinted that the Pinckney brothers, Thomas and

[1] *Letter from Alexander Hamilton, concerning the Public Conduct and Character of John Adams, Esq., President of the United States.* There were five printings of this in 1800, possibly more. One of these editions was a reprint made by William Duane at Philadelphia, who wrote that it had done more mischief to the parties concerned "than all the labors of The Aurora." See P. L. Ford's *Bibliotheca Hamiltoniana*, 57. There were several answers to Hamilton's railings, which are also enumerated by Ford in *ibid.*, 59–63. Another example of the vituperation to which Adams was subjected was John Ward Fenno's *Desultory Reflections on the New Political Aspects* (New York, 1800, p. 41): "Because the man [Adams] was obliged to sculk in Holland in the habiliments of a sailor, from the pursuit of Sir Joseph Yorke's messengers, at a time when he was acting in Holland the part of Genêt in America . . . are we to be made the sport of his prejudice and private pique?"

Charles Cotesworth, were susceptible to British influence.
The British representative at Philadelphia agreed with
Adams that the circumstance of Thomas Pinckney's education at Westminster School and his long residence in England had tended to give him a predilection for that country
"and a desire of rendering his conduct satisfactory." [1]
All these strivings and dissensions between the Hamiltonians, the Adamsonians, the Pinckneyites, and other group-
ings among the Federalists might well have cost Adams the
election. They do not seem to have done anything of the
kind, for outside of New York he received more electoral
votes in 1800 than he had in 1796, receiving none from South
Carolina on either occasion, — he was stronger with "the
people" in 1800 than he had been in 1796.

Adams and Jefferson were the two candidates for the
first place in the coming election ; but the issues upon which
there might be waged a logical and vigorous party contest
were very hard to find. Was the object of all this political
activity merely the putting out of Adams, Pickering, and
their comrades and the bringing in of Jefferson, Madison,
Gallatin, Samuel Smith, and the rest? Jefferson and his
friends had tried one thing after another to destroy Hamiltonianism, and every time had met failure. At last the
Alien and Sedition Acts seemed to Jefferson to open a
better path of attack. Federalist hostility to foreigners,
other than natives of Great Britain, was largely due to
the French propaganda of recent years and to the persistent attempts of French authorities to separate Americans
from their government. There were very many fugitives in
the United States. Most of them were Frenchmen, some
from San Domingo, others from Paris, — Royalists,
Girondists, and Jacobins. Then there were English refugees

---

[1] *Dropmore Manuscripts*, ii, 250.

like Joseph Priestley, who "joining chemic with religion's hate, try'd to decompose the church and state," and the foul-penned J. Thomson Callender. There were some exiles from Ireland, and there would have been more of them had not Rufus King induced Lord Grenville to divert a ship-load or two to other shores after the Battle of Vinegar Hill.[1] Many of these newcomers were extreme radicals and expressed their opinions by speech or pen with a venomous facility that has few counterparts in these milder times. In their old homes, they had detested kings and governors, but had been compelled to keep their thoughts more or less to themselves. In America, they contemned whatever magistrate they found in power without fear of guillotine, axe, Bastille, or Tower. These outpourings have been looked upon as harmless if only they had been left unnoticed; but it is impossible to take this view at the present day when one is constantly witnessing the effects produced upon public opinion by speeches, by letters, and by public appeals of all kinds and varieties. It was inevitable that in 1798, some one should ask by what right a lot of foreigners came over here and malignantly reproached those whom the voters had placed in high station? If these foreigners did not like the men and things that appealed to the majority of American voters, let them keep away, or if they had come over, let them get out.

The Federalists passed four laws [2] dealing with this situation (June and July, 1798). The first of these, the Naturalization Act, prolonged from five years to fourteen the period required for complete admission to the rights of

---

[1] This later brought trouble to King; see the denunciations hurled against him in the *Baltimore American* in April, 1807, which were copied from the *New York American Citizen*.

[2] *Laws of the United States* (Philadelphia, 1799), iv, 133, 143, 160, and 202; *Annals of Congress*, 5th Cong., iii, 3739, 3744, 3754, 3776.

citizenship. Exceptions were made in favor of those persons who were actually in the country in January, 1795;
but the mass of foreign immigrants were disfranchised for
years to come. The two Alien Acts gave the government
power to deal with alien enemies and authorized the President to order any alien, whether an enemy or not, out of the
country, or license him to reside within the United States,
at whatever place he might designate. The Sedition Act
dealt with all persons, native or foreign, who conspired
against the government, or, through writing or printing,
did anything to bring it or any one of its officers into dis-
repute. Jurisdiction under these laws was given to the
federal courts, but punishment was limited to five years'
imprisonment and five thousand dollars' fine. The defendant in any libel suit brought under the Sedition Act might
give in evidence the truth of the matter and the jury was
intrusted with the determination of both law and fact.
The Sedition Act was a distinct modification of the existing
State laws as to libel, but it really extended the jurisdiction
of the federal courts, for it was unlikely that the federal
judges would proceed very far in exercising a criminal jurisdiction without direct legislative authorization.[1]

A recent case that had been tried in Pennsylvania gave
point to the Federalist contention that the Sedition Act in
reality was a mitigation of the law of libel as administered
by the State courts. This case arose over certain criticisms
that had been aimed at the Spanish minister, Don Carlos
Martinez d'Yrujo. He had married a daughter of Chief
Justice McKean, who presided at the trial. McKean laid
down the law with a vigor that would not have shamed Lord

[1] See F. M. Anderson's "The Enforcement of the Alien and Sedition
Laws" in American Historical Association's *Reports*, 1912, pp. 15-126. Professor Anderson's papers on the subject
of these acts of Congress are among the
most satisfying things of the kind that
have appeared in recent years.

Mansfield himself. He declared that it was for the judge to decide as to what did or did not constitute a libel, that the jury had nothing to do with the law, and that the truth of the statements could not be given in evidence as in any way justifying the libellous writing. The jury's duty, indeed, was only to decide whether the publication then in question had been written, uttered, or published by the defendant. McKean's attitude takes one back to the days of John Peter Zenger, which is noteworthy, considering that politically McKean was an ardent Democrat and a supporter of Jefferson for the presidency.

There were a few prosecutions under the Sedition Act, but not many. The trials aroused indignation, partly because the people were unfamiliar with the action of the federal judiciary in criminal cases, but more especially because of the overbearing and brutal conduct of Samuel Chase of Maryland, one of the Associate Justices of the Supreme Court, who happened to preside at nearly all these trials. There was also a good deal of scandal aroused by the lack of any national law for the drawing of jurors which gave rise to the charge that juries were "packed." Chief Justice Ellsworth declared that the Sedition Act did not create an offence. On the contrary, by permitting the truth to be given in justification, in some cases it caused that "not to be an offence which was one before." The act restricted the power of judges as to punishment. It did not abridge the freedom of speech or of the press. It only negatived the right to publish slander. If the law were to be destroyed, the preamble of the repealing act might well run as follows:[1] "Whereas, the increasing danger & depravity of the present time require that the law

---

[1] "Pickering Manuscripts," xxiii, 362. This is printed substantially the same in William G. Brown's *Oliver Ellsworth*, 271.

against seditious practices should be *restored to its former vigor*," the present act should be repealed. In 1798 John Marshall was a candidate for the national House of Representatives. In the course of the campaign, he was asked whether he was "an advocate for the Alien and Sedition Bills"? He replied that he was not, because they are useless and "are calculated to create unnecessarily, discontents and jealousies at a time when our very existence, as a nation, may depend on our union." [1] He would not agitate for the repeal because the laws would expire by limitation at the end of the term of the present chief magistrate, but he would oppose their being reënacted. As a matter of fact when the question came up in Congress, Marshall voted in favor of repeal and was the only Federalist representative who did so.[2]

When legislation against aliens was first proposed Hamilton was lukewarm in approbation, to say the least. He thought that even if the aliens were expelled from the country, "the provisions in our Treaties in favour of Merchants ought to be observed & there ought to be *guarded* exceptions of characters whose situations would expose them too much if Sent away & whose demeanour among us has been unexceptionable. . . . Let us not be cruel or violent." [3] Adams exhibited slight interest in the Alien Acts.[4] He did not veto them, but he never compelled the departure of a single person out of the country or licensed any alien to restricted residence. The acts produced considerable result, however, for many French refugees fled while they

[1] *Columbian Centinel*, October 20, 1798; see also the *Aurora*, December 22, 1798, and St. George Tucker's *Letter to a Member of Congress respecting the Alien and Sedition Laws;* Mr. Albert J. Beveridge in collecting material for his life of John Marshall came across the above-mentioned letter in the *Columbian Centinel* and very kindly called my attention to it.

[2] *Annals of Congress*, 6th Cong., p. 419, and *Journal of the House of Representatives*, iii, 567.

[3] "Pickering Papers," xxii, 196.

[4] Adams's *Work of John Adams*, ix, 14 and note.

were still masters of their own movements. There was undoubtedly some harshness and some injustice to individuals as the result of the passage of the laws, but it was trifling in comparison with the harm done by Frenchmen in setting on foot expeditions against the Spanish dominions and in seeking to separate the American people from their chosen rulers.

Jefferson was not afraid of Frenchmen or of French ideas. He disbelieved in the dangers that were so much talked about and thought that the strengthening of the central government was much more to be dreaded than the loss of one or two hundred ships or the most malignant writings of a dozen Callenders.[1] He was in direct communication with leading men in Kentucky and had no fear of the separation of the western country. The secrecy with which Jefferson concealed his political motions makes it very difficult to say exactly what he did or did not do in any particular case. He was in the habit of gathering his political friends about him for confidential week-ends at Monticello, selecting times when court was held at the neighboring county seat so that Madison, Monroe, and Wilson Cary Nicholas might have some ostensible reason for being in his neighborhood, other than visiting him. On one occasion he made Mrs. Madison the bearer of an invitation to her husband to come and confer with him and Nicholas and informed Madison that his wife did not know the object of the meeting.[2] Later he enclosed a draft of some paper to

[1] In 1803, Jefferson wrote confidentially to McKean of Pennsylvania that the Federalists were pushing the licentiousness of the press to such a degree of prostitution he thought a few prosecutions of the most prominent offenders under State laws would have a wholesome effect. *Writings of Jefferson* (Ford ed.), viii, 218. In 1804, Hamilton had the satisfaction of securing the acquittal of Harry Croswell, a New York printer, on the charge of libelling Jefferson. See Lodge's edition of Hamilton's *Works*, vii, 336 and note.

[2] Letter dated Monticello, August 26, 1799 in "Jefferson's Private Papers" in Massachusetts Historical Society. A similar invitation was sent to W. C. Nicholas, and is printed in *Writings of Jefferson* (Ford), vii, 389.

a correspondent reminding him that he had promised to copy it himself and not to let it be seen by any one in the original, nor to permit the least idea to escape as to the "quarter from which it comes." At this time he was doubly cautious. He drew up a series of resolutions condemnatory of the Alien and Sedition laws and gave them to Nicholas in the expectation that they would be put forth by the North Carolina Assembly. In October, 1798, John Breckinridge was in Virginia and visited Nicholas. The latter gave him a copy of Jefferson's Resolutions and informed Jefferson that Breckinridge was confident "the legislature of Kentucky (of which he is a member) will adopt them." [1] Nicholas added that Breckinridge was very anxious to pay his respects to Jefferson, but "we both thought it best that he should not see you, as we believed if he did the resolutions would be attributed to you. I ventured to inform him that they came from you."

Kentucky was certainly a fruitful soil in which to plant seed of this kind. Public meetings had been held there in the preceding two months, at which memorials had been adopted severely condemning the Alien and Sedition Acts as well as the other measures that the national government had recently taken against France; but it is by no means certain that these memorials meant anything whatever except that Jefferson had been very successful in his endeavors to stir things up. The Kentucky governor fathered the Resolutions which were adopted in November, 1798, with the exception of two that probably went too far

---

[1] W. C. Nicholas to Jefferson, Oct. 4, 1798 in "Jefferson's Public Papers" ("Miscellaneous Letters to Jefferson") in Library of Congress. Jefferson's answer of Oct. 5 is in Ford's *Writings of Jefferson*, vii, 281. Jefferson approves of Nicholas's confidence in Breckinridge, although he "had imagined it better those resolutions should have originated with N. Carolina. But perhaps the late changes in their representation may indicate some doubt whether they could have passed. In that case it is better they should come from Kentucky."

for the legislature in that year, although the substance of the omitted sections was incorporated in a second set of resolutions that was passed in 1799. In the Kentucky Resolutions of 1798 the theory is set forth that the general government exists by compact, certain definite powers being delegated to it, "the residuary mass of right" being reserved to each State; and that whenever the general government assumes undelegated powers "its acts are unauthoritative, void, and are of no force." The remainder of the Resolutions declares that the Alien and Sedition laws and an act to punish frauds on the Bank of the United States are void and of no force and call for their repeal by Congress. Finally, the governor of Kentucky is authorized to communicate the Resolutions to the legislatures of the several States, assuring them that Kentucky is faithful to the compact, but is determined "tamely to submit to undelegated and consequently unlimited powers in no man or body of men on earth," and calling upon its "Co-states" to express their sentiments whether the acts are or are not authorized by the Federal Compact.[1]

The Virginia Resolutions which were adopted a month later (December, 1798) were much briefer in form and not so outspoken. At the outset the General Assembly of Virginia solemnly declared its "warm attachment to the union of the states" and its firm resolution to defend the Constitution of the United States and the constitution of Virginia against every aggression. It then went on to declare the general government as resulting from compact and limited by the plain sense and intention of that compact. "In case of a deliberate, palpable, and dangerous

---

[1] The Resolutions of 1798 are widely printed. The words quoted here are taken from the copy transmitted to Massachusetts and now in the archives of that State, from which they and the Virginia Resolutions of 1798 are printed in *American History Leaflets*, No. 15.

exercise of other powers" the States are in duty bound to interpose. The General Assembly expressed its deep regret at the application of the doctrine of implied powers and particularly protested against the Alien and Sedition Acts, which it described as "palpable and alarming infractions of the Constitution." In conclusion the General Assembly called upon the legislatures of the other States to concur in declaring these acts unconstitutional and to take the necessary measures for "maintaining unimpaired the authorities, rights, and liberties, reserved to the states respectively, or to the people."

As was the case in Kentucky, so in Virginia, these resolutions followed upon the adoption of memorials by voters in several of the administrative units of the State. From this it has been argued that the resolutions passed by the legislatures of Kentucky and Virginia reflected the wishes of considerable fractions of the voters of these two States. There is no doubt as to the adoption of the memorials, for they may still be read in the newspapers of that time. The spontaneity which has been ascribed to them may well be doubted by one versed in the Jeffersonian method of political management. It will be noticed that these memorials were confined almost entirely to the two States in which Jeffersonian organization was most fully developed, or perhaps it would be better to say in which Jefferson was most amply supplied with faithful political lieutenants. The voters in other States, even in North Carolina and Maryland, adjoining Virginia on the south and the north were silent; and in Pennsylvania and New York, where the Republicans were strong, not much opposition to the Alien and Sedition laws had been manifested. Probably Jefferson's expectation was that the Resolutions would arouse public excitement throughout the country and bring forth expressions of agreement. If he had any such expectation, he must have been grievously disappointed. No response was made to them at all from the States to the southward of Virginia. In New York, the Federalist majority had apparently no expectation of paying any attention to them and was induced to do so only by the suggestion that if it did not condemn them in so many words, it would be regarded as assenting to the sentiments contained in them. The greatest interest in the matter was displayed in Maryland, Massachusetts, and Vermont. In all, the Resolutions were condemned in no measured terms. In Massachusetts the only Republican Senator, Bacon by name, stood up for his cause. His speech was published in the "Chronicle," a Boston paper, which prophesied that his name would be handed down with high respect and gratitude "while the names of such as have aimed a death wound to the constitution of the United States will rot above ground and be unsavory to the nostrils of every lover of republican freedom." Exactly how a name could rot and stink might perhaps be doubted, but this statement and others aroused the ire of Chief Justice Dana of Massachusetts. In a charge to the grand jury, he stigmatized these articles as traitorous. Thomas Adams, the publisher of the "Chronicle," and Abijah, his younger brother, who was employed in the office, were indicted under State law for encouraging sedition. The elder brother was dying and was not brought to trial. The younger was tried under "the common law of the State" which was ruled to recognize as libellous that which was so recognized in England. He was found guilty and sentenced to thirty days' imprisonment. Possibly no better comment could have been found as to the desirability of some change in the law of libel, similar to that of the Sedition Act, than this indictment, trial, and conviction of

Abijah Adams, for the publication of this article in his brother's newspaper.

In every answer that was voted to the Resolutions that had come from Kentucky, the idea of State nullification was denounced in no measured terms; but little attention was paid to the question of the constitutionality of the Alien and Sedition Acts or the Act for punishing frauds on the Bank.[1] On the other hand, in the speeches and legislative protests and newspaper articles published on the Republican side, not much was said as to the remedies proposed in the Kentucky Resolutions, but a great deal was said about the impolicy and unconstitutionality of the laws under discussion. When this body of adverse opinion reached Kentucky and Virginia, the legislatures of those States were very differently affected. The Kentuckians passed a second set of resolutions,[2] declaring that the principle and construction contended for in these answers, that the general government (through the federal judiciary) is the exclusive judge of the extent of the powers delegated to it, is despotism, and that the several States being sovereign and independent have the unquestionable right to judge of infractions of the Constitution and that "a nullification, by those sovereignties, of all unauthorized acts done under color of that instrument, is the rightful remedy." It proceeded to declare under the most deliberate reconsideration that the Alien and Sedition laws are palpable violations of the Constitution. The Kentucky legislature did not again declare the reprobated laws altogether void and of no force as it had done in 1798, but weakly contented itself with entering against them its solemn protest.

[1] See Frank Maloy Anderson's "Contemporary Opinion of the Virginia and Kentucky Resolutions" in *American Historical Review*, v, 45–63, 225–252.

The replies of the States are printed in Ames's *State Documents on Federal Relations*, No. i, pp. 16–26.

[2] *American History Leaflets*, No. 15.

Virginia rejoined to Northern condemnation by adopting,
January, 1800, a paper laboriously compiled by Madison
and often cited as the "Report of a Committee" [1] appointed
to examine into the constitutionality of the Alien and
Sedition Acts. As a reasoned statement of the legal position of a State when brought face to face with what appears to be an infraction of the Constitution, this paper is
remarkable; but as a document intended to influence public
opinion, it had little value even in those days of patient
readers. There is no doubt as to the excitement that prevailed in Virginia during these years, or in certain parts of
the State. The legislature went so far as to vote money for
the purchase of arms and military supplies, and to build
an armory.[2] Washington was greatly disturbed. In a
memorable letter to Patrick Henry written on January 15,
1799,[3] he deplored the lead that Virginia had taken against
the federal government. He still believed that Virginians,
for the most part, were well affected to the Union, but found
it difficult to reconcile this with the election of Congressmen
and members of the State Assembly who were opposed to
the general government. He implored Henry to come forward and fight for a seat either in Congress or in the State
legislature. By this time Henry's conversion to Federalism
was complete. He was too feeble to stand the strain of the
congressional contest, and attendance at the seat of the
general government would take him away from his house
and family and from the practice of his profession and
management of his business affairs. He consented to stand

---

[1] *Writings of Madison* (Hunt), vi, 341–407.

[2] S. Shepherd's continuation of Hening's *Statutes of Virginia* (1835), ii, 87;
and D. R. Anderson's *William Branch
Giles*, 70 and note.

[3] *Writings of Washington* (Sparks ed.),
xi, 387. In October, 1795, Henry had
written to Washington that he had "bid
adieu to the distinction of federal and
antifederal ever since the commencement of the present government."
Henry's *Henry*, ii, 559.

for the Assembly and made his last memorable speech from the porch of the tavern at Charlotte in March, 1799. He had seen with regret, he said, the unlimited power over the purse and the sword consigned to the general government. He had been overruled and it was now necessary to submit to the exercise of that power. If a people were intolerably oppressed, they had the right to overturn the government, but should wait until some infringement is made upon their rights which cannot otherwise be redressed. "United we stand, divided we fall. Let us not split into factions which must destroy that union upon which our existence hangs. Let us preserve our strength for the French, the English, the Germans, or whoever else shall dare invade our territory, and not exhaust it in civil commotions and intestine wars." If Virginians opposed the general government, Washington would lead the army against them. Where is the American "who will dare to lift his hand against the father of his country"? "No, you dare not do it; in such a parricidal attempt, the steel would drop from your nerveless arm!"[1]

The Alien and Sedition laws were distasteful to many people in the country, entirely apart from the question of their constitutionality. They infringed, or seemed to infringe, the rights of man that lie at the very root of American governmental conceptions. Yet, on the other hand, Patrick Henry had struck the true note. There was danger from France; there had been and might be danger from Britain. The Alien and Sedition Acts and any other laws

---

[1] These bits of Henry's last speech are taken from William Wirt Henry's *Patrick Henry*, ii, 608–610; on p. 611 of the same book W. W. Henry states that it "is taken almost entirely" from a manuscript in the handwriting of John Randolph, dated March, 1799, and addressed to Patrick Henry, which apparently was written for publication in the newspapers. A somewhat shorter abstract of the speech from the same source is in the closing pages of William Wirt's *Life of Patrick Henry*.

passed by Congress, or anything done by the general government, could be ameliorated or repealed by lawful agitation and by the ordinary working of constitutional machinery. Moreover, these laws, that were complained of, were limited in point of time and at the worst would continue for only a few months. This reasoning, or something akin to it, certainly appealed to very many persons.

It is impossible to trace any connection whatever between the Alien and Sedition laws and the Virginia and Kentucky Resolutions, on the one hand, and the defeat of Adams, on the other. Kentucky and Virginia gave Jefferson twenty-four votes in 1796 and twenty-five votes in 1800. South Carolina gave her eight votes to Jefferson and Thomas Pinckney in 1796 and her eight votes to Jefferson and Burr in 1800; but the refusal of the electors at Columbia to vote for Charles Cotesworth Pinckney cannot in any way be attributed to the Alien and Sedition laws or to the Virginia and Kentucky Resolutions, none of which aroused much interest in that State. South Carolina was the Hamiltonians' hope. Pickering thought that if the electors of that State and some of those of North Carolina were to vote for Charles C. Pinckney, he would be elected, provided the New England States voted solidly for him and John Adams.[1] The other Carolina votes would be given to Jefferson, who would probably be elected President; but this does not seem to have troubled Pickering. What did trouble him was the possibility that some of the Massachusetts electors might omit Pinckney from their ballots and thus relegate him to third or fourth place. General Pinckney declined to be a party to any underhand attempt to secure votes for himself at Adams's expense.[2] The elec-

[1] Letter to William Laughton Smith, dated May 7, 1800, in "W. L. Smith Papers" in the Library of Congress.

[2] See C. C. Pinckney's *Life of General Thomas Pinckney*, 155; C. F. Adams's *John Adams*, ix, 579, 584; and Charles

tion in South Carolina turned on very different issues, the most important of which was the personal political advancement of Charles Pinckney.

Charles Pinckney had been a delegate from his State in the Old Congress and had suggested limiting John Adams's term as minister to England to two years, — which had aroused that statesman's distrust of all Pinckneys, however named. Charles Pinckney had been a member of the Federal Convention and his name is associated with the mysterious "Pinckney Plan." He had sought a diplomatic appointment from Washington, but without success, although his application was reënforced by a letter from Henry Laurens.[1] Since then he had been governor of South Carolina and was now one of the two Senators from that State. He had invested largely in rice plantations and had so far been unable to pay all the purchase money.[2] Like so many Southerners, including Jefferson himself, he was land and negro poor, and had come to distrust banks, national debts, and all the appurtenances of Hamiltonianism. In May, 1799, we find him in charge of the Jeffersonian campaign in South Carolina and trying to impress upon Madison [3] the absolute necessity of changing the mode of choice of presidential electors in North Carolina and Virginia from the district system to appointment by the leg-

---

Pinckney's letters in *American Historical Review*, iv, 112, 127; and especially De Saussure's letter to John Rutledge, Dec. 2, 1800, quoted in *ibid.*, iv, 113, from the *Providence Journal* of Dec. 24, 1800.

[1] See "Madison Manuscripts" in the Library of Congress, xviii, 55, and a manuscript volume entitled "Applications for Office" in the same repository, under date of August 20, 1791.

[2] Charles Pinckney to the Editors of the *Carolina Gazette*, October 9, 1800. In the *Gazette*, for October 13, Pinckney

denied that "he had made any bargain with Jefferson to aid him in his election."

[3] Charles Pinckney to James Madison, May 16 and September 30, 1799 in "Madison Manuscripts" in Library of Congress, xvi, 117; xvii, 34. He enforced his argument by asserting that Adams had been elected President in 1796, owing to the fact that one Virginia elector and one North Carolina elector had voted for him instead of for Jefferson; owing, presumably, to the district system.

islature. The South Carolina elections were held in October, 1800. Federalist assemblymen were generally chosen from the older settled parts of the State [1]; but the Republicans were strong in the upper regions. There is no obtainable information as to what actually happened at Columbia, but when the votes for presidential electors were counted, it was found that the Republicans had been chosen by safe majorities. On December 3rd, the eight electors voted for Jefferson and Burr.[2] It had been expected that one elector would vote for Clinton instead of for Burr, and thus make it certain as to which of the Republicans should be President.[3] But they all cast the straight ticket and thus threw the actual designation of the new occupant of the presidential mansion into the House of Representatives. Jefferson somewhat grudgingly appointed Charles Pinckney minister to Spain, where he blundered as he had at home.

The Pennsylvania electors in the first three presidential campaigns had been chosen by the voters on one general ticket. In 1800, the matter came up again. It was now proposed that the electors should be chosen by districts. The political situation in the Assembly was peculiar, the Senate being Federalist and the House Republican; both by small majorities. No agreement could be reached as to the appointment of electors and the legislature adjourned. When it met again in November, it was too late to do anything except to appoint the electors themselves. On a joint ballot the Republicans would have outnumbered the

[1] The Federalists secured 11 out of the 15 members of the Assembly from Charleston. Pinckney wrote that the election had been disorderly and illegally conducted and that he intended to contest the right to their seats of 8 or 9 of the 11 Federalist members.

[2] See Charles Pinckney to Thomas Jefferson, October 12, 16, 26, November 22, December 2, 6, 23, 1800; March 5, 1801, in the "Jefferson Papers" in the Library of Congress, in a volume marked "Letters Received after his Retirement, Second Series," vol. 66. Most of this material with some other is printed in *American Historical Review*, iv, 111–129.

[3] Peter Freneau to Jefferson, December 2, 1800; *ibid.*, iv, 120.

Federalists, and the Senate, therefore, refused to accede to that method. Finally it was arranged that each House should nominate eight persons, or sixteen in all, from whom the fifteen Pennsylvania presidential electors should be selected by joint ballot. When this process was completed, it was found that eight of the fifteen were Republicans and seven Federalists. This compromise, as it is called, is sometimes regarded as a base trick on the part of the Federalists to secure what did not belong to them; but it would seem that the merest tyro in politics could have foretold the results when the scheme was first suggested. Besides, the electoral vote as cast — eight for Jefferson, seven for Adams — probably represented public opinion in the State.

An analysis of the electoral vote of 1800 dispels many illusions, especially when it is compared with the vote of 1796.[1] The apportionment was the same in both years. In each election, Adams received the whole thirty-nine votes of New England. Omitting for the moment the vote of New York, Adams received in 1796, twenty electoral votes from New Jersey and the States to the southward; in 1800, he received twenty-six votes from those States. It appears, therefore, that omitting New York, John Adams had more electoral votes in 1800 than he had in 1796, notwithstanding Alien and Sedition Acts,

[1] VOTE FOR ADAMS, OUTSIDE NEW YORK IN 1796 AND 1800

	1796	1800		1796	1800
North Carolina	1	4	Connecticut	9	9
Virginia	1	–	Rhode Island	4	4
Maryland	7	5	Massachusetts	16	16
Delaware	3	3	Vermont	4	4
Pennsylvania	1	7	New Hampshire	6	6
				59	65
New Jersey	7	7	New York	12	–

Benton's *Abridgment of the Debates of Congress*, ii, 62, 487.

Virginia and Kentucky Resolutions, Hamiltonian and Pickeringite intrigues, and all the opposition of Republican politicians and immigrant newspaper writers. The downfall of the Federalists was due entirely to the transference of the twelve electoral votes of New York from Adams to Jefferson. Indeed, had only one-half of them been given to Adams in 1800, instead of all of them as in 1796, he would have been elected President; for in 1800, Jefferson had seven fewer electoral votes from States outside of New York [1] than he had in 1796. The presidential election of 1800 turned entirely upon the election in New York and that depended upon Burr's manipulation of New York City politics. To him, therefore, the downfall of Federalism was ultimately due.

Around Aaron Burr hangs the smoke of the duelling ground at Weehawken and the disgrace of the treason trial at Richmond; to which must be added the writing of the most disgraceful journal in existence. Whether or not he has been much sinned against by statesmen and historians from Jefferson down, he certainly was a most efficient political manager. By the exercise of his great personal charm, and by his unvarying political successes, Burr had drawn to himself energetic and ambitious politicians in the city of New York. He had devised new methods of political action by which his party workers could bring to the polls every voter who would support Burr's candidate. Owing to the closeness of party majorities in 1800, it was evident that if a complete set of Republican assemblymen could be sent to the legislature from the city of New York,[2]

---

[1] JOHN ADAMS   THOMAS JEFFERSON
1796 = 59 + 12 N.Y. = 71   68 (No N.Y.)
1800 = 65 (No N.Y.)   61 + 12 N.Y. = 73

See *Annals of Congress*, 6th Cong., p. 744, and *ibid.*, 4th Cong., 2nd Sess., p. 2096.

[2] For a detailed account of the election in the city of New York in 1800, see Charles A. Beard's *Economic Origins of Jeffersonian Democracy*, 382–387.

the control of that body would pass from the Hamiltonians to the Jeffersonians, New York's twelve presidential electors would be all Republicans, and Jefferson would be elected President. Burr, thereupon, framed a ticket for the city, which included men of great popularity and distinction, as Clinton and Livingston, and induced them to consent to serve in the Assembly, by showing them how necessary it was at this crisis for men to do whatever they could for their party and their country. Of course, it is entirely possible that some influences not so legitimate were used, but it is easy to make assertions of this kind that cannot be disproved. Burr's efforts met with complete success; the thirteen members of the Assembly from New York City were all Republicans by a majority of about five hundred votes. These thirteen members gave the Republicans control of the Assembly on joint ballot.[1] It is perfectly truthful, therefore, to say that a change of less than two hundred and fifty votes in the city of New York in the May election of 1800 would have given New York's vote to Adams [2] and made him President with seventy-seven votes to sixty-one for Jefferson, — of such was the Revolution of 1800.

Hamilton had taken little interest in the canvass, but when the telling nature of this blow became apparent, he bestirred himself and wrote a letter to Jay, who was still governor of the State. The New York legislative year then ended on the first of July. The existing Assembly had a

[1] The total number of votes for the highest candidates for both sides in New York City was 5757 or a majority of 2879. Clinton stood first on the poll and obtained 3092 votes to 2665 for his nearest Federalist opponent. A change of 214 votes would have placed Clinton in the minority. Charles A. Beard's *Economic Origins of Jeffersonian Democracy*, 383, citing the *New York Spec-* *tator*, May 7, 10, 1800.

[2] There were 84 Republican Senators and Representatives and 67 Federalists in the New York Assembly that appointed the 12 presidential electors of that State. Had the 13 Representatives from New York City been Federalists, the numbers would have been 71 Republicans and 80 Federalists.

Federalist majority. Hamilton suggested, therefore, to Jay that he should call it in extra session with a view to the passage of a law providing for the choosing of presidential electors by districts. If this were done, there was a good chance that the Federalists would secure at least five of the twelve electors, which would give Adams the majority. General Schuyler, Hamilton's father-in-law, also wrote to Jay in the same strain and more in detail, stating that John Marshall agreed with him as to the necessity and propriety of the proposed action. Jay seems to have made no reply to either of these letters; but he indorsed on that of Hamilton's these words: "Proposing a measure for party purposes, which I think it would not become me to adopt." [1]

An interesting problem in connection with Adams's defeat in 1800, and one difficult to solve, is, How far was it due to the dwellers in towns and how far to the farming and pioneer population? Secretaries of State in those days had loose ideas as to the sacredness of election returns, and the newspapers at that particular time were well supplied with other forms of "padding." Fortunately the newspapers of April and May, 1800, printed detailed accounts of the elections in New York and Massachusetts.[2] These will repay a moment's study, although one must not argue too strongly from two instances, especially as the Massachusetts figures are those of the vote for governor and not for the members of the legislature.[3] The results, however,

---

[1] H. P. Johnston's *The Correspondence and Public Papers of John Jay*, iv, 271, 273.

[2] See the *Aurora* for April 17, and following, 1800; "Ebeling Collection of Newspapers" in the Harvard University Library, no. 151. Similar figures are also in the *Columbian Centinel* for April 9, 12, 16, 19, 23, 26, 30, May 3, 7, 10, 17, 1800; *Independent Chronicle* for Apr. 21, 1800; and the *Massachusetts Mercury* for May 9, 1800. For these latter citations I am indebted to Mr. Lewis D. Stilwell.

[3] In 1799, Massachusetts went overwhelmingly Republican; in 1800 a Federalist governor was chosen by a large majority and the legislature appointed sixteen Federalist electors. There are no returns in the Massachusetts archives as to the political affiliations of the members of the legislature.

are so contrary to one's expectations that they are worth
stating. There were one hundred and fifty-one Senators
and Representatives in the New York Assembly. Of
these, the Republicans elected eighty-four, the Federalists
sixty-seven. Of the Federalists only five came from New
York City and near-by counties, the other sixty-two were
from up the Hudson and the newly settled western country.[1]
In Massachusetts, Caleb Strong, the Federalist candidate,
and Elbridge Gerry, the Republican nominee, were nearly
equal in the old settled part of the State; but in the western portion Strong had twice as many votes as his opponent,
— in the westernmost counties he received 3748 votes to
only 937 for Gerry.[2] In other words — if these figures mean
anything — they show that the Republicans were strongest
in the commercial towns on the seaboard and the Federalists
among the farmers of the interior.[3]

The government moved to Washington City in the summer of 1800 and Adams seized the opportunity to deal out
some sort of retributive justice to his treacherous advisers,
James McHenry and Timothy Pickering. McHenry
promptly handed in his resignation when asked for it by

Nevertheless Professor Libby, arguing
from the geographical distribution of
the gubernatorial vote, writes: "The
Massachusetts Federalists in 1800 are
from precisely the same general region
as the Anti-Federalists in 1788 and the
Shays rebels of 1786" (*Quarterly
Journal* of the University of North
Dakota, ii, 227).

[1] The Federalists were especially
strong in the Upper Hudson country —
adjoining western Massachusetts. Of
the 33 Representatives from this region
only 6 were Republicans.

[2] Anson E. Morse's *Federalist Party
in Massachusetts to the Year 1800* is a
careful, comprehensive account of this
movement. He attributes the per-
sistence of colonial prejudices and practices to the "leadership of the Congre-

gational divines."

[3] Opposed to this view is the declaration of Professor William E. Dodd
of the University of Chicago (*Statesmen
of the Old South*, 53); Jefferson "had
drawn a line from northeast to southwest, from the town of Portsmouth in
New Hampshire to Augusta in Georgia,
west and north of which almost every
man was his devoted admirer. . . . Jefferson had changed the first sectional
line separating North from South to one
separating the older from the newer sections of all the states." Somewhat agreeing with this is H. C. Hockett's statement in *Frederick Jackson Turner Essays* (p. 123) that "the West" — apparently the western part of New York
— carried the election for Jefferson.

Adams (May 6, 1800). Three weeks later, he drew up a memorandum of a conversation he had had with the President on the evening before that day. In this paper, Adams is represented as saying that Hamilton had been opposing him in New York, had caused the loss of the election, and that all the Secretaries were subservient to him, all of which McHenry denied. Continuing, Adams asserted that Hamilton was as much a foreigner as Gallatin, and added, "Mr. Jefferson is an infinitely better man; a wiser one, I am sure, and, if President, will act wisely." Four days after the resignation of McHenry, Adams invited Pickering to go (May 10, 1800). He declined on account of his ill financial condition and was thereupon dismissed.[1] Pickering attributed his turning out to his opposition to Colonel Smith's appointment as adjutant general and also to the fact that Adams had determined to coalesce with Jefferson that he might secure for himself another term as President or Vice-President. On the other hand, if Adams had seen any one of several letters that Pickering had written to "leading Federalist characters" [2] as to his chief's limitations, he might

[1] In Pickering's letter to Adams, declining to resign, he said that he hoped to save enough money while in office to "aid me in transporting them [his family] into the woods, where I had land, though all wild and unproductive, and where, like my first ancestor in New England, I expected to commence a settlement on *bare creation*." Upham's *Life of Pickering*, iii, 487.

On the other hand, Adams's sending five hundred dollars anonymously — with the help of Wolcott — for the relief of distressed persons in Philadelphia, again scourged by the yellow fever (September, 1798), deserves to be noted.

[2] See Pickering to Timothy Williams, May 19, 1800; rough draft in "Pickering Manuscripts," xiii, 514. The letter as sent is in *ibid.*, xxxviii, 24. In this letter Pickering suggests that a combination of circumstances proves beyond

a doubt, "that the new arrangements [the appointment of his and McHenry's successors] have been made in concert with Mr. Jefferson, under whom, be assured, Mr. Adams, rather than not be in office, would serve as vice-president. And mark my words, That whatever interest Mr. Adams shall take in the choice of electors in Massachusetts, it will be to secure Mr. Jefferson's election, and to exclude General Pinckney. He will not pay the smallest regard to federal principles; but be governed wholly by personal considerations." On May 28, Pickering wrote to W. L. Smith that the morning he sent in his refusal to resign, "Mr. Jefferson was seen to go into the President's house." This, added to what McHenry had doubtless told him, might have confirmed his suspicions as to Adams.

well have expelled him from office in a burst of indignation.

Pickering's successor, as Secretary of State, was John
Marshall of Virginia. Like Jefferson, Marshall was descended from a Randolph, and like him had grown up on
the frontier. With these two circumstances resemblance
between these great Virginians ceases. Ellsworth resigned
the chief justiceship in November, 1800. Adams first
offered the place to Jay, and, upon his refusal, appointed
Marshall. For some weeks, the last named occupied two
offices. As Secretary of State, he attested the President's
signature to the last commissions given to Federalist appointees, among others to William Marbury, as commissioner in bankruptcy for the District of Columbia, and
Elizur Goodrich, as collector at New Haven. From the
mass of papers preserved at Washington, it would seem that
the pressure for office in the last two months of Adams's
administration was very keen. His yielding to it was
most unfortunate, but it should be attributed to the goodness of his heart rather than to any selfish desire to defraud
Jefferson of any of his rights.

The equal votes for Jefferson and Burr seemed to many a
despairing Federalist to be an opportunity once again to refuse the highest office in the country to the man of Monticello, who possessed in their eyes, if their utterances may
be believed, all the evil qualities that could have been gathered into one human being. They determined to elect Burr
and came very near doing it. The Federalists possessed a
majority in the House of Representatives, as ordinarily
counted, and, also, when voting by States as the Constitution required, in case of a tie for the two highest offices.
Ballot after ballot was taken, sick men were brought to the
capitol or such of it as was then erected, and the excitement

increased with each day. All kinds of rumors ran through the boarding houses and swamps of the infant city. Among other reports it was said that the Federalists were going to postpone any choice until after the 4th of March, when, there being no President or Vice-President legally elected, the administration would devolve upon the Speaker of the House, or a "President pro tempore of the Senate" might be chosen by that body. Hamilton protested against the elevation of his New York rival. Burr, he wrote,[1] had formed himself on the model of a Catiline, and was too cold-blooded a conspirator to change. James A. Bayard, Representative from Delaware and casting the entire vote of that State, could have at any moment elected Jefferson, by simply changing to him from Burr. He wrote to Hamilton that the means existed for electing Burr, but this required his coöperation. The little use that Burr made of this opportunity gave Bayard "an humble opinion of the talents of an unprincipled man."[2] On the other hand, in

[1] Hamilton also wrote to John Rutledge (New York, Jan. 4, 1801) that Burr is "in every sense a profligate" with "uncommon habits of expense"; he is "without doubt insolvent for a large deficit"; at a "critical period of the war, he resigned his commission"; he "has constantly sided with the party hostile to fœderal measures before and since the present constitution of the U States"; he is "of a temper bold enough to think no enterprise too hazardous and sanguine enough to think none too difficult"; and though "possessing infinite art cunning and address — he is yet to give proofs of great or solid abilities." Allan McL. Hamilton's *Alexander Hamilton*, 386–389. For another view, see Isaac Jenkinson's *Aaron Burr, his personal and political relations with Thomas Jefferson and Alexander Hamilton* (Richmond, Ind., 1902).

[2] *Annals of Congress*, 6th Cong., 1008, 1021–1033; Randall's *Life of Jefferson*, ii, 576–588; Adams's *Life of Albert Gallatin*, 248–263; *Papers of James A. Bayard*, under date (American Historical Association's *Reports*, 1913, vol. ii); *Documents relating to The Presidential Election in the Year 1801: containing A Refutation of Two Passages in the Writings of Thomas Jefferson, aspersing the character of the late James A. Bayard, of Delaware* (Philadelphia, 1831). The passages complained of are in Jefferson's "*Anas*," under date of Feb. 12, 1801 and April 15, 1806, and *Writings* (Ford ed.), i, 291, 311. See also M. L. Davis's *Memoirs of Burr*, ii, 69–75; J. C. Hamilton's *Works of Alexander Hamilton*, vii, 490 and fol.; Lodge's *Works of Hamilton*, viii, 565 and fol.; C. R. King's *Rufus King*, iii, 356, etc. An excellent contemporary account of the election of 1800 is in a letter from R. G. Harper, Representative from South Carolina, to his constituents dated "Washington, February 24, 1801" and printed in the *Papers of James A. Bayard*, 132.

1814, — long after the event to be sure — Jefferson remembered that Mr. Erving came from Boston to Virginia to inform him of the dangers resulting from Burr's intrigues.[1] On the sixth day and the thirty-sixth ballot, the Federalists at last brought themselves to confirm what was the plain wish of the Republicans and designated Thomas Jefferson as President. This momentous decision was reached on February 17, 1801. On the 4th of March following, a note was handed to Jefferson from the custodian of the "President's House" informing him [2] that "at four o'clock this morning the late president left this house which, by order of the Secretary of the Treasury, I took possession of immediately."

The "Reign of Terror" was no more. To the tune of "Adams and Liberty" Republicans sang : —

> "Rejoice ! Columbia's sons, rejoice !
> To tyrants never bend the knee,
> But join with heart, and soul, and voice,
> For JEFFERSON and LIBERTY."

[1] Jefferson to Gideon Granger, March 9, 1814, in the "Granger Manuscripts" in the Library of Congress. Samuel Smith on January 11, 1801, wrote to Burr that "a Mr. Ogden" had been at Washington trying to induce the New York Representatives to vote for him; he thought it a Federalist attempt to disunite the "Democrats." In September, 1800, Burr, in writing to Smith, had utterly disclaimed "all competition for the presidency with T. J." Smith met Burr in Philadelphia, while the matter was still undecided, and was surprised when he declared that the House of Representatives ought not to adjourn without designating either Jefferson or himself as President.

[2] The reason for Adams's seemingly discourteous departure was the recent death of his son, Charles, at New York, and the consequent dislike to any public appearance; see Charles F. Adams's *Life of John Adams*, ii, 354. Jefferson, forwarding to Adams some papers relating to the affairs of the dead son, which came to Washington after Adams's departure, caused the latter, in thanking his successor, to refer to this "greatest grief" and "deepest affliction" of his life. He added that there was nothing in the condition of affairs in New England "to obscure your prospect of a quiet & prosperous administration which I heartily wish you." See letter under date of March 24, 1801, in C. F. Adams's *Works of John Adams*. From this it would seem that in March, 1801, Adams had no particular feeling of grievance against Jefferson which would have compelled him to refuse common civilities to his successor on the day of his inauguration.

NOTE

Apportionments. — In 1790, Pendleton County in the "Upper Regions" of South Carolina had a population of about 2000 white males and 834 slaves; it sent three Representatives and one Senator to the Assembly. In the same year St. Bartholomew, on the seaboard, with 625 white males and 10,338 slaves, likewise sent three Representatives and one Senator. Professor W. A. Schaper states the matter as follows: "The low country controlled the house, 70 to 54, while its white population was 28,644, as against 111,534 of the up country. Its colored population was 79,216 as compared with 29,679 of the up country." [1]

In Virginia, twenty counties in the western portion of the State, with 31,000 white men of military age, sent 40 delegates to the Assembly or one to 775 fighting men; on the other hand, 18 counties in the eastern part of the State, with 13,000 fighting men, sent 36 delegates, or one to every 361. Stating the matter in terms of taxation, the upper counties sent one delegate for every one thousand dollars contributed, the seaboard one for every one hundred and twenty-six dollars paid in taxes. [2]

[1] "Sectionalism and Representation in South Carolina" in American Historical Association's *Reports*, 1900, vol. i.

[2] St. George Tucker's *Blackstone's Commentaries* (Philadelphia, 1803), i, Pt. i, Appendix 95–106, especially table on p. 104. Professor Tucker had already worked this out in a letter to Dr. Bentley of Salem, dated Williamsburg, June 30, 1797, in manuscript in the Harvard Library. Still earlier, Jefferson had called attention to the disproportionate representation of the tide-water region as compared with the country between the falls and the Ohio in his *Notes on Virginia* (Paris edition), p. 212. He gives a table in § 13.

CHAPTER IX

THE REVOLUTION OF 1800

AT twelve o'clock on the fourth day of March, 1801, Thomas Jefferson left Conrad's boarding house and walked across the open space between it and the unfinished capitol.[1] The day had been ushered in by a discharge of artillery, at ten the Alexandria Riflemen had paraded, and at noon the cannon again roared as the President-elect proceeded to the installation. All this militarism seems rather undemocratic, but the scene inside the Senate Chamber was simplicity itself. Indeed, life at Washington City was primitive. There were then some thirty-two hundred human beings within its limits, and of these at least six hundred were negro slaves. Only one wing of the proposed capitol[2] was sufficiently advanced to be occupied.

[1] There is a story to the effect that Jefferson had intended to go to the inauguration in a coach and four; but that his grandson did not get to Washington with them in time. Esther Singleton's *Story of the White House*, i, 28, quoting Mrs. Upton's *Our Early Presidents*. Another story has it that Jefferson rode on horseback to the capitol, and hitched his horse to the fence outside. This comes from John Davis's *Travels of Four Years and a Half in the United States of America* (London, 1803). There seems to be no probability in either of these stories, as Conrad's was less than an eighth of a mile from the capitol and contemporary letters and newspapers all have it that Jefferson came on foot. See Henry Adams's *United States*, i, 196–198; B. L. Ray-

ner's *Sketches of the Life, Writings, and Opinions of Thomas Jefferson*, 403, 404. Robert Goodloe Harper, a Federalist, informed his South Carolina constituents that the inauguration "was conducted with the utmost propriety."

[2] Glenn Brown's *History of the United States Capitol*, 2 vols., Washington, 1900. Dr. William Thornton, a West Indian by birth, designed the capitol; but the details were worked out by Benjamin H. Latrobe. His plans had been the first in the competition, but Thornton had later presented so much better a design that Washington adopted this method to satisfy all parties and secure the best possible building. A plan showing the capitol as it was first occupied is in the above, i, 24 and plate 38.

245

Near at hand were seven or eight boarding houses, a tailor's shop, a shoe-maker, a printer, a washerwoman, a grocery, a dry goods store, and an oyster house. A mile away, where the Eastern Branch joins the Potomac, there were a few large houses, more smaller ones, an empty ware-house, an unused wharf, and a block of twenty buildings that the Greenleaf and Morris syndicate had left uncompleted. A swamp divided this settlement from the capitol and another swamp and the Tyber River [1] separated that eminence from the high ground toward Georgetown, where were the President's House, a few public office buildings, one hundred brick dwellings, and two or three hundred wooden structures of one sort or another.[2] Pennsylvania Avenue, running through the alder swamp, eventually connected these two settlements, but in 1801, it was hardly more than a clearing except that stone chips, from the public buildings, had been used to make a walk or causeway for part of the distance. The President's mansion was still unfinished, the principal staircase was not even begun, only a part of the house was plastered, the roof leaked, and the floors had begun to sag, owing to the unseasoned timbers that had been used in its construction. Life at Washington in those early years was not easy and was more expensive than at Philadelphia.[3] Accommodations were so scanty

---

[1] This stream's earlier name was Goose Creek; later it became a canal, and today, instead of being the recipient of a city's sewage like its namesake, is itself a sewer. L'Enfant had conceived the pleasant project of bringing this stream on a higher level at the front of the Capitol and there turning it into a cascade or waterfall.

[2] See *American State Papers, Miscellaneous*, i, 257; and W. B. Bryan's *History of the National Capital*, i, 358.

[3] *Writings of Jefferson* (Ford), viii, 95. It is interesting to run over the itinerary prefixed to this volume and the

next to see how persistently Jefferson sought Monticello. The details in the preceding paragraph are taken from a letter from Albert Gallatin to his wife, dated "Washington City, 15th January, 1801" (Adams's *Gallatin*, 252). Other descriptions of early Washington are those of Mrs. Adams (*Letters of Mrs. Adams, the Wife of John Adams*, Boston, 1840, p. 432), and of Oliver Wolcott (Gibbs's *Memoirs of the Administrations of Washington and John Adams*, ii, 376). These descriptions and others are repeated more or less at length in Esther Singleton's *Story of the*

that Jefferson was the only one at his boarding house who had a room to himself, and Gallatin, who also lodged at Conrad's, wrote that had it not been for the presence of two ladies, the dining-room would have looked like a "refectory of monks." In this "city" the distances from one village to another were so great and the roads so poor that an afternoon call was a good deal of an undertaking. Moreover, the situation was so unwholesome that new-comers dwelling there in the late summer and early autumn seldom escaped fever and ague. Even Jefferson, Virginian though he was, resolutely refused to reside there in these months, if it could possibly be avoided.

The new President was in his fifty-eighth year. He was long, thin, and awkward. Margaret Bayard, wife of Samuel H. Smith, founder of the "National Intelligencer," relates how she admitted a stranger in her husband's absence, how he sat with his arm on the table, and how he so charmed her with his conversation that she forgot that he was a stranger, and was dismayed when her husband, on his return, addressed him as Mr. Jefferson, — for she had grown up in a Federalist home. Major Beckwith also tells us of his awkwardness; but he was not charmed by his conversation. Jefferson was one of those men who could talk a great deal without saying much, when he so desired; and could charm man or woman when he wished. In his home life, he was a good deal of a recluse, withdrawing to his study after breakfast and remaining there until dinner

White House; Anne H. Wharton's *Social Life in the Early Republic;* Allen C. Clark's *Life and Letters of Dolly Madison; Memoirs and Letters of Dolly Madison* (edited by her grand-niece) ; and *Dolly Madison* by Maud Wilder Goodwin. The most interesting account of life at the capital in the early days is *Forty Years of Washington Society Portrayed by the Family Letters of Mrs. Samuel Harrison Smith,* edited by Gaillard Hunt. Unfortunately, many interesting bits of information in this work are printed from Mrs. Smith's "Reminiscences," which were written in 1837. Washington life and the approaches thereto are vividly described by Irving in a letter dated "Jany. 13th 1811" (*Letters of Washington Irving to Henry Brevoort,* p. 19).

at three or four o'clock. To his family and neighbors, he was a Virginia planter of the olden type, but in public intercourse, he was the exemplar of democracy.[1] He came to Washington in 1801 determined to break down distinctions, there should be no more levees, birthdays, royal parades, and the arrogation of precedence in society should be "buried in the grave of federalism." In spirit, Jefferson was an optimist; there was always fair promise for the future.

Jefferson's first Inaugural Address is one of the most noteworthy documents[2] that ever came from his pen, and even now deserves the careful attention of every one, because the principles therein enunciated underlie democratic government in every age and clime. Justice to all men, he proclaimed, "honest friendship with all nations, entangling alliances with none,"[3] the support of the State governments as the "surest bulwarks against anti-Republican tendencies," the preservation of the general government, jealous care of the "right of election by the people," and acquiescence in the decisions of the majority. Proceeding, Jefferson demanded economy in the public expenditures,

---

[1] Occasionally Jefferson reverted to type and showed an aristocratic strain. On December 13, 1801, in writing to Monroe as to "cleansing the Post office" at Richmond, he said he desired to appoint to the place a "gentleman of respectable standing in society; and to such I would wish to give office, because they would add respect and strength to the administration."

[2] The address is printed in countless places; among others in *Messages and Papers of the Presidents*, i, 321 and from the original draft, with all the peculiarities of spelling, punctuation, and arrangement in Paul Leicester Ford's *Writings of Jefferson*, viii, 1.

[3] This phrase "Honest friendship with all nations, entangling alliances with none" is in Jefferson's First Inaugural Address (*Messages and Papers of the Presidents*, i, 323). The equivalent phrase in Washington's "Farewell Address," which was probably written by Hamilton, is "Why, by interweaving our destiny with that of any part of Europe, entangle our peace and prosperity in the toils of European ambition, rivalship, interest, humor, or caprice? "It is our true policy to steer clear of permanent alliances with any portion of the foreign world." *Ibid.*, 223.

Hamilton's examination of Jefferson's first Annual Message is in Lodge's edition of his *Works*, vii, 200; it is really a defence of the Federalist administrations.

reasoning that governmental assessments ultimately fall on the laboring man. This assertion was hardly more than an iteration of his statement in a previous paragraph that a wise government was one which restrained men from injuring one another, but otherwise left them free to regulate their pursuits, and did not take "from the mouth of labor the bread it has earned." In other words, there should be as little governmental regulation as possible, the individual otherwise being left free to work out his own salvation. He concluded this statement of political faith by calling for the "honest payment of our debts and sacred preservation of the public faith; encouragement of agriculture, and of commerce as its handmaid," diffusion of information, pitiless publicity, and freedom of religion, of the press, and of the person. These principles formed "the bright constellation" which had guided the nation's steps through revolution and reformation. He spoke in so low a tone that few heard him, but the speech having been given to the printer early in the morning was ready for distribution to the audience as it left the hall. Distinguished citizens waited upon the new President at his lodgings, and the remainder of the day was given to festivity, ending with "a pretty general illumination" at night.

After three or four weeks in Washington, mostly spent at Conrad's boarding house, Jefferson journeyed to Monticello. At the end of April, he returned to the seat of government, and for the next few months led a peripatetic existence, spending all the time he could at Monticello, but being necessarily at Washington every now and then.[1]

[1] In the course of the eight years of his administrations, Jefferson was absent from Washington 771 or 796 days or the equivalent of about two years and six weeks. The absences of all the Presidents down to the year 1868 may be found in an executive document presented to Congress by President

For months, indeed, the government was administered mainly by Samuel Dexter, — the relict of Adams's administration, — whom he had left at the head of the Treasury, and by Levi Lincoln, who was on the spot and was confirmed as Attorney General on March 5. Jefferson had kept to himself his wishes as to his principal advisers until after the election had been settled in the House of Representatives on February 17. The Senate that was in existence in these first weeks was still in the control of the Federalists. It was not thought best, therefore, to send in Gallatin's name as head of the Treasury. Madison was nominated for the State Department and was confirmed, but personal affairs demanded his immediate presence in Virginia, and it was some time before a commission was given to Gallatin as a vacancy appointment.

The South was in the saddle. To many a Virginian and Carolinian, March 4, 1801 seemed to be the dawn of a perfect day.[1] Again, as in 1789, a Virginian occupied the chief magistracy and a Virginian was at the head of the State Department. And, now, the majority in the new Congress was distinctly Southern and representative of

---

Grant, May 4, 1876, and printed in *Messages and Papers of the Presidents*, vii, 364. See also J. D. Defrees's "A Record of the Absence of President Grant and Cabinet from the Seat of Government to the Neglect of the People's Business," dated July 27, 1872.

[1] In November, 1801, Doctor Cunningham wrote to Jefferson from Washington stating that he had failed in the brewery business, partly from having trusted an Englishman and partly because his political opponents in the city had introduced "beer from other places in opposition to mine." He therefore asks for a loan of fifteen hundred dollars from the government to be secured by a mortgage on his property. Jefferson

in reply states that he cannot order the payment of public money except in conformity with an act of Congress, and adds, "These considerations will doubtless be a sufficient apology for the not doing in the present instance what you had deemed might be done." "Jefferson Papers" under date of November 10 and 12, 1801.

Another instance as to prevailing ideas of the use of public money comes out in a letter from Benjamin Lincoln, collector at the port of Boston, to Jefferson (April 7, 1804), stating that certain packages which had come addressed to Jefferson had been "stored in the public store and reshipped by the public boat men so that the only expence was the duties."

slave-holding interests. Jefferson realized that his victory, such as it was, had been merely accidental. Unless
the Republicans could win Northern support, they could
not retain their possession of the government for more than
four years. New England susceptibilities must be consulted. Too much reformation would alienate the friends
the administration already had in the North: "We are
all Republicans, we are all Federalists," Jefferson declared,
although brethren of the same principles have been called
by different names. Some Hamiltonian misdeeds must
be corrected and the Republicans given a share in the
governmental service; but this would be all. This mod-
eration in reform distressed many of his followers; but
there was no one to whom they could transfer their support with any hope of success, — as they and Jefferson
well knew.

For the first time, there was a complete change in the
control of the administration. It soon appeared that very
many Republicans favored extensive changes in the offices.
Applications came from all directions and from all conditions of men and women.[1] Wilderness and distance protected the embryonic capital from invasion by office-seekers;
but the mails were open, and personal solicitation to local
luminaries was easy. One letter came to Jefferson from
Mary Glenholmes of Winchester, Virginia.[2] She addressed
him as "Great Monark" and solicited a place for a neighbor, an elder in the "Metho-Republican Church" who had
been persecuted by the aristocrats. He had remained

---

[1] Gaillard Hunt's "Office-Seeking
during Jefferson's Administration" in
American Historical Review, iii, 271.

[2] "Jefferson Papers," March 11, 1801.
The kind of pressure that was brought
to bear on the new President is seen in
a letter from Thomas Lomax of "P!

Tobago" (May 28, 1801), saying that
he will be extremely thankful for any
aid that Jefferson can give in securing
an appointment for a youthful Lomax
"as a writer in some of the Public
Offices."

firm in his Republicanism, had "alumanated sixty lites of glass" for Jefferson's success, and had been turned out of house and home by his Federalist landlord. She was a poor widow and could do nothing for the family, but hoped that Jefferson might. Newspaper editors, Duane of Philadelphia, and James Cheetham of New York, declared that readjustments in the offices must be made or Republicans would be disheartened. They wanted customs collectors of their own party appointed, who would turn over the printing, advertising, and stationery business to them. Charles Pinckney of South Carolina suggested that no arrangements should be made in his State until he could personally lay certain facts before the new President. From all sides came communications leaving no shadow of doubt as to the expectations of Republican politicians and voters.

Jefferson thought that public offices should be open to all and distributed according to merit.[1] For years, only Federalists had been appointed to positions under the government, to be known as a Republican had been equivalent to official ostracism. In September, 1801, there were only thirty Republicans in the two hundred and twenty-eight principal offices.[2] Now was the chance to effect a

---

[1] Illustrating the workings of Jefferson's mind from a different angle is the case of Allen or Allan McLane, collector at Wilmington. There are papers innumerable relating to him in the files of the State Department and twenty-five more in the "Jefferson Manuscripts." McLane had been a soldier of the Revolution, was collector at Wilmington, Del., and had supported Adams in the campaign of 1800. On the fifth day of the voting for President in February, 1801, Bayard had asked two of Jefferson's political friends as to what would be done with the less important office-holders, instancing McLane. The next morning, Samuel Smith — one of the go-betweens — reported that "Mr. J." said he did not think such officers ought to be dismissed on political grounds only. "As to McLane he had heard of him and he would not or ought not to be displaced." Bayard, on February 17, 1801, wrote McLane, "I have taken good care of you, and think if prudent, you are safe," and he was. For years the Democratic-Republican politicians of Delaware tried to get him removed. They resolved that he ought no longer to be continued collector; they addressed the President, urging that offices of profit "should circulate among the People"; but nothing could be done; McLane continued in office year after year.

[2] A Reply to Lucius Junius Brutus's Examination of the President's Answer to the New-Haven Remonstrance . . . By

reëstablishment of party equilibrium in the governmental service. Looking about him, Jefferson determined to regard as nullities the appointments that Adams had made in the last few months of his term even as late as nine o'clock on the evening of March 3, 1801.[1] He drafted a letter to the holders of the "midnight appointments," stating that "officers who are to begin their course as agents of his administration should be persons on whom he has personal reliance"; the recipient, therefore, will kindly look upon his appointment as if it had never been made. He soon became convinced that he must go farther and make removals to satisfy the just demands of his own followers and to encourage Federalists to change their party allegiance. In 1804 and 1805, when the ill-judged appointments of Adams no longer stirred him to wrath, Jefferson stated his ideas as to the appointment of officials. All dishonest men and those called Federalists and land-jobbers must be rejected [2] and the principle of geographic distribution should be borne in mind, but, so he wrote a little later, the appointment of a woman was "an innovation for which the public is not prepared; nor am I."

Leonidas (New York, 1801), Appendix.

[1] The story of Levi Lincoln, with Jefferson's watch in hand, ordering Marshall to stop countersigning commissions is in Sarah N. Randolph's Domestic Life of Thomas Jefferson, 307. Doubtless it was the family tradition, but the details are absolutely contrary to fact. Jefferson's earliest thoughts on the subject are contained in a letter, dated March 24, 1801, and addressed to Benjamin Rush in Old Family Letters copied for Alexander Biddle, Series A, 466. "Midnight appointments, to wit, all after Dec. 12" is a definition given in a memorandum in Jefferson's handwriting and dated 1801. Between February 1, 1801, and March 3, Adams sent

216 nominations to the Senate. Senate Executive Journal, i, 378–390.

[2] "Jefferson Papers," April 28, 1805. Among the reasons given for removal in the memorandum of 1801 in Jefferson's handwriting are "ill treatment of Lyon, packing of juries, Federalism, non-residence and drink, extortion, . . . profligacy, and notorious delinquency." In thirteen cases no reason is stated. In 1814, Jefferson wrote to H. G. Spafford who had applied for an office that had long been occupied by another that "the principle of rotation is not that of our constitution." He added that there had never been an instance of removing an officer merely because he had been long enough in office.

One of the reproaches that was heaped on Adams was his proneness to give public place to members of his family.[1] It is true that his son, John Quincy Adams, had been put into the diplomatic service by Washington without any promptings from either father or son. It is also true that the appointment of his son-in-law, William Stephens Smith, to be Adjutant General had likewise been suggested by Washington, and Adams, while President, had distinctly refused to have Smith ordered to a particular post that would have been pleasant to him. On the other hand, it must be said one of the last appointments made by John Adams was that of Smith to be surveyor of customs at New York, and he contributed to the comfort of Mrs. John Quincy Adams's father by giving him the office of super-intendent of stamps at Washington. Jefferson did not fall into exactly the same pit. He had no son, his two sons-in-law were provided for by election to Congress, and his kinsmen, John Randolph of Roanoke and John Marshall, were otherwise cared for. Jefferson, however, did all that he could to contribute to the support of Fulwar Skipwith, who was connected with him by marriage. His distant cousin, George Jefferson, acted as his agent at Richmond. While President, Jefferson felt it would be improper to give him a place.[2] At the very end of his term, in 1808, he invited the younger man to pass a week-end at Monticello. He wrote that he would solicit his successor for him and for him alone. There were some offices "exercisable in Richmond, & compatible even with the continuance of your present business . . . but on this

---

[1] See C. F. Adams's *Works of John Adams*, viii, 529 note, 545, 652. On one occasion John Adams wrote to a kinsman that it was impossible "to appoint my own relations to any thing, without drawing forth a torrent of obloquy." *Ibid.*, viii, 636; see also *Writings of J. Q. Adams*, ii, 179.

[2] See letter of March 27, 1801; *Writings of Jefferson* (Ford), viii, 38.

subject the necessary explanations are mutuably incom-
municable but verbally." In due time, Madison appointed
George Jefferson to a consulship.

The most notorious of Jefferson's reformations of the
civil service was the dismissal of Elizur Goodrich from the
collectorship at New Haven and the appointment of Samuel Bishop to that office. Goodrich had been nominated
on February 18, 1801, so that he came within the category
of Adams's late appointments, but Jefferson felt some
doubt in this case, for Goodrich was a man of consideration
among the people of Connecticut and of New England. He
wrote to Gideon Granger, the newly appointed Postmaster
General, and to Pierrepont Edwards, a leading Connecticut
Republican, stating that there might be reasons for continuing Goodrich in the office, but if that would do more harm
than good, it would be well to appoint some one who, from
his character and standing in society, would most effectually
silence clamor. It was in Connecticut that Jefferson had
been most fiercely attacked on account of his religion and
there was ground for this because he was a Unitarian —
whose theological opinions were certain to be ill received
in that State.[1] After consulting with prominent men of
the neighborhood, they wrote to Jefferson that continuing
Goodrich in office would only strengthen Federalists in their
opposition.[2] Edwards suggested as his successor "Samuel
Bishop Esq. of this town, Mayor of our City, Chief Judge
of our County Court, and a Decon in one of our established
churches" for in him were combined "respectability, integrity, religion, steady habits, and firm republicanism."
A committee of New Haven merchants at once remonstrated,

[1] For Jefferson's religious opinions,
see *Writings of Jefferson* (Ford), viii, 223
and note. See also Jefferson's invocation
to the "infinite power which rules the
destinies of the universe" at the end of
his first inaugural speech.
[2] *American Historical Review*, iii, 272,
274, 277.

stating that Mr. Goodrich was satisfactory to them and that Bishop's eyesight was so poor he could scarce write his name and that he was too feeble in body and mind to master the revenue laws of which he was totally ignorant.[1] Jefferson seized the opportunity thus afforded to expound his views as to the civil service. During the late administration, he wrote, all the offices under the national government had been monopolized by a particular sect. It was true that he had declared in favor of political tolerance, but was it intolerance to claim a proportionate share in the direction of public affairs? And who could more justly be displaced than one who was about to begin his career with a new administration which could expect from him no cordial coöperation. "If a due participation of office is a matter of right, how are vacancies to be obtained? Those by death are few; by resignation none. Can any other mode than that of removal be proposed?" As to Bishop's qualifications, it is true that he was seventy-seven years of age, but Franklin had been an ornament of human nature at a much more advanced period, and, at the time of his appointment, Bishop held no less than five local offices, to two of

[1] March 27, 1802, Samuel Bishop wrote to Jefferson thanking him for the appointment, saying, "I retain my handwriting sufficiently to express this gratitude. Being recovered from a long season of sickness, I shall endeavor to perform personally some official acts and to cause the rest to be done to acceptance." The feebleness of the chirography goes far toward justifying the attitude of the New Haven merchants.

The New Haven Remonstrance and Jefferson's reply are in the Norwich, Connecticut, *Courier* of July 29, 1801. The reply is dated July 12, 1801, and is in every edition of Jefferson's writings. Samuel Bishop's son, Abraham, had prepared an oration "On the Extent and Power of Political Delusion." It was to have been delivered before the Phi Beta Kappa Society of Yale College in 1800. The committee of the Society, getting sight of a printed copy before the day of delivery, cancelled the appointment, but the pamphlet was disseminated with the original title-page. The last paragraph of it invited those who had bowed the knee to the political Baal, or were slavishly devoted "to the *self-stiled* friends of order and good government," to prepare their necks for the yoke. See F. B. Dexter's article in Massachusetts Historical Society's *Proceedings*, xxxix, 190. Abraham Bishop stated his views of the "Remonstrance" in five and a half columns of the *Sun of Liberty* which is reprinted in the Petersburg, Virginia, *Republican* of October 5, 1801.

which he had been appointed by the Connecticut legislature, only three months before.

The details of removals and appointments made by Jefferson and the Heads of Departments will never be known. Of the offices filled by the President with the consent of the Senate, one-half changed hands during his first term. In addition, the repeal of the Judiciary Act of 1801 and the destruction of the internal revenue system brought about the removal of a considerable number of Federalists; but no Republicans profited by this destruction.[1] Every change in the civil service incited would-be office-holders — M. L. Davis, James Cheetham, William Duane — to greater activity and caused more anxiety and trouble to Jefferson and his advisers. Burr had already prepared a list of New York Federal office-holders for decapitation and suggested good Burr Republicans for their places.[2] Before taking action, Jefferson seems to have consulted George Clinton or some Clintonian leader. It was one of the latter who had suggested to his chief that "in some collateral way" he might hint to Jefferson as to the probable effect of appointing New York Burrites to office. Jefferson had distrusted Burr for years, but he was so powerful that the President pursued a more than usually tortuous course in dealing with this matter. Burr's most

---

[1] It is impossible to give more than a rough approximation of the extent of removals from office made by Jefferson. July 24, 1803, he drafted a letter to William Duane defending his course — which had been much too moderate for the Pennsylvania radicals; *Writings of Jefferson* (Ford), viii, 255–261. In it Jefferson states that of 316 officers subject to removal and appointment by him, 130 only are Federalists. The figures in the text are repeated from J. M. Merriam's essay (American Historical Association's *Papers*, ii, no. 1, p. 51) which were taken from the *Ex-* *ecutive Journal of the Senate;* for another estimate, see Jefferson to Short, May 19, 1807, in *Writings of Jefferson* (Ford), ix, 51. The most detailed discussion of the subject is C. R. Fish's *The Civil Service and the Patronage* in *Harvard Historical Studies*, xi. Miss L. M. Salmon's "History of the Appointing Power of the President" in American Historical Association's *Papers*, i, No. 5, has little definite information on this part of the subject.

[2] *American Historical Review*, iii, 290; Adams's *Life of Albert Gallatin*, 282.

intimate friend and his biographer, Matthew L. Davis, actually penetrated to Monticello in search of a job; and great pressure was put upon Gallatin, whose father-in-law was prominent in New York politics; but nothing that any one could do helped a Burrite, — "Nothing is determined" was the only satisfaction they got.

James Cheetham, an English radical, had escaped with difficulty from his own country, had found life in America unpleasant during what he was pleased to call "The Terror," and was now editing a Republican paper in New York. In 1801, when he was twenty-eight years of age and had been three years in the United States, he exhorted Jefferson to exclude "obnoxious characters" from office. He had been friendly with Burr, but by December, 1801, had fallen out with him. He journeyed to Washington to warn Jefferson and Madison against the Vice-President because there had been a plan for one of the New York electors to give his vote for Burr and some one other than Jefferson and thus relegate the latter to second place. This plan had been thwarted by the Clintonians, so Cheetham said.[1] Duane was born in Canada, Vermont, or Ireland, and came to America from India, whence he had been expelled by the government. Settling in Philadelphia, he became intimate with the family of Benjamin Franklin Bache, editor of the "General Advertiser," or "The Aurora" as it was more often called, and ere long succeeded to the paper and to the widow, and became a loving father to the little Baches. Jefferson's advent seemed to open a boundless vista of offices, subscriptions to the paper, and contracts for printing. It turned out quite otherwise, for two Republican papers struggled for every new subscriber, and secretaries and collectors were deaf to appeals for advertising and

[1] Massachusetts Historical Society's *Proceedings*, vol. 41, pp. 41–64.

for profitable contracts. Duane declared that the Philadelphia collector even discouraged importers and auctioneers from advertising in his paper.[1] He laid the blame for these disappointments on Gallatin's shoulders and, on account of his facile pen, became no despicable enemy. Most unfortunately, Jefferson temporized with Duane, instead of standing as a barrier between him and his Secretary of the Treasury, who had troubles enough of his own. The scoldings and intriguings of Duane and his tribe, now they were perfectly free, are possibly the best justification of the Sedition Act.

Jefferson was an experienced administrator. He gathered about him an able set of men and with them worked the governmental machine carefully and well until prosperity created dissensions among his followers. Some months after entering upon his duties, he sent a circular letter to his principal advisers announcing his intentions to return to the system that Washington had pursued.[2] In the future the President would keep the control of business in his own hands, the departmental heads submitting all important matters to him, either orally or in writing. At Washington he was accessible every day, and in his long absences at Monticello he arranged for a reasonably constant postal

[1] For Duane, see Allen C. Clark's sketch of William Duane in Columbia Historical Society's *Records*, vol. 9, p. 14; also printed separately. For other material on Duane, see *Writings* of Jefferson and of Gallatin, Henry Adams's *Life of Gallatin*, and the "Letters of William Duane" in Massachusetts Historical Society's *Proceedings*, vol. 40, pp. 257–394. See also the "Letters of James Cheetham" in *ibid.*, vol. 41, pp. 42–64. From a letter from Gallatin to Jefferson, dated December 15, 1801, it would seem that Gallatin approved of awarding contracts for public printing and for supplying public stationery to Duane. On this general subject see also Worthington C. Ford's "Jefferson and the Newspaper" in Columbia Historical Society's *Records*, vol. 8, p. 78.

[2] *Writings of Jefferson* (Ford), viii, 99. In another respect, Jefferson broke away from the practice of his predecessors in opening Congress in person with a speech. In transmitting his first message, Jefferson stated that "the circumstances under which we find ourselves at this place rendering inconvenient the mode" of personal address, he had substituted a written message for the spoken word to which a reply had been made, at the expense of time.

service, to and from the capital. Only the most important matters were submitted to the Secretaries and the Attorney General in joint meeting.[1] Jefferson seems to have felt doubts as to the constitutionality of this mode of proceeding and to have believed that written reports were much more consonant to the letter and spirit of the Constitution. Jefferson's relations with his advisers were remarkably close and intimate, especially with Madison and Gallatin. For years he had believed that many things could be arranged in personal intercourse, especially at the dining table. Madison and Gallatin frequently dined at the President's without any formality, and concerted measures with him, and came to decisions. Where relations were so close and confidence so secure it was possible for the President to take a leading hand in many strictly departmental matters; and this Jefferson did, often writing with his own pen letters that one would have expected would have been written and signed by one of the great officers of state. On the other hand, he was in the habit of turning over to them, especially to Madison and to Gallatin, many things which most Presidents would have seen to themselves. Where there was so much freedom and so much confidence, this system worked admirably. Indeed, it would be difficult to find a more effective bit of administration than that of our national affairs in Jefferson's first term.

The new chief magistrate and his great financier were firm believers in the perfectibility of mankind. They proceeded to take the whole American people into their confidence, precisely as Jefferson took his leading advisers into his. This accounts for the mass of explanatory matter that poured forth from the national capital in these years.

---

[1] Jefferson's minutes of Cabinet meetings are printed in the "Anas" in   *Writings* (Ford), i, 291 and fol.

An example of this is Jefferson's reply to the "New Haven Remonstrance"; but this is only one of countless emanations from the President, Secretary of the Treasury, the Postmaster General, and other members of the administration. It was a time of openness combined with the utmost secrecy, — such as had been marked features of Jefferson's political campaigning. To read some of these effusions, one would place Jefferson among the simple minded and confiding idealists; but in reality, they were the result of design and of subtle principle. Whatever the reason, it must be admitted that, somehow, Thomas Jefferson managed to hold together for a series of years the diverse and warring elements that composed the Republican party and made it possible for men so differently constituted as Albert Gallatin, Samuel Smith, and William Duane to work together for what he considered to be the best interests of the nation.

When the Republicans took charge of affairs, they found the national treasury overflowing with gold and silver and the annual income of the government ten and one half million dollars in comparison with less than four millions in 1791. Gallatin's first report as Secretary of the Treasury was presented to Congress in December, 1801.[1] It appeared that the national debt had increased some eight or nine million dollars since 1792. These figures did not take into account the sinking fund that might well have been subtracted from the gross debt, for Gallatin thought that until the debt was actually wiped off the books it should be reckoned as a liability. He estimated the average annual income for the next eight years at $10,600,000 and the

---

[1] It is widely printed as in *American State Papers, Finance*, i, 701. With it should be studied the "Report of the Committee of Ways and Means, pursuant to a Resolution of the 2d March, 1803," and "Letter from the Secretary of the Treasury" of April 16, 1810, in *ibid.*, ii, 37, 423.

annual expenditures at $3,500,000, leaving $7,100,000 free for the payment of the interest and principal of the national debt. About one-half of this must be used for the payment of interest; but the rest could be applied to the extinguishment of the principal, which, if everything turned out as planned, would be paid off in 1817. Everything did not turn out exactly as planned, but in 1810, the net decrease of the debt was no less than twenty-seven and one-half millions, or, counting in the money that was paid for Louisiana, forty-two and one-half millions.

The country owes a great debt of gratitude to Hamilton for his financial constructiveness; but Federalist organization of the details of financial administration was too much tinged with conservatism, — it followed too closely on colonial precedents. Moneys had been voted in bulk to the several departments, leaving the actual expenditures very much to the discretion of the higher officials. It fell out, in this way, that large expenditures had been made without legal authority and money appropriated by law for one purpose had been applied to another. A committee of the House of Representatives was appointed to examine into these matters and did so with thoroughness. It reported that money still remained to be accounted for by Federalist officials;[1] but found almost no wrong doing.

---

[1] Timothy Pickering was charged on the treasury books with $380,675.27 "for want of an appropriation by congress." According to a "Letter from the Comptroller of the Treasury," dated December 1, 1809, Pickering's accounts as Quartermaster General in the Revolutionary War had only recently been settled. This lax accountability continued, if a statement in the *Columbian Centinel* for March 31, 1810 is correct, for then nine persons were debited on the treasury books with over one million dollars; six collectors of the customs had nearly four hundred thousand in unpaid balances; and the residences of one hundred and three persons who had unsettled accounts in the Navy Department were then unknown.

Oliver Wolcott, in *An Address to the People of the United States, on the Subject of the Report of a Committee . . . presented on the 29th of April, 1802*, analyzed the figures presented in the report, which he prints at length with Gallatin's letter and other documents.

The money ($32,872.34) that had been paid for the trans-
portation of the personal and private goods of governmental employees from Philadelphia to Washington City
was the only clear case of unlawful expenditure. It
was evident, nevertheless, that Gallatin was right in demanding stricter accountability and especially in arguing
for specific appropriations. The accomplishment of this
design was a matter of time and difficulty, but it is to
the credit of Gallatin and the Republicans that they
entered so heartily into the task of securing a more
stringent accountability in the expenditure of the nation's
money.

Of Federalist abominations, after the Alien and Sedition
laws and the Judiciary Act, none loomed larger in Republican eyes than the excise tax on distilled liquors.[1] The
methods of collection were necessarily inquisitorial and
exceedingly expensive, amounting to no less than one-fifth
of the total sum collected, as against only two or three
per cent for the customs revenue. Nothing had done
more to arouse Jefferson's suspicion of Hamilton's motives
than this excise tax. Now, of course, the motives of those
in high office were entirely pure and untainted with mon-
archism; but the tax was of hateful memory and bore with
undue weight on the western agriculturalists. Jefferson
demanded its repeal and Gallatin resisted, for he wanted
the half-million that it brought in. But Jefferson secured
promises of economy from the spending departments and
the tax was swept away. His relations with his greatest
follower do not seem to have been in any ways affected.
In the end, Gallatin's estimates of income proved to be

[1] See tables accompanying Gallatin's
letter of December 21, 1801, in *American
State Papers, Finance*, i, 718, and the
report of the committee of the House in
the *History of the Last Session of Congress, which commenced on the Seventh of
December, 1801*, p. 82.

so much under the mark that his plans as to the reduction of the national debt were carried out.

On March 3, 1801, the day before his exit from the chief magistracy, John Adams approved an act for the reduction of the naval establishment, at the President's discretion, to thirteen vessels, nine captains, and a proportionate number of other officers.[1] As soon as Jefferson found a Secretary of the Navy, which proved to be a rather hard undertaking, he set about the reduction of the navy according to this law of the last Federalist administration. He then looked about for something for the remaining vessels to do and soon found it in the regulation of the beys and bashaws of the North African coast. For generations, powerful and proud Christian countries had truckled to these potentates, who were supposedly tributary to the Turkish sultan. Really, they acknowledged only the necessity of keeping their subjects' good will, which could most easily be accomplished by plundering Christian shipping instead of levying taxes.[2] For years, Great Britain had purchased immunity by the payment of an annual tribute. With independence, American vessels and crews were exposed to these marauders, who hailed with joy the coming of a new flag and sailed out into the Atlantic to gather fresh booty in ships and slaves. In 1784, Adams at London and Jefferson at Paris had been ordered to do what they could to abate the nuisance.[3] Adams thought the only way would be to buy off the corsairs, but Jefferson argued for the establishment of a navy. He wrote that one hundred and fifty guns on the Barbary coast[4] would be more efficacious

---

[1] *Annals of Congress*, 6th Cong., 1557; *Statutes at Large*, ii, 110.

[2] On early conditions in the Barbary States, see Gardner W. Allen's *Our Navy and the Barbary Corsairs*, chs. i and ii.

[3] See Gardner W. Allen's *Our Navy and the Barbary Corsairs*, 28 and fol., and the authorities cited on the pages.

[4] *Writings of Jefferson* (Memorial ed.), v, 364, 365. In 1802, Jefferson declared that peace was "the most im-

and cheaper than paying money to the pirates; a naval force belonging to the United States in Congress Assembled would also be useful to coerce the States that were behindhand in the payment of their requisitions. Jefferson even suggested negotiations to induce European commercial countries to blockade the Barbary ports; but the time was not yet ripe for any such concerted action. In 1786, therefore, a treaty was concluded with the ruler of Morocco for the payment of money and the giving of presents in exchange for captive Americans and future immunity, and this treaty was still in force in 1789. One of Jefferson's earliest acts as Secretary of State was to compile two reports on our relations with the North African powers. Again he advocated the use of force and a coöperative blockade, this time (1791) under the command of the redoubtable Paul Jones. Washington hearkened, however, to the moans of the captives and entered into agreements with Algiers, Tunis, Tripoli, and Morocco; and Adams kept up the sending of tribute.

Once in the presidential chair, Jefferson was in a position to test the efficacy of force in bringing the Barbary freebooters to a realizing sense of their position in the world. May 15, 1801, he proposed the questions in cabinet meeting "Shall the squadron now at Norfolk be ordered to cruise in the Mediterranean" etc.? and how far could an American commander go in waging war?[1] It seemed clear that they could resist attack even without a constitutional declaration of war by Congress and might sink and destroy the attacker. Five days earlier, Yusuf Caramelli, Bashaw of Tripoli, had taken matters into his own hands by cutting

portant of all things to us, except the preserving an erect & independent attitude." *Writings* (Ford), viii, 173.

[1] Jefferson's "Anas" in *Writings* (Ford), i, 293.

down the flag-staff in front of the American consul's residence, for that was his method of declaring war.[1] When the American squadron entered the Mediterranean, one of the vessels, the *Enterprise*, was attacked by a Tripolitan cruiser. In a couple of hours the enemy yielded. As Captain Sterrett of the *Enterprise* could not capture her, he stripped her of her sails except one and left her and her crew to drift home as best they might. They arrived at Tripoli with such tales of the fighting qualities of the Americans that the Tripolitans were more careful after this in their treatment of American warships. Other fleets followed, and in 1803, the war took on a more active form, with Edward Preble in chief command. In these earlier stages of the conflict and, indeed, throughout its course, the American commanders were seriously hampered by the niggardliness of Congress and of the Secretary of the Treasury. Albert Gallatin had no ethical scruples against warfare. He had fought in our Revolution and on sundry occasions in the following years was quite willing to go to war when others wished for peace; but he was an economist before all. He was intent upon paying the public debt: Congress had deprived him of the internal revenue, and administrative officers out of his own department were careless spenders. His idea and, possibly, Jefferson's was to utilize the existing naval force and when more money was necessary, he induced Congress to levy an extra five per cent on imported goods to pay for these expenses under the name of the Mediterranean Fund. Even with this added resource, the naval officers were hard put to it to maintain the efficiency of their ships and to preserve their fighting qualities. Robert Smith, the Secretary of the

---

[1] Events at Tripoli at this critical time are best seen in the "Letter Book" of J. L. Cathcart, our consul at that port, in J. B. C. Newkirk's *Tripoli. First War with the United States* (La Porte, Ind., 1901).

Navy, brother of Samuel Smith, head of one of the leading commercial houses of Baltimore, and a member of Congress, was in a difficult position between Gallatin and Preble.[1] Discretion in spending had to be given to a commanding officer on a distant station, and supplies had to be bought at home in emergencies at whatever price was demanded. The Naval Department accounts seem to have been kept better than those of any of the other disbursing departments, but Gallatin, with one eye fixed on the national debt and the other on specific appropriations and knowing nothing of the costs of warfare, was inexorable.

In the Mediterranean, Commodore Preble planned to keep his squadron employed to the utmost. He had under his orders the *Constitution*, the *Philadelphia*, and half a dozen smaller vessels with officers of the type of Bainbridge, Burrows, Decatur, Porter, and MacDonough. On his arrival, he learned of the loss of the *Philadelphia*, the second strongest ship of his squadron, and soon met with even worse news in the announcement that she had been floated from the reef where she had struck and had been taken into the harbor of Tripoli.[2] As his smaller vessels would be unsafe in her presence, unless the *Constitution* were at hand, the first thing to be done was to bring about her destruction. This was most gallantly accomplished by Lieutenant Stephen Decatur (February 16, 1804). With a few men, he sailed into the anchorage off the town of Tripoli, laid his vessel alongside the *Philadelphia*, drove her crew overboard, set fire to her in several places, and rowed away by the light of her blazing spars and to the thunder of scores of guns on ship and shore. It was a feat which Lord Nel-

[1] In gathering material for these paragraphs I have been greatly aided by Mr. G. H. Davies, who is engaged on a study of General Smith's career.

[2] See T. Harris's *Life and Services of Commodore William Bainbridge* (Philadelphia, 1837, p. 80, etc.).

son is said to have declared the most bold and daring act
of the age. The *Philadelphia* out of the way, Preble laid
siege to the town and fortress; [1] he had bought, borrowed,
or hired half a dozen gun-boats and bomb-ketches and
six heavy guns for the spar deck of the *Constitution* and
ninety-six Neapolitan gunners. All in all, he had one
thousand and sixty officers and men. Unfortunately, estimating his task at its true magnitude, he had urgently
asked for reënforcements. These were sent, but with them
came in command Captain Samuel Barron, who held an
appointment senior to that of Preble. Barron was ill at
the time of his arrival and the responsibilities of his position
and the Mediterranean climate compelled him to remain in
port. After Preble sailed for home, therefore, the command
of the squadron off Tripoli devolved on John Rodgers,
who naturally did not feel like taking desperate chances
in the absence of his commanding officer. The interest
now turned to affairs on land and to one of the most extraordinary figures in our history, William Eaton, a Connecticut Yankee, formerly consul at Tunis.

There were two Caramelli brothers, Hamet and Yusuf;
Yusuf was the younger, but he usurped the rightful place
of the elder as Bashaw of Tripoli and drove him away. Any
one might have thought of using Hamet against the reigning bashaw, but Eaton actually proceeded to carry the idea
into execution. In 1805, Hamet was an exile in Egypt.
Eaton pursued him thither, induced him to join with him
in an attack on the Tripolitan city of Derne, which was
difficult to reach overland from Tripoli and still more

[1] See Ira N. Hollis's "The Constitution at Tripoli" in *Papers* of the Military
Historical Society of Massachusetts,
vol. xi, no. 3; and "The Hull-Eaton
Correspondence during the Expedition
against Tripoli 1804–1805," edited by
C. H. Lincoln in *Proceedings* of the
American Antiquarian Society, vol. xxi,
pt. 1.

difficult to get to from Egypt across the Libyan Desert. Hamet, once securely in place at Derne, might make Yusuf more tractable and save the expenditure of naval gunpowder. With a dozen Americans, twenty-five or thirty Europeans, forty Greeks, one hundred Tripolitans including Hamet, and a body of Arabian horsemen led by a Sheik, Eaton started on his adventure, — and succeeded after fatigues, hardships, and mutinies in the midst of the desert. Almost a month after this accomplishment, Bashaw Yusuf signed a treaty, and Eaton was directed to evacuate Derne, which proved to be a more perilous undertaking than its capture had been, and he spent the rest of his life in trying to secure recompense from Congress.

There is a great deal that is doubtful about the Tripolitan Treaty of Peace of 1805. The negotiator was Tobias Lear, once Washington's private secretary and later a consul. He bore the title of Colonel, which he had obtained not in war, but as Washington's military secretary in 1798. Lear had most pacific intentions which were seconded by Captain Rodgers. The Bashaw had suggested a payment of two hundred thousand dollars and the restoration of all his property as the price of peace. Lear cut this down to sixty thousand dollars and a mutual exchange of prisoners and then signed the treaty. It has been said that these easy terms were accorded Yusuf because the crew of the *Philadelphia*, prisoners in Tripoli, were in danger of their lives. In commenting on it, Preble wrote to Robert Smith that every American must be gratified to have peace established with Tripoli "on more honorable terms than any other nation has ever been able to command."

Gun-boats and row-galleys were in common use in the

Mediterranean for defence and offence.[1] Preble had employed them in his attacks on Tripoli. As early as April 19, 1804, he had written from Syracuse advising the construction of ten or twelve large-size gun and mortar boats to be sent across the Atlantic to be used in future attacks on Tripoli. Several were built and sent to the Mediterranean, one disappearing on the voyage over. They did good service and were well spoken of by British naval officers who saw them. Gun-boats had been authorized even before this by an act of Congress that had been approved by Adams on May 4, 1798; but none seem to have been built at that time. Jefferson laid the subject before Congress in November, 1804, and again in February, 1807. The problem of coast defence had troubled the federal authorities. Before 1789, the question of building forts and arming them had been left to the States. Whenever the subject was approached at Washington, its magnitude and costliness appalled the legislators.[2] In his 1807 communication to Congress, Jefferson spoke of land batteries, movable artillery, floating batteries, and gun-boats. The last in the crude conditions of land transportation and the great extent of the coast seemed to be the best solution of the problem. Commodore Barron and Captain Tingey, super-

[1] Dr. Gardner W. Allen most kindly placed at my disposal notes that he had made as to the origin of the gun-boat policy from "the Preble Papers" in the Library of Congress, the *Writings of Jefferson*, the *American State Papers, Naval Affairs*, and Goldsborough's *Naval Chronicle*. See especially letters of Barron and Tingey in *American State Papers, Naval Affairs*, i, 164, and the *Naval Chronicle*, 323.

[2] This question may be further examined in the report of Henry Dearborn, Secretary of War, of February 13, 1806 (*American State Papers, Military Affairs*, i, 192), and the speech of Josiah Quincy, delivered in the House of Rep-

resentatives on April 15th of the same year.

The collateral question of naval protection is well treated in *An Address to the People of the United States on . . . a Permanent Navy* (Philadelphia, 1802). An appendix (pp. 44–46) contains a study of the effect of war on maritime insurance of neutral vessels — with figures for the years 1793–1799. In 1801 Wm. Caruthers wrote to Jefferson from Lexington, Ky., suggesting that a "receiver highly charged with electricity, hermetically sealed, and violently projected" would, on breaking, give a violent shock to the enemy.

intendent of the Washington navy yard, as well as Commodore Preble advocated their construction. It is probable that the supposed cheapness of these small vessels appealed to Jefferson. At any rate he suggested building two hundred of them "merely for defensive operations" and not for the protection of commerce at sea or even on the coast. This was the origin of the gun-boat policy which also appealed to administrators as affording numerous small commands. In the prosecution of the war on the Barbary corsairs, several small sea-going naval vessels were also built and did good service. Whatever the merits or demerits of Jeffersonian naval warfare in the first half dozen years of his presidency, it must be admitted that these cruises afforded admirable training for young and enterprising naval officers and turned out a remarkable number of distinguished captains and commodores, as the War of 1812 was presently to demonstrate. In April, 1804, Jefferson wrote to Robert Smith expressing mortification at the conduct of American officials in Europe, on the occasion of the loss of the *Philadelphia*, who have hawked us about as begging alms at every court ; they appear to suppose that all is lost and that the United States is without resource, all of which seemed to him to be most unpardonable. Jefferson's bellicose attitude in the early years of his presidency is well worth bearing in mind in view of his later determination to keep the United States out of the world-wide war regardless of what seemed to many persons to be the national honor.

NOTES

I. Bibliography. — Henry Adams has made the period covered by this and the succeeding chapters of this volume the subject of an historical masterpiece: *History of the United States* (9 vols., New York, 1889–1891). As published the set was divided into four groups, each dealing with an administration. The ninth volume contains a general index of over a hundred pages and there is an index at the end of each of the first three administrations. This work is founded on a most patient research, which brought to light masses of hitherto unused material, and Mr. Adams used to the full his almost unrivalled historical judgment. The volumes are oftentimes not easy to read because of the mass of detail in the text, — giving, indeed, all of the more important parts of the documents that had been copied for him in foreign archives. The work is, therefore, an original source as well as an historical comment. Adams naturally found it impossible to divest himself of his great grandfather's distrust of Jefferson, but in general the work is impersonal. The same author's *John Randolph* in the *American Statesmen* series is a brilliant, historical study of a remarkable man. Henry Adams's *Documents Relating to New-England Federalism* (Boston, 1877) is made up of original matter on this period.

Vying with Adams's great work, and in some respects surpassing it, are Captain Alfred T. Mahan's studies of the influence of sea power on the fortunes of the world in these twenty-five years ending in 1815. The books are *The Influence of Sea Power upon the French Revolution and Empire, 1793–1812* (2 vols., Boston, 1894) and *Sea Power in its Relations to the War of 1812* (2 vols., Boston, 1905). These works display great learning and profound critical insight. The first half of the first volume of the *War of 1812* is a masterly analysis of the commercial warfare preceding the outbreak of naval and military conflict. Mahan's insistence upon " preparedness " finally jars upon the reader, but his judgment is marvellous, although sometimes in conflict with that of Henry Adams. The *War of 1812* is in many respects Mahan's greatest contribution to historical science, but it often lacks the readable qualities of his earlier productions.

II. President Jefferson. — Jefferson's manuscripts are preserved in several different places. The " Official Papers " are in the Library of Congress, the " Private Papers " are in the cabinet of the Massachusetts Historical Society. The separation was not skilfully done, so that some papers that might fairly be called official are at Boston. Besides, there are still several small collections in private hands. Jefferson was a most voluminous writer; he used either a wet copying press or a machine, called the polygraph, that wrote two copies at once. He filed away masses of papers with an unstinted hand and destroyed others for various reasons. The Department of State printed a *Calendar of the Correspondence of Thomas Jefferson* in 1894, but a complete list of the private papers has never been printed. There are three sets of the *Writings of Jefferson*. The most complete is the " Memorial edition " in twenty volumes, Washington, 1903. Ford's edition in ten volumes (New York, 1892–1899) is more usable, but unfortunately does not repeat all the matter printed in the nine-volume " Congress edition " (Washington, 1853–1854).[1] A selection from the private papers forms volume 1 of the 7th series of the *Collections* of the Massachusetts Historical Society. A mass of material that Jefferson put together in his old age under the title of " Anas " is printed in the first volume of the Ford edition and by itself as *The Complete Anas of Thomas Jefferson* (New York, 1903). Some of this matter may fairly be called original material, but much of it is simply the recollections of an old man with a somewhat unreliable memory. There have been numerous biographies and papers relating to all or a part of Jefferson's varied career. Of these, the biography by H. S. Randall (3 vols., New York, 1858) is markedly prejudiced and valuable for that reason. George Tucker's *Life of Thomas Jefferson* (2 vols., Philadelphia, 1837) is interesting as giving a Virginia view, and Cornelis de Witt's *Thomas Jefferson, Etude Historique sur la Démocratie Américaine* [2] is important as being a distinctly foreign, but sympathetic analysis. Schouler's brief biography perhaps best expresses the man, Thomas E. Watson's little sketch gives the view of a

[1] This was edited by H. A. Washington and is often cited under his name. It was reprinted at Philadelphia and New York. An early four-volume work by Jefferson's grandson, T. J. Randolph, entitled *Memoir, Correspondence, and Miscellanies, from the Papers of Thomas Jefferson*, was printed at Charlottesville, Va., in 1829 and at Boston in 1830. B. S. Catchings arranged the *Master*

[2] Published at Paris in 1861 and again in 1862. It was translated by R. S. H. Church with some extra matter as *Jefferson and the American Democracy* (London, 1862).

Thoughts of Thomas Jefferson under seventeen heads in a book with that title; it is useful for those who do not wish to see the man for themselves.

modern southern radical, and Parton's one-volume biography (Boston, 1874) is by far the most readable of them all. Paul Leicester Ford's *Thomas Jefferson* (*Monographs of the American Revolution*) is a beautiful bit of book-making and written by one who was thoroughly conversant with his theme. [1]

L. H. Boutell privately printed at Chicago in 1891 an interesting study of *Thomas Jefferson, the Man of Letters* and there is a stimulating paper on "Jefferson as a Naturalist" in *Magazine of American History*, xiii, 379. Jefferson's granddaughter, Sarah N. Randolph, wrote a volume entitled *Domestic Life of Thomas Jefferson* and also printed an analysis of his private character in the *North American Review*, xci, 115. There is a book by H. W. Pierson entitled *Jefferson at Monticello*, which represents the recollections of an old man who, some years earlier, had been Jefferson's superintendent, — many of the anecdotes are plainly impossible. B. L. Rayner's *Sketches of the Life, Writings, and Opinions of Thomas Jefferson* is most favorable to him and often seems to be authentic. Of hostile views, those by William Sullivan in his *Familiar Letters on Public Characters* and by Theodore Dwight in a book entitled *The Character of Thomas Jefferson, as exhibited in His Own Writings* are thoroughly antagonistic, and the same may be said of two volumes which were written by Stephen C. Carpenter and printed at New York in 1809 with the title of *Memoirs of the Hon. Thomas Jefferson, . . . with a View of the Rise and Progress of French Influence and French Principles in that Country* [the United States].

C. H. Hart's Browere's *Life Masks of Great Americans* has a representation of Jefferson which is undoubtedly the most authentic of many attempts to preserve his lineaments for future ages.

---

[1] Ford also printed an article on "Thomas Jefferson in Undress" in *Scribner's Magazine*, xii, 509.

CHAPTER X

THE FLOOD TIDE

THE most significant achievement of Jefferson's first administration was the procurement of Louisiana; but this is so intricate a matter to elucidate, and so important withal, that it would better be treated by itself in a separate chapter. Next in significance to this was the attack on the federal judiciary. Nothing in the constitutional settlement had so aroused the suspicions of Jefferson and his followers as the rapid extension of the activity and jurisdiction of the judges of the United States courts. They honestly believed that the individual States were the most important political entities and only tolerated the federal union as a painful necessity. Moreover, the federal judiciary had been established to compel the payment of debts by the people of one part of the United States to creditors living in other parts or in other countries. The Kentucky Resolutions of 1798 had declared null and void a recent act of Congress giving federal courts jurisdiction in certain cases.[1] One of the last acts[2] passed by the Federalist Congress and approved by John Adams had materially extended and improved the judicial system, and the outgoing President had appointed Federalists to the new offices that were thus created.

[1] *American History Leaflets*, no. 15.
[2] The reformation of the Judiciary was referred to a committee of the Senate, December 15, 1797, and of the House, December 24; but nothing further was done at this time.

A change in this system was certainly most desirable in 1801, if it was to be worked to the best advantage. The compensation of the justices stood next to that of the President of the United States and on an equality with that of the highest placed administrative officers, but it was not equal to the earnings of the foremost lawyers in the different parts of the country. The honor of being a member of so august a tribunal was very great; but the constantly recurring journeys to hold sessions of the circuit courts made the position unattractive to gentlemen of middle life, sustained reputation in their profession, and large earning capacities. The honor and lack of adequate compensation balanced one another, but the hardships of travel weighed greatly against acceptance, and, indeed, against continuance in office. The Judiciary Act of 1789 had provided a set of district courts, and between them and the Supreme Court a series of circuit courts that were to be held by the justices of the Supreme Court and the district judges. This meant that there would be a good deal of travelling between the places of holding the sessions of the Supreme Court and the different parts of the country. At first the circuits were dealt out permanently to pairs of justices of the Supreme Court, and this proving distasteful, it was arranged that they should ride by turns the least and the most eligible circuits.[1] No matter how it was fixed, the riding horseback, travelling by stagecoach, lodging at uncomfortable and overcrowded taverns certainly interfered with the energies of men who were no longer in vigorous life and deterred desirable candidates from taking the position.

---

[1] See Act of April 13, 1792, § 3, conveniently found in *Annals of Congress*, 2nd Cong., 1358. As to the distastefulness of circuit riding, see the representation of Jay and his associates in *ibid.*, 2nd Cong., 1318. The Judiciary Act of 1789 is in *ibid.*, 1st Cong., vol. ii, 2182; the act of 1801 is in *ibid.*, 6th Cong., 1534; and the repealing act of 1802 is in *ibid.*, 7th Cong., 1st Sess., 1305.

On the other hand, there were many arguments against the reconstruction or enlargement of the federal judiciary. Apart from circuit riding, the Justices of the Supreme Court had very little to do. They held two sessions in each year which occupied only five or six weeks of their time in each twelve months.[1] Very few cases came before the Supreme Court in the first dozen years of its existence, and the Justices refused steadily to leave the strict judicial path. At one time, it had seemed probable that there would be much litigation between individuals and the several States; but this had been ended by the Eleventh Amendment. There had also been a likelihood of business in connection with the enforcement of debts due to British creditors; but this was all referred to a board of Commissioners by one of the clauses of Jay's Treaty. The Sedition Act had given the justices something to do, but that, too, would cease with the ending of the law in March, 1801. The advocates of the reorganization had argued for an increase in the number of the district courts and for the establishment of circuit courts with permanent circuit judges, on the ground that these improvements would make resort to federal tribunals more easy and hence would increase federal judicial business. But this was a line of argument that did not in any way appeal to the separatist minds of the southern gentlemen. They certainly had a good deal in their favor, when they declared that there was no reason for establishing two district courts in Virginia instead of one, when that one had so little business that in 1800, after sitting ten days, it had "actually decided on several [cases] returnable at the ensuing term."

[1] See W. G. Brown's *Life of Oliver Ellsworth*, 244. On this general subject of the amount of work performed by the Justices of the Supreme Court in these years, see H. L. Carson's *Supreme Court of the United States*, pp. 158–194. In April, 1802, it was stated in debate that in the "last June term, there were only eight [cases] before the Supreme Court."

Adams brought the matter before Congress in 1799 in his third Annual Address; but, beyond arousing debate, nothing came of it at the moment. Two bills were introduced, one in 1799 and the other in 1800, to improve the method of procuring jurors for the federal courts [1] and to prevent the appointment of any more Chief Justices to important diplomatic positions. The former was enacted, but the latter was defeated. A year later (December, 1800), a bill was brought in for the reorganization of the federal judiciary that commanded sufficient support to bring about its enactment and its approval by the President on February 13, 1801.[2] This law provided for a rearrangement of the district courts and for the establishment of six circuit courts. Each of the latter was to have a distinct set of judges who would have nothing to do except to hold sessions in different parts of their circuits. What with the new judges, sixteen in all, additional marshals, clerks, and messengers, there would be an added annual expenditure of some thirty-six thousand dollars, besides the fees. Connected in a measure with this reorganization was an act for the administration of justice in the District of Columbia, which was approved on February 27, 1801. It established a circuit court for the District, an Orphan's Court, and authorized the appointment of registrars of wills and as many justices of the peace as the President deemed best, these last to hold office for five years.[3] Taking them all together, there were nineteen new life appointments and an indeterminate number of other appointments authorized by these two laws. Moreover, by promoting district judges, some places would be open to outgoing Congressmen who would be ineligible for appointment to the newly created positions.

[1] *Journal of the Senate* (Washington, 1821), iii, 66. See *Speeches of Charles Pinckney in Congress* (printed in 1800).

[2] See *Annals of Congress*, 6th Cong., 1534.

[3] *Annals of Congress*, 6th Cong., 1552.

Considering how desirable it was to conciliate opposition to the federal judiciary, it would seem that Adams should have left these places open for appointment by the new President.[1] On the contrary, he employed himself most busily in considering how he could utilize this great power for good or evil. He filled every one of these offices with Federalists and appointed no less than forty-two "Justices of the Peace," with five-year terms, for the District of Columbia.

The Republicans came into control of the government face to face with nearly a score of new life judicial appointees, many of whom had not even taken the oath of office, and led by a Chief Justice of the Supreme Court, who had been confirmed by the Senate on January 27th of this year. They were especially irritated at the moment by a series of trials which had been presided over by Samuel Chase, one of the Associate Justices, in what was termed at the time the "bloody circuit." Jefferson determined to regard the commissions of the forty-two justices of the peace as not having been issued, for these appointments had only been confirmed on March 3. The commissions were still on the table of the Secretary of State, when the office was transferred, and they were withheld by the President's order. As to the other judges, they could only be reached by repealing the act of Congress that created their offices. At once a nice question arose. Could a judge who held an office during life be deprived of that office by legislative process? Jefferson seems to have doubted the rightfulness, or possibly the expediency of such drastic action, and even made six appointments under the Judiciary Act to take the places of those of Adams's "midnight judges" who had either de-

---

[1] See, however, Professor Max Farrand's article on "The Judiciary Act of 1801" in *American Historical Review*, v, 682.

clined to serve or had resigned.[1] The Republicans in Congress had no scruples and were so numerous that they could practically pass any legislation they wished. The Federalists were greatly alarmed, for the repeal of the Judiciary Act of 1801 seemed to them to throw down the barrier that had been "erected round our persons, liberty, and property." One of them even declared that many persons now living would "spill their blood to defend that Constitution. . . . Will they [the Republicans] risk civil dissension, will they hazard the welfare, will they jeopardize the peace of the country" by passing the repealing bill?[2] The law was finally enacted by the votes of only fifty-nine members, or five more than one-half of the total membership of the House. It was approved by Jefferson on March 8, 1802.[3] It repealed the whole of the preceding law and revived all the legislation previous to that act, and was to take effect on the first day of July, 1802. Before that time, only seven and a half weeks after the passage of the repealing law, and nine weeks before the old judiciary system would be revived, Jefferson put his name (April 29, 1802) to a law practically continuing the twenty-two district court system of the discarded act and also providing for six circuits. There were to be no new circuit judges and the old arrangement of the Justices of the Supreme Court holding these circuits with the district judges was revived. The peculiar feature of the April act was its interference with the sessions of the Supreme Court, putting the next meeting off until Feb-

[1] See *Executive Journal of the Senate* under January 6 and April 6, 1802.

[2] *Annals of Congress*, 7th Cong., 1st Sess., 982. See *Debates on the Bill for repealing the Law "For the More Convenient Organization of the Courts of the United States"* (pp. 796, Albany, 1802). The debates are also given in the *Annals of Congress*, 7th Cong., 1st Sess., and in isolated pamphlets as *Debates in the Senate of the United States on the Judiciary during the First Session of the Seventh Congress* (Philadelphia, 1802) and *The Speeches of Mr. Giles and Mr. Bayard in the House of Representatives . . . February, 1802* (Boston, 1802).

[3] *Ibid.*, 7th Cong., 1st Sess., 1306.

ruary, 1803.[1] The Federalists asked whether this was done because the Republicans were afraid the Supreme Court would declare the repealing act unconstitutional; [2] to which the reply was made that they could declare it unconstitutional in February, 1803, as well as in June, 1802 ! [3] John Marshall and his associates made no attempt to reinstate the displaced judges. They nevertheless expressed their opinion of executive, legislative, and judicial power under the Constitution in the case of Marbury against Madison.

William Marbury was one of the forty-two Justices of the Peace of the District of Columbia nominated by Adams on March 2, and confirmed by the Senate on March 3, whose commissions had been retained by the express direction of President Jefferson. Marbury and three others, whose commissions had likewise been retained, had applied to the Supreme Court in the December term of 1801 for a rule requiring Madison, the new Secretary of State, to appear in court and show cause why a writ of mandamus, ordering

[1] By the Judiciary Act of 1789 the sessions of the Supreme Court were held in February and August. The sessions were changed by the act of March, 1801, to June and December. This last law was repealed by the act of March 8, 1802, which revived the act of 1789, thus returning to the February and August arrangement. Finally the act of April 29, 1802, abolished the August session or rather changed it into a session for receiving motions, etc. The result of all these enactments was that the Supreme Court sat in December, 1801, and did not hold a complete session again until February, 1803. This matter is well worked out by J. B. Thayer in his *John Marshall (Riverside Biographical* series), p. 74.

[2] *History of the Last Session of Congress, which commenced on the Seventh of December, 1801,* p. 152. It is said that the number of suits then on the docket of the Supreme Court did not exceed eight. In connection with his first message to Congress, Jefferson transmitted what he described as "an exact statement of all the causes decided since the first establishment of the courts, and of those which were depending when additional courts and judges were brought in to their aid." This and other papers are not ordinarily printed with the message. The table is given in *ibid.*, 35. From this table it appears that the number of cases instituted in eleven years in the circuit courts was 8358, of which no less than 2162 were brought in the Eastern District of Virginia. At the time this recapitulation was made, there were 1629 suits depending, of which 331 were entered in the same district in Virginia. This undue proportion of Virginia suits in the federal courts is worth bearing in mind, as one goes through the history of these years.

[3] *Annals of Congress,* 7th Cong., 1st Sess., 1229.

him to hand over these commissions, should not issue. Marbury's application was mentioned in the debate on the act of April 29, 1802. It was not until February, 1803, that Chief Justice John Marshall had a chance to state the opinion of the Supreme Court on the matter. By the Constitution, he said, the Supreme Court had original jurisdiction as to a few specified subjects and appellate jurisdiction as to others. The Judiciary Act of 1789 had undertaken to give the court original jurisdiction as to objects not mentioned in the Constitution. Among these would come the issuing of a mandamus as asked for by Marbury. This part of the Judiciary Act was, therefore, unconstitutional, and the demand was refused. Instead of confining himself to this statement, the Chief Justice prefaced it by a long discourse as to the character of appointments and commissions, as to remedies, and as to the rights of Marbury.[1] As to the first of these, he laid down the general proposition that when the President had made an appointment and it had been confirmed by the Senate, the appointee is authorized to perform the duties of the office. The commission is merely evidence that the appointment has been made, as is clear from the fact that if a person loses his commission and continues to perform his duties the performance is not invalid. A commission must be signed by the President and must be sealed and recorded. Marshall said nothing about its being authenticated by the signature of the Secretary of State, — possibly because his own commission lacked this teste, if the Appointments Book at Washington for that year is correct. The delivery of the commission was not a necessary part of the authorization, for any man could go and get a copy of the record for a small payment. For these and other considerations, it was clearly the opinion

---

[1] For the books on this case see Note I at end of chapter.

of the court that Marbury was a duly appointed justice of
the peace for the District of Columbia for five years ; but the
remedy for Madison's refusal to deliver the commission was
not a mandamus from the Supreme Court. Twenty years
later, Jefferson defended his own conduct and reprobated
that of his cousin, the Chief Justice, by claiming that delivery was necessary to the completion of the deed.[1]

Having disposed of the new circuit judges, the justices
of the peace for the District of Columbia, and sundry other
judicial officials by legislation or removal, the Republicans
turned their attention to the Justices of the Supreme Court,
who could be got rid of only by an amendment to the Constitution or by conviction after impeachment. No one
seems to have seriously thought of legislating Marshall and
his associates out of office by constitutional amendment. At
the moment impeachment was rife. This process takes us
back to far-off times in English history. Our ancestors, so
far as they came from England, could look back with more
or less satisfaction to the impeachments of Strafford and
Manwaring, and at the moment of making the Constitution
that of Warren Hastings was still in the imagination. In
the older days, impeachment had been a species of publicity
for political enemies who had gone contrary to public desire.
It had required not over-much legal proving, and when this
mode of dealing with an unpopular personage had proved to
be ineffective, recourse could easily be had to an act of
attainder. The injustice of this process and the cruelty of
the Hastings prosecution had led the makers of the Constitution to prohibit bills of attainder and to limit the impeachment of federal officials to treason, bribery, and other "high
crimes and misdemeanors." There had been some impeachments in colonial days and a few in the States before the

---

[1] *Writings of Jefferson* (Ford), x, 230 note.

establishment of the federal government. Since that time, there had been some prosecutions of the kind, notably in the most recent years.[1] In Massachusetts, impeachments were a rarity, because under the constitution of that State judges could be removed by the governor on address from both Houses of the legislature.[2] It was in Pennsylvania that impeachment was first used to purge the bench of political enemies. The indiscreet utterances of Judge Addison of that State and his discourtesy toward his associates on the bench had led to his impeachment and to his removal on conviction (January, 1803). This success had emboldened the Pennsylvania Republicans to try to get rid of all but one of the judges of the Superior Court. The result was not favorable to their design, for the Republican judge asked to be impeached with his brethren, and Jefferson's district attorney for Pennsylvania joined other leading lawyers of the State to defend the impeached judges. They succeeded so well that the State Senate refused to convict, and this process of punishing one's political enemies came to an end in the States.

The first use of impeachment in national affairs was in the case of William Blount, Senator from Tennessee.[3] He

---

[1] To the subject of impeachment, Roger Foster has devoted considerable space in his *Commentaries on the Constitution of the United States*, i, 505–713. Possibly the most valuable of this matter is the Appendix containing "State Impeachment Trials."

[2] In 1803, the question of the continuance of Paul Dudley Sargent and William Vinal in their offices came before the Massachusetts legislature on the motion to address the governor for their removal. Henry Knox appears to have been chairman of a committee to consider the matter and he referred to John Quincy Adams. Adams's reply was dated Boston, 14 February, 1803. He dissented from the vote in the State Senate because he thought that no judicial officer should be removed by address on the ground of offences for which the Constitution had expressly provided the mode of impeachment and because the decision of the Senate ought not to have been taken without giving the two judges an opportunity to be heard in their own defence. All of which, with some changes, Knox seems to have embodied in a report, "Knox Papers," 45, fo. 82, 84. Adams refers to this matter in his diary under the date of February 10 and 12, 1803 (*Memoirs*, i, 262).

[3] *Report of the Committee of the House of Representatives of the United States*

was accused of furthering the organization of an expedition to attack the territories of a friendly country. The Federalists in Congress undertook to see what could be done to reprove Blount and those who were likewise minded. The Senate promptly expelled him (July, 1797), so promptly, indeed, that he was no longer a member when the House sent up a committee to impeach him. As the Constitution states that "civil officers" may be impeached, the question at once arose as to whether Blount was a civil officer after his expulsion, and for this or some other reason or reasons, the Senate declined to vote him guilty (January, 1799).[1] The first federal impeachment that resulted in conviction was that of John Pickering, judge of the United States District Court for New Hampshire. In the fulness of time Pickering had become mentally unbalanced and had taken to excessive drinking, possibly to alleviate his mental distress, and these had reacted on one another. His behavior while on the bench had become unfitting. Pickering's enemies sent the papers to Jefferson. He, without thought, turned them over to the House of Representatives and Judge Pickering was impeached.[2] When the case came before the Senate, Robert Goodloe Harper, a Federalist Representative from South Carolina, asked to be permitted to present a petition from Judge Pickering's son. After some demur, this was acceded

---

appointed to prepare and report Articles of Impeachment against William Blount, a Senator of the United States . . . Printed by John Fenno, pp. 16, clx ; Proceedings of the Impeachment of William Blount (Philadelphia, 1799). These proceedings are in the Annals of Congress, 5th Cong., indexes under William Blount and ibid., vol. ii, 2245–2416; and Wharton's State Trials of the United States during the Administrations of Washington and Adams, 200–321. See also "Documents on the Blount Conspiracy, 1795–1797" in American Historical Review, x, 574.

[1] Annals of Congress, 5th Cong., ii, 2245–2416.

[2] See Message from the President of the United States enclosing Sundry Documents relative to John Pickering (Washington City, 1803). The proceedings in the House and the Senate may be followed in Annals of Congress, 8th Cong., 1st Sess., 315–367. The vote removing Pickering from office was given on March 12, 1803; he died a little more than two years later, April 11, 1805. Possibly the best statement of the facts of this impeachment is that in J. Q. Adams's Memoirs (i, 297–310).

to, when it appeared that the judge was insane and had been for some time. It was impossible, therefore, for him to appear, to employ counsel, or in any way to defend himself. Nevertheless, the Senate proceeded to vote on the impeachment. Nineteen Senators out of twenty-six, being more than the two-thirds necessary for conviction, voted him guilty as charged by the House of Representatives, March 12, 1804 — and he was removed from office.

On the day that the Senate voted an insane judge guilty of the acts charged against him, the House of Representatives decided to attack the Supreme Court by impeaching Samuel Chase of Maryland, one of the Associate Justices of that tribunal, and a veteran of the Revolutionary contest, — a signer, indeed, of the Declaration of Independence. Originally, Chase had been an extreme radical, but the disorder of the period of confusion following independence had converted him as it had so many other eminent men. He had taken the conservative side, and being of ardent temper and active disposition had thrown himself into this cause as strenuously as he had into that of separation from the British Empire. In 1796, Washington had appointed him an Associate Justice of the Supreme Court. It fell to his lot to preside at the trials of Cooper and Callender under the Sedition Act and at the second trial of Fries for treason, as the ringleader in the opposition to the collection of the direct tax levied in 1798 to provide funds for the warfare against France. More recently, in 1803, addressing a grand jury, Chase had pointedly reflected upon the course of the Jeffersonians in destroying courts and in providing universal manhood suffrage. These changes, he said, would "take away all security for property and personal liberty. . . . And our republican constitution will sink into a mobocracy, the worst of all possible governments;" there would be nothing left in the State constitution "worthy the care or support of freemen." [1] Delivering political addresses in the guise of charges to grand juries is so unlike present-day methods that it seems very improper. It had been, however, a common practice. There are political charges to juries [2] connected with the name of John Jay, and Judge William H. Drayton's charge to the grand jury of Charlestown, South Carolina, in 1776 is one of the most stirring of Revolutionary political pamphlets. In 1803, the time had gone by for things of this kind, because the exaltation of the judiciary had removed judicial officers from ordinary spheres of human activity. Chase in other words was an anachronism; but was that a sufficient reason for straining the Constitution to remove him from the bench, embitter the last days of the life of a Signer of the Declaration of Independence, and set a precedent that would destroy the greater part of the protective efficiency of the federal judiciary and greatly injure that of the State judiciaries? Bench and bar rallied to the support of Chase as the legal profession had gathered to that of the Pennsylvania judges. An array of counsel appeared in his defence that has seldom been equalled in any court, and it had the support of Chief Justice John Marshall and the Associate Justices of the Supreme Court. The committee of managers of the House was led by the ablest congressional debater of the day and one of the half-dozen greatest men of his time, John Randolph of Roanoke. [3] But in a contest at law, he was distinctly out of place. His strength lay in seizing upon the salient point in a contest and arguing all around that and overthrowing his opponent by vituperative eloquence.

[1] See *Answer and Pleas of Samuel Chase* (Salem, 1805), 65, 66.

[2] Johnston's *Correspondence and Public Papers of John Jay*, i, 158; and John Drayton's *Memoirs of the American Revolution*, ii, 259-274.

[3] For a lifelike description of the man see "Diary of Edward Hooker" in American Historical Association's *Reports*, 1896, vol. i, p. 924.

These faculties availed him little in legal argumentation.
Perusing the evidence presented against Chase and in his
favor,[1] the lay reader is impressed with the very slight
grounds for accusation. Chase was abrupt and overbearing
in his manner, but this was not a misdemeanor, much less a
high misdemeanor or a high crime. He had tried to hasten
matters that did not seem to him as important as they had
to the defendants who were in court before him. There were
no settled federal regulations as to summoning jurors and
witnesses, and the federal judges were, perforce, obliged to
follow State laws and precedents as well as they could. It
was no easy matter to do this, and a failure accurately to
comply with all the requirements of local practice argues
simply for ignorance of that practice and does not in any
way come under the description of impeachable offences
in the Constitution. These were high crimes and misdemeanors. The accusers sought to separate the misdemeanor from the "high" and to argue that any irregularity
was a misdemeanor. Any one reading the Constitution
with impartial eye can hardly help being conscious that the
"high" goes with misdemeanors as well as with crimes. A
man accused of petty larceny could not be deprived of
trial by jury because he happened to be a civil officer on
any such ground, or because he had been guilty of an
offence against good taste, which was about all that could
be justly charged against judges making political harangues
from the bench. Randolph had, no doubt, been stirred by
Burke's wonderful outbursts of eloquence in the Hastings
impeachment; but his closing address was far away from a
successful imitation of Burke's orations. He took refuge

[1] See *Trial of Samuel Chase taken in
short-hand by Samuel H. Smith and
Thomas Lloyd* (printed in several forms,
most conveniently in *Annals of Congress,*
8th Cong., 2nd Sess., 81–676); *Report*
of the *Trial of the Hon. Samuel Chase . . .
taken in short hand by Charles Evans*
(Baltimore, 1805). Other titles may
be found in A. P. C. Griffin's *Select List
of References on Impeachment.*

in his health, in the impossibility of adequate preparation, and than launched forth into a torrent of inaccuracies and calumnies that must have seemed pitiable after the masterly arguments of the defenders. The Senators certainly were impressed very much in this way. The Republicans could not hold their members faithful to party allegiance on any one count. The highest number that voted for conviction was nineteen out of thirty-four, or four less than the two-thirds demanded by the Constitution (March, 1805). The process of impeachment as a mode of getting rid of a political opponent or a disagreeable judge was plainly one not to be easily used, — in point of fact, it has proved to be little more than an inconvenient and cumbersome mode of securing publicity.

Randolph was bitterly disappointed by the result of the Chase impeachment and his feelings of resentment against those around Jefferson had been growing stronger and stronger every month for a year and more. As his later life was to show, Randolph was not more scrupulous as to the conversion of public money to private uses [1] than the ordinary run of politicians of his day, but he ferociously reprobated financial irregularities in others. He had been in Georgia in 1796 at the height of the scandal over the corrupt granting of lands in the Yazoo region by the legislature of that State. The Yazoo matter is one of those historical tangles that are impossible of elucidation in a few paragraphs. It is enough to say that the Georgia legislature voted quantities of wild land — to which the State

---

[1] John Randolph spent ten days in Russia as special minister, and most of a year in England without official business. Returning to the United States he drew $21,407 from the national treasury and paid off a long-standing debt on his estate. Henry Adams in his *John Randolph*, p. 296, says: "This act of Roman virtue, worthy of the satire of Juvenal, still stands as the most flagrant bit of diplomatic jobbery in the annals of the United States government."

possessed very slight claim — to companies of speculators, and these promptly sold their claims to subordinate companies. These were organized in all parts of the country and, in one way or another, leading men everywhere became interested in the scheme. Senator James Gunn of Georgia, Wade Hampton, and R. G. Harper of South Carolina, and James Wilson of Pennsylvania, one of the Associate Justices of the Supreme Court, to mention no others, were involved in them and there were few members of the Georgia legislature who were not pecuniarily interested in the grants that they had voted. When the matter became public, there was great indignation in the State. The legislature of 1796 repealed all the grants, but did not return the money that had been paid for them, some of it by persons who were entirely innocent of wrong-doing and were possessed of power and influence. Complicated with this matter was a question as to whether Georgia had any right whatever to these lands, whether they did not, as a matter of fact, belong to the United States. Some equitable settlement was so clearly desirable, that Jefferson referred the whole affair to Madison, Gallatin, and Lincoln for investigation and report. They arranged with the State its present western boundary, thereby giving the United States a clear title to the disputed Yazoo tracts. This accomplished, the commissioners suggested that Congress should award five million acres of Yazoo lands to the claimants under the forfeited Georgia charters, in place of the fifty million acres that had been corruptly voted in 1795.[1] In this way, ceaseless law suits would be

---

[1] See *Report of the Commissioners appointed in pursuance of an act for the amicable settlements of limits with the State of Georgia published by order of the House of Representatives, 29th November, 1804.* This with the accompanying documents occupies 140 pages. This matter is repeated in *American State Papers, Public Lands*, i, 132–155. The repealing act is given in the last publication, i, 156, and other matter is given on pp. 165–179. The articles of agreement and cession between the United States and Georgia are in *ibid.*, i, 125, and also printed separately with the President's Message of April 26, 1802.

avoided and the claims of innocent purchasers equitably adjusted. In January, 1805, the question of ratifying this arrangement by legislation came before Congress and aroused the greatest indignation in Randolph's soul. He outdid himself in vituperation.[1] "Orgies of Yazoo speculation," "monstrous sacrifice of the best interests of the nation," "abomination," "dread of tyrants and of villains," and "guilty of gross and wilful prevarication," — these and like epithets and phrases were applied by him to the foremost men of the country who were trying to do justice. For years Randolph talked to death every resolution on the subject; but in 1814, when he was temporarily relegated to private life by his constituents, the bill was passed. He appears to have been totally unconscious of the effects of his words; he seems to have thought that he could call the highest placed men in the government liars and despots and continue to work in harmony with them. From this time on, he drifted away from the Jeffersonians, or they drifted away from him. With a few, very few faithful comrades — the "Quids," as they were called — he stood for the old Republicanism that had been right yesterday, was right today, and would be right tomorrow.

The question whether the federal union should live or die and the exact moment of its demise came up for discussion in nearly every year from 1789 on; but it was not until 1804 that any attempt was made to give the idea practical application. To many persons in the North, the acquisition of Louisiana, which was consummated in the

---

The best compendious account of the Yazoo matter is C. H. Haskins's "Yazoo Land Companies" in American Historical Association's *Papers* for 1891. See also *Report of the Secretary of the South-Carolina Yazoo Company. In Three Parts* (Charleston, 1791); *Report from the Committee of Claims of Sundry*

Citizens of Massachusetts, etc. (Washington City, 1805). Harden's *Life of George M. Troup* and Shipp's *Life of William H. Crawford* give the views of Georgia politicians on the affair.

[1] *Annals of Congress*, 8th Cong., 2nd Sess., 1024–1026.

autumn of 1803, seemed to be directly contrary to the original compact at the base of the federal system. Jefferson, himself, had thought that an amendment to the Constitution would be necessary to legalize the purchase; but in this, as in some other things, he yielded to the judgment of others. Northerners were now questioning as to the effect of the Louisiana Purchase upon the political equilibrium in view of the "federal ratio," which gave to a Southern planter owning fifty slaves as much voice in the federal affairs as thirty Northern freemen. The opening up of new lands in the Southwest would mean an extension of slavery and an increase of slave power. The purchase had been made without consulting the States who were the original partners to the federal pact, and this in itself justified the ending of that agreement in any way that seemed best. This feeling comes out in a letter from Senator Timothy Pickering of Massachusetts to Judge Richard Peters of Pennsylvania (December 24, 1803). He will "not yet despair," he writes, as he anticipates "a *new confederacy*, exempt from the corrupt and corrupting influence and oppression of the *aristocratic democrats* of the South. . . . A continued tyranny of the present ruling sect, will precipitate that event. The patience of good citizens is now nearly exhausted."[1] By this Pickering meant that his patience was nearly exhausted, which was perfectly true. He had lost hope of the Federalists regaining hold of the government and had even abandoned faith in Alexander Hamilton. Secession seemed to him to be the only chance of salvation. Pickering ap-

[1] See "Pickering Papers" in the cabinet of the Massachusetts Historical Society, vol. 14, fo. 68. On the general subject of this conspiracy, see Samuel E. Morison's *Harrison Gray Otis*, i, 264–270, and the authorities therein cited, especially *Life of William Plumer* by his son William Plumer, Jr., pp. 283– 311. I have also received several suggestions from an unpublished paper by Elwyn Gage. Federalist feeling is well shown in a pamphlet entitled "*Look Before You Leap.*" *An Address To the People of Massachusetts, and the County of Essex in Particular. By a Washington Federalist* (Newburyport, 1805).

prized the selectmost politicians of New England of his views, and, to give the movement more substance, an attempt was made to include New York. This was to be accomplished by enlisting the sympathy and services of Aaron Burr, who was to be chosen governor of New York as a first step in the enterprise, for he was now thoroughly discouraged by the treatment that he had received at the hands of the Virginians. The thought of Aaron Burr as the president of a Northern Confederacy was repellant to Hamilton, who resented being pushed to one side by his New England co-workers in favor of this most disreputable of politicians. He gave instances of Burr's ill behavior and was understood to have others in reserve. This three-cornered fight ended in Burr's defeat, for about one-half of his former following in the lower Hudson counties deserted him for the Jeffersonian candidate and he and his allies did not gain enough votes in the other parts of the State to overcome this handicap.[1] Burr thereupon called upon Hamilton to make good his charges against his honor. On the 11th of July, 1804, on the western bank of the Hudson, just opposite New York City, at Weehawken, they met, and Burr shot Hamilton through the heart.[2] The secret of the Burr-Pickering coalition and the attendant secession conspiracy was well kept, but inklings of the project seeped through the newspapers.[3] Jefferson followed the intrigues with solicitude, receiving "daily and confidential reports" of the proceedings from Gideon Granger,[4] the Postmaster General and a Connecticut

[1] See the figures in Cheetham's *Republican Watch Tower* (New York), June 30, 1804. These returns are stated to be taken from the official records.

[2] See Note II at end of chapter.

[3] See the *Eastern Argus*, published at Portland, Me., June 21, 1804 and *Independent Chronicle* (Boston, June 28, 1804), quoting the Newark, N. J. *Centinel*. The following toast is said to have been given at Boston. "May the dominion of Virginia be limited by the constitution, or at least by the Delaware."

[4] Jefferson's statement to Granger was dated March 9, 1814, and is in the "Granger Papers" at Washington. He writes that the combination of the seven States was made either to overawe the Union by the mere fact of coalition or

man. In the outcome, the whole affair seems to have helped the Republicans; for in the autumn of 1804, Jeffersonian presidential electors were chosen in Massachusetts.[1]

The election of 1800 with its equality of votes for Jefferson and Burr had pointed plainly to a change in the Constitution as to the election of the two first officers. As with the duties of the Vice-President, so with the mode of his election there had been much discussion in the Federal Convention. It had been suggested that he should be appointed by the State governments or chosen by the national House of Representatives. The settlement was complicated by the necessity of placating the small States and by the wish of many members of the Convention to have an executive council instead of a single executive. The device of the electoral college and of the peculiar voting by the electors for two persons without stating which one should be President had been devised to give or to seem to give the small States a share in the government.[2] After a good deal of debate, an amendment was formulated which finally became the Twelfth Amendment.[3] It provided that each elector should vote separately for President and Vice-President. An attempt was still made to do something for the smaller States by providing that in case no candidate for the presidency should obtain a majority of the electoral

---

"by threats of separating themselves from it."

[1] Below are figures of Massachusetts elections, 1800–1804 : —

Vote	Year	Federal (Strong)	Republican (Gerry)
Governor	1800	20,003	16,966
"	1803	30,255	14,047
			(Sullivan)
"	1804	29,673	24,134
Presidential		(Pinckney)	(Jefferson)
Electors	1804	25,585	29,637

These figures are taken from the newspapers of the time. Slightly different figures are given in William Burdick's *Massachusetts Manual*, p. 26. In 1806, the Federalist majority for governor dwindled to 176 and the council and legislature were both Republican. See paper by Edward Stanwood in the *Proceedings* of the Massachusetts Historical Society for January, 1906, p. 12.

[2] The history of this clause of the Constitution may be readily followed in the "Index by Clauses" in Farrand's *Records of the Federal Convention*, iii, 642.

[3] See Lolabel House's *A Study of the Twelfth Amendment* (Philadelphia, 1901).

votes, the House of Representatives, voting by States, should choose one of the three having the largest number of electoral votes. It had been at one time proposed to vote on the five candidates having the largest number, but this had ultimately been defeated. The opposition to the change is well shown in letters from Senator Pierce Butler of South Carolina to the governor of his State. He wrote that if the alteration were agreed to, the smaller States "never will give either a President or a Vice-President to the Union." The doctrine of chance was against there being another equality of votes as in 1800. "Under the specious garb of republicanism [a few States were attempting] to rob other states of their rights & ranke in the confederation." He wished South Carolina to save the smaller States from this degradation by refusing to ratify the amendment.[1] It was ratified, however, by a sufficient number of States to be in force for the presidential election of 1804. Jefferson's reëlection had never been in doubt, but the size of his electoral vote, 162 out of 176, came as a surprise to many people. In 1804, indeed, only Connecticut and Delaware gave all their votes to Charles Cotesworth Pinckney of South Carolina, to which should be added two stray votes from Maryland. None of our Presidents, except Washington and Monroe, ever received a more decisive electoral indorsement than this.

[1] Butler's letters are dated December 6, 1803, and April 3, 1804, and are in the Library of Congress. His prophecy as to the working of the Twelfth Amendment, in case it were adopted, has been abundantly borne out by the facts. The Vice-President, he wrote, instead of being the second most estimable character in the Union will be the "offspring of intrigue." He adds, in the event of the death of the President how dreadful would the situation of the country become under the government of such a Vice-President as this arrangement will nineteen times in twenty give the Union.

NOTES

I. Marbury *vs*. Madison. — Cases in which the courts declared laws null and void have been already noticed in the present work (iii, 498 and following), down to the organization of the federal government. The early history of the doctrine after 1789 is treated by Professor Max Farrand in " The First Hayburn Case, 1792 " in *American Historical Review*, xiii, 281. A case involving this point was decided by the Virginia judges in 1793, they adhering to the overruling power of the judiciary (L. G. Tyler's *Letters and Times of the Tylers*, i, 177). Marbury against Madison is reported in the first volume of W. Cranch's *Reports of Cases argued and adjudged in the Supreme Court of the United States*, and repeated thence in J. P. Cotton's *Constitutional Decisions of John Marshall*, i, 7–43; J. H. Perkins's *Writings of John Marshall upon the Federal Constitution*, 1–28, and partially in Thayer's *Cases on Constitutional Law*. Writing to Mrs. John Adams, Sept. 11, 1804, Jefferson says that she seems to think it devolved on the judges to decide on the validity of the sedition law. " But nothing in the Constitution has given them a right to decide for the Executive, more than to the Executive to decide for them. . . . But the opinion which gives to the judges the right to decide what laws are constitutional, and what not, not only for themselves in their own sphere of action, but for the Legislature & Executive also, in their spheres, would make the judiciary a despotic branch." *Writings of Jefferson* (Ford), viii, 311 note. The Marbury case is mentioned in every work on American constitutional law. E. S. Corwin (*The Doctrine of Judicial Review, its Legal and Historical Basis*) has written a clear and succinct essay on the subject; but it deserves fuller treatment.

II. Duelling. — The Burr-Hamilton duel occasioned a revulsion of public opinion that set a limit to duelling in the North. At the time, 1804, duelling was an ordinary mode of settling personal differences. It was rife in the navy, in Congress, and in society. Benton's description of James Jackson, Senator from Georgia, is well known: " honest, patriotic, brave . . . the bold denouncer of crime in high as well as in low places; a ready speaker, and as ready with his pistol as his tongue." Benton says that he died of wounds received in the last of his many duels, but John Quincy Adams records that he died of dropsy. The duel between Campbell and Gardenier occurred in 1808; after wounding his man, it was believed mortally, Campbell at once went to attend the session of the House of Representatives, as if nothing had happened.   Twelve years later, Commodore Barron killed Admiral Decatur on the duelling ground at Bladensburg.

   The details of the Burr-Hamilton tragedy are set forth at length in William Coleman's *Collection of the Facts and the Documents relative to the Death of Major-General Alexander Hamilton* (New York, 1804).   They are also to be found in any of the lives of Hamilton or Burr.   According to the ideas of that day, a man who had reflected upon another, as Hamilton had upon Burr, knowingly laid himself open to a challenge, which, indeed, Hamilton himself seemed fully to realize.   Of the sermons brought forth by this tragedy, one preached by Timothy Dwight, President of Yale College, on September 9, 1804, possibly best expresses the abhorrence of New England.

   Hamilton's eldest son had been killed in a duel in 1801, when he was only nineteen years of age.   On the general subject of duelling see L. Sabine's *Notes on Duels and Duelling* and B. C. Truman's *Field of Honor*.   In 1776 the rules of war forbade any officer or soldier to send a challenge; in 1806 the rules forbade him to send or accept a challenge.   See John F. Callan's *Military Laws of the United States* (Philadelphia, 1863), pp. 66, 179.   As late as 1838, John Lyde Wilson published at Charleston, S. C., his *Code of Honor; or Rules for the Government of Principals and Seconds in Duelling.*

CHAPTER XI

IN 1763, at the close of the great war, Louis of France ceded to his cousin of Spain all of Louisiana that he had not been compelled to relinquish to Great Britain as the price of peace. In this way Spain acquired all of America west of the Mississippi and, in addition, the island on which the city of New Orleans stands on the eastern side of that stream. Spain deferred taking possession until 1769. Since that time, Louisiana had been a constant source of expense, with very few compensating advantages. The new masters tried to convert the Creoles into good Spaniards; but the French colonists loved their mother land, their mother tongue and their old customs. They resolutely refused to become Spaniards, and the few Spanish colonists who went to the Mississippi Valley found it necessary to learn French, because all commercial transactions were carried on in that language. The Spanish domination retarded the growth of the province. No new settlers came from France, few from Spain, and the hostility of both the French and the Spaniards toward Englishmen was so strong that not many English traders or settlers found their way to New Orleans. In addition to all this, the prosperity of the colony was greatly hampered by the Spanish commercial system, which restricted trading to half a dozen ports in the Iberian peninsula, although there was no place in Spanish markets for the products of Louisiana. The two most important of these were indigo and furs, but American indigo could not compete with that produced in Spain and the Spaniards made no use of furs.[1]

With the coming of the American Revolution the future of Louisiana looked more hopeful. In the course of that conflict the Spaniards conquered the adjoining British provinces of East and West Florida, and they acted more or less in harmony with the Americans in wresting the country northwest of the Ohio River from the English. These years also saw the coming of American pioneers into the territory between the Alleghanies and the Mississippi. Kentucky was the first to receive colonists from the Atlantic seaboard; then followed Tennessee and Ohio; and with these might be included the settlements in the western part of Pennsylvania.

In 1790, there were more than one hundred thousand American settlers west of the Alleghany Mountains. Their only way to reach the markets of the outer world with their surplus products was to take them down the Mississippi to New Orleans and there transfer them from the river craft to sea-going vessels.[2] The expense of maintaining the

---

[1] Charles Gayarré's *History of Louisiana* in four volumes (3rd ed., New Orleans, 1885) reproduces the local idea of the history of that State. The same may be said of Alcée Fortier's *History of Louisiana* also in four volumes (Paris, 1904). All the histories of Louisiana necessarily owe much to the earlier work of F. X. Martin, which was originally printed at New Orleans in 1827–1829, and was reprinted with new matter in 1882. J. W. Monette's *History of the Discovery and Settlement of the Valley of the Mississippi* (New York, 1846) is still useful.

Besides the volumes on *Foreign Relations* in the *American State Papers*, there is much interesting matter in the volumes entitled *Miscellaneous*, i, and *Public Lands*, v. Masses of papers relating to Louisiana in its widest aspect are noted in J. A. Robertson's *List of Documents in Spanish Archives relating to the History of the United States, which have been Printed or of which Transcripts are Preserved in American Libraries* (Washington, 1910). There is much useful and out-of-the-way information in Joseph M. White's *New Recopilacion of the Laws of Spain and the Indies* (2 vols., Philadelphia, 1839).

[2] In 1802, and the next few years, shipwrights at Pittsburg and elsewhere in the Ohio Valley built many sea-going vessels. These were passed over the falls, — at high water, — were freighted

administration of Louisiana and the poverty of the people, coupled with the constantly increasing commerce with the interior, led the Spanish government and its colonial officials to relax its commercial restrictions and, at the same time, to try to bring the trans-Alleghany American settlements within the scope of Spanish policy. The trade of Louisiana was also no longer confined to a few Spanish ports. In the future, goods might be sent from New Orleans to any part of Spain that was open to commerce and also to France and to Spanish America as well as to the United States.[1]

Indigo and rice were the principal products of Louisiana down to the closing years of the century. Every decade there was more intercourse with the Indian tribes of the interior and consequently a larger quantity of furs for exportation. The cultivation of tobacco also increased; the cypress and cedar trees of the swamps were cut down, sawn into boards, and sent to Havana, where the lumber was utilized in the manufacture of boxes for the transportation of sugar to Spain. By 1794, the end of the production of indigo was plainly in sight, owing to the ravages of a

with cotton, tobacco, and peltry, and were sent to sea by way of New Orleans. One of them, the brig *Deane*, is reported as arriving at Liverpool in 1803; the largest was the ship *Louisiana* of 300 tons. Mr. Demass E. Barnes, searching western newspapers for material on the early commerce of the Ohio, counted 5 ships, 8 brigs, and 6 schooners as launched in the years 1803 and 1804 in the Valley. See *Kentucky Gazette*, May 17, Oct. 4, 1803; *Guardian of Freedom*, April 14, 21, 1804; and *Palladium*, April 14, 21, May 12, 19, 1804. See also Thaddeus M. Harris's *Journal of a Tour* (Boston, 1805), p. 52; and Archer B. Hulbert's "Western Ship-Building" in *American Historical Review*, xxi, 720.

[1] See the "Real Cedula" of January 22, 1782 and the "Real Orden" of June 9, 1793 in the Archives at Seville ("Papeles Procedentes de la Isla de Cuba," Legajo No. 2317–1 and Legajo No. 184). Good working synopses of these documents are given in Martin's *Louisiana*, 68, 118; the paper of June 9, 1793 is dated February, 1793 in Martin. Dr. Jameson of the Carnegie Institution most kindly permitted Dr. R. H. Hill to oversee the copying of these and other documents relating to the commerce of Louisiana in the Archives at Seville. These transcripts are now deposited in the Library of Harvard University, where they are accessible to students.

most destructive insect, and to the growing competition of East Indian indigo in the markets of Europe. At this moment, when everything looked darkest for Louisiana, a mode was found by which sugar could be profitably produced in the lower Mississippi Valley. Cultivation of the sugar cane had been tried a generation before, but without success. Now, Etienne de Boré discovered by experimentation that it was possible to grow sugar cane that would mature sufficiently in one season to yield syrup. The further discovery was made that if the canes were cut, piled in heaps, and covered with straw, they would keep for some time without turning sour. In 1795, Boré sold his crop at a good profit and thereby gave new life to the province.[1]

The ever increasing pressure from the American settlers in the Ohio Valley gave rise to a series of intrigues. Don Diego Gardoqui, Spanish representative in the United States between 1785 and 1789, entered into dealings with several persons of prominence to lead colonists to upper Louisiana. Among these was Colonel George Morgan, who actually founded a settlement on the western bank of the Mississippi at New Madrid. Other prominent men who were concerned in these schemes were Baron Steuben, who meditated leading a colony of Revolutionary veterans to the Spanish province, and William Duer, who had some hazy idea of promoting a settlement in that region. The Spanish authorities at New Orleans engaged in a series of intrigues with James Wilkinson and other dwellers in

---

[1] On the general condition of Louisiana in the years around 1800, see the documents printed in James A. Robertson's *Louisiana under the Rule of Spain, France, and the United States*, and Pontalba's "Memoir," which was submitted to Napoleon and is printed in lengthy extracts in Gayarré's *Louisiana*, iii, 411–445, and Alcée Fortier's *History of Louisiana*, ii, 189 and fol. On the sugar culture in that State, there is an excellent article by Edward Hogan in the *International Review*, xi, 597.

Kentucky.[1] Wilkinson had no official connection with the United States when he appeared at New Orleans with a cargo or cargoes of Kentucky produce and induced the governor to permit him to market the goods without payment of duties. Bearing in mind that Kentucky was half independent and was quite likely to become entirely so, these early intrigues of Wilkinson and others would seem to have been perfectly consonant with their obligations to Kentucky and to the United States. After the inauguration of Washington, commerce between the American settlements and New Orleans became more important every year. It aroused an increasing jealousy of American influence in the minds of Spanish officials and led to renewed intrigues with Wilkinson and others that can no longer be regarded as innocent.

The Spaniards, furthermore, sought to win over the Indians living between the settled parts of Georgia and the plantations on the Mississippi. If these could be converted into good Spanish Indians, they would serve as a buffer against the swarms of settlers that were certain to come from the southernmost United States. From this point of view, the French and the Spanish idea that the Appalachian mountain system was the natural eastern boundary of Louisiana was entirely sound; but the carrying into effect of any such theory, or any attempt to carry it into effect, was certain to meet with considerable opposition. The Spanish hold upon Louisiana was so weak, the province had so much potential importance, and its possession by a strong colonizing power would be so inimical to the interests of others, that projects were certain to be set on

---

[1] See Daniel Clark's *Proofs of the Corruption of Gen. James Wilkinson* (Philadelphia, 1809); Wilkinson's *Memoirs of My Own Times*, vol. ii; "Papers on Wilkinson's Relations with Spain" in *American Historical Review*, ix, 748 and fol.; and I. J. Cox's " Wilkinson and his Later Intrigues" in *ibid.*, xix, 794.

foot for its acquisition by the United States, by Great Britain, and by France.

The first suggestion of an attempt to change the status of Louisiana after the organization of the government under the Constitution was in connection with the supposed attack by the British at the time of the Nootka Sound controversy.[1] Very likely this existed only in the imaginations of Thomas Jefferson and Phineas Bond; it certainly amounted to nothing. A more formidable conspiring against the integrity of the Spanish colonial empire was Genêt's plan to send a force against New Orleans composed of western frontiersmen, led by the redoubtable George Rogers Clark[2] and financed by money not yet due from the United States to France.[3] The whole scheme came to an innocuous ending as did the rest of Genêt's plottings. In 1796, Citizen Pierre Auguste Adet, then representing the French Republic at Philadelphia, sent General Collot and an associate or two to explore the western country and report as to its value. Collot's journeyings resulted in a book that was largely copied from Pitman's "Present State of Proceedings on the Mississippi." His journey caused uneasiness to General Wayne, who could not understand what he was doing. Wayne suspected that Wilkinson, his second in command, was somehow connected with Collot, and at the moment there was a great deal of discontent in the western country over the

---

[1] See above p. 118. On December 21, 1786, Louis Otto, the French representative, sent to Jay the following extract from a despatch, written by the Count de Vergennes on August 25: "The exchange of Louisiana for a French possession in the West Indies has never been in question." *Diplomatic Correspondence, 1783–1789*, i, 336.

[2] Clark had already been engaged in schemings for separation. See F. J. Turner in *American Historical Review*, iii, 652.

[3] See Professor Turner's contributions to the elucidation of the diplomatic contest for the Mississippi Valley in *American Historical Review*, ii, 474; iii, 490, 650; vii, 706; viii, 78; x, 249, 574, and American Historical Association's *Reports*, 1896, vol. i, p. 930, and 1897, p. 569.

collection of the whiskey tax. Wayne got possession of some letters that had been sent from Adet to Collot. These he forwarded to the Secretary of War. Adet's conduct and Collot's had already aroused misgivings in the administration. Charles Lee, the Attorney General, reported to President Washington (May, 1796) that there was reasonable ground for believing that France had serious expectations of obtaining all or part of the Spanish North American possessions, that she contemplated a separation of the western and eastern parts of the Union, and that Collot and his confederates were paid by France and instructed by her minister at Philadelphia and had already begun their operations.[1] Five months later, John Quincy Adams, then American minister at the Hague, confirmed these suspicions in a letter, stating that the obtaining Louisiana from Spain was then under consideration by the Directory.[2]

The first effective impulse to the rebuilding of the French colonial empire in North America was given by Talleyrand and may be dated, well enough, from the year 1798. In any such scheme the reconquest of San Domingo and other French sugar islands from the blacks and the obtaining Louisiana and the Floridas from Spain were essential features which might, or might not, be combined with the addition of the western American settlements and with the establishment of French rule in some part of South America. Talleyrand had not proceeded very far in the carrying out of this plan, when Napoleon Bonaparte became the chief power in France and began his conquering career in Europe. In 1800, Napoleon put intense pressure upon the Spanish monarchs to induce them to give up their territories in North America and made what seemed to be

---

[1] See "John Adams Manuscripts, Executive, War, Attorney General" under date May 20, 1796.

[2] Adams to Pickering, Oct. 16, 1796. *Writings of J. Q. Adams* (Ford), ii, 31 note.

adequate preparations for the reconquest of San Domingo. Spain was then in the hands of Don Carlos IV, the king, Doña Luisa, his spouse, and Manuel Godoy, Principe de la Paz, a name which is usually and incorrectly translated into English as the "Prince of Peace." Don Carlos was respectable enough in his personal life, was excessively fond of mechanics and hunting, and left most of his political duties to the queen and Godoy. Their personal lives were anything but respectable; but Godoy had abilities and a tenacity of purpose that were entirely lacking in the king. Whether in office or out, he possessed great influence and was really the ruler of Spain. The bait held out to the trio as the price of Louisiana was a throne in Italy for Don Carlos and Doña Luisa's daughter and her husband, the titular Duke of Parma. Recently Napoleon had overrun large districts of Italy. He now proposed to give up enough to make a kingdom for the son-in-law in exchange for Louisiana, the two Floridas, and six ships-of-the-line. The Spaniards were willing enough to part with Louisiana, which was a constant source of expense to them.[1] It had only recently been acquired, and was French to begin with. The case of Florida was very different. That had been an old Spanish possession and was bound up with the memories of Ponce de Leon and Menendez. As to the six battle-ships, history is silent; but the Spaniards always had plenty of them and never knew what to do with them. After negotiating for a while, Napoleon consented to receive Louisiana, alone, in exchange for the Italian kingdom, and the bargain was struck at San Ildefonso on the first

---

[1] According to a table in Villiers du Terrage's *Les Dernières Années de la Louisiane Française*, 370, the total receipts of the Spanish government at New Orleans in 1801 amounted to 950,000 livres; the expenditures to 2,841,000 livres, leaving in round numbers a deficit of 1,888,000 livres to be made good by Spain.

day of October, 1800.[1]   He designated Tuscany or Etruria, as he was pleased to call it, for the throne of the son-in-law and his wife.   He invited them to Paris, paid them marked attention, and sent them to Florence, where they soon realized that they were expected to sit on the throne, while the taxes were collected and the kingdom administered by successive French generals.   The Spaniards stiffened. They refused to convert the preliminary agreement of October 1 into a definitive treaty or to give the order for the surrender of the province.   The Peace of Amiens, March 25, 1802, freed Napoleon's hands from the English war, and a turn of affairs in the West Indies seemed to open the way to the actual reoccupation of the Mississippi Valley.   The Spaniards still refused to complete the transaction, until Gouvion St.-Cyr, who was representing Napoleon in Spain, in July, 1802, gave a written pledge that France would never alienate Louisiana.[2]   This seemed to content Don Carlos and the queen; but they still delayed giving the formal order for the delivery of Louisiana, as if they doubted the reality and continuity of Etruria.   For a moment, Napoleon did not press the matter, as he suddenly had added to his desires a renewed wish for the Floridas, or for West Florida, at any rate.   He even offered to give the old Duchy of Parma outright to the Etrurian king in return for this additional territory; but the Spaniards were obdurate.   They had gone as far as they would go.   Napoleon was obliged to content himself for the time being with the surrender of Louisiana, according to the terms of San

----

[1] The document signed at San Ildefonso on October 1, 1800, was only a "traité préliminaire." The negotiations were to be completed within one month.   See D. Luis de Onis's *Memoria Sobre las Negociaciones entre España y los Estados-Unidos de América, que dieron Motivo al Tratado de 1819* (Madrid, 1820).   The treaty in Spanish is on p. 3 of the appendix and in English in the translation of the above *Memoir*, which was printed at Baltimore in 1821.

[2] *American State Papers, Foreign Relations*, ii, 569; Madison to Monroe, *Writings of Madison* (Hunt), vii, 67.

Ildefonso.[1]   On October 15, 1802, this order was signed by his Catholic Majesty at Barcelona.[2]

The fact of the negotiations for the retrocession of Louisiana was known in governing circles in Europe in the winter of 1800–1801, — eighteen months before the agreement was completed.   The first intimation of the probable shift of the ownership of Louisiana came to Madison in May, 1801.   One letter was from Rufus King.   He wrote from London that the cession of Tuscany to the Spaniards gives credit to the opinion which was prevalent both at Paris and at London that Spain had actually ceded Louisiana and the Floridas to France.[3]   In all probability it was this communication from King that Jefferson had in mind when he wrote, on May 14, 1801, that it is feared that "Spain is ceding Louisiana to France, an inauspicious circumstance to us." [4]   The probability of a change in ownership of the western half of the Mississippi Valley certainly was an inauspicious circumstance, but it does not seem to have aroused any great amount of excitement in governmental circles.   Rumors of the kind had been rife

---

[1] For the treaty of October 1, 1800 and the subsequent agreements, see Alejandro del Cantillo's *Tratados, Convenios y Declaraciones de Paz y de Comercio* (Madrid, 1843), pp. 692, 697, 698.   The last of these is the "Real cédula espedida en Barcelona á 15 de octubre de 1802 para que se entregue á la Francia la colonia y provincia de la Luisiana."   This document does not refer to the preliminary articles of San Ildefonso by title, but repeats the phraseology as to the limits of the colony to be retroceded.

[2] Henry Adams's *History of the United States*, i, chs. xv–xvii.   This part of Adams's work is based on transcripts which he had made at great expense in time, thought, and money.   They are now in the State Department at Washington.   J. A. Robertson used them extensively in his *Louisiana under the Rule of Spain, France, and the United States, 1785–1807*.   Other documents are in *American State Papers, Foreign Relations*, ii, 506–583 ; Villiers du Terrage's *Les Dernières Années de la Louisiane Française* (Paris, 1904), pp. 366 and fol. ; Barbé–Marbois' *Histoire de la Louisiane* (Paris, 1829).   This was translated and published at Philadelphia in 1830 as *The History of Louisiana*.

[3] Rufus King to Madison, London, March 29, 1801 (C. R. King's *Rufus King*, iii, 414).   William Constable sent the same information to Hamilton about a week earlier.   Hamilton forwarded this letter to Madison, May 20, 1801 ; J. C. Hamilton's *Works of A. Hamilton*, vi, 524.

[4] Massachusetts Historical Society's *Collections*, Seventh Series, i, 95.   See also Jefferson to Monroe, May 26, 1801, *Writings* (Ford ed.), viii, 58.

ever since 1796 and had not ripened into fact. Madison thought the matter was of sufficient importance, however, to open the subject to Charles Pinckney, who was then representing America at Madrid. Madison wrote that information had lately been received through several channels, that France was about to recover, or had recovered, some part of her old possessions on the Mississippi. The English government also was solicitous as to the probable result of the resuscitation of the French colonial empire.[1] The British foreign secretary conversed on the subject with Rufus King. He dilated on the extensive influence which the cession might give France and stated that Great Britain must be unwilling to have the territory pass into Napoleon's hands. In reply, King quoted Montesquieu to the effect that God had permitted Turks and Spaniards to be in the world, to possess great empires with insignificance. He added that the United States government was content to have the Floridas remain in the hands of Spain,[2] but would be unwilling to see them pass into the possession of any one else except themselves. Six months later, in November, 1802, we find William Windham, who was then out of office, but was nevertheless a man of influence, declaring that the retrocession of Louisiana gave the French nothing less than the command of two continents. It could easily be rescued from their hands, and this, he thought, would be pleasing to America.[3]

Robert R. Livingston was now American minister at Paris. He belonged to one of the three or four great New York manorial families. A quarter of a century earlier,

[1] *Writings of Madison*, vii, 48, 49.
[2] C. R. King's *Rufus King*, iii, 469.
[3] *The Windham Papers*, ii, 201. See also *Speeches in Parliament of William Windham*, ii, 11, 66. On the other hand, Jefferson hinted that the United States might be forced to make an alliance with England, *Writings of Jefferson* (Ford), i, 298; Sawvel's *Complete Anas of Thomas Jefferson*, 219.

he had served with Jefferson on the historic committee that
had drafted the Declaration of Independence. Long-tried
friendship and the desirability of securing his political aid
— and that of his family connections — had induced Jefferson to offer him several posts, from which Livingston selected that of diplomatic representative in France. For
this particular position, his deafness and lack of training
would seem to have unfitted him. As one thing after another came up in regard to Louisiana, Madison sent him
instruction after instruction. He was directed to press for
the payment of American claims on the French government,
to obtain the cession of New Orleans and the Floridas, to
call the attention of the French authorities to the impolicy
of what they were doing; at the same time he was not to
arouse anybody's anger or to make any pecuniary offer
that was likely to be effective. At Paris, Livingston felt
the excitement that ran through French society as to the
reëstablishment of colonial power in the Mississippi Valley.
He could hardly help it, for the gatherings which he fre-
quented were filled with chatter as to the glory of things
to come in America. He also was cognizant that preparations were going forward to make the retrocession an actu-
ality. Following out his instructions, he sought to edu-
cate ministerial public opinion and through it to suggest an
idea or two to the First Consul, himself. He wrote letters
to influential gentlemen in Paris, and finally presented a
memoir that was lengthy enough to give him the opportunity to state his ideas in detail. The reacquisition of
Louisiana, he argued, would be harmful to France, for it
would bring her territories in America again into contact
with those of Great Britain which would give rise to end-
less disputes. Moreover, the ownership of the mouth of
the Mississippi River would involve her in continuing con-

troversies with the American government. The navigation of the river and the right of deposit at New Orleans, or
at some other suitable spot within convenient reach of sea-
going sailing vessels, was essential to the prosperity of the
trans-Alleghany settlers; but the administration of any
rules that might be adopted to regulate this commerce was
certain to arouse friction between French officials and the
river traders. All these difficulties might be avoided by
ceding New Orleans and the island on which it stands, on
the eastern side of the Mississippi, to the United States.
If to this were added all of Louisiana, west of the great
river, and north of the Arkansas, French and British
dominions would be separated by a block of American territory; and there would remain a large extent of French
Louisiana to protect Spanish Mexico from contact with
radical America. Livingston's efforts would seem to have
been well suited to the purpose he had in mind,[1] although
he lacked the light touch and literary effectiveness that had
stood Franklin in good stead in similar educational efforts.
It was while affairs were in this train in France that the
Spanish intendant, or finance officer at New Orleans, by
proclamation, closed that port to American commerce.

From the cold historical standpoint, it is difficult not to
sympathize somewhat with the Spaniards, both with the
royal government at Madrid and with the officials at New
Orleans; for an examination of the custom house books shows
conclusively that Louisiana was coming more and more
under American influence and that this danger of Ameri-
canization proceeded in great part from the Treaty of 1795
which conferred upon Americans the right to deposit goods
at New Orleans free from all government exactions, while

---

[1] See Livingston's "Memoirs" in   ii, 520–524, 534–537.
American State Papers, Foreign Relations,

awaiting transshipment to ocean-going vessels.[1] Before 1795, whatever privileges Americans enjoyed in Louisiana were the results of special relaxations which were due either to the scarcity of food or to the cupidity of some high official. These could be taken away at any time, — and they were constantly changed. Under these conditions no stable commerce could develop. All this was altered by the Treaty of 1795, which recognized the right of the American traders to avail themselves of the facilities offered by the peculiar position of New Orleans. The effect was startling. In 1794, only thirty-one vessels were entered at the custom house there as coming from New York, Philadelphia, and other Atlantic ports; and only twenty-three barges, keels, and flat-boats from the American settlements in the Ohio Valley. Five years later, in 1799, no less than seventy-eight vessels entered from the Atlantic seaboard of the United States and one hundred and eleven river craft from Pittsburg, Kentucky, Natchez, and other up-river settlements. As to clearances outward to Atlantic seaports the number increased from twenty-six in 1794 to sixty-six in 1799. In the same years, the number of vessels clearing from New Orleans for Havana, Santa Cruz, and other American ports had actually decreased. In the next three years, American commerce grew with great rapidity and Spanish remained stationary.[2]

[1] Statistics of the trade of Louisiana are given in a digest of information that Jefferson caused to be printed in 1803 under the title of "An Account of Louisiana." It is reprinted in *Old South Leaflets*, no. 105, without the statistics; these are most conveniently found in the copy in *American State Papers, Miscellaneous*, i, 354–356. On the general subject, see Monette's "Progress of Navigation and Commerce on the . . . Mississippi" in Mississippi Historical Society's *Publications*, vii, 479, and Louis Pelzer's "Economic Factors in the Acquisition of Louisiana" in Mississippi Valley Historical Association's *Proceedings*, vi, 109.

[2] An idea of the rapidity with which the province was growing can be gathered from the following figures that have been compiled from transcripts of the New Orleans custom-house books that were made for me at Seville. The export of sugar rose from nothing in 1794 to over 1,000,000 pounds in 1799, and to 45,000 casks valued at over

According to the Treaty of 1795, the right of deposit at New Orleans was given for three years. In 1798, the initial period came to an end. No definite renewal of it was made, but after a few months, the right was restored in practice and continued in effective and constantly increasing operation until 1802. In June of that year, Daniel Clark, a successful and influential merchant at New Orleans, wrote [1] to Madison that the Spanish Intendant had for some time been trying to impede American commerce by all kinds of restrictions, bonds, and fees. There must have been a good deal of correspondence between the officials in Louisiana and the home government, because on the 14th day of July, 1802, the king of Spain directed the Intendant to put an end to the introduction and deposit of American merchandise at New Orleans without express order from Madrid. In carrying out this direction, he was not to justify himself by referring to the royal order, but was to allege that on consulting the Treaty of 1795, he found that the limit of three years fixed by that instrument bound his hands so that he could not allow the further enjoyment of the right of deposit without the express permission of the king.[2]

October 16, 1802, Don Juan Ventura Morales, the Spanish Intendant of Louisiana, by proclamation declared that

---

$300,000 in 1802. Cotton increased from 243,000 pounds in 1799 to 20,000 bales in 1802, valued at over $1,000,000. Large amounts of tobacco were sent out, much of it from up the river. In 1799, 121,000 pounds of tobacco came down the river and about double that amount was exported. In the same year, 9333 barrels of flour were brought in from up the stream; 22,000 pounds of hemp; 504 barrels of cider; 520 gallons of whiskey; and, among other things, kettles and other iron utensils. Practically none of these commodities came

down the river in 1794. In 1802, goods descending the Mississippi to the value of over $1,000,000 were entered at the custom house at Natchez. Commerce between the United States and the Floridas and Louisiana is given in the "Report of the Secretary of the Treasury," dated October 24, 1803, Tables F and G (*American State Papers, Finance*, ii, 56).

[1] Clark's letter to Madison, dated New Orleans, 22 June, 1802, is in the "Monroe Papers" at Washington.

[2] See Note at end of chapter.

the right of deposit at New Orleans, having been introduced
during a war and the war having come to an end, he could
no longer permit Americans to enjoy the privilege conferred
by the treaty without the express order of his royal master.
This proclamation was posted on the walls and printed in
the newspapers. The news travelled slowly upstream, arousing the greatest excitement throughout the western settlements. New Orleans was open to attack by a few hundred
men. There were no Spanish soldiers to speak of in the
province and there was no fort above the city or below
that was capable of offering any extended resistance. The
Republicans and the administration, when the news came
to Washington, affected to minimize it and sought delay.
The Federalists thought that the hour had struck for taking
their revenge on Jefferson. Their brief glare of popularity
had been won as champions of America against Gallic aggression. It now seemed perfectly evident that Spain,
having retroceded Louisiana to France, was not to hand
over that province burdened with the servitude of the
right of deposit at New Orleans. The Federalists wished
to rouse the Westerners to fury and send them to seize
New Orleans.[1] Once there, they could dare Spaniards and
Frenchmen, both, to do their worst. What Jefferson and
Madison would have done, if they had been let alone, no
one can say. Assailed on the flank by the Federalists and
likely to forfeit their hold on the western Radicals, they were
obliged to take some steps to hold themselves up before
the eyes of the American people as maintaining their rights
in the face of both France and Spain. On January 11, 1803,

[1] See *Annals of Congress*, 7th Cong.,
2nd Sess., Pt. i, 83–97, 106–256, etc.;
*The Mississippi Question fairly Stated,
and the Views and Arguments of those
who Clamor for War, Examined . . . by
Camillus* [Willliam Duane], Philadelphia,
1803; and *Mississippi Question. Report on Certain Resolutions concerning
the Violation of the Right of Deposit in
the Island of New Orleans* (Philadelphia, 1803).

Jefferson nominated James Monroe of Virginia as Minister Plenipotentiary and Envoy Extraordinary to France [1] and Spain to negotiate a settlement of these difficulties in conjunction with the resident ministers at Paris and at Madrid. Samuel Smith, then a Representative from Maryland and in confidential relations with the administration, at the same time introduced a resolution appropriating two million dollars to enable the United States to settle the whole business, once for all. This activity did not at all convince the Federalists that they were beaten in their attempted combination with the frontiersmen. Senator Ross of Pennsylvania, who represented a good deal of pioneer fervor in his own person, introduced a resolution calling for military activity on the part of the government (February 16, 1803). Nothing came of this effort; but any turn in events might at any time bring sufficient strength to the opposition seriously to affect the State elections and, through them, give the Federalists victory in the national campaign of 1804. Jefferson recognized to the full the perilousness of the situation, and the next few months were months of anxious and watchful waiting.

James Monroe was one of those men of persistent mediocrity from whom useful and attractive Presidents have been made. For years he had been in intimate relations with Jefferson and Madison and was one of the three or four Virginia politicians to be habitually consulted by them. Up to this time, Jefferson had had great confidence in Monroe's judgment. At the moment this was somewhat shaken. Monroe possessed a facility for poking into

---

[1] The commission to Livingston and Monroe denominated Livingston Minister Plenipotentiary and Monroe, Minister Extraordinary and Plenipotentiary. When Livingston objected to this distinction, Madison informed him that it was merely an error on the part of a clerk in his office; but Livingston might well have felt annoyed and did feel so.

the personal affairs of great men.　Having exploited the Hamilton-Reynolds scandal, he now had on his mind the connection between Mr. Jefferson and a certain Mrs. Walker. It may be that the time seemed rather opportune to get him out of the country.　Certainly, neither his past history as a diplomatist nor his potential capacity for settling difficult problems could have marked him out as the best candidate for this extremely critical situation.[1]

It took Monroe almost exactly three months from the time of his nomination to reach Paris, — which must be regarded as commendable speed under the existing circumstances of transportation.　In the interval, affairs in France had been moving with Napoleonic swiftness and unexpectedness.[2]　Events had not progressed in Europe at all to Bonaparte's wish.　His position for the present and for the future depended upon "glory"; but there was no glory in peace. Everywhere — at home in France and abroad in Prussia, Austria, and England — forces were at work for his undermining.　It was only in war that he could be secure.　On March 12, 1803, at Madame Bonaparte's reception, he turned violently on the British ambassador and declared that England must give way or there would be war.[3]　This was the signal for the renewal of the conflict, but it was not answered by England by a formal declaration until May 18, more than two months later.　Napoleon's pronuncia-

---

[1] See Madison to Monroe, Washington, April 20, 1803, in *Writings of Madison* (Hunt), vii, 48 note.

[2] Besides the documents cited on p. 307, note 2, see *State Papers and Correspondence bearing upon the Purchase of the Territory of Louisiana* (Washington, 1903, "House Documents," 57th Cong., 2nd Sess., No. 431).　Unfortunately all the printed collections of documents dealing with this matter are marred by typographical errors at important points.　See also the writings of Jefferson, Madison, Monroe, and Rufus King.　It is to be regretted that no collection of the writings of Robert R. Livingston has ever been printed. The lack is by no means made good by E. B. Livingston's *The Livingstons of Livingston Manor*, which is in many respects an exceedingly useful book.

[3] *American State Papers, Foreign Relations*, ii, 547.

mento was not merely the beginning of another decade of European warfare, it was the announcement of the ending of French colonial aspirations for a century. Great Britain maintained her colonial ascendency in war and strengthened it because she was the ruler of the oceans. France was nothing of the sort; peace was necessary for the rehabilitation of her colonial empire. In war with Britain, colonies were a burden to her rather than a source of strength as they were to her enemy. When the occupation of Louisiana had appeared to be easy of accomplishment, General Victor had been ordered into colonial exile for this purpose, and, earlier, Napoleon's brother-in-law, General Leclerc, had been sent to San Domingo with a formidable force for its subjugation. Toussaint Louverture and his blacks — with the yellow fever — had put an ending to Leclerc's conquering career by destroying him and most of his soldiers.[1] In Europe, the ice of winter had prevented Victor's departure, so that Louisiana had not actually come into French hands. It might still be easy to take possession of it, but it was certain to be difficult and expensive to maintain its connection with France. On the other hand, judging from Livingston's letters, from his conversations, and his memoirs, money was likely to be forthcoming from the Americans provided a sufficiently attractive *quid pro quo* was suggested.

It was under circumstances something like those detailed in the preceding paragraph that Napoleon (April 10, 1803) summoned two of his ministers, Barbé Marbois, who had charge of the finances, and Denis Decrès, the Minister of Marine, and asked them what they thought of selling Louisiana to the United States. Decrès opposed the proj-

---

[1] See T. Lothrop Stoddard's *French Revolution in San Domingo*, 296–350; and T. G. Steward's *Haitian Revolution, 1791 to 1804.*

ect. He pointed out that at the close of the approaching
struggle the question of the ownership of Louisiana, as of
every other part of the world, would depend on the outcome of the war in Europe. Marbois had lived in America
during our Revolution and had married an American wife.[1]
As head of the Treasury, he was conscious of the great
difficulty of financing a new war in its earlier stages before
conquered countries could be levied upon. Here was an
opportunity to gain money by the simple process of selling
what a modern stockbroker would term a "call" for the
delivery of certain goods, which in this case consisted of one
town and an indefinite amount of wilderness. The conference soon came to an end; but the next morning at break
of day, the First Consul sent for Marbois. He ordered him
to open negotiations at once with Livingston for the sale of
Louisiana, New Orleans and all, for fifty millions of francs,
on condition that the Americans would take care of the
claims of their citizens on the French government. He
told him not to wait for the coming of Monroe, whose
arrival at Havre had already been heliographed to Paris,
but to push the matter through without delay of any kind.[2]

Napoleon had also spoken of the sale of Louisiana to
Talleyrand, who still had charge of foreign affairs and the
negotiations would naturally be in his department; but

---

[1] Elizabeth Moore, daughter of William Moore, once President of Pennsylvania.

[2] Monroe's statement is interesting:
"I could not but disapprove of M.ʳ
L.ˢ conduct in communicating with M.ʳ
Marbois on a subject committed to us
jointly, after I arrived at Paris, especially as M.ʳ Marbois's agency was
then only in contemplation, referred to
or rather grew out of a decision taken
after my arrival at Havre was known,
to cede the territory, which decision
was actually produc'd by my arrival,

and the more so as I was at his house
when M.ʳ Marbois called on him, when
if an interview at that time was at all
proper, under the then circumstances,
it wo.ᵈ have been as easy to have arranged a joint as a separate one."
Writings of Monroe (Hamilton), iv,
148.

The account in the text follows that
in Barbé Marbois's *Histoire de la Louisiane*, 247–339; translation, *History of
Louisiana*, 225–316. This forms the
basis of the account in Adams's *United
States.*

Napoleon had given him no directions as to conducting the affair. Nevertheless, Talleyrand surprised Livingston beyond measure by inquiring what the United States would give for Louisiana, the whole of it, including New Orleans and the country above the Arkansas, as well as below it. The next day, April 12, Livingston saw Talleyrand again, who then remarked that his proposition was only personal and, indeed, that Louisiana was not theirs to sell. By this time Monroe had reached Paris and he and Livingston passed the greater part of the next day, April 13, in looking over the papers relating to their mission. That afternoon Livingston entertained some friends at dinner to meet Monroe. While at table, Marbois was seen walking in the garden. He came in for coffee, was introduced to Monroe, and suggested to Livingston that he should come to his office that evening when they could talk over the subject of American claims about which something had been said at St. Cloud, — where Napoleon was then in residence. Marbois had taken two days to consider as to the best means of approaching the subject, or he may have been busy about other things. At any rate when he and Livingston were alone together he told him that the First Consul had said to him "Let them [the Americans] give you one hundred millions of Francs, and pay their own claims, and take the whole country" of Louisiana. According to his own account, Livingston looked surprised at the exorbitancy of the demand, whereupon Marbois said that he had told the First Consul that it was too much, and asked him what the United States would pay? Livingston replied that he and Monroe would have to confer together on the subject. Upon this, Marbois declared that he was not authorized to make any especial inquiry of Livingston, but if he would name any sum that came near the mark, he would mention it to his chief. In the end, Marbois suggested that if the Americans would name sixty million francs and take upon themselves the claims upon the French treasury to the amount of twenty millions more, he would try how far this would be acceptable. After more conversation, Livingston returned to his house and wrote a letter to Madison recounting what had occurred.[1] He finished his writing at three o'clock in the morning and, apparently, despatched the missive on its way to America before he had any conversation with Monroe as to Marbois's propositions.[2] The rest of the negotiation was a mere matter of haggle which all came to nothing, for Marbois's terms were finally acceded to. There were three documents. They were completed on different days, but were all dated back to April 30, 1803, and are often loosely referred to as the Louisiana Purchase Treaty. After Marbois, Monroe, and Livingston had affixed their names to these instruments, they shook hands and Livingston announced: "We have lived long, but this is the noblest work of our whole lives. The treaty which we have just signed has not been obtained by art or dictated by force. . . . From this day the United

[1] See Livingston's letters of April 11, 13, and 17, in *American State Papers, Foreign Relations*, ii, 552–555. Monroe's sourish account of the negotiations is in Hamilton's *Writings of Monroe*, iv, 9–17. These documents are repeated in *State Papers bearing upon Louisiana*. With these should be read Monroe's letter to Madison, dated Paris, July 6, 1805, in *Bulletin* of the New York Public Library, iv, 50.

[2] As the weeks went by Livingston and Monroe grew more and more jealous of one another, especially as to the credit due for this acquisition. Livingston's side is stated in his letter to Madison of November 15, 1803 in *American State Papers, Foreign Relations*, ii, 573 and in Madison's letter to him of February 7, 1804 in *Writings of*

Madison (Hunt), vii, 114 note. Monroe's side of the case is in his letters of April 15, 1803, to Madison and of May 25 to the Virginia Senators. These may be found in the *Writings of Monroe* (Hamilton), iv, 9 and 31; they with his journal or memorandum have been widely printed, as in the *State Papers*.

It is not difficult to apportion the credit for this transaction. Napoleon, for reasons having nothing whatever to do with the United States, suddenly determined to get whatever he could for whatever title to Louisiana he had. He threw the province, so to speak, at Livingston, Monroe, Madison, and Jefferson; and they share between them — equally — whatever credit there was in catching it and holding it — that is all.

States take their place among the powers of the first rank. . . .
The instruments which we have just signed will cause no
tears to be shed : they prepare ages of happiness for innumerable generations of human creatures."

The treaty of cession provided for the delivery of Louisiana to the United States with all its rights and appurtenances as fully and in the same manner as they have been
acquired by the French Republic in virtue of the treaty of
San Ildefonso.[1] By this the Spanish king had engaged to
cede to the French Republic that province "with the same
extent that it now has in the hands of Spain, and that it
had when France possessed it ; and such as it should be
after the treaties subsequently entered into between Spain
and other states." The inhabitants of this territory were
to be incorporated in "the Union of the United States"
and admitted, "according to the principles of the Federal
constitution" to the enjoyment of all rights of American
citizens. The other articles provided for the observance
of treaties that had been made between Spain and the
Indians and for certain privileges for French commerce for

---

[1] Article I of the treaty recites that,
whereas the king of Spain and the
First Consul made a treaty by which
the Spanish king on certain conditions
promised to retrocede to the French
Republic "La Colonie ou Province de
la Louisiane, avec la même étendue
qu'elle a actuellement entre les mains
de l'Espagne, et qu'elle avoit lorsque
la France la possédoit, et telle qu'elle
doit être d'après les traités passés
subséquemment entre l'Espagne et
d'autres Etats."

In English the quoted sentence
states that his Catholic Majesty engages
to cede to the French Republic, on
certain conditions, "the colony or
province of Louisiana, with the same
extent that it now has in the hands of
Spain, and that it had when France
possessed it ; and such as it should be
after the treaties subsequently entered

into between Spain and other states."
And, whereas, in pursuance of this
treaty the French Republic had an
incontestable title to the domain and
to the possession of the said territory,
with all its rights and appurtenances,
the First Consul doth hereby cede to
the United States, in the name of the
French Republic the said territory as
fully and in the same manner as it
had been acquired by the French Republic, in virtue of the above-mentioned
treaty.

The above text is printed from the
copies of the treaty in the State Department at Washington. The text
has been printed in countless places:
over and over again in the *Public
Documents, State Papers, Statutes at
Large,* and in various histories of
Louisiana, especially in Barbé Marbois's,
it is given in both French and English.

twelve years.[1] By the first of the two conventions, the
United States engaged to pay eleven millions two hundred
and fifty thousand dollars in six per cent stock which was
irredeemable for fifteen years. And this stock must be
transferred to the government of France within three
months after the exchange of the ratifications of the treaty.
The second convention provided that the debts due by
France to American citizens contracted before September
30, 1800 should be paid by the United States so far as
twenty millions of francs would discharge them, both
principal and interest.[2] Such in brief was the famous settlement by which the United States obtained for a sum of
money, entirely incommensurate with its potential value,
the rights of preëmption to the western half of the North
American continent. The limitations of this great tract
were vague. Marbois said if they were not indefinite, it
would have been well to have made them so; and Talleyrand told the Americans that they had made a noble bargain which, he assumed, they would make the most of.
Delay after delay now occurred. Napoleon and his lieutenants were busily employed in getting ready for the on-

[1] For the later history of this clause,
see Max Farrand on "The Commercial
Privileges of the Treaty of 1803" in
American Historical Review, vii, 494.

[2] Commissions were appointed according to the two Conventions that
supplemented the Louisiana treaty, but
the later history of the claims by American citizens on France is not pleasant
reading. The Commissioners disputed
with the Ministers, first with Livingston and then with Armstrong; they
and the French authorities disagreed
as to the interpretation of vital phrases
in these documents. The result was
that no claimants were fully paid;
that some were half paid, and others
not paid at all. To phrase it differently
the United States obtained Louisiana

by casting to three of the four winds
of Heaven the righteous claims of its
own citizens on France. As one of the
sufferers wrote, if the United States
does not want to pay its own citizens
what it ought, let it give Louisiana
back to France, which would very
likely compensate them by the grant
of one-fifteenth of that province.
See *View of the Claims of American
Citizens, which were . . . assumed by the
United States, In the Louisiana Convention of the 30th April, 1803. By a
Citizen of Baltimore* (1829); *To the
People of the United States* [statement
by one of the Commissioners at Paris
of the transactions under the Convention of April, 1803], Philadelphia,
1807.

coming war. Moreover, the First Consul, having obtained more money than he had expected to get for a mere scrap of paper, was rather inclined to wish that he had demanded more. In the enthusiasm of military preparation, it is entirely possible that he realized how closely the fate of Louisiana was bound up with French success or failure in Europe. Possibly, for this reason, the Americans could not secure the necessary official papers for carrying out the agreement. Instead, Marbois presented a letter to the American delegates declaring that if the six per cent stock were not delivered on time, the whole transaction would be ended. Livingston and Monroe protested with dignity. The letter was withdrawn and a courier started for America bearing the official copy of the conventions, an order to Pichon, the French agent at Washington, to ratify the treaty in case the Americans did, and an order to Laussat, the French representative at New Orleans, to turn over the province to the United States.[1]

Pierre Clément Laussat, who had been appointed to represent the French authorities in Louisiana, had been at New Orleans since March, 1803. He found life there rather trying, for the resident Spaniards thoroughly disliked the thought of retrocession to France, and the French colonists were by no means enthusiastic. Recently, they had been making good money from their commerce with Spain, had been trading freely with the rest of the world, and viewed with apprehension the stricter rule that was certain to follow French occupation. Americans residing at New Orleans also deplored the handing Louisiana back to France, for they supposed that this meant that the temporary closure of the port would be made permanent. Laussat, having nothing else to do, wrote letter after letter to his

[1] See letter of Livingston and Monroe to Madison under date of June 7, 1803.

superiors at Paris, giving them much information and suggesting various plans for the future. When the first rumors came of the sale of the province to the Americans, he would not credit them and did not even believe the official intelligence that was sent to him by way of Washington. The Spanish minister, the Marqués de Casa Irujo, or Yrujo, believed the evidence of despatches, but the greater the probability that they were true, the greater became his wrath. After communicating with his government, he informed Madison that the cession was not good. The conditions upon which the retrocession was to have been made to France had never been fulfilled and France had promised not to alienate the province. Madison reminded Yrujo that the Spanish government itself had suggested to Charles Pinckney that the United States should go to France with its demand for Louisiana. Moreover, he also told him, the whole question was one for France and Spain to settle between them, it did not concern the United States. And so it fell out, for Yrujo in May, 1804, stated that the explanation which France had given to Spain and the amicable disposition of Don Carlos toward the United States had determined him to abandon all opposition to the transference of Louisiana.

The news of the great purchase came as a distinct shock to the government at Washington (July, 1803). Livingston and Monroe had been instructed to pay not more than ten million dollars for New Orleans and West Florida, or a part of it. They had agreed that the United States should pay fifteen or sixteen million dollars for New Orleans and the whole of Louisiana.[1] For years Jefferson and

---

[1] The sum to be paid is stated in the two "particular conventions" which were dated the same day as the treaty itself. By the first of these, sixty million francs were to be paid independent of the sum fixed by the other convention for the payment of the debts due by France to citizens of

his friends had been declaiming against the outrageous behavior of Federalists and Monocrats in interpreting the Constitution most liberally to suit their own evil purposes. It should be strictly construed, for the Union was a mere pact between independent States. Yet here was a proposition to add at one blow a territory larger than the original domain. Its settlement and division into States would unhinge the whole balance of the original agreement; it would bring in conditions that had been unthought of in 1787 and 1788. On the other hand, the acquisition of the province would be of tremendous benefit, and would put an end to many extremely awkward conditions. Plainly the way to get the necessary authority was to amend the Constitution. Jefferson drew up amendments declaring "Louisiana, as ceded by France . . . is made a part of the U. S.," but reserving the lands north of the Arkansas for the Indians. He also summoned Congress, that the Senate might consent to the ratification of the treaty, and the two Houses vote the necessary money and also adopt an amendment for submission to the States. Then came letters from Livingston and Monroe, warning against anything that could justify the First Consul in drawing back. As the possibility of losing the prize became greater, Jefferson's anxiety took a new turn.[1] It was then that Wilson Cary Nicholas came to the rescue. Five years before, he had handed over Jefferson's draft of the Kentucky Resolutions

the United States. The second convention fixed this sum at not exceeding twenty million francs. In Gallatin's report of October 25, 1803, it appears that $11,250,000.00 was payable in six per cent stock to the French government and "a sum which cannot exceed, but may fall short of, 3,750,000 dollars" was payable in specie at the United States treasury to American citizens on account of their claims against the French government.

[1] See Jefferson to John Dickinson, Aug. 9, 1803 (Ford's *Writings of Jefferson*, viii, 262). He writes, "In the meantime [while securing an amendment to the Constitution] we must ratify & pay our money, as we have treated, for a thing beyond the constitution, and rely on the nation to sanction an act done for its great good, without its previous authority."

to Breckinridge. Now he wrote that the Constitution was not intended to confine Congress in the admission of new States to the existing territory of the thirteen that had made that instrument. Nor were there any restraints on the treaty-making power, except the general limitations of the organic law and the objects for which the government was instituted. As one of the objects for which the government had been instituted was the promotion of the general welfare, under this interpretation of the Constitution, it was difficult to conceive of any limitation on the treaty-making power. Jefferson replied that if the grant of that power was boundless, there was no Constitution. However, if "our friends shall think differently, certainly I shall acquiesce with satisfaction; confiding, that the good sense of our country will correct the evil of construction when it shall produce ill effects." Well might he have recalled Portia's reply to the suggestion that the law, in its administration, might be twisted — to do a great right, do a little wrong : —

> "It must not be. . . .
> 'Twill be recorded for a precedent,
> And many an error, by the same example,
> Will rush into the state : it cannot be."

NOTE

The Closure of the Mississippi. — Different statements have been made as to the ending of the right of deposit under the Treaty of 1795 and by the two persons who would seem to be well informed. One of these, Barbé-Marbois, the negotiator of the Louisiana treaty on the part of France, states that Moralès, the Spanish Intendant at New Orleans, suddenly imagining that an indulgence introduced during the war should cease with peace, contrary to the opinion of the governor, put an end to the enjoyment of a privilege which he was afraid to see perpetuated by a sort of prescription. See Barbé-Marbois's *Histoire de la Louisiane* (Paris, 1829), pp. 232, 233; or English rendering (Philadelphia, 1830) pp. 212, 213. Henry Adams (*History of the United States*, i, 419, 420) follows Barbé-Marbois and fortifies his statement by referring to a letter from Laussat to Decrès, written in April, 1803, in which the French prefect of Louisiana states that Moralès explained to him that defying the opposition and even the threats of the government, he had proclaimed the right of deposit to be at an end.

Villiers du Terrage (*Les Dernières Années de la Louisiane Française*, 367) gives a quotation from the very rare volume of memoirs of Laussat which was published at Pau in 1831, to the effect that " Le gouverneur Salcedo le supprima contre l'avis de l'intendant." Laussat suggests that this was probably due to the rivalry that existed between the two, and states that Moralès was his authority. He represents himself as expressing his astonishment to the governor who replied, " qu'il n'avait voulu que se mettre en règle auprès de son Gouvernement, duquel il avait cru prévenir les intentions, mais, qu'ayant rendu compte au capitaine général à La Havane, il s'en tiendrait là, tant qu'il n'y aurait pas une décision supérieure."

In the archives at Seville is the royal order of July 14, 1802, directing the Intendant to close the port to Americans. A transcript of this was kindly procured for me by Dr. Roscoe H. Hill of the Carnegie Institution of Washington. The wording is as follows: " Conviene que el Intendente de la Luisiana se oponga à la introduccion y deposito de mercancias de los Americanos en Nueva-Orleans, no escudandose para esta novedad con la orden del Rey, sino alegando que para inquirir la estension de sus facultades, y sus obligaciones en esta materia consultò el referido tratado de 1795, y hallò que il termino prefisado de tres años en el articulo 22 le ataba las manos para no poder permitir la introduccion y deposito de mercancias americanas sin orden espresa del Rey." This was translated for me by Dr. Julius Klein as follows: " It is advisable that the Intendant of Louisiana should oppose the introduction and deposit of goods of the Americans in New Orleans, not excusing himself for this innovation with the order of the king, but alleging that in order to investigate the extent of his powers and his duties in this matter he consulted the above mentioned treaty of 1795 and found that the limit of three years fixed by article xxii bound his hands so that he could not allow the introduction and deposit of American goods without the express permission of the king."

CHAPTER XII

The Louisiana treaties were delivered at the Department of State at Washington on July 14, 1803. Two days later, Jefferson summoned Congress to meet on October 17, and departed for Monticello for his annual summer retreat. Promptly, on time, the treaties were sent to the Senate, which at once advised ratification. As the French ratification was already in the hands of the representative of that Republic at Washington, the transaction was at once concluded (October 21). The whole matter was now laid open to the public by the printing of the presidential message with the treaties and the accompanying documents.

Considering the rapidity with which the actual negotiation had been conducted at Paris, one is impressed with the slowness with which the later steps were taken. It was a long way from Washington to New Orleans, and the order for the transfer could not be sent by Pichon until the ratifications had been exchanged. When the Spanish order for delivery to the French authorities arrived at New Orleans, the condition there was critical. It was known that Spain had protested vigorously against the sale, and Laussat, the French Intendant, had no force behind him to make good the orders of his consular master or to maintain the peace at New Orleans after the transfer, provided it should be made. It was not until November 30, therefore, that the

Spaniards were ready to hand over the province to him and he felt sufficiently assured of approaching American aid to make it desirable to accept the burden.[1] On that day the Spanish flag was hauled down from the staff at New Orleans, and the tri-color of France hoisted in its place.

For twenty days Louisiana was again a province of France. Laussat made the most of his brief opportunity. He upset the Spanish régime, disposing of the hereditary council, or cabildo, which had been a feature of the Spanish rule and instituting a municipal council. Then he reëstablished the French legal system as it was before the reformations of the Code Napoléon. He also substituted French officers for the Spaniards, who were in command of the small native military forces. For the rest, he took part in a round of social gayeties and awaited the coming of Governor William C. C. Claiborne of Mississippi Territory and General James Wilkinson, who were to take over the province for the United States.

On the twentieth day of December, 1803, the final transfer was effected. There could not be much ceremony because there were no French troops and only a handful of Americans, Wilkinson having left at Natchez most of the few soldiers he had brought down the river. At noon, the French flag was hauled down for the last time, — a patriotic sergeant of the Republican armies seizing it and wrapping it around his body. The American flag slowly ascended, obstinately sticking for a while about half way up the mast. When it reached the top, a cheer burst forth from the dozen or so Americans gathered in the square and the transfer was accomplished. Laussat issued the usual proclamation releasing the inhabitants from their allegiance to the French

[1] See F. X. Martin's *History of Loui-siana* (New Orleans, 1827), ii, 194–200 and Charles Gayarré's *History of Louisiana*, iii, 599–620.

Republic; but the Americans were in no position to issue a similar proclamation directing the newly made American citizens to take the oath of allegiance to the United States because there was no accurate information obtainable as to the bounds of the new acquisition.

In point of fact, beyond Laussat's confidential statement,[1] no one knew anything as to the bounds of Louisiana. Livingston and Monroe had been directed to purchase New Orleans and West Florida together with East Florida, if they could get it. Before the original negotiations began, Livingston knew perfectly well that the Spaniards had obstinately refused to part with any portion of the Floridas on any terms that Napoleon's agent had suggested. He and Monroe had concluded the purchase of Louisiana with that idea firmly fixed in their minds. The latter, indeed, was on the point of starting for Spain to negotiate for the Floridas in conjunction with Charles Pinckney, the American Minister at Madrid, when he was deterred by the advice of the French authorities that the present was not a good time to push that undertaking.[2] Instead he went to London, for King had returned home, leaving no one in charge of American affairs in England. It was under these circumstances that Livingston pored over the words of the treaty of San Ildefonso, which were repeated in the Louisiana Treaty: "Louisiana,

---

[1] Madison to R. R. Livingston, March 31st, 1804: "In mine of January 31, I informed you . . . that *Mr. Laussat had confidentially signified that it* [Louisiana] *did not comprehend any part of West Florida; adding at the same time that it extended westwardly to the Rio Bravo otherwise called Rio del Norde.*" *Writings of Madison* (Hunt ed.), vii, 123. See also Madison's letter of Jan. 31, 1804 in *ibid.*, p. 117. "Both the commissioner of the French Republic and the commissioners of the United States understand that the line is to begin or to conclude at the point where the Rio Bravo [Brabo] empties into the Gulf of Mexico." Casa Calvo to Cevallos, Jan. 13, 1804 in Robertson's *Louisiana, 1785–1807,* vol. ii, 163. See also Talleyrand to Decrès, October 2, 1802, "The Rio Bravo, from its mouth up to the 30th degree, serves as the line of demarcation." *Ibid.*, ii, 141 note.

[2] Monroe to Madison, London, July 20, 1803. Consul Cambacérès said, "You must not go to Spain at present. . . . It is not the time; you had better defer it." *Writings of Monroe*, iv, 45.

with the same extent . . . that it had in the hands of
France." To him these words were clear enough. French
Louisiana had extended eastwardly to the Perdido River.[1]
The other phrase, "it [Louisiana] now has in the hands of
Spain" meant that Spain was obliged to restore only as
much of the old French Louisiana as was then in her hands.
It was all in her hands up to the thirty-first parallel and
therefore so much of it was plainly included in the tract
that Spain retroceded to France and that France sold to us.
The third clause, "and such as it should be after the treaties
subsequently entered into between Spain and other States,"
simply meant that Spain was not obliged to hand over to
France any of the old Louisiana east of the Mississippi and
north of the thirty-first parallel, for she had acknowledged
that that was the southern limit of the United States; but
the rest of French Louisiana east of the river was clearly
included within the tract just purchased. Livingston therefore wrote to the authorities at Washington that Florida
between the Iberville and Perdido rivers was within the
Louisiana Purchase, and advised that that territory be
occupied, or a claim to its possession be set up.[2]

From this point, the matter of the bounds of Louisiana
passed into the hands of the diplomatists, and when they got
through with it, by the Florida treaty of 1819, the historians
took it up and have been at it ever since. In the long diplo-

---

[1] It is often said that this river
which flows into the Gulf of Mexico,
midway between Mobile and Pensacola,
was selected by the French and Spanish
commanders at those places as a con-
ventional boundary on account of its
position. Monroe wrote to Talleyrand
(November 8, 1804), "The river Perdido
is the ancient, and, of course, present
boundary of that province [Louisiana]
to the east." *American State Papers,
Foreign Relations*, ii, 634. See also

Robertson's *Louisiana*, ii, 162, 295,
331; LePage du Pratz's *History of
Louisiana* (London, 1774), p. 130; and
Martin's *Louisiana*, ii, 202. Peter J.
Hamilton in his *Colonial Mobile* (ed.
1910, p. 181) wrote: "Perhaps no
distinct paper ever regulated the
boundary, but the French claim east
to Perdido River became a *fait accom-
pli*."

[2] May 20, 1803. *American State
Papers, Foreign Relations*, ii, 560, 561.

matic wrangles that went on, the Americans were at a sad disadvantage. Whatever information they could glean was got painfully and, much of it, surreptitiously from books and maps. For every new argument that they advanced the Spaniards were always able to bring abundant proof to the contrary. They had the whole archives of the Indies at their disposal, could produce maps unheard of before, and disinter records of expeditions and missions that no one except Spanish officials had the least inkling of. It was all in vain and absolutely fruitless. Napoleon sold to us the right to call upon the Spaniards for the delivery of certain territory. That territory was described in the instructions that were issued to General Victor long before any thought of selling the province to the United States or to anybody else had entered the mind of Napoleon or any other Frenchman, and show conclusively what the French government understood was the meaning of the treaty of San Ildefonso. These instructions were repeated to Laussat, and it was this territory that he received from the Spaniards and passed on to Claiborne and Wilkinson as representatives of the United States. According to these instructions, the eastern boundary of Louisiana was the Mississippi from its source to the thirty-first parallel and thence to the Iberville. Down that river the line ran to Lakes Maurepas and Pontchartrain and so to the Gulf of Mexico. On the west, the boundary was the Rio Bravo — the Rio Grande as we now call it — from its mouth to the thirtieth parallel and thence it was undefined.[1] On the north it was coterminus with British America and, in the unknown region between, it

---

[1] Victor's instructions were copied for Henry Adams from the archives in Paris. The important clauses are translated by him (*History of the United States*, ii, 6). The whole document is translated in Robertson's *Louisiana* under the *Rule of Spain, France, and the United States*, i, 361. In the first line of the sixth paragraph of this document, Robertson substituted "east" for "west," thus making the Rio Grande the eastern boundary of Louisiana.

extended to the water-parting of the Rocky Mountain system and, perhaps, even to the Pacific Ocean, — such was the Louisiana that we bought from France in the year 1803.

On the 22nd of October, 1803, the question of legislation for carrying the Louisiana Purchase treaty into effect came before the House of Representatives. Jefferson, the apostle of the right of man to govern himself according to certain unalienable laws, had negotiated through his representatives a treaty acquiring some thousands of Spaniards and French-men together with an entirely unknown quantity of North American Indians. Government "existed by consent of the governed," but the consent of not one of these persons had been asked. Moreover, in the existing condition of affairs with the world at war and a very large proportion of these recently purchased human beings by no means enthusiasti-cally affected to their new owners, whatever government was established, must be somewhat autocratic. What right, indeed, had the United States to buy lands and rivers without the consent of the inhabitants or with it? Was the Constitution a pact between sovereign States and limited to the area of 1783 or did the American people form a nation? Jefferson and his co-workers had declaimed loudly against the idea that the United States was something more than a bunch of sovereign States working together under an agreement for certain limited purposes and had demanded that this compact should be strictly construed that the rights of the co-States should suffer no impairment. Possibly the most interesting thing that came out of the Louisiana Purchase was the statement by Jefferson to Breckinridge, August 12, 1803,[1] that after the treaty was ratified and executed an appeal must then be made to "the nation" for a confirmation of an act which "the nation" had not previously authorized,

---

[1] *Writings of Jefferson* (Ford), viii, 244.

— only five years after the Kentucky Resolutions and their author was writing about "the nation"!

By the Louisiana Purchase the United States acquired something under one million square miles of territory, if we limit its area to its smallest possible extent, or over two million square miles, if we give it its greatest possible extension, doubling or trebling the original area of the United States. Whatever its size, it has proved to be a land of riches : animal, vegetable, and mineral — beef and mutton, wheat, corn and cotton, gold, silver, copper and zinc.[1] Its population in one hundred years grew from one hundred thousand or possibly two hundred thousand — counting in the Red Men — to from eighteen to twenty-seven millions as one excludes or includes from its area Texas and the Pacific slope. Supposing for the moment that Louisiana had not been acquired in 1803, what would have become of the trans-Mississippi region in the nineteenth century ? Would it have become another Mexico or another Canada ? Or supposing that Napoleon had remained obdurate[2] and we had "married the British fleet and nation," — as Jefferson had hinted we might. Would not today the peace of the world be beyond disturbance ? Coming more strictly within the confines of American annals : had there been no

[1] In 1914, individuals and corporations within the original area of the United States contributed $51,041,-688.99 to the total income tax ; the whole trans-Mississippi country and Louisiana east of the river $9,466,749.08, of which $5,144,347.88 came from the country between the Mississippi and the mountains and north of Texas!

[2] A South Carolina Rutledge, writing to H. G. Otis in 1803, animadverted on "the purchase of a tractless world . . . for our fifteen millions. This seems to me a miserably calamitous business — indeed I think it must result in the disunion of these States." This was communicated to me by D. Huger Bacot, Jr., of Charleston, who found it in the "Otis Papers" that were kindly opened to him by Dr. S. E. Morison. J. P. Quincy's article on "The Louisiana Purchase" in the *Proceedings* of the Massachusetts Historical Society for November, 1903, renews interestingly the Federalist objections to the acquisition. Professor W. M. Sloane has some important suggestions on this general theme in an article entitled "The World Aspects of the Louisiana Purchase" in *American Historical Review*, ix, 507–521.

Louisiana Purchase there would have been no Missouri Compromise, no Texas annexation, no Mexican War, no Oregon boundary! The Kansas-Nebraska Act would never have been passed and there would have been no struggle for Kansas! Indeed there would have been no War for Secession with its attendant orgies of Reconstruction. But the star of destiny otherwise determined, and it is not the function of history to question.

The years immediately following the Louisiana Purchase were among the most troublous in our annals. That acquisition had removed the danger which had brought the United States and Great Britain into some sort of harmony. France had got all from America that she could expect to gain, except from a renewal of the seizures of American shipping. Spain was so thoroughly irritated by Napoleon's action in selling Louisiana, when it did not belong to him, by the claims put forward by the United States as to boundaries, and by her fears of the results certain to flow from the proximity of American democracy to her colonies in Florida and in Mexico that she almost seemed to be willing to go to war.

The western settlers were vigorous outstanding democrats, for whom commercial advantages and the possibility of the acquisition of cheap and fertile lands had great charm. They were deeply tinged with ideas akin to those of the French radicals and looked upon themselves somewhat in the light of emissaries of freedom and at the same time were determined to uphold the rights of the United States against Spanish aggression. The time and the country were ripe for an explosion or for several of them. Aaron Burr, disgraced by the killing of Hamilton and ostracized by the Jeffersonians and by most of the Federalists, thought he saw a new field for his activities in the southwest and in Mexico.

His last words as Vice-President were among the most
affecting ever spoken in the Senate and among the most
pitiful ever uttered anywhere in America.[1] His old reputation was gone; he was eager to make a new one somewhere
and somehow.

Deeply seated in hatred of Jefferson and his following,
Burr already had found a congenial spirit in the person of
Anthony Merry,[2] the British minister who was at Philadelphia in midsummer, 1804, when Burr reached that city
after the killing of Hamilton. Almost exactly two weeks
later, Merry wrote to his superiors at London that Burr had

[1] J. Q. Adams in his diary (*Memoirs*,
i, 367) states that Burr's speech was
listened to with the most earnest and
universal attention. "Many of the
members appeared deeply affected,
and two of them, Mr. Wright and Mr.
Smith, of New York, were moved even
to tears." The speech as Adams took
it down differs somewhat from that
given in the *Annals of Congress* (8th
Cong., 2nd Sess., 71), which was taken
from the *Washington Federalist* of
March 13, 1805, and is the original of
that given in Davis's and Parton's
biographies and Benton's *Abridgement*.
Writing to his daughter, on March 13,
and enclosing a copy of this paper, Burr
states that "tears did flow abundantly."
On the other hand, John Randolph,
referring to what he termed "the
vehement puff of B." declared that
"this is overstepping the modesty of
nature. Besides, we were in Washington at the time, and heard nothing
of the miraculous effects of his valedictory," (Adams's *John Randolph*,
155). For two very hostile criticisms
of Burr as a politician, see James
Cheetham's *A View of the Political
Conduct of Aaron Burr* (New York,
1802) and his *Nine Letters on the Subject
of Aaron Burr's Political Defection* (New
York, 1803). Among other things
Cheetham asserted that Burr intrigued
against Jefferson in 1801. A friendly
view is *An Examination of the various
charges exhibited against Aaron Burr* . . .

By Aristides [W. P. Van Ness], New
York, 1803.

[2] Anthony Merry was a good-natured,
honest gentleman, who was "popped
into a diplomatique situation," to use
the language of an English contemporary writer, and he possessed a
punctilious wife. Jefferson, being a
widower and given to simplicity in
public, had established the rule of pell
mell at his functions, — a rule that was
observed in many European courts.
Attending a dinner at the President's
Mansion, Mr. and Mrs. Merry found
themselves together following President
Jefferson and Mrs. Madison into the
dining room where no seats were assigned. The Merrys were greatly put
out. Nathaniel Macon wrote that the
British minister "had kicked up a little
dust about his and his wife's rank . . .
and this prank of the Briton has acted as
a spur to the Spaniard." There was no
moving Jefferson on a matter of this kind,
and the Merrys trying to do it, found
themselves in a difficult situation. At
any rate, Merry listened to Burr's propositions, — and was recalled. Extracts
from his letters are printed in Adams's
United States, ii, 395, 401, 403; iii, 229,
and in McCaleb's *Aaron Burr Conspiracy*, 20, 42, 69. "Rules of Etiquette"
that apparently were adopted in 1803
are in Jefferson's *Writings* (Ford), viii,
276; Jefferson described the Merry
incident in a letter to Monroe in *ibid.*,
viii, 291.

offered his assistance to bring about a separation of the western and eastern parts of the Union. Again, in the spring and, finally, in the autumn of 1805, he addressed his government on the subject. In the last letter, the scheme had expanded to include an attack on Spanish territories in America. Burr needed money and suggested, so Merry wrote, that the British government might contribute half a million dollars or so to the carrying out of his plans.

Far away to the southwest in Louisiana, especially at New Orleans, there was deep dissatisfaction over the immediate outcome of the transfer of Louisiana to the United States. The Creoles looked upon themselves as fully the equals of the loose-ended pioneers, whom the flat boats brought down the great river, and even of such official specimens as William C. C. Claiborne or James Wilkinson. They resented being governed more absolutely by Americans than they had been by Spaniards or Frenchmen. They sent a deputation to Washington in December, 1804, and Congress modified the original arrangement by authorizing Claiborne to summon an assembly of twenty-five delegates, and furthermore provided that the inhabitants of the Territory of Orleans — for that was the official name of the southern part of the Purchase — should send a delegate to represent them on the floor of Congress. Burr met the deputies, Messieurs Sauvé, Derbigny, and Destréhan, learned from them of the discontent at New Orleans, and determined to go there and see for himself what prospect there was to rehabilitate his political fortunes and his finances by removal to the western country.[1]

[1] The best books on this part of Burr's career are Adams's *United States* and W. F. McCaleb's *Aaron Burr Conspiracy, a History largely from Original and hitherto Unused Sources* (New York, 1903). Dr. McCaleb had already stated his views in briefer form in the *Report* of the American Historical Association for 1903, vol. i, p. 131. These two authors reach very different conclusions, — Adams laying the greatest stress on the separation from the Union,

Journeying down the Ohio, the ex-Vice-President was
everywhere received with acclaim. He made the acquaintance of Harman Blennerhassett, an Irish gentleman, who
was living on an island in the Ohio River. He talked to
him of the conquest of Mexico, of the establishment of an
empire there, of which he, himself, should be emperor, with
remainder to his daughter, Theodosia, and with Blennerhassett presumably one of the high officers of the court.
In Tennessee, he met and charmed Andrew Jackson; in
Kentucky, he likewise made friends with Henry Clay. At
New Orleans, his reception was most cordial. Returning
upstream, Burr conversed with General James Wilkinson,
the commander-in-chief of the United States army of thirty-
five hundred men. In the course of the journey, he also
renewed his intimacy with John Smith, formerly one of the
Senators from Ohio, who kept a general store at Cincinnati.
What Burr told these people, no man knows; probably he
could not have said himself.

In the late autumn of 1805 Burr was back at Philadelphia
and Washington. Merry, the British minister, was still
most receptive, but he had received no response to his
communications with his superiors. No money was forthcoming from the British treasury. Thereupon Burr and
ex-Senator Dayton, who was very close to him at this time,

McCaleb on the proposed attack on
the Spanish dominions. Adams had
not the use of material drawn from
Spanish-American archives as McCaleb
had. It is impossible to believe that
a trained diplomatist, like Anthony
Merry, should have fabricated such a
proposition from the man who was
actually holding the office of Vice-
President of the United States. Barclay, the British consul, also wrote to
Lord Howick that it appears to be "the
opinion of the best informed in these
States, that Mr. Burr's views extend
to a division of the United States of
America, and creating a new Government in the Western part thereof"
(*Barclay Correspondence*, 251). Recently Burr had been privy to a plan
to separate the northeastern States
from the rest of the Union and there is
in the archives at Paris a plan for a
French invasion of the United States
which was drawn up by Burr whose
mind at this time might be described
as chaotic and devoid of the patriotic
impulse.

opened communications with the Marquis of Casa Yrujo. They represented to him how imminent was an attack on the Spanish possessions in America, and that Burr was the only person who could prevent it or render it innocuous. They had tried to get half a million from Great Britain, but recognizing the difference in the financial resources of the two kingdoms, they only asked for a hundred thousand dollars from Spain, and might even do the job for less. Yrujo swallowed the bait as easily as Merry had taken it, and transmitted faithfully to his superiors at Madrid all that he got from Burr and Dayton. He even gave the plotters ten thousand dollars without orders from home. The Spaniards replied to Yrujo's letters which was more than the British had done to those of Merry. They told him not to pay any money and either for this or for some other reason directed the Viceroy of Mexico to increase the military force on the border between Texas and Louisiana.[1]

In the summer of 1806, Burr was again in the western country. He had gathered a little money in one way or another and procured a little more from the ill-fated Blennerhassett. The whole amount was very small; but it was enough to justify Burr in ordering fifteen or twenty flat boats to be built and provisions, tools, and arms to be got together. He also purchased some shadowy claims to several hundred thousand acres of wild lands in Louisiana, some miles to the west of the Mississippi.[2] The politicians

---

[1] There may possibly have been some connection between these events and the Miranda expedition. The parallelism may be discerned in papers printed in the *American Historical Review*, vi, 508 and American Historical Association's *Report* for 1907, vol. i, p. 193.

[2] Burr's agents gathered recruits far and wide. Among them was Silas Brown of Onondaga, New York. Writing home (October, 1807), after the failure of the scheme, he says, that the expedition "was bent upon an agricultural and commercial intercourse." At Blennerhasset Island "all was peace and harmony . . . All persons, whether neighbors or strangers were at liberty to pass to and from the Island when they pleased; no guards were placed on the Island," and they had no military stores.

now got hold of the scheme. Up to this time, Jefferson had scoffed at the idea of danger. The United States District Attorney in Kentucky happened to be a Federalist; he saw a chance to make capital for his party and laid Burr's doings before the grand jury. Burr courted the fullest investigation, but the District Attorney could not produce his witnesses. The inquiry fell flat. Later another effort was made; this time evidence was produced, but it was unsatisfactory to the grand jurors who reported no bill and the preparations for the expedition went on.

Unfortunately for himself, Burr had not dealt squarely with Wilkinson. That personage was engaged in all kinds of mysterious adventures from his youth in the Revolutionary War to his disappearance as a military factor in the War of 1812. And mysterious as his doings were, he contrived in his "Memoirs" [1] by a combination of truths and tergiversations to shroud them in almost impenetrable darkness. Acting on orders from Washington, he now descended the Mississippi and personally directed the defence of the American dominions against the Spaniards.

---

[1] *Memoirs of My Own Times by General James Wilkinson* (3 vols., Philadelphia, 1816). Previously, in 1810, he had printed at Washington a slender volume entitled *Memoirs of General Wilkinson, volume ii,* and had reprinted this with a second title page in 1811 as *Burr's Conspiracy Exposed; and General Wilkinson Vindicated against the Slanders of his Enemies on that Important Occasion.* No volume i of this edition ever appeared. Wilkinson throve on courts martial and committees of inquiry and they added to the mass of printed matter. See *Report of the Committee appointed to inquire into the Conduct of General Wilkinson* (Washington, 1811, forming a volume of the "Reports of the 11th Cong., 3rd Sess."). This volume contains the most important documents that had come to light down to that time. Later searches in the Spanish and Mexican archives have produced other letters and documents which have been printed under the editorship of W. R. Shepherd (*American Historical Review,* vols. ix and x), and I. J. Cox in *ibid.* vol. xix and in *Mississippi Valley Historical Review,* vol. i. The first charges against Wilkinson were laid before Congress by John Randolph of Roanoke, December 31, 1807, and included the documents that had come from Daniel Clark of New Orleans; See *Annals of Congress* (10th Cong., 1st Sess., vol. i, 1257 and on); *Proofs of the Corruption of Gen. James Wilkinson, and of his Connection with Aaron Burr by Daniel Clark of the City of New Orleans* (Philadelphia, 1809).

Wilkinson talked very loudly of what he was going to do to
the Spaniards, but when he got to the frontier, he found that
they had retired.   As it takes two to make a war, it was
quite clear that there would be no war with Spain.   There
were rumors, ugly rumors, of the coming of Burr with one
thousand men, with two thousand men, with eight thousand
men ; and Wilkinson, himself, received some kind of communication from the former Vice-President.   What it was,
no man knows, for our only knowledge of what the letter
contained is Wilkinson's own version.   At all events, he
became panic stricken, made truce with the Spaniards,
returned to New Orleans, arrested Burr's agents, shipped
them off by sea, and made all manner of preparations to
hold down the Louisianians, and to repel Burr and his army
when they should come.

Wilkinson's reports, the activity of the western Federalists,
and the rumors that incessantly came from the Ohio Valley
as to what was going on there at length convinced Jefferson
that something must be done.   On November 27, 1806 he
issued a proclamation requiring all good citizens to appre-
hend and secure the persons of Aaron Burr and his followers.
The Westerners now aroused themselves.   The militia embodied and descended upon Blennerhassett's Island to find
it deserted.   The proclamation travelled most slowly and
somehow, wittingly or unwittingly, Burr kept just ahead of
it.   The gathering excitement, however, impelled him to
start down the river when only half the preparations were
completed.   With nine or ten boats and sixty or eighty men
scantily armed and poorly supplied, he passed one American
post after another and finally tied up at Bayou Pierre, about
thirty miles above Natchez.   There, more judicial inquiries
and grand juries awaited him.   He also was forced to give
bonds to appear when wanted and Wilkinson and his men

were coming up the river. It was then that in disguise
with a single companion, Burr left his party and for a
month wandered in the wilderness, finally to be captured
by a United States soldier, who was eager for the two
thousand dollars reward that had been placed on Burr's
head. He was taken to Richmond and brought before
Chief Justice Marshall in the United States Circuit Court
on a charge of treason in levying war against the United
States.[1]

The mountain had labored and brought forth nothing;
the secession of the western country, the conquest of Mexico,
and possibly of Central America and of South America had
all turned into an expedition of sixty to one hundred persons
to settle in the western part of the Territory of Orleans.
The outcome to Burr was painful; it was even more so to
Wilkinson, for it covered him with ridicule, the last clothing
that was suitable to that general; and it filled Jefferson
with loathing that he should have lost his head just at the
moment when he should have kept it. The only persons
who came out with any show of triumph were Chief Justice
John Marshall and John Randolph of Roanoke, Virginians
both, and now intensely hostile to their fellow Virginian and
kinsman, the President of the United States. The Chief
Justice ruled that an overt act of treason must first be shown,
and then Burr connected with it. No evidence was produced, or could be produced, to show that there had been
any treasonable act by any one, except possibly by Wilkinson. Randolph, as foreman of the jury, refused to bring in

[1] Documents showing the excitement occasioned in Mississippi Territory by Burr's approach and material
as to his arrest are printed at length
in Dunbar Rowland's *Third Annual
Report* (1903–4) as Director of the
Department of Archives and History
of the State of Mississippi. A. J.

Pickett wrote out an account of the
"Arrest of Aaron Burr" for a local
paper. It is to be found, greatly ab-
breviated, in his *History of Alabama*, ii,
ch. xxix. See also the "Letters of
William T. Barry" in *American Historical Review*, xvi, 327.

any bill. Next the prosecutors tried to secure an indictment
for misdemeanor against the ex-Vice-President.[1] Wilkinson
was summoned from New Orleans and the President of the
United States was ordered to appear and produce all the
documents that were in the government's possession relating to the whole affair. Jefferson refused to attend. He
sent the documents and Wilkinson, and the trial turned
into an attempt to convict that personage out of his own
mouth of high crimes and misdemeanors. That was as
vain as the rest and is the one thing in Wilkinson's career
that arouses admiration for his mental endowment and his
courage. In the end Burr sought exile in France. After
suffering discomforts ever attendant on penury and an
entire lack of recognition, he returned to the United
States and passed a long old age in semi-oblivion at New
York.[2]

From all the evidence it seems that in the beginning, Burr
was quite willing to head an attempt to split the Union into
its component parts, to bring about the secession of the
Northern States, or the secession of the western country.
Those ideas having no chance of fulfillment, his mind turned
to thoughts of Mexican revolution and freeing the continents

[1] The proceedings in the Burr inquiry and trial were reported at length
in the *American and Commercial Daily
Advertiser* of Richmond for the summer
of 1807 and were reprinted thence,
more or less completely, in countless
newspapers. The most complete account in book form is David Robertson's
*Reports of the Trials of Colonel Aaron
Burr for Treason, and for a Misdemeanor*
(2 vols., Philadelphia, 1808) ; and see
also W. H. Safford's *Blennerhassett
Papers* (Cincinnati, 1891).

[2] Luther Martin of Maryland, who
defended Burr, came in for much
objurgation from Jefferson and the
Jeffersonians. The "impudent Fed-

eralist bull-dog" they termed him.
Martin replied to his enemies by demanding why his critics, if they had the
most perfect knowledge of Burr's
guilt, "had not come forward and informed your government"? See *Vermont Centinel*, August 26, 1807.

The feeling toward Marshall in
some quarters is shown by the following
pretended execution by the common
hangman on Gallows Hill: "1. Chief
Justice M———, for repeating his XYZ-
tricks ; which are said to have been
much aggravated by his felonious capers
in open court under plea of irrele-
vancy." *Albany Register*, November 24,
1807.

from the burden of Spanish misrule; that again being hope-less, he essayed the rôle of western pioneer and started to develop the Bastrop lands, hoping, no doubt, that the future might have some more active and more glorious career in store for him.

NOTE

Limits of Louisiana. — The words of the treaty have already been given in the note to page 320. The official papers that passed between the governments of the United States and Spain are printed in the *American State Papers, Foreign Relations* vols. ii and iv; especially in connection with the negotiation of the Florida treaty of 1819.[1] Of the almost countless articles and essays that have been written on this theme, see especially Professor John R. Ficklen's " Was Texas included in the Louisiana Purchase? " in Southern History Association's *Publications* September, 1901. Professor Ficklen argues against the inclusion of Texas and bases his argument very largely upon maps. I. J. Cox has three articles on " The Louisiana-Texas Frontier " in the Texas State Historical Association's *Quarterly* for July, 1906, and in the Southwestern Historical Association's *Quarterly* for July and October, 1913. See also Lester G. Bugbee's " The Real Saint-Denis " in Texas State Historical Association's *Quarterly*, April, 1898; Anne E. Hughes's " The Beginnings of Spanish Settlement in the El Paso District " in *University of California Publications in History*, i, 295–392; and E. M. Violette's " Early Settlements in Missouri " in *Missouri Historical Review*, October, 1906. Marbois (*Histoire de la Louisiane*, 308 or *History of Louisiana*, 284) states that, according to old documents, the Bishopric of Louisiana extended to the Pacific Ocean. In 1804, Jefferson drew up " An Examination into the boundaries of Louisiana," which is published in *Documents relating to the Purchase and Exploration of Louisiana* (Boston, 1904).

[1] Many of these documents are to be found in Wait's *State Papers of the*   *United States* (3rd ed.) vol. xii.

CHAPTER XIII

A CHANGED OUTLOOK AT HOME AND ABROAD

FOR four years since March, 1801, Jefferson had passed from one triumph to another. His second Inaugural was a hymn of praise for things that were gone and of hope for those that were to come. Spain had withdrawn her objections to the transfer of Louisiana and our friendship with European nations was undisturbed. There was no need to augment the military forces; affairs were going well in the Mediterranean, and the building of gunboats was in the course of execution. The finances had fulfilled all expectation. There would be a balance for the redemption of the funded debt, notwithstanding the extraordinary expenditures for Louisiana and for the extinction of the claims of British citizens against those of the United States. In a few weeks, Jefferson betook himself to Monticello. From that time on, scarcely a month passed away without some untoward happening on one side of the Atlantic or the other. In January, 1809, he practically abdicated in favor of James Madison, his elected successor, and in March fled from Washington, leaving the new President for six years to bear the full weight of misfortune, and then, for the rest of his term, to enjoy a popularity that was quite as undeserved as was most of the ignominy that he had so patiently borne.

Jefferson's misfortunes were partly due to himself, but they were more especially the result of circumstances over which he had or could have little control. His idealism and the actualities of American political life had no continuing points of contact. In the beginning, as is the case with every President, he had enjoyed the ardent support of those who looked to him for power and place. He had done something toward rewarding them, but not as much as they hoped. When he announced that political parity had been reached and that there were no more places to be parcelled out, they lost their interest. He had also grievously disappointed those who had looked to him as the incarnation of republicanism as applied to the individual and to the States. In a moment of great irritation, he had declared that undelegated power could be conceded to no man or body of men on earth; but he had not defined undelegated. Some years earlier, he had advised Washington as to the limits of executive functions. According to this opinion,[1] the President was "the sole competent judge" as to what foreign missions should be established, the Senate's power being limited to the confirmation or rejection of nominees. The recognition of revolutionists was an executive act, he maintained, and it was for the commander-in-chief to prescribe the purposes for which armies should be used. And, finally, the legislative branch could not refuse to carry into effect treaties which had been negotiated by the President and ratified with the advice and consent of the Senate. Of course, Jefferson's supporters had been ignorant of this interpretation of executive affairs. Some of them were amazed when he, with Gallatin and Madison, established what was practically an executive

[1] See "Appendix" to *Speech of Hon. Henry Cabot Lodge, of Massachusetts,* in the Senate of the United States, *January 5, 1904.*

directory. Ostensibly, he drew a sharp line of demarcation between the exercise of executive and legislative functions; but he repeatedly forced his will on Senators and Representatives as amply as Hamilton had ever done. Among his former followers, who had not shifted their points of view upon coming into political prosperity, were John Randolph[1] and his scanty following, William Duane and his democratic friends, and William B. Giles, Senator from Virginia.[2] These were soon joined by malcontents of one kind or another, like the Smiths of Maryland. The recalcitrants within the camp were not numerous; but they were sufficient in number and in strength to give Jefferson and his friends many an unhappy hour.

Randolph's rebellion became patent to the congressional world in 1805 in the Florida affair. As a species of retributive justice for the violation of the Constitution in the procurement of Louisiana and the immorality of receiving stolen goods from the greatest cutthroat of modern times, the limits of the purchase proved to be other than Jefferson had expected. He had desired the Floridas with a bit of nearby Louisiana; he bought Louisiana without any Floridas and without that part of Louisiana that the Spaniards were ruling as a portion of West Florida. Jefferson turned to France for aid to consummate his purpose, to

[1] No adequate collection of John Randolph's writings has ever been printed, nor is there a memoir of him commensurate to his services. Henry Adams's biography in the *American Statesmen* series is an admirable and unsympathetic study. H. A. Garland's *Life of John Randolph* (2 vols., New York, 1850) is a good specimen of an old time southern biography; Powhatan Bouldin in 1878 printed at Danville, Va., a volume entitled *Home Reminiscences of John Randolph of Roanoke;* and a volume entitled *Letters of John Randolph, to a Young Relative* was printed at Philadelphia in 1834. Of the four, the last named brings one nearest to the man.

[2] In 1811, Giles had come to look with scorn on the Gallatin-Jeffersonian system of debt-reduction. He declared that cutting the debt in halves from eighty millions to forty "had never been felt by society. It had produced no sensible effect upon the common intercourse amongst men in their pecuniary affairs." *Annals of Congress*, 12th Cong., 1st Sess., Part i, pp. 51, 84, etc. See also Dice R. Anderson's *William Branch Giles.*

Napoleon and Talleyrand — to two of the most unscrupulous and far-seeing men who ever lived. They understood Jefferson and his problem much better than he ever did and proceeded to make whatever they could of his desire. Imperialism and militarism were far afield from Jefferson's political and social theories; but the necessity of French aid and consent in the gaining of any part of the Floridas unconsciously tinged his every move and powerfully affected those of his successor. The French side of the balance was weighted from beginning to end, for to break with France was to abandon all hope of acquiring any part of the Floridas. In 1805, Jefferson hit upon the scheme of repeating the Louisiana stroke. In open message, he breathed war on Spain. In a confidential communication, he asked for a secret vote of two million dollars. Randolph had acquiesced in the earlier bit of jugglery and, indeed, had helped it on. Now he seized this occasion to break with the administration. If the President wanted money, let him say so openly. The President had said that war was in the air. As chairman of the Committee of Ways and Means, Randolph proposed to vote money for the protection of the southwest frontier. Jefferson got his two millions, but they did him no good. Randolph was dismissed from the Ways and Means Committee at the first opportunity, and his faithful follower, Nathaniel Macon, the Speaker, was relegated to private place.

Jefferson's domestic difficulties were trifling in comparison with those that befell in connection with international affairs, — and for these he was only partly responsible. In 1793, the European war, which up to that time had been confined to the European continent, extended to Great Britain. It became world-wide and took on a maritime aspect. From that year until 1812, with the exception of eighteen months (October, 1801–May, 1803), fighting was continuous, and during all that time the United States was the most prosperous neutral ocean-carrier. American tonnage employed in foreign trade increased from 363,110 tons in 1791 to 669,921 in 1800, and to nearly 1,000,000 in 1810. In the same years imports and exports grew marvellously, because the United States had come to be the foremost trans-Atlantic commerce carrier. With the extension of the war to Great Britain in 1793, direct commerce between France and her colonies was at first greatly hampered and then practically destroyed and, after Spain joined the other powers under Napoleon's rule in the conflict with Great Britain, direct trade between her home ports and those of her colonies also ceased. The United States, owing to her situation and to the enterprise and vigor of her shipowners and seamen, became the entrepot for the carrying on of this vast commerce in subtropical products. England by colonial blockades sought to put an end to this traffic, and failing to do much in that way, resuscitated an old rule that is always referred to as the Rule of War of 1756.[1] This forbade a neutral to prosecute in time of war a trade that was closed to him in time of peace. It was easy enough to say that carrying on this commerce was to perform an unneutral act, because thereby the United States increased the power of resistance of a belligerent. On the other hand, it is easy to point out that while the Rule of 1756 might or might not be a part of international law, as the United States was the only trans-Atlantic neutral and was the only commerce carrier to possess no colony, it was a rule that worked only one way so far as she was concerned and, therefore, was not equitable. Moreover it was a rule that could not apply rigidly to American commerce

---

[1] See J. B. Moore's *International Law Digest*, vii, 383.

with the French West Indies, for in time of peace a certain restricted commerce with these islands and also with a few Spanish American ports had been allowed. One way out of this particular difficulty was for American vessels to bring West Indian products of French and Spanish origin to United States ports, pay the duties there levied, and transship the goods by the same or other vessels to France or to Spain, receiving a drawback of the import duties at the time of exportation. It soon became customary, instead of paying the duty, to give a bond for its payment, paying down only enough money to cover the difference between the drawback and the nominal amount of the duty; and often the goods were carried across the Atlantic by the same ship that had brought them from the West Indies.[1] In a similar way, commerce was carried on from France and Spain to the United States and thence to the West Indies. A great carrying trade was developed, some sixty millions of the increase in importations and exportations being fairly attributable to this one cause alone. During the greater part of this time also, staple North American products — flour, tobacco, and cotton — sold at Liverpool, Hamburg, and Amsterdam for approximately double what they cost at Philadelphia, Richmond, and Charleston.[2] And this was

[1] November 24, 1801, Gallatin sent a circular letter to the collectors of the customs, stating that information had been received that a practice prevails at some ports of permitting vessels to enter, of securing the duties on their cargoes, and afterwards allowing them to proceed to foreign ports without unlading the merchandise. He informed them that this practice was contrary to law and must not be permitted except in case of necessity.

[2] Trade with Hamburg grew rapidly in these years. In 1791 only 35 vessels entered at that port from the United States, in 1794 the number rose to 91 and in 1799 to 192. When Hamburg was closed to American commerce in 1804 the vessels sought the nearby Danish port of Tönning, no less than 119 entering there in 1809. See E. Baasch's "Beiträge zur Geschichte der Handelsbeziehungen zwischen Hamburg und Amerika" in *Hamburgische Festschrift zur Erinnerung an die Entdeckung Amerika's*, vol. i, no. 3, pp. 67, 91. I have to thank Professor C. H. Hull for calling my attention to this work.

As to Amsterdam, no less than 160 vessels arrived there from the United States in 1801. On the return voyage they carried valuable cargoes — 100,000 florins sometimes — Dutch gin, Ger-

also a great excitation to commission dealers and forwarders.

It must not be supposed that the belligerents stood calmly by and permitted this commerce to be carried on without hindrances of all kinds. The British seized ships carrying provisions to the Islands and to France and the government of the French Directory undertook to put pressure on Great Britain by seizing vessels bound to and from her harbors. It was these endeavors that brought about the spoliations and international conflicts that have been related in preceding chapters. George Cabot, who was a much sounder merchant than he was politician, deplored the over-protection of American shipping. The more risk the neutral vessel ran in crossing the Atlantic, the greater would be the price that could be charged for her cargo, if she succeeded in making port. The real key to profit, he declared, was the difference in price between what the goods could be bought for in America and sold for in Europe, — the cost of the ship being rather an incidental factor. When spoliations, sequestrations, and confiscations were at their height, the merchant made money if one vessel in three landed her cargo. Moreover, the greater the peril of capture, the higher would be the freight. Orders in Council and decrees seem to have been welcomed by the adventurous traffickers of those years.

Sentiment played a large part in dictating the discussions and acts of that day as well as of our own. The sayings "The flag covers the cargo," "Free ships make free goods," "The freedom of the seas," and others of the kind have given a false glint to the whole debate. Property that is rightfully spoken of as private and neutral, while on the

man ironware, French cutlery, and odds and ends from all over Europe. This commerce rapidly declined after 1801 and still more rapidly after 1803.

land in a neutral country, ceases to be such the moment
it finds itself on the ocean on the way to a belligerent, no
matter how directly or indirectly it may go. On the contrary, such property partakes of a semi-military character, however inoffensive it may seem in itself to be, provided it can in any way be used for the support of civilians
engaged in supplying military forces with recruits, munitions, or food.[1] A neutral ocean commerce carrier engaged
in the transportation of goods to a belligerent in ninety-
nine cases out of a hundred is giving aid and comfort to one
country at the cost of lives and treasure to the other, and
in so far is performing an un-neutral act.

The ten years ending in 1805, with Jefferson's first term,
marking well enough the life of Jay's Treaty, had been singularly harmonious so far as the relations between the
United States and Great Britain were concerned, especially
during the years of our quasi conflict with France. The
British had acted arbitrarily every now and then, but most
of the matters in dispute had been smoothed out or arranged
by Rufus King, one of the most effective representatives
the United States has ever had at London. Before leaving
his post in 1803, he negotiated three conventions. One of
these, as to impressments, at the last moment failed of acceptance at London.[2] A second was actually signed, but
being ratified only in part by the Senate was refused further
consideration by the British government.[3] The third convention put an end to the long drawn out contest over the
payment of debts due by Americans to British creditors.
This provided that the United States should pay a lump sum
of nearly three million dollars in satisfaction of all these

---

[1] See Mahan's *War of 1812*, i, 144.
One branch of the subject is treated
in J. F. W. Schlegel's *Neutral Rights;
or an Impartial Examination of the Right*
of Search of Neutral Vessels under Convoy
(Philadelphia, 1801).

[2] See below, p. 363.

[3] See Note II at end of chapter.

claims, and further provided that the amount that had been awarded by a commission under Jay's Treaty to Americans for British spoliations should likewise be paid. According to Oliver Wolcott, this convention [1] was ratified by the President and Senate because claims amounting to eight and a half million dollars had been filed by British creditors against inhabitants of the State of Virginia. With the ending of this acrimonious dispute, there would seem to have been good ground for continuing harmonious relations between the two countries. It fell out otherwise, for British ship-owners brought an ever-increasing pressure upon the ministry to put an end to the growing American commerce that seemed to them to be jeopardizing their financial prosperity.

Washington and Jefferson had repeatedly warned their countrymen not to become entangled with foreign countries; but now it seemed impossible to keep out of the sweep of world-wide war. Napoleon realized to the full that the one hope for permanent peace was to conquer England, and to add the British kingdoms with attendant

---

[1] See *American State Papers, Foreign Relations*, ii, 382–428, and King's *Rufus King*, iv, 17, 25, 54, 92.

Wolcott compiled the following table as to the claims of British creditors against American debtors (*British Influence on the Affairs of the United States, Proved and Explained*, Boston, 1804, p. 12).

	Sterling
The claims exhibited against the *New-England* states amounted to . .	£23,000
The states of *New-York* and *New-Jersey*, ...	180,000
The states of *Pennsylvania* and *Delaware*, ...	15,000
The whole amount of claims against the states north of *Maryland*, amounted therefore to no more than	£218,000

	Sterling
While those against the five southern states, amounted to	£3,869,000

Of this 8,500,000 dollars, or one half of the whole amount, was claimed of the single State of *Virginia*.

See also J. B. Moore's *Digest of International Arbitrations*, i, 271–298. King explained that under the convention those having "what is now a bona fide Debt, that is what is a legal subject" will not depend upon the interpretation of treaties, but will stand on the footing of any other case at law. What he called a full and exact account of the whole matter is in *American State Papers, Foreign Relations*, ii, 390.

colonies, navies, and fleets of merchantmen to his own wide-embracing sway. Then would there be peace, — a peace in which all regions of the earth and all its peoples would be submissive to the least nod of the Emperor. In the way of the realization of this dream was the sea-power of England. The invasion and conquest of the British Islands was the only way to universal dominion. Only thirty miles across the Channel was the British strand; a thousand flat-boats issuing from Boulougne and near-by harbors might row and drift across this watery space and disembark one hundred thousand men with Napoleon at their head on English soil, — not very far, perhaps, from the very spot where William, the Norman, had landed, nearly seven hundred and fifty years before. The boats were ready and the soldiers waiting, when Nelson at Trafalgar on October 21, 1805, put an end to these imaginings. Baffled by the winds, the waves, and the men of the ocean, Napoleon turned eastwardly and at Austerlitz (December 2, 1805) made himself master of Austria and of all Europe, except Prussia and Russia. Britain's one hope of saving herself from a similar fate and in that of saving the world depended upon the preservation of a vigorous and profitable commercial life. Up to 1800, she had thriven on war, for the policy of the Directory, in levying commercial war upon her, had ended in the destruction of the French mercantile marine and in the crippling of French manufacture and trade. The two great essentials of English maritime supremacy were the naval stores of the Baltic and the tropical products of the Indies. The handling of these and the tobacco of Virginia formed the backbone of her commercial life, which was fed by the products of her factories. With the proceeds of her woolens and hardware, she was able to pay for her imports and have something over. It was under these circumstances that the United States began to interfere with her trans-Atlantic commerce and also with that to the Continent and to the East. British ship-owners became more and more alarmed. They found an effective advocate in James Stephen; he published in 1805, a remarkable tract on trade under the title of "War in Disguise; or The Frauds of the Neutral Flags."[1] In this he argued that the Americans, by prosecuting the carrying trade between colonies belonging to belligerent powers and the mother countries, had been guilty of unfriendly acts. They had taken part in the war on the side of Britain's enemies, had committed breaches of neutrality, and should be treated accordingly. At almost the same time that this book appeared and some three months before the battle of Trafalgar, at the moment of greatest peril, England shifted her policy toward America. Her admiralty court declared that to give a neutral carrier immunity from the operation of the Rule of 1756, there must be more than an artificial breaking of the voyage, that the intent of the voyage was a fact of principal importance.[2] The meaning of this decision seemed

---

[1] See also Nathaniel Atcheson's *American Encroachments on British Rights; . . . A Defence of the Shipping Interest* (London, 1808, containing many interesting papers, printed in whole or in part); Alexander Baring's *An Inquiry into the Causes and Consequences of the Orders in Council* (London, 1808); and Macall Medford's *Oil without Vinegar, and Dignity without Pride: or British, American, and West-India Interests Considered* (London, 1807).

[2] The case of the *Essex:* Robinson's *Reports of Cases . . . in the High Court of Admiralty*, v, 368–372. Previous cases were those of the *Polly* and the *Immanuel*, also reported in *ibid*. Discussions of the new policy are Madison's *Examination of the British Doctrine, which subjects to capture a Neutral Trade, not open in Time of Peace* (published anonymously in 1806, and reprinted in Hunt's edition of *Writings of Madison*, vii, 204); *Speech of the Hon. J. Randolph, . . . on a motion for the non-importation of British merchandise*. With *An Introduction by the Author of "War in Disguise"* (London, 1806); *American Arguments for British Rights; being a republication of The Celebrated Letters of Phocion* [*William L. Smith*] *on the subject of Neutral Trade* (Charleston, S. C. and London, 1806). In this connection may also be read the "Memorials" from the merchants and traders of Baltimore, Philadelphia, and Boston presented to Congress in January and February, 1806. Smith points out that Madison in various writings had been rather disingenuous in his treatment of Sir William Scott's decisions and that the distinction between the doctrines propounded in the deci-

somewhat shadowy, but there was no doubt whatever of a sudden increase in the activity of British cruisers and in condemnations by admiralty courts throughout the British Empire. Such precipitancy in confiscation without notice can hardly be described by any other word than robbery, no matter what the necessity, no matter what the technical rights and wrongs, — and it may be said that such treatment of neutrals was unusual for Britain.

> "While Europe's mad powers o'er creation are ranging,
>   Regardless of right, with their bloodhounds of war;
> Their kingdoms — their empires, distracted and changing;
>   Their murders and ruins resounding afar," [1]

what should be the part of the United States? Should it be war, armed war, with Great Britain or with France — with one or with both? Or was there any expedient by which compulsion could be had without actual shedding of blood? In 1793, when war with England had seemed on the point of breaking out, Jefferson, who was then Secretary of State, and Madison, then the foremost man in the House of Representatives, sought to put pressure on England by commercial restriction. Jefferson recalled the success of the non-importation agreements in securing the repeal of the Stamp Act and the Townshend Acts. He prepared an elaborate report on commerce [2] and instigated Madison to bring forward in Congress a measure restricting British trade with the United States, — which was defeated in the Senate by the casting vote of Vice-President

sions as to the *Polly* and the *Essex* did not exist. Madison, he states, had omitted the words "for his own use" in repeating Scott's language in the earlier of these cases, and thereby gave a wholly wrong construction to the decision in the case of the *Essex*. See *ibid.*, pp. 57, 72.

[1] From poem entitled "Freedom and Peace, or The Voice of America" printed in *The Reporter* of Lexington, Kentucky, October 3, 1808. This poem had been awarded a prize medal by the Philadelphia Military Association.

[2] *Writings of Jefferson* (Ford) vi, 470–484.

Adams.[1] Such a policy would work well in many ways, he thought, and "introduce between nations another umpire than arms. It would relieve us too from the risks & the horrors of cutting throats."[2] When the British pressure[3] began to be severely felt in the winter of 1805–1806, Jefferson reverted to the policy of commercial restriction as being a most eligible weapon to bring her to terms. The precise connection between the President's House and the Capitol in 1806 is extremely vague, but vagueness of information does not in any way imply absence of connection between Jefferson and a law passed by Congress. On April 18, 1806, he approved the Non-Importation Act[4] that brought the United States into the commercial warfare that was then raging in Europe. It provided that after the 15th day of November next, it should not be lawful to import certain enumerated goods of British manufacture into the United States, from any part of the British Empire or from anywhere else. The law was plainly designed as a club to be used by the American negotiators in London. Upon their representations, the time was further extended and the act did not go into operation until December, 1807.

William Pitt died on one of the last days of January, 1806. A new government was formed comprising men of different parties and known in history as the "Ministry of All the Talents." Charles James Fox, whose friendship for America had always been pronounced and always in-

[1] Learned's "Casting Votes of the Vice-President" in *American Historical Review*, xx, 574.

[2] Jefferson to Madison, March, 1793; *Writings of Jefferson* (Ford) vi, 192.

[3] Several cases of capture by British cruisers are given in the *Memorial of the Merchants of the Town of Boston, February 3, 1806*. One ship, the *Indus*, was captured while on the point of entering Boston harbor, and was con-demned because of the instructions of the owners directing the captain to insert the words "and Embden" in the manifest after the ship had come within the port. She was condemned on the ground that she was bound for a port included in Fox's blockade. See also Christopher Gore to Madison, November 18, 1805 in *Monthly Anthology*, iii, Appendix, p. 18.

[4] See Note III at the end of chapter.

effective, had charge of foreign affairs. To him Monroe
went to seek justice for America. He found Fox cordial
and friendly; but, in 1806 as in 1783, the ship-owners soon
got his ear and his good-will, such as it was, went for little.
To meet infringements of neutral obligations by Danes
and Dutchmen, to quiet America's objections to the enforcement of the Rule of 1756, and also to satisfy their
own supporters, the British government declared the coast
of continental Europe from the mouth of the German river
Ems to the great French naval arsenal at Brest to be blockaded: but for the time being, the blockade would be effective only between Havre and Ostend.[1] Since the
battle of Trafalgar, French privateers had distressed British commerce at sea and Napoleon's agents had interfered
with it on land, so that the process of strangulation of
British trade had visibly begun. On the other hand, the
substitution of British manufactures for those of France
throughout the Continent was steadily progressing. Napoleon decided to meet the issue raised by the British
blockade in his own imperial fashion. In the preceding
October, he had crushed Prussian military opposition to
his will on the battlefield of Jena. November 21, 1806,
by the Berlin Decree, he declared the British Islands to be
in a state of blockade, prohibited all intercourse with them,
and decreed that all merchandise coming from them was
good prize and so was any vessel that sought to evade his
orders by means of false papers or otherwise. It was while
affairs were in this trim, but before knowledge of the Berlin Decree reached England, that Monroe and his colleague,

---

[1] See Note III for a synopsis of the
Decrees and Orders through 1807.
Englishmen were then as much irritated by the devices employed to evade
the precepts of international law by
Danes and Dutchmen as they were by
those of Americans. See *The Mysteries
of Neutralization . . . By John Brown
of Great Yarmouth* (London, 1806).

William Pinkney, negotiated a treaty with the British government; but just before signing the instrument news of Napoleon's action reached London.

The appointment of William Pinkney as a colleague to Monroe is veiled in Jeffersonian mistiness.[1] Pinkney was a Maryland lawyer of high reputation and had already represented the United States at London on one of the commissions appointed under Jay's Treaty. He was a mild Federalist and it is sometimes thought that the appointment was made to conciliate that party. In announcing to Monroe the coming of a colleague, Madison laid stress upon Monroe's expressed desire to return home; but the latter seems to have felt that there was some reproach in the mere fact of giving him a colleague. At a later time, when the whole venture was shrouded in failure, some people argued that Jefferson and Madison had purposely bound Monroe with impossible restrictions [2] and had provided him with a running mate to diminish his chances as a presidential candidate, if the negotiation should unexpectedly turn out well. This explanation seems to be somewhat far-fetched and demands an abatement of the affection that Jefferson felt for Monroe at almost every other time in their joint lives. As to binding him and Pinkney with impossible instructions, that is unquestionable. They were required to lay down certain principles as affecting international relations and to get these recognized by the medium of a treaty. At London, the Americans found

---

[1] Henry Adams (*History of the United States*, iii, 169) found a letter from Samuel Smith dated April 1, 1806 to his brother-in-law, Wilson Cary Nicholas, giving the impression that the Smiths wished to go to England for this negotiation and that Jefferson, of his own motion, substituted William Pinkney for General Smith. There are two biographies of Pinkney, one by his nephew, the Rev. William Pinkney, D.D., New York, 1853; the other by Henry Wheaton, Boston, 1826, neither very satisfying.

[2] Madison's instructions to Monroe and Pinkney are in *American State Papers, Foreign Relations*, iii, 119.

themselves in a predicament, for the only principle that
affected England at the moment was that of self-preservation, — the necessity that knows no law above or below,
divine or human, and in the light of which paper agreements
have no meaning. The authorities at London would have
gladly adopted any one or two of several lines of compromise to soothe America; but as to yielding anything on
principle, they were absolutely steadfast. The life of
England depended on manufacturing and trade, and her
safety upon the forcible employment of all British-born
sea-faring men in the national defence. In the outcome,
Monroe and Pinkney broke their instructions, as American
negotiators generally did in those days, and signed a treaty
containing a number of compromises. Every one of them
improved the actual position of the United States, but did
not abandon the principles underlying British ocean tyranny.
In the course of the negotiations, the Americans informed
the British commissioners that they were acting against
their instructions [1] and that their government could not be
pledged to ratification. The treaty was signed at London,
December 31, 1806.[2] By that time, the Berlin Decree
had reached England. At the moment of signing, the
British negotiators handed to the Americans a note to the
effect that, owing to the aggressions of Napoleon, the British government would not ratify the treaty unless the
"United States, by its conduct or assurances, will have
given security to His Majesty that it will not submit to
such innovations on the established system of maritime
law." [3]

[1] Monroe and Pinkney to Madison, November 11, 1806, see *American State Papers, Foreign Relations*, iii, 139; see also Jefferson's Seventh Annual Message, October 27, 1807, *Annals of Congress*, 10th Cong., 1st Sess., vol. i, 15.

[2] *American State Papers, Foreign Relations*, iii, 147; *Annals of Congress*, 10 Cong., 1st Sess., vol. ii, 2523.

[3] *American State Papers, Foreign Relations*, iii, 152.

The American government was absolutely free to accept or reject the treaty as best suited its purposes. Jefferson did not even think it worth while to submit it to the Senate.[1] He pigeon-holed the instrument and Madison wrote to the commissioners at London that no treaty would be ratified which did not contain a guarantee acceptable to America as to impressment. The over-attentive, not to say eavesdropping, Timothy Pickering gives the impression that Jefferson thought it mattered little whether we had or had not a treaty with Great Britain, because "the measures pursued & pursuing by Bonaparte are of such a nature, that the Government of England cannot much longer exist."

It could hardly be expected that England would stand quietly by, while a power that could not keep a battle fleet on the ocean, declared her coasts blockaded. On January 7, 1807, the London government issued an Order in Council prohibiting the coasting trade of France and her allies to neutral shipping. This order bore severely on American commerce, as it was not always easy for a ship to find a homeward cargo at the port where the outward cargo could be disposed of to good advantage. For the first half of 1807, Napoleon was employed in bringing Russia to terms. Having accomplished this by the battles of Eylau and Friedland,

[1] For the administration's view of this negotiation, see Jefferson to Monroe, March 21, 1807 and to James Bowdoin, April 2, 1807 in *Writings* (Ford ed.) ix, 35, 39; and Madison to Monroe and Pinkney, February 3, 1807 and May 20, 1807 in *American State Papers, Foreign Relations*, iii, 153, 166; and *Writings of Madison* (Hunt ed.) vii, 395, 407.

Monroe's defence of the negotiation is to be found in his letter to Madison of February 28, 1808 in *American State Papers, Foreign Relations*, iii, 173. It is reprinted in a separate publication entitled *Mr. Monroe's Letter on the Rejected Treaty, between the United States and Great Britain ; concluded by Messrs. Monroe and Pinkney. Also the Treaty Itself* (Portland, 1813). See also a pamphlet entitled *The British Treaty*. It is supposed to have been printed in Philadelphia in 1807, and was reprinted at London in 1808, with an Appendix of State papers. This tract is dedicated to "Those Members of Congress who have the sense to perceive and the spirit to pursue the true interests of their country." For a hostile British view, see *Observations on the American Treaty, in Eleven Letters. First published in "The Sun" under the signature of Decius* (London, 1808).

he conferred with Czar Alexander on a raft anchored in the
River Niemen at Tilsit (June 25, 1807). There, the two
emperors came to an agreement obliging the Czar to enforce
Napoleon's commercial system in all parts of his dominions
and to aid in imposing it on all Europe. Up to this time
the Berlin Decree had not been enforced but, on Napoleon's
return to Paris, seizures and confiscations became the
order of the day, not only in France, but throughout continental Europe. In November, England replied by more
Orders in Council, prohibiting all trade with ports from which
the British flag was excluded, unless a vessel first called at
a British port, paid duties upon her cargo, and obtained a
fresh clearance. Napoleon promptly rejoined by a decree
issued at Milan (December 17, 1807) threatening confiscation to every ship that had been visited by an English naval
officer, had paid any duty to the British government, or had
come from or was bound to any British port anywhere in
the world. To sum up the whole matter, no American
vessel could go to a French port, without first paying tribute
to a British custom-house to the amount of three cents on
each pound of tobacco, sixteen cents on each pound of cotton, and two dollars on each barrel of flour; and if the
French got hold of an American vessel that had done this,
or had even been stopped by a British ship, or had any
British goods on board she was liable to capture and condemnation.[1]

---

[1] This summary is paraphrased from
an electioneering address of John G.
Jackson which was probably written
by his brother-in-law, James Madison.
Two cases will serve to show the spirit
of the execution of the French decrees.
One of these was of the ship *Margaret*
which sailed from Boston for Tunis in
1809 with a general cargo, including
pepper, silks, and brocades from India.
She was captured by a French privateer
and taken to Naples where her captain
found twenty-six other American merchantmen awaiting the action of the
French prize authorities. There was
so much doubt as to whether the pepper
and silks actually came from British
India that the ship was released on
condition of paying to the captors one-
half of the proceeds of the cargo;
("Dane Papers" in Massachusetts Historical Society). The other case is that

One of the most astonishing spectacles of these years was the way in which belligerent war vessels and fleets made use of American harbors and bays and patrolled the coasts of the United States. For weeks at a time, British men-of-war, singly or in groups, lay off the bar at Sandy Hook, stopping vessels bound in or out and firing upon them in case they did not at once obey orders to heave to. Some of these warships came to New York at the request of Thomas Barclay, the British Consul General there. He had understood the president of the Marine Insurance Company of that city to request him to take measures to protect American ships going in and out from predatory corsairs that appeared on the coast as soon as British vessels left them "unprotected," to use Barclay's phrase. He was an American Loyalist, a man of ability, and, from the language of his letters, appears to have thought that the British had been successful in the Revolutionary War. The captains of British war vessels likewise looked upon America as under their protection, or as helpless.[1] When short of provisions the patrolling vessels would run into the nearest port and remain there until they had procured food, wood, and water, or had made whatever repairs they needed. One captain undertook to punish a shipwright whom Barclay had sent off to him, because he had preached desertion to the crew.[2] Another asserted that the privileges

of the *Victory*, which sailed from New York for Cherbourg in 1807. She was seized by an English privateer, carried into Plymouth, England, was released, and permitted to resume her voyage. She was condemned in France because of having entered this British port; L. Goldsmith's *Exposition of the Conduct of France towards America: Illustrated by Cases decided in the Council of Prizes in Paris* (London, 1810) p. 51.

[1] Captain Basil Hall's *Fragments of Voyages and Travels* (Philadelphia, 1831) i, chap. xi; reproduced in 1895 as *Voyages and Travels*. See also *Selections from the Correspondence of Thomas Barclay*, edited by George L. Rives (New York, 1894). On the activity of the British cruisers in pursuing French naval ships, see pp. 164, 192 and the index under Didon, Ambuscade, Cybèle, Eole, Poursuivant.

[2] On one occasion, in 1808, the British brig-of-war *Sandwich*, on being ordered out of the Savannah River,

of his ship as a man-of-war did not stop with her bulwarks, but extended for a cable's length around her. The British pursued French vessels into territorial waters, captured them within the three mile limit,[1] battered and burned a French warship when stranded on the Carolina coast,[2] and anchored inside of the Capes of the Chesapeake while blockading a French vessel higher up the bay. In short, they paid no attention to international rules and very little to the king's instructions regulating the capture of prizes.[3] The French were hardly behind the English in their disregard of neutral rights, whenever they had the opportunity, and there are instances of outrages by French privateers that were fully as bad as anything that was done by any British cruiser. The difference was that when the French seized a deserter from one of their own war vessels,[4] they were not likely to take an American-born citizen, and as to the plunderings, so few French vessels sailed the seas, that these were necessarily few in number.[5]

Britain's tyranny on the sea was not confined to the regulation of commerce, but extended to the seizure of seamen from the decks of American vessels and their imprisonment

fired on a pilot boat and committed other misdeeds; see E. J. Harden's *Life of George M. Troup*, 44 and note.

[1] J. Stewart's *Cases determined in the Court of Vice-Admiralty at Halifax*, 101. In 1803, just before war broke out, Captain Douglass of the British ship *Boston* removed a sailor from a French vessel in Hampton Roads, according to a report made to Albert Gallatin.

[2] See Madison to George H. Rose, March 5, 1808.

[3] Dr. Croke, the British admiralty judge at Halifax, declared in one case that "not one of His Majesty's instructions relating to proceedings upon prize have been observed."

[4] In 1806, the French admiral Willaumez wrote to his minister at Washington, General Turreau, that he had just apprehended four seamen, deserters from the *Valeureuse* frigate whom he found on board an American brig and suggested that Turreau should make the American government "pay down a compensation for this misconduct in seducing" French seamen. The letter in English is printed in John Lowell's *Peace without Dishonour — War without Hope*, 21. For another instance of this, see *Columbian Centinel* for December 23, 1807.

[5] See the case of the ship *Othello* in the *Farmers' Register*, September 15, 1807. She was boarded by an officer from a French war vessel while at anchor in Chesapeake Bay, and was ransacked by the crew of a privateer from Guadaloupe, also within the Capes.

among the crews of British men-of-war from which there was no release except by death or by the cessation of maritime conflicts.[1] The British naval service was a purgatory on the seas owing to the brutality of the officers, to the wretched food, and to the crowded and unsanitary quarters of the ships. The British army was composed of men hired for the purpose, the navy was manned by conscription, which took the form of the seizure of all available men when necessity demanded. In the stress of the Napoleonic Wars, with the blockades of Brest and Toulon, the defence of the Channel, and the destruction of privateers and their places of refuge, the demand for seamen was great and the supply unusually limited. One reason for this was the comparatively high wages and good conditions of employment on American vessels, which had been necessary to attract men from the land to the sea and from the forecastles of British ships.[2]

As the years went by, the demand for seamen in the British navy grew and the supply diminished. The case became so desperate that the government opened the forecastles of British merchantmen to neutral sailors of any nation, and did not enquire closely as to their nativity. American ships not only competed with British for the carrying of trans-Atlantic commerce, they also offered an

---

[1] See Mahan's admirable historical summary of the impressment question in his *War of 1812*, i, 114–127.

[2] In 1803, Nelson estimated that in the first part of the great war 42,000 seamen deserted from the fleet. (J. R. Hutchinson's *The Press-Gang*, 326, from a memorandum in the "Admiralty Records"). It was said at the time that between 30,000 and 40,000 British seamen — at one time or another within this period — shipped on American vessels, public or private. February 29, 1808, the Secretary of State reported to Congress that 19,139 seamen had received certificates of citizenship from the collectors of the customs and been registered as American seamen, or an average of 9568 in each of these years. To this number should be added 1425 for the seamen authorized to be employed in the naval service, or 10,993 for each of these years. The *Columbian Centinel* of September 24, 1808 gives the total number of so-called American seamen as 65,000, of whom 48,000 belonged to New England and New York.

asylum to British seamen deserting from merchant vessels or men-of-war. American naturalization was easy. Any one after a few months residence could secure State citizenship papers legitimately. Soon the demand for these documents outgrew the supply which was increased by various means : farmers and laborers took them out and sold them to ship brokers at the nearest seaport for a dollar apiece who, in turn, matched them as well as they might with deserting British sailors. There was, undoubtedly, a great deal of fraud, but the possession of a certificate of citizenship seemed to be the only practicable mode of identification of American seamen. The right of British naval authorities to seize British-born sailors wherever found went back far behind the American Revolution, but the colonists had been exempted from its operation by an act of Queen Anne's time. There are few recorded cases of impressment in America before the Revolution and there was a feeling of something akin to horror at the practice as being alien to the rights and liberties of mankind.

The British government accepted the independence of the United States as redeeming from the press-gang all those who were American citizens in 1783, whether born within the limits of the United States or not, but refused to recognize any change of allegiance made since that time. There was nothing new or strange in the idea of indelible allegiance; it had been maintained by Chief Justice Ellsworth in the Circuit Court at Hartford in 1799.[1] More-

---

[1] The case of the United States against Isaac Williams is in Francis Wharton's *State Trials of the United States*, 652–658, to this is appended a long historical note; Van Santvoord's *Sketches of the Lives, Times and Judicial Services of the Chief Justices* (2nd ed. Albany, 1882) pp. 305–310. The case is summarized in W. G. Brown's *Oliver Ellsworth*, 257–260. It was not until years later that the United States by law recognized the right of an American-born citizen to renounce his allegiance. See also Kent's *Commentaries on American Law* (ed. 1873) ii, 45 ; John Lowell's *Review of a Treatise on Expatriation by George Hay, Esquire* (Boston, 1814), p. 33.

over, there was no doubt of the right of the British authorities to seize their own subjects on American merchant vessels within British harbors and within gunshot of British coasts. Whether they were equally at liberty to remove them from the decks of American merchantmen on the high seas, was a more delicate matter. A belligerent cruiser had a perfect right to stop a neutral merchant vessel to ascertain its true character and search it for contraband or for goods carried contrary to the Rule of War of 1756. Had the boarding officer an equal right to summon the crew and arrest a fellow subject and remove him to his own ship for service there? The matter was further complicated by the fact that Americans and British looked very much alike, had very much the same manners, and spoke very much the same language. It was difficult to tell whether a particular sailor was British born or American born, and his certificate of citizenship [1] was not of much use, when, as frequently happened, he had lost it or had fogotten the precise details as to name and appearance given in the document. In view of the well-known frauds practised in this matter and the need of hands on most British cruisers, it was entirely within the course of human nature that a British boarding officer should regard as British or Irish any well-set-up sea-dog who did not talk through his nose, or say "paise"

[1] Below is a copy of a "certificate" preserved in the "Pickering Papers" vol. 9, 33.

(Office copy)   Woolwich July 13th 1798.
   These may certify that Thomas Snell Junior of Woolwich in the County of Lincoln, State of Massachusetts, was born in said Town of Woolwich Height about five feet seven inches, light complection, dark eyes, about twenty three years of age.

Jaˢ Winship
                Minister of Woolwich
Abner Wade   ⎫
David Gilmore ⎰
        Select men of Woolwich

This certifies that the above said Thomas Snell Junior's birth is on the Town Records agreeable as above.
        Attest
        Joshua Farnham Town Clerk
A true copy from the original filed in my office
        In testimony whereof I have hereto set my hand and Official Seal at Philadelphia the 31ˢᵗ day of July 1798
        Timothy Pickering
        Secretary of State.

for peas, order him into the boat alongside, and strike him down if he offered the slightest resistance. The practice was an abominable one; if the searcher had found a bale of supposedly contraband goods on board, he would have sent the ship into port where the question would have been decided by an admiralty judge; but if he found a man, he seized him on the ground that he was British born and condemned him to nautical slavery without submitting the matter to any judge save the captain of his ship who was himself an interested party.

The British impressed American seamen constantly and with vigor. In February, 1798, Timothy Pickering, who was then Secretary of State, transmitted a report on the subject to the House of Representatives,[1] giving page after page of seamen impressed, with the particulars of impressment. In the same year Commodore Loring, commanding the British squadron off Havana, caused certain seamen to be removed from the United States man-of-war, *Baltimore*, Captain Phillips, and no redress ever seems to have been made.[2] The question of impressment naturally occupied much of the time of successive American ministers at London. In 1803, Rufus King thought that he was on the point of entering into a satisfactory arrangement [3] with

[1] See *Letter from the Secretary of State accompanying* . . . *[abstracts of returns of] Registered American Seamen* . . . *and Impressed Seamen 1797-1798.*

[2] See Gardner W. Allen's *Our Naval War with France*, 76-81. From a letter written by Benjamin Stoddert (October 17, 1798) it appears that Phillips received his appointment "because the ship at that place [Baltimore] required the attention of a Captain, and the merchants there knew of no person to recommend in preference"; "Allen Transcripts 1798-1801," fo. 4. See *Impartial Examination of the Case of Captain Issac Phillips.*

[3] The proposed convention contained these words : "No Person shall be impressed or taken upon the high seas out of any Ship or vessel belonging to the subjects or Citizens of one of the Parties, by the private or public armed Ships or men of War belonging to, or in the service of the other Party, and strict orders shall be given for the due observance of this Engagement." This is enclosed in a note from Rufus King to Lord Hawkesbury, dated May 7, 1803, in which King brings to his recollection "the article relative to our seamen, to which we agreed a little before the close of the late war" and flatters himself that there will be no objection to its being formally agreed to before his departure.

the British government that would put an end to similar difficulties in the future. But the project fell through at the last moment. The Tripolitan War found American naval vessels largely manned by native-born Britons. At the time there was the best of feeling between the American and British naval services and, until October, 1803, there was a reciprocal return of deserters. In that month, Captain Gore of the British ship *Medusa* refused to return certain sailors who had deserted from Preble's squadron and had claimed the protection of the British flag.[1] As throwing a side-light on the whole subject, it may be noted that in December, 1803, Captain Bainbridge, who was then a prisoner at Tripoli, reminded Preble that "the greater part of our [the *Philadelphia's*] crew consists of English subjects not naturalized in America." [2] Two years later, in 1805, boats from Admiral Collingwood's squadron removed three seamen from the American *Gun Boat No. 6* while she was off the Spanish coast. Thereupon Captain John Rodgers, who commanded the American fleet in the Mediterranean, directed that in the future no seamen should be surrendered from an American war vessel; but if the commander found himself in the presence of an irresistible force, he should haul down his flag and surrender his vessel and crew.[3]

Two more years passed away and then, on June 22, 1807, the British fifty-gun ship *Leopard* stopped the United States frigate *Chesapeake* off the Virginia coast, outside of the three mile limit, demanded the surrender of seamen who

King's account of the failure of this negotiation was written after his return to America. See King's *Rufus King*, iv, 259, 271; Mahan's summary, written from this material, is in his *War of 1812*, i, 124.

[1] "Allen Transcripts, 1802–1816," fo. 66, Edward Preble to Captain Gore,

17th October, 1803.

[2] "Allen Transcripts, 1802–1816," fo. 86.

[3] "Allen Transcripts, 1802–1816," 232–239; and Allen's *Our Navy and the Barbary Corsairs*, 225; Paullin's *John Rodgers*, 145.

were said to be deserters from the British naval service, and on refusal, fired into her.[1] The *Chesapeake* was fresh from port, her decks were littered with all kinds of stores, and many of her guns were still unmounted. After twenty-one of her men had been killed or wounded, one gun was discharged by a coal brought from the galley fire and her flag was hauled down. The British took from her four seamen who were alleged to be deserters from the British fleet that was then enjoying the hospitality of Chesapeake Bay. The captain of the *Leopard* refused to accept the surrender of the *Chesapeake,* and both vessels returned to the anchorages whence they had sailed a few hours before.[2] The citizens of Norfolk and Portsmouth in Virginia promptly met and adopted sixteen resolutions, the inhabitants of Hampton destroyed hogsheads of water that were on their way to a British warship, and the governor of the State ordered out a troop of cavalry to watch the movements of the fleet.[3] On the second day of July, President Jefferson

[1] On August 23, 1807, Mr. John Cowper wrote from Norfolk to Commodore Truxton that "our government" in regard to its dignity and perhaps to its safety ought to discourage desertion. He had been an eye-witness of the conduct of the men who had deserted from the *Halifax,* the very men whose surrender was demanded by the captain of the *Leopard.* They had risen on the officer who had charge of the boat, openly insulted their captain in the public street, and enlisted in the service of the United States on the same day. A little earlier, when the captain of a French frigate which was interned at Norfolk had demanded the restoration of some seamen who had deserted from his ship and had likewise enlisted with an officer of the United States, they were delivered to an armed force sent from the frigate. This had caused British officers to "conceive there was partiality shown, to their prejudice." Pickering copied this letter from the original and

it is now in the "Pickering Papers" vol. 54, p. 124. See also *The Trial of John Wilson, alias Jenkin Ratford, for Mutiny, Desertion and Contempt: to which are subjoined, a Few Cursory Remarks,* Boston, 1807.

[2] See Mahan's *War of 1812,* i, 155; Adams's *United States,* iv, 7–26; James's *Naval History of Great Britain,* (ed. 1859) iv, 249; Cooper's *History of the Navy of the United States,* ii, 12.

[3] The excitement of the moment comes out in a letter from Jefferson to his son-in-law, dated July 5, 1807. He wrote that one could believe nothing that comes from any one connected with a vessel. The latest report was that the Vice-President had had twenty-five shots fired at him from men-of-war boats as he passed out of the Capes. The local newspapers are full of references to the outrage: "War existed by the act of the British which was only a proper ending to the malignant jealousy with which Great Britain had regarded the

issued a proclamation,[1] which seemed to John Dickinson, and doubtless to many other persons, to be singularly appropriate. He ordered British men-of-war out of the waters of the United States, forbade others to enter, and prohibited all intercourse with the warships of that nation. He summoned Congress to meet on October 26, postponing the day of the meeting that passions might have time to quiet down. He also arranged with the Governor of Virginia to call out the militia to prevent the British landing anywhere within the Capes.

When the news of the *Chesapeake-Leopard* affair came to Canning, he at once wrote to Monroe telling him what had happened, so far as he knew it, expressed "the sincere concern and sorrow" that he felt, and assured him that if the British officers had been culpable, the most prompt and effectual reparation would be afforded. When instructions reached Monroe from Washington, he found that he was directed to accept no reparation that did not include a change of British policy on the whole subject of impressment. Instead of treating the *Chesapeake* incident as something entirely apart from the removal of British seamen from American merchant vessels, he was to use it to bring about a settlement of the whole question. Nothing could be done at London under these instructions.[2] Canning thereupon

---

progress of the nation whom she had once held in bondage."

The reality of impressment is brought out in a letter from Stephen Pindell to his father, Gassaway Pindell of Ann Arundel County, inspector of tobacco at Pig Point Warehouse, Maryland. It appears that the younger Pindell had been impressed from a schooner and was now on the *Bellona*, a British man-of-war actually at anchor in Hampton Roads. The boy implored his father to come to his relief, writing "I would indeed sooner drown myself than

continue where I am." *Petersburg Intelligencer*, July 21, 1807.

[1] The Proclamation is in *Messages and Papers of the Presidents*, i, 422; *Writings of Jefferson* (Ford ed.) ix, 89. The letters to the governor of Virginia as to employment of force are in *ibid.*, ix, 87 and notes to following pages.

[2] The official correspondence in this matter is contained in *American State Papers, Foreign Relations*, iii, 183, 187 and fol. *The Letter from the Secretary of State to Mr. Monroe on the subject of the Attack on the Chesapeake, . . . Printed*

sent a special envoy to Washington, George Henry Rose. He directed him, before even opening discussions as to the *Chesapeake* affair itself, to secure the revocation of Jefferson's proclamation ordering British naval vessels out of American territorial waters.[1] Still further to make its position clear, the British government issued a proclamation (October 17, 1807) directing officers of the royal navy to exercise the right of impressing British subjects from neutral merchant vessels to its fullest extent. The special envoy with these instructions, the proclamations, and unofficial news of the British Orders in Council of November, 1807, reached Washington at almost the same time. An emergency had arisen that plainly called for most drastic treatment.

by order of the House of Representatives, Washington, 1808; and *Papers relating to America. Presented to the House of Commons, 1809* (London, 1810, pp. 5–110). See also *Annals of Congress,* 10th Cong., 1st Sess., ii, 2618.

The determination of the Washington government was probably strengthened by the action of the captain of the British ship, *Columbine,* in ordering a United States revenue cutter to be searched for a deserter while both vessels were at anchor within Sandy Hook, and while the *Columbine* had been given special privileges by the

collector of customs at New York. *Correspondence of Thomas Barclay,* 270; McMasters' *United States,* iii, 267.

[1] The British admiral at Halifax in ordering the demand to be made on the *Chesapeake* had acted entirely on his own responsibility, for the government at London had never pretended to the right to impress anybody from a neutral war vessel. Jefferson's proclamation was unfortunate in that it forbade American ports to British warships, while permitting their use by French. It was this partiality that affected Canning and his colleagues.

NOTES

I. Bibliography. — Adams's *United States* (vols. iii–vi) is the standard authority upon the subject matter of this chapter and the next two or three. These volumes of Adams's monumental work are not merely instructive as a narrative, but must be regarded as a " source " because so much original material is printed either in the text or in foot-notes.[1] On the whole, Adams takes a rather optimistic view of the diplomatic doings of Jefferson, Madison, and Monroe while jeering at the system by which they sought to put pressure on Great Britain and France. Admiral Mahan takes a gloomy view of the diplomatic achievements of Madison [2] while agreeing with Adams as to the general fallaciousness of the Jeffersonian system as a whole. As between two such experts, it is not for the layman to decide; but it certainly does seem that the facts of the case are rather with Mahan than with Adams. Possibly the best compendious account of the commercial troubles leading to the War of 1812 is O. T. Howe's " Introduction " to *The Autobiography of Capt. Zachary G. Lamson* which states in brief form the leading facts and is clear and unencumbered with extraneous matter.

II. Boundary Convention, 1803. — May 12, 1803, King signed at London a convention for the settlement of the northeastern and northwestern boundaries.[3] A commission was to define the northeastern boundary, but the northwestern limit was described in Article V of the instrument: " The shortest line which can be drawn between the northwest point of the Lake of the Woods and the nearest source of the river Mississippi." The impolicy of doing anything at the moment of the probable cession of Louisiana does not seem to have

[1] Henry Adams has deposited with the government at Washington the transcripts from foreign archives on which so much of his work was based. They are accessible, therefore, to students who owe a deep obligation to Mr. Adams.

[2] *The Influence of Sea Power upon History, 1660–1783.* (Boston, 1890; 24th ed. Boston, 1914); *The Influence of Sea Power upon the French Revolution and Empire, 1793–1812* (Boston, 1893; 10th ed. 1898); *Sea Power in its Rela-*

tions to the War of 1812 (Boston, 1905). The discussion of this subject occupies the first half of the third of these works. Mahan spent the closing years of his life in the preparation of the *War of 1812*. His statements in this book are sometimes not easy of perusal, but the historical judgments are remarkable.

[3] The documents are given in connection with the President's Message of October 24, 1823; *American State Papers, Foreign Relations*, ii, 584–591.

occurred to King; but when the convention came before the Senate it was seen that it compromised the whole northern limit of Louisiana. The articles as to the northeastern boundary were unexceptionable. The Senate, therefore, advised the ratification of the convention without the article relating to the northwestern boundary. The British government refused to accept the mutilated instrument and the whole arrangement fell to the ground.[1] Writing to Monroe, on February 14, 1804,[2] enclosing the conditional ratification, Madison stated that there was reason to believe that the northern boundary of Louisiana had been settled by the Commissioners appointed under the Treaty of Utrecht, as running from the Lake of the Woods " westwardly in lat. 49."

III. Acts, Orders, and Decrees, 1806–1807. — The American Non-Importation Act of April 18, 1806 provided that from and after the 15th day of November next [3] no articles of which leather, silk, hemp, flax, tin, brass, or wool is the material of chief value shall be brought into the United States from any port or place within the British Empire except the cheaper grades of articles made from tin, brass, or wool. Furthermore, no glass whatever, no silver or plated wares, paper, nails, spikes, hats, ready-made clothing, millinery, playing cards, beer, ale, porter, pictures, and prints shall be brought into the United States from the British Empire and none of these goods produced within the British Empire shall be brought indirectly from any other foreign port.

The Orders and Decrees of the belligerent powers of Europe, passed since 1791, affecting the commercial rights of the United States were transmitted to Congress by President Jefferson on December 23, 1808.[4]

---

[1] *Executive Journal of the Senate*, i, 451–463; *Treaties and Conventions* (ed. 1873) p. 1016.

[2] See *Letters from the Secretary of State to Mr. Monroe . . . . Part II. Accompanying the message of the president of the United States, received on the 22d of March 1808* (Washington City, 1808).

[3] The time was further extended by act of December 19, 1806, until the "first day of July next" and thereafter not later than the second Monday in December, 1807, at the discretion of the President. It will be noted that a gap of something more than a month existed between the time that the act

of April 18, 1806 was to have gone into force and this continuing act of December 19, 1806. The second section of this latter act, therefore, provided for a remission of all fines and penalties that might have been incurred through the non-observance of the earlier law. See *Statutes at Large*, ii, 379, 411; *Annals of Congress*, 9th Cong., 1st Sess., 1259, *ibid.*, 2nd Sess., 1249.

[4] *Message from the President of the United States, transmitting Copies of all Acts, Decrees, Orders, and Proclamations affecting the Commercial Rights of Neutral Nations, issued since 1791: in Pursuance of a Resolution of the House, of

Below are a few leading sentences from some of them and synopses of some more important portions: —

[Fox's Blockade.] April 8, 1806, C. J. Fox, British Secretary of State, acquainted Mr. Monroe that it had been judged expedient to " establish the most rigorous blockade at the entrances of the Ems, the Weser, the Elbe and the Trave, and to maintain and enforce the same in the strictest manner." May 16, 1806, Fox informed Monroe that the king, taking into consideration " the new and extraordinary means resorted to by the enemy for the purpose of distressing the commerce of his subjects," has directed the blockade of " the coast, rivers, and ports, from the river Elbe to the port of Brest, both inclusive," but that such blockade shall not prevent neutral vessels, laden with goods not being the property of His Majesty's enemies and not being contraband of war, from entering and leaving the said rivers and ports, except those from Ostend to the Seine, provided that the said ships shall not have been laden at an enemy's port, nor shall be destined to such port, nor have previously broken the blockade.[1]

[Berlin Decree, November 21, 1806.] " Napoleon, emperor of the French, and king of Italy, considering: 1. That England does not admit the right of nations as universally acknowledged by all civilized people "; imprisoning crews of merchant vessels, seizing private property in such vessels, blockading ports not fortified and mouths of rivers and declaring places blockaded before which she has not a single vessel of war. The evident design of England being to extend her commerce and industry upon the ruin of those of the continent, " We have resolved to enforce against England the usages which she has consecrated in her maritime code." The Decree: Article I.

---

the Eleventh Ultimo. December 23, 1808 (City of Washington, 1808) ; Annals of Congress, 10th Cong., 2nd Sess., 1685–1760; American State Papers, Foreign Relations, iii, 262–294. In the two last books, it is stated that the Message was communicated on December 28th instead of the 23rd as in the official Journal. A convenient summary of embargo laws, British orders, and French decrees is The Embargo Laws . . . to which is added, an Appendix (Boston, 1809). The two last from 1793 to 1809 are arranged in parallel columns in W. J. Duane's The Law of Nations, Investigated in a Popular Man-

ner. Addressed to the Farmers of the United States (printed by William Duane, Philadelphia, 1809), pp. 71–73. A convenient series of documents is the volume entitled American State Papers, and Correspondence . . . &c. &c. &c. (Philadelphia, printed, London, reprinted, 1812).

[1] September 25, 1806, Monroe was notified that the blockade from the Elbe to the Ems, both inclusive, "is for the present discontinued." On June 26, 1807, the British minister at Washington notified the American government that this blockade had been reestablished.

" The British islands are declared in a state of blockade." II. Commerce and correspondence with them are prohibited and letters and packages addressed to England, to an Englishman, or in the English language shall be seized. III. Every subject of England found in countries occupied by our troops shall be made a prisoner of war. IV. All property belonging to an English subject shall be lawful prize. V. Trade in English merchandise is forbidden. VII. No vessel coming from England or the English colonies shall be received in any port; but VIII. shall be seized as if they were English property.

[Order in Council, January 7, 1807.] In consequence of the Berlin Decree the British king orders " that no vessel shall be permitted to trade from one port to another, both which ports shall belong to or be in the possession of France or her allies " and His Majesty's ships of war and privateers are instructed to warn or capture any vessel coming from any such port which together with her cargo shall be condemned as lawful prize.

[Orders in Council, November 11, 1807.] A long preamble recites the Berlin Decree and orders all places and ports of France and her allies — including the colonies — and all places in Europe from which the British flag is excluded to be subject to the same restrictions as if they were actually blockaded in the most strict and rigorous manner. All trade in articles, the produce and manufacture of the said country or colonies shall be deemed unlawful and every vessel trading from or to such countries or colonies together with their cargoes shall be good prize. The king being " desirous not to subject neutrals to any greater inconvenience than is absolutely inseparable from the carrying into effect His Majesty's just determination " will still allow neutrals the opportunity of furnishing themselves with colonial produce and even leave open, for the present, such trade with His Majesty's enemies as shall be carried on directly with the ports of His Majesty's dominions, provided that it shall not be to or from any port actually blockaded.

Another Order in Council of the same date provided that goods might be imported into England in vessels of countries at amity with His Majesty on paying certain duties enumerated in acts of Parliament.

The duties referred to in the above order are given farther on in the same publication. Among them are the following: cotton wool was taxed nine pence per pound, molasses five shillings per cwt., rice two shillings per cwt., brown sugar ten shillings per cwt., tobacco one and one-half pence per pound.   Flour was taxed five shillings per cwt. on exportation.   These duties might be suspended by the king or the exportation of any of the articles might be prohibited by him. No drawback was allowed on any of the goods exported under these circumstances.

[Milan Decree, December 17, 1807.]   Napoleon, observing the measures adopted by the British government on the 11th of November last, by which neutral vessels are made liable to be searched by English cruisers and to have a tax laid on the cargo by the British legislature and observing that by these acts the British government denationalizes ships and asserts as a right the infamous principle that the flag of a nation does not cover goods, decrees, I. that every ship that shall have been searched by an English ship, or voyaged to England, or paid any tax to the English government is thereby and for that alone declared to have become English property.   II.   Such " denationalized " ships entering " our ports " or those of our allies or those captured by our ships shall be good prize.   III.   The British Islands are declared to be in a state of blockade both by land and by sea.   Every ship of whatever nation that sails from or to an English port or port occupied by English troops is good prize.   IV.   These measures shall continue as long as the British government does not return to the principle of the law of nations.

CHAPTER XIV

WAR between the United States and Great Britain seemed to be inevitable in the last half of 1807. Men as far apart geographically and politically as Jefferson, Gallatin, Samuel Smith, John Quincy Adams, and Rufus King expected to be deep in war before the first snow-storm. "If England does us ample justice in the *Chesapeake* affair it will be a war saved. But I do not expect it," so Jefferson wrote to his son-in-law on July 12. Gallatin thought it was their duty to avert war if it could be done honorably; but he had no such aversion to war at this time as he had in 1812. Adams stated, sometime in the spring of 1808, that he hoped the declaration of war against England by Russia and Austria would deter the ministers at Downing Street from rushing into a foolish and extravagant war against us, which he believed they had determined upon in 1807. As between England and France, Jefferson wrote in August, 1807 that he never expected to wish success to Bonaparte; but "the English being equally tyrannical at sea as he is on land and that tyranny bearing on us in every point of either honor or interest, I say 'Down with England', and as for what Bonaparte is then to do to us, let us trust to the chapter of accidents." Before actually beginning a war from which it would be difficult to withdraw, the administration determined once more to try the efficacy of commercial pressure to bring Great Britain to a realizing sense of the impolicy of her actions; but these were "experimental measures"[1] adopted in part because the country was unprepared for war.

On December 18, 1807, Jefferson sent a message to Congress showing the dangers that beset American ships, merchandise, and seamen. The safety of "these essential resources" being of the greatest importance, Congress "will doubtless perceive all the advantages which may be expected from an inhibition of the departure of our vessels from the ports of the United States" and "their wisdom" will also see the necessity of preparing for whatever events may grow out of the present crisis.[2]   Gallatin would have preferred to recommend some definite restriction as to the duration of the proposed embargo, but Jefferson and Madison thought otherwise.   With the message came many documents reciting the misdeeds of foreign governments and also, but occultly, there came a bill, which Jefferson is supposed to have drawn, for the immediate establishment of an embargo for an indefinite period of time; but no ready-drawn bill for a regular army or an enlarged navy appears to have come with it, invisibly or otherwise.

Congress took fire at once.   The Senate led.   One day sufficed for putting the bill through all the stages and sending it to the House.   Of the Senators, John Quincy Adams suggested very strong doubts as to the propriety of the measure; but consented to it upon General Smith's stating the reasons which had influenced the President.   In conclusion, Adams argued that letting "our ships go out without arming them and authorizing them to resist the decrees," is merely swelling the plunder of the contending parties.[3]

---

[1] This phrase is used in a letter written by Madison to Henry Wheaton in 1824; *Writings of Madison* (Hunt ed.) ix, 194.

[2] *Messages and Papers of the Presidents*, i, 433.

[3] J. Q. Adams's *Memoirs*, i, 491; Ford's *Writings of J. Q. Adams*, iii, 168

In the House, John Randolph of Roanoke jumped on to his feet at the first possible moment, insisted on recognition, and proposed a bill of his own. The next day, when the bill came down from the Senate, he opposed its passage with as much vigor as he had advocated the adoption of his own. The Representatives accepted the Senate bill with some changes, the President signed it on December 22, and it went into force at once. No sooner was it passed than loop-holes to its enforcement appeared, and Congress passed two supplementary acts, one on January 9, the other on March 12, 1808. Taking them all three together, they practically prohibited sending out of the United States, by sea or by land, any goods either the produce of the United States or reëxportations. The means adopted for carrying this policy into effect were bonds to be given by the owner of the ship to double or treble the value of his vessel, and double the value of the cargo, obliging the ship to return to the United States. Following the old English system, the bonds had to be filed with the collectors of the customs and, later, certificates had to be placed in their hands showing that the conditions contained in the bonds had been complied with.

As the year 1808 drew towards its close, it became increasingly evident that the desired pressure was not being exerted upon Great Britain. Jefferson and Madison thought that this failure was due to the lax enforcement of the embargo in America. Gallatin, while agreeing with them,

and notes. Timothy Pickering gave a different account in his letter of April 22, 1808, to Governor Sullivan of Massachusetts. In this, he says, Mr. Adams denied his request for time exclaiming: "I would *not consider:* — I would *not deliberate:* I would *act.* Doubtless the *president* possesses such further information as will justify the measure!" See *Interesting Correspondence* between . . . *Governour Sullivan and Col. Pickering* (Boston, 1808) p. 11. Henry Adams followed Pickering's account in his *History of the United States,* iv, 173. J. Q. Adams's contradiction of Pickering's statement was written after the event. It was first printed in 1824; see Henry Adams's *Documents relating to New-England Federalism,* 174 note.

wished to declare war. The embargo policy was producing unlooked for and undesirable results in compelling administrative officials to exercise powers that were not authorized by the Constitution or by the laws. Collectors had forbidden the loading of vessels and had refused to issue clearances without any legal authority and only on instructions from the Secretary.[1] Gallatin even offered to finance a war for one year without resorting to loans or new taxations. Jefferson and Madison preferred to make one more trial with the embargo and the Enforcement Act of January, 1809, was passed. This gave Gallatin the power he needed to make it impossible to ship goods outside of the United States. It authorized collectors to seize merchandise or other movable property which was apparently on the way to the frontier, to refuse permits to load merchandise on vessels, and to detain them almost at will, — it conferred upon them almost the same kind of power that had been so strongly reprobated in Otis's arguments against the Writs of Assistance. Moreover legal coasting trade was made impossible and the burden of proving innocence was placed on the owner or shipper. With this engine of efficiency in Gallatin's hands, the administration enforced the embargo laws and thereby compelled their repeal.

There are interesting topics connected with the history of the days of the embargo : by what devices was it evaded ? what was its effect upon the different parts of the country ? Notwithstanding the speed with which the first embargo law was enacted, there was time to give advance information

---

[1] There is an interesting letter from Moses Myers, dated Norfolk, November 25, 1808, describing the difficulties of shipping agents, in the "Ellis and Allan Papers" at Washington. See in this connection, Judge Johnson's decision, given in 1808, in the case of "Ex parte Adam Gilchrist and others *vs.* the Collector of the Port of Charleston," that administrative officers could exercise such powers only as were conferred upon them by law ; *The Embargo Laws with the Message from the President* (Boston, 1809, p. 23) ; Adams's *United States*, iv, 263.

to shippers in the Middle States and New England. At once cargoes were poured into the holds of vessels and they departed half loaded and half provisioned. Many of those that were out, and could be communicated with, remained away carrying cargoes for other neutrals or for the belligerents, greatly to the profit of their owners. Coasting vessels cleared for remote United States ports and were driven by "stress of weather" into a Nova Scotian harbor or to an anchorage in the West Indies. So many of them left without taking out clearance papers that the British government directed their naval officers not to molest any American ship found on the high seas on the routes from the United States to the West Indies, no matter how devoid of official documentation she might be. British manufacturers and forwarders aided in the evasion of the embargo and non-importation. They packed up superfine broadcloths and invoiced them at five shillings per yard, for these cheap cloths were permitted while expensive weaves were forbidden; they shipped Scottish "threads" in trunks or boxes, carefully concealed under a layer or two of muslins.[1] Sometimes a vessel cleared coastwise with foreign commodities entered upon the manifest, or cargo list, that were not in her hold and received them at sea from another vessel, or possibly took them on board at Passamaquoddy or at some foreign port. British goods were also brought in from "Spanish and Swedish ports" in vessels with Spanish or Swedish flags and registers, and were invoiced as goods of Spanish or Swedish origin.

As to exportation from the United States to foreign countries, there is abundant evidence that this trade was constantly going on, but the evidence is also abundant that it

---

[1] "Letter" of the Secretary of the Treasury to the collectors of the customs October 1, 1808.

was prosecuted with difficulty. The commerce of Lake Champlain, Lake Ontario, and Lake Erie grew by leaps and bounds; flour and beef moved from central New York and Vermont to the St. Lawrence Valley and thence to Europe, and there was a corresponding return movement of British manufactured goods to the shops and warehouses of New York, whence distribution to towns along the coast was comparatively easy.[1] The government tried to crush out this commerce and bloodshed, civil war, and a presidential proclamation followed. Nothing troubled Jefferson more than the large quantities of flour that were being carried along the coast, much of it presumably for shipment to foreign ports. After the embargo was in working order, not a barrel of flour could go from Philadelphia or Richmond to New Bedford or Boston, without a governmental permit, but permits were easy to obtain. These were issued by the Treasury authorities upon the recommendation of the governor of a State. In this embargo year, James Sullivan was governor of Massachusetts. He was a Republican in politics, but seems to have been more interested in the continued success of the party in his State than in putting into practice Jefferson's commercial theories. At any rate he affixed his approbation to quantities of certificates of the towns on the coast as to the amount of flour required by their citizens and accompanying testimonials as to the good character of the merchants and captains who proposed to do the importing.[2] It was said that these papers were issued so lavishly that they were openly bought and sold in New York. There is no question whatever that a very large quantity of flour was brought to New England,

---

[1] See David Anderson's *Canada: or a View of the Importance of the British American Colonies* (London, 1814, Appendix).

[2] Some of these certificates are preserved in the cabinet of the Massachusetts Historical Society.

for the difference in the selling price at Boston and Philadelphia was less in 1808 than in 1807. A great deal of it was shipped out of New England by way of Nova Scotia. An inhabitant of Eastport, who had been caught in the act of transporting two barrels of flour across the boundary, was fined one thousand and twenty-five dollars and costs; — the size of the fine bearing eloquent testimony to the frequency of the practice.

Turning to the South, the marketing of tobacco and cotton was much more seriously affected by the embargo than was the selling of flour, which was then the great export industry of the Middle States. This is shown by the fact that the prices of tobacco at Richmond and of cotton at Charleston declined materially in the embargo year. Tobacco went from six and a half cents to five at Richmond, and Georgia upland cotton went from twenty or twenty-two cents to fourteen at Charleston.[1] As both of these products could be kept without deterioration the loss was not permanent, but undoubtedly caused a good deal of temporary distress on many plantations.

The British government in no way assisted the Jeffersonians to carry out their part of the commercial war. Quite the contrary. It did whatever it could to break down the embargo and to promote the importation of staple products of the United States. American vessels were admitted to its ports without clearance papers, and goods were accepted contrary to the requirements of the navigation laws and the acts of trade. Commercial letters of the time bear witness to some commerce with America. In March 1809, Logan and Lenox, a Liverpool firm engaged in American trade, wrote to their correspondent at Richmond that "the

[1] Many interesting particulars are given by G. W. Daniels in an article on "The American Cotton Trade with Liverpool under the Embargo" in *American Historical Review*, xxi, 276.

Sally from City Point," on the James River, was the only "embargo breaker" that had recently arrived with tobacco from Virginia, but a "considerable number" had come in from New York and Savannah with cotton and naval stores, and added "the ships that come this way find capital employment in the Baltic trade." Another letter, this time from a New York forwarding house, stated that high freights were being paid for vessels to go to the Azores. There, the flag of the ship was changed and a consular certificate obtained for a trifle stating that the cargo had been relanded, although not a single hogshead had been moved. The British government was exceedingly liberal in giving licenses both to import all articles of American produce into Great Britain and also to carry on prohibited trade from that country to the Continent. How many American vessels took advantage of these various opportunities, one cannot say, but, in 1809, the British government issued fifteen thousand licenses as against less than three thousand in 1807. Of course, there was nothing like the number of vessels employed in trans-Atlantic commerce as in normal times, but those that remained at work earned high freights, for the rate on cotton rose from one and one-half pence per pound to four pence in the first part of 1809, and the cost of sending other goods must have been proportionately high. The third embargo act contained a clause that greatly helped American vessels to gain the high seas by permitting them to sail in ballast for the purpose of bringing home property stored in European warehouses but belonging to citizens of the United States. Eight hundred vessels went out on this errand, and only a small proportion of them had returned to America before March, 1809. Once out of sight of land, a vessel might easily be captured or injured in a storm, or, gaining a foreign port, might be sold.

Another interesting inquiry is as to the effect of the embargo on the different sections of the country. One reads of hundreds of vessels laid up at the wharves at Philadelphia, at New York, and elsewhere, their decks covered over by temporary wooden roofs. John Lambert, a British traveller who visited New York in the spring of 1808, gives a gloomy picture of restricted commercial dealings there, and tells us that the grass was growing on the wharves in the month of April![1] The newspapers give lists of vessels in port, over six hundred of them at Boston, Salem, and New Bedford; two-thirds being harbor and coasting craft. These figures have little value, for the coastwise trade was then seasonal, being confined to the eight or nine warmer months of the year and it was still carried on in square-rigged vessels. Moreover, one finds in the New York *Mercantile Advertiser* that foreign arrivals at that port and clearances were practically continuous throughout the year. On May 2, 1808, there were three arrivals from foreign ports, on June 27, likewise three, on September 5, there were five, and on December 19, two. These vessels came from all over the world, — Havana, St. Kitts, Campeachy, Madeira, Batavia, Liverpool, and Londonderry. That there was a considerable slackening up of commerce is evident from the migration of hundreds and thousands of British seamen from the forecastles of American ships and from the wharves of Philadelphia and other ports to Canada and Nova Scotia. Idle and starving sailors wandered about the streets for a time being employed by the authorities at starvation wages and then departed. Some of them, probably, enlisted on British men-

---

[1] John Lambert's *Travels through Lower Canada and the United States,* ii, 157; this passage is quoted at length in Adams's *United States,* iv, 278. Confirmatory evidence is in the "Reports of John Howe" in *American Historical Review,* xvii, 87 and fol.

of-war. At any rate the embargo justified itself in part by relieving America of the men whose presence on her ships was one of the greatest causes of international irritation.[1] And there was a demand for their services at Halifax and Quebec, for one hundred and fifty vessels are said to have been at the latter port at one time awaiting cargoes of products from across the line. Once in the crimping houses of Liverpool and London, many of these sailors were rounded up by naval press gangs and in so far, the embargo may be said to have benefited Great Britain.

It is as to the effect of the embargo on Virginia and New England that most discussion has arisen, it being a favorite thought with some of the older writers that it bore very heavily upon New England and ruined Virginia. There is abundant proof that the commercial towns along the New England seacoast were severely affected for a time. Buildings were advertised for rent at embargo rates and, while it lasted, at least one Boston dentist offered his services at half price except when gold was used; but it is uncertain whether these advertisements and others like them were catch-penny devices or indicate severe retrenchment. Then there were instances of drownings of seamen in Salem harbor that have sometimes been regarded as suicides on account of lack of employment; but it might mean nothing more than lack of expertness in handling small boats that is often found in those that traverse the sea in ships. Soup kitchens were opened at Portland, Maine,[2] and at some other places; but in other seaport towns, where records are accessible, there was an absence of demand for increased relief, if the amount of money voted for the care of the poor can be taken as presumptive proof.[3] The constructive effect

[1] Mahan's *War of 1812*, i, 192, and "Secret Reports of John Howe, 1808," in *American Historical Review*, xvii, 89, 92.

[2] W. Goold's *Portland in the Past*, 426.

[3] See, however, Samuel E. Morison's *Harrison Gray Otis*, i, 324.

of the embargo on New England has been quite overlooked. There was a good deal of manufacturing in that section during the Revolution and in the years immediately following its close. The demand for labor in the fields and on the ocean, the difficulty of securing the raw materials, and the keen competition from outside had later caused the closing of most mills and shops. The small amount of protection afforded by the early tariff acts had not been enough to stimulate the renewal of these industries. Now, the high price of imported goods, owing to the cost of evading the laws, gave would-be manufacturers their chance. Old factories were reopened; new factories were built and equipped, and the making of textiles and hardware was undertaken with vigor and success. These enterprises demanded labor and must have done something to relieve the distresses of embargoed seamen and of those who were otherwise dependent upon navigation for their bread and butter. The extension of manufacturing in New England and in other States north of Maryland, went on throughout the period of commercial warfare; and thereafter was greatly stimulated by the conflict with England. Northern manufacturing owed its rebirth to the Jeffersonians, an outcome of their policy that was certainly very far from their desire.

South of Pennsylvania, there were some feeble attempts to emulate the growing industry of the North. In Virginia, a committee appointed by the friends of the "Manufacturing Association" issued an address to the people advocating the establishment of mills and factories. It was signed by some of the leading men of the State: William H. Cabell, William Wirt, William Foushee, Sr., Peyton Randolph, and Thomas Ritchie.[1] Nothing came of the attempt because there was no capital in the Old Dominion seeking

---

[1] *Virginia Argus*, July 26, 1808.

employment. In South Carolina, too, public interest was stimulated; this time by Charles Pinckney, who was then governor of the State, in a message to the legislature. He announced the formation of the South Carolina Homespun Company with a large capitalization of which one thousand shares were reserved for members of the legislature, "if they think proper to take them." Whether the legislators subscribed for their reserved shares does not appear, but the Homespun Company must have been incorporated by act of the Assembly for a little later it was authorized to establish a lottery or lotteries for its benefit.[1]

The embargo unquestionably bore with distressing weight on Virginia, for the old social organization of that State was nearing dissolution in 1802, and the commercial warfare and the actual conflict of arms gave it the death stroke. Jefferson, in letters to his intimate correspondents,[2] pointed out more than once that the slave system, as it existed in Virginia, was inevitably fatal to the planters. Slaves were tied down to the plantations and to the State; there was no mobility of labor. The slaves that were adequate to the effective use of a one-thousand acre plantation, in thirty, forty, or fifty years, by natural increase, would overstock the plantation with labor and begin the process of eating the owner out of his house and lands. Labor and land had reached an equilibrium in the settled part of Virginia in the middle of the eighteenth century, and ever since plantation economy had yearly become a more serious matter. There was something charming about the old Virginia life [3]

---

[1] Cooper's *Statutes of South Carolina*, v, 619. A copy of Pinckney's message is in the Library of Congress. See also C. S. Boucher in *Washington University Studies* for April, 1916, p. 244.

[2] See, for instance, a letter to Mrs. Paradise, dated Monticello, Sept. 11, 1792: "As negroes double in about 25 years, yours may by this time be too many for the lands. Whenever this is the case, they lesson instead of increase the profits of an estate."

[3] The scholastic side is well set forth in William P. Trent's "English Culture

with its barbaric largeness, its lavish hospitality, and its
self-sufficiency. The planter was a law unto himself, his
family, and his slaves; and the whole little community
lived on the product of its land and labor. Even the greatest planters bought astonishingly little; but the little that
they did buy was their undoing, because they went on from
year to year, always buying and never paying. They never
paid because the net return from their annual crops was less
than the interest on debts and the cost of the few things that
they did purchase. Jefferson with five thousand acres,
eighty-six negroes, and twenty-six horses went behind hand
steadily, year after year; and so did Washington with
Mount Vernon and all its outlying farms.

At Richmond, there were eight or ten large mercantile
firms, which were practically branches of British commercial houses, having generally one partner who was a native-
born Briton and another who was a Virginian. One of
these firms was Ellis and Allan, whose history in health and
decay extends from before the Revolution until after the
War for Secession.[1] Their letter books and ledgers have
come down to us and serve as a searchlight into the family
life of the Old Dominion in the time of its first decay.
Among their accounts was one with a Randolph, not otherwise known to fame. It began in 1804 and was presented
for payment early in 1809. There are three hundred and
sixty entries. These included pins, putty, silk twist, and
bar iron, "osnabrigs" for slave clothes and a camels-hair
shawl for the lady of the house, a spelling book for the

in Virginia" in the *Johns Hopkins
Studies*, vii, nos. v and vi.

[1] Among the "Ellis and Allan
Papers" is an account that was presented to John Hoomes Jr., on September 1, 1812. It ran from September,
1805. On May 1, 1810, it amounted
to £125 and some shillings, Virginia
money, of which nearly £21 was interest.
On that day, they credited him with
£32 12s. 4d. received for two hogsheads
of tobacco. By the 1st of September
1812, the total amount due from Hoomes,
including £13 interest money, was £105
15s. 3d.

children, and an umbrella for the master, — the latter at the price of two pounds, five shillings, Virginia. In these five years the charges totaled about four thousand dollars. The amount was reasonable for a person in this Randolph's walk of life; it was far less than a family of the same grade in Philadelphia or New York would have spent for similar articles, for a good deal of it was invested in reproductive material for the plantation. The difference between the planter and the city dweller was that the latter bought and paid, while the former in these years paid for less than one-half of what he bought.

The diminution of the exportation of tobacco and flour in 1808 made it even more difficult for Virginia debtors to pay anything on these "open" plantation accounts. Ellis and Allan began to feel uneasy and their uneasiness was increased by the Virginia Assembly reviving an earlier law for the protection of debtors. This provided that if goods taken in execution could not be sold for three-fourths of their value, the debtor might keep the goods on giving a bond to pay the debt within twelve months, or the goods might be sold on twelve months credit.[1] Ellis and Allan declared that this action by the legislature shook public and private credit and paralyzed the confidence between the merchant and his country friends which was so essential to both of them. They decided to refuse further credit and to expedite the collection of outstanding debts. It was this that induced them to make out this bill to this particular Randolph and to present it with a statement that their own necessities were very urgent and a prompt payment was desirable. By the end of 1809, Ellis and Allan decided to charge interest on the unpaid balances of these old accounts. This was the last straw, for to many a planter the compound-

---

[1] Shepherd's *Statutes of Virginia*, iii, 364.

ing of interest every twelve months seemed no better than usury, one might as well go to a bank. In 1810, Ellis and Allan placed many of their overdue accounts in the hands of attorneys for collection and received in return many plaintive letters and assignments of debts due to the writers from other planters. If the experience of other firms was anything like that of Ellis and Allan, which presumably it was, the embargo, by taking away from the Virginia plantation owner his sole source of credit by greatly restricting the exportation of tobacco and flour, brought about a crisis from which he did not recover. His one hope of escape from bankruptcy was to sell his surplus slaves.[1] In 1809, or 1810, John Peyton conducted a coffle of Virginia slaves to New Orleans for sale. This particular venture did not turn out very well owing to the poor character of the Louisianian agent; but the way had been pointed out for economic recuperation.[2]

The embargo in its operation aroused irritation in most

[1] See J. Burton Harrison's "Slavery Question in Virginia" in *The Harrisons of Skimino*, 352. This article is reprinted from the *American Quarterly Review* of December, 1832.

The decline of Virginia compared with other States, as Massachusetts and New York, is evident from a study of the figures of "Exports from the Several States" (Webster's *Compendious Dictionary*, ed. 1806, p. 383, and *American State Papers, Commerce and Navigation*, i, 722): —

	1791	1796	1801	1804	1807
Massachusetts .	$2,519,650	$ 9,949,345	$14,870,565	$16,894,379	$20,112,125
New York . . .	2,505,465	12,208,027	19,851,136	16,081,281	26,357,963
Virginia	3,131,865	5,268,615	6,483,028	5,790,001	4,761,234
Totals of Original Thirteen States	$19,012,040	$67,064,097	$93,020,513	$77,699,074	$102,030,395

[2] Charles Ball's *Slavery in the United States : A Narrrative of the Life and Adventures of . . . a Black Man* (Lewistown, Pa., 1836). Ball was a Maryland negro who was carried to South Carolina and then to Georgia as a slave before the War of 1812. Some passages are reprinted in *Documentary History of American Industrial Society*, ii, 59–66.

unexpected quarters. Jefferson's agent at Philadelphia wrote to Gallatin that the requirement of a bond of three hundred dollars per ton could "answer no other purpose than to create enemies to the government." He instanced a flatboatman who had a three hundred dollar craft on which only one-half had been paid, and now the man was required to give a bond of nine thousand dollars to keep his boat going or he and his family would starve. Dr. Logan, a familiar correspondent of Jefferson and Madison, declared that the embargo system amounted to "dastardly attacking the humble cottage, the comforts, the subsistance of unoffending women & children, instead of meeting in an open & honorable conflict the armed battalions of your enemy,"[1] — rather curious language to come from a Quaker. Moreover, the embargo seemed to be producing slight effect upon England. The manufacturers of cotton and tobacco were hard pressed for their raw material; but, on the other hand, British shipping was benefited by being relieved from some of the American competition. It was at this time, providentially for Britain, that the ports of Spanish America were opened to British commerce. After bleeding the Spanish monarchy as long as there was any blood or money left, Napoleon decided to take possession of Spain and Portugal, too. The Portuguese royal family saved itself by timely flight to Brazil. The Spanish royal family was removed to France and a Napoleonic brother substituted. In May, 1808, the Spaniards rebelled. The British saw their opportunity. They sent soldiers to the Peninsula, and cargoes of goods to Spain and Spanish America to the temporary relief of British manufacturers and forwarders.

The session of Congress of 1808–1809 was a time of continuing excitements. Ostensibly, the members might be

---

[1] Deborah N. Logan's *Memoir of Dr. George Logan*, 170.

considering the enforcement of the embargo, or the holding
of an extra session; always, the real question at issue was
when should the embargo be ended? Day after day, and
week after week, the same arguments were repeated and
the same manœuvres practised: Should there be war or
no war, embargo or no embargo, or non-intercourse with
France added to that with England and trade with the rest
of the world thrown open? Whenever France was mentioned, a charge that the Republicans were acting under
French influence or truckling to the Emperor was made or
suspected and indignantly repelled. In December, 1807,
French bankers had written to John Derby of Salem that
an immediate embargo will be the best means effectually to
protect American property and prevent the United States
from being involved in the "Broils of Europe."[1] No
doubt there were other letters of a similar import and every
such suggestion coming from Frenchmen must have seemed
confirmatory of the general Federalist theory that Jefferson
and the Republicans were acting in consequence of imperial
mandate; it was even hinted that the Louisiana Purchase
had been a mask to hide the payment of tribute to France.[2]

As long as the embargo policy had not been carried out,
New England had remained reasonably quiet; but as soon
as the administration began to execute the Enforcement
Act, town meetings were held, resolutions adopted, and Committees of Correspondence appointed, that the commercial
towns and States might act as one.[3] Jefferson realized that

[1] This letter was found in the "Derby
Manuscripts" in the Essex Institute
at Salem by Mr. Paul D. Evans, who
communicated it to me.

[2] See *Address to the People of the
County of Hampshire,* [Massachusetts]
in 1809, pp. 6, 7.

[3] See "Secret Reports of John Howe,
1808," *American Historical Review,* xvii,
332. Adams summarizes many of the
resolutions adopted by the towns in his
History of the United States, iv, 409–416.
The petitions adopted in the Boston
town meetings are in the *Boston Records,* xxxv, 238, 240. The resolutions
adopted by the legislatures of Massachusetts and Connecticut are in Ames's
State Documents on Federal Relations,
No. 1, 26–44.

some change must be made, but he felt that his own justification demanded the continuance of the embargo through
the spring of 1809. When Congress came to the actual
discussion of the date of repeal, one of those sudden moblike
ebullitions of fear carried it off its feet. The act substituting
non-intercourse with Great Britain and France for the embargo was approved by Jefferson on March 1, 1809, four
days before the close of his public career. To the end of
his life, he unceasingly pointed to this catastrophe as resulting from the strength of the New England town system.
It was, indeed, an occasion when the town-meeting democracy of the North had overthrown the plantation democracy of the South, — something that the "best men" and
those possessed of the "first principles" had been quite
powerless to accomplish.

During this embargo year of ever-growing disorder and
irritation, George Henry Rose, the new British envoy, had
failed to offer any effectual reparation for the *Chesapeake*
outrage, and Madison had been chosen as Jefferson's successor
to the chief magistracy. Rose's instructions were of a type
peculiar to George Canning and James Madison. As Monroe
and Pinkney had been ordered to do the impossible, so Rose
was directed to begin arranging the reparation for the attack
on the *Chesapeake* by demanding the withdrawal of the proclamation closing American ports to British naval ships.
When that was done he was to offer a disavowal of the act
of the British admiral, provided the Americans would likewise disavow the doings of their own commander; but he
was not to make these demands known until after the proclamation had been withdrawn. Jefferson and Madison
were anxious for accommodation. They even proposed that
a document withdrawing the proclamation should be signed
by the President and placed in Rose's hands and that he

should then disclose the conditions of reparation. When this little farce had been played it was found that the American government was required to disavow Captain Barron whose only fault had been in not fighting. The negotiation came to an end and Rose went back to England, carrying with him letters from Timothy Pickering and other Federalists that were unpatriotic and treasonable.

In 1805 Jefferson had determined not to stand for a third term.[1] He selected Madison as his successor; but there were Virginians like Randolph and his friends, who distrusted Madison and would have preferred to see the succession go to Monroe. The Madisonians in Virginia stole a march on their opponents by securing a vote from the Assembly in favor of Madison, so that he might fairly be regarded as the Virginia candidate. Under these circumstances, it would seem that the Federalists might have joined with anti-Jeffersonian Republicans and have chosen enough presidential electors to have carried the day. The chances of success were especially good, because the New York Republicans were divided in their allegiance between two Clintons, George and De Witt. The former was the old governor and Vice-President in succession to the recreant Burr. The other, De Witt, was his nephew, and one of the ablest and most selfish of American politicians. Could the Federalists have coalesced with George Clinton, they might possibly have destroyed the Virginia dynasty; but they could not bring themselves to support him for the presidency. Most of the members of the assemblies that were to appoint presidential electors were chosen in the spring of 1808, when resentment against the Jeffersonian embargo policy was only in

[1] Letter to John Taylor of Jan. 6, 1805 in *Writings* (Ford) viii, 339. Originally he had preferred a seven-year term and ineligibility thereafter, but had come to realize that "there should be a peace-able way of withdrawing a man in mid-way who is doing wrong. The service for 8. years with a power to remove at the end of the first four" now seemed to him to be best.

the beginning. As it was, the regular Federalist ticket, Charles Cotesworth Pinckney and Rufus King, received forty-seven electoral votes, instead of fourteen that had been given them in 1804; of the rest Madison received one hundred and twenty-two for President. The New York electors were not united in their voting. There were nineteen in all; of these six voted for George Clinton for President, dividing their votes for Vice-President between Madison and Monroe, — three to each. Jeffersonianism was still supreme, but unless there was a modification in its policies, the political future was by no means secure.

NOTES

I. Acts, Orders, and Decrees. — [First Embargo Act, December 22, 1807.] This law [1] laid an embargo on all vessels within the limits of the United States bound to any foreign port; no clearances were to be furnished to any vessel so bound except under the immediate direction of the President: provided that any foreign vessel might depart in ballast or with the cargo actually on board. No coasting vessel could leave port without giving bond to double the value of the vessel and cargo that the cargo shall be landed in some port of the United States "dangers of the seas excepted." A certificate from the collector where the goods were relanded must be transmitted by him to the Secretary of the Treasury.

[Supplementary Embargo Act, January 9, 1808.] Coasting vessels must give bonds in double the value of vessel and cargo that the vessel shall not proceed to any foreign port and that the cargo shall be landed in some port of the United States. Fishing vessels were to give a bond to four times the value of vessel and cargo, and small river and harbor craft to give bonds for three hundred dollars for each ton not to engage in any foreign trade. No vessel shall leave port without a clearance. The remainder of the act provided penalties for the infraction of this and the act of December 22, 1807.

[Additional Embargo Act, March 12, 1808.] In some respects this act modified the requirements of the preceding laws as to bonds; in others increased them and extended them to inland waters and to exportation by wagon or sleigh. The seventh section authorized the President to grant permission to citizens to send vessels in ballast for property which they may have in foreign ports. [2]

[Bayonne Decree, April 17, 1808.] It exists in the form of a letter from Napoleon to M. Gaudin, Minister of Finance, directing him to give orders for the seizure of all American vessels which should enter the ports of France, Italy, and the Hanseatic towns. [3]

---

[1] *Statutes at Large*, ii, 451, 453, 473, 506, 528; *Annals of Congress*, 10th Cong., 1st Sess., ii, 2814, 2815, 2839; *ibid.*, 10th Cong., 2nd Sess., 1798, 1824.

These and later laws, circulars, certificates, and Orders and Decrees were published at Boston in 1809 under the title *The Embargo Laws, with the Message from the President . . . [and] an Appendix*.

[2] By act of April 22, 1808, the President was authorized, practically at his discretion, during the recess of Congress to suspend in whole or in part the Embargo Acts. *Statutes at Large*, ii, 490.

[3] *Correspondance de Napoléon I*, vol.

[Enforcement Act, January 9, 1809.] This prohibits any person, directly or indirectly, placing any merchandise or specie on any conveyance with a view to its exportation under penalty of confiscation and punishment of any one aiding therein ; and that no goods shall be laden on any vessel without a previous permit. The penalties under this act were very severe. Power was given to customs officers to seize articles found on board any water craft " when there is reason to believe that they are intended for exportation, or when in vessels, carts, wagons, sleighs, or any other carriage, or in any manner apparently on their way towards the territories of a foreign nation, or the vicinity thereof, or towards a place whence such articles are intended to be exported."

[Non-Intercourse Act, March 1, 1809.] This act interdicts United States waters to all public vessels belonging to Great Britain or France and after the 20th day of May next interdicts all vessels sailing under the flag of Great Britain or France or owned in part by a citizen or subject of either from entering the waters of the United States and the importation of goods from those countries is forbidden. Section 12 of this law raised the embargo except as to Great Britain and France after March 15, 1809, and Section 17 repealed the Non-Importation Act after May 20. The other sections related to the mode of enforcement and provided that this act and all the embargo acts should cease from and after the end of the next session of Congress.

II. **Controversial Writings.** — Besides the voluminous writings of Timothy Pickering,[1] J. Q. Adams's *Letter to Harrison Gray Otis*,[2] and Henry Adams's *Documents relating to New-England Federalism, 1800–1815*,[3] the student will go to the tracts that are associated with the

17, p. 16. April 23 and April 25, 1808, Armstrong reported the orders for the seizure of American vessels and the reasons given therefor in this letter. In December, 1808 this was "the only authentic information" that had been received at Washington relative to the Bayonne Decree. *American State Papers, Foreign Relations*, iii, 291.

[1] Timothy Pickering's "Papers" are in the cabinet of the Massachusetts Historical Society. Large excerpts from them are printed in C. W. Upham's *Life of Timothy Pickering* (4 vols., Boston, 1867–1873) ; *A Letter from the Hon. Timothy Pickering . . . to His Excellency James Sullivan* (Boston, 1808) ;

and see also *Interesting Correspondence between His Excellency Governour Sullivan and Col. Pickering* (Boston, 1808).

[2] For hostile views, see William Coleman's *Remarks and Criticisms on the Hon. John Quincy Adams's Letter to the Hon. Harrison Gray Otis*, of which Coleman asserts one hundred thousand copies had been circulated through the country ; and John Lowell's *Remarks on the Hon. John Q. Adams's Review of Mr. Ames's Works* (Boston, 1809).

[3] The beginning of this work was in "The Correspondence between John Quincy Adams, Esq. . . . and several

name of John Lowell: *Thoughts upon the Conduct of our Adminis-tration . . . concerning the Attack on the Chesapeake by a Friend to Peace* (Boston, 1808); *Peace without Dishonour — War without Hope being a calm and dispassionate Enquiry into the Question of the Chesa-peake . . . by a Yankee Farmer* (Boston, 1807); *Analysis of the late Correspondence between our Administration and Great Britain & France* and *Supplement to the late Analysis,* both published in 1808; *The New-England Patriot being a Candid Comparison, of the Principles and Conduct of the Washington and Jefferson Administrations* (Boston, 1810). This was addressed to the " honest and well disposed part of the People of Massachusetts. An Answer to the Question, Why are you a Federalist? " Other essays by Mr. Lowell are, *Mr. Madison's War. A Dispassionate Inquiry into the Reasons alleged by Mr. Madison for declaring an Offensive and Ruinous War against Great-Britain by a New-England Farmer* (Boston, 1812); and *The Im-partial Inquirer . . . of the Conduct of the President of the United States* [under the act of May 1, 1810].

Of somewhat different character, but containing suggestive matter are the following: Jno. Thierry Danvers, of Virginia, *A Picture of a Republican Magistrate of the New School, being a full length likeness of His Excellency Thomas Jefferson* (New York, 1808); Francis Blake's *Examination of the Constitutionality of the Embargo Laws* (Worcester, 1808). The *Annals of Congress* necessarily give a great deal of space to the speeches delivered on both sides of the Senate and the House at this time. Many of these were reprinted, sometimes over and over again, as *The Speech of Mr. Giles, Member of the Senate of the United States from Virginia on the Resolution of Mr. Hillhouse for the Repeal of the Embargo Laws* (Northampton, Mass., 1808); Josiah Quincy's *Speech of January 19, 1809,* and Mr. Bayard's *Speech of February 14, 1809.*

Citizens of Massachusetts, concerning the charge of a design to dissolve the Union alleged to have existed in that State." This was printed in 1829 as a broadside, "Supplement to the Boston Daily Advertiser" and was twice re-printed in pamphlet form in the same year.

CHAPTER XV

INTRICACIES, FOREIGN AND DOMESTIC

JAMES MADISON [1] began the eight years of his presidential office on March 4, 1809, with a colorless Inaugural Address. There was some friction in the arrangement of his cabinet, but otherwise the next six months were of hopeful augury. The Federalists of the North and commercial men everywhere were fully occupied in sending to market — or as near to it as they could get — the accumulated surplus products of the last two years. Even George Canning adopted a less irritating tone, and for a time it looked as if Great Britain and America would compose their differences. The bare possibility of any such harmony aroused in Napoleon some thoughts as to the desirability of treating American commerce with greater fairness. Everything at home and abroad seemed to favor justice and tranquillity, when the horizon darkened. The British refused to accept the provisional agreement that had been made with their minister at Washington, Napoleon took the back course, and

[1] William Cabell Rives published three volumes entitled *History of the Life and Times of James Madison* (Boston, 1859–1868). It is an admirable example of its type, but unfortunately stops, owing to the death of the author, with the inauguration of Adams on March 4, 1797. There are two editions of the *Writings of Madison*, one in four volumes published by order of Congress in 1865 and generally known as the "Congress edition"; the other in nine volumes under the editorship of Gaillard Hunt (New York, 1900–1910). All the citations in the present work are to the latter. There is a "Calendar of the Correspondence of James Madison," now in the Library of Congress (*Bulletin of the Bureau of Rolls and Library of the Department of State*, No. 4) with an elaborate index in a "Supplement."

the Federalists once again complained of the subservience of the government to France. Month by month, the strain grew greater, until, in June, 1812, the breaking point was reached and war was declared upon England.

Naturally, to Madison, the first thing and the most important, in the existing state of world politics, was the filling of the position of Secretary of State which had been made vacant by his own elevation to the presidency. He designated Gallatin for this most critical office and found himself confronted by the Smiths, John Randolph of Roanoke, William Branch Giles, and their scanty but devoted bands of followers in both Houses of Congress.[1] Year after year, Gallatin had charged Robert Smith with extravagance and waste in the administration of the navy. There was, no doubt, much inefficiency in that department, especially in the navy yards; but the Mediterranean cruises show that the vessels themselves were kept fully up to the mark when away from home. The Smiths and their allies pointed to the fact of Gallatin's foreign birth as being distinctly against his having the management of the international relations of the United States. After a struggle Madison gave way. Gallatin retained his old post; Robert Smith became Secretary of State, and for a few months there was a reasonable amount of harmony. In June, however, it came to Senator Samuel Smith's ears that Gallatin had accused the commercial firm of which he was the head with indefensible financial transactions with the Navy Department, while his brother Robert was in charge.[2] Gallatin's

---

[1] See Henry Adams's *Life of Gallatin,* 389, his *History of the United States,* v, 4, and Dice R. Anderson's *William Branch Giles,* ch. x.

[2] Gallatin thought that the trouble was caused by Smith and Buchanan drawing bills on their foreign correspondents without sending funds with which to pay the drafts. Smith pointed out that commercial bills were drawn against goods shipped and the accompanying policy of marine insurance. Some of these bills had been purchased by an employee of the Navy Department entirely without pressure from or knowledge of the Secretary and in the regular

explanations were rather lame and betrayed considerable ignorance of the course of actual commercial transactions, — the breach between the Smiths and Gallatin was irreparable. For John Randolph, it was quite enough that Gallatin had advocated justice for the Yazoo men; but just why Giles broke with the administration is not clear. The feud between the two sets of politicians affected Gallatin's later career most unfortunately and had an influence upon the course of American history.

The embargo had aided France in her commercial war with Britain, Jefferson's proclamation forbidding the waters of the United States to British naval vessels while sheltering French warships was distinctly discriminatory and war seemed to be plainly impending. John Henry, a British spy at Boston, reported that disunion was a delicate subject of debate [1] but could be brought about by an unpopular war. Canning decided to reopen negotiations at Washington through David M. Erskine, the resident minister there, with a view to sending some one else with full powers to conclude a definite bargain.[2] In his instructions to Erskine, Canning dropped the demand for a disavowal of Commodore Barron, but did not renew the offer to disavow the British admiral. He instructed Erskine that the London government would withdraw the Orders in Council, provided that contemporaneously the United States would

course of business. Smith declared it was a common commercial proceeding, while Gallatin described it as the most extraordinary transaction that had fallen within his knowledge. Smith's letter of June 26 and Gallatin's of the 29th are printed in Adams's *Life of Albert Gallatin*, 402, and the latter is also printed in Adams's *Writings of Albert Gallatin*, i, 454. On the other hand, the relations of Gallatin with the Barings of London, with Astor and Girard and Parish would make an inter-

esting study. See Vincent Nolte's *Fifty Years in Both Hemispheres*, 139.

[1] Adams's *United States*, v, 14, citing the Henry letters in *American State Papers, Foreign Relations*, iii.

[2] The letters between Canning and Erskine are printed in *Correspondence between Mr. Secretary Canning and The Hon. D. Erskine* (London, 1810); and in *Correspondence Relating to America, presented to Parliament In 1810.* (London, 1811).

withdraw its interdiction of American territorial waters to British men-of-war, permit intercourse between the two countries while refusing it to France, recognize the rightfulness of the Rule of 1756, and allow the British to enforce the non-intercourse with France. These conditions, that were to precede the real negotiation, Erskine was authorized, but not directed, to read to the American negotiator. David M. Erskine was a Whig by birth and, therefore, out of sympathy with Canning and the existing government at London. He may have been influenced by his wife, who was an American, or by association with her friends. Whatever the reasons that actuated him, he did not read the instructions to the American Secretary of State, or inform him that he was allowed no option whatever. He simply outlined them and proceeded to agree to a provisional arrangement. By this, the interdict against British war vessels being already withdrawn and the non-intercourse with France continuing for the time being, Erskine announced that the Orders in Council of January and November, 1807, "will have been withdrawn as respects the United States on the 10th day of June next." [1] Thereupon, (April 19, 1809) Madison issued a proclamation renewing trade with Great Britain on the same 10th day of June.

While these negotiations were progressing at Washington and the Erskine treaty was crossing the Atlantic, the London government had withdrawn the old Orders in Council and issued a new one, declaring a blockade from the River Ems to northern Spain and of the Mediterranean ports of France and northern Italy. Madison and Robert Smith were puzzled by this action of the British govern-

[1] This provisional arrangement, including the proclamation, is embodied in a series of notes which passed between Smith and Erskine; *Documents accompanying The Message from the President of the United States, May 23, 1809; American State Papers, Foreign Relations*, iii, 295, and *American Register, or General Repository of History, Politics and Science*, v, 117.

ment, but Erskine assured them that the arrangement, that had been so recently and so happily concluded, would be "strictly fulfilled" by his royal master. Directly the opposite proved to be the case, for Canning disavowed it as soon as he saw it and recalled Erskine. At this point of time, far removed in space and chronology from those days, it is difficult to understand the motives of Canning's action. The Erskine arrangement practically secured all that England could ask for with any prospect of success; but no technical avowal and disavowal had been secured, according to Canning's instructions. Moreover, in one of the letters addressed by Smith to Erskine, the Secretary had informed the Minister as to what "would best comport with what is due from His Britannic Majesty to his own honor." This was extraordinary language to use in a diplomatic communication, and it may be this sentence that impelled Canning to disavow his Whiggish subordinate. When he communicated the disapproval to William Pinkney, now sole American minister at London, Canning read to him the actual instructions that had been sent to Erskine and informed him that Erskine had no others. Meantime, believing that the President had acted on good grounds in restoring commerce with England, vessels by the hundreds left American ports for that country deeply laden with flour, tobacco, cotton, and rice. These the British government permitted to enter freely, to unload and to depart; and the enormous mass of American products that found their way to British warehouses and factories took from Madison whatever coercive power the Jeffersonian commercial system might have had, had it continued in strict operation. He also had to issue another proclamation reviving non-intercourse with Great Britain; and the whole unhappy affair left the United States in a much

worse position than it was in at the time of his inauguration.

To succeed Erskine as British representative at Washington, Mr. Canning picked out Francis James Jackson, a
man of good family, who had seen diplomatic service, and
had a Prussian wife. Canning and Jackson evidently
thought that Erskine had been too susceptible to American
blandishments. It was improbable that Jackson would be
thus affected, for to him all Americans proved to be alike
"except that some few are less knaves than others." [1] The
idea now was to set the American government in its proper
place and, this being done, listen to whatever proposals the
President might have to make. Gallatin and Madison easily
divined the purpose of the incoming diplomat, and, even
before he landed, decided to bring him to the point at once
and send him home. Jackson seems to have suspected that
something of the kind might befall him, as he stipulated
for a year's emoluments before he embarked.

The new minister arrived at Washington at the time of
the summer cessation from business. He declined an invitation to go to Montpelier, Madison's plantation, where
the President then was, and awaited his return to the
capital in October, meantime reading Erskine's correspondence and conversing with him. When October came, the
President returned and so did Robert Smith, Secretary of
State. For a couple of days, Smith and Jackson talked together, the Secretary endeavoring to find out what the
envoy had been told to do. He had poor success in this
and on the third day Madison seems to have taken the

[1] *A Further Selection from the Diaries
and Letters of Sir George Jackson, K.C.H.*,
i, 29. This publication is often referred
to as the *Bath Archives* and sometimes as
the *Bath Archives, Second Series*, from
the fact that two other volumes entitled the *Diaries and Letters of Sir
George Jackson, K. C. H.*, deal with the
years before 1809; but the words "The
Bath Archives" do not occur on the
title pages of these earlier volumes.

matter upon himself, although Smith signed the letters that were directed to the British minister. In the first letter, the President, or Secretary, declared that he learned with no less surprise than regret that Jackson had no explanations to make as to the Erskine disavowal and was instructed to proceed on practically the same lines that had proved to be impossible in the case of his predecessor. He added, "to avoid the misconceptions incident to oral proceedings," it is thought expedient that further discussions be in a written form. This called from Jackson an "enormous despatch" deprecating the cessation of verbal communications. Continuing, he wrote that it appeared Erskine had not communicated in full his original instructions and declared to Smith and through him to the President that the despatch which Canning had read to Pinkney, containing the three conditions, is the only desspatch in which these conditions were prescribed to Erskine. He sought to minimize the absence of instructions to explain the disavowal, by the fact that Canning had stated the reasons of it to Pinkney. He himself had no proposals to make and explained why at great length; but he was open to proposals from the American government. In reply, Smith and the President recalled to Jackson's mind — what he had probably never known — that Pinkney had been shut off from verbal communications by Canning in almost the exact circumstances of Smith's recent suggestion and then went on for many pages, concluding with the statement that the President is ready to favor any mode of bringing about a final and comprehensive accommodation between the two nations. After some more rather recriminatory writings, Smith informed Jackson that no further communications would be held with him. Madison and Gallatin had divined truly that Jackson had no propositions to make that would interest the American government or improve the existing situation; they were undoubtedly right in bringing him to the point and getting rid of him. Mahan points out, however, that the means adopted will not bear close investigation,[1] because a careful perusal of Jackson's inordinately long communications show that he was very careful to use diplomatic language and to make no such improper allusion as that with which he was charged. He demanded his passports; but getting them did not leave the country, for he wished to serve his year out.

The congressional session of 1809–1810 was peculiarly impotent.[2] It is associated largely with the names of Giles, Samuel Smith, and Nathaniel Macon. Projects of armament and disarmament, of spending money, or retrench-

---

[1] *Sea Power in its Relations to the War of 1812*, i, 223–228. Mahan's point is that Jackson carefully said that it was he, himself, who had the honor to inform the American government that Erskine had only one set of instructions. He never implied directly that the American government knew Erskine was not authorized to make the arrangement. In a similar way Mahan shows that offence was taken where none was meant in the interpretation of Canning's own language by changing Canning's phrase "purpose of securing the operation of the embargo, and of the bonâ fide intention of America to prevent her citizens from trading with France" to read "the purpose of *securing the bonâ fide intention* of America" etc. Considering that Madison stated in an unpublished writing, composed sometime in 1811, that the correspondence in Jackson's case "in a manner" fell into his own hands, it is possible that these particular bits of maladroitness or ill-faith belonged to the Secretary and not to the President. See Hunt's *Writings of James Madison*, viii, 142. It is well to compare Adams's account of this episode (*History of the United States*, v, 123–131); Madison's statement is also in the "Congress Edition"

of his works, ii, 499. A contemporaneous Federalist view, anticipating Mahan's criticisms, is John Lowell's *Interesting Political Discussion. The Diplomatick Policy of Mr. Madison Unveiled.*

[2] This paragraph is based upon Adams's *United States*, v. ch. ix. See also W. E. Dodd's *Life of Nathaniel Macon*, 249–260. The cabal on this measure is noted in Robert Smith's *Address to the People of the United States*, 9 and in Madison's *Writings* (Hunt) viii, 140.

Henry Adams declares that no man in American history left a better name than Macon, and John Randolph of Roanoke said that he was the best, purest, and wisest man he ever saw; but of him, as of so many Southern statesmen, only inadequate memoirs exist. Of Macon, beside Dodd's little book, there is an earlier one by E. R. Cotten (Baltimore, 1840) and a memoir by Edwin Mood Wilson in *James Sprunt Historical Monographs*, No. 2. The same number and the succeeding one No. 3, contain letters and explanatory matter which throw some light on the life and career of this comparatively unknown politician.

ing expenditures were brought forward and voted down, or passed with little regard to anything save personal animosities and petty politics. The one alleviating fact was the appearance of Henry Clay, fresh from the West whence he brought ideas of patriotism and national honor that seem to have deserted the old-time politicians. The principal work of the session was the production of an act that was usually referred to at the time as Macon's Bill No. 2. The reason for this measure was the termination of the Non-Intercourse Act with the session of Congress. What should be done? Should the whole matter be dropped and trade thrown open with the world? A committee of which Macon was chairman reported a bill, that is said to have been devised by Gallatin and accepted by the cabinet, for the exclusion of all British and French vessels from the ports of the United States, while admitting British and French products when imported from their place of origin in American bottoms. This was really a navigation act, and was an entirely intelligible measure. It passed the House, went up to the Senate, and came back minus everything except the enacting clause and the interdiction of warships. This was the result of the fight between Gallatin and the brothers Smith; it was Gallatin's plan, it would aid the Treasury, therefore it must be killed. Why it was necessary to do anything, is not clear, for the foreign trade was again being vigorously carried on [1] and the finances were recovering

---

[1] The following figures are taken from *American State Papers, Commerce and Navigation*, i, 733, 877: —

Date	Registered Tonnage	Enrolled and Licensed	Total Tonnage of Vessels Over 20 Tons Each
1807	848,306 $\frac{55}{95}$	379,787 $\frac{8}{95}$	1,228,093 $\frac{93}{95}$
1810	984,269 $\frac{5}{95}$	397,704 $\frac{32}{95}$	1,381,973 $\frac{37}{95}$

from past difficulties.[1] But Macon and those who worked
with him thought that something must be done. Therefore he brought in Bill No. 2. This opened trade with the
world, but went on to provide that if one of the belligerents
should see reason and, before the 3rd day of March, 1811,
remove its restrictions on neutral trade and the other belligerent should not do this, then the President by proclamation
shall revive non-intercourse against the recalcitrant power.
While the bill embodying this scheme was passing through
the House an amendment was made to increase the duties
on all products of Great Britain or France by fifty per cent.
When it came to the Senate, the Smiths and Giles did not
kill it, as they had Bill No. 1. They struck out the fifty
per cent extra duty clause, added one providing convoy for
American merchantmen, and sent it back to the House.
That body insisting on its amendment, a conference was
held and the bill in its original form was passed and approved by the President.

In 1810, Napoleon took part in the fray and added to the
embarrassment of the administration at Washington. In-
tentionally or unintentionally, the United States by the
embargo had taken sides with the French and by the Non-
Intercourse Act had broken this tacit alliance. In the
future, French national vessels as well as English were to
be excluded from American harbors; and the ability of an
American merchantman to sail to any part of the world

[1] Amounts collected at the custom houses, *ibid.*, *Finance*, ii, 551, 552: —

DATE	GROSS AMOUNT OF DUTIES	PAYMENTS FOR			NET REVENUE
		Drawbacks on Merchandise Re-exported	Bounties and Allowances	Expenses of Prosecution and Collection	
1807	$27,323,227.19	$9,995,559.15	$188,668.20	$646,110.77	$16,493,434.75
1810	16,898,539.40	3,689,863.17	3,914.79	447,868.16	12,757,988.29

was equivalent to commerce with Britain, whether direct trade with that country was permitted or not.[1] In the summer of 1809, Napoleon was busily employed with the Austrians. The Non-Intercourse Act stirred his interest for a moment and so did Erskine's arrangement and its disavowal. Reprisals on America were projected and so was a repeal of the Berlin Decree; but nothing was done. On March 23rd, 1810, in the midst of his second marrying, he found time to issue a decree which goes by the name of Rambouillet. The first part of it recites the provisions of the Non-Intercourse Act and the penalties provided for attempts to evade it, and proceeds by denouncing similar treatment to vessels of the United States entering French ports. They shall be seized and sold and the proceeds deposited in the surplus fund, which in French phrase is denominated the "caisse d'amortissement" [2] — a phrase that somehow carried a connotation of hopelessness with it. This edict had scarcely gone into effect, when news came of the ending of the Non-Intercourse Act and the substitution of the Macon Bill No. 2. To French eyes, this was hardly less than entering into alliance with Great Britain, as the new law took away all restraints on commerce between the United States and that country while British cruisers saw to it that the similar freedom of commerce with France

---

[1] The course of commerce between America and Great Britain comes out in a letter from Logan and Lenox of Liverpool, November 2, 1809, to their American correspondents. Tobacco, cotton, naval stores, and flour "will pay well," they write. "There will be ships in great abundance at Amelia Island and Lisbon to bring forward such articles of American produce as may be shipped through those channels." Amelia Island was in Spanish Florida, just south of the Georgia boundary; Lisbon was in Portugal, a country not tabooed by the Non-Intercourse Act or by Macon's Bill No. 2.

[2] *American State Papers, Foreign Relations*, iii, 384. Mr. Waldo G. Leland of the Carnegie Institution writes me that the words as to the disposal of the amount realized from the sale of the confiscated vessels were added to the original draft by the hand of Napoleon, himself.

The *Columbian Centinel* of June 27, 1810 has a list of 133 vessels that had been sequestered in French harbors or in ports of countries subservient to France, since the 1st of April, 1809.

should amount to very little. For months there followed a distressing correspondence and series of conferences between John Armstrong, American envoy at Paris, and French ministers of one sort or another. Napoleon's activity at this epoch was startling. He was making peace and war, divorcing and marrying, extending his continental system here and contracting it there, all at one time. The student with painful toil seeks to unravel and correlate; but, really, it is of little use. A few facts stand out and a statement of these will be quite enough for the present purpose.

At London, Pinkney dangled before the British government the offer of Macon's Bill No. 2 to revive non-intercourse against either France or Great Britain, provided the other one withdrew its obnoxious orders or decrees before a stated day. As the matter stood, the Londoners were getting about all they wanted, in fact rather more, for American products were pouring into Great Britain in so great a stream as to force prices down below cost. Moreover, the British administration was going to pieces. In 1810, it was at its weakest phase, no one minister daring to take upon himself much of any responsibility, — not even the high-handed Marquess of Wellesley, who had succeeded George Canning at the Foreign Office. To Napoleon's scrupleless disposition and Corsican imagination Macon's Bill No. 2 seemed to offer a clear road for the hoodwinking of the United States, and, perhaps, forcing her into war with Great Britain. He swept up all the sequestered ships and cargoes, wherever he could reach them — in Holland, in Italy, and in France [1] — and ordered the products of the sales to be turned into the treasury. On August 5, 1810, two decrees, or rather minutes, were signed by the Emperor;

[1] See his order of July 22, 1810, in Adams's *Writings of Gallatin*, ii, 211.

one of these was communicated by Champagny, Duc de Cadore, to Armstrong in a letter of the same date. It announced that the new state of things, the abandonment of non-intercourse and the adoption of Macon's Bill No. 2, had led to a new determination on the part of the Emperor, who loved the Americans whose prosperity and commerce were within the scope of his policy. Therefore, the Foreign Minister was authorized to declare "that the decrees of Berlin and Milan are revoked, and that after the 1st of November they will cease to have effect"; — as a member of Congress paraphrased it, they were dead on August 5 and will cease to live on November 1 — it being understood that in consequence the English shall revoke their orders, or the United States have compelled them to respect their rights. The other minute, which is referred to as the "Decree of the Trianon," ordered the sale of sequestered ships and cargoes and payment of the proceeds into the imperial treasury.

Years afterward in 1821, Albert Gallatin, when United States Minister at Paris, accidentally got a sight of the Trianon Decree, copied it, and sent it to John Quincy Adams [1] who was then Secretary of State, stigmatizing it as "a glaring act of combined injustice, bad faith, and meanness." No one could suppose, so he wrote, that if it had been known in 1810 the United States would have taken grounds with respect to the promised revocation of the French decrees that led to war with Great Britain. On the other hand, it must be said that the Trianon Decree was merely a repetition of that of July 22, which in turn was only an imperial authorization of what had been going on for some time and what was then being prosecuted with vigor; namely, the seizure and condemnation of American property in coun-

---

[1] See Note at end of the Chapter.

tries under Napoleon's control. The injustice and diabolical
ingenuity of Napoleon in robbing Americans was perfectly
well known to any one who had any eyes to see before the
5th of August as well as after. His imperial ingenuity in
handling Jeffersonian Americans was also perfectly patent
to every one except the victims. The language of the
Duc de Cadore's letter was also open to doubt. Were the
decrees revoked or were they to be revoked in consideration
of something to be done by the British or by the American
government? But these uncertainties sat lightly on Madison's mind. On November 2, 1810, he issued a proclamation
declaring that the edicts of France having been "so revoked"
as to cease to have effect on the 1st day of the present month,
all the restrictions on commerce with France shall cease.
Moreover, if Great Britain shall not within three months
thereafter modify her edicts in the same manner, then the
Non-Intercourse Act shall be revived against her.[1]

Meantime in these years of controversies over neutral
rights, the question of the Floridian boundary and of the
acquisition of Spanish Florida had tinged every thought of
the administration and affected its action in regard to France
and Great Britain. In 1804, as a part of the Louisiana
settlement, Congress had passed an act for laying and collecting duties on imports and tonnage within the limits of
the new acquisition. The eleventh section of this law
authorized the President to erect Mobile and its neighborhood into a separate collection district, for Mobile was
within the limits of Louisiana as it had been in the hands
of France. It had not been received by Spain from France
in 1763, but had come from England as a part of the settlement of 1783.[2] The Spaniards regarded it as in West Florida

---

[1] *American State Papers, Foreign
Relations*, iii, 392.

[2] On this exceedingly difficult subject,
see Henry E. Chambers' "West Florida

and not as in Louisiana. When a copy of the Mobile Act came into the hands of the Marquis del Casa d'Yrujo, he hastened with it to Madison's office and indulged in quite undiplomatic language to the Secretary of State. Some months later, it occurred to him to appeal to the people through the public press. He sought Major Jackson, formerly Washington's secretary and now the editor of a Federalist newspaper. He asked Jackson to receive and print "elucidations" from him for which he would make "any acknowledgement." Washington's erstwhile major domo thought he saw a bribe in this and promptly apprised Jefferson of the nefarious attempt of the Spanish minister. This was the end of Yrujo, but his office would have ceased before long owing to the disturbed conditions in Spain.

At first, after the cession of Louisiana, Napoleon took a somewhat neutral attitude as to the extension of the eastern bounds of Louisiana into Spanish West Florida. When he seized the Spanish kingdom, and interned its royal family in otherwise unused French castles, he refused to listen to any suggestion of alienating any part of Spanish America. His determination to retain that Spanish American empire intact continued for some time after British soldiers and Viscount Wellesley of Talavera had made his hold on Spain decidedly precarious. As the British extended their protection over the Spaniards, they too, refused to listen to the slightest whisper of the cession of Florida and even began to exhibit doubts as to the morality of the Louisianian procurement. Spanish colonists and governors were uncertain as to whom they owed obedience. Should they obey the Spanish king or the Emperor or his agents, or should

and its Relation to the Historical Cartography of the United States" in *Johns Hopkins University Studies*, xvi, No. 5 (bibliography on p. 57); H. B. Fuller's *Purchase of Florida: its History* *and Diplomacy*, ch. iv; P. J. Hamilton's *Colonial Mobile*; and J. F. H. Claiborne's *Mississippi, as a Province, Territory and State*.

they follow the exhortations of British emissaries and naval commanders? In that part of West Florida lying on the Mississippi River between the thirty-first parallel — the old southern boundary of the United States — and the River Iberville — the northern boundary of the Louisiana Purchase — was a stretch of Spanish territory inappropriately termed West Feliciana.[1] Its inhabitants were of all sorts and their Spanish ruler did not know who was his master. Accordingly, when they grew discontented and demanded a convention, he permitted them to hold one. They adopted a declaration of independence of the State of West Florida, and demanded the surrender of Baton Rouge, the only remaining Spanish town in this region.[2] There was a fort at that place, with a garrison of thirty men, and a gallant commander, Louis Grandpré. He refused to surrender and the conventioners marched into the fort over his dying body. Madison acted in this concatenation without regard for the feelings of the West Felicianians. By proclamation of October 27, 1810, the President included within Orleans Territory all of the lands east of "the lakes" that had been acquired by the Louisiana Purchase Treaty. And, to run forward eighteen months, in April, 1812, Congress by law included within the limits of the newly formed State of Louisiana so much of this territory as lay to the westward of the Pearl River.

In April, 1809, Jefferson wrote that Bonaparte's policy

[1] See "Some of the Causes and Conditions that brought about the West Florida Revolution in 1810" by Henry L. Favrot in *Publications* of the Louisiana Historical Society, i, Pt. ii, p. 37.

[2] An attempt was also made to revolutionize Mobile. See documents printed in *American Historical Review*, ii, 699–705. Thomas M. Owen has contributed bibliographies of Alabama and Mississippi to the *Reports* of the American Historical Association for 1897, No. xxii, and for 1899, No. xxi. An interesting "Speech of Gov. Fulwar Skipwith" to the Senate and House of Representatives of the "State of West Florida" on Nov. 20, 1810, is in *The Susquehanna Democrat* for January 25, 1811. It is followed by a proclamation which also elucidates the rebellion of 1810.

was "so crooked that it eludes conjectures."[1] His object was to dry up the sources of British prosperity and opening European ports to American vessels would defeat this because they would bring British goods to the continental market. By 1810, Napoleon had extended his policy to the sapping of Russia's military strength by destroying her commercial life. To accomplish these endeavors and keep on terms of amity with the United States, possibly forcing her into war with Great Britian, was a game worth playing. And Napoleon played it very well, except that he did not push Madison over the line into war with England until his own military power had passed the zenith and entered upon a rapid tropical twilight.

By his proclamation of November 2, 1810, Madison, conformable to the terms of the Macon Act, had given England three months to withdraw her blockade. For three months, therefore, he awaited news from France and England showing that the decrees really were annulled and that the British government was withdrawing the blockade orders. Nothing happened on either side of the Channel. For a time no American vessels were sequestered, but those that were in French clutches before August 5, were not set free. Then came the seizure of an American vessel at Bordeaux. Explanations were difficult, because there was no American minister, only a chargé at Paris, and Napoleon, after his wont, had closed possibilities of awkward discussion by ordering that no more reports of these cases should be made public. It became perfectly obvious that the Berlin and Milan Decrees remained fundamental laws of the empire, regardless of whether they were repealed or suspended as to America. For in this very year Napoleon was forcing his Continental System upon the Baltic powers

---

[1] *Writings of Jefferson* (Cong. ed.) v, 444.

and getting ready to punish the Czar of Russia for his failure to enforce it within his domains.

At London, William Pinkney wrote sundry letters to the Marquess of Wellesley, growing ever more determined in tone.[1] He found it impossible to make the British Foreign Secretary admit that the French decrees were revoked. The utmost that Wellesley would do was to promise that whenever France returned to her ordinary modes of action England would do likewise. For weeks at a time, Pinkney did not even get this measure of satisfaction. He could not even induce the Marquess to answer his letters. The reason was simple enough and might well have induced both Pinkney and his employers at Washington to pause in their careers. In one of the first days of November, George III lost his reason for the last time, and it was not until February, 1811, that the regency was formed and the government again in working order. And then another three months might well have been allowed to elapse while the administration was recovering from the strain of this interregnum. Apart from regal difficulties, the British ministry was torn with dissension. The Prime Minister, Spencer Perceval, was little regarded by any one. His colleagues did not respect him and had little esteem for one another. Wellesley was the greatest of them, but whatever strength he had he necessarily gave to his brother

---

[1] *Correspondence of the Marquess Wellesley, the Earl of Liverpool, and Viscount Castlereagh with the American Ministers in London. January 1810 to July 1812* in four parts marked A. B. C. D. presented to Parliament in February, 1813 and printed in that year, and *Correspondence Relative to the French Decrees, and the Orders in Council subsequent to 20th May 1812*, also presented to Parliament in 1813 and printed in that year. The books relating to Wellesley necessarily give most of their space to his career in India, but some American matter is contained in the third volume of R. R. Pearce's *Memoirs and Correspondence of the Most Noble Richard Marquess Wellesley*. The *Wellesley Papers* (London, 1914), while covering the years at the Foreign Office, have almost nothing relating to America — they are mainly occupied with squabblings for office — like so many English memoirs.

— the Duke of Wellington — in Spain.   As he could not write to Pinkney what the latter wanted and, very likely, what he himself wished, he made no reply, or when he did, only repeated what he had said in earlier letters.   It was about the same with Pinkney.   His business was to prove that Napoleon's decrees had been rescinded.   But scarcely a week went by without giving evidence that while they might be suspended as to America, they certainly were not ended as to Great Britain.   Wellesley was inclined to be friendly, but he insisted upon the rightfulness of his position and the ancient and established prerogatives and interests of his country.[1]   Moreover no successor to Jackson had been sent to Washington.   This was partly due to the promise of a twelve-month term that had been made to Jackson and, when he had returned to England, the disordered condition of the government and the royal illness put off consideration of this appointment for months. When Wellesley again felt reasonably firm in office, he informed Pinkney that Augustus J. Foster had been selected for the Washington mission.   But Pinkney had lost all patience and had already asked for his audience of leave. Nothing that Wellesley could do or say could turn him from his purpose.   He had his audience of leave on February 28, 1811, and sailed for home.

Matters had also been running swiftly to a conclusion in America.   Having proclaimed to the world that the French decrees were repealed, Madison was obliged to adhere to his declaration.   This he did with all the pertinacity of his nature.   He and his following concocted a precious theory.   The United States, they said, was bound to Na-

[1] See Wellesley to Pinkney, December 29, 1810.   Lord Milton, afterwards the fifth Earl Fitzwilliam, regarded Wellesley as "a great calamity inflicted upon England."   It was the imperious language of the "Conqueror of the East" to which he especially objected. See *The Creevey Papers*, i, 118.

poleon to enforce its rights in the face of British opposition and, per contra, the British must repeal their orders, Napoleon having revoked his decrees. The whole thing went around in a circle. Any one who wishes can read the debates in the "Annals of Congress" and there is an abundance of letters to satisfy the most inordinate desires. When all is done, the reader will inevitably arrive at the conclusion or lack of conclusion stated in the preceding sentences. The Madisonians felt that they were obliged to do something and the thing that they did was to pass the Non-Intercourse Act of March 2, 1811, which was nothing more than a legal recognition of the fact that the Non-Intercourse Act of March 1, 1809, by the failure of Great Britain to repeal her orders, was revived as against her.

For several years, there had been an equilibrium in the world-wide commercial warfare. On the face of it, the United States was the only one of the three that was gaining anything. Since the ending of the embargo, American commerce and navigation had experienced a marvellous revival. The exports had gone up to a figure only exceeded by those of the last years preceding the laying of the embargo. The ship yards of New England and the Middle States had resounded with the making of new ships and the repairing of old. The tonnage leaving United States ports for foreign parts had come back almost to that of the earlier period and the returns at the customs houses had made it possible to pay the expenses of the year and have something over. This activity and success were not confined to the North; the Southern States shared in it as their stored crops found a way to market. It was an indirect way, to be sure, but the extra expense of indirectness was borne by the foreign consumer. Jeffersonian policy seemed to have succeeded despite the repeal of the embargo. A shrewd ruler and one whose every thought was bound up with the prosperity of the country might well have gone on developing American industry, commerce, and navigation regardless of the niceties of international law and the agonies of trans-Atlantic countries.

On the European continent, Napoleon apparently was supreme. His military strength was never greater than in 1811. It is true that Wellington's resistance in the "Lines of Torres Vedras" was like the proverbial cloud no bigger than a man's hand that portends the coming storm. A man of Napoleon's military instinct must have recognized the meaning of the portent. To the world in general, it simply meant that, for the moment, the success of Napoleonic armies was limited, or that Wellington and his expedition were saved from disaster. Over all the rest of continental Europe, no emperor or prince dared say his soul was his own, or was willing to say it. For any such pronouncement meant the speedy appearance of one hundred thousand soldiers with a Napoleonic marshal at their head, or even the Emperor, himself. Around the whole Continent, there was an impenetrable barrier to British commerce. Soldiers, three deep, guarded the most likely means of ingress, and bales of British goods, discovered in French and German cities, were the signal for a textile *auto da fé*. Napoleon had said he would enforce the Continental System if he had to overturn the world, and he came very near doing it to accomplish the downfall of Great Britain. It was the difficulty of enforcing this ruthless exclusion of British manufactures that made it impossible for the Emperor to accede to the American demand for the revocation of the decrees for any real revocation would mean an inundation of British goods. So, he contented himself with saying they were repealed as to America and with admitting

such American vessels as were certified to have loaded in
American ports nothing but American products; and these
were obliged to carry away from France only French goods.
Napoleon thought he saw the ruin of Great Britain in the
destruction of markets for her products. He forgot to take
account of what would happen to French and German industry when British and American markets had been
closed to them for any length of time. The incessant warfare on the Continent had killed off or maimed the manhood of the warring nations. The practical extinction of
large lines of industry had destroyed the means of living
of thousands and thousands. How long human beings
could withstand this treatment, how long they would permit their lives and hopes to be thus played with, — these
were questions for the future and the future was to answer
them very soon. They were urgent in 1811, but only those
gifted with prophecy could see the urgency.

In England the condition of things outwardly was more
critical than on the Continent. There had been a great
deal of distress there in 1810, bankruptcies, closing of factories, and starvation. The next year, 1811, was even worse,
more bankruptices, more closings of factories, and wider
spread starvation. It is an interesting inquiry as to what
cause or causes were at the bottom of this commercial and
industrial disaster. For one thing a failure of crops in 1811
had driven the price of wheat up to almost prohibitory figures, to three dollars and a half a bushel. How much of
this could be attributed to the Continental System? How
much to the American commercial war? How much to a
temporary lessening of the rainfall or to an unusual distribution of moisture? Napoleon's system undoubtedly
was a powerful contributory cause to the suffering and distress in England. He had closed to British industry a very

large part of its natural market, although he could not close it absolutely. But, on the other hand, it was continental flour imported by special license that maintained England in this very year! It is one of the curiosities of this time that every act of American commercial war against England was checkmated by some alleviating circumstance in Europe. Thus the embargo was contemporaneous with the Spanish Revolution, so that, as American ports closed, Iberian and Spanish-American colonial ports opened; but British goods were sent to South America in such quantities that they lay for months without cover on the streets and wharves. The colonists could not pay for more than a fraction of what was sent them, they could not even use much of what was unloaded upon them. Bankruptcy necessarily followed this ill-thought-on enterprise and, where insolvency was not the penalty, there was an impairment of credit and capital. The repeal of the embargo and the opening of indirect trade between Great Britain and the United States were likewise the signal for dumping great quantities of American products on British wharves. In the embargo years speculation in rice, cotton, tobacco, and flour had forced up the prices. In the autumn of 1809, tobacco and cotton were selling at Liverpool at shillings per pound; at its highest point tobacco brought fifteen and one-half pence, and cotton, — upland cotton — twenty-four pence and more. Prices then rapidly fell to four and a half pence for tobacco and twenty pence for cotton. As to flour, that was selling for fifty-six shillings a barrel at Liverpool in the autumn of 1809 and rose to sixty, to sixty-six, shillings in 1810 and 1811. The letters of Ellis and Allan show how they and their English correspondents were caught with large stocks of American produce in English warehouses. They were able to hold it until the outbreak of war made it salable at almost any price; but for many a firm the over-speculation of 1809 and 1810 spelled disaster.

In 1811, commercial and industrial conditions on the island of Great Britain were in a very dangerous state. All the enemies of the government rallied to discredit its policy and demanded the repeal of the Orders in Council and the reëstablishment of living commercial conditions with the United States. The ship-owners alone remained firm in their opposition to any relaxation and their voices were heard at Downing Street. An inquiry was held by the House of Commons. The evidence that was taken then, as well as that which was received in 1808, has been printed and is accessible to any one who cares to read it.[1] He will get very little tangible information as the result of his endeavor; but he will get enough to understand that the administration was obliged by discontent, no matter what its cause, to take the back track. Henry Adams tells us that if a strong man had been representing America at London in the winter and spring of 1812, war might then have been averted. Possibly, it might have so fallen out, had Pinkney remained at his post; but there was no one there who could take advantage of circumstances as they arose.

[1] See *Minutes of Evidence, Upon taking into Consideration several Petitions, Presented to the House of Commons, respecting The Orders in Council*, ordered printed in 1808, and reprinted in 1812; and *Minutes of Evidence, taken before the Committee of the Whole House* . . . *relating to The Orders in Council*, printed in 1812; (in *Parliamentary Papers*, Nos. 231 and 210). This matter, in a condensed form, will be found in *An Abstract of the Evidence lately taken in the House of Commons, against the Orders in Council* (London, 1812).

NOTES

I. Acts, Orders, etc. — [Proclamation of April 19, 1809.] It [1] recites the eleventh section of the Non-Intercourse Act which provided that in case either France or Great Britain so modifies her edicts as that they shall cease to violate the neutral commerce of the United States, the President is authorized to declare the same after which trade with that nation may be renewed.   The British minister having declared that the Orders in Council of January and November, 1807, will have been withdrawn as to the United States on June 10 next; after that day American trade with Great Britain may be renewed.

[Order in Council, April 26, 1809.]   It recites [2] the Orders of November and December, 1807, and March 30, 1808.   In consequence of events which have since taken place, it is expedient that parts of these Orders shall be altered or revoked.   It is therefore ordered that all ports and places from the River Ems southward, under the government of France and Holland and plantations of those governments, and also of the northern parts of Italy shall be subject to the same restrictions " as if the same were actually blockaded by His Majesty's naval forces in the most strict and rigorous manner."

[Proclamation of August 9, 1809.]   After reciting the Proclamation of April 19 and stating that the Orders in Council had not been withdrawn, it [3] proclaimed this fact and stated that consequently " the trade renewable on the event of the said orders being withdrawn, is to be considered as under the operation of the several acts by which such trade was suspended."

[Macon's Bill No. 2, May 1, 1810.]   " An Act concerning the commercial intercourse between the United States, Great Britain and France " etc.   No British or French armed vessel shall be permitted to enter the harbors or waters under the jurisdiction of the United States, except when forced in by distress or when charged with despatches.   All pacific intercourse with any interdicted foreign, armed vessel is forbidden.

Section 4 provides " that in case either Great Britain or France shall, before the third day of March next, so revoke or modify her edicts as that they shall cease to violate the neutral commerce of the

---

[1] *Annals of Congress*, 11th Cong., 1st and 2nd Sessions, Pt. 2, 2060.

[2] *American State Papers, Foreign Re-* lations, iii, 241.

[3] *Annals of Congress*, 11th Cong., 1st and 2nd Sessions, Pt. 2, 2076.

United States " the President shall proclaim the same and if the other nation shall not within three months thereafter similarly revoke her edicts, then the Non-Intercourse Act shall be revived against that nation. And the restrictions imposed by this present act (in sections 1 and 2) shall from the date of the proclamation be discontinued in relation to the nation so modifying her decrees.

["Rambouillet" Decree, March 23, 1810.] Considering that the United States by act of March 1, 1809 announced non-intercourse with France, Napoleon decrees [1] that all vessels navigating under the flag of the United States or possessed in whole or in part by American citizens which shall enter into any French port after May 20, 1809, shall be seized and sold, and the proceeds deposited in the " caisse d'amortissement."

[The Duc de Cadore's Letter [2] to Armstrong, August 5, 1810.] Congress having revoked its steps (the act of March 1, 1809) the ports of America are open to French commerce. " In this new state of things, I am authorized to declare to you, sir, that the decrees of Berlin and Milan are revoked, and that after the 1st of November, they will cease to have effect; it being understood that, in consequence of this declaration, the English shall revoke their orders in council, and renounce the new principles of blockade . . . or that the United States . . . should cause their rights to be respected by the English."

[Proclamation of November 2, 1810.] It recites [3] the provisions of Macon's Bill No. 2. " And whereas it has been officially made known to this Government, that the edicts of France violating the neutral commerce of the United States have been so revoked as to cease to have effect on the 1st of the present month " : the President proclaims that the said edicts of France have been so revoked and that from this day all the restrictions imposed by the aforesaid act shall cease in relation to France.

II. The Trianon Decree. — Gallatin's letter to Adams with the decree enclosed is dated Paris, September 15, 1821. The letter and enclosure are printed in Adams's *Writings of Gallatin* (Philadelphia, 1879) ii, 196, and in *The Diary of James Gallatin* (New York, 1914) p. 187; and an English translation is given in Appendix iii of the latter book. Article vi of this decree or minute of August 5, 1810, provides

---

[1] *American State Papers, Foreign Relations*, iii, 384.
[2] *American State Papers, Foreign Relations*, iii, 386.
[3] *Annals of Congress*, 11th Cong., 3rd Sess., 1248.

that for the future and until the 1st of November "les navires améri-
cains pourront entrer dans nos ports ; mais leur déchargement ne pourra
avoir lieu, à moins qu'ils ne soient munis d'une license signée de notre
main, que sur un rapport fait en conseil de commerce, constatant qu'ils
n'ont pas été dénationalisés par leur soumission aux arrêts du conseil
britannique, et qu'ils n'ont point contrevenu à nos décrets de Berlin et
de Milan." Mr. Waldo G. Leland of the Carnegie Institution writes
me that the original reading of the latter part of Article vi was " Les
batiments Americains entrés dans nos ports ni seront pas confisqués s'ils
n'ont pas été dénationalizés par leur soumission aux arrets du Conseil
Britannique et s'ils n'ont point contrevenu à nos decrets de Berlin et
de Milan de l'application desquels aucun batiment ne peut être dis-
pensé que par une license signee de notre main." The amended form
is inserted in the margin of the minute and is signed by Napoleon.

CHAPTER XVI

NEW MEASURES, NEW MEN

THE population of the United States in 1810 was a little under seven millions and a quarter as compared with five million three hundred thousand in 1800, and less than four millions in 1790.[1] A study of these first three censuses shows that, while there was a constant pushing into the interior, the increase in population west of the water-parting between the Atlantic and the Mississippi was very slow. Nearly one half of the State of New York was still unsettled and there were great quantities of wild land in the northern part of Pennsylvania. The acquisition of Louisiana, while adding territory of immense economic possibilities, increased the immediate population by only some sixty thousand human beings, excluding the wild Indians of the plains. Studying map and population tables together, one is surprised at the sparseness of settlement at the beginning of the nineteenth century. The country was agricultural with a few commercial towns and fewer manufacturing villages. In 1810, the urban population, including in that designation every town with ten thousand people or over, was something over three hundred thousand in comparison with two hundred thousand in 1800, and approximately one hundred thousand in 1790. These figures are trifling in comparison with what

---

[1] Contrary to the general idea of the paucity of women in newly settled countries, the census of 1790 shows that there were 509 men to every 491 women, taking the country through.

constitutes a town or city to-day. They are none the less interesting because comparing the growth of the urban population with that of the country as a whole, it is at once seen that there was no pressure from the land to the town — in point of fact the movement is one of dissemination rather than of concentration.

Another significant fact that comes out in these early enumerations is the disproportionate growth of the black population. In the first ten years from 1790 to 1800, the black population increased thirty-two per cent, the white thirty-five; but in the next decade, from 1800 to 1810, the black population increased thirty-seven and a half per cent, the white thirty-six.[1] This increased rate of growth reflects the great demand for labor in the cotton fields of the South, following on the introduction of the short-staple upland cotton as a profitable commercial crop.

Eli Whitney's adaptation of the existing machinery for separating the cotton seed from the cotton fibre came at one of those psychological moments that are constantly met with in historical study. The inventions of Crompton, Arkwright, and others in England in combination with the introduction of steam power led to an epoch-making development of cotton manufacturing and to an accompanying, insistent demand for cheap fibre. The existing sources of supply of the long staple cotton — India, the West Indies, and the Carolina sea-islands — were not able to meet this demand. The upland of the Lower South was fitted by nature with soil, temperature, and moisture entirely congenial to the growth of the short-staple, green-seed cotton plant. Two things stood in the way of its cultivation : the lack of suitable labor and the difficulty of separat-

---

[1] A noticeable thing about the increase of the black population is that the free blacks between 1790 and 1800 increased from 59,000 to 108,000; this decade marking the first period of emancipation.

ing the seed from the fibre. Many attempts had been
made to solve this difficulty. None of them had been
successful until Whitney in 1794 devised a machine that
could be used commercially. He and his partners rented
these machines, or "gins," to producers, and they also
bought cotton and ginned it themselves. Probably, they
were actuated partly by desire for gain and partly by a
wish to properly separate the cotton from the seed.[1] As
almost any good mechanic could duplicate the Whitney
cotton-gin, the attempt to regulate its use led to law suits,
disputations, and disappointments. Had not Whitney hit
upon the idea of manufacturing firearms on a large scale
with interchangeable parts, thereby making himself independent of the cotton-gin, his later life might have been
another tragedy of the American inventor. The cultivation of cotton rapidly overspread the Southern uplands.
There was a market for every pound that could be produced; there was a field and a hoe for every negro slave
who could be procured.

It is almost impossible to give any tangible idea of the
increase in the amount of cotton cultivation. If one puts
it in pounds, the number at once becomes so large that
it is beyond ordinary comprehension. And what is a
pound of cotton? What does it signify? How much
ordinary cotton cloth does it make? There is no compre-
hensible answer to any of these inquiries. Perhaps the
best way to give some comprehension of the extension of

[1] "Correspondence of Eli Whitney relative to the Invention of the Cotton Gin" in *American Historical Review*, iii, 90. M. B. Hammond's introduction to these letters is the best summary of the controversy as to this notable invention, and is abundantly supplied with citations. The same author's *Cotton Industry*, published by the American Economic Association, New Series, No. I, also goes over the whole field. W. P. Blake's "Sketch of the Life of Eli Whitney" in New Haven Colony Historical Society's *Papers*, v, 109, gives some local color; but Whitney's career deserves much fuller notice than it has yet received.

the industry is to say that practically no North American-grown cotton was imported into Liverpool from the United States in 1790, and that almost two hundred thousand bags of it were imported in 1810; but how many pounds of cotton there were in a bag or what impression it would convey to us if we knew, is an entirely different question. The cultivation of upland cotton increased with marvellous rapidity and, could the necessary labor have been found, it would have increased much faster had not commercial warfare restricted exportation. This lessening of foreign demand was in part made good by a great increase in cotton spinning in the North. In 1807, according to Gallatin,[1] there were fifteen mills with about eight thousand spindles in the United States; in 1811, there were eighty-seven mills with eighty thousand spindles, and they used 3,600,000 pounds of cotton in twelve months.

By this time the Northern States had generally rid themselves of negro slavery or were in a fair way to end it by some scheme of gradual emancipation. A large number of free blacks had been introduced into the population of that section and had aroused jealousy and fear. In the South, the wave of sentimental emancipation had spent its force. The revolution in San Domingo, the objections that were felt toward the Northern free blacks, and the increasing profitableness of slave labor resulting from the extension of cotton cultivation, put an end to all thoughts of emancipation in that part of the country. Quite the reverse was true,[2] for South Carolina, in 1803, repealed the law prohib-

---

[1] *American State Papers, Finance,* ii, 427; see also on the general subject, Tench Coxe's *Statement of the Arts and Manufactures of the United States . . . 1810* (Philadelphia, 1814).

[2] Possibly the high water mark of South Carolinian opposition to the slave trade is to be seen in the State law of December 1800. This forbade the importation of negro slaves by land or water — except that newcomers from other States might bring in not exceeding ten slaves who had been his or her property for at least two years.

iting the importation of slaves into that State and re-awakened the apprehensions of the Northern friends of the blacks.[1]

The Constitution provided, as one of the famous compromises, that no prohibition of the slave trade could be made by Congress before 1808, but a tax, not exceeding ten dollars for each negro imported, might be imposed at any time. In 1804 and in 1805, bills for levying this tax were introduced into Congress, but without anything being accomplished. In 1807 an act was passed prohibiting the introduction of slaves from abroad on the first day permitted by the Constitution (January 1, 1808). Apart from the question of the prohibition of the oversea slave trade there were several points of interest in the debate. Could the foreign slave trade be stopped, if the coastwise slave trade were permitted to go on? And what should be done with slaves captured on vessels breaking the law? Also what should be done with the vessel, her captain and owners? If the interstate slave trade was to continue, how could the coastwise trade be stopped? On the other hand, if that were permitted, how would it be possible to prohibit the importation of slaves from Florida, Texas, and Cuba? The matter was arranged by confining the domestic sea-

---

Probably dread of San Domingan insurrectionists had as much to do with it as dislike of the slave trade in general.

A list of vessels importing slaves into Charleston, in 1804 to 1807 inclusive, with the country of the owners and number of slaves brought in is given in the speech of Senator Smith of South Carolina on the admission of Missouri in *Annals of Congress*, 16th Cong., 2d Sess., 72–77, and is reprinted in Dawson and De Saussure's *Census of Charleston for the Year 1848*, 136–142. From Jan. 1, 1804 to Dec. 31, 1807, 202 slave ships entered at Charleston bringing 21,027 negroes. Seventy of the vessels were British, 61 belonged to Charleston,

and 59 to Rhode Island. Somewhat larger figures are given in John Lambert's *Travels* ii, 405. The Charleston *Times* of Jan. 5, 1807, advertised nine lots of freshly imported slaves for sale. There were 1815 in all, ranging from "Very Prime Congo" to "Choice Gold Coast" negroes. Many similar entries can be found in the newspapers of Charleston and Savannah.

[1] There was so much interest in 1804 on the general subject of slaves and the slave trade that the debates in the House of Commons on the slave trade were reprinted at length as in Cheetham's *Republican Watch-Tower* for August 4, 1804.

borne traffic to vessels of over forty tons, for it would be easier to keep an eye on these than on smaller boats. As to the disposal of the captured slaves, that was a more difficult problem. The logical thing seemed to be to take them back to Africa and land them free and unfettered on their native continent. The trouble was that practically no slaves were kidnapped by the slaver. They were bought of coastal slave dealers who, in turn, procured them from black or Arab slavers, who had originally bought them in the interior. Slavery was the usual condition of things in Africa. Any captive taken in war was a slave. One tribe raided another tribe for the purpose of getting slaves. The American slave trade only intensified the general slave-making habit. Any slaves landed on the coast of Africa, therefore, would be seized by the nearest tribe and either used for its own purposes or sold to the next slave dealer who happened to come along. Under these circumstances, why not found a negro state on the African shore to which liberated slaves might go or be taken. This project had already attracted notice in England and America; and had led to the chartering of the Sierra Leone Company in 1791 by George III. In America, several persons, among them Dr. William Thornton, the designer of the national capitol, believed that in deportation lay the solution of the difficulties that surrounded negro slavery; but in this as in some other things, he was ahead of his time, and the American Colonization Society was not formed until after the close of the War of 1812.[1] Repatriation in Africa being

---

[1] W. E. B. DuBois has gone over with care the early history of this subject in his *Suppression of the African Slave-Trade to the United States* (*Harvard Historical Studies*, No. I). Related material is in Mary S. Locke's "Anti-Slavery in America (1619–1808)" in *Radcliffe College Monographs* No. II. For early negro deportation projects, see a paper by Dr. H. N. Sherwood in *Mississippi Valley Historical Review*, ii, 484–508 and Archibald Alexander's *History of Colonization on the Western Coast of Africa* (Philadelphia, 1846).

plainly out of the question, it was proposed to sell the captured negroes to the highest bidder. To the friends of the blacks the proposition that the United States could have a title to black men and women that could be transferred by sale seemed to be in the highest degree incongruous. Possibly, the captured negroes might be indentured for a term of years. To this it was easy to reply that already there were too many free blacks in the country. Finally, it was decided, as the only way out of the dilemma, that the slaves should be disposed of according to the law of the State in which the vessel was condemned.

It is interesting to note in concluding this subject, that Jefferson and Randolph held different views. Jefferson had always had very decided ideas as to the wrongfulness of the slave trade and had brought forward the matter in a message to Congress. In 1803, a petition had been presented to him for the pardon of a man who had been imprisoned for bringing slaves into the United States. In reply the President declared that the prisoner's situation, so far as respects himself, merits no commiseration, but that of his wife, children, and mother does as also does "the condition of the unhappy human beings whom he forcibly brought away from their native country, and whose wives, children and parents are now suffering for the want of their aid and comfort." To Randolph, the matter presented itself in very different guise. Slaves were property and the rights of slave owners were recognized by the laws of Virginia. What right had the Congress of the United States to legislate as to what disposition a Virginian should make of his property? He, therefore, was opposed to any such legislation and when the bill was passed, he proposed that the whole Virginia delegation should wait on the President and demand its veto. In all this, John Randolph of Roanoke forecasted the future and used language that seemed not a trifle extraordinary coming as it did from a man who thought negro slavery to be wrong and who emancipated his own slaves by will.

The phenomenal extension of cotton culture determined the history of the Lower South and, in the existing ignorance of bacterial life, fastened negro slavery on that region;[1] the application of steam to water transportation made possible the rapid settlement of the West in time to counteract in a measure the growing strength of the Slave States. A dozen patents[2] had been given for the propulsion of vessels by power other than sails, and a dozen vessels and more had been successfully moved by steam[3] before the *Clermont* left her dock on August 9, 1807.[4] The names of John and Robert L. Stevens, Oliver Evans, John Fitch, James Rumsey, Nathan Read, and Nicholas L. Roosevelt in America, and William Symington, Lord Stanhope,[5] and Patrick Millar in Great Britain are all associated with vessels that were moved by steam before that day. Of them all the younger Stevens, only, produced a boat that repaid the cost of operation, and this vessel, the *Phœnix*, came from the shop only a month after the *Clermont* made her trial trip.

Of Scottish-Ulster-Irish-Presbyterian extraction, Robert

---

[1] Had the malarial mosquito and the hookworm been eliminated before the invention of the cotton-gin, white and not black labor might have been employed in the South.

[2] See "List of Patents transmitted to Congress" in 1805.

[3] Commodore Preble's *Chronological History . . . of Steam Navigation*, 20–52.

[4] See Fulton to Livingston, August 10, 1807, in E. B. Livingston's *The Livingstons of Livingston Manor*, 385; Dickinson's *Robert Fulton*, 216.

[5] Lord Stanhope thought that the "side-wheel" would not be so well suited to the broad American rivers as the "ducks-foot" because in the high seas which are common on those rivers, one of the wheels would be out of water while the other would be too deeply immersed. "Barlow Manuscripts," No. 17, Barlow to Fulton, May 11, 1803. In 1790, Stanhope had actually taken out a patent to operate a double-ended vessel which was to be driven by "a propeller operating like the foot of an aquatic bird."

Fulton [1] was born in Pennsylvania and at an early age removed to England where he studied art and painted pictures. Suddenly he abandoned art and took to engineering, making plans and writing about canals and canal diggers. He next went to France where he fell in with Joel Barlow and later with Robert R. Livingston. While there he busied himself with "torpedoes" which were really floating mines, with a plunging boat, and finally with a steamboat. All of these were real things, but none was thoroughly successful. An ordinary splinter net hung away from the ship's sides would protect against the torpedo; the submersible went under water with Fulton and three men in her and stayed under water with them, but it could not be moved to any practicable extent with a screw propeller worked by two men at a crank; the boat propelled by fire went up and down the Seine, but it was not commercially useful. In France, Fulton had sight of Fitch's plans. He knew of all or nearly all preceding boats. He studied the formula for calculating resistance of wetted surfaces, and experimented with something like a modern marine engineering tank. Livingston, with Stevens and Roosevelt, had been experimenting on steam navigation in New York before his appointment as minister to France. He had a grant from the State legislature giving him exclusive rights to the navigation of the Hudson for a term of years, provided he produced a workable steamboat within

[1] The latest and best work on Fulton is H. W. Dickinson's *Robert Fulton, Engineer and Artist : His Life and Works* (London, 1913). See also Cadwallader D. Colden's *Life of Robert Fulton* (New York, 1817) and criticisms of it as *An Examination of Cadwallader D. Colden's Book, entitled A Life of Robert Fulton. By a friend of John Fitch, deceased, 1818:* and *A Vindication by Cadwallader D. Colden, of the Steam Boat Right granted by the State of New York* (Albany, 1818). An excellent family biography is the memoir by Fulton's great granddaughter, Mrs. Alice Crary Sutcliffe, entitled *Robert Fulton and the "Clermont."* As to the validity of Livingston and Fulton's monopoly of the navigation of New York waters by state grant, see opinion of W. A. Duer in his *Lectures on Constitutional Jurisprudence*, 505–512.

a certain time. He now enlisted the services of Fulton, who with opportunity in his hands at once proceeded to order an engine to be built in England for a boat to be constructed in America. The combination proved successful.

At the time, there was almost no excitement over either the *Clermont* or the *Phœnix*. The newspapers are painfully barren of notice of these momentous voyages and most of the stories that have come down to us are of later birth. The steamboat came into the world as quietly as the telephone or the trolley car, but with even more far-reaching effects. The cost of a ticket, which was seven dollars from New York to Albany, not including meals, may have damped the enthusiasm of most intending voyagers. It was some time before the public began to utilize the new mode of conveyance. By the end of the season, the steamboat was carrying seventy passengers on a trip. In the winter, she was entirely reconstructed. In a few years, three boats were running on the Hudson; a ferry service had been established with the Jersey shore; and Stevens's boat, which had gone outside from Sandy Hook to the Delaware, was running from Philadelphia to Burlington, thus shortening the time of the journey from New York to Philadelphia. The next conquest was Long Island Sound and then the steamboat appeared on western waters where its effect was immediate in sending the price of freight down twenty-five per cent and making possible the cultivation of the soil on the rich prairie lands far away from the markets of the East.

The booming prosperity of the Lower South, following on the cultivation of the upland short-staple cotton, showed itself in the growing spirit of nationalism and a belief in the prowess of America. This became visible in Congress with the entrance of Calhoun and his colleagues into public life.

Since 1801 the Jeffersonians had lost a great deal of their particularistic tendencies. Jefferson had written about the "Nation" and Madison in the settlement of the Olmstead case, had upheld the authority of the national government in a way that one would hardly have expected from the author of the Virginia Resolutions of 1798. Years before, in 1778, Gideon Olmstead, a native born Connecticut seafarer with three companions had captured a British sloop, the *Active*, with thirteen seamen on board. Before he could get his prize into a New Jersey harbor, two Pennsylvania vessels, one of them a State ship, took her away from him and a Pennsylvania jury decided that the Pennsylvanians and not Olmstead had captured her. He appealed to the Continental Congress and commissioners appointed by it reversed the judgment of the Pennsylvania court, but the prize money had already been paid over to the State treasurer. Year after year, and decade after decade, Gideon Olmstead fought on. In 1808, when over eighty years of age, he secured an order or mandamus from the Supreme Court of the United States directing the marshal of the Pennsylvania federal court to take possession of the prize funds and turn them over to Olmstead. When the marshal tried to do this he found his way barred by State militia commanded by the Pennsylvania General Bright. A little later the marshal tried again and this time he secured the persons of the custodians of the money. Then came a writ of *habeas corpus;* but the Chief Justice of Pennsylvania saw that the time had come to yield and returned the prisoners to the marshal. Meantime, the State legislature had appropriated eighteen thousand dollars to be expended at the discretion of the governor. Upon receiving this money, the marshal released his victims and paid it over to Olmstead. General Bright had been dealt

with for obstructing federal processes and sentenced to
imprisonment and fine and so, also, had some of his men.
It was in the course of these later transactions that the
Pennsylvania legislators "as the guardians of the State
rights," resolved that they could not permit an infringement
of those rights by an unconstitutional exercise of power,
and so on for five paragraphs. Governor Snyder of Pennsylvania sent these resolutions to President Madison,
expressing the hope that he would "adjust" the present
"unhappy collision of the two Governments in such a
manner as will be equally honorable to them both" and
told him of the eighteen thousand dollars. Madison
replied (April 13, 1809) that the executive of the United
States is not only unauthorized to prevent the execution
of a decree of the federal court "but is expressly enjoined,
by statute, to carry into effect any such decree where opposition may be made to it." It was a propitious circumstance, he wrote, that the legislature had made adequate
provision for the removal of the existing difficulty ; and he
felt "great pleasure" in assuring himself that the authority
given in it would be exercised in a patriotic spirit. On his
part, the President, after an interval, pardoned General
Bright and his militiamen on the ground that they had acted
under a mistaken sense of duty.[1]

In 1811, it became clear that a large part of the people
of the United States was wearying of inaction, was content
no longer to submit to insults, and was conscious of a growing spirit of nationalism. In May, an American frigate

[1] See *Annals of Congress*, 11th Cong.,
Pt. 2, 2253–2269. There is an excellent
account of this case, with citations to
the legal authorities, by H. L. Carson
in *Pennsylvania Magazine of History
and Biography*, xvi, 385. The amendment to the Constitution proposed by
Pennsylvania, and Virginia's action
thereon are in *ibid.*, xviii, 194. For
extracts from the resolutions with a
good paragraph on the case itself, see
Herman V. Ames's *State Documents on
Federal Relations*, No. ii.

fired on a British ship-of-war; in November, the battle of
Tippecanoe expressed western protest against British interference with the Indians south of the boundary line; and
in December new men filled with aggressive nationalism
came into prominent political positions.

Paul Hamilton, Secretary of the Navy, on June 9, 1810,
directed commanders of American naval vessels to resist
any attack on the national dignity by the British or any
one else. Now that commerce with France was again
permitted British warships reappeared off the American
coast. Again, American vessels were stopped and searched
and seamen taken from them. Commodore John Rodgers,
with a small squadron including the frigates *Constitution*
and *President*, was directed to cruise off the coast from
Montauk Point to Cape Henry. Following the Secretary's
instructions, Rodgers ordered his commanders to submit
to no insult of any kind and, if fired on, to return two shots
for one. Nothing happened in 1810, but in 1811, the
British frigate *Guerrière* impressed a seaman from an American vessel off Sandy Hook. Thereupon, the Secretary ordered Rodgers, who was in port at the moment, to put to
sea and carry out his former instructions. It thus happened
that the lookout on the *President* sighted a ship-rigged
vessel that in the distance looked like the *Guerrière* (May 16,
1811). Rodgers set all sail in pursuit, but did not come up
with the chase until after sundown. She was plainly a
man-of-war, and in the uncertain light appeared to be a
frigate. Both commanders hailed at the same time without
answer. When on the point of hailing a second time, a
gun was fired from the stranger. The *President* at once
replied, and the firing became general and continued, with
an intermission, until there plainly was no probability of
any further aggressive action on the part of the other ship.

Rodgers then hailed and this time received an answer that the stranger was the British sloop-of-war, *Little Belt.* Around this conflict, there has gathered controversy, as the American and British accounts were very different. Two things are perfectly plain. One is that the *President* should have sent the *Little Belt* to the bottom of the sea in the smallest time given in the American account. The other is that an American frigate had taken up the challenge of a British warship and given her at least as good as she sent. The affair soothed the wounded feelings of the American people and made them quite indifferent as to reparation for the outrage on the *Chesapeake.*[1]

The growing friction with the natives of the Northwest resulted from the nervousness of the settlers of the Mississippi Valley over the increasing assertiveness of Tecumseh and the Indian tribes that he was welding into an association with the good-will of the British authorities in Upper Canada. Tecumseh was one of those rare Indians of whom there are not more than half a dozen within the limits of American annals. He strove to reconstruct the rapidly deteriorating habits of the natives on the frontier. He labored hard to make them self-sustaining, to drive away the drink demon, and to limit their selling of lands to the whites. He was opposing the march of human history, but his efforts were praiseworthy and his success remarkable. It was inevitable that white settlements should spread into the wilderness, that the authorities at Washington should listen to the plaints of the pioneers, and should not always inquire too closely into the methods employed by their agents to enforce peace. William Henry Harrison

[1] C. O. Paullin's *Commodore John Rodgers,* 211–212; Mahan's *War of 1812,* i, 257; James's *Naval History of Great Britain,* v, 274; Thomas Clark's *Naval History of the United States,* i, 167; *American State Papers, Foreign Relations,* iii, 473, 477.

had charge of the region between the State of Ohio and the Mississippi River. He was a Virginian by birth. He had lived long in the western country and had come to express in thought and action the aspirations of the frontier people. Putting himself at the head of an armed force, he marched toward the model Indian town of Tippecanoe. Tecumseh was absent at the moment or, possibly, there would not have been a battle. As it was, the Indians attacked Harrison and his men in their encampment not far from the town. They were beaten off and deserted their habitations (November 7, 1811). Around this battle of Tippecanoe, there has grown a good deal of doubt.[1] To some modern writers it does not appear creditable from military or humanitarian points of view; to the western people of that time it appealed strongly as marking the end of a pusillanimous chapter in our history. They hailed it as a victory and the man in command as a hero. It was the first of a chain of events that ultimately made William Henry Harrison President of the United States.

In this same year, 1811, that seemed to mark a turning point in our history, a political revolution took place in Massachusetts that heightened the spirits of the warlike section of the Republican party. For the first time, the Federalists lost control of both the executive and legislative branches of the government of that State. The victory was not so complete as the Republicans persuaded themselves, for the defeat of the Federalist candidate for governor was due to personal unpopularity and the margin of Republican strength in the Senate was very small, being only one on a full vote. It was enough, however, to secure the retirement of Timothy Pickering from his seat in the

[1] The Harrison side is fully represented in Moses Dawson's *Historical Narrative of the . . . Services of Major-* *General William H. Harrison, and a Vindication of his Character and Conduct* (Cincinnati, 1824) ch. xxii.

national Senate. Otherwise, the Republicans used their power very ill. They redistricted the State for the election of Senators. In doing this they followed evil examples from New York and Virginia. They arranged the boundaries of the new electoral districts so that strong Federalist towns were placed by themselves. It was hoped by this arrangement that Republican minorities in two of the old districts might be converted into a Republican majority in one. To accomplish this, some of the new senatorial districts were shaped in a manner that violated geography, natural interest, and pretty much everything else.[1] By adding a few details to this cartographical monstrosity, it assumed the form of a strange looking beast, which was dubbed a "gerrymander," thus consigning Elbridge Gerry the Republican governor, who was guilty of approving the law, to everlasting political infamy. And the scheme did not have the measure of success that covers many sins. In the next election, the Federalists brought forward their old popular candidate, Caleb Strong, and elected him, and also a Federalist legislature. Gerry found solatium in being chosen Vice-President of the United States.

The twelfth Congress came together in December, 1811, and did not adjourn until July, 1812. Henry Clay entered the House of Representatives for the first time, having already served a term in the Senate, and was at once chosen Speaker. Behind him was a remarkable group of young men, as the ages of legislators go, — John C. Calhoun, Langdon Cheves, William Lowndes, and David R. Williams of South Carolina, Felix Grundy of Tennessee, Richard M. Johnson of Kentucky, and Peter B. Porter of New

---

[1] E. C. Griffith's *Rise and Development of the Gerrymander;* J. W. Dean's "Gerrymander" in *New-England His-* *torical and Genealogical Register* for October, 1892; also privately printed.

York. At the time their fame and position were much the same; but now, none, save historians, remember any of them, except Clay and Calhoun. They stood for a different generation than that represented by Jefferson and the reformers of 1801. Excepting Porter, they all came from the South and expressed agrarian protest against commercial domination, — the restiveness of producer against distributor, — in this case represented by British capitalists and their American partners in the general crime of defrauding agriculture of its just share in the profits rightly belonging to the tillers of the soil. Henry Clay was a native of Virginia and had grown up under the influence of Chancellor Wythe, who moulded so many of the great men of the Old Dominion. At the age of twenty, Clay had gone to Kentucky and there taken up the practice of the law and entered politics. He ardently believed in the "eternal principle of self-preservation" that justifies any measure which seems to be necessary and knows no limitation of time or place. Probably no man in our political annals achieved conspicuous political success so early in life, or failed so utterly to win the largest measure of fame. Clay brought into Congress the confidence of the pioneer in himself and in his neighbors. He believed in the Nation and in "the Fathers." His eloquence was such that he and his hearers were carried away with it and he proclaimed as facts, without reservation, things that some slight study would have shown him were wrong. John Caldwell Calhoun was of that Scottish-Irish-Presbyterian stock that has so powerfully wrought on the destinies of the United States. Born in South Carolina, he graduated at Yale College in New Haven in 1804, passing another year and a half in Connecticut in the study of law. He possessed remarkable mental gifts, reading Locke's "Essay on the

Human Understanding" at the age of thirteen. He had not the oratorical power of Clay or of Webster, but he argued logically and boldly, convincing men by reason rather than by eloquence. He immediately took a foremost place in Congress, arguing for the power of the country to enforce its rights. To Clay and Calhoun must be added Daniel Webster, although he did not enter Congress until 1813. He was born in New Hampshire, the son of a simple farmer who had fought at Bennington. As a boy, Webster was physically weak, which marked him out — in those days — for education. He went to Dartmouth College, taught school, and became a lawyer. In 1800, while Webster was still an undergraduate, the citizens of Hanover, his college town, invited him to deliver the Fourth of July oration.[1] He did so and it was printed. It breathes the spirit of flamboyant nationality. He proclaimed the "present grandeur [of] the empire of Columbia." At the name of "our father Washington," now "consigned to dust," the sympathetic tear glistens in the eye of every youthful hero. Ending, Webster invoked "the God of our Fathers" to preserve secure Columbia's freedom. The hypercritical may find fault with the exuberance of the phrasings of Webster and Clay and of the early nationalistic utterances of Calhoun. To the historical student, they come as rays of sunshine out of the dastard debates of the preceding decade.

Meantime, the coming of James Monroe into the administration as Secretary of State and the departure of Robert Smith (April 1, 1811) changed the whole tone of the executive department as to the expediency of fighting with carnal weapons. Monroe had returned to Virginia

---

[1] *An Oration, pronounced at Hanover, New-Hampshire, the 4th Day of July,*   *1800 . . . By Daniel Webster* (Hanover, 1800).

from England, disgusted with everything and everybody, for he had been humiliated at Paris, Madrid, London, and Washington. After brooding over his misfortunes and dabbling with the schemes of John Randolph of Roanoke, he accepted the friendly hand held out to him by Madison and again became a figure in national life. Into the tangled play of politics in Congress, of diplomacy in the executive department, and of intrigues everywhere it is profitless to venture. Monroe came into office with a serious and firm conviction that the American government must resent the usage which it had received and was receiving from foreign powers, not by arguments and protests merely, but by an appeal to arms. These opinions he held forth day and night and was more responsible than any one else for the declaration of war.[1]

A very little concession at this time would have turned the scale toward conciliation with Britain, for the actions of Napoleon were most harassing. Were the Berlin and Milan Decrees repealed or were they in force? How could any one tell? Some American vessels were admitted to French ports and treated hospitably; others were burned on the high seas by French armed vessels. General Serurier, the French representative at Washington, found it impossible to satisfy the American government on these matters, for his instructions directed him to make no pledges as to

[1] See "Joseph Gales on the War Manifesto of 1812" in *American Historical Review*, xiii, 303–310. This article contains entirely new matter on the history of this time. The recollection of Mr. Gales was written out somewhere about 1850. It is strongly confirmed by a letter written by Monroe to some unknown person in England in "the fall of 1811" (*Writings*, v, 191). In it Monroe states the case of the United States as it lay in his mind at the time. The English, he wrote, demanded of the United States "not that they should protest their neutral rights against France in a commerce with G. Britain and her dominions, but that they should open the continent to British manufactures" or that Great Britain should retain the Orders in Council and America withdraw the prohibition to import British goods. Such a demand, he thought, showed a determined hostility on the part of the British government to the United States.

the Decrees. Unfortunately, at this time, the United States was not adequately represented at Paris. Armstrong had long since returned home, leaving the legation in charge of Jonathan Russell, who did not know how to make disagreeable charges in diplomatic language. Madison decided to send Joel Barlow as minister to Paris, where he was well known, and where he had spent many profitable years. He was nominated, was confirmed by the Senate; his departure was delayed, was determined on, and was again put off, — all to the uneasiness of Serurier. The Frenchman could not understand Monroe at all. Neither could the new British envoy, Augustus J. Foster, who held to the regular British Tory view that the misunderstanding had flowed entirely from Jefferson's proclamation ordering British men-of-war out of American waters, while permitting French naval vessels to remain in them. Foster had been instructed not to give way at all as to the Orders in Council, but he was authorized to make reparation for the *Chesapeake* outrage without requiring any disavowals or inquiries. When Foster conversed with Madison and Monroe, they appeared to have forgotten all about the *Chesapeake*. The general subject of impressment interested them keenly, but they seemed to have abandoned all hope of redressing that except by resort to force. Foster heard a great deal of the talk as to the conquest of Canada which was rife at Washington at the time. He lost his temper and thus played directly into the hands of those who wished for war with his country.

Into the atmosphere of doubt and anger at Washington in the winter and spring of 1812, there was interjected a curious complication which is known as the affair of the "Henry Letters." John Henry was an actual person, a British subject. He had visited Boston and had written letters to the Governor General of Canada, detailing conversations that he had had with leading Federalists of New England. He had followed up his letters with demands for money to the amount of more than one hundred and twenty-five thousand dollars. One British official after another refusing payment, he had sailed for the United States with copies or paraphrases of his letters. Ultimately, after intricate negotiations these "Henry Letters" were sold to the government for fifty thousand dollars. Madison sent them to Congress (March 9, 1812). He prophesied that "the discovery of such a procedure [as shown in the letters] . . . will not fail to render more dear to the hearts of all good citizens that happy union . . . which, under Divine Providence, is the guarantee of their liberties, their safety, their tranquillity, and their prosperity."[1] Upon seeing the letters and finding them quite commonplace, the Federalists laughed at the simplicity of Republican officials who had paid fifty thousand dollars of the taxpayers' money for them.

Joel Barlow reached Paris in September, 1811. In due course he asked for information as to whether the Decrees were repealed as to the United States or were still in full vigor. In reply the "Decree of St. Cloud" was placed in his hands. It was dated April 28, 1811, and stated that the earlier decrees "are definitively, and to date from the 1st day of November last, considered as not having existed in regard to American vessels."[2] This document had never been promulgated; it had not been sent to Russell and no copy had reached Serurier. Was it an after-thought drawn up at the moment and ante-dated to placate America at

[1] Niles's *Weekly Register*, ii, 19–27; *Annals of Congress*, 12th Cong., Pt. i, 1162–1181; Henry Adams's article on "Count Edward de Crillon" in *American Historical Review*, i, 51; Morison's *H. G. Otis*, ii, 43.
[2] See *American State Papers, Foreign Relations*, iii, 603.

the outset of the Russian campaign? It matters little, for almost at the moment this paper came into Barlow's possession, Napoleon left Paris for Moscow, Elba, Waterloo, and St. Helena. American history was no longer to be dominated by him.

Two things that might have caused the administration and the war party in Congress to pause in their belligerent careers were the news that came from Russia and the growing kindness of tone of the government in England. John Quincy Adams arrived at St. Petersburg, as representative of the United States, in October, 1809. The outlook seemed most disheartening and remained so for a time. The Russian Czar was deeply involved in the alliance with Napoleon, and the French minister at St. Petersburg appeared to be carrying all before him. The only thing that Adams could do was to cultivate the acquaintance of those in power, do what he could for his countrymen, and watch the course of events. These tasks he performed admirably. He met many old friends and made new ones. American vessels sailing to the Baltic had been seized by Danish privateers and sequestered or condemned as good prize. The same thing had happened in Sweden. Adams tried to get the Russian government to interfere in behalf of the owners. As the winter of 1810 wore on, it became evident that the attitude of the Czar towards his French ally was undergoing a change. This may have been due to the natural fickleness of the Czar Alexander or, more likely, it was due to a growing consciousness on his part that Napoleon, through his Continental System, was undermining the economic and military strength of Russia. It happened, therefore, that when Adams applied for instructions to be given to the Russian agents at Copenhagen and Stockholm to put pressure upon the authorities to hasten the disposition of

American prize cases the orders [1] were issued to the surprise of every one. Moreover, the Czar refused to keep American vessels out of Russian ports, with the result that they thronged to them, bringing in American products and likewise some things that were not American, and they took away large quantities of Russian goods. Napoleon determined to strike, but a whole year was necessary for the requisite preparations to be completed. And it was not until the summer of 1812 that he began the campaign that meant so much for the interests of civilization. Adams detailed all these things in long, well-written despatches to Washington, but they seem to have produced slight impression upon Monroe or the President. They may not have reached Washington before the declaration of war.

As to England, the change that was coming over the governing class might well have been understood by the Secretary of State, who had resided so long at London and certainly would have been accurately reported by Pinkney, had he been still in residence at the British capital. Wellesley's instructions to Foster were by no means conciliatory; but compared with those issued to Rose and to Jackson, might be described as friendly. In January, 1812, Wellesley gave up his office, which fell to Castlereagh. Perceval remained at the head of the re-constituted government and the Orders in Council continued in force. The economic condition of England was serious, and was becoming more so all the time. Riots and petitions were the order of the day, and then came an inquiry into the results of the Orders in Council. At the same time the debates in Parliament took on more asperity. It was recognized that a warlike

---

[1] See Adams's letter dated St. Petersburg, 14 February, 1810, in Massachusetts Historical Society's *Proceedings* for December, 1895. The first paragraph is omitted from the letter as printed in Ford's *Writings of John Quincy Adams*, iii, 397.

spirit was rising in America and that it was no longer a mere pretence. Would an American war be worth while as the cost of maintaining the Orders? Even with non-intercourse and non-importation, there was some access to American markets, both for the raw material of British manufactures and for the sale of British goods. How much of this commerce would be left with the British navy adding its efforts to the American government in the enforcement of non-intercourse? The end of the Orders was plainly in sight, when a crazy man assassinated Perceval as he was entering the House of Commons, May 11, 1812. Time was needed to make over the ministry, so that it was not until the end of May or the middle of June that the question of suspending the Orders in Council was ready for settlement. At length, on June 16, Castlereagh announced in the House that the Orders would be immediately suspended, and the next day the suspending Order in Council was agreed to, but it was not actually issued until the 23rd.

At Washington, affairs had proceeded almost as if nothing had been going on in the last six months in Europe, as if no great change in the alignment of nations was impending, as if the government at London were not already beginning to be amenable. On January 28, 1812, after his resignation had been handed in, but before his successor had taken office, Wellesley wrote a despatch to Foster which is regarded as having brought about the American declaration of war. In it he deprecated the arming of neutral merchant vessels because it "announces a system which, if carried into practice, must occasion acts of hostile violence . . . as may tend to produce the calamity of war between the two countries."[1] Foster was also directed in

<hr />

[1] *Correspondence and Treaties with*   vol. xiv, C, p. 22.
Foreign Powers, Session, 1812-1813,

instructions that were to remain secret to avoid any suggestion of compromise as to the Orders. Thus spurred on, he assumed an even more decided tone. On April 1, 1812, Madison, on his part, sent a message [1] to Congress suggesting that a general embargo be laid for the period of sixty days. Congress fell in with this, although the time was lengthened from sixty days to ninety days. It was a little more than one month after this that the Federalists gained greatly in strength in New York and in Massachusetts; also these Northern States showed distrust in the warlike policy of the Southern majority in Congress by small subscriptions to the loan that was offered. Proceeding onward with eyes blinded by a happy Fate and acting under the influence of Monroe, on June 1, Madison recommended a declaration of war.[2] Day after day, the matter was debated in the Senate and in the House; on June 18, the act declaring war was finally adopted and was at once approved by the President. Of the one hundred and five Republican members of the House, only seventy-nine voted in favor of war, and in the Senate the bill was carried nineteen to thirteen, the three Republican Senators, Smith, Giles, and Leib, who habitually acted against the administration, on this occasion, voting with it.

In 1812, Madison was the Republican nominee for the chief magistracy and was elected. For many years historical students have given credence to a story that the war message was the price of his re-nomination. There is no evidence worth consideration in support of this position

---

[1] *Annals of Congress*, 12th Cong., Pt. ii, 1587.

[2] The case for the administration was skilfully set forth by Alexander J. Dallas in *An Exposition of the Causes and Character of the Late War*. J. Q. Adams's *The Lives of James Madison and James Monroe . . . with Historical Notices of their Administrations* (Boston, 1850) may be regarded as defences of their conduct — and of his own. On July 6, 1812 Madison sent to Congress a list of vessels captured by Europeans since 1803. By this it appeared that the French had seized 558 vessels since November, 1807, the British 389.

and the stimulus to war came equally from the administration and from Congress. His reëlection was due in great measure to the fact that there was no strong opposition candidate with a definite line of policy. De Witt Clinton was the only man who seemed to have any chance of success against the southern ascendency. The Federalists held a meeting, or convention,[1] of leading men and determined to support him; but there was no vigorous, whole-souled campaigning, and the election went almost by default. It is astonishing that it should have been so, when there were so many issues upon which the North might well have stood as one man : the admission of Louisiana destroying the equilibrium of States, the blindfolded policy of the administration as to commerce and impressment, and the undue truckling to France, — at almost any other time in our history might well have brought on political revolution. But so it was, and the United States plunged into war with Great Britain at the moment when the fate of humanity was hanging in the balance, — when it depended on her resistance to the all-embracing ambitions of the conquering Corsican.

[1] This is often regarded as the first national nominating convention. See article by J. S. Murdock in *American Historical Review*, i, 680, and S. E. Morison's *H. G. Otis*, i, 308; and articles in the *Review* by J. S. Walton and M. Ostrogorski (ii, 262; v, 253). Morison (*ibid.*, xvii, 744) assigns priority to the meeting of 1808.

NOTE

Torpedoes. — Two opinions were held as to the use of the underwater boat. In 1798, Fulton declared that " the destruction of the English Navy will ensure the independence of the seas and France, the Nation which has most natural resources and population, will alone and without a rival hold the balance of power in Europe." At another time, he appears to have doubts, for he wrote, "This manner of making war on an enemy carries with it such reprobation, that the persons who undertook it and failed would be lost. Certainly it is not a gallant death" (Dickinson's *Fulton*, 79, 118). A drawing of Fulton's submarine, *Nautilus*, is in *ibid.*, p. 82. In 1807, at the time of his public demonstration of the efficacy of what he termed " dumb Torpedoes," Fulton wrote that their general use would " lead to the destruction of military marines, and the establishment of the liberty of the seas," (*Baltimore American*, July 20, October 22, 1807).[1] See his *Torpedo War and Submarine Explosions* reprinted in *Magazine of History with Notes and Queries* (Extra Number, 35). The utility of the device was submitted to a board of naval officers, including Rodgers and Decatur, who reported that there was nothing to it. See Paullin's *John Rodgers*, 204. Fulton's letter to President Madison on torpedoes is reprinted in *American State Papers, Naval Affairs*, i.

[1] For Jefferson's opinion of torpedoes, see his letter to Fulton of August 16, 1807; *Writings of Jefferson* (Ford), ix, 125.

CHAPTER XVII

THE YEAR 1812 ON LAND AND SEA

LOOKING backward, it is clear — as so many things are in retrospect — that America had more than an even chance of conquering Canada in 1812. Calhoun prophesied that within four weeks from the declaration of war, Upper Canada and a portion of Lower Canada would be seized; Clay maintained that "the militia of Kentucky are alone competent to place Montreal and Upper Canada at your feet." [1] It must not be inferred that in advocating conquest the Westerners were actuated merely by desire for land; they welcomed war because they thought it would be the easiest way to abate Indian troubles. The savages were supported by the fur-trading interests that centred at Quebec and London. Conquering Canada would put an end to this pressure and thus relieve the western frontier of its cruelest enemy. The Southerners, on their part, wished for Florida, and they thought that the conquest of Canada would obviate some Northern opposition to this acquisition of slave territory. There was abundant cause for making war on Great Britain, and once begun the conquest of Canada was the natural thing to undertake. In population, in men of military age, in partly trained soldiers, and in supplies of muskets, gun-powder, and other necessities of military

---

[1] *Annals of Congress*, 11th Cong., Pt. i, 580.

conflict, the United States vastly exceeded Canada.[1] There were approximately three-quarters of a million militiamen enrolled in the United States and about one-tenth as many in Canada. There were four or five thousand "regulars" in Canada and more — possibly twice as many — in the United States. Great Britain might give some aid to her colony, but it could not be much in 1812, for she was then deeply engaged in the Peninsular War. In both the United States and Canada, there was opposition to the war or luke-warm support of it. The New Englanders hoisted the flag at half-mast on receipt of the news of the declaration of war, and the New York militiamen were only half-hearted. In Upper Canada there were many recent settlers from the

[1] In February, 1811, President Madison sent to Congress a return of the enrolled militia of the United States. This had been compiled at the War Department from returns made in the years 1805 to 1810 (*American State Papers, Military Affairs*, i, 298). It does not represent an absolutely accurate statement for one moment of time; but is sufficient for our purposes. The third census, taken in 1810, divides the white male population conveniently under persons of 16 and 26 years and from 26 to 45. From these two sources, the following table has been compiled: —

SECTION OF COUNTRY	WHITE MALES BETWEEN 16 AND 45	ENROLLED MILITIA
New England	274,463	140,538
Middle States	382,698	231,484
Southern States, including Dist. of Columbia	294,574	223,462
The West	167,859	99,251
	1,119,594	694,735

From other reports, sent to Congress at about the same time (*ibid.*, i, 300, 303, 307, 317) it appears that at the time these returns were compiled there were 2753 pieces of heavy ordnance in the United States; 611,339 cannon balls, 513,939 pounds of gun-powder, and 475,555 stands of arms. The national armories at Harpers Ferry and Springfield were turning out 22,000 muskets in each year. Going a little further into detail, the militia of Massachusetts numbered 70,710, and the State probably had in store 48,908 muskets, and 1076 rifles, besides those in service; New York with 95,324 militia had 45,232 muskets and 4100 rifles; and Virginia with 79,429 militia had 13,417 muskets and 2965 rifles.

Melish, the geographer, gives the total population of the British possessions at 330,000 on the face of the first map in his *Military and Topographical Atlas*, published at Philadelphia in 1815.

United States, and in Lower Canada there were the French whose feelings had been greatly irritated within recent years. The letters of Canadian officials are full of statements as to the ill behavior of large numbers of Canadian colonists. They would not turn out when summoned, and when embodied in companies and regiments, deserted and disappeared into the wilderness.[1] The Indians rendered great service to the British, but at the outset it was by no means certain which side they would take,[2] for the memory of Wayne's campaign was still fresh in their recollection. Tecumseh and his immediate following would necessarily fight on the British side and so would the families of loyalist exiles from the United States; but numerically and materially the balance was heavily weighted against the British on land. The difficulties that thwarted American hopes had not to do with men or material, but were administrative and geographical. The Washington government was ignorant of the meaning of war on a large scale. For half a dozen years or so war had been imminent — although it was not certain with whom it would be waged — but nothing had been done to prepare for it, not even continuing

---

[1] E. A. Cruikshank's *Documents relating to the Invasion of Canada* (*Publications of the Canadian Archives*, No. 7), pp. 99, 107, 191, etc. In 1809 Brock wrote: "The idea prevails . . . that Napoleon must succeed, and ultimately get possession of these provinces. The bold and violent are becoming every day more audacious; and the timid . . . think it better and more prudent to withdraw altogether from the society of the English." Brock thought that if the positions were precisely reversed, the English would act as he expected the French-Canadians would in the existing circumstances. See F. B. Tupper's *Life and Correspondence of Major-General Sir Isaac Brock* (London, 1847), pp. 75, 76.

[2] The cynicism with which both parties viewed the Indian problem comes out in the following extracts. In February, 1811, Brock wrote that "Our cold attempt to dissuade" the Indians from making war on the United States could scarcely be expected to prevail "after giving such manifest indications of a contrary sentiment by the liberal quantity of military stores with which they were dismissed." See F. B. Tupper's *Sir Isaac Brock*, 95.

Jefferson, also, argued for liberal treatment of the border tribes "by taking their pelts & furs at higher prices, and selling them goods at lower prices than the trade will bear without loss to let them see their own interest in an exclusive adhesion to us." Jefferson to Harrison, Washington, January 16, 1806.

the Bank of the United States, that most efficient financial engine. Congress had voted to raise men by the score of thousands, but had not provided for their support, and, indeed, had not provided for their enlistment. The War Department included a Secretary and ten or twelve subordinates. These, with a few accountants in the Treasury Department and the commanding officers in the field, constituted the whole military staff of the United States. The administrative force was so meagre that the most active and the most efficient Secretary of War who ever lived could have accomplished very little. The existing incumbent was an amiable man and an efficient politician, — Dr. Eustis of Boston, — but he was not fitted for this job. In 1811, Congress bestirred itself somewhat and provided for the establishment of the beginning of a general staff, — an adjutant general with suitable deputies, — which was almost immediately changed to a rather different system. Commissary generals, quartermaster generals, and wagon masters were provided and taken away and the army was organized on one basis as to companies and regiments, and six months later reorganized in quite another way. All in all, it was nearly impossible to get five or ten thousand soldiers together at one place, to feed them, when collected, and to move them to any other spot.

The natural military boundary between the United States and British North America stretched in a long, bow-like line from Michilimackinac and the Sault St. Marie, on the northwest, by Detroit, Niagara, and Montreal to Quebec on the northeast. This region was divided into two provinces by the Ottawa River, which was the boundary between Upper and Lower Canada, and into several military zones : the Lake Erie Region, the Niagara Peninsula, Lake Ontario, and the Lake Champlain route from New York

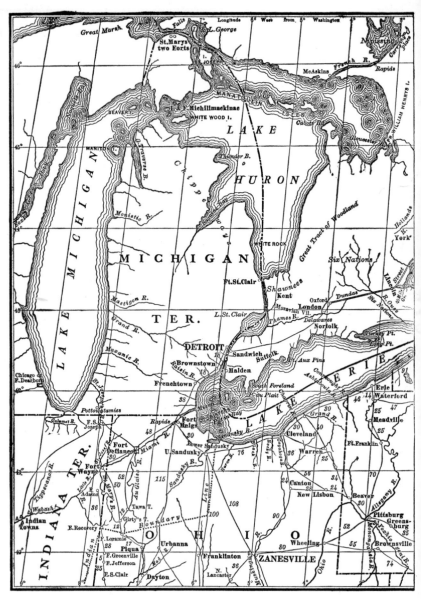

THE SEAT OF WAR

(From John Melish's *Military and Topographical*

460

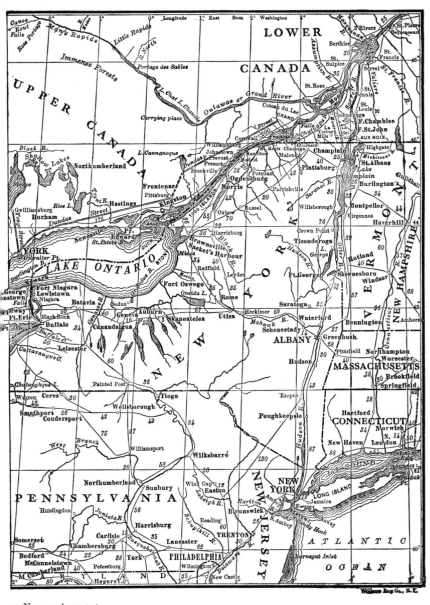

IN NORTH AMERICA

Atlas of the United States, Philadelphia, 1815)

461

to the St. Lawrence. An attack anywhere along this line, except at its far western end, implicated every part of the line to the westward of the point where the attack was made. The Niagara Peninsula marked a transferring point of food and supplies from one lake to the other; the occupation of it was vital to Upper Canada. The permanent conquest of any part of the St. Lawrence by the Americans would necessitate the abandonment of all Canada above that point. Evidently, from a military point of view, a quick and fierce stroke at Montreal, or the river between that city and Quebec, was the thing to do; but political considerations compelled attention to the western end of the line. Few administrations could have afforded the loss of Mackinac, Chicago, and Detroit at the outset of a war confessedly waged for the conquest of Canada. And yet, all these places were outside of ordinary supporting distance from the settled parts of the United States, except with complete control of Lakes Erie, Huron, and Michigan.

The possession of Detroit depended primarily upon the control of Lake Erie. As far back as June 15, 1811, Governor William Hull of Michigan Territory informed Madison that "a naval force on Lake Erie superiour to the British, and sufficient to preserve your communication" would be the most expedient measure of war. Some six months later, General Armstrong reënforced Hull by declaring that the position of Detroit "would be positively bad unless your naval means have an ascendancy on Lake Erie." The Miami River, or rather the Maumee, flows into Lake Erie at almost its westernmost point. Detroit was about sixty miles northward; Cleveland seventy or more to the eastward, on the southern shore; and in the heart of Ohio one hundred and thirty miles to the southward was Urbana. There were some other little settlements, as the Sandusky village and Frenchtown on the River Raisin, but Cleveland and Urbana were the nearest points of supply for Detroit. Across this line of march, as one approached the Maumee River, was the Black Swamp. This was a rectangular space of land, which was then and for a long time afterwards unoccupied, because its clayey soil would not permit of cultivation until a system of drainage was established. It was this difficulty of land transportation that made conveyance by water so necessary for Detroit. On the British side, the situation was not dissimilar. There were almost no roads westward from Montreal and communication was mainly by water. If the control of Lake Ontario and Lake Erie passed away from the British, or was even seriously in danger, Upper Canada was lost to them. As the case stood, the Americans possessed great advantages, for shipwrights by the thousand could be easily and speedily transported from the seaboard ship-yards to the towns on the American lake shores and there set to work to construct a fleet or fleets of war vessels. The greatest trouble was the difficulty of transporting heavy ordnance over a few limited bits of almost impassable road between the Hudson and the town of Pittsburg and the Lakes; [1] but even then the Americans were in so much greater numbers and possessed so much greater resources that the invasion of Canada seemed to be almost certainly successful.

As the war came nearer, no effective measures were taken by the Washington government to gain the superiority on Lake Erie, but Governor Hull was placed in command of a force of a couple of thousand men and ordered to Detroit. In making this assignment, the government possibly expected, by the occupation of Upper Canada from Detroit, to gain

[1] Andrew Ellicott surveyed the road to Presqu' Isle, or Erie, in 1793–1795. See C. Van C. Mathews's *Andrew Ellicott*, ch. v.

control of Lake Erie without having a fleet there. It was also the intention to follow up this first force with other detachments, and steps were at once taken to recruit them and send them on. Finally, it was expected that another army operating from New York would seize the Niagara Peninsula and thereby greatly aid Hull in his march from the Detroit River eastwardly. General William Hull had served bravely and well in the Revolutionary War. He was nearly sixty years of age, not old as modern generals go, but he had seen no military service for many years. Leaving Urbana on June 10 or 11, 1812, he made a rapid march of some one hundred and thirty miles, more or less, amid "heavy & incessant Rains," cutting roads through the Black Swamp as he went and reached the Maumee on the 29th day of the month.[1] Hull had received no news of the declaration of war, and believing that the two countries were still technically at peace, he placed a quantity of medical supplies, officers' baggage, and the sick of the expedition on a little schooner and despatched her for Detroit, while the soldiers marched over land. John Jacob Astor, the head of American fur-trading interests in the Northwest, had apprised his agents of the act of Congress declaring war, and had sent this news in an envelope that was said to bear the frank of the Secretary of the Treasury.[2] Astor's message was forwarded with the greatest possible speed and sent across the line to his partners and employees in Canada. When the schooner with the sick, the stores,

---

[1] An account of the march of a portion of the troops is given in the opening pages of the *Robert Lucas Journal of the War of 1812*, published by the State Historical Society of Iowa.

[2] Mr. R. G. Trotter of Toronto informs me that Astor bought furs at Montreal and was in partnership with some members of the Canadian North-west Fur Company. As Astor and Gallatin were on friendly terms, it is entirely possible that the Secretary should have given him the earliest possible notice of the declaration of war and Astor would certainly have used every effort to apprise his agents on both sides of the boundary line.

and Hull's private papers appeared in the river below Detroit, she was seized by the British, who thus gained a
knowledge of Hull's plans and forces. On July 12, Hull
crossed into Canada, and the next day by proclamation to
the inhabitants announced the invasion of their country
and tendered to them the invaluable blessings of civil,
political, and religious liberty, and emancipation from
tyranny. If they, contrary to their interest, took part
with the British, they would be treated as enemies and
"the horrors, and calamities of war will Stalk before you." [1]
The Americans had no difficulty in occupying the little
town of Sandwich on the Canadian side of the river and
they were joined by many Canadian colonists. But for
reasons similar to those one so often finds in accounts of
military occupations — the cannon would not fit their carriages, or the carriages the cannon, or the combination was
too heavy for the bridges — Hull did not attempt the
capture of the fort at Amherstburg, and thus left a rallying
point for the enemy.

Three men at this juncture saved Canada for the British
Empire: Sir George Prevost, General Isaac Brock, and
Captain Charles Roberts. Prevost was governor general
in succession to Sir James Craig. Of Swiss parentage, he
was born in New Jersey in 1769, his father, Augustine Prevost, of the British army, being stationed there at the time.
The son had served with distinction in the West Indies,
had come to Canada at a most difficult hour, when the
French inhabitants were irritated at the rough treatment
some of their leading men had received at the hands of
British officials.[2] The year 1812 was a time of severest

[1] *Publications of Canadian Archives,*
No. 7, p. 58.
[2] *Some Account of the Public Life of
the late Lieutenant-General Sir George*

*Prevost, Bart. particularly of his services
in The Canadas; including a Reply to
the Strictures on his Military Character
contained in an Article in the Quarterly*

strain for Britain. No money and no men could be spared
for the Canadian defence; Prevost was directed to be very
cautious, and he passed on his orders to his subordinates
with added emphasis. He has received hard measure at
the hands of history. Canadian writers and British writers
have not always realized the great responsibility that
was placed upon him by the course of events, and by his
employers; and American writers have added their scorn
on account of his failure at Plattsburg, entirely regardless
of Wellington's dictum that without the naval control of
Lake Champlain capture of forts and occupation of Plattsburg and any other place on the lake would have been useless. Isaac Brock [1] was a man and a soldier of whom any
nation might be justly proud and is rightly looked upon as
the savior of Canada. He was born on the island of
Guernsey of a long line of ancestry, mainly French. He was
a trained soldier, but had seen little actual service and had
never exercised independent command in the field. Soon
after his appointment as administrator of Upper Canada
and commander of the troops there, he evolved the scheme
of giving special training to the "flank companies" of the
militia regiments and thus developed a small, highly trained,
and enthusiastic body of soldiers, who can only technically

Review for October, 1822 (London, 1823).
The *Quarterly Review* article — which
was printed in the July, not the October number — repeated charges that
had been made in *Letters from The
Montreal Herald* by an author who
concealed his identity under the pseu-
donym of "Veritas."

[1] There are several lives of General
Brock. F. B. Tupper's *Life and Correspondence of Major General Sir Isaac
Brock, K. B.* was published at London
in 1845. It is the second edition,
published in 1847, and containing
about one-third more matter than the
original, that is usually referred to.
This book consists largely of the writ-

ings of General Brock and is still most
useful. Of the later books, D. B.
Read's *Life and Times of Major General Sir Isaac Brock, K. B.* is possibly
the best; but Lady Edgar's *General
Brock* in the *Makers of Canada* series
is certainly much more interesting.
There are other books as Nursey's
Brock; but after all, Brock's life was
so largely that of Canada's from June
to October, 1812, that any work on this
portion of the war is almost necessarily
a memoir of him. In point of fact little
else is known of him; his life before
coming to Canada occupies only 23 of
the 463 pages of Tupper's biography.

be called militia. Of Captain Roberts, next to nothing is known except what is related in the following paragraph.

Brock received information of the declaration of war on June 26, 1812, only eight days after the vote in Congress. He at once ordered Captain Roberts, commanding at St. Joseph's Island [1] at the Sault Ste. Marie, to attack and capture the American post at Michilimackinac in the Strait of Mackinaw. Following this letter came one from Prevost directing Roberts to proceed with great caution and to do nothing to irritate the Americans. And on top of this came a third letter, being the second from Brock, telling him to act on his own discretion. He did so ; collecting four or five hundred men, — white and red, — a heavy gun or two, he embarked in a motley fleet of boats and canoes, gained Michilimackinac Island unannounced, hauled one gun up to the top of the hill overlooking the post, and summoned the garrison to surrender. Lieutenant Porter Hanks commanded the American outposts in this remote region. He had received no notice of the declaration of war, had only fifty-seven "effectives" in the fort, and could do nothing but surrender (July 17, 1812).[2] It was

[1] The British handed over the post at Mackinac Island to the United States in 1796, having held it for thirteen years against the provisions of the Treaty of Peace. They then established a new fur-trading post at St. Joseph's Island in the entrance to the Sault St. Marie. This new location was clearly debatable, for the international boundary line followed the channel between Lakes Huron and Superior. It was determined in 1822 by the Commission appointed under the Treaty of Ghent that the line should run "between the island of St. Joseph's and the American shore," thus making the island definitely British. "Message from the President of the United States, transmitting a Report . . . of the Commissioners under the 6th and 7th

articles of the Treaty of Ghent" in *Executive Reports of Seventh Congress*, 2nd Sess., vol. vi, No. 91. In 1796 and 1812, however, it was by no means clearly on the British side of the line.

A good account of the loss of Mackinac is in "The Dobbins Papers" (*Publications* of the Buffalo Historical Society, viii, 300).

[2] Fort Dearborn (Chicago) was abandoned by its American occupants, August 15, 1812, — to the accompaniment of the usual Indian massacre. M. M. Quaife's *Chicago and the Old Northwest* (Chapter X and Appendixes) is the only authoritative account of "Chicago's grimmest tragedy." See also documents printed in *Mississippi Valley Historical Review*, i, 563. Quaife maintains that Mrs. Kinzie's *Wau Bun,*

this disaster that turned the Indians of the Northwest
definitely away from the American side. It was, therefore,
one of the decisive events of the war ; but, so far as is known,
no notice of this important service of Charles Roberts was
ever taken by the British government.

At the first news of Hull's crossing the Detroit River,
Brock was able to do very little to checkmate him except
to send Colonel Procter to take over the command at Amherstburg and do what he could to organize resistance.
Brock had to guard the Niagara frontier and to meet the
assembly at York, for disaffection was rife in Upper Canada.
In letter after letter, he describes the pernicious effects of
Hull's proclamation and he issued one of his own.[1] The
Canadians, he said, had been invited to submit to the
enemy ; but "where is the Canadian Subject who can truly
affirm to himself that he has been injured by the Government in his person, his liberty, or his property?" Were
they prepared to become "slaves to the Despot who rules
the nations of Europe with a rod of Iron?" Gradually,
he felt himself stronger, so far as his own people were concerned, and there was no appearance of an early American
attack across the Niagara River. He determined to strike
a blow at Hull and Detroit.[2] Assembling all the soldiers

---

the *Early Day in the Northwest* is largely
imaginative. Reuben Gold Thwaites,
in printing a sumptuous edition of
Wau Bun in 1901, declared that "it
has been accepted by historians of
Illinois as substantially accurate."
An elaborate bibliography concludes
Quaife's book.

[1] *Publications of the Canadian Archives*, No. 7, p. 81.

[2] Richardson's *War of 1812* contains
a chapter on Brock's capture of Detroit, giving the recollections of a
participant on the British side. Henry
Adams's account (*History of the United
States*, vi, ch. xv) is full and discrimi-

nating. The publications of the Michigan Pioneer and Historical Society
reproduce large quantities of documents (vol. viii, 620 and fol.), and there
is some original matter in C. W. Robinson's *Life of Sir John Beverley Robinson*, ch. ii, and in J. A. Macdonell's
Sketches of Glengarry in Canada, 173–
200. The conditions on the British
side of the line are set forth in the
"Journal of William K. Beall, July–
August 1812" in *American Historical
Review*, xvii, 783–808. Beall was an
officer of Hull's expedition and was
captured in the *Thames* schooner on July
3 and held as prisoner on board of her.

that he could safely take from Niagara and gathering some militiamen, he placed them in whatever vessels he could find, voyaged along the northern shore of Lake Erie, and landed at Amherstburg on August 13, after five days of journeying. He found Amherstburg and Malden in British hands and the Americans back on their side of the river. Meantime Procter had done what he could to break up the communications between Detroit and the Maumee River, and a party of Hull's men was actually trying to reopen them. Without loss of time Brock crossed to the American side and summoned Hull to surrender, which that commander refused to do in most emphatic language. Realizing that he was between two parts of Hull's forces and in a rather dangerous position, Brock determined to at once attack Detroit. Upon advancing, August 16, he was met by a flag of truce with a proposition to surrender from General Hull.[1] The capitulation was speedily put into form and thus ended the first paragraph or chapter in the history of the War of 1812.

We turn now to the main field of action, to New York, the strategic centre of North America, and to the Northern

[1] The surrender of Detroit has aroused great interest. Hull was tried by court martial, the presiding general being Henry Dearborn, whose conduct in the campaign might well have been examined into at the same time. See *Trial of Brig. Gen. William Hull, for Treason, Cowardice, Neglect of Duty and Unofficer-Like Conduct* (Boston, 1814); *Report of the Trial of Brig. General William Hull, taken by Lieut. Col. Forbes* (New York, 1814); *The Defence of Brigadier General W. Hull Written by Himself* (Boston, 1814). Some years later, Hull obtained copies of the report and other documents relating to the campaign and printed them with explanatory matter as *Memoirs of the Campaign of the North Western Army of the United States,* *A.D. 1812* by William Hull (Boston 1824). An exhaustive family biography and justification was printed in 1848 as *Revolutionary Services and Civil Life of General William Hull by his daughter, Mrs. Maria Campbell: together with the History of the Campaign of 1812 . . . by his grandson James Freeman Clarke,* — the two having a common pagination. Henry Adams's analysis of the case is in his *United States,* vi, 311. Mahan takes a rather severer view in his *War of 1812,* i, 347–350. See also H. A. S. Dearborn's *Defence of Gen. Henry Dearborn, against the Attack of Gen. William Hull* (Boston, 1824). The case against Hull is well stated by A. C. McLaughlin in his life of Lewis Cass in the "American Statesmen" series.

Army and its commander, General Henry Dearborn. Like Hull, Dearborn was a veteran of the Revolution. For eight years he had been Secretary of War in the Republican administrations and had succeeded General Lincoln as collector of the port of Boston. Madison had served with Dearborn in Jefferson's cabinet, was acquainted with his many good qualities, and possibly was influenced by the fact that he was a New Englander and therefore might arouse interest where enthusiasm was entirely lacking, to say the least. Dearborn accepted his appointment and at once set about organizing the forces to operate in the direction of Niagara, Kingston, Montreal, and Quebec. He appears to have had as little misgiving as to the immediate result of Hull's campaign as had Clay or Calhoun. He seems to have expected Hull to march victoriously through Upper Canada and to afford him material assistance in an attack on Niagara. And there is a great deal to be said for all this expectation, for the militiamen of Upper Canada needed only an American victory or two in that region to induce them to join the victor, and in that case the Northwestern Indians would have remained immovable, — with the exception of Tecumseh and his immediate following. At once, Dearborn began to find troubles in his path.

The news of the declaration of war brought forth peace memorials and resolutions at New York and Boston; but New York and New England, in the course of the next two years and a half, did their duty proportionately to the performance of the people of any other part of the Union.[1] At

---

[1] Henry Adams has collected figures relating to the proportionate shares of Massachusetts and Virginia in the war (*History of the United States*, viii, 233–236). In 1810, Massachusetts including Maine had a population of 700,745; Virginia, 974,622. There were no slaves in Massachusetts and 392,518 in Virginia, who are included in the total population. Virginia had 23 Representatives to 20 from Massachusetts, under the federal ratio. The total revenue derived from Massachusetts in the year 1814

the same time the war was unpopular in the northeastern
part of the country. The soldiers came slowly to the
colors and money was hard to get. There can be no question that Dearborn was greatly hampered by the reluctance
with which New York and New England put their forces
into the field. He was also troubled by the refusal of the
governors of Massachusetts and Connecticut to heed his
requisitions. In New York a Republican governor was in
office, but the rank and file of the New York militia appear
to have had very little heart in the campaigns of 1812.[1]

In colonial days, each colony had looked out, more or
less, for its own defence; Massachusetts had built and
maintained a fort in Boston harbor, and New York had,
from time to time, fortified positions leading up to the city.
During the Revolution, the new States had protected themselves as well as they could and, when attacked, had been
defended by the armies of Congress and the Confederation
together with local levies. Before 1783, before 1789, there
had been no obligation of local defence on the part of
the general government. After the establishment of the
new nation, attempts had been made, from time to time, to
direct national attention to securing the safety of the leading seaports. Something was done, but the smallest possible amount of money that could be named for any valid

was $2,123,698.95; from Virginia,
$566,577.30 (*American State Papers,
Finance*, iii, 44–48; Pitkin's *Statistical
View*, 368, 415). The only index of
men supplied by the two States that
Adams adduced was the letter of the
paymaster dated October 26, 1814,
and given in *American State Papers,
Military Affairs*, i, 519. According to
the law of January 27, 1814, each soldier who enlisted for five years or during the war was entitled to a bounty of
$124 and perquisites were paid to pro-
curers of recruits to the extent of $8

per head. The paymaster reported
that $2,012,439 had been paid out by
him as bounties and premiums. Of this
$237,400 had gone to Massachusetts,
$495,320 to New York, and only
$160,962 to Virginia.

[1] The *Public Papers of Daniel D.
Tompkins, Governor of New York* (3
vols., Albany, 1898–1902) do not contain any direct evidence bearing out
this statement; but every now and
then one comes across suggestions of
dissatisfaction on the part of those
mentioned in the letters.

plan of coastal fortification was prohibitive. It was only
necessary to get a report to secure the shelving of the whole
subject. Jefferson suggested the possibility sometime of
a system of movable fortifications, of guns that could be
transported from place to place where they could be protected by earthworks and natural objects. Somewhat in
combination with these, he inclined to a gun-boat system,
whereby a heavy gun on a small vessel could be moved
from place to place. But this palliative amounted to almost
nothing when it came to the test. War declared, Dearborn,
by order of the President, called upon the governors of
New York and the New England States to protect their
borders. Caleb Strong of Massachusetts consulted the
Council and the justices of the supreme court of the State
and replied that no invasion existed justifying the calling
out of the militia, and the two governors of Connecticut in
succession, Roger Griswold and Cotton Smith, declined to
do anything whatever. Under circumstances such as these
and without any efficient organization, Dearborn took several months before he was able to place any considerable
body of troops on the Canadian border. There had been
a regular army of the United States ever since the formation
of the Continental Line, but it was impotent in proportion
to the task placed upon it. Congress had done something
in the way of preparedness by authorizing the enlistment
of soldiers by the thousands, but had refused to provide
the necessary funds for carrying any such organization into
effect. The President and his advisers had commissioned a
good many officers. These for the most part were not
superior, to say the least, to Dearborn and to Hull; but
their capacities will appear in the following pages. In the
lower ranks, there were good men; but it took time to bring
them to the front. Whenever a promising soldier appeared

the government lost no time in recognizing his abilities and
giving him responsibility and rank.

For whatever reason, whether one attributes it to Dearborn's age and incapacity or to the lack of a feeling of
national unity, the process of recruiting the Northern
Army and placing it in the field was long drawn out. At
the end of July, 1812, Dearborn was still at the beginning
of his task. On August 8, Colonel Baynes, a British officer,
who had been sent by Sir George Prevost to arrange an
armistice while negotiation for the ending of hostilities
was going on, appeared at Dearborn's headquarters. The
American commander acceded to the governor general's
suggestion, but insisted that the armistice should not extend to Upper Canada beyond Niagara, as he had no doubt
of Hull's success. As Brock was already on his westward
journey and did not learn of the armistice until after the
surrender of Detroit, it had no effect in bringing about
that disaster. The arrangement was exceedingly favorable
to Dearborn because it enabled him to move troops and
supplies to the frontier without fear of attack. Of course
the same measures were open to the Canadians; but they
could not take advantage of the opportunity because they
had no troops or supplies to move to the front. The government at Washington disapproved of the cessation of
hostilities. On August 15, the Secretary of War wrote to
Dearborn that a diversion in favor of General Hull was
urgent and that not a moment should be lost in gaining
possession of the British post at Niagara and aiding
the force operating from Detroit. The next day Hull
surrendered and a week or so later, Brock was back at
Niagara with Hull's army in his clutches, as prisoners
of war. From now on, soldiers and supplies rapidly accumulated on the American side of the Niagara River and

it was determined to make an attack before winter closed in.

The first offensive movement from the American side came from the navy, and not from the army; it was the work of Lieutenant Jesse D. Elliott, who had been sent to Lake Erie to select a site for a naval station. On the morning of October 8, 1812, he noticed two armed brigs anchoring under the guns of the British Fort Erie on the opposite side of the lake. One of these was the *Caledonia*, which had earlier convoyed the expedition from St. Joseph's to Mackinac; the other was the American brig *Adams*, that had been surrendered on the ways where she was repairing at Detroit, and had been rechristened *Detroit*.[1] On board the two vessels were furs, heavy guns that were no longer needed at Amherstburg and Detroit, munitions of war, and American captives. At that very moment, there arrived overland at Black Rock, which Elliott had picked out for the naval arsenal on Lake Erie, some one hundred men. Giving them the least possible time to rest, Elliott armed them, placed them on boats, and in the night time attacked the enemy's vessels as they lay at anchor in fancied security and captured them both. He managed to take the *Caledonia* safely to Black Rock; but the *Detroit* or *Adams* ran aground and was destroyed by gun fire from both shores. The affair was trifling in itself, but most important in restoring something of the American morale and in very greatly lessening the British offensive naval strength on Lake Erie.

---

[1] See Mahan's *War of 1812*, i, 354–356. Adams's *United States*, vi, 347, and *Biographical Notice of Com. Jesse D. Elliott*, p. 20. In 1835 there was a correspondence between Colonel Towson, whose men formed the bulk of the expedition, and Captain Elliott as to where the credit belonged. This was printed at Philadelphia in 1843 as *Correspondence in Relation to the Capture of the British Brigs Detroit and Caledonia.* British writers have suggested that as these ships bore something of the nature of cartels, the attack was hardly justified; but that Mahan did not even think it necessary to notice the circumstance. See Casselman's *Richardson's War of 1812*, 87–90.

It was Elliott's success that led directly to the attack on
Queenston or Queenstown. The American military forces
in the Niagara region were divided between the New York
militia Major General Stephen Van Rensselaer, and Brigadier General Smyth of the United States Army. Van
Rensselaer's titular rank was the higher and he was a leading New York Federalist politician. Alexander Smyth
was an immigrant from Ireland, who had received a commission from Jefferson in 1808, and had exercised the office
of inspector general. He and his soldiers, mostly regulars,
were stationed above the Falls, while Van Rensselaer and
his, among whom were some regulars, were at Lewiston
and at Fort Niagara. He thought the attack should be
made on his front and Smyth was equally decided that it
should be made on his. On the morning of October 13,
Van Rensselaer launched his boats. A body of his regulars crossed the river in the early morning, scrambled up
the bluff overlooking Queenston, seized a battery there,
and began to establish themselves. This was the time for
Smyth to have attacked on his front; but he stood still.
Brock, on learning of the assault, at once rode to the scene
of action, placed himself at the head of whatever troops he
could get hold of, led them into the fight, and was fatally
shot. The British from Fort George now came to the succor of their comrades, while the Americans refused to attack or, as was the case with Van Rensselaer's New York
militia, refused to cross the Niagara River and thus go outside of the State of New York. They would not move
and saw their comrades driven down the bluff and forced to
surrender on the beach below. Van Rensselaer resigned
and Smyth took command of all the troops in that region.
On November 28, he carried out his plan of an attack by
the upper river. In the beginning it was successful, but

not being followed up, it ended in failure and surrender.
Smyth returned to his home and disappeared from view.
And this was the end of the conquest of Upper Canada and
Montreal which Jefferson had predicted would be mainly
a question of marching.

On the land, with its overwhelming superiority of numbers and resources, the United States was immeasurably more
powerful than its opponent in 1812. The sea frontier, on
the contrary, was defenceless and was open to attack by the
naval forces of the greatest sea power in existence. The
outcome of the land campaigns had been most unfortunate,
while on the sea the Americans had been successful. The
wars with the Barbary corsairs and the recent cruisings
for the protection of American vessels on the coast, together
with the indignation excited by the *Chesapeake* outrage, had
resulted in a high state of efficiency on the vessels that constituted the diminutive navy of the United States, as it
might well be termed in comparison with that of its opponent. There were three heavy frigates, — "forty-fours" they
were termed, but what this means is quite incomprehen-
sible to a landsman. The *Constitution*, the most famous
of them, carried a varying number of guns from thirty-
eight to fifty-five, and the other "forty-fours," the *United
States* and the *President*, at one time or another had even
more numerous batteries, running up as high as sixty guns.
These figures are of no great importance and are only
given because no one has ever written about these battles
without attempting to magnify or minimize the disparity
of force between the American "forty-fours" and their
British victims. These ships had been designed by Joshua
Humphreys expressly to outclass the existing type of frigate
in the British and French navies and now performed admirably the tasks for which they had been built. When one

has said this, it is hardly necessary to go any farther, but so much argument pro and con is to be found in the books that possibly a few more things should be said. Not only were these heavy frigates superior in the number of guns, but they were much more heavily timbered than their antagonists; so much so, indeed, that the balls from the lighter English guns sometimes rebounded from their sides, while their own projectiles went crashing home. These ships were furthermore designed for speed, so that other things being equal, they were enabled to take and maintain positions that would give them every advantage. Finally, they carried much larger crews than the largest British frigates, and these crews were volunteers and not the prey of the press gangs. When all is said, therefore, unless some accident supervened, these ships ought to have sent their opponents to the bottom in about the time that they did.[1] So wonderful was the reputation of the British navy, especially after the battles of St. Vincent, and the Nile, and Trafalgar, that one expected nothing but defeat at the hands of British sea-dogs. It was the regular thing. When, therefore, the *Constitution* sailed into Boston Harbor with the captive crew of the *Guerrière* on board, and the *United States* brought in the *Macedonian*, ship and crew, and the *Constitution* sent the *Java* to the bottom, there was rejoicing, such as a nation knows once in a century, — and in England there was amazement and indignation, such as few nations know in any century. When one has

---

[1] Captain Dacres of the *Guerrière* asserted that his gunners fired three shots to the *Constitution's* two. A peaceful historical student finds himself inquiring as to whether the 24 broadside guns of the British ship firing three times in a given period did not really outweigh the 28 of the *Constitution* firing only twice in the same time. A computation of this kind would give the following results: —

Three broadsides of the
Guerrière .... 1578 lbs.
Two broadsides of the
Constitution .... 1520 lbs.

Possibly calculations like this might find their place in showing the fallacy of the elaborate arguments to be found in American and British books.

figured up all the dimensions of the ships, the weights of the broadsides, the goodness or the badness of the gunpowder, how many of the crews were American, how many were British, and has been through the court martial and the court of inquiry records, one thing stands out, and that is, that the Americans ships were much better fitted for the job on hand than were their opponents. Besides giving an artificial filip to American patriotism and sending up the rate of British insurance, these single-ship actions produced few valuable results. Admiral Mahan, indeed, points out that they were really unfortunate, in that they led the American people to place an entirely false estimate upon the necessity of naval preparedness.

Apart from raising the spirits of the people bowed down by the burden of the Canadian campaigns, the navy performed a most useful mission in drawing British naval forces away from American shores at the precise time when returning merchantmen were seeking their home ports at Boston, New York, Philadelphia, and the Chesapeake. The senior officer in command of the American vessels was John Rodgers. He and Stephen Decatur, with the *President* and the *United States* and two smaller vessels, were patrolling the coast from Long Island southward to protect American merchantmen from visitation by British cruisers. At the moment that the declaration of war was known at New York, Rodgers, who happened to be within the port, weighed anchor and stood out to sea, thus missing orders from the government that he might have regarded as limiting his freedom of action. Sailing eastwardly, he chased a British frigate, the *Belvidera*, which carried the news of the war into Halifax, and then disappeared from sight off the banks of Newfoundland. As a matter of fact the American ships crossed the Atlantic and then re-crossed again. They made few prizes, missing the British convoys and meeting mostly their own countrymen. The effect of this bit of naval strategy was to draw the British squadron on the coast away from the shores of the United States to the crossing points of the ocean routes. Ingress into American harbors was therefore free during the autumn of 1812, a fact of immense importance from many points of view.

The declaration of war had been hardly approved by Madison, and the Orders in Council suspended, than negotiations began looking toward the suspension of hostilities and the continuance or restoration of peaceful relations. Jonathan Russell, after Barlow's arrival in Paris, had crossed the Channel to England to take charge of the affairs of the American legation at London. Before long, he and Castlereagh, who was then at the head of the British Foreign Office, found themselves engaged in negotiating for an armistice.[1] The Englishman was amenable enough on the subject of the Orders in Council, for the British government on economic grounds was exceedingly anxious to regain the American markets. Russell, however, was obliged by his instructions to bring forward the matter of impressment, demanding that seamen already impressed should be restored, that impressment should cease during the armistice, and that negotiations should be conducted to bring about a permanent cessation of the practice on condition that the United States should in some way by law provide that no British-born seaman should serve on American ships, whether public or private. This brought from Castlereagh the time-worn response (August 29, 1812) that he could not give up the "ancient and accustomed practice" of impressing British subjects into the king's service, wherever found. Again, two weeks later (September 12, 1812), acting under

---

[1] *American State Papers, Foreign Relations*, iii, 585–595.

new instructions, Russell made similar propositions, this time suggesting a somewhat more specific plan for the prohibition of British subjects serving on American ships. Castlereagh was now much more affable and was distinctly conciliatory. He went into a long disquisition to show Russell how impossible it was for the British government to give up the practice of impressment, and stated that this would have been done at the time of Rufus King's abortive negotiation, if any way could have been found to do it, because Mr. King was so highly thought of. Further discussions would conveniently be transferred to America, as Sir John Borlase Warren had been instructed to open communications with the American government on that point and had been given command of all British ships in American waters.

Warren wrote from Halifax to the Secretary of State at Washington on September 30, 1812,[1] proposing that there should be an immediate cessation of warfare. Monroe replied on October 27th, nearly a month later, refusing the suggested suspension of hostilities on the ground that it appeared Warren's overtures were based on the repeal of the Orders in Council. He stated that the President had seen with regret the rejection by the British government of the propositions made by Mr. Russell in regard to impressment. That question being satisfactorily adjusted, the way would be open to a general pacification. It will be seen from this that Madison and Monroe continued the war on the question of impressment alone,[2] for the conquest of

---

[1] *American State Papers, Foreign Relations*, iii, 595; Monroe's reply is on the next page.

[2] Writing to John Taylor of Caroline in November, 1813, Monroe sought to justify himself and the President. "To the latest moment, before the decln of war, Mr. Foster assured me," so he wrote, "that the orders in council would not be repealed, and nothing was recd from Engld which induc'd a different hope. I had written to the friends of Mr. Fox and had they come in, under the Regent, I have no doubt that an accomodation would have ensued. Not being brought into the

Canada, by the end of October, 1812, must have seemed rather dubious even to them.   It will be well, therefore, for a moment to consider the reality of impressment.   As has already been pointed out, the hardships of the British naval service had driven thousands of British seamen to the American merchant marine and, at one time, considerable portions of the crews of some American warships were composed of native-born subjects of the British king. Many of them had become naturalized and many of them, whether naturalized or not, had procured protections, oftentimes for a few dollars each.   On January 16, 1812, Madison laid before Congress a report [1] of the Secretary of State giving particulars as to impressments which had come under the notice of the Department since April 4, 1810, and lists that had been forwarded by the American agent at London of American seamen and citizens who have been "impressed and held in bondage" from April, 1809 to September, 1810. These returns cover only a portion of the impressment period, but they are portentous in themselves, with those that had already been presented adding up to 6057 cases reported, some of which may be duplications.   This tabulation stirred the Massachusetts House of Representatives.   A committee was appointed to examine the message and the whole sub-

Ministry, they had nothing to say to me. Impressment having long been a ground of complaint, and a principal cause of the war, the British claim would have been confirm'd, as it was thought, if the war was terminated without some adequate provision for it. I was satisfied, that, had we caught, at the modified repeal of the orders in council, made afterwards without an arrangement of other questions particularly that of impressment, the British govt. would have concluded that it had gained a victory, and maintained its whole system in full vigor, even the principles of the orders in council in the form of blockades, against the U states. Having gone to war, it seemed to be our duty, not to withdraw from it, till the rights of our country were plac'd on a more secure basis." Massachusetts Historical Society's *Proceedings*, May, 1909 p. 331.

[1] This report in forty-seven tables gives details as to 2000 cases of the 6057 seamen impressed : the towns of which they represent themselves to be citizens, date and place of impressment, name of ship, from whence taken and on board of which vessel detained, the evidence of citizenship, and the result of representations made on their behalf.

ject.[1] They found not only duplications in these lists, but, sometimes, the same name to be "reckoned three and four times." It was moreover impossible to determine how many were "Americans" and how many were foreign born. They thereupon summoned fifty-one ship-owners and took their sworn depositions. These men employed about 1560 seamen or about 18,720 for the twelve years of the French war. These witnesses could remember only thirty-five cases of impressment within their personal knowledge. Of these only twelve were Americans, and of them nine had been discharged and one escaped. Among the deponents was William Gray of Boston, the largest ship-owner in New England and a Republican in politics. He testified that for the last fifteen or twenty years he had employed about three hundred seamen annually. He remembered only two cases of impressment from his vessels, which were from the ship *Rachel* while she was at Leith, Scotland. He had knowledge of other cases, but not from his own ships. Of course he had had whole crews taken when his vessels were captured, but refused to say that the men in those cases were impressed. Coming from so great a master of navigation and a Republican withal, the statements are certainly remarkable. James Perkins and Thomas Handasyde Perkins, his partner and brother, employing from a hundred to a hundred and fifty seamen annually, also deposed. They could recollect only three men who had been impressed from their vessels, and these were foreigners. Thomas H. Perkins deposed that foreigners repeatedly had applied

---

[1] *Report of the Committee of the House of Representatives of Massachusetts, on the subject of Impressed Seamen* (Boston, 1813). See also a "Letter from the Secretary of State, accompanying Statements and Abstracts relative To the Number of American seamen . . . impressed" dated January 23, 1805; and a similar letter of the following year, dated March 8, 1806. Thomas Barclay, the British consul general at New York, strove manfully and successfully to mitigate the hardships of impressment; see his *Correspondence* edited by G. L. Rives, using index under "impressment," and p. 218.

to him for employment, stating that they had no protections, but would get them, and that the prices paid were two dollars each at the shipping offices. The friends of peace of Rockingham County in New Hampshire met together in August, 1812, listened to an oration, and adopted a memorial and resolutions, the former of which is supposed to have been drawn by Daniel Webster. In this the New Hampshire men reiterated the facts stated by the Massachusetts committee that the number of cases of impressment has been "extravagantly exaggerated." Some of the members present had been constantly employed in navigation since 1783 and had never suffered the loss of one native American seaman by impressment. The deposition of William Gray is certainly startling in its incompatibility with the evidence laid before Congress by Madison and believed by him to be a complete justification of war on land and sea with all its killings, and burnings, and pillagings, and doubtfulness of result that attends any exercise of arms.

NOTES

I. General Military Bibliography. — The official papers relating to the military side of the war have never been collected and printed in an authoritative manner.   Documents are printed in the *American State Papers, Military Affairs*, i, 337 and fol.; *Annals of Congress*, 13th Cong. (vols. ii and iii, Appendixes); Niles's *Weekly Register*, vols. ii to vii; and John Brannan's *Official Letters of the Military and Naval Officers of the United States . . . in the Years 1812, 13, 14, & 15* (Washington City, 1823) and in many other places. The proof-reading of many of these papers often gives rise to suspicion of their accuracy.   The best collection that has been made is that by Lieutenant Colonel E. A. Cruikshank, which was printed by the Lundy's Lane Historical Society, but this covers only the campaigns on the Niagara frontier.   A similar volume, also edited by Colonel Cruikshank, and printed in the *Canadian Archives*, is devoted to Hull's Detroit campaign.[1]   A good bibliography is given in Winsor's *Narrative and Critical History*, vii, " Critical Essay " appended to J. R. Soley's chapter on " The Wars of the United States," but this has titles of books only that were printed before 1888.

The chapters in volumes vi, vii, and viii of Adams's *United States* and Mahan's *Sea Power in its Relations to the War of 1812* form — taken together — the best modern account of the conflict.   Both Adams and Mahan had prejudices against the Jeffersonian-Madisonian policy which obscured their vision to some extent; otherwise their accounts are marvels of research and scholarly acumen, and Mahan's naval chapters have professional interest also.   B. J. Lossing's *Pictorial Field-Book of the War of 1812* gives a skilled historical student's view of the conflicts and reports with pen and pencil local tales and topography — so far as 1860 can represent 1812.   Of the more compendious accounts, C. P. Lucas's *Canadian War of 1812* is the best; but the subject has had slight interest for American historical students — possibly owing to the harrowing details of military incompetence.   Accounts of contemporaries are invariably of a disputatious character.   Of them may be mentioned John Armstrong's

---

[1] *Documents relating to the Invasion of Canada and the Surrender of Detroit, 1812 (Publications of the Canadian Archives*, No. 7, Ottawa, 1913); *Parliamentary Papers, 1814–1815*, containing three groups of papers which were ordered to be printed February 9 and 10, 1815.

Notices of the War of 1812 (2 vols., New York, 1840); C. J. Ingersoll's historical writings on the war [1] reflect the opinions of an ardent Madisonian who was in political life at the time; and William James's *Military Occurrences* [2] equally reflect the views of a British subject who suffered imprisonment at the hands of his American enemies.

Of the older books, and mainly valuable as expressing the opinions of the times in which they were written, are J. L. Thomson's *Historical Sketches of the Late War* (Philadelphia, 1818); Samuel Perkins's *History of the Political and Military Events of the Late War* (New Haven, 1825); and Henry M. Brackenridge's *History of the Late War* (Baltimore, 1816). The edition of this work printed at Philadelphia in 1844 has some most remarkable pictorial representations of military and naval events.

II. General Naval Bibliography. — A. T. Mahan's *Sea Power in its Relations to the War of 1812* (2 vols., Boston, 1905) has supplied the long-felt want of a history of the maritime part of the last war with England. Theodore Roosevelt's *Naval War of 1812* (New York, 1882) is less scientific in character, and the author had not then acquired the stylistic swing that characterizes his later writings. He treated the same subject in briefer form in 1901 in W. Laird Clowes's *Royal Navy*, vol. vi. William James, the British naval writer, printed at London in 1817 *A Full and Correct Account of the Chief Naval Occurrences of the Late War between Great Britain and the United States of America.* [3] He repeated much of the same matter in the fifth

[1] C. J. Ingersoll's *Historical Sketch of the Second War between the United States of America and Great Britain* (Philadelphia, 1845); a thin double-columned volume bearing the same title brings the story down through 1814. See also his *History of the Second War between the United States of America and Great Britain* (2 vols., Philadelphia, 1852).

[2] *A Full and Correct Account of the Military Occurrences of the Late War between Great Britain and the United States of America* by William James (2 vols., London, 1818).

[3] James's other works on the single-ship naval actions are "An Inquiry into the Merits of the principal naval actions between Great Britain and the United States" (Halifax, 1816); and "Warden Refuted; being a Defence

of the British Navy against the Misrepresentations of a work . . . entitled 'A Statistical . . . Account of the United States . . . by D. B. Warden'" (London, 1819). James's mission, so he conceived it, was to dissipate "the vile compound" of the tables in Warden's book (iii, 426) which "but for this early notice, might have spread contagion over the land," and, he might have added, the water also. In the tables in this work James gives Warden's figures and the correct ones, as he deems them, in consecutive lines, — a table compiled from this is given on p. 545 of the present volume. Kingsford reprints James's original table, without the American figures and without stating that James was the compiler, in his *History of Canada*, viii, 426.

and sixth volumes of his *Naval History of Great Britain* (London, 1837). James Fenimore Cooper, in 1839, published in Philadelphia and London a *History of the Navy of the United States*, which is as one-sided as James's, and represented the current American ideas. Volume ii contains an account of the War of 1812. Roosevelt points out the difficulty of reaching any conclusion as to a great many details of this naval episode. Probably the best thing for most students will be to accept Mahan's analysis without more ado. Original accounts were printed at the time in the newspapers and gathered into the magazines as *The Naval Monument, The Examiner*, Niles's *Weekly Register*, and *The Historical Register of the United States*, etc. The *American State Papers, Naval Affairs*, vol. i, contain much the same information. Citations to specific accounts of particular actions have been placed in footnotes to this and the following chapters.

CHAPTER XVIII

THE WAR IN 1813 AND IN 1814

THE year 1813 was marked by one brilliant success that had far-reaching consequences, — Perry's victory over the British squadron on Lake Erie; otherwise it was filled with disappointments. Hull's defeat and the difficulty of doing anything on the Niagara frontier convinced the authorities at Washington that the control of the Lakes was necessary to the prosecution of the northern campaign to any satisfactory conclusion. They detached Captain Chauncey from the seaboard, ordered him to take command on the Lakes, fit out a fleet, and gain the upper hand. With the efficiency that characterized the navy in this war, Chauncey at once undertook the purchase, transportation, and assembling of adequate forces, carpenters, sailors, and their food supplies, and the materials for their ship-building programme. When Chauncey reached his command in October, 1812, and looked over the situation, he realized that he had undertaken by no means an easy task. Lake Ontario and Lake Erie, although only a few hundred miles away from the ship-building yards and gun foundries of the Atlantic seacoast, possessed almost no ports on the American shores that were accessible by overland transportation. Lieutenant Elliott had selected the little harbor at Black Rock as the site of naval construction on Lake Erie; but this was within reach of the enemies' guns on the opposite bank of the Niagara River and was therefore difficult to enter and to leave. On Lake Ontario Chauncey picked out Sackett's Harbor as best adapted to his purpose. It could be defended against any ordinary attack, but had no direct connection with the existing lines of transportation through New York. The easiest way, indeed, to transport guns and heavy material, was to take them by the Mohawk route to Lake Oneida and thence down the Oswego River and along the lake shore to Sackett's Harbor. There were many difficulties to overcome on this route and the last part of the way was within reach of enemy's ships on the lake. On Lake Erie matters were worse, if anything. Black Rock was clearly an impossible naval base, but the only other harbor on the American shore within practicable reach of the seaboard was Presqu'Isle, or Erie, as it later became. The harborage here was good and it was fairly accessible to Pittsburg and Philadelphia. The great disadvantage of Presqu'Isle as a naval port was a sand-bank or bar that closed the harbor to vessels drawing more than four or five feet of water. Sackett's and Presqu'Isle were the most available ports and were selected. Chauncey worked with vigor and inspired enthusiasm in others. He soon had a new set of warships afloat on Lake Ontario and cruised about upon the lake. He claimed to have gained a superiority over the enemy; but, really, he had accomplished very little when the winter set in and his vessels were blocked by the ice in Sackett's Harbor. The British, too, were not idle, and labored so effectively that throughout the whole of 1813 there was a question as to which side held the supreme position on Lake Ontario; but there was no doubt whatever on this point on Lake Erie after September 10.

Lieutenant Elliott had at first been in charge of affairs on Lake Erie, but Commander Oliver Hazard Perry, de-

siring more active service than he was likely to get as chief
of a gun-boat flotilla, was sent there. He removed the
naval base from Black Rock to Presqu'Isle and drove on
the construction of two brigs and several smaller vessels.
Everybody worked with a will and the squadron was ready
late in July, 1813. Perry's greatest want was for seamen.
Chauncey, naturally, kept as many as possible with him.
In early August, the relations between the two became so
strained that Perry asked the Secretary of the Navy to
remove him from the station. This was refused and he
remained in command of the little fleet. The difficulties
facing the British were greater, if possible, than those that
Perry overcame. Their naval base was at Amherstburg,
at the western end of the lake, at the mouth of the Detroit
River. Captain Barclay, an able officer of the British
navy, was in command of the naval forces on Lake Erie.
He found it almost impossible to get workmen, materials,
and food. Gathering whatever vessels he could, he blockaded Presqu'Isle. The bar at that place was so shoal that
the larger American vessels could not cross it until their
guns were removed, which of course, made them helpless
until they were re-shipped on the outside of the bar. In
other words, it was impossible to get the ships out of the
harbor while the entrance was watched by the enemy
even with an inferior force. At length Barclay was obliged
to quit his blockade and before he could get back Perry
had carried his two largest vessels safely over the sand-
bank, August 5, and with his fleet sailed up the lake to the
Bass Islands. He anchored there in Put-in-Bay, thus
securing for the time being, the control of the lake.

Barclay realized that he should not meet the American
squadron until a new ship, the *Detroit*, was completed.
But he had no proper equipment for her or guns with which

to arm her. Thousands of soldiers, settlers, and Indians were congregated at Amherstburg and in the vicinity. They had almost no food on hand and could get no adequate supply except by water. It was necessary for Barclay to strike a blow at the American fleet. If skill and chance should give the victory to the inferior force, the lake would be open to the British; if Barclay were defeated, Detroit and Amherstburg would necessarily be abandoned, as they would have to be if Perry simply maintained his control of the water communications without a battle. It is well to recognize that in number of guns, homogeneity of battery, and weight of broadside, the Americans were greatly superior to the British, — the *Detroit*, indeed, was partly armed with guns from the ramparts of Fort Malden. There was not much difference between the crews of the two squadrons; Perry had some practiced gunners and more militiamen among his men, and Barclay had soldiers and Canadian voyageurs, as well as sailors. None of the crews had worked together in battle. Indeed, on Lake Erie and at Plattsburg, green-timbered, hastily built, and inadequately armed ships navigated by untrained crews won two victories that were more decisive of the fate of the United States than any others in the War of 1812. Perry was quite as anxious to meet Barclay as Barclay was to meet him, for the defeat of the British squadron would restore the Northwest to the United States and open Upper Canada to Harrison's army that had been held motionless for the greater part of a year on the lower Maumee and near-by rivers.

It was September 10, 1813, when the two fleets came together to the northward of Put-in-Bay. There was none of that manœuvring for the weather gauge that is so puzzling to the land writer and so gratifying to the nautical

historian. The wind settled the matter for them by giving
Barclay the windward position until the two fleets came
near to firing distance and then turned directly around
and put him to leeward. Perry in the *Lawrence*, a brig of
twenty guns, sailed headlong into the fight, the mark for two
of Barclay's three heavy ships. The green crews fired away
as rapidly as they could, and hit their marks, for the vessels
were very near together. The two flagships, the *Lawrence*
and the *Detroit*, became hardly more than wrecks, the
latter having been the target also of some of Perry's smaller
vessels which carried one or two long guns apiece. While
this was going on, Perry's other heavy vessel, the *Niagara*
under Lieutenant Elliott, favored by the wind, took a position at some distance away from her British antagonist, the
Queen Charlotte, firing her thirty-two pounders without
receiving much damage from her lighter armed opponent.
Seeing his own ship out of the combat and the *Niagara*
practically fresh, Perry stepped into a boat, gained her
deck, took her into the thick of the fight, and won the day.
Not one British vessel escaped. "We have met the enemy;
and they are ours"[1] was literally true. All the enemy's
force on Lake Erie or that could get there was eliminated.
Not only this, the victory gave a free hand to Harrison's
army and compelled the British to retire eastwardly from
the Detroit River.

No sooner had Hull started on his march than the federal
government and the States of Ohio, Kentucky, and Tennessee pushed forward preparations to reënforce him.
The recruiting and organizing of an expedition, containing
a few thousand men, was then a matter of time and the
supplying even such a small party in the existing lack of
transportation and the absence of storage warehouses filled

---

[1] Niles's *Weekly Register*, v, 60.

with food was well nigh impossible. Hull had surrendered before the expedition under General William Henry Harrison [1] began its march through the wildernesses of central and northern Ohio and Indiana. Harrison thought it best to proceed by three lines, so as not to exhaust the limited facilities of any one route. It was the ever-recurring story of rains and mud, incapable commanders, and disorderly starving militiamen. For weeks and months, the army struggled on without making any appreciable advance. In mid-winter, the ground froze so hard that artillery and heavy wagons could be hauled over it; and then Harrison found himself with his three units on the Sandusky, the Portage, and Maumee rivers. In January, 1813, the commander of the westernmost division, General Winchester, was induced by his Kentucky officers to send a large portion of his troops to succor the American inhabitants of Frenchtown on the River Raisin, which was then occupied by a Canadian force from Amherstburg. Colonel Henry Procter had been left in charge of affairs in Michigan and western Canada by Brock on his return to Niagara. Procter's military ending was most humiliating; but in this middle period of his career, he showed himself a brave, energetic, and resourceful commander. Learning of the Americans at Frenchtown, he organized an expedition of whites and Indians, surprised the Kentuckians on the River Raisin, and killed or captured nearly all of them, including General Winchester who was himself a Tennesseean.[2]

---

[1] Moses Dawson in his *Historical Narrative of . . . William H. Harrison*, ch. xxiv and fol., has gone at length into the campaigns of 1812, 1813, from the point of view of an admirer of that general. This portion of our history is treated from a local standpoint in C. E. Slocum's *Ohio Country* and his *History of the Maumee River Basin* (Defiance, Ohio, 1905).

[2] Owing to the massacre of the American wounded after the affair of the River Raisin, there was a good deal of recrimination which led to several publications, as William Atherton's *Narrative of the Suffering & Defeat of the North-Western Army under General Winchester* and Elias Darnell's *Journal . . . of those heroic Kentucky Volunteers and Regulars commanded by General*

Harrison had planned to cross the ice to attack the British posts on the northern side of Lake Erie. On the contrary, it was Procter who did the attacking. He came twice, once to Fort Meigs that had been built at the rapids of the Maumee, and at another time to a fort on the lower Sandusky. In the expedition to Fort Meigs (May, 1813) he was provided with heavy artillery for battering ramparts and a large number of Indians under the redoubtable Tecumseh. He captured a division of the American forces that disobeyed Harrison's commands,[1] but returned without accomplishing anything more. The attack on Sandusky (August) was an even greater failure, for he did not then pick up any disobedient militiamen and suffered a considerable proportionate loss of his own army. All these things convinced Harrison that there was nothing except peril in advancing further towards the recovery of Michigan, until the Americans could gain command of Lake Erie. Furthermore, it was very difficult to keep his soldiers supplied where they were and it was the critical condition of his affairs that induced Perry to strike at the enemy before his fleet was in really first-class condition. His success left the field open to Harrison and he lost no time in taking advantage of the opportunity thus given him.

There was but one thing for Procter to do after Perry's victory on Lake Erie and that was to save his troops and as much of his material and equipment as he could. The Indians were greatly opposed to the abandonment of Detroit and Amherstburg, having slight knowledge of the influence of sea power on land affairs. It was only with

Winchester. There is some interesting matter in Richardson's *War of 1812* and chapter iv of volume vii of Adams's *United States* is one of the most careful bits of that author's historical writing.

[1] A vivid description of this un-necessary disaster is Captain Leslie Combs's official report printed at Cincinnati in 1869 as *Col. Wm. Dudley's Defeat opposite Fort Meigs, May 5th, 1813.*

difficulty that Procter gained the consent of Tecumseh to the retirement, and then only on some kind of an agreement that the retreat would be only to Moravian Town, about halfway from the Detroit River to the outpost of the British Niagara army. These preliminaries and packing up took time, so that the British did not start until ten days or two weeks after Perry's victory. They delayed so long that Harrison entered Fort Malden three days after they left, September 27, 1813. The first part of the retreat was parallel to water communications, so that the heavy goods and food supplies could be carried by boat. Harrison had a considerable body of mounted soldiers. Any one familiar with stories of wars and retreats can easily understand what was certain to happen, especially as the road from the Detroit River to Moravian Town was hardly more than a "trace." Before many days, the Americans caught up with the foe in a bit of open woodland to the west of Moravian Town. The British fired a couple of volleys before the cavalrymen rode over them and compelled surrender. Tecumseh and his Indians had been stationed at an angle to the British line in another patch of woods. The idea, apparently, was that they should assail the flank and rear of the Americans when they were engaged with the British in front. Harrison had so many men that he told off part to take care of the Indians. This they did, Tecumseh being killed in the fight. Procter saved his life by rapid flight on horseback, only to incur censure and disgrace. After the battle of the Thames,[1] October 5, 1813, the Americans followed the fleeing enemy as far as the Moravian Indians' town, which they burned. Harrison then returned to the Detroit River and with the main part of his soldiers went

---

[1] American authors usually term this conflict the battle of the Thames; the Canadians call it the battle of **Moravian Town**.

by water to the Niagara frontier.   This was the end of
operations on a large scale in Michigan Territory and
uppermost Canada,—and Lake Erie passes out of historical
narrative.

The story of the war in the country to the eastward
of Lake Erie — on the Niagara River, on Lake Ontario,
and on the St. Lawrence — is one of the most depressing
and monotonous tales in American history, — and led to
nothing in the end. A fair beginning was made in 1813 by
the capture of Fort George on the British side of the outlet
of the Niagara River. Then followed weeks of waiting for
the coöperation of Chauncey's fleet and of sudden and
distressing attacks by the British, who had abandoned the
Niagara Peninsula and established their headquarters at
Burlington Heights at the western extremity of Lake Ontario. The naval situation on the lower lake was very
peculiar throughout the war. There were two able naval
captains in command of the opposing fleets, Commodore
Isaac Chauncey on the American side and Sir James L.
Yeo on the British; they were supplied with men and
materials in abundance compared with what Perry and
Barclay had on Lake Erie, and yet throughout the war, with
occasional intervals, the condition on Lake Ontario was
one of stalemate. The Americans there had the advantage
of priority of opportunity. In the late autumn of 1812,
Chauncey gained control of the lake and held it in the spring
of 1813. Nothing more resulted from this except the occupation of York, the capture of a few British soldiers, and
the destruction of a ship or two on the stocks. When Yeo
finally got his fleet into fighting trim, he and Chauncey sailed
up and down the lake, first one and then the other being
pursuer. There were other American attacks across the
St. Lawrence and there were British invasions of American

soil at Sackett's Harbor, when Chauncey was absent at the other end of Ontario, and at Ogdensburg. From these somewhat random encounters and operations, three soldiers of merit emerged, — Jacob Brown, Winfield Scott, and Eleazar Ripley. These were providential finds to the government at Washington, were promptly recognized as such, and given rank which they would not have obtained in twenty or fifty years of peace. Jacob Brown, Pennsylvanian born of Quaker parents, was a New York militia officer who had seen nothing of war, but when the time came, refused to be frightened. Scott and Ripley had risen rapidly from lower grades in the regular army. With these three men in upper commands on the Niagara frontier, and a great improvement in the quality of the regimental officers, the soldiers were much better led in 1813 than in 1812.

In April, 1813, General Dearborn and Commodore Chauncey sailed forth from Sackett's with the most formidable expedition that had yet been seen on the Great Lakes. The town of Kingston at the northeastern end of Lake Ontario was the most important Canadian naval and military station west of Montreal. It was the strategic point of attack, second only to Montreal, for if either of these places were seized by the Americans and held, all Canada to the westward was lost to the British. Instead, Dearborn and Chauncey sailed westward and attacked York, now Toronto, at the northwestern end of the lake. There was a ship there and soldiers and magazines, but it was distinctly subordinate from a military point of view to Kingston. The Americans were in such force that the British made off without attempting any resistance to speak of. A most unfortunate incident of the affair was the explosion of a large powder magazine, which resulted in the death of Brigadier General Zebulon M. Pike, who had charge of the land operations and was near by at the time of the explosion. This disaster incited the Americans to vengeance and led to the destruction of the capitol of Upper Canada and other buildings. Abandoning York, the expedition next went to Fort George at the mouth of the Niagara River. The troops were landed, the fort captured (May 27), the British driven off, and then the vigor and success that had so far marked the expedition came to an end, and everything relapsed into the conditions of the preceding year. Dearborn was old and ill, and the death of Pike had removed an officer of indomitable courage, who was familiar with wilderness life. Whether he had the other qualities that would make a military commander had not been demonstrated. Certainly, his successors showed none of these traits and lacked the fearlessness in danger that Pike had shown on many occasions. The names of these commanders and the scenes of action are best forgotten. American forces were broken up and captured and destroyed or put to flight. It was the old story of the Harrison campaign and was doubtless due in large part to the employment of large bodies of Indians by the British. These not only stole through the forest and came upon their white foes unawares, but the fear of them induced surrender, while there was opportunity to place one's self or one's brigade or army under the protection of the British white contingent.[1] In July, the British became so emboldened that they actually crossed the Niagara River and attacked Fort Schlosser on the American side not far above the Falls.

[1] Some British writers have suggested that the sudden surrendering of the British at the "Battle of the Thames" was likewise due to fear of Indian outrage, — this time from their own erstwhile allies.

The best that can be said for one of these unpleasant happenings is to be found in J. P. Boyd's *Documents and Facts Relative to Military Events during the Late War.*

At the other end of Ontario, almost a similar story could be told of the British. Commodore Yeo and Sir George Prevost, or properly speaking, Sir George Prevost and Commodore Yeo, seeing that the American fleet and army were busily employed at Niagara, thought the moment a good one to attack Sackett's Harbor, burn the vessels on the stocks there, and carry off whatever provisions and stores could be taken away. The place had been left almost defenceless, but fortunately Jacob Brown lived in the neighborhood. He had been asked by Dearborn to take charge of affairs in case of trouble. When the British appeared, Brown took command. His troops were mostly militia, but he was one of those men who do not know when they are beaten, and militiamen can often be rallied and brought back by a courageous commander in whom they have confidence. The British got on shore May 29, 1813, and occupied the town ; fire destroyed a nearly completed warship and the barracks ; but the fighting went on and Sir George Prevost, seeing that nothing useful could be accomplished without great hazard, ordered the expedition back to his own side of the lake. The affair had an important consequence in recalling Chauncey from his dreams of conquest to the westward, and the destruction of materials lessened his offensive power. Such was the condition of affairs in August, 1813, when General James Wilkinson arrived at Sackett's Harbor from New Orleans and assumed direction of the campaign.

General James Wilkinson was another Revolutionary soldier who had done well enough in a minor place. Since that war he had risen to the command of the United States army after the death of Anthony Wayne. For years, he had lived on the frontier, engaged in intrigue and the sale of flour and constantly losing in morale and efficiency. He had an effective force, when combined with those that came from the Niagara River, — even Harrison's men from the Maumee and Detroit were brought to Sackett's. The plan, which seems to have been of Armstrong's devising, for he had now taken the office of Secretary of War, was to concentrate for an attack on Montreal. Wilkinson was to descend the St. Lawrence or march along its banks to Isle Perault, where he would be joined by another force under General Wade Hampton coming from Plattsburg on Lake Champlain. General Wilkinson and Wade Hampton had little in common, except their dislike and distrust of one another. Wilkinson was an adventurer, ever in want of a dollar; Wade Hampton was one of the half-dozen richest planters in the South. What their private griefs were is unknown, but they certainly were an ill-assorted pair of commanders, their only merit being that up to the present time they had not been associated with the fiascos of the Lakes.

There were the usual delays inevitable on such occasions, so that Wilkinson did not begin his evolution until the first of November, 1813. His movements down the river were well enough conducted, but they were slow, as was natural and perhaps necessary. On November 11, a British pursuing force caught up with a body of flankers on the British side of the river at Chrystler's Farm, and handled them so sternly that the expedition was brought to a standstill for the time being. The next day, November 12, Wilkinson received a letter from General Wade Hampton saying that he had turned back from Châteauguay. Wade Hampton's march had been made on time. He had advanced about halfway from the Canadian line to the St. Lawrence when his van was vigorously assailed, October 26, by a mixed body of French Canadians and Indians under De

Salaberry.[1] Instead of pushing right into the enemy and acting with vigor, Hampton turned about and left Wilkinson to himself.[2] That commander then retired to French Mills, on American soil, where his army went into winter quarters.[3] In December, the tale of American adversity was finished by the retirement of the Americans from the Niagara Peninsula after wantonly burning the little town of Newark, hard by Fort George; and a few days later, December 18, the British followed them across the river and took possession of Fort Niagara, — which they retained until the execution of the Treaty of Ghent.

The campaigns in the year 1814 closely resembled in many particulars those of 1813. There were the same indecisive naval operations on Lake Ontario, the same advance and retreat on the Niagara Peninsula, a similar abortive invasion of Canada, but in the outcome a counter British invasion of the United States came to naught. The turn of affairs in Europe following on the Battle of Leipsic in October, 1813, and the invasion of France by the allies in the following winter and spring, culminated in April, 1814, with the abdication of Napoleon. This set free soldiers and ships for America; but they did not begin to arrive in any considerable force until the campaigning season was half gone. The American force that was designed to invade the Niagara Peninsula was commanded by Jacob Brown, now a major general in the regular army. He had under his orders Scott, Gaines, and Ripley, three

---

[1] This affair has naturally interested the Quebec historians. Benjamin Sulte printed in 1899 at Quebec a brochure entitled *La Bataille de Châteauguay*. See also W. D. Lighthall's *Account of the Battle of Châteauguay*; and W. F. Coffin's *1812; The War, and its Moral: A Canadian Chronicle*, 244–251.

[2] *American State Papers, Military Affairs*, i, 462.

[3] The third volume of James Wilkinson's *Memoirs of My Own Times* is occupied entirely with the evidence and arguments presented at the court martial with his own interpretation of his doings contained in chapters x–xv. He was acquitted on all the charges presented against him, and the finding of the court was approved by President Madison.

men of more than ordinary military ability, and he expected
to have the coöperation of the naval force on Lake Ontario.
He crossed the Niagara River to Fort Erie, which was
abandoned by the British, and moved down the Canadian
side of the river, fighting a memorable battle at Chippewa
or Street's Creek, July 5, 1814.[1] But when he reached Lake
Ontario, he found no American fleet to meet him and, in
fact, Commodore Chauncey was unwilling to go out on to
the lake for the purpose of coöperating with the military.
American writers have reprobated this conduct of the
naval commander, and certainly Chauncey was not one of
those men who seize the vantage moment; but it may well
be that he knew more about the naval possibilities than did
General Brown or his critics of a later time. At all events,
he refused to coöperate at the moment when his coöperation might have been decisive. Brown, therefore, retired
to the westward, and in retirement fought an action at
Lundy's Lane, July 25, 1814, within sound of Niagara Falls,
that has made his campaign memorable. It was one of
those combats, beginning late in the day and continuing
into the night, that are marked by forward and backward
movements, by mingling troops and captured guns that are
left on the field. In the end the Americans retired to Fort
Erie, and the British were entitled to claim a victory.[2]
There were regular British troops in this action, but they
were not the veterans of the Peninsular War, of Wellington's
training, for these had not yet been long enough in Canada
to get so far away from ocean navigation. At Fort Erie,
the Americans entrenched themselves within a long range
of works, which were assaulted by the British in a night

[1] See *Documentary History of the
Campaign on the Niagara Frontier in
1814*, i, 38, 47, 54, etc. (publications of
the Lundy's Lane Historical Society).

[2] See *Documentary History of the
Campaign on the Niagara Frontier in
1814*, i, 97, etc. (publications of the
Lundy's Lane Historical Society).

attack with disastrous results to the storming parties. A
later sortie by the garrison in September led to the retirement of the British ; upon which the Americans sought their
own side of the river, leaving Fort Erie to its former owners.

By this time, many of the higher officers had been wounded.
Brown had been replaced as commander-in-chief by General George Izard, who had originally commanded one
part of Wade Hampton's innocuous army. The Niagara
campaign, turning out to be so much more strenuous than
had been expected, Izard almost abandoned the works and
camps at Plattsburg, marched across the country to Sackett's
Harbor, withdrew the army from Fort Erie, and then followed Hull, Dearborn, Wilkinson, Hampton, etc., into
retirement.[1] As to Commodore Chauncey and Sir James
Lucas Yeo, they were still competing in building and arming vessels for the control of the Lakes. For some unknown or unexplained reason, Chauncey had provided
himself with a fleet of large vessels and small vessels, with
so much disparity of size that they could not sail the water
together, so that the larger ships took the smaller ones in
tow. Yeo, on the other hand, began the construction of a
leviathan of the Lakes to carry one hundred and two guns.
Her construction was delayed, as was natural with a vessel
of her size, and the American privateer *Fox* added to the
delay by capturing on the Atlantic a British ordnance brig
with sixty-six twenty-four pounders that were destined for
her battery. It was well into October, 1814, therefore,
before Yeo's great ship, the *St. Lawrence*, sailed out of
port and shut Chauncey and his motley fleet in Sackett's
Harbor, where they were when peace was proclaimed.

[1] Adams's account is very unfavorable
to General Izard. In the *Magazine of
American History*, for December, 1891,
G. E. Manigault of Charleston, S. C.
has stated the other side. In a preceding number of the same magazine
(xix, 462) he had already printed an
article on Izard's career.

One more operation on the northern frontier, this time on Lake Champlain, and the story of battles, advances, and retreats in that part of the country is done. In all former wars, Lake Champlain had borne the most conspicuous part, but in this conflict, hitherto, it had seen little worthy of remark. In 1813, there had been some desultory fighting. The British had occupied Plattsburg for a few days, and had then returned to the northern end of the lake. In the course of this episode, two armed American sloops had been captured, thereby seriously detracting from the American force on Champlain and adding to that of the British. The Wellington veterans began arriving at Quebec in June, 1814, and, by August, Sir George Prevost found himself at the head of a force of more than 10,000 seasoned, disciplined troops — apart from those that were defending the province above Montreal. It was the strongest, best appointed army that had ever appeared in America, — with the possible exception of that which Howe led to the Brandywine in the Revolutionary War. In September, Prevost set out to invade the United States by the way of Lake Champlain. His movements were timed necessarily by that of the work on a thirty-seven gun ship, the *Confiance,* that was fitting out on the British end of Lake Champlain. Prevost might have passed down either side of the lake. He chose the western side because an invasion by that route would not interrupt the flow of cattle and provision northward through Vermont. In this way he came to Plattsburg on the evening of September 6, 1814. When General Izard had marched off to Sackett's Harbor with four thousand men, a few days before Prevost started southward, he had left General Macomb with fifteen hundred troops in the extensive fortifications. Macomb and the New York authorities showed admirable energy.

In a short time, the militia began coming in, and every day
added to their numbers; but they were not able to prevent
Prevost occupying the village which then stood on the
northern side of the Saranac River. The Americans destroyed the bridge or bridges behind them and retired into
a series of forts that crowned the hills on the southern side
of the stream, extending from it to Lake Champlain.

On the lake, Commodore Macdonough had assembled a
small squadron.[1] The larger vessels he had built on the
Vermont side of the lake and had carried them rather
unknown to the British from their launching-place. He
anchored these vessels across the mouth of Plattsburg Bay
in such positions that any hostile force entering the port
was obliged to fight on his own terms. The British naval
commander was Captain George Downie of the regular
navy, who had been detailed by Yeo for this service. He
had hardly taken command, when Prevost pressed him to
action, for the commander-in-chief rightly felt that as long
as the Americans had control of the lake, conquest or advance was ill-advised and out of the question. The large
ship was somehow delayed, as ships were on the Lakes,
owing to distance from magazines and paucity of material
and men. At length, after urging, as soon as the *Confiance*
was ready, Downie sailed and entered Plattsburg Bay.
The battle that followed reminds one in a way of Perry's
exploit of the preceding year. To understand them, one
must try to conceive of vessels of the size of small coasters

[1] Mahan, in his *War of 1812*, ii, 360–
382, has described the Battle of Lake
Champlain at great length. In a
note on page 382, he apparently regrets
that no dispute like that between Perry
and Elliott provided material for the
future historian, but says that the
"Record of the British Court Martial"
contains the most complete and satisfactory evidence. Rodney Macdonough's *Life of Commodore Thomas
Macdonough* (Boston, 1909) sets forth
the facts of the naval battle at great
length, with records in an appendix.
There seems to be some doubt as to the
precise location of the fleets' anchorage,
but the discrepancies are of no vital
importance. Three different plans are
given in Adams, Mahan, and Macdonough.

with hardly any bulwarks, the deck of each ship crowded with men firing at one another at point blank range. That any of them were left alive to tell the story of victory and defeat is a marvel. As the British advanced, the Americans opened fire, and shots carried away the *Confiance's* anchors and chains, so that she was unable to take up the position that had been designed for her. Nevertheless, she was so superior in force to Macdonough's ship, the *Saratoga*, that matters seemed to be going hard with the latter, when she was turned completely around by means of springs on her cable and a fresh broadside opened on the enemy! The death of Captain Downie in the early part of the fight and the failure of the British galleys to join in the fray materially contributed to give victory to the Americans. Excepting the refractory galleys, every British vessel was captured or destroyed. On shore, Prevost's men had advanced to the attack. Those that tried to cross the river near the lower bridge failed in the attempt; but another body forded the stream at a higher point and pushed away the American force guarding it. At this moment, the loss of the fleet becoming certain, Prevost called off his men and rapidly retreated to Canada. No one on either side has received harder measure of blame than Sir George Prevost. In this instance, it would appear to be most undeserved. The British fleet seemed superior to the American and a partial defeat of the latter would have placed Champlain under British control. Why, then, because he had veterans of Salamanca and Torres Vedras should he hurl them at strong redoubts, even if they were defended by militia-men, when by remaining perfectly still the Americans must retreat? On the other hand, the loss of the British fleet, and with it the control of Lake Champlain, made the occupation of Plattsburg or of any other place on the lake shore perfectly useless and worse than useless, a positive incumbrance. At any rate the Duke of Wellington, when refusing to go to America, wrote that without British control of the Lakes his going there would only "prove the truth of Prevost's defence." [1]

Turning, now, to the Middle States and the Chesapeake, the year 1813 had seen some disjointed and pestiferous performances of the British Admiral Cockburn in Chesapeake Bay. At the slightest provocation, houses and villages along the shores were burned and property destroyed; and, without any reason, except love of pilfering, all kinds of household belongings were torn from their owners and stored aboard ship. Only one serious attack was made, this was an attempt to seize Norfolk and Portsmouth and the United States naval establishment there. The affair was most seriously mismanaged and resulted in a rather disgraceful return to the ships. A more successful descent was made on the village of Hampton on the opposite side of the James River. On this occasion there was outrageous pillaging and rapine. The British asserted this was the work of a foreign regiment, which it was agreed in the future should be elsewhere employed.

The release of British troops in 1814 enabled the government at London to send very considerable reënforcements to the Chesapeake. Some were embarked at Bordeaux and were joined at Bermuda by another contingent. The combined expedition under Admiral Sir Alexander Cochrane

---

[1] *Correspondence, Despatches, . . . of Viscount Castlereagh*, x, 188; *Supplementary Despatches . . . of Wellington*, ix, 426. On December 22, 1814, Wellington wrote to Lieutenant General Sir George Murray: "Whether Sir George Prevost was right or wrong in his decision at Lake Champlain, is more than I can tell; but of this I am very certain, he must equally have retired to Kingston [Canada] after our fleet was beaten, and I am inclined to believe he was right.

"I have told the Ministers repeatedly that a naval superiority on the lakes is a *sine quâ non* of success in war on the frontier of Canada, even if our object should be solely defensive." *Despatches of Wellington*, xii. 224.

sailed thence for the Chesapeake where it was joined by
Cockburn and his expeditionary force. The design was
primarily to effect a diversion in favor of Prevost's attack
upon New York. The military leader of the combined
forces was Major General Robert Ross, who is said to have
"possessed the happy talent of conciliating by his disposition
and instructing by his example." Apart from the naval
vessels blocked in the Elizabeth River, there was an American gun-boat flotilla commanded by Captain Joshua Barney, a veteran sea-fighter of the Revolution. He could do
nothing, of course, against so great a squadron as that which
was now in the Chesapeake. He retired up the first available river, the Patuxent, — which unfortunately led in the
direction of Washington. To gain unrestricted control of
Chesapeake Bay and its rivers, the British seamen pursued
the flotilla up the Patuxent and the soldiers, landing,
marched parallel to the river. When they reached the little
village of Nottingham, they heard explosions and found
that Barney had blown up his gun-boats and retired with
some of his guns and gunners towards Washington. Up
to this point, it is not clear that the British had any well-
defined intention of attacking Washington at that time.
The land force numbered about eight thousand of all arms,
an insignificant army to invade the heart of a great nation.
Ross and his men went on to Bladensburg on the eastern
bank of the stream, where the upper road crosses the Eastern Branch of the Potomac, four or five miles above the
capital.

At Bladensburg, the British found the Americans drawn
up in two or three lines on an open hillside with Barney and
his battery on another hillside. No preparations had been
made for defence because the city of Washington had no
strategic value, had no importance from a military point of

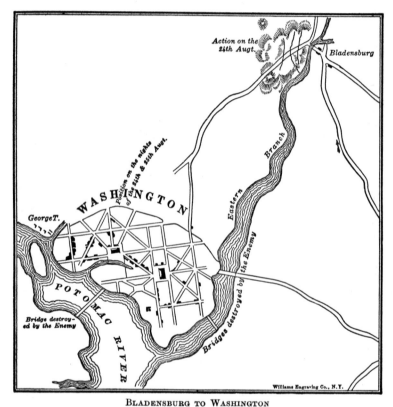

BLADENSBURG TO WASHINGTON

(From E. D. Ingraham's *Sketch of the Events which preceded the
Capture of Washington*, 1814)

view to either Americans or British. And it does not seem
to have entered the head of any one in control of national
affairs that the British would seize the capital for political
effect, and much less does it seem to have occurred to Madison, or Monroe, or Armstrong that they would capture
it for the sole purpose of devastation and plunder. When
the British suddenly appeared in force on the land, soldiers
and militiamen were hastily gathered from the sparsely
settled surrounding country and hurried to the post of
danger, while Madison and Monroe followed. With the
exception of Barney, they seem to have been innocent of
war and unmindful of its method. At all events, the
British tired and worn with their day's exertion had no
difficulty in putting them to flight, notwithstanding a most
skilful and valorous artillery practice by the gun-boat crews.
After the disappearance of the militiamen, the British
pushed on to Washington, arriving there on the evening of
August 24, 1814. As the British entered the city a few
muskets were discharged at them. They seized the capitol
and set it on fire. Some of the officers ate the dinner they
found ready at the President's Palace and then set fire to
the mansion. The Americans, themselves, applied the
torch to the buildings at the Navy Yard and the vessels
there. Private property seems to have been respected by
the British and there were no outrages to persons. The
next day the destruction recommenced and was brought to
a sudden conclusion by the bursting of a hurricane which
darkened the sky, threw down walls, tore off the roofs of
houses, while torrents of rain put an end to the fires and
filled the British with desire for return. That evening they
set out, and the next morning (August 26), without a shot
having been fired at them during their whole retreat, regained touch with the fleet. They reëmbarked quietly

and sailed down the river to the bay. From that day to this, writers have tried to palliate and justify this destruction of a national capital. The latest and the best of the British writers declares that the burning of Washington was an event in the "colonial history of Great Britain," was no "wanton outrage," but was done deliberately under definite instructions and was justifiable as a direct reprisal in kind, — for the burning of the hamlet of Newark and village of York in Canada. It gave notice that "the wrongs of the colonies should be requited upon the wrongdoers" as if they had been inflicted upon the mother land.[1] Monroe, on the other hand, wrote that one "must go back to distant and barbarous ages to find a parallel"; and Madison declared that it exhibited "a deliberate disregard of the principles of humanity and the rules of civilized warfare."

Out in the bay, the naval commanders decided that it was too soon to go to the West Indies as the hurricane season had only just begun. It was determined, therefore, to continue the diversion in favor of Sir George Prevost. Baltimore was selected as the next victim, for there there would be plenty of booty and the destruction of the shipping in the harbor and provisions in the storehouses would be a severe blow to the Americans. Baltimore is situated on Patapsco River, which at that point is really an arm of Chesapeake Bay. It had not then been dredged and was too shallow for the heavier ships of war. It was decided, therefore, to land the army on the peninsula that

---

[1] C. P. Lucas's *Canadian War of 1812,* 229–233. In somewhat different vein, Admiral Cochrane wrote to Sir George Cockburn — August 28, 1814 — "I am sorry you left a house standing in Washington, depend upon it it is mistaken mercy." In writing to Monroe, September 19, 1814, Cochrane declared that he would persist in his destructive measures until remuneration was made to the Canadians for the injuries they had sustained "from the outrages committed by the troops of the United States," until he received instructions otherwise. *American State Papers, Foreign Relations,* iii, 694.

makes out on the northern side of the Patapsco estuary
and march overland to the city, while the men-of-war
reduced the forts below the town and opened the navigation
for the smaller ships of war and the supply vessels. There
was no trouble in getting on shore, any more than there
had been at the Patuxent; but after that the stories of the
two enterprises are very different. General Winder, who had
so thoroughly bungled at Bladensburg, came to Baltimore
to take command, but he was set aside by Senator Samuel
Smith, who had had some experience in the Revolution and
must have been aided by persons of military capacity.
Fortifications were thrown up, defending the town from approach by the route the British were to take and a small
body of troops was sent forward to observe the roads.
These were militiamen and did not stand their ground for
any great length of time when they came into contact with
the foe, but they staid long enough to kill and wound a good
many of the enemy, among them General Ross. After
this encounter the British advanced to within sight of the
defences, when they paused and opened communication
with the fleet. The war vessels had made no impression
on Fort McHenry, where the star spangled banner waved
through the smoke of battle. Until that fort was silenced,
the obstructions in the channel could not be removed.
The whole attempt was, therefore, abandoned. The expedition remained at anchor in the bay until October,
when it sailed for Jamaica and New Orleans.[1]

The British did not land for the attack on New Orleans
until well into December. In the South, the providential

---

[1] Documents printed at the end of
*The Citizen Soldiers at North Point and
Fort McHenry, September 12 & 13, 1814*
(Baltimore, 1862), give the most satisfactory picture of the defence of Baltimore. John C. Carpenter's article
entitled "The Star-Spangled Banner"
in *The Century* (xlviii, 358), has interesting details as to the episode itself.

departure of General Wilkinson to gather laurels on the
St. Lawrence had left affairs in the hands of General Andrew Jackson. This extraordinary man was born in Carolina
on the boundary line between the two States. He had
studied law, had gone to Tennessee in early manhood, and
had gained a living by the practice of his profession and by
farming. It is one of the curiosities of history that he had
aroused the distrust of Thomas Jefferson, but the two had
little in common, except their faith in common clay. Jackson was a duellist; he befriended Burr; and possessed the
courage and confidence of a man of the frontier. When
war broke out he was a general officer of the Tennessee
militia, but his leadership of men was so conspicuous that
he had at once won his way to high place in the United
States army. In 1813 and in the early months of 1814,
he was engaged in the arduous service of fighting the Creek
nation. As the British in the Northwest intrigued with
Indians within the limits of the United States or, at any
rate, made no distinction between their treatment of those
Indians and the tribes living within British territories, so
in the South, they made friends with the Indians living
over the boundary line of Spanish Florida. Tecumseh, too,
had visited these southern Indians and inoculated them
with some of his fear and hatred of the Americans. The
result was an Indian war with its accompaniments of
massacre of white men, women, and children, and retributive justice in the shape of expeditions of frontiersmen,
who were quite as ruthless as their Indian neighbors. The
massacre at Fort Mims of hundreds of white people brought
out the frontiersmen from Tennessee, Carolina, and Georgia.
The Indians, as always, retreated; the militiamen pursued
ineffectually, and their terms of enlistment expiring, went
home. Jackson remained in the field with a few faithful

followers, and recruits came to his aid. The whole story is a marvellous one of the effect of one iron will in overcoming lack of numbers, lack of food, and one might almost say, the forces of nature. When the time for action came, Jackson moved with celerity. He traced the Creeks to their fortified town at Tohopeka or Horse-shoe Bend.[1] Jackson attacked the fortifications on the land side, while General Coffee, with a body of troops, crossed the river and attacked it from the open side. Five hundred or eight hundred warriors were killed. Very few escaped; but only four or five women and children lost their lives. The power of the Creek nation was broken and Jackson was the leader of the Southwest.

The British expedition for the conquest of New Orleans comprised the troops that had operated in the Chesapeake with additional regiments and one body of negro soldiers, that had been recruited in the British islands. They found the task which had been set for them of no common kind. The shallow mouths of the Mississippi and the four mile current of that mighty stream made it impossible for the heavy ships of war to ascend, or even to enter the river; and the lighter armed vessels were not sufficient to overcome the forts that guarded the channel fifty miles or more below the city. It was necessary, therefore, to approach New Orleans from the rear by way of Lake Borgne and some of the numerous bayous and canals that led from the lake to the river. When the execution of this project was attempted, it was found to be more arduous than had been conceived possible. The sea-going vessels could not traverse the shallow lake and the men had to be transported in open ships' boats for eighty miles or so.[2] A few Ameri-

[1] Jackson's report to Governor Blount of Tennessee is in *Magazine of American History*, xix, 45.

[2] In 1817, or thereabouts, according to the later recollections of Sir Harry Smith, the Duke of Wellington declared

can gun-boats disputed the control of the water for a time,
but were captured. Arrived at the bayous there was more
boating and when at last the men found themselves on firm
land, the solid ground was of narrow width for marching
thousands. Not only did these physical obstacles inter-

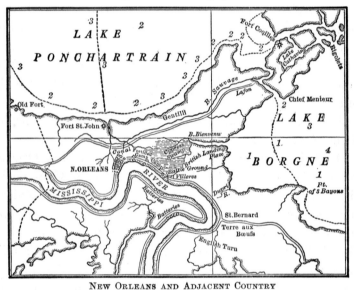

NEW ORLEANS AND ADJACENT COUNTRY
(From John Melish's *Military and Topographical Atlas of the United States*,
Philadelphia, 1815)

fere with the movement of troops; they also made the
supplying them with military stores and food a matter of
great difficulty. It was the great hazard of the enterprise
to an invader by this route that made Jackson slow to
believe that such a thing could be in contemplation. He
proposed, instead, to attack a British force at Pensacola,
and to defend Mobile for the latter was the natural base
for an attack on New Orleans from the Gulf of Mexico.

that the troops should never have landed
where they did. He had been consulted "about those lakes" and, learning
that they were not used for purposes
of trade, had said: "Then it is in-
judicious to use them to land an army,
and craft of any size will never get up to
land the troops." *Autobiography of Sir
Harry Smith*, i, 304.

The authorities at Washington got early information of the
project and ordered Jackson to desist from his proposed
expedition and go to the defence of New Orleans; and they
made such provision as they could in the way of soldiers
and arms. Even then Jackson hesitated; he actually
captured Pensacola and proposed to defend Mobile. He
arrived at New Orleans, however, on December 2, eight
days before the British sighted the islands off Lake Borgne.
Once at New Orleans, he acted most energetically. He
expected the British to come by the Chef Menteur Road,
which led from Bayou La Fon directly to the city, and his
chief anxiety was to defend this approach. Instead, the
British came by a chain of bayous that led to the Mississippi some eight to twelve miles below the city. A guard
had been posted at the mouth of one of these bayous; but
the men were captured before they could retreat or even
fire a gun. This misfortune enabled the British to advance
unmolested and, indeed, without Jackson's knowledge, to
the bank of the river itself,[1] — sixteen hundred of them in
broad daylight, and to capture Major Villeré and his entire
company (December 23, 1814).

Once apprised of his danger, Jackson acted with all the
vigor and pertinacity that marked his character. At the
moment the British reached the Mississippi, they might
have marched into New Orleans unmolested. They chose
to stay where they were until other regiments could come
up, — and giving Jackson an hour, or six, or twelve, under
circumstances such as these, was a fatal error. As night

[1] Henry Adams's comment on this
affair runs thus: "The record of
American generalship offered many
examples of misfortune, but none so
complete as this. Neither Hull nor
Harrison, neither Winder nor Samuel
Smith, had allowed a large British army,
heralded long in advance, to arrive
within seven miles unseen and unsus-
pected, and without so much as an
earthwork, a man, or a gun between
them and their object. The disaster
was unprecedented, and could be repaired only by desperate measures."
History of the United States, viii, 339.

fell, the British saw a vessel drawing near to the camp; she anchored under the opposite bank, furled her sails, and no answer was returned to repeated hailings and even to musket shots. Then her broadside swung directly over against the camp and six or eight guns loaded with grape were discharged, sweeping down numbers of the British standing on the levee or lying around the fires. As soon as they could, they got under the shelter of the embankment. In about half an hour, the picket toward New Orleans fired, and a straggling fire began up the river which came nearer. The night was dark; the soldiers were collected in haphazard groups; in bands and companies they went forth to meet the enemy. Not long after, another body of Americans suddenly appeared on the side of the battle-field away from the river. For an hour or an hour and a half, the fighting raged, when Jackson and Coffee withdrew their men because the smoke of combat collecting in the night fog made it impossible to distinguish friend from foe. Jackson retired up the river, two or three miles, and then entrenched himself behind one of the numerous canals that led from the river to the swamp which here was only about seven hundred yards away. The British grew stronger and stronger each day. On December 28, 1814, General Pakenham, the British commander, successor of the "amiable" General Ross, marched up the river and found himself face to face with the half-finished redoubts. At the moment, the Americans were drilling, but as soon as the foe appeared, they manned the embankment and Pakenham commanded a retreat. Now, the British spent more days in bringing up guns from the fleet with which to batter down the American defences. When the guns were in position and the artillery duel began, it became apparent that the Americans were more expert at that game than were their opponents. The firing went on until the British guns were silent, partly perhaps from lack of ammunition. They were left in position but as Jackson's men did not remove them, the British managed to recover most of them in the following night. By this time, Jackson had got together as many soldiers as he could provide with arms and ammunition; in fact, rather more. After his position on the east bank of the river was made good a force was sent over to the west bank to erect a battery that could sweep the ground in front of the American redoubt, for the *Carolina*, the armed vessel that had done such execution, had been set on fire by a red-hot shot.

It was now apparent that the only way by which General Pakenham could retrieve the day was, first of all, to take possession of the western bank. Doing this, he could turn the guns on to Jackson's men, or, marching up the river bank, he could bombard New Orleans itself and thus compel Jackson to leave his fortification.[1] The only way that this could be accomplished was to get the ships' boats into the river and use them to ferry across the men. A canal in the rear of the British position which connected with the bayou along which they had come was deepened and the boats brought into it. Then a dam was thrown across it, behind the boats, and the levee separating it from the Mississippi was cut. All this work was done without the knowledge of the Americans, although Jackson, expecting an attack on the west bank, had reënforced the troops there. The night of January 7th, 1815, was selected by Pakenham for this enterprise and fourteen hundred or sixteen hundred of his men were told off to make the attempt. One accident

---

[1] Charles Francis Adams has severely criticized Pakenham's failure to seize the western bank of the Mississippi and turn Jackson's position (Massachu- setts Historical Society's *Proceedings* for January, 1900) with additional matter in *Studies, Military and Diplomatic, 1775–1865*, p. 174.

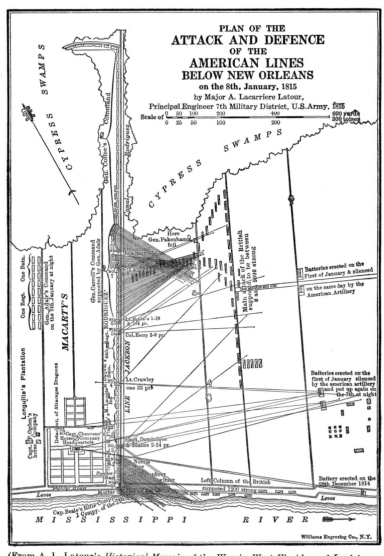

(From A. L. Latour's *Historical Memoir of the War in West Florida and Louisiana*, Philadelphia, 1816)

518

after another occurred. The banks of the canal, of soft, spongy earth, gave way in places filling in the channel. It was with difficulty and a great expenditure of time that the boats were hauled through the mud to the river. It fell out in this way that instead of fourteen hundred men landing on the western bank in the darkness only a few hundred got across by daylight of January 8. Meantime, the main attack was made ready and every one listened for the firing on the western bank. The sun rose, the mist cleared away, the American redoubt came into view, but no signal sounded. Pakenham, not knowing what to do, was spurred on by a jeer from Admiral Cochrane, that with a thousand of his sailors, he could take the redoubt, so it is said. Whether this anecdote is true or false, Pakenham ordered his men forward. They went; and a terrific fire burst from the American position.[1] Twenty guns and a thousand muskets and more concentrated on two columns of assailants. They went down by tens, by twenties, by hundreds. The

[1] The standard account of the New Orleans campaign is still that written by Major A. Lacarrière Latour, Jackson's engineer officer in the campaign. It was written in French and translated into English by H. P. Nugent and published at Philadelphia in 1816 as *Historical Memoir of The War in West Florida and Louisiana in 1814–15. With An Atlas.* An appendix of over one hundred pages contains documents, and the maps which are sometimes bound with the printed matter are of great value. The important ones have been reproduced many times as in Adams's *United States*, viii. The best modern accounts are those in Adams and in J. S. Bassett's *Life of Andrew Jackson* (1911), i, 126–207. Bassett had the use of Jackson's manuscripts which are now in the Library of Congress. Another recent American account is *The Battle of New Orleans* written by Z. F. Smith and published, with very wide margins, by the Filson Club (*Publications* No. 19, Louisville, 1904); of course Smith gives attention to the charge of misbehaviour on the part of Kentucky troops. James in his *Military Occurrences* gives the British documents. Three most graphic accounts from that side are in Gleig's "Narrative," in J. E. Cooke's *Narrative of Events . . . in 1814 and 1815* (London, 1835, pp. 224–237), and in the *Autobiography of Sir Harry Smith*, i, 226–255. Letters that Captain E. Codrington wrote to his wife when in America have much interesting comment on the New Orleans campaign and also on the capture of Washington (Lady Bouchier's *Memoir of the Life of Admiral Sir Edward Codrington*, i, 309–343). Alexander Walker's *Jackson and New Orleans* reproduces at great length practically all the information that was available in 1856. Major P. M. Davis's *An Official and Full Detail of the Great Battle of New Orleans* (New York, 1836) gives in fifty-nine pages a succinct and good account.

generals strove to drive them on; Pakenham was killed;
Keane, the next in command, was badly wounded; and
Gibbs, the third general, died the next day of his injuries.
Meantime, on the western bank, the British had been completely successful.   No preparations had been made to
resist the attack on that bank by a force coming up the
river, and the defenders were militiamen for the most part,
many of them unarmed.   But General Lambert, the fourth
and last of the British general officers, was unwilling to
take the responsibility of any further attack.   He recalled
the men from the western bank and leisurely and without
molestation made his way in a week or two down the bayous
and so to his ships.   Thence he sailed to Mobile, where he
captured the poorly garrisoned Fort Bowyer, when news
arrived that peace had been made.

NOTES

I. The Credit for the Victory on Lake Erie. — Perry in his report dated September 13, 1813,[1] lauded Elliott; Captain Barclay states that the *Niagara* " kept so far to windward as to render the *Queen Charlotte's* 20 pound carronade useless." Not long afterwards, conversations in the fleet began to be adverse to Elliott's action, and, on the other hand, Elliott's partisans and he, himself, claimed that it was his orders that carried the *Niagara* into the position which decided the battle. A court of inquiry was held in 1815.[2] In 1818, Perry formulated charges against Elliott. These President Monroe pigeonholed, and Perry dying in 1819, the charges were never examined under oath. Admiral Mahan states the matter thus: " The author's conclusion upon the whole is that, as Perry's action in first standing down insured decisive action, so by him was imparted to the ' Niagara ' the final direction which determined victory" (*War of 1812*, ii, 98). The Perry side of the controversy is maintained in the biographies of him by John M. Niles (Hartford, 1820), Alex. Slidell Mackenzie (2 vols., New York, 1840), and J. C. Mills (Detroit, 1913); in Tristam Burges's *Battle of Lake Erie with Notices of Commodore Elliott's Conduct in that Engagement*. This book, which was published at Boston in 1839, has a most useful appendix of documents, all of which can be obtained elsewhere.[3] George Bancroft has also taken Perry's part in his *History of the Battle of Lake Erie* (New York, 1891).

On the Elliott side, J. Fenimore Cooper opened the combat in his *History of the Navy*, ii, 452–469. It was this account that led Mackenzie to make unpleasant strictures, which in turn incited Cooper to put out a little pamphlet entitled *The Battle of Lake Erie, or Answers to Messrs. Burges, Duer, and Mackenzie* (Cooperstown, 1843). In 1835, there was published at Philadelphia *A Biographical Notice of Com. Jesse D. Elliott; containing a Review of the Controversy between him*

[1] Perry's official report is printed in innumerable places, among others in *American State Papers, Naval Affairs*, i, 294, 295.

[2] The report of the Court of Inquiry convened at the request of Captain Jesse D. Elliott, in 1815, is printed in Niles's *Weekly Register*, viii, 236.

[3] See also a letter of Dr. Usher Parsons printed in Rhode Island Historical Society's *Publications*, vii, 245. Modern accounts of the naval campaign are an article by P. L. Haworth in Mississippi Valley Historical Association's *Proceedings*, v, 207, and O. L. Lyman's *Commodore Oliver Hazard Perry and the War on the Lakes* (New York, 1905).

and the late Commodore Perry . . . by a Citizen of New-York, and Elliott, himself, delivered a *Speech . . . in Hagerstown, Md., on 14th November, 1843*. This was published by the Committee of Arrangement (Philadelphia, 1844), pp. 5–15.

II. Bladensburg and Washington, 1814. — The official papers are printed in the *Report of the Committee . . . to inquire into the Causes and Particulars of the Invasion of the City of Washington*.[1] The best modern account of the burning of Washington is in Adams's *United States*, viii, 120–148, which is abundantly supplied with citations and extracts from the manuscript records. Lossing's *Field Book of the War of 1812*, ch. xxxix, has a detailed account with much local color, and makes the matter more real than Adams. Most lifelike and interesting contemporaneous narratives are those of the Rev. G. R. Gleig.[2] John S. Williams, an American militia brigade major, in his old age wrote a *History of the Invasion and Capture of Washington* (New York, 1857).[3] John Armstrong's *Notices of the War of 1812* (ii, ch. v) gives the Secretary of War's views as to the actions of Winder and others.

The burning of the nation's capital and the tragic or ludicrous flights of the chief magistrate and his following have been the theme of tradition and recollection. The books on Washington City and on Mrs. Madison[4] naturally deal with this subject at length with copious citations. An account by an American contemporary is Dr. James Ewell's reminiscences that were originally printed in the *Planters' and Mariners' Medical Companion* (3rd ed., Philadelphia, 1817) and reprinted in Columbia Historical Society's *Records*, i, 55–88. An excellent compendious narrative is Horatio King's " Battle of Bladensburg " in *Magazine of American History*, xiv, 438.

---

[1] "State Papers," 3rd Sess., 13th Cong., No. 24. The Appendix, pp. 51–370, contains ample material.

[2] These exist in several forms; *A Narrative of the Campaigns of the British Army at Washington and New Orleans by an Officer who served in the Expedition* (London, 1821) ; *A Subaltern in America; comprising his Narrative*, etc. (Philadelphia, 1833) ; *The Campaigns of the British Army at Washington and New Orleans by the author of the Subaltern* (4th ed. corrected and revised, London, 1836). An edition of the "Narrative," published at Philadelphia in 1821, has an Appendix of "Corrections and Remarks" from the American standpoint. See also the *Autobiography of Sir Harry Smith*, i, 195–208 and Lady Bouchier's *Memoir of Sir Edward Codrington*, i, 313–318.

[3] The Appendix to this book contains six communications from American officers, beginning with a narrative of General Winder. A briefer American account is E. D. Ingraham's *Sketch of the Events which preceded the Capture of Washington* (Philadelphia, 1849).

[4] Allen C. Clark's *Life and Letters of Dolly Madison*, ch. iv and citations.

CHAPTER XIX

BESIDE the single-ship actions on the oceans and the fleet combats on the Great Lakes, which have already been mentioned, there were many other conflicts between English and American ships — generally one vessel on each side on the open sea. At the end of this chapter is a list of them in which the estimates of British and American writers are placed together. The table makes a pretty study, and any one who wishes to go farther can read Admiral Mahan's book or Theodore Roosevelt's. American naval men won glory and renown, which was sadly needed at home, and diverted a considerable part of Britain's naval strength from other objects. Of the later conflicts that which attracted most attention was the capture of the *Chesapeake* by the British frigate *Shannon*. The *Chesapeake* was a luckless ship from her launching, and her commander, James Lawrence, was unfortunate. He was a gallant seaman and she was a good ship, but mischance befell them both. The *Chesapeake* was at Boston in May, 1813, when Lawrence took command of her. Most of the men had been in her several weeks before she sailed on June 1, 1813. The precise officers and crew then in her had not worked together at sea, but they had worked together in harbor, and most of them were experienced seafighters. The *Chesapeake* proceeded to sea, the intention being to run past the blockading squadron, as Rodgers had done a few weeks before.

She was then to seek the Gulf of St. Lawrence to intercept store ships and troop ships going to Canada. It was a most important mission, — far more important than the destruction of any frigate in the British navy. Boston was then blockaded by the British ships *Shannon* and *Tenedos*. The former was commanded by Philip Bowes Vere Broke. Commodore Codrington, writing to his wife as to the capture of the British ship *Epervier*, stated that the worst part of the story was that the British sloop was cut to pieces and the other vessel scarcely scratched. He goes on to declare that the system of favoritism and borough influence prevailed so very much at the Admiralty that officers who should have been dismissed were promoted in the service. Indeed, "the few Americans chosen for their merit" might be expected to win except when they meet "with our best officers on equal terms." [1] Captain Broke was one of these, and his ship, the *Shannon*, was one of the best appointed and best kept in the service. He sent away the *Tenedos* in the hope that when the *Chesapeake* should come out, Lawrence, finding the *Shannon* alone, would seek rather than avoid a combat. Broke had written a letter making a suggestion of the kind, but it was never delivered to Lawrence. The two vessels came together ; in nine minutes the *Chesapeake* was beaten, the crew driven from the deck, and Lawrence mortally wounded. These combatants were more equally matched as to numbers of men and weights of broadsides than the earlier ones. The *Chesapeake* had from three hundred and fifty to four hundred men and the *Shannon* about the same. The broadside of the *Chesapeake* was under six hundred pounds and that of the *Shannon* somewhere near it. The victory delighted Englishmen ; they knighted Broke for a gallant and well-fought action,

---

[1] *Memoir of . . . Admiral Sir Edward Codrington*, i, 310.

and did what they could to minimize the strength of the
Shannon and to increase that of her opponent. At the
time, Lawrence's last words, "Don't give up the ship. Blow
her up," were an inspiration to many an American, as to
Oliver Hazard Perry and his gallant companions on Lake
Erie. Later, it became the custom to find fault with Lawrence for fighting his ship unprepared. In reality, the
Chesapeake did very well, for in six or ten minutes her crew
killed or wounded as many of the *Shannon's* ship's company
as the *Constitution* did of the *Guerrière's* in over twenty.[1]
It was chance, that settles so many things in war, that
made the *Chesapeake* unmanageable almost at the outset of
what otherwise might have been a long, hard-fought action.
She was placed at the mercy of her antagonist, who rightly
took advantage of her helplessness as Hull did of that of
the *Guerrière*. James Lawrence died the death of a hero
and should have his place in our history, however unfortunate he and his ship may have been on this and other
occasions.[2]

A commander and a ship to make a longer cruise than
Lawrence in the *Chesapeake* and to meet the same unhappy
fate was Captain David Porter in the *Essex*. In 1813, she
sailed for an Atlantic cruise; but not meeting her consorts

---

[1] This is Mahan's statement, *War
of 1812*, ii, 144. He says that it needs
slight qualification, as some of the
Shannon's men were hurt in the boarding, not by the cannonade, but, he
adds, "The general statement is substantially accurate."

[2] Besides the regular accounts in
Mahan, Roosevelt, and James, see
*Biography of James Lawrence, Esq.
. . . together with . . . Interesting Papers
relative to the Action between the Chesapeake and Shannon* (New Brunswick,
N. J., 1813); Albert Gleaves' *James
Lawrence* (New York, 1904); and two
articles in *The United Service* for October, 1879 and February, 1905. On the
British side is J. G. Brighton's *Admiral Sir P. B. V. Broke, Bart.* (London, 1866). A much more interesting
account from the British standpoint
is in the same author's *Admiral of
the Fleet Sir Provo W. P. Wallis* (London, 1892). Wallis was second lieutenant of the *Shannon* at the time of
the battle.

Mahan's verdict (*War of 1812*, ii,
145) is that Lawrence had no right,
under the conditions of efficiency of
the two ships, to take the *Chesapeake*
into action; but "had some luck
favored him . . . there was a fighting
chance of victory."

made her way into the Pacific[1] to destroy the British whaling industry there. This accomplished, instead of returning home by the Cape of Good Hope, she put back to Valparaiso on the western coast of South America, and there was attacked by two British ships and captured.

In one of his most instructive passages, Admiral Mahan discussed the strategy of commerce destroying. American seamen in the War of 1812 were compelled to seek British commerce carriers on the open sea and to hover about the coasts and harbors of the British Islands. The loss they inflicted upon individuals was grievous but, apart from the outcry it compelled, it had no military effect. So great was the profit to be gained from trade between Great Britain and the outer world that it went on increasing every year of the war. On the other hand, the British blockaded the American coast so effectively that by the end of 1814 there was no legitimate American sea-borne commerce either foreign or coastwise. Probably in all nautical history, no above-water commerce destroyers were ever so successful as the American privateers of this time. The early privately owned war vessels were makeshift affairs, — fishermen and coasting schooners armed with a gun or two. Some of the later privateers were fine, large vessels carrying crews of one hundred and fifty men or more, and quite capable of lying alongside of a British sloop-of-war. Such a ship was the *America* belonging to the Salem Crowninshields. She was a razeed East Indiaman; her upper deck had been removed, her sides filled in solidly, and longer spars placed in her on which larger sails were bent.

---

[1] See *Journal of a Cruise made to the Pacific Ocean, by Captain David Porter, in the United States Frigate Essex,* (2 vols., Philadelphia, 1815). This most interesting journal was foully abused in the English *Quarterly Review* for July, 1815. Porter's comment on the review is printed as a preface to the second edition of the *Journal* (New York, 1822). Mahan has a succinct account of this cruise in his *War of 1812,* ii, 244–252.

She was faster than anything she was likely to meet in the way of small British warships or merchantmen; and in voyage after voyage she made valuable returns for her owners and crews, — in one sixteen months' period at sea, she netted over a million dollars.[1] The most successful American privateer of this war is supposed to have been the brig *Yankee*[2] that sailed from Bristol, Rhode Island. In six cruises she captured more than five million dollars of British property and brought to her owners and crews over a million. These two examples are of the most successful ships. On the other side of the account, there were captures of privateersmen by the British and recaptures of prizes made by the Americans; but the absolute loss of British property was great although only a part of the gross privateer-captured tonnage ever reached port. The business was a speculative one, but was conducted on business lines like other speculations, and only when so conducted was it successful. Much damage was done to British commerce and the expense of overseas transportation was greatly increased by the necessity of taking convoy or paying extremely high insurance premiums. But, after all, the effect was largely psychological, for the thought of serious interruption of commerce between Bristol or Liverpool and Cork or Belfast, that is to say between two home ports, was disturbing to the English commercial and underwriting mind.[3]

[1] B. B. Crowninshield's "Account of the Private Armed Ship 'America' of Salem" (Essex Institute's *Historical Collections*, xxxvii).

[2] American Antiquarian Society's *Proceedings* for April, 1913, pp. 12–62.

[3] Adams takes a rather harsh view of the war value of the privateering; but he devotes many pages to the privateers, (*History of the United States*, vii, 12, 309–338; viii, 194–209; ix, 228. Mahan gives considerable space to the subject (*War of 1812*, i, 392–398; ii, 20–24, 215–242, 267). He estimates that the Americans seized four British ships for every three lost by themselves, and contrasts with this the arrival in the British Channel of a convoy from the West Indies numbering 226 sail or about one-half of the total British losses from American privateers and national ships in one year of the war. In the whole war 526 privateers captured 1344 vessels or 2.7 prizes per vessel. Mahan compiled his information from Niles'

On the other side of the picture, the British waged war against American commerce in a vastly more effective manner, — which her naval superiority permitted. Instead of attacking American commerce on the open sea, the British sought it at its base. They blockaded large portions of the American coast and, finally, the whole coast itself. In the first part of the war, this blockade was limited to the Mississippi[1] and to the Atlantic coast south of Narragansett Bay. Savannah and Charleston, the Chesapeake and the Delaware, New York, and Long Island Sound lent themselves to naval blockade, even in the days of sailing vessels. A squadron at anchor in the lower reaches of Chesapeake Bay effectually barred it to commerce, except when a strong northwester blew the blockaders from their moorings and at the same time drove a blockade runner, flour or tobacco laden, out between the Capes to the Atlantic and the Gulf Stream where she was reasonably safe. The same conditions held for the other ports below Rhode Island and were very different from those that had attended the blockade of coasts of France and Holland, where the fleets were obliged to lie in the open. There, an oncoming westerly gale obliged them to tack to sea to gain an offing; but the same wind kept the enemy's warships and merchant vessels secure in harbor. In 1813, the blockade of the greater part of the United States was effective. Ships did get out, and did get in, but the former were in many cases engaged in collusive

Weekly Register and G. F. Emmons's The Navy of the United States, . . . 1775 to 1853 (Washington, 1853), pp. 170–201. The standard detailed account is George Coggeshall's History of the American Privateers during our War with England (New York, 1856). See also "An Account of the Private Armed Vessels belonging to Salem, Mass., during the War of 1812" in Essex Institute's Historical Collections,

ii, 57; and "The War of 1812" in Rhode Island Historical Society's Publications, v, 143–183.

[1] In November, 1812, Captains Mugford and Wardwell with some forty ships' officers arrived at Salem overland from New Orleans, there being no chance of getting home with their vessels, as the British had control of the mouth of the Mississippi. Salem Gazette, November 20, 1812.

commerce. In 1814 the British blockade was extended to New England. North of Cape Cod, the wind conditions were unlike those of the southern ports, for there the easterly gales blew with great violence directly on shore. It was impossible to maintain a close watch of Boston and ports to the northward, except in the summer months. In the stormier seasons of winter, the blockading fleets were entirely withdrawn. During the whole war, privateers from the British provinces aided in the blockading operations by lying offshore and seizing American vessels bound in or out. By the summer of 1814 American navigation was brought to a practical standstill, with the exception of the trade with the enemy which went on throughout the war.

American commerce had been so harassed by the embargo and non-intercourse and non-importation, that markets were somewhat bare of European productions. Prices were high and the demand was keen. It was under these circumstances that the forwarders and commission merchants of London, Bristol, Liverpool, and Glasgow, believing that the suspension of the Orders in Council meant a resumption of American trade, packed great quantities of goods on the first vessels they could get hold of and sent them off for the United States. When these shipments reached American ports non-importation was still in force as to Great Britain and, war having been declared, these goods were very largely enemy property, — because, under the existing conditions of British interest in American commercial houses, it was impossible to say what part of the partnership property was American and what part British. Congress and Gallatin looked with eager eyes on these incoming cargoes which were seized by the customs collectors. Technically, the importers had broken several laws, but had they not had good reason for supposing that when the

Orders in Council were ended commerce with Great Britain would be free? The importers petitioned for relief and made out a strong case; they also "lobbied" vigorously.[1] Finally, the importers were permitted to receive the full profits on the transactions, after paying the cost of prosecution.[2] This was directly contrary to Gallatin's wish, for he had advocated confiscating the war profits that would be made on these goods beyond what the merchants had reasonably expected. He was overruled on this subject as he was on many others; and the Treasury was lighter by a considerable sum of money which might have made good some of the deficiencies in the equipment of the northern armies.

The experience of the importers with the bringing in of enemy's goods did not lessen in any way their appetite for further profits. As they could not trade directly with their British partners and financial backers, they traded with them indirectly. Some of them fitted out privateers to capture vessels laden with goods that had been shipped after the war was known in England. These privateers brought in their prizes which were condemned and sold greatly to the profit of the owner or the privateer, who was also, in some cases, the owner of the ship and the cargo, or was interested in the last on a commission basis. In 1812, the war was still going on in Spain and Portugal and the British soldiers there were dependent upon America for their food. Vessels, that were loaded at the signal of war, made their way to sea half-manned and badly supplied with

[1] The importers of New York in October, 1812, drew up a memorial to Congress which was "strengthened" by the appearance at Washington of "a delegation of intelligent and respectable merchants." Baltimore and Richmond were also represented. Among them was Charles Ellis who listened to "one of the most eloquent speeches . . . from the chaste lips of Mr. Cheeves" in favor of remitting the penal bonds.

[2] See act of January 2, 1813 in *Annals of Congress*, 12th Cong., 2d Sess., 1316.

food and water.   In Canada there were small garnered stores of food.   As soon as the war took the farmers away from their fields in seed time or harvest, soldiers and settlers fed on bread and meat that came from the United States or from across the Atlantic.   British fleets, operating on the coast, were also in need of supplies and manufacturers in Britain lacked cotton and tobacco.[1]   These necessities were met in various ways.   The farmers of Vermont and northern New York furnished Canadian commissaries and contractors with droves of beef cattle and tons of flour. So large was the supply that Sir George Prevost [2] declared his own army was fed chiefly from the United States, and the people on the border sorrowed rather than rejoiced at the news of peace.

As to the ocean trade, it was carried on by collusion between the shippers, the handlers of products, and the British authorities.   Lord Sidmouth, the First Lord of the Admiralty, signed hundreds of licenses permitting the holder to go with his vessel across the Atlantic to Lisbon, the voyage to be completed before a certain designated date.[3]   These licenses were bought and sold openly at brokers' offices in New York and, probably, also at Philadelphia and Boston. As the danger of capture lay principally in coastal waters, one of these licenses was about as good for a voyage to Gothenburg as it was to Lisbon, for it would pass its possessor and his ship through the lines of blockaders and by any

---

[1] Smuggling across the Niagara frontier had been going on ever since 1803 according to a letter written by Joseph Ellicott in March, 1812; it did not stop with the declaration of war. This letter was copied for me by Mr. Paul D. Evans.

[2] *Canadian Archives*, 1896, p. 37. See also General Z. M. Pike's proclamation of January 15, 1813, calling attention to the Articles of War (No. 56)

threatening court martial and death for any one relieving the enemy or communicating with them.   (*Plattsburg Republican*, under date.)

[3] A "Sidmouth" is printed at length in Stewart's *Cases in the Admiralty Court at Halifax*, 499.   About six hundred of them were issued when the Peninsular campaigns being ended no more were given out — to the grief of American exporters.

roaming squadron on the Atlantic. In 1813, a "Sidmouth license" having three months to run was worth nearly a thousand dollars. Another batch of licenses was given by Admiral Sawyer, the commander of the British fleet on the Atlantic station in the early months of the war. These licenses were local in their terms, permitting the holder to take his vessel to some port, generally Halifax in Nova Scotia or to Newfoundland. The person to whom one of these licenses was issued was vouched for as a friend to Britain by one of the erstwhile British consuls in New England.[1] Besides these two comprehensive sets of licenses others were issued by local squadron commanders for the supplying of their own needs. Coupled with this license system was a widespread denationalizing of American vessels. Before the days of commercial and naval warfare, the number of Swedish and Spanish vessels in North American harbors was distinctly limited. In 1813, they were plentiful and were provided with officers and crews, speaking the language required. Until 1814, New England was practically clear of blockaders, although provincial privateers lay off Cape Cod and Cape Sable, intercepting vessels that were not protected by licenses or passes.

New England was especially favored by the British in the first part of the war, in the hope of detaching that part of the country from the rest. It happened, therefore, that commerce between Massachusetts, New Hampshire, and Maine and the nearby Maritime Provinces was extensive and contributed greatly to the enrichment of New England, very largely at the expense of the rest of the country. There

---

[1] See the "Dearborn Letters" in *Mississippi Valley Historical Review*, ii, 422 and Stewarts' *Cases*, where a certificate is printed. The governor of Barbadoes issued licenses to import provisions into that island. One of these could be bought for $500 in May, 1813 and "would perhaps answer . . . not to go to Barbadoes but to go to Porto Rico from thence where our agent or purchaser might deem it proper." John Allan to Charles Ellis, May 14, 1813.

was a constant inflow of British manufactures into New England and an outflow of the same goods from New England to the southward. These had to be paid for in gold and silver or in goods. There was urgent demand at Boston and other shipping ports for flour and for tobacco. There was an abundance of these commodities in the Delaware and the Chesapeake regions. To get them to the northern market overland was a matter of great expense, as they had to be carried on wagons drawn by horses and oxen. The disadvantage of Virginia's position as a producer of flour and tobacco and a would-be consumer of manufactured goods was peculiar. The British were their best customers, but the Virginia planters having been largely in debt to Britain for many years and being still largely beholden to her merchants and capitalists felt an instinctive aversion to her and her ways. In September, 1811, John H. Cocke, a well-to-do planter, declared that a people was never more determined to exist in a state of commercial slavery than were the Virginians; "but thanks to the British spirit of domination, we are about to be kick'd & cuff'd out [of] this servile state of things." The mercantile outlook in Virginia, however, was very different and was like that of New York or Boston. This is reflected in the letter-books of the Richmond firm of Ellis and Allan. Allan was an Englishman by birth who had long lived in Virginia. Ellis was a native of the Old Dominion. The business of this firm centered in Virginia, but their outlook was so affected by the complication of their interest with British bankers and manufacturers, that in 1812 they looked upon the war as most unnatural. "Let Kings & Presidents war and fight but not old friends" so they wrote to one of their best customers at Bristol, England. As war became imminent, they felt it desirable to have a representative on the eastern side of the Atlantic. John Allan, the junior partner, sailed for Lisbon. In June, 1812, the firm wrote to their London agents that if any of their friends in England could send out a ship under Portuguese or Spanish colors, they might "make a handsome speculation" in the exporting of provisions. The threat of war had put up the freight rates fifty per cent, even before the actual declaration, which accounts for this suggestion that a ship should be sent out from England. The Virginians were not so fortunate as were the New Yorkers in getting their vessels away before the embargo of April, 1812 went into effect, for they were so near to the seat of government that they could not get news much in advance of the collectors of the customs. Ellis and Allan must have read with regret a letter from their New York agent stating that he "was happy to say that an immense number of vessels have escaped its operation here." By September, 1812, hardware had more than trebled in price at Richmond, and flour and tobacco were still selling at high prices; but the next year the decline was rapid. Vessels under foreign flags at Norfolk and ports up the bay commanded exorbitant figures. This induced Ellis and Allan, in 1813, to try to send a cargo of flour by way of Albemarle Sound and Ocracoke Inlet. They sent the flour by small boats through Deep Creek and the Dismal Swamp canal, connecting James River with the sound. It was then placed on board the brig *Olivia* which was provided with a Sidmouth license that had only three weeks to run, although it cost eight hundred dollars at New York. The collector at Elizabeth City, North Carolina, obligingly antedated the clearance papers to make the proposed voyage to Lisbon under British license appear possible. In passing the bar, the *Olivia* "thumpt and thumpt as if every nail had been started. Being very strong she will in 7 or 8 days be in Boston where she is directed to put in in distress." On reaching port, it was found that the agents had orders to sell every barrel of flour out of the vessel which was "leaking." The expenses of the voyage were great, but the difference in the price of flour, five dollars at Richmond and from twelve to thirteen at Boston, made up for much expenditure and much leakage, — a gross profit of one hundred and fifty per cent would only net twenty-five.

Somewhat later in the year 1813, a man named Mitchell entered into a contract with Captain Oliver, commanding the British blockading squadron off the Chesapeake, to supply him with two cargoes of flour for the use of his crews. There was some delay and trouble and when Mitchell appeared, with one cargo instead of two, he found that Oliver's squadron had been replaced by another, commanded by Sir Thomas Hardy. The American ship was captured, but Mitchell had no difficulty in explaining the matter to Commodore Hardy, who gave him a pass to go to Halifax, where he sold his flour.[1] In point of fact, it seemed to be impossible, even in Virginia, the home of the war party and almost within reach of Washington, to keep American vessels from running flour and other provisions out of the Capes with a practical certainty that the cargo would go straight to the aid and comfort of the enemies of the United States. It was under these circumstances, that President Madison invited Congress to take measures to prevent the continuance of the practice of trading with the enemy. He told of the condition of affairs in two messages, one dated February 24, 1813; the other December 9, 1813.[2]

[1] Stewart's *Cases decided in the Admiralty Court at Halifax*, 551.
[2] *Annals of Congress*, 12th Cong., 2nd Sess., 1116; 13th Cong., i, 549. The circular of the colonial office transmitting the Order in Council and the proclamation of the Governor of Bermuda publishing the Order are printed with the first of these messages.

In these two messages, Madison described the traffic with the enemy succinctly and with authority. It appears that in October, 1812, a British Order in Council had been issued to provide for supplying the British plantations under special licenses. These were in addition to those that have already been noted and the circular from the colonial office directed the governor to confine licensed importations from the United States "to the ports in the Eastern States exclusively." To guard against the demoralizing and disorganizing tendencies of this system which was intended to dissolve the ties of allegiance and against the effect of individual cupidity and treachery, Madison recommended the prohibition of any trade whatever under special licenses by citizens of the United States and also a prohibition of all exportations from the United States in vessels flying foreign flags, which were almost entirely counterfeit. In the latter of the two messages, he informed Congress, December 9, 1813, that supplies of the most essential kinds find their way to British armies with which we are contending and even the fleets and troops infesting American waters are by like supplies encouraged in their incursive warfare. The other way round, British fabrics and products come into American ports often in British vessels disguised as neutrals. Besides, illegal importations were openly made and the practice of ransoming is a cover for collusive captures. To remedy these, he proposed an effectual embargo on exports. Congress was not ready to take any drastic step in the spring of 1813, and nothing was done at that time.

Madison being disappointed in the failure of Congress to pass an embargo law, orders were issued to the officers of the navy and of the army directing them to stop all vessels "proceeding or apparently intending to proceed toward the

enemy's vessels" either under guise of being neutrals or of
prosecuting coasting voyages. This prohibition worked
havoc with the "license ships" which were now for a time
obliged to keep close to their anchorages.[1] In December,
1813, Congress at length passed an act laying an embargo
on all vessels then in United States ports with the exception of foreign neutral vessels which could depart with
whatever they had on board and necessary sea stores. This
law was modelled in part on the Enforcement Act of 1809,
in extending its prohibitions to authorize collectors to seize
anything which they believed intended for exportation, or
when in any conveyance in any manner apparently on the
way towards a foreign country. In interpreting this law,
the treasury department issued most stringent instructions
by which permission to perform coasting voyages was not
to be granted in case the vessels even for a short space would
leave "what is properly called a bay, river or sound" and
be at sea.[2] With treasury officials in the ports refusing to
permit vessels to leave, with the naval officers and the
army officers ready to fire at any vessel bound apparently
in the direction of an enemy's ship, and with the British
blockaders waiting to seize any vessels that eluded these
prohibitions, commerce came to an end in the first months
of 1814, excepting at the two ends of the line, — the eastern-
most ports of Maine and the Spanish harbor just over the
Georgia boundary in Florida. There was some doubt at
first as to whether the act prohibited coasting voyages, but
it was soon so interpreted by United States authorities and

---

[1] Niles' *Weekly Register*, iv, 370, 386;
and letter of Charles Ellis, dated Norfolk, Aug. 3, 1813, in "Ellis and Allan
Papers."
[2] The act of December 17, 1813, is in
Annals of Congress, 13 Cong., ii, 2781,
and in Niles' *Weekly Register*, v, 273.
The treasury circular is in *ibid.*, v, 353.

The only exceptions, other than foreign
vessels, were vessels in ballast which
might be cleared "under the immediate direction of the President of the
United States." Later, in January of
the next year, the President was authorized to make certain exceptions in
case of the inhabitants of Nantucket.

the British, too, made every effort to put an end to any such commerce. In consequence land transportation soon was at a premium. With the existing condition of roads, and the modes of propulsion that were in vogue, for as yet there were not a dozen steamboats in the whole country, this was a very expensive and slow mode of transferring goods, especially bulky and heavy articles, from one part of the country to the other. So expensive was it that Andrew Ellicott, removing from Lancaster, Pennsylvania, to West Point on the Hudson, sold his furniture at Lancaster and bought a new outfit at New York whence it could be transported to his new home by water. Prices of food rose in New England and fell in the agricultural districts. Flour sold for seventeen dollars a barrel at Boston in the winter of 1813–1814 and at once fell to seven dollars and a half when peace was proclaimed.[1] Flour was selling at Richmond for ten dollars in 1812, when the demand for export to Lisbon was keen, and for three dollars and fifty cents in the spring of 1814, when the embargo and blockade were at their highest efficiency. Tobacco in these years sold at from three to five cents per pound at Richmond, from six to thirteen cents at Boston, and from three and a half pence

[1] This table shows the rise and fall of prices in Boston and New York:—

		Flour (bbl)	Beef (lb.)	Coffee (lb.)	Molasses (gal.)	Jamaica Rum (gal.)	Tobacco (lb.)	Upland Cotton (lb.)	Fuel Coal (ton)
Boston	1812	$11		.07–.10	.15–.16	.52– .75	$1.12	.06	.11	$14
	1813	13 –17		.07–.10	.20–.30	.75–1.47	1.33	.09 –.13	.18	14
	1814	14 –15		.07–.10	.24–.37	.85–1.08	2.00	.06½–.13	.27	27
	1815	9.25– 7.50		.07–.13	.24–.27	.70–1.60	1.70–1.20	.07	.20	20
New York	1812	7 –11		—	.13–.18	.52– .75	1.50–1.75	.07 –.08	.09–.11	—
	1813	8.50–12.50		—	.21	.70– .94	1.56–1.70	.07 –.10	.11–.18	—
	1814	8 –12.		—	—	—	—	—	—	—
	1815	9		—	.24–.26	.92– .75	1.50	.18 –.22	.27–.30	—

to even as high as forty-eight pence per pound at London. This last was in September, 1814, and was "without precedent." Cotton in the same years sold at from eight to fourteeen cents per pound at Charleston, eleven to twenty-seven cents per pound at Boston, and at thirty pence per pound at London which was the highest price of the whole war. The effect of the war on imported articles that were costly in proportion to weight or size was not nearly so great at Boston or New York. Coffee sold at sixteen cents per pound at Boston in 1812, and at twenty-five cents per pound in 1814. And, undoubtedly, if one could trace the prices of the finer textiles, a similar result would be reached; but these articles greatly increased in price as one proceeded southward. Possibly the most interesting of any of these effects of the embargo and blockade was to put up the price of Virginia coal at Boston from fourteen dollars a ton to twenty-seven; but fortunately heating was generally done by wood which was by no means inexpensive in those days in the larger towns, costing about as much as it does at the time of writing.

The effect of embargo and blockade on New England was not to stop trading with the enemy, but only to make it more expensive. In the winter of 1813–1814, when the blockaders were withdrawn, vessels obtaining clearances from one coastwise port to another in Massachusetts Bay could square away for Passamaquoddy or Halifax. As the months went by and the customs officials were spurred to greater efforts, commerce along the coast practically ceased. Goods then were brought to the Kennebec, either along the coast or partly by boat and partly by wagon, and were thence transported overland to Boston. Possibly, in part to promote this commerce, which was so essential to the British, Sir John Sherbrooke, governor of Nova Scotia,

was ordered by the British government to seize and occupy
the eastern part of Maine, — which would not only aid the
illicit traders but would also be a convenient bit of land for
the British to have whenever negotiations for peace should
be entered on in earnest.   The British had little trouble in
taking possession of the country between the St. Croix
and the Penobscot.   No doubt their operations were facilitated by sympathizers among the inhabitants.   It is reported that the citizens of Eastport exhibited great joy at
the surrender of the fort at that place to the British and one
man is said to have held the customs collector by the collar
until a British officer came up and took him prisoner.[1]

At the other end of the line, Amelia Island hard by Fer-
nandina in Spanish Florida and just to the southward of
the St. Mary's River that marks the boundary line, was the
centre of the southern trade.   The anchorage was good
within the islands.   In July, 1814, an Englishman, William Burgess, acted as agent there for several English firms
and for several American firms of Richmond, Norfolk,
and Charleston.   He reported then that there were not
less than fifty square rigged vessels in the port.   The course
of trade was by small vessels from the plantation wharf on
a Maryland or Virginia river to Elizabeth City, North
Carolina, by way of the Dismal Swamp Canal.   From that
place, the tranportation was by coasting craft, running
through the sounds and creeks to Charleston, and from
that point by craft "that use the inside navigation to
Amelia Island."   It cost thirty-eight dollars to transport
one hogshead of tobacco from Elizabeth City to Amelia
Island by this route and a varying sum from the plantation
to Elizabeth City; but the profits were so great that ex-

---

[1] Professor Anson E. Morse called   *Essex Register* for Aug. 3, 1814.
my attention to this entry in the

porters were willing to pay almost any sum to get their goods on the high seas. A hogshead of tobacco that cost a hundred dollars, or so, at Richmond, might well cost another hundred to get to the London warehouse, but there, while prices held, it could be disposed of for a thousand dollars, more or less. What did it matter — a hundred dollars in freight money or the loss of one cargo in five? At all events, forwarders and commission merchants at Baltimore, Richmond, and Norfolk were sending a constant stream of tobacco and flour through the sounds of North Carolina, and the merchants of Charleston were doing a similar business with cotton by the way of Amelia Island.

This trade with the enemy had been the safety-valve that kept New England and New York by the side of their sister States in these years of war, mostly disastrous. With the stiffening of regulations under the embargo and the ever-tightening British blockade, discontent with the doings of the Madisonians became more and more acute. It did not make much difference what the government and Congress did at Washington, it was all bad. Whether it was floating a new loan or the enlistment of minors or, failing to do this or doing that, it was just the same; it was directed against New England rather than against the enemy. Governor Martin Chittenden of Vermont was an exponent of the anti-national spirit. Vermont militiamen had been marched out of that State into New York and placed under the command of an officer of the United States army. Thereupon, on November 10, 1813, the governor issued a proclamation ordering the Vermont militiamen to return to their State forthwith, and to hold themselves "in constant readiness to march on the shortest notice, to the defence of the frontiers" of Vermont, or to join with other good citizens in repelling invasion. It is quite evident that some Vermonters were not with their governor for the officers of this regiment refused to obey his orders [1] and declared they were not going to desert their fellow-citizens in the defence of New York. In Massachusetts, as the ocean-borne commerce became less and less profitable and trade with the enemy dwindled, manufacturing came nearer to the hearts and purses of the people. They sold their goods, whether of foreign or domestic manufacture, such of them as they did not want, to their neighbors to the southward. There was a constant inflow of specie into New England to pay for these goods, for the Middle States and the South had few transportable commodities that could be used to extinguish their debts to New England. It fell out, therefore, that the war which was distinctly unpopular in New England and was the work of the Virginia, South Carolina, and Kentucky groups of politicians made greatly toward the material advancement of Massachusetts and Connecticut. The change is well exemplified in the careers of Patrick T. Jackson and Francis Cabot Lowell of Massachusetts. Jackson accumulated his first capital in the prosecution of trade to India in the years 1800 to 1808. He then engaged in commerce with Havana which of course came to an ending at the outbreak of war. It was at about this time that Lowell returned from a long visit to England and Scotland. While there, he had been struck with the fact that although labor was cheaper in Great Britain, the advantages as to the raw product and water power, in his own country, might overbalance those things that favored Great Britain. On his return, Lowell and Jackson built a mill at Waltham, not far from Boston, at the falls of the Charles River. There they manufactured shirtings and sheetings from the raw material to the finished product, all in one establishment, —

---

[1] See Adams's *United States*, vii, 366; Niles' *Weekly Register*, v, 212, 230.

the first time in the history of the industry that this was
done. They were successful from the very start and almost
at once began the erection of another mill, twice the size
of the first. A few years later, to get more power, this
enterprise was transferred to the banks of the Merrimac
where the town of Lowell was founded, which has ever
since been one of the centres of New England manufacturing interests.

Prosperous though Massachusetts and the New England
States were, especially in contrast with other members of
the Union, they were far from contented. The United
States government did nothing to defend them except to
try to employ their militiamen — expecting the State to
pay for them. On the other hand, a very large part of the
taxes that were collected were gathered in New England
and were used elsewhere to pay the expenses of the United
States. Nevertheless, there was a constant drain of specie
into New England and the richer that section became the
louder grew the complaints. In April, 1814, the closing
days of the embargo were reënacted at Washington. New
England had evidently reached the limit of her suffering
and her patience. The cessation of conflict in Europe had
opened the ports of the Continent to American trade.
Was it right that the American government should aid
the British government in confining commerce with these
countries to British merchants? That was practically what
the embargo was doing. The indignation grew to such a
height that repeal was the only possible thing. In April,
therefore, Congress repealed the embargo and not only that
but possibly, as some sort of vengeance upon New England
for compelling this action, likewise repealed the non-importation laws and opened American markets, so far as the
war permitted, to trade with the neutral world. This

relieved the situation somewhat, but by the autumn of 1814 discontent had again reached an acute stage in New England. On the 17th day of October the Massachusetts legislature issued a circular letter summoning a convention of all the New England States to meet at Hartford in Connecticut to take into consideration the existing condition of affairs and suggest a remedy. Seven days before, President Madison had transmitted to Congress most serious communications from the Commissioners at Ghent, stating that the British negotiators demanded extensive cessions of lands and the formation of an Indian state as the price of peace, — conditions so grave that public attention everywhere was at last concentrated upon the war. These documents were published immediately and with the vote of the Massachusetts General Court and with the approaching bankruptcy of the Washington government seemed to be "big with consequences of direful import" and to portend the disruption of the Union.

NOTE

Naval Battles.—This table is compiled from William James's *Warden Refuted; being a Defence of the British Navy* (London, 1819) p. 13. Against each action the upper line is that of Warden, the lower that of James whenever he differed from the American view. The totals of losses are those given by James.

Actions between (American)	Actions between (British)	Duration H.M.	American							British						
			Number of guns mounted	Weight of metal (Broadside)	Number of men	Killed	Wounded	Prisoners	Total	Number of guns mounted	Weight of metal (Broadside)	Number of men	Killed	Wounded	Prisoners	Total
Essex	and Alert	0.8	46	676	328					26	180	86		3	150	150
										20						
Constitution	and Guerrière	0.30	54	736	400	7	7		14	49	517	350	15	64	287	350
		2.12	56	768	468		13					263				
Wasp	and Frolic	0.43	20	268	102	5	5		10	22	292	135	30	40	105	135
					137	8				19	274	110	15	47		
United States	and Macedonian	1.30	54	876	400	5	7		12	49	561	350	36	68	312	350
		2.0	58		478							292				
Constitution	and Java	1.45	54	677	400	9	25		34	49	605	400	60	101	340	400
		3.40	55	754	480		46			47	535	377	24		353	
Hornet	and Peacock	0.15	20	300	135	1	2		3	20	262	139	5	33	134	139
		0.25			165	2				19	198	122				
Chesapeake	and Shannon	0.15	48	581	350	49	98	300	350	53	613	396	26	58		84
			49	590	391	58	115	333	391	52	538	330				
Argus	and Pelican	0.43	20	228	130	6	16	124	130	21	274	150	2	5		20
					125							116				7

Actions between (American)	Actions between (British)	Duration H.M.	American — No. of guns mounted	American — Weight of metal (Broadside)	American — Number of men	American — Killed	American — Wounded	American — Prisoners	American — Total	British — No. of guns mounted	British — Weight of metal (Broadside)	British — Number of men	British — Killed	British — Wounded	British — Prisoners	British — Total
Enterprize	and Boxer	0.45	16	135	130 / 123	1	13		14	18 / 14	153 / 114	130 / 66	20 / 4	14 / 17	110 / 62	130 / 66
Am. & Br. squadrons on Lake Erie		3.0	54	928	350 / 580	27	96		123	63	459	450 / 345	90 / 41	94	320	450
Essex	and Phoebe & Cherub	2.30 / 2.15	46	676	255 / 265	58	65	132 / 161	255	81 / 77	913 / 862	500 / 421	5	10		15
Peacock	and Epervier	0.43	22	329 / 338	160 / 185		2		2	18	288 / 274	128 / 117	8	15	113	128
Wasp	and Reindeer	0.19	22	329 / 338	160 / 175	5 / 11	21 / 15		26	19	204 / 190	118	23	42	95	118
Wasp	and Avon	0.41	22	329 / 350	175	2	1		3	18	262	117	11 / 10	33 / 32		44 / 42
Am. & Br. squad. on L. Champlain		2.20	86	1012 / 1194	820 / 950	52	58		110	95 / 87	975 / 765	1050 / 537	84 / 54	110 / 116	367	500
President	and British squadron	4.30 / 2.30	53 / 58	916	400 / 477	25 / 35	53 / 70	375 / 434	400 / 477	50	676	346	17 / 11	15 / 14		32 / 25
Chasseur	and St. Lawrence	0.14	12	72 / 99	89 / 117	5	8		13	15 / 13	98 / 81	75 / 51	15 / 6	23 / 18	60	75
Hornet	and Penguin	0.22 / 0.42	14 / 20	300 / 306	165	1	11 / 16		12	21 / 19	306 / 274	158 / 122	17 / 6	28	118	158

CHAPTER XX

THE CLOSING SCENE

ON June 26, 1812, only eight days after Congress had declared war against Great Britain, Monroe directed Jonathan Russell, who was in charge of American affairs at London, to open the matter of a termination of hostilities with the British government. At nearly the same time, the British Secretary of State ordered Sir John Borlase Warren, the admiral on the American station, to begin negotiations with the administration at Washington with a view to bringing about the same result. On both sides there were similar obstacles to peace. Lord Castlereagh, the British Foreign Secretary, was surprised, so he said, that the American government should expect Great Britain to desist from its "ancient and accustomed practice" of impressing British seamen from merchant ships. Monroe, on his part, informed the admiral that a suspension of the practice of impressment was a necessary preliminary to a cessation of hostilities.[1] If, during the armistice, the two countries could come to some permanent arrangement, peace would be the result. Monroe regarded his offer as the beginning of a negotiation; but the British looked upon it as putting an end to anything of the kind. Alexander, the Russian Czar, next intervened. His interest was partly

[1] See Warren to Monroe, Sept. 30, and Monroe to Warren, Oct. 27, 1812, in *American State Papers, Foreign Relations*, iii, 585, 586, 589, 590, 595; and Niles' *Weekly Register*, iii, 153.

aroused by the economic difficulties of his empire and partly by a tendency towards republicanism that he had received from his tutor, La Harpe, the Swiss, and from his perusal of the works of Jean Jacques Rousseau. His interference was more fruitful; but the period of fruition was protracted. The year 1812 was signalized in Europe by Napoleon's invasion of Russia. On the 15th day of September, he entered Moscow, the ancient capital of Russia, and five days later the Russian chancellor, Count Rumiantsov, requested Mr. Adams, our minister at St. Petersburg, to meet him in conference. On September 21 they met. It appeared that the Czar was greatly concerned with the outbreak of hostilities between America and Britain which would interfere with the economical benefits Russia had hoped to secure by her recent change from friendship with France to friendship with England. Would a proffer of Russian mediation be well received in the United States? Adams had not a word of instruction on this point; he had not even received official notice from Washington that war had been declared against Great Britain. As a good diplomatist he replied that he was certain that such an offer would be cordially received at Washington and he, himself, could foresee no obstacle to its acceptance. Three days earlier, September 18, Rumiantsov had already written to the Russian representative at London directing him to make this offer in almost the same words to the British government.[1]

Madison accepted the Russian offer precipitately (March 11, 1813). By this time, the whole face of war in Europe had changed. Napoleon's grand army had disappeared and he, himself, had fled from the Beresina to Paris. The

[1] See letter found in the Russian archives by Professor Frank A. Golder of the State College of Washington and printed in *American Historical Review,* xx, 109.

relief to England was great and diminished the desire for ending the American war. Of course there was no telling what the fortunes of future battles might bring forth. Nevertheless, the British government declined the Russian proposal. The disputations with the United States had to do with the internal government of Great Britain and, therefore, were not proper subjects of negotiation. In other words, the quarrel with the United States was a sort of family affair which the British and Americans would better settle for themselves. The further history of the mediation episode is indistinct. Russia renewed her good offices which Great Britain again declined; but, in declining, offered to appoint representatives to meet those from the United States directly. Madison had appointed three commissioners to negotiate with the British under the imperial mediation. These were Albert Gallatin, Secretary of the Treasury, James A. Bayard, Senator from Delaware, and J. Q. Adams, American minister at St. Petersburg. Gallatin and Bayard had left America before the Senate had acted on their nominations. They were at St. Petersburg, but had no authority to negotiate directly with Great Britain. And then came the news that Gallatin's enemies in the Senate had taken advantage of his retention of the secretaryship to refuse to confirm his nomination as envoy. The battle of Leipsic, October 16–19, 1813, was a crushing defeat for Napoleon; from that time his power was confined to France, and in April of the next year he abdicated. It was under these circumstances that Castlereagh offered the United States government to enter into negotiations for peace with its representatives directly, either at London or at Gottenburg, a seaport of the neutral country of Sweden. Adams and Bayard were appointed to this new mission and to their number Henry Clay and Jonathan

Russell were added. Madison had not named Gallatin, thinking he was on his way home to resume the charge of the Treasury Department. When it was found that he had definitely resigned that employment, he was nominated and at once confirmed by the Senate. The delay resulted in his being the fifth instead of the first on the commission. Clay and Russell promptly sailed for Sweden; but various contingencies prevented the assembling of the commission until midsummer by which time the scene of negotiation had been removed to Ghent in Belgium. Gallatin had favored accepting the British suggestion of London. He argued that it would be very difficult to give any conciliatory instructions to British peace commissioners because these would have to be made public. If, however, the Americans could meet the British Secretary of State face to face at London, they very possibly might agree to some modus vivendi that would bring about peace and preserve the credit of both British and American politicians. Clay refused point blank to negotiate at London, but was willing to meet the British representatives at Ghent, a decision which in the event seemed a little peculiar in view of the fact that that town proved to be garrisoned by the British army; but Clay thought that the Americans had condescended enough already.

By the summer of 1814, the whole problem of international politics had taken a new twist. On May 13, of this year, the first Peace of Paris put a temporary end to the Napoleonic Empire, provided for the residence of the deposed Emperor on the island of Elba, and released thousands of British soldiers and sailors for service in America. There was every reason, therefore, for the British to delay the negotiations in the hope that a fortunate blow or two in America would make the Americans more amenable. On

the other hand, the attitude of the Czar Alexander, of the
King of Prussia, and of the restored French monarchy did
not point toward the continuance of European peace.   In
June, the Czar and the King visited London to try to come to
some arrangement as to the division of the spoils, which was
to be definitely settled at a Congress to be held at Vienna.
In France, matters were not going at all well, as the French
people were crushed under a load of poverty and death.
For the last few years they had been living by plunder.
Would not a return to that system be their only hope?
Napoleon was at Elba to be sure, but that island was not
far removed from the shores of France.   The outlook in
Paris seemed so dangerous that the British government
sought a pretext for removing the Duke of Wellington from
his command there.   Later, Talleyrand, now again French
foreign minister, plunged the allies into disorder by declaring that France retained her old limits with some few exceptions, therefore that the spoils would be much less than had
been expected.   It was these anxieties and uncertainties
that fully occupied Lord Castlereagh's energies and those
of the other members of the British government.   The
appointment of British commissioners was put off and put
off; but at the same time the American negotiation must
be continued; so they were finally sent to Ghent, where
they arrived on August 7, 1814.

The peace commissioners at Ghent were eight in number,
five Americans and three British.   The three British are
unknown to fame except of the minutest sort.   There was
Lord Gambier, a seaman, Henry Goulburn, an under-secretary, and William Adams, who was sent because he knew
something of international law.   Of the five Americans four
of them were of the ablest in the land and indeed of the ablest
in the world.   Albert Gallatin has few equals in history as a

man of accomplishment.   He had that invaluable capacity
of bringing things to pass.   He was a foreigner, but that in
the present instance was no disqualification.   The nominal
head of the commission was John Quincy Adams, a perennial
office-holder, — from his entrance into public office in 1794
until his death in 1848, hardly a whole year elapsed when he
was without public employment.   He had all the qualities
of the Adamses and all the defects of those qualities.   He
was the most experienced diplomatist at Ghent and was
a man of the greatest ability and integrity.   The third
member was Henry Clay, Speaker of the House of Representatives, and for half a century a quadriennial candidate
for the presidency, — and unsuccessful.   He represented
the spirit of the rising West and played a remarkable part
in these negotiations by preserving his hopefulness and
buoyancy in the darkest hour.   Of Bayard, not much
need be said except to refer to the part that he had played
in the election of Jefferson.   He was still technically a
Federalist, but he had lost touch with the sterner leaders
of that sect.   Jonathan Russell was appointed because of
his commercial knowledge, so it was said.   His last years
were embittered by a lingering libel suit that he had brought
against a New York editor who had accused him of using
his knowledge of the transactions at Ghent for purposes of
speculation.   No verdict was ever reached owing to Russell's death.   He remains in memory mainly from the
letters that he wrote or caused to be published with a view
to destroying the political fortunes, first of John Quincy
Adams and later of Henry Clay.[1]   The American commission made up in ability for the lack of it on the British side
of the table.   In fact, as Henry Adams has pointed out,

[1] See Massachusetts Historical So-   *Duplicate Letters* [of J. Russell], pp.
ciety's *Proceedings* for January, 1911,   64–113.
pp. 305–322 ; and J. Q. Adams's *The*

when they couldn't contend with their British opponents, they fought among themselves.

Why the British should have entered on peace negotiations in 1814 seems very difficult to understand, for they certainly had no intention of bringing anything to a conclusion before the campaign of 1814 had resulted, as they most fondly expected it would, in success for British arms. The expectations of ardent British men are best seen on a map which accompanies Nathaniel Atcheson's "Compressed View of the Points to be Discussed in Treating with the United States." [1] Atcheson had acted as the penman for the British "Society of Ship Owners" which was at the bottom of nearly every act complained of by the American government. The proposition now put forward was to form an Indian state to the west of the Muskingum and Lake Erie and north of the Ohio and Missouri rivers. To the eastward, a new boundary should be run including in the British domains all the territory of the St. Lawrence basin, northern Maine, and eastern Maine between the Penobscot and the St. Croix. This would give the Great Lakes, all the bordering lands, and Lake Champlain to the British. Atcheson's "Compressed View" was dated in March, 1814, and was doubtless printed soon afterwards. What influence, if any, it had on the ministers is unknown, but

[1] This was printed at London in 1814 and reprinted as a number of The Pamphleteer, vol. v, London, 1815. On pages 24 and 25 of the original edition, Atcheson sums up his recommendations under nine heads. The first four relate to the boundary line, the fifth provides for the exclusion of Americans from the coast fisheries of British North America; the sixth from all intercourse with the British West India Islands and the seventh from the British East India possessions and from the northwest coast of America. By the eighth, they were not to be allowed to acquire Florida and, on the other hand, the cession of New Orleans to Great Britain might be required, and finally, no commercial treaty should be entered into with the United States. Some of these views had already been set forth by the same author in a tract in 1808. This is entitled *American Encroachments on British Rights* and was reprinted in the sixth volume of *The Pamphleteer* in 1815, without the Appendix of documents.

when the instructions to the British commissioners were drawn up, they were directed to contend for the status of possession at the date of the Treaty of Peace and to demand of the Americans as a *sine qua non*, or condition precedent to any negotiation, that "a full and express recognition of their [the Indian tribes] limits as shall take place."[1]

The instructions issued to the Americans in January 1814 and to the British, half a year later, have a curious family resemblance — perhaps all instructions look alike. In this case the Americans were directed to argue for a cession of Canada, or Upper Canada, to the United States;[2] the British, on their part, were to demand the establishment of an Indian dominion or territory under the guarantee of the British government, a rectification of the boundary, and a prohibition of the building of any fortifications on the American shores of the Lakes. The Americans were to discuss blockades and impressment and all the other time-worn topics; the British were to limit or decline the discussion of such subjects. In June, in the intermission of European warfare, the American cabinet voted it to be expedient to conclude peace without a surrender of impressment on the part of Great Britain; but these modified instructions were not in the hands of the American commissioners when the discussions began.

At the outset, the Englishmen made a sad blunder in misinterpreting the meaning of their own instructions and the policy of their own government. They demanded as a

---

[1] Castlereagh's *Correspondence*, x, 70.

[2] This paragraph was omitted from the despatch as printed in *American State Papers, Foreign Relations*, iii, 701. Henry Adams suggested that this and other paragraphs were omitted because the Ghent commissioners decided not to act upon them. These paragraphs are printed from the documents in the State Department at Washington in F. A. Updyke's *Diplomacy of the War of 1812*, pp. 178–182 and from the "Bayard Manuscripts" in American Historical Association's *Reports*, 1913, ii, 263–265. There are minor differences between the two drafts, but none of them vital.

sine qua non the establishment of an Indian Territory in the Northwest and declared it to be equally necessary to have definite boundaries assigned under mutual guarantee. The answer of the Americans was that they had no power to negotiate as to any such disposal of United States lands. Gallatin inquired of the British commissioners as to what would happen to the one hundred thousand white settlers on the land which it was proposed to allocate to the savages and was answered cheerfully that they must look out for themselves. After having drawn from the British the full extent of their Indian demands, the Americans replied in a formal letter refusing them without waiting to consult their employers at Washington. In writing home, they one and all expressed themselves as hopeless of the continuance of the negotiation. When the doings of the British commissioners came before the government in England with the replies of the Americans and the statement of their pronounced attitude, the ministers were conscious of the ill-result of employing such inferior persons. It would never do to break off the conferences and prolong the war on the issue of the acquisition of territory. The British people were not prepared to pay and fight for the aggrandisement of Canada and, however honorable it was to look out for their Indian allies, the war could not be continued for them. These propositions disappeared or melted into one for amnesty toward the Indians. Instead of breaking off the negotiations, the British government seemed determined to protract them, and the Americans were held immovable at Ghent, somewhat against their wishes.

British expectations of military success in America ran high at London. Thirteen thousand Peninsula veterans or more were in Canada; another five thousand were in the Chesapeake region effecting an important diversion to

facilitate the march of the first band southward into New
York.   Other thousands were on the point of embarkation
to aid these.   Toward the end of October news of the
British disaster at Plattsburg, and the retirement of the
Peninsula veterans northward, the repulse of Drummond
in the assaults on Fort Erie, the death of Ross in front of
Baltimore, and the withdrawal of the British army from the
Chesapeake, all came to London within a week.   To these
untoward tidings from America, there were added others,
equally disheartening, from Vienna.   For a whole month
"The Powers" had been unwilling to face the issues in
public conference at that city.   The Russians had put forward claims to central Poland and the city of Warsaw, —
to be formed into a Grand Duchy with the Emperor and
his successors as grand dukes.   The proposed ducal domain
formed a salient thrust into the heart of Europe between
Hohenzollern lands on the north and Hapsburg lands on
the south.   Alexander's Germanic allies were disposed to
be refractory and France, under Talleyrand's lead, was not
at all inclined to smooth matters over.   It certainly seemed
a time when England's hand should be free for whatever
contingency was likely to arise.   Each succeeding letter
that came from London to the British commissioners at
Ghent, therefore, was more tolerant of American pretensions.   To this conclusion the British government had
been impelled by the Duke of Wellington.   It had been
suggested that he might be sent to America to take the
chief command and to make peace, if the event of war should
be favorable.   But Wellington, in replying, had declared
his going would suggest that affairs in America were in a
much worse state than they really were.   Moreover, in
another letter, he wrote that it was not a "general" that
they needed in America, but a naval superiority on the

Lakes; if he crossed the Atlantic without such an ascendancy being first assured, it would be only to prove the truth of Prevost's defence and to sign a treaty of peace which might just as well be signed at Ghent. Up to this time, there had been no hint of Napoleon's return from Elba, but the fire was ready laid in France, waiting to be kindled, — that much was certain.

The negotiations now went rapidly forward, the British withdrawing one demand after another until a point was reached where all five Americans could sign. This was done on December 24, 1814, the day after Jackson's night attack on the invading British army below New Orleans. The treaty as signed conceded nothing. There was no mention of impressment or blockades, and whatever boundary troubles there were were pushed over to the future.[1] It was a treaty of peace to free Britain's hands for the coming conflict with Napoleonism that was to end on the battle-field of Waterloo. Three copies were made. One of them went to England with the secretary of the British commission who was to carry it and the British ratification to America. Other copies of the treaty were sent by other messengers. In the condition of ocean transport then existing, it was certain to take weeks, and it might take months, for the documents and the news to cross the Atlantic; and, meantime, events seemed to be moving toward a crisis in America.

The stoppage of New England commerce in the winter and spring of 1814 and the subsequent seizure of the eastern

---

[1] While in the Chesapeake, and again in the New Orleans campaign, the British incited negro slaves to leave the plantations and take refuge in camp or on board ship. There were also stories of enlistments in British forces, and of these fugitives being sold into West Indian servitude; but these stories lack evidence. Great Britain ultimately was obliged to pay heavily for the removal of these slaves. See books cited in Note I at end of chapter. There is some information on this subject in Charles Ball's *Slavery in the United States: A Narrative*, 363.

counties of Maine by Sir John Sherbrooke greatly intensified
the feeling of discontent that had been steadily rising in
Massachusetts and New England ever since the election of
Jefferson in 1801. The acquisition of Louisiana in 1803
and the admission of the Territory of Orleans as the State of
Louisiana in 1812 brought home to the New Englanders
their present helplessness and the still greater humiliations
that their children and grandchildren were to bear in future
years. The feelings of the most strenuous of them were
expressed by Josiah Quincy in the national House of Representatives on January 14, 1811,[1] in one of the early stages
of the discussion on the conferring of statehood on Louisiana. The passage of this bill is virtually a dissolution of
this Union, he said. It will free the States from their
moral obligation, "it will be the duty of some to prepare
definitely for a separation — amicably if they can, violently
if they must." Further on in the same speech, he asked if
any one supposed that the people of the Northern and
Atlantic States will look on with patience and see "Representatives and Senators from the Red river and Missouri
pouring themselves upon this and the other floor, managing
the concerns of a seaboard fifteen hundred miles at least
from their residence?" Quincy was most outspoken and
persistent. The war and everything about it was wrong.
In 1813, he induced the Massachusetts Senate to resolve
that in a conflict like the present, "waged without justifiable
cause, . . . it is not becoming a moral and religious people
to express any approbation of military or naval exploits
which are not immediately connected with the defence of
our sea-coast and soil." As the war went on, the general
government collected money by the hundreds of thousands
of dollars in Massachusetts and New England, used most of

[1] *Annals of Congress*, 11th Cong., 3d Sess., 524, 540, and numerous other places.

it outside their borders for purposes of which they did not
approve, and left them to defend themselves as well as they
might. The irritation grew and was utilized by the politicians who fanned the flame of discontent by reports and
resolutions and communications to the newspapers. In
January, 1814, a circular letter was sent out to the select-
men of the towns of the old Hampshire county inviting their
fellow citizens to consider whether a convention of the
commercial States would better be held "for procuring such
alterations in the federal constitution as will give to the
Northern States a due proportion of representation, and
secure them from the future exercise of powers injurious to
their commercial interests." [1] The newspapers of Boston
and other New England towns in the autumn of 1814, after
the publication of the first letters from the peace commissioners, contained communications openly justifying
secession. In one is the declaration that "the federal
constitution is nothing more than a treaty between independent sovereignties." A State cannot rebel, nor can any
citizen of such a State acting under its authority "be guilty
of treason against the United States." The Constitution
was ratified by the States, "it was by the assent of nine
states, considered as such, that it became a compact," and
it is for the States, therefore, to decide whether the stipu-
lations of the compact have been fulfilled or violated. If
it becomes necessary to resort to force, the conflict will be
a war between one sovereign State and "that power, whatever it might be, which should come with hostile intentions";
the citizens of such a State taken in arms would be prisoners
of war, not traitors. Our duty to the general government is

[1] Quoted from paragraphs of the circular given in a letter from Noah Webster
to Daniel Webster, dated New Haven,
Sept. 6, 1834, and printed in *American
Historical Review*, ix, 96–104. The
words quoted are on p. 102. The best
account, by far, of these years in
Massachusetts is that given in S. E.
Morison's *Harrison Gray Otis*, ii, 52–
124.

founded on express compact and treaty. So long as the general government adhered to the provisions of the original compact, a qualified allegiance was due to them but "if they violate the terms of that compact, its validity is annihilated, and the parties to it are released from their obligations." [1] How far this spirit of secession had permeated the hearts of the people and how near fruition such sentiments were, are questions that can never be answered. So much always goes on under the surface that is unknown to contemporaries and to historians that in a case of this kind one is forced to descend from fact to deduction; but here the deduction is entitled to a good deal of consideration. Secession was openly considered and talked about. It was also the topic of private letters, as one from Gouverneur Morris to H. G. Otis written as far back as April, 1813, in which he advocated the holding of a convention to mark out a course of conduct, and suggested that the question should be examined whether it was for the interest or the happiness of the "Northern and Eastern States to continue in Union with the Owners of Slaves." [2]

A convention was the good old English and American way of political action. Sometimes one might be entirely unofficial as the Suffolk Convention of 1774, or it might have some legal recognition as the Massachusetts constitutional convention of 1780. There had been movements in earlier years looking toward the holding of a convention to consider Northern grievances, but it was not until February, 1814, that an official standing was given to the proposition by the

[1] These quotations are taken from papers printed in Professor Frank Maloy Anderson's article entitled, "A Forgotten Phase of the New England Opposition to the War of 1812" in Mississippi Valley Historical Society's *Proceedings*, vol. vi. This article is a good example of what can be accomplished by painstaking research; we need many more of the kind.

[2] These words are quoted from Morris's letter as printed in Morison's *Otis*, ii, 84. Morison points out that Sparks "discretely omitted" the secession portion in the letter as given in his *Gouverneur Morris*.

adoption of a report by the Massachusetts House of Representatives advocating the passage of laws nullifying the existing embargo and also the holding of a Northern convention to obtain amendments of the Constitution to secure the people of that part of the country against future abuses of power. From that time, there was long procrastination, but in October, 1814, the Massachusetts legislature adopted a resolution for the appointment of delegates to confer with delegates from the other New England States on their grievances, on the best means of preserving their resources, and, also, to take measures for securing a convention of delegates from all the United States to revise the federal Constitution upon the basis of fair representation. Hartford in Connecticut was suggested as the place of holding the preliminary conference. The next day the Federalist members of the Massachusetts State legislature met together and selected the State's delegates to the proposed gathering. At the head of them was the venerable George Cabot, who accepted this call from retirement saying, "We are going to keep you young hot-heads from getting into mischief." So also Nathan Dane is represented as attending the convention to prevent mischief and for that purpose only.[1] Connecticut and Rhode Island responded to the invitation, and two counties of New Hampshire and one of Vermont sent representatives. There were radically disposed revolutionists in the convention, but it was distinctly in the control of the conservatives as its rules of procedure and resolutions show. As to the first, inviolable secrecy was to be observed as to all propositions, debates, and proceedings; but the day of secret conclave had passed in America. The "Report" in its final form attributed the troubles in America to the duplication

---

[1] Lodge's *George Cabot* (ed. 1878), 519, 602.

on this side of the Atlantic of the "fierce passions which have convulsed the nations of Europe." The Constitution under "a wise and virtuous Administration" — that of Washington — had proved itself competent to all the objects of its framers, but the "lust and caprice of power, the corruption of patronage, the oppression of the weaker interests of the community by the stronger" are the natural offspring of bad administration and a change in public opinion seemed to be "already manifested." If the Union were to be dissolved, it should be done in times of peace. Paragraphs of argumentation followed of similar import, all tending to uphold the "farewell address of the Father of his country." After twenty-four pages of printed report, the Convention resolved that acts of Congress in violation of the Constitution are void, but it was not necessary for a State to fly to open resistance upon every infraction of the Constitution. "In cases of deliberate, dangerous, and palpable infractions of the Constitution, affecting the sovereignty of a State, and liberties of the people; it is not only the right but the duty of such a State to interpose its authority for their protection. . . . When Emergencies occur . . . States, which have no common umpire, must be their own judges, and execute their own decisions." [1] The Convention, furthermore, recommended an earnest application to the government of the United States, requesting their consent to some arrangement whereby the said States, separately, or in concert, may assume the defence of their territory and receive a reasonable portion of the taxes collected within their limits. Seven amendments to the Constitution were proposed. Among them was one to do away with the federal ratio. Another required a two-thirds

---

[1] *Public Documents [of the Massachusetts Senate] containing Proceedings of the Hartford Convention of Delegates;* *Report of the Commissioners while at Washington,* etc. (Boston, 1815) p. 9.

majority in each House of Congress for admitting new States, passing non-intercourse laws, and declaring war. A third provided that no person hereafter naturalized shall be eligible to Congress or to civil office under the general government. Massachusetts and Connecticut sent commissioners to Washington to make arrangements with the national government for the separate defence of these States. There were three commissioners for Massachusetts, the first being Harrison Gray Otis. In sending them their commission and instructions, Governor Strong informed them that on request from General Dearborn, the State had returned to the United States authorities the ordnance, stores, and munitions that had been borrowed from the federal government in the preceding September and October for the defence of the frontier,—an act which would seem to preclude all intention of secession by violence on the part of the Massachusetts authorities. At Baltimore on their southward journey, the commissioners heard of "the miraculous success of our arms at N Orleans" which Otis thought would put the administration on stilts.[1]

Hardly ever has there been a more anxious period in our history than these early days of February, 1815. The situation at New Orleans was most alarming, greatly compli-

[1] Samuel E. Morison in the *Life and Letters of Harrison Gray Otis* (Boston, 1913) has devoted a large part of the second volume to the Hartford Convention. To the documents there printed should be added Governor Strong's letter of January 31, 1815 (Massachusetts Historical Society's *Proceedings* for March, 1915). A convenient set of documents is in H. V. Ames's *State Documents on Federal Relations*, No. ii, p. 10 and fol. Dr. Morison holds that the Hartford Convention was not a secession conspiracy as was maintained by J. Q. Adams in a letter dated Washington, 30th December, 1828, and printed with an "Appeal to the Citizens of the United States" by leading Federalists as "Supplement to the Boston Daily Advertiser" of February 7, 1829, and reprinted with much other matter in Henry Adams's *New-England Federalism;* and see also Lodge's *George Cabot*. The account in Adams's *United States*, viii, 287–310, is a moderate statement of the family view. Hermann von Holst treats the episode from a more detached standpoint in his *Constitutional and Political History of the United States*, i, 237 and fol. The student will find abundant citations for further research in the footnotes to these volumes.

cated by Jackson's slowness to believe that the British could intend to attack from the lakes, and not from Mobile. On February 4, 1815, news came of "the most decided victory" of Jackson on January 8. This anouncement, glorious though it was, did not entirely remove the despondency that pervaded society. On February 11th the withdrawal of the British from below New Orleans was announced at Washington to the firing of rockets. Three days later, February 14, 1815, Henry Carroll, charged with the Treaty of Peace, rode down Pennsylvania Avenue. The Senate advised ratification on the 17th; the next day the ratifications were exchanged and the war was over.[1] The revulsion of feeling was tremendous. Without waiting to look into the treaty "every one passed from gloom to glory" and drinking and congratulations were the order of the afternoon and the evening. The ratified treaty was at once made public. Within twenty-three hours a copy of it went from Washington to New York, — an unexampled swiftness of transit. Everywhere as the news came "Peace — Security — Prosperity" was the cry; scholars were dismissed from school, flags were exhibited, even Harvard University was "splendidly illuminated in the evening, on this happy occasion." Prices of staple American products bounded up to the gratification of farmer and planter; prices of imported goods were cut in halves, greatly to the sorrow of merchant and importer. Everywhere, throughout the land, interest in foreign affairs and in home politics ceased. The American Nation, with its back to Europe and its face to the West, addressed itself to the solution of the problems of the Nineteenth Century.

[1] Nicholas Murray Butler, now President of Columbia University, brought together a number of facts as to the effect of the War of 1812 upon the consolidation of the Union in *Johns Hopkins University Studies*, Fifth Series, vii, pp. 26–30.

NOTE

Bibliography of the Negotiations at Ghent. — Mahan has treated the negotiations at Ghent with acumen and industry,[1] unusual even in him (*War of 1812*, ii, ch. xviii). Henry Adams's account (*United States*, ix, 1–53) is not so ample as one would expect and not nearly so detailed as the earlier matter in his *Life of Albert Gallatin*, 493–546. Professor F. A. Updyke has necessarily devoted most of his work on *The Diplomacy of the War of 1812* to the negotiation at Ghent.

There is no adequate collection of documents relating to this negotiation. Official papers are printed in *American State Papers, Foreign Relations*, iii, 695–726, 730–748; and in Wait's *State Papers*, ix, 310–446; and in Niles's *Weekly Register*, vol. vii. The diary of James Gallatin that was published in 1914 under the title of *A Great Peace Maker* adds little to our knowledge of this negotiation beyond an entry as to letters received by Gallatin from the Duke of Wellington in which the latter plainly hints that Gallatin being " a foreigner " could be absolutely relied on. In one of these Wellington writes that he has brought all his weight to bear to bring about peace. Quantities of letters have been printed in the *American Historical Review* and elsewhere, but they still lack coördination. The *Memoirs* of John Quincy Adams (ii and iii) and his *Writings* (vol. v.) printed under the editorship of Worthington C. Ford have a mass of matter on this subject, some of which is given from other drafts in the American Antiquarian Society's *Proceedings* for 1913, pp. 110–169. The " Papers of James A. Bayard " in the *Report* of the American Historical Association for 1913, and Gallatin's *Writings* (vol. ii) contain much material from another standpoint, but without adding much to the sum total of our knowledge.[2] Instructions and despatches of the British Ghent Commission are printed from the British archives in the *Proceedings* of the Massachusetts Historical Society for December, 1914; and other material from that point of view is in *Correspondence, Despatches, and Other Papers, of Viscount Castlereagh*, vol. x, and in the 9th volume of *Supplementary Despatches, Correspondence, and Memoranda of . . . Duke of Wellington*, see index volume to whole set under " America."

[1] The same account word for word, except a concluding paragraph, is printed in the *American Historical Review*, xi, 68–87.

[2] Bayard's letters to Cæsar A. Rodney in *Bulletin* of the New York Public Library, iv, 228, supplement this matter.

INDEX